John Larkin Lincoln, Ovid

Selections from the Poems of Ovid

John Larkin Lincoln, Ovid

Selections from the Poems of Ovid

ISBN/EAN: 9783337006082

Printed in Europe, USA, Canada, Australia, Japan

Cover: Foto ©Thomas Meinert / pixelio.de

More available books at **www.hansebooks.com**

Appletons' Classical Series.

SELECTIONS

FROM THE

POEMS OF OVID

WITH NOTES AND VOCABULARY

BY

J. L. LINCOLN, LL. D.

PROFESSOR OF LATIN IN BROWN UNIVERSITY

NEW YORK
D. APPLETON AND COMPANY
1, 3, AND 5 BOND STREET
1894

PREFACE TO THE NEW EDITION.

In the preparation of a new edition of these "Selections from the Poems of Ovid," the work has undergone a careful revision. A chief result of the revision has been the insertion of words in the Vocabulary, which were omitted in the first edition. Corrections, too, have been made in the Vocabulary, and also in the text and the notes. I hope, therefore, that the book will now be found to be a better one, and more worthy of use. I take this occasion to make my acknowledgments to the many teachers who have expressed a favorable opinion of the work, and have adopted it as a text-book. I have especially to express my sense of obligation to my friends who have pointed out defects in the work, and have called my attention to words omitted in the Vocabulary; particularly am I indebted for such service to Professor C. N. Dougherty, Superintendent of Public Schools in Peoria, Illinois, and to my former pupils, Messrs. William T. Peck, of the Providence High School, Enoch Perrine, of the Peddie Institute, Hightstown,

New Jersey, William C. Joslin, of Belleville, New York, and James P. Kelley, of the Connecticut Literary Institution, Suffield. I shall be thankful to any teachers, who may use the book with their classes, for suggestions or criticisms, which may help to make the work a more useful one in the study of Latin, and of Ovid as a Latin poet.

— " Si quid novisti rectius istis,
Candidus imperti."

J. L. LINCOLN.

BROWN UNIVERSITY, *August* 22, 1884.

PREFACE.

This selection is intended as an introduction to the reading of Latin poetry. It is the opinion of experienced teachers (and it is at the request of such that this volume has been prepared) that the poetry of Ovid is better fitted for the uses of beginners than that of Vergil. It is in accordance with such an opinion that, in the course of Latin study pursued in the schools of Europe, and especially of England and Germany, the reading of Ovid precedes the reading of Vergil. It is desirable that the student become familiar in Ovid, both by theory and practice, with the structure of the Latin hexameter, and with the peculiarities of poetic Latin, before he comes to the statelier numbers and the loftier diction of Vergil. And, certainly, in respect to the subjects treated by the two poets, it seems fitting that those immortal stories from the Greek and Roman mythology, which, largely through Ovid's charming versions, have entered as an enduring possession into the literature of modern times, should have an earlier place in a course of Latin study than Vergil's great national epic, which traces, in finished heroic verse, the grand fortunes of Rome, its destined universal dominion, and all that was noblest and best in its life—political, moral, and religious.

Some selections from the "Amores," the "Fasti," and the "Tristia" have been added to those made from the "Metamorphoses," not only on account of the interesting themes of which they treat, but also for the sake of giving the student an opportunity of becoming acquainted with Latin elegiac verse, of which, in Latin poetry, Ovid is the acknowledged master.

If this volume should be found to contain more than can be conveniently read in an introductory course of Latin poetry, perhaps the following pieces may be preferred, from their superior interest, and from the superior illustrations they present of Ovid's genius and style: From the "Metamorphoses," The Golden Age, Deucalion and Pyrrha, Phaethon, Pyramus and Thisbe, Arachne or the Spider's Web, Latona's Revenge, The Golden Fleece, Philemon and Baucis, Atalanta's Race, Alcyone, and the Epilogue; and from the remaining selections, the three from the "Amores," and especially the three from the "Tristia."

The text of the selections is that of Merkel (1873), with an occasional variation, in the "Metamorphoses," adopted from Siebelis, or from Haupt. In preparing the Notes, the editor has been indebted to the edition of Siebelis, Leipsic, 1873, edited by Dr. Fr. Polle; of Moritz Haupt, Berlin, 1876, edited by Dr. Otto Korn; and of William Ramsay, 1868, edited by Prof. George G. Ramsay.

PREFACE.

The grammatical references (H. or Gr.) are to the Latin Grammar of Professor Albert Harkness, revised edition of 1881.

J. L. LINCOLN.

Brown University, Providence, R. I.,
August 22, 1882.

THE LIFE OF OVID.

The poetry of Ovid, like that of his predecessor, Horace, contains many incidental notices of his own life and fortunes. One of his elegiac poems, indeed (Tristia, iv. 10), which is included in this collection, is a brief autobiography in verse. We may thus gather from the poet's works all that is needful for the knowledge of his life.

Publius Ovidius Naso was born on the 20th of March, in the year 43 b. c. The day he has himself marked * as the second of the festival of the Quinquatria, and the year † as the one made memorable by the death of both the consuls, Hirtius and Pansa. His native place was Sulmo, now Sulmone, a town among the moist hills of the Peligni, about ninety miles from Rome.‡ He belonged to a family which for many generations had held equestrian rank, a fact which the poet has repeatedly recorded in verse.# His father lived to the advanced age of ninety; and Ovid, while mentioning this fact,‖ as well as the death of his mother,△ and the grief he felt for their loss, yet counted himself happy that they did not live to know the calamity which afterward befell himself.◊ The poet had a brother, born just twelve months before him, but who died at the age of twenty, when he was giving

---

* Tristia, iv. 10, 14. † Ib. 6. ‡ Ib. 3, 4.
\# Amores, iii. 15, 5; Tristia, iv. 10, 7 and 8; Ex Ponto, iv. 8, 17.
‖ Tristia, iv. 10, 77 and 78. △ Ib. 80. ◊ Ib. 81 and 82.

promise of rising to distinction in public life.* The father, who seems to have been a man of practical Roman character, early brought his sons to Rome, and gave them the best advantages of education, and especially the choicest instruction in law and eloquence, that thus they might, like all Roman youth, be trained to the service of the state. To these Roman pursuits the elder brother developed an inborn tendency; but the younger, marked in his very nature by the Muse for her own, was even in his boyish years drawn into her service. Even in his declamations in the rhetorical schools, which he attended in compliance with his father's will, he betrayed his poetic instincts; and, as we learn from the rhetorician Seneca,† his prose diction had in it something of the rhythm of verse. He tells us also himself, in a characteristic passage, that when, to please his father, he tried to write prose, "the verse came of its own accord into fitting numbers." ‡

Soon after assuming the manly gown, our student-poet, when about seventeen years of age, entered upon a course of foreign travel and study, visiting Sicily, and then the chief cities of Asia, in the company of his friend, the poet Macer,# and especially resorting to Athens,∥ and there quickening his genius and increasing his literary resources by congenial communion with the master spirits of Greek literature, and especially of Greek poetry.

On his return to Rome, in his twentieth year, he held in succession several of those humbler offices △ with which

---

* Tristia, iv. 10, 10; ib. 17 and 18; ib. 31 and 32.

† Controversiae, ii. 11: Memini me videre Nasonem declamare.—Oratio ejus jam tum nihil aliud poterat videri quam solutum carmen.

‡ Tristia, iv. 10, 25 and 26. # Ex Ponto, ii. 10, 21-30.

∥ —quas quondam petii studiosus, Athenas. Tristia, i. 2, 77.

△ Tristia, iv. 10, 33; ib. ii. 93; Fasti, iv. 384; Tristia, iv. 10, 35-38.

young Romans of his rank were wont to open for themselves a career of statesmanship. But he had no taste for either the labors or the rewards of public life; it was distinctly a case of Horace's *invita Minerva*, quite contrary to the native bent of his mind; and so, never aspiring to the higher offices which would have entitled him to senatorial rank, he readily yielded his will to the gentle persuasions of the Muses,* and gave himself exclusively to their service as a poet.

He was in just opening manhood, when he began to read his poetry in public; so he records it himself in a passage in the Tristia (iv. 10, 57 and 58):

> Carmina cum primum populo juvenilia legi,
> Barba resecta mihi bisve semelve fuit.

He soon won his way into favor as a poet, not only with the people, but also with all his brother-poets then living in Rome, to most of whom he became united by ties of personal as well as of literary companionship. These he mentions in an interesting passage in that poem † in which he tells us so much of his life; some of them, now unknown except in such passages as this, as Macer, Ponticus, Bassus; but others of a world-wide fame, as Horace and Vergil, and especially the three who with himself make now, as they then made, the quartette of Roman elegiac poets, Tibullus, Gallus, and Propertius:

> Successor fuit hic (Tibullus) tibi, Galle; Propertius illi;
> Quartus ab his serie temporis ipse fui.

As the companion and friend of such literary men as these, and also of the chief political characters of the time, and sharing with his brother-poets the favor and

---

* Et petere Aoniae suadebant tuta sorores
  Otia, judicio semper amata meo.—Tristia, iv. 10, 39 and 40.
† Tristia, iv. 10, 41–56.

patronage of the emperor; in possession of a comfortable home near by the Capitol, and a fortune with it, which made him independent, he developed, amid all these fortunate circumstances, a genius distinctively poetic in quality, and also far more productive than that of most of his contemporaries in Roman poetry. Yet the fruitfulness of production and the singular facility which Ovid had as a writer, seem never to have betrayed him into careless composition. On the contrary, the style of no poet in that highly cultivated Roman society, unless it be that of Horace, shows the traces of a more assiduous culture, of more patient toil in the exercise of his art, than that of Ovid in all the various efforts of his Muse.

In respect to the family relations of Ovid, we learn from himself that he was thrice married: first,* when very young, to one whom he describes as "neither worthy nor useful," a union which was a very brief one; the second time † to one who was of blameless character, from whom, however, he was also soon divorced. His third wife was of the noble Fabian family; ‡ and with her the union seems to have been long and happy, their mutual affection continuing through all the many weary years of the husband's exile from country and home. The poet had one daughter, the Perilla to whom he wrote one of the most touching of his Tristia (iii. 7); she was twice married, and was the mother of two children. #

Ovid's life flowed on undisturbed in a current of prosperous fortune till his fifty-first year. Then it was that, when his genius was mature and was yielding its best fruits, there fell upon it, as upon his whole life, a sudden blight, in the order of the emperor, that he

---

* Tristia, iv. 10, 69 and 70.   † Ib. 71 and 72.
‡ Ib. 73 and 74; Ex Ponto, i. 2, 138; ib. ii. 11, 13.
\# Tristia, iv. 10, 75 and 76.

should leave Rome forthwith and for ever, and go into banishment at Tomi, a colony planted among the Getae, on the western shore of the Black Sea. This imperial order was inexorable and ultimate, and had to be instantly obeyed; and the grief it brought to the poet in parting from his wife and daughter, and from all his happy surroundings in the metropolis, is touchingly described in one of his most characteristic elegies.* It was not a formal exile, a Roman *exsilium*, which was always a result either of a judicial sentence or of a decree of the senate; it was a Roman *relegation*, which emanated simply from the emperor's will. Many have been the labored and curious discussions of ingenious writers touching the cause of this relegation; but they have all left it an unsolved problem. In several passages the poet lays the blame of his misfortune upon his poetry. For instance, in the Ex Ponto, iv. 13, 41, he says:

Carmina nil prosunt; *nocuerunt carmina quondam:*
Primaque tam miserae causa fuere fugae.

He refers here to one of his early poems, the "Ars Amatoria," as having brought upon him, by its immoral character, the emperor's displeasure; this he himself makes clear in the Ex Ponto, ii. 10, 15, where he says:

Naso parum prudens, *artem dum tradit amandi,*
Doctrinae pretium triste magister habet;

and he speaks with equal clearness on this head in several passages † of the second book of the Tristia; indeed, the burden of that book is an elaborate defense of that youthful and licentious poem. It were easy to believe that Augustus, who had sent away into hopeless exile, for their profligacy, his only daughter Julia, and his daugh-

---

* Tristia, i. 3.   † Tristia, ii. 211, 240, 345.

ter's daughter, the second Julia, would visit a like punishment upon a poet whose writings might directly minister to such profligacy; but apart from the fact that this poem was published ten years before Ovid's banishment, there are other passages in the poet's writings which clearly show that there was another and probably the direct and chief cause of the emperor's severe displeasure. This cause, of which the poet always speaks in a cautiously reticent tone, he yet insists was no *crime* of his, but rather a blameless *error*. Thus, when addressing the *manes* of his parents in Tristia, iv. 10, 89 and 90, he says:

> Scite, precor, *causam*—nec vos mihi fallere fas est—
> *Errorem* jussae, non *scelus*, esse *fugae*.

In another passage * he couples this cause with the other, which has just been mentioned:

> Perdiderint cum me duo crimina, *carmen et error,*
> Alterius facti *culpa silenda mihi.*

While, however, he does not venture to reveal what this error was, lest he should further displease the emperor,

> Quem nimio plus est indoluisse semel,†

yet he says distinctly in two passages ‡ that it consisted in his having been a witness of *something*, though quite unintentionally, and by mere accident, and that thus *his having had eyes* constituted his only offense. In the first passage his words are these:

> Cur *aliquid* vidi? cur noxia lumina feci?
> Cur *imprudenti* cognita culpa *mihi?*
> Inscius Actaeon vidit sine veste Dianam:
> Praeda fuit canibus non minus ille suis.

---

* Tristia, ii. 207, 208. † Tristia, ii. 210.
‡ Tristia, ii. 103–106; ib. iii. 5, 49 and 50.

And in the other, as follows:

> Inscia quod crimen viderunt lumina, plector:
> *Peccatumque oculos est habuisse meum.*

What that *something* was which *his eyes unwittingly saw*, he nowhere reveals; but in one place* he gives his readers to understand that it was something of a *deadly bad quality:*

> Nec breve nec tutum, *quo* sint mea, dicere, *casu*
> Lumina *funesti* conscia facta *mali.*

What this very evil thing was, it is of course impossible to determine; but there is an air of probability in the conjecture made by several writers, and well put by Professor William Ramsay, that Ovid "had become accidentally acquainted with some of the intrigues of Julia, the granddaughter of the emperor, whose well-known sensibility in all matters affecting the honor of his family rendered him unable to tolerate the presence of a man who had been an eye-witness to the infamy of one of its members." This view is more friendly to the self-love of Augustus than to his sense of justice and right; but if he cared to defend his decree of the poet's banishment, he could readily defend it by the consideration of the immoral influence of Ovid's "Ars Amatoria." But whatever were the grounds on which the poet was punished, it was a punishment greater than he could bear. Imperial power in its most ingenious exercise could hardly have devised a more exquisite penalty than to doom to a dreary existence on the bleak shores of the Euxine, and to companionship with the rude soldiers of a frontier garrison and with the yet ruder barbarian natives, a highly cultivated Roman, who had always lived in the midst of the most polished society of

---

* Tristia, iii. 6, 27 and 28.

the metropolis of the world, where all was congenial to his cherished tastes and pursuits, and where he was loved as a man, and admired and honored as a poet. Yet to this strange solitude into which he was thrust, his genius went with him (as he writes in his poem to his daughter), to be his company and his joy;* over that, he exclaims, even Caesar could have no jurisdiction;

> Ingenio tamen ipse meo comitorque fruorque:
> Caesar in hoc potuit juris habere nihil.

Poetry was now both his chief occupation and his exceeding great reward, though his Muse, whom he gratefully thanks for the rest and solace she gave him,† now with his changed fortune wore only the garb of mourning, and sang in the tones of sad elegy. It is a token of the kindliness of his nature, and of his intellectual activity, that he came to love the people of Tomi,‡ though he hated the place itself; and that he mastered the language of the Getae, and wrote poetry in it. Siebelis, one of the German editors of Ovid, notes the curious fact that Jacob Grimm, who held the Getic and the Gothic race and tongue to be one and the same, speaks of Ovid, in his "History of the German Language," # as the oldest German poet! Of one of these Getic poems Ovid makes mention in his epistle to his friend Carus,∥ a poem written after the death of Augustus, in which he sang the praises of the deceased emperor. Singularly enough, he recited this poem to an assembly of the Getae, and by it stirred to a quite demonstrative admiration the rude na-

---
* Tristia, iii. 7, 47 and 48.
† Tristia, iv. 10, 115–120.
‡ Ex Ponto, iv. 14, 23 and 24:—Tomitae,
   Quos ego, cum loca sim vestra perosus, amo.
Second edition, p. 137.   ∥ Ex Ponto, iv. 13, 19–38.

tures of his barbarian hearers, so that one of them shouted from the crowd: "As you can write such things about Caesar, you ought to have been restored by Caesar's command." The people of Tomi were not slow to recognize and requite the poet's friendly spirit and conduct. They granted him exemption from all taxes or other civic burdens, a favor which Ovid records as done never before to any one else;* and yet more, they honored him with a civic crown,† thus making him, in a sense, their poet-laureate, a strange distinction for a Roman poet to achieve, on that far-off Euxine shore, at the hands of a half-civilized race !

Ovid died at Tomi in the year 18 A. D., in the sixtieth year of his age, and the tenth of his banishment. In an elegy ‡ which he addressed to his wife, he had begged that his ashes might be brought to Rome and there interred, with the following inscription on his tomb :

> Hic ego qui jaceo, tenerorum lusor amorum,
>   Ingenio perii Naso poeta meo.
> At tibi, qui transis, ne sit grave, quisquis amasti
>   Dicere: Nasonis molliter ossa cubent!

Thus it appears from the *tenerorum lusor amorum* in this epitaph—an expression which also occurs in the first line of the autobiography # — that Ovid wished to be known to posterity by his erotic poetry; and yet it was this part of his poetic work which probably wrought the ruin of his fortunes, as it has certainly fixed an indelible stain upon his fame as a writer. It were not just, however, in the absence of evidence from contemporary writers, to infer, from the licentious character of his "Ars Amatoria," the licentious character of the poet. It is fair,

---

* Ex Ponto, iv. 14, 51–54.   † Ib. 55 and 56.
‡ Tristia, iii. 3, 73–76.   # Tristia, iv. 10, 1.

too, to put into the case his own testimony, that he was himself better than his poetry:

> Crede mihi, distant mores a Carmine nostro.
> Vita verecunda est, Musa jocosa mea; *

that *no talk of the town* had ever *made any strictures upon his name:*

> Strinxerit ut nomen fabula nulla meum; †

and that his *character* would be found, *upon inquiry, to be free from blemish:*

> Sive velis, qui sint, *mores inquirere nostros,—*
> Errorem misero detrahe—*labe carent.*‡

But we have to bear in mind that, in putting forth this claim of unblemished morals, the poet is judging himself, as the people of his time would judge him, by the low moral standard which then prevailed in Roman society. He may have been, in his personal life, no worse than most men of his rank and position in Rome; he may have been free from the dominant vices of a dissolute age; but it is an abiding reproach to his fame that, richly gifted and cultivated as he was, and possessed of such a faculty of graceful and finished poetic expression, he allowed himself, like other men of genius in modern as well as in ancient times, to minister by his writings to the low and vicious tastes of his age, when he might have elevated and purified them. But let us not forget that, when he was in his best years, he bade farewell to love-poems; and that his other works, more numerous and of larger compass, and nowise inferior in poetic and literary merit, are not obnoxious to moral censure. We have his "Metamorphoses," that marvelous wonder-book of Roman let-

---

* Tristia, ii. 353 and 354.   † Tristia, ii. 350.
‡ Ex Ponto, iv. 8, 19 and 20.

ters, in which the old myths of Greek and Italic fable were made young again by the creative touch of Ovid's imagination, and enriched by his literary genius with a new and precious wealth of poetical adornment; his "Fasti," in which his patriotic spirit brought his Muse into the service of the religion of his country; and his "Tristia," and the "Epistolae ex Ponto," which, though seldom varying from the monotone of sad complaint over his sufferings in exile, yet reveal fine sensibilities of nature, and especially a tenderness of pathos, which the writer's gay Roman life had never made known. It is such merits as these that won for Ovid as a poet the admiring recognition of his own countrymen, and have made him ever since one of the favorite and most read of the ancient classic writers; so that his own prediction of his fame has been fulfilled:

—in toto plurimus orbe legor.*

To this sketch of our poet's life, I add here a complete list of

THE WORKS OF OVID.

I. AMORES, published probably in the year 9 B. C. This work consists of forty-nine poems in elegiac verse, originally arranged in five books, and afterwards reduced to three, as we learn from the Prologue to the work:

Qui modo Nasonis fueramus quinque libelli,
    Tres sumus. Hoc illi praetulit auctor opus.

II. HEROIDES, a collection of twenty-one letters, also in elegiac verse, purporting to have been written by famous heroines of classic mythology to their absent husbands. Published 4 B. C.

III. ARS AMATORIA, a poem in three books, in the same kind of verse as the two preceding works. The date of the poem is 2 B. C. This was followed in the year 2 B. C. by—

* Tristia, iv. 10, 128.

IV. REMEDIA AMORIS, a poem, consisting of eight hundred and fourteen elegiac verses.

V. METAMORPHOSES, in fifteen books, in dactylic hexameters, forming a collection of those fables of the ancient mythology which involved, as the title indicates, *transformations*, or changes of form. The poet was occupied with this work during the seven years following the publication of his "Remedia Amoris"; and, as we learn from himself,* he had not completed it when he was ordered into exile. In his despair, on receiving this order, he burned † his manuscript of the poem, as well as of some other compositions. But, fortunately, other copies of the "Metamorphoses" had been circulated among his friends, and so the destruction of the work was prevented.

VI. FASTI, in six books of elegiac verse, containing an exposition of the holy days in the Roman calendar, with the rites and ceremonies of the Roman religion pertaining to their observance. The plan of the work was to take up the holy days in succession by months, and to have a book devoted to each month. It was carried out, however, only to the end of June. This work also was unfinished at the time of the poet's banishment, as we learn from Tristia, ii. 549-552.

VII., VIII. These are the TRISTIA, in five books, and the EPISTOLAE EX PONTO, in four books—all in elegiac verse. They are here classed together, because they are the chief works belonging, in their composition and publication, to the period of the poet's exile, and are devoted to themes which all have to do with that event.

IX. IBIS. An elegiac poem in six hundred and forty-six lines, consisting of reproaches against some enemy of the poet, whose name, however, does not appear. It was written immediately after the banishment.

X. HALIEUTICA, a fragment of one hundred and thirty-two lines, in hexameters, of a "Natural History of Fishes."

XI. MEDICAMINA FACIEI, a fragment, in elegiac verse, of a poem on "Cosmetics." Only one hundred lines are extant.

Ovid also wrote a tragedy called "Medea," which is mentioned by Quintilian in terms of praise; but this is not extant.

* Tristia, i. 7, 13 and 14. † Ib. 15 and 16.

VERSIFICATION.

For a general view of the subject of Latin versification, the student is referred to Harkness's Latin Grammar, articles 596-608.

Ovid uses in his poetry two kinds of verse, the dactylic hexameter, and elegiac, verse.

I. The Dactylic Hexameter Verse.

In this verse the "Metamorphoses" are composed. A full account of it is given in the Grammar, 609-613. To that account, which contains all that is necessary for the metrical reading of the "Metamorphoses," I subjoin, from Siebelis,* some curious details touching the technics of Ovid's versification.

1. Words having a dactylic ending suffer elision † when the dactyl occurs in the second and third places in the verse. An apparent exception exists in the word *nescio;* but this always is used by Ovid with *quis* (*nescio quis*), and the two words are treated as a single word.

(1.) Dactyls occur in the second place twelve times, and in the third only five times.

(2.) The following is a view of the number of times in which in the other places the dactyls are elided, and of the number of times in which they occur as pure dactyls:

a. Elided:

First foot.	Fourth foot.	Fifth foot.
68	6	57

b. Pure:

First foot.	Fourth foot.	Fifth foot.
2,535	1,288	5,435

* "Wörterb. zu Ovid's Metamorphosen," von Dr. Johannes Siebelis. 3te Aufl., besorgt von Dr. Fr. Polle. Leipzig, 1879.   † See Gr. 608, I.

VERSIFICATION.

2. From Ovid's aversion to the ecthlipsis,* or elision of a final *m* with the preceding vowel, he does not use words having a dactylic ending in *m*. A single exception to this remark, however, occurs in Metam. vi. 524—virgin^{em} et unam.

As this course on the part of the poet leads him to exclude many words, he resorts to various devices by which to make good such losses:

(1.) In the case of substantives like *terminus*, only *nus* and *ne* are used, and the acc. sing. is not used at all. Here the resort is to synonymes. For instance, *fīlĭŭm* is supplied by such words as *nātum, sătum, prōlem,* and the like.

(2.) For the neuter substantives in *um*—as *Palātĭŭm, vocābŭlŭm*—the plural is used—as *Palātĭă, vocābŭlă*—or the vowel is treated as a consonant; e. g., *i* as *j*—as *Antjum*.

(3.) In such words as *insula*, only this form is used; hence such an unusual expression as *insula* (Marsya) *nomen habet*.

(4.) In adjectives like *horridus*, only *dus, de,* and *da* are employed; hence occur such expressions as *lactea nomen habet*, and *cui fecimus aurea nomen*.

(5.) In such words as *spiritus*, this form only is used. *Impete* also occurs instead of *impetu*.

(6.) The genitive plural of participles in *ns* is used without the *i;* as *dicentum;* so also *agrestum*, and the like.

3. Of the words *abominor, auguror, comprecor, suspicor, glorior, gratulor, pigneror*, only the forms in *or* and *er* are employed.

4. Verse-endings.

The "Metamorphoses" contain 11,959 verses. The words that end the lines occur, as to metrical form, as follows:

⌣	65	times.
– ⌣	7,062	"
⌣ – ⌣	4,788	"
– – ⌣	7	"
⌣ ⌣ – ⌣	8	"
– – – ⌣	27	"
– ⌣ ⌣ – ⌣	2	"
	11,959	"

* See Gr. 608, I., Note 4.

II. THE ELEGIAC VERSE.

This verse Ovid employs in the "Amores," the "Fasti," and the "Tristia." It is called the elegiac distich, and consists of the hexameter, as above, and the pentameter (see Gr. 614), so that a poem composed in elegiac verse consists of alternate hexameters and pentameters.

Ovid shares with Vergil the palm of excellence in the composition of Latin hexameters; and in the composition of elegiac verse he holds the highest rank among Latin poets.

INDEX OF SELECTIONS.

I. METAMORPHOSES.

		PAGE
1.	The Creation. I. 1–88	1
2.	The Four Ages of the World. I. 89–150	4
3.	The Flood. I. 244–312	6
4.	Deucalion and Pyrrha. I. 313–415	8
5.	Python. I. 434–451	12
6.	Daphne. I. 452–567	12
7.	Phaethon. I. 748–779. II. 1–339	16
8.	The Heliades. II. 340–366	28
9.	Cycnus—Grief of Phoebus. II. 367–400	29
10.	The House of Envy. II. 760–796	30
11.	Cadmus and the Dragon's Teeth. III. 14–137	32
12.	Pyramus and Thisbe. IV. 55–166	36
13.	Cadmus and Hermione. IV. 563–603	39
14.	Andromeda's Release. IV. 663–752	41
15.	Proserpine. V. 338–571	44
16.	Arachne, or the Spider's Web. VI. 1–145	52
17.	Niobe, or Latona's Revenge. VI. 146–312	56
18.	The Lycians; and Marsyas. VI. 313–400	62
19.	The Golden Fleece. VII. 1–158	65
20.	The Death of Icarus. VIII. 183–259	70
21.	Philemon and Baucis. VIII. 616–724	73
22.	The Wooing of Deianira. IX. 1–97	76
23.	The Death of Hercules. IX. 134–272	79
24.	Orpheus and Eurydice. X. 1–77	84
25.	Hyacinthus. X. 162–219	87
26.	Atalanta's Race. X. 560–680	89
27.	The Death of Orpheus. XI. 1–84	93

	PAGE
28. MIDAS; OR, THE KING OF THE GOLDEN TOUCH. XI. 85-193	96
29. CEYX AND ALCYONE. XI. 410-748	99
30. THE HOUSE OF FAME. XII. 39-63	110
31. ACIS, GALATEA, AND THE CYCLOPS. XIII. 750-897	111
32. THE EPILOGUE. XV. 871-879	116

II. AMORES.

1. THE POET'S DEFENSE. I. 15	117
2. THE DEATH OF TIBULLUS. III. 9	118
3. FAREWELL TO LOVE-SONGS. III. 15	121

III. FASTI.

1. ROMULUS AND REMUS. II. 383-422	122
2. THE DEIFICATION OF ROMULUS. II. 475-512	123
3. LUCRETIA. II. 710-758	125
4. THE BUILDING OF ROME. IV. 809-862	126

IV. TRISTIA.

1. THE POET'S DEPARTURE FROM ROME. I. 3	129
2. TO HIS DAUGHTER PERILLA. III. 7	132
3. THE POET'S LIFE. IV. 10	134

METAMORPHOSES.

1. THE CREATION.

I. 1-88.

The Proem, 1-4. Chaos, 5-20. The Elements, and living things in them, 21-75. Man, 76-88.

In nova fert animus mutatas dicere formas
Corpora. Di, coeptis—nam vos mutastis et illas—
Aspirate meis, primaque ab origine mundi
Ad mea perpetuum deducite tempora carmen.
   Ante mare et terras et, quod tegit omnia, caelum,   5
Unus erat toto naturae vultus in orbe,
Quem dixere Chaos; rudis indigestaque moles,
Nec quicquam nisi pondus iners, congestaque eodem
Non bene junctarum discordia semina rerum.
Nullus adhuc mundo praebebat lumina Titan,   10
Nec nova crescendo reparabat cornua Phoebe,
Nec circumfuso pendebat in aëre tellus
Ponderibus librata suis, nec bracchia longo
Margine terrarum porrexerat Amphitrite.
Utque erat et tellus illic et pontus et aër,   15
Sic erat instabilis tellus, innabilis unda,
Lucis egens aër: nulli sua forma manebat,

Obstabatque aliis aliud, quia corpore in uno
Frigida pugnabant calidis, umentia siccis,
Mollia cum duris, sine pondere habentia pondus.   20
   Hanc deus et melior litem natura diremit;
Nam caelo terras et terris abscidit undas
Et liquidum spisso secrevit ab aëre caelum.
Quae postquam evolvit caecoque exemit acervo,
Dissociata locis concordi pace ligavit.   25
Ignea convexi vis et sine pondere caeli
Emicuit summaque locum sibi fecit in arce.
Proximus est aër illi levitate locoque;
Densior his tellus, elementaque grandia traxit
Et pressa est gravitate sua: circumfluus umor   30
Ultima possedit solidumque coërcuit orbem.
   Sic ubi dispositam, quisquis fuit ille deorum,
Congeriem secuit sectamque in membra redegit,
Principio terram, ne non aequalis ab omni
Parte foret, magni speciem glomeravit in orbis.   35
Tum freta diffundi rapidisque tumescere ventis
Jussit et ambitae circumdare litora terrae.
Addidit et fontes et stagna immensa lacusque,
Fluminaque obliquis cinxit declivia ripis,
Quae, diversa locis, partim sorbentur ab ipsa,   40
In mare perveniunt partim, campoque recepta
Liberioris aquae pro ripis litora pulsant.
Jussit et extendi campos, subsidere valles,
Fronde tegi silvas, lapidosos surgere montes.
Utque duae dextra caelum totidemque sinistra   45
Parte secant zonae, quinta est ardentior illis;
Sic onus inclusum numero distinxit eodem
Cura dei, totidemque plagae tellure premuntur.
Quarum quae media est, non est habitabilis aestu;

1. THE CREATION.

Nix tegit alta duas : totidem inter utramque locavit, 50
Temperiemque dedit mixta cum frigore flamma.
  Imminet his aër ; qui, quanto est pondere terrae
Pondus aquae levius, tanto est onerosior igni.
Illic et nebulas, illic consistere nubes
Jussit, et humanas motura tonitrua mentes 55
Et cum fulminibus facientes frigora ventos.
His quoque non passim mundi fabricator habendum
Aëra permisit : vix nunc obsistitur illis,
Cum sua quisque regant diverso flamina tractu,
Quin lanient mundum ; tanta est discordia fratrum. 60
Eurus ad auroram Nabataeaque regna recessit
Persidaque et radiis juga subdita matutinis.
Vesper et occiduo quae litora sole tepescunt,
Proxima sunt zephyro : Scythiam septemque trionem
Horrifer invasit boreas : contraria tellus 65
Nubibus assiduis pluvioque madescit ab austro.
Haec super imposuit liquidum et gravitate carentem
Aethera nec quicquam terrenae faecis habentem.
  Vix ita limitibus dissaepserat omnia certis,
Cum, quae pressa diu massa latuere sub illa, 70
Sidera coeperunt toto effervescere caelo.
Neu regio foret ulla suis animantibus orba,
Astra tenent caeleste solum formaeque deorum,
Cesserunt nitidis habitandae piscibus undae,
Terra feras cepit, volucres agitabilis aër. 75
  Sanctius his animal mentisque capacius altae
Deerat adhuc, et quod dominari in cetera posset.
Natus homo est : sive hunc divino semine fecit
Ille opifex rerum, mundi melioris origo,
Sive recens tellus seductaque nuper ab alto 80
Aethere cognati retinebat semina caeli ;

Quam satus Iapeto, mixtam fluvialibus undis,
Finxit in effigiem moderantum cuncta deorum.
Pronaque cum spectent animalia cetera terram,
Os homini sublime dedit, caelumque videre 85
Jussit et erectos ad sidera tollere vultus.
Sic, modo quae fuerat rudis et sine imagine, tellus
Induit ignotas hominum conversa figuras.

2. The Four Ages.
I. 89-150.

Aurea prima sata est aetas, quae vindice nullo,
Sponte sua, sine lege fidem rectumque colebat. 90
Poena metusque aberant, nec verba minacia fixo
Aere legebantur, nec supplex turba timebat
Judicis ora sui, sed erant sine judice tuti.
Nondum caesa suis, peregrinum ut viseret orbem,
Montibus in liquidas pinus descenderat undas, 95
Nullaque mortales praeter sua litora norant.
Nondum praecipites cingebant oppida fossae;
Non tuba directi, non aeris cornua flexi,
Non galeae, non ensis erant: sine militis usu
Mollia securae peragebant otia gentes. 100
Ipsa quoque immunis rastroque intacta nec ullis
Saucia vomeribus per se dabat omnia tellus;
Contentique cibis nullo cogente creatis
Arbuteos fetus montanaque fraga legebant,
Cornaque et in duris haerentia mora rubetis, 105
Et quae deciderant patula Jovis arbore glandes.
Ver erat aeternum, placidique tepentibus auris
Mulcebant zephyri natos sine semine flores.
Mox etiam fruges tellus inarata ferebat,

2. THE FOUR AGES.

Nec renovatus ager gravidis canebat aristis : 110
Flumina jam lactis, jam flumina nectaris ibant,
Flavaque de viridi stillabant ilice mella.
   Postquam Saturno tenebrosa in Tartara misso
Sub Jove mundus erat, subiit argentea proles,
Auro deterior, fulvo pretiosior aere. 115
Juppiter antiqui contraxit tempora veris,
Perque hiemes aestusque et inaequales autumnos
Et breve ver spatiis exegit quattuor annum.
Tum primum siccis aër fervoribus ustus
Canduit, et ventis glacies astricta pependit. 120
Tum primum subiere domus. Domus antra fuerunt
Et densi frutices et vinctae cortice virgae.
Semina tum primum longis Cerealia sulcis
Obruta sunt, pressique jugo gemuere juvenci.
   Tertia post illam successit aënea proles, 125
Saevior ingeniis et ad horrida promptior arma,
Non scelerata tamen. De duro est ultima ferro.
Protinus irrupit venae pejoris in aevum
Omne nefas : fugere pudor verumque fidesque ;
In quorum subiere locum fraudesque dolique 130
Insidiaeque et vis et amor sceleratus habendi.
Vela dabant ventis, nec adhuc bene noverat illos
Navita ; quaeque diu steterant in montibus altis,
Fluctibus ignotis insultavere carinae.
Communemque prius ceu lumina solis et auras 135
Cautus humum longo signavit limite mensor.
Nec tantum segetes alimentaque debita dives
Poscebatur humus, sed itum est in viscera terrae,
Quasque recondiderat Stygiisque admoverat umbris,
Effodiuntur opes, irritamenta malorum. 140
   Jamque nocens ferrum ferroque nocentius aurum

Prodierat: prodit bellum, quod pugnat utroque,
Sanguineaque manu crepitantia concutit arma.
Vivitur ex rapto; non hospes ab hospite tutus,
Non socer a genero; fratrum quoque gratia rara est;
Imminet exitio vir conjugis, illa mariti;
Lurida terribiles miscent aconita novercae;
Filius ante diem patrios inquirit in annos.
Victa jacet pietas, et Virgo caede madentes,
Ultima caelestum, terras Astraea reliquit. 150

3. The Flood.

I. 244-312.

Dicta Jovis pars voce probant stimulosque frementi
Adiciunt, alii partes assensibus implent. 245
Est tamen humani generis jactura dolori
Omnibus, et, quae sit terrae mortalibus orbae
Forma futura, rogant: quis sit laturus in aras
Tura, ferisne paret populandas tradere terras.
Talia quaerentes, sibi enim fore cetera curae, 250
Rex superum trepidare vetat, subolemque priori
Dissimilem populo promittit origine mira.
  Jamque erat in totas sparsurus fulmina terras:
Sed timuit, ne forte sacer tot ab ignibus aether
Conciperet flammas, longusque ardesceret axis. 255
Esse quoque in fatis reminiscitur, adfore tempus,
Quo mare, quo tellus correptaque regia caeli
Ardeat et mundi moles operosa laboret.
Tela reponuntur manibus fabricata Cyclopum.
Poena placet diversa, genus mortale sub undis 260
Perdere et ex omni nimbos demittere caelo.
  Protinus Aeoliis Aquilonem claudit in antris

3. THE FLOOD.

Et quaecumque fugant inductas flamina nubes,
Emittitque Notum. Madidis Notus evolat alis,
Terribilem picea tectus caligine vultum: 265
Barba gravis nimbis, canis fluit unda capillis,
Fronte sedent nebulae, rorant pennaeque sinusque.
Utque manu late pendentia nubila pressit,
Fit fragor, inclusi funduntur ab aethere nimbi.
Nuntia Junonis, varios induta colores, 270
Concipit Iris aquas, alimentaque nubibus adfert.
Sternuntur segetes, et deplorata coloni
Vota jacent, longique perit labor irritus anni.
  Nec caelo contenta suo est Jovis ira, sed illum
Caeruleus frater juvat auxiliaribus undis. 275
Convocat hic Amnes. Qui postquam tecta tyranni
Intravere sui, "Non est hortamine longo
Nunc" ait "utendum. Vires effundite vestras,
Sic opus est. Aperite domos, ac mole remota
Fluminibus vestris totas immittite habenas." 280
Jusserat. Hi redeunt, ac fontibus ora relaxant,
Et defrenato volvuntur in aequora cursu.
Ipse tridente suo terram percussit; at illa
Intremuit motuque vias patefecit aquarum.
Exspatiata ruunt per apertos flumina campos, 285
Cumque satis arbusta simul pecudesque virosque
Tectaque, cumque suis rapiunt penetralia sacris.
Siqua domus mansit potuitque resistere tanto
Indejecta malo, culmen tamen altior hujus
Unda tegit, pressaeque latent sub gurgite turres. 290
  Jamque mare et tellus nullum discrimen habebant:
Omnia pontus erant. Deerant quoque litora ponto.
Occupat hic collem: cumba sedet alter adunca
Et ducit remos illic ubi nuper ararat;

Ille super segetes aut mersae culmina villae 295
Navigat, hic summa piscem deprendit in ulmo ;
Figitur in viridi, si fors tulit, ancora prato,
Aut subjecta terunt curvae vineta carinae.
Et, modo qua graciles gramen carpsere capellae,
Nunc ibi deformes ponunt sua corpora phocae. 300
Mirantur sub aqua lucos urbesque domosque
Nereïdes, silvasque tenent delphines, et altis
Incursant ramis, agitataque robora pulsant.
Nat lupus inter oves, fulvos vehit unda leones,
Unda vehit tigres, nec vires fulminis apro, 305
Crura nec ablato prosunt velocia cervo.
Quaesitisque diu terris, ubi sistere detur,
In mare lassatis volucris vaga decidit alis.
Obruerat tumulos immensa licentia ponti,
Pulsabantque novi montana cacumina fluctus. 310
Maxima pars unda rapitur : quibus unda pepercit,
Illos longa domant inopi jejunia victu.

4. Deucalion and Pyrrha.

I. 313–415.

Separat Aonios Oetaeis Phocis ab arvis,
Terra ferax, dum terra fuit : sed tempore in illo
Pars maris et latus subitarum campus aquarum. 315
Mons ibi verticibus petit arduus astra duobus,
Nomine Parnasus, superantque cacumina nubes.
Hic ubi Deucalion, nam cetera texerat aequor,
Cum consorte tori parva rate vectus adhaesit,
Corycidas nymphas et numina montis adorant, 320
Fatidicamque Themin, quae tunc oracla tenebat.

4. DEUCALION AND PYRRHA.

Non illo melior quisquam nec amantior aequi
Vir fuit, aut illa metuentior ulla deorum.
  Juppiter ut liquidis stagnare paludibus orbem,
Et superesse virum de tot modo milibus unum,   325
Et superesse videt de tot modo milibus unam,
Innocuos ambos, cultores numinis ambos,
Nubila disjecit, nimbisque aquilone remotis
Et caelo terras ostendit et aethera terris.
Nec maris ira manet, positoque tricuspide telo   330
Mulcet aquas rector pelagi, supraque profundum
Exstantem atque umeros innato murice tectum
Caeruleum Tritona vocat, conchaeque sonanti
Inspirare jubet, fluctusque et flumina signo
Jam revocare dato. Cava bucina sumitur illi   335
Tortilis, in latum quae turbine crescit ab imo,
Bucina, quae, medio concepit ubi aëra ponto,
Litora voce replet sub utroque jacentia Phoebo.
Tunc quoque, ut ora dei madida rorantia barba
Contigit, et cecinit jussos inflata receptus,   340
Omnibus audita est telluris et aequoris undis,
Et quibus est undis audita, coërcuit omnes.
Flumina subsidunt, collesque exire videntur:
Jam mare litus habet, plenos capit alveus amnes,
Surgit humus; crescunt loca decrescentibus undis.   345
Postque diem longam nudata cacumina silvae
Ostendunt, limumque tenent in fronde relictum.
  Redditus orbis erat. Quem postquam vidit inanem
Et desolatas agere alta silentia terras,
Deucalion lacrimis ita Pyrrham adfatur obortis: 350
"O soror, o conjunx, o femina sola superstes,
Quam commune mihi genus et patruelis origo,
Deinde torus junxit, nunc ipsa pericula jungunt:

Terrarum, quascumque vident occasus et ortus,
Nos duo turba sumus: possedit cetera pontus. 355
Haec quoque adhuc vitae non est fiducia nostrae
Certa satis; terrent etiamnunc nubila mentem.
Quid tibi, si sine me fatis erepta fuisses,
Nunc animi, miseranda, foret? quo sola timorem
Ferre modo posses? quo consolante doleres? 360
Namque ego, crede mihi, si te quoque pontus haberet,
Te sequerer, conjunx, et me quoque pontus haberet.
O utinam possem populos reparare paternis
Artibus atque animas formatae infundere terrae!
Nunc genus in nobis restat mortale duobus; 365
Sic visum est superis: hominumque exempla manemus."
  Dixerat, et flebant. Placuit caeleste precari
Numen, et auxilium per sacras quaerere sortes.
Nulla mora est, adeunt pariter Cephisidas undas,
Ut nondum liquidas, sic jam vada nota secantes. 370
Inde ubi libatos irroravere liquores
Vestibus et capiti, flectunt vestigia sanctae
Ad delubra deae, quorum fastigia turpi
Pallebant musco stabantque sine ignibus arae.
Ut templi tetigere gradus, procumbit uterque 375
Pronus humi, gelidoque pavens dedit oscula saxo.
Atque ita "Si precibus" dixerunt "numina justis
Victa remollescunt, si flectitur ira deorum,
Dic, Themi, qua generis damnum reparabile nostri
Arte sit, et mersis fer opem, mitissima, rebus." 380
  Mota dea est sortemque dedit: "Discedite templo,
Et velate caput, cinctasque resolvite vestes,
Ossaque post tergum magnae jactate parentis."
  Obstipuere diu, rumpitque silentia voce
Pyrrha prior, jussisque deae parere recusat, 385

4. DEUCALION AND PYRRHA.

Detque sibi veniam, pavido rogat ore, pavetque
Laedere jactatis maternas ossibus umbras.
Interea repetunt caecis obscura latebris
Verba datae sortis secum, inter seque volutant:
Inde Promethides placidis Epimethida dictis 390
Mulcet et " Aut fallax " ait " est sollertia nobis,
Aut pia sunt nullumque nefas oracula suadent.
Magna parens terra est: lapides in corpore terrae
Ossa reor dici: jacere hos post terga jubemur."
Conjugis augurio quamquam Titania mota est, 395
Spes tamen in dubio est: adeo caelestibus ambo
Diffidunt monitis. Sed quid temptare nocebit?
Descendunt velantque caput tunicasque recingunt
Et jussos lapides sua post vestigia mittunt.
Saxa—quis hoc credat, nisi sit pro teste vetustas?— 400
Ponere duritiem coepere suumque rigorem,
Mollirique mora, mollitaque ducere formam.
Mox ubi creverunt, naturaque mitior illis
Contigit, ut quaedam, sic non manifesta, videri
Forma potest hominis, sed uti de marmore coepto, 405
Non exacta satis rudibusque simillima signis.
Quae tamen ex illis aliquo pars umida suco
Et terrena fuit, versa est in corporis usum:
Quod solidum est flectique nequit, mutatur in ossa;
Quae modo vena fuit, sub eodem nomine mansit: 410
Inque brevi spatio superorum numine saxa
Missa viri manibus faciem traxere virorum,
Et de femineo reparata est femina jactu.
Inde genus durum sumus experiensque laborum,
Et documenta damus, qua simus origine nati. 415

5. Python.

I. 434–451.

Ergo ubi diluvio tellus lutulenta recenti
Solibus aetheriis almoque recanduit aestu,   435
Edidit innumeras species, partimque figuras
Rettulit antiquas, partim nova monstra creavit.
Illa quidem nollet, sed te quoque, maxime Python,
Tum genuit, populisque novis, incognite serpens,
Terror eras; tantum spatii de monte tenebas.   440
Hunc deus arcitenens, et nunquam talibus armis
Ante nisi in dammis capreisque fugacibus usus,
Mille gravem telis, exhausta paene pharetra,
Perdidit effuso per vulnera nigra veneno.
Neve operis famam possit delere vetustas,   445
Instituit sacros celebri certamine ludos,
Pythia perdomitae serpentis nomine dictos.
His juvenum quicumque manu pedibusve rotave
Vicerat, aesculeae capiebat frondis honorem.
Nondum laurus erat, longoque decentia crine   450
Tempora cingebat de qualibet arbore Phoebus.

6. Daphne.

I. 452–567.

Daphne, the daughter of the river-god Peneus, having rejected Apollo's love, is changed by him into a bay-tree.

Primus amor Phoebi Daphne Peneïa, quem non
Fors ignara dedit, sed saeva Cupidinis ira.
Delius hunc nuper, victo serpente superbus,
Viderat adducto flectentem cornua nervo,   455

6. DAPHNE.

"Quid" que "tibi, lascive puer, cum fortibus armis?"
Dixerat; "ista decent umeros gestamina nostros,
Qui dare certa ferae, dare vulnera possumus hosti,
Qui modo pestifero tot jugera ventre prementem
Stravimus innumeris tumidum Pythona sagittis.   460
Tu face nescio quos esto contentus amores
Indagare tua, nec laudes assere nostras."
Filius huic Veneris "Figat tuus omnia, Phoebe,
Te meus arcus;" ait "quantoque animalia cedunt
Cuncta deo, tanto minor est tua gloria nostra."   465
Dixit, et eliso percussis aëre pennis
Impiger umbrosa Parnasi constitit arce
Eque sagittifera prompsit duo tela pharetra
Diversorum operum; fugat hoc, facit illud amorem.
Quod facit, auratum est et cuspide fulget acuta: 470
Quod fugat, obtusum est et habet sub harundine plumbum.
Hoc deus in nympha Peneïde fixit; at illo
Laesit Apollineas trajecta per ossa medullas.
Protinus alter amat; fugit altera nomen amantis,
Silvarum tenebris captivarumque ferarum   475
Exuviis gaudens innuptaeque aemula Phoebes.
Vitta coercebat positos sine lege capillos.
Multi illam petiere, illa aversata petentes
Impatiens expersque viri nemorum avia lustrat,
Nec quid Hymen, quid Amor, quid sint conubia, curat.
Saepe pater dixit "Generum mihi, filia, debes."
Saepe pater dixit "Debes mihi, nata, nepotes."
Illa, velut crimen taedas exosa jugales
Pulchra verecundo suffunditur ora rubore,
Inque patris blandis haerens cervice lacertis   485
"Da mihi perpetua, genitor carissime," dixit
"Virginitate frui: dedit hoc pater ante Dianae."

Ille quidem obsequitur, sed te decor iste quod optas
Esse vetat, votoque tuo tua forma repugnat.
Phoebus amat, visaeque cupit conubia Daphnes, 490
Quodque cupit, sperat; suaque illum oracula fallunt.
Utque leves stipulae demptis adolentur aristis,
Ut facibus saepes ardent, quas forte viator
Vel nimis admovit, vel jam sub luce reliquit,
Sic deus in flammas abiit, sic pectore toto 495
Uritur et sterilem sperando nutrit amorem.
Spectat inornatos collo pendere capillos,
Et "Quid, si comantur?" ait. Videt igne micantes
Sideribus similes oculos, videt oscula, quae non
Est vidisse satis; laudat digitosque manusque 500
Bracchiaque et nudos media plus parte lacertos:
Siqua latent, meliora putat. Fugit ocior aura
Illa levi, neque ad haec revocantis verba resistit:
"Nympha, precor, Peneï, mane! non insequor hostis:
Nympha, mane! sic agna lupum, sic cerva leonem, 505
Sic aquilam penna fugiunt trepidante columbae,
Hostes quaeque suos; amor est mihi causa sequendi.
Me miserum! ne prona cadas, indignave laedi
Crura notent sentes, et sim tibi causa doloris.
Aspera, qua properas, loca sunt; moderatius, oro, 510
Curre, fugamque inhibe; moderatius insequar ipse.
Cui placeas, inquire tamen; non incola montis,
Non ego sum pastor, non hic armenta gregesque
Horridus observo. Nescis, temeraria, nescis,
Quem fugias, ideoque fugis. Mihi Delphica tellus 515
Et Claros et Tenedos Patareaque regia servit.
Juppiter est genitor: per me quod eritque fuitque
Estque, patet: per me concordant carmina nervis.
Certa quidem nostra est, nostra tamen una sagitta

6. DAPHNE.

Certior, in vacuo quae vulnera pectore fecit. 520
Inventum medicina meum est, opiferque per orbem
Dicor, et herbarum subjecta potentia nobis.
Ei mihi, quod nullis amor est sanabilis herbis,
Nec prosunt domino, quae prosunt omnibus, artes!"
Plura locuturum timido Peneïa cursu 525
Fugit cumque ipso verba imperfecta reliquit,
Tum quoque visa decens. Nudabant corpora venti,
Obviaque adversas vibrabant flamina vestes,
Et levis impulsos retro dabat aura capillos;
Auctaque forma fuga est. Sed enim non sustinet ultra
Perdere blanditias juvenis deus, utque movebat
Ipse amor, admisso sequitur vestigia passu.
Ut canis in vacuo leporem cum Gallicus arvo
Vidit, et hic praedam pedibus petit, ille salutem;
Alter inhaesuro similis jam jamque tenere 535
Sperat, et extento stringit vestigia rostro:
Alter in ambiguo est, an sit comprensus, et ipsis
Morsibus eripitur tangentiaque ora relinquit:
Sic deus et virgo, est hic spe celer, illa timore.
Qui tamen insequitur, pennis adjutus amoris 540
Ocior est requiemque negat tergoque fugacis
Imminet et crinem sparsum cervicibus adflat.
Viribus absumptis expalluit illa, citaeque
Victa labore fugae, spectans Peneïdas undas, 544
"Fer, pater," inquit "opem, si flumina numen habetis!
Qua nimium placui, mutando perde figuram!" 547
Vix prece finita, torpor gravis occupat artus,
Mollia cinguntur tenui praecordia libro,
In frondem crines, in ramos bracchia crescunt: 550
Pes, modo tam velox, pigris radicibus haeret,
Ora cacumen obit. Remanet nitor unus in illa.

Hanc quoque Phoebus amat, positaque in stipite dextra
Sentit adhuc trepidare novo sub cortice pectus,
Complexusque suis ramos, ut membra, lacertis 555
Oscula dat ligno: refugit tamen oscula lignum.
Cui deus " at quoniam conjunx mea non potes esse,
Arbor eris certe" dixit " mea. Semper habebunt
Te coma, te citharae, te nostrae, laure, pharetrae.
Tu ducibus Latiis aderis, cum laeta Triumphum 560
Vox canet et visent longas Capitolia pompas.
Postibus Augustis eadem fidissima custos
Ante fores stabis, mediamque tuebere quercum.
Utque meum intonsis caput est juvenale capillis,
Tu quoque perpetuos semper gere frondis honores." 565
Finierat Paean. Factis modo laurea ramis
Adnuit, utque caput visa est agitasse cacumen.

7. Phaethon.

I. 748–779. II. 1–339.

"When drove, so poets sing, the Sun-born youth,
Devious through Heaven's affrighted signs his sire's
Ill-granted chariot."—Milman's " Samor."

Huic Epaphus magni genitus de semine tandem
Creditur esse Jovis, perque urbes juncta parenti
Templa tenet. Fuit huic animis aequalis et annis 750
Sole satus Phaëthon. Quem quondam magna loquentem
Nec sibi cedentem Phoeboque parente superbum
Non tulit Inachides, " matri" que ait " omnia demens
Credis, et es tumidus genitoris imagine falsi."
Erubuit Phaëthon, iramque pudore repressit, 755
Et tulit ad Clymenen Epaphi convicia matrem:
"Quoque magis doleas, genetrix," ait "ille ego liber,

Ille ferox tacui. Pudet haec opprobria nobis
Et dici potuisse et non potuisse refelli.
At tu, si modo sum caelesti stirpe creatus,   760
Ede notam tanti generis, meque assere caelo."
Dixit et implicuit materno bracchia collo,
Perque suum Meropisque caput taedasque sororum,
Traderet, oravit, veri sibi signa parentis.
    Ambiguum, Clymene, precibus Phaëthontis, an ira 765
Mota magis dicti sibi criminis, utraque caelo
Bracchia porrexit, spectansque ad lumina solis
"Per jubar hoc" inquit "radiis insigne coruscis,
Nate, tibi juro, quod nos auditque videtque,
Hoc te, quem spectas, hoc te, qui temperat orbem,   770
Sole satum. Si ficta loquor, neget ipse videndum
Se mihi, sitque oculis lux ista novissima nostris.
Nec longus patrios labor est tibi nosse penates.
Unde oritur, domus est terrae contermina nostrae.
Si modo fert animus, gradere, et scitabere ab ipso."   775
    Emicat extemplo laetus post talia matris
Dicta suae Phaëthon et concipit aethera mente,
Aethiopasque suos positosque sub ignibus Indos
Sidereis transit patriosque adit impiger ortus.

Regia Solis erat sublimibus alta columnis,
Clara micante auro flammasque imitante pyropo;
Cujus ebur nitidum fastigia summa tegebat,
Argenti bifores radiabant lumine valvae.
Materiam superabat opus. Nam Mulciber illic   5
Aequora caelarat medias cingentia terras
Terrarumque orbem caelumque, quod imminet orbi.
Caeruleos habet unda deos, Tritona cănorum,

Proteaque ambiguum, ballaenarumque prementem
Aegaeona suis immania terga lacertis, 10
Doridaque et natas, quarum pars nare videtur,
Pars in mole sedens virides siccare capillos,
Pisce vehi quaedam; facies non omnibus una,
Nec diversa tamen; qualem decet esse sororum.
Terra viros urbesque gerit silvasque ferasque 15
Fluminaque et nymphas et cetera numina ruris.
Haec super imposita est caeli fulgentis imago,
Signaque sex foribus dextris, totidemque sinistris.
  Quo simul acclivo Clymeneïa limite proles
Venit et intravit dubitati tecta parentis, 20
Protinus ad patrios sua fert vestigia vultus
Consistitque procul: neque enim propiora ferebat
Lumina. Purpurea velatus veste sedebat
In solio Phoebus claris lucente smaragdis.
A dextra laevaque Dies et Mensis et Annus 25
Saeculaque et positae spatiis aequalibus Horae
Verque novum stabat cinctum florente corona,
Stabat nuda Aestas et spicea serta gerebat,
Stabat et Autumnus, calcatis sordidus uvis,
Et glacialis Hiems, canos hirsuta capillos. 30
Inde loco medius rerum novitate paventem
Sol oculis juvenem, quibus aspicit omnia, vidit,
"Quae" que "viae tibi causa? quid hac" ait "arce petisti,
Progenies, Phaëthon, haud infitianda parenti?"
  Ille refert: "o lux immensi publica mundi, 35
Phoebe pater, si das hujus mihi nominis usum,
Nec falsa Clymene culpam sub imagine celat,
Pignora da, genitor, per quae tua vera propago
Credar, et hunc animis errorem detrahe nostris."
  Dixerat. At genitor circum caput omne micantes 40

7. PHAETHON.

Deposuit radios, propiusque accedere jussit,
Amplexuque dato, "nec tu meus esse negari
Dignus es, et Clymene veros" ait "edidit ortus.
Quoque minus dubites, quodvis pete munus, ut illud
Me tribuente feras. Promissi testis adesto   45
Dis juranda palus, oculis incognita nostris."
 Vix bene desierat, currus rogat ille paternos
Inque diem alipedum jus et moderamen equorum.
 Paenituit jurasse patrem. Qui terque quaterque
Concutiens illustre caput, "temeraria" dixit   50
"Vox mea facta tua est. Utinam promissa liceret
Non dare! confiteor, solum hoc tibi, nate, negarem.
Dissuadere licet. Non est tua tuta voluntas.
Magna petis, Phaëthon, et quae nec viribus istis
Munera conveniant nec tam puerilibus annis.   55
Sors tua mortalis. Non est mortale, quod optas.
Plus etiam, quam quod superis contingere fas est,
Nescius adfectas. Placeat sibi quisque licebit,
Non tamen ignifero quisquam consistere in axe
Me valet excepto. Vasti quoque rector Olympi,   60
Qui fera terribili jaculatur fulmina dextra,
Non agat hos currus. Et quid Jove majus habemus?
Ardua prima via est et qua vix mane recentes
Enitantur equi. Medio est altissima caelo,
Unde mare et terras ipsi mihi saepe videre   65
Fit timor, et pavida trepidat formidine pectus.
Ultima prona via est, et eget moderamine certo:
Tunc etiam, quae me subjectis excipit undis,
Ne ferar in praeceps, Tethys solet ipsa vereri.
Adde quod assidua rapitur vertigine caelum,   70
Sideraque alta trahit, celerique volumine torquet.
Nitor in adversum, nec me qui cetera, vincit

Impetus, et rapido contrarius evehor orbi.
Finge datos currus: quid ages? poterisne rotatis
Obvius ire polis, ne te citus auferat axis? 75
Forsitan et lucos illic urbesque deorum
Concipias animo, delubraque ditia donis
Esse? per insidias iter est formasque ferarum.
Utque viam teneas, nulloque errore traharis,
Per tamen adversi gradieris cornua Tauri, 80
Haemoniosque arcus violentique ora Leonis,
Saevaque circuitu curvantem bracchia longo
Scorpion, atque aliter curvantem bracchia Cancrum.
Nec tibi quadrupedes animosos ignibus illis,
Quos in pectore habent, quos ore et naribus efflant, 85
In promptu regere est. Vix me patiuntur, ubi acres
Incaluere animi, cervixque repugnat habenis.
At tu, funesti ne sim tibi muneris auctor,
Nate, cave, dum resque sinit, tua corrige vota.
Scilicet ut nostro genitum te sanguine credas, 90
Pignora certa petis? do pignora certa timendo,
Et patrio pater esse metu probor. Aspice vultus
Ecce meos. Utinamque oculos in pectora posses
Inserere, et patrias intus deprendere curas!
Denique quicquid habet dives, circumspice, mundus, 95
Eque tot ac tantis caeli terraeque marisque
Posce bonis aliquid. Nullam patiere repulsam.
Deprecor hoc unum, quod vero nomine poena,
Non honor est. Poenam, Phaëthon, pro munere poscis.
Quid mea colla tenes blandis, ignare, lacertis? 100
Ne dubita, dabitur—Stygias juravimus undas!—
Quodcumque optaris; sed tu sapientius opta."

Finierat monitus; dictis tamen ille repugnat,
Propositumque premit, flagratque cupidine currus.

Ergo qua licuit, genitor cunctatus, ad altos 105
Deducit juvenem, Vulcania munera, currus.
Aureus axis erat, temo aureus, aurea summae
Curvatura rotae, radiorum argenteus ordo.
Per juga chrysolithi positaeque ex ordine gemmae
Clara repercusso reddebant lumina Phoebo. 110
Dumque ea magnanimus Phaëthon miratur, opusque
Perspicit, ecce vigil rutilo patefecit ab ortu
Purpureas Aurora fores et plena rosarum
Atria. Diffugiunt stellae, quarum agmina cogit
Lucifer, et caeli statione novissimus exit. 115
Quem petere ut terras mundumque rubescere vidit,
Cornuaque extremae velut evanescere lunae,
Jungere equos Titan velocibus imperat Horis.
Jussa deae celeres peragunt, ignemque vomentes
Ambrosiae suco saturos praesepibus altis 120
Quadrupedes ducunt, adduntque sonantia frena.
Tum pater ora sui sacro medicamine nati
Contigit, et rapidae fecit patientia flammae,
Imposuitque comae radios, praesagaque luctus
Pectore sollicito repetens suspiria dixit: 125
 "Si potes his saltem monitis parere paternis,
Parce, puer, stimulis, et fortius utere loris.
Sponte sua properant: labor est inhibere volentes.
Nec tibi directos placeat via quinque per arcus:
Sectus in obliquum est lato curvamine limes, 130
Zonarumque trium contentus fine, polumque
Effugit australem, junctamque aquilonibus Arcton.
Hac sit iter. Manifesta rotae vestigia cernes.
Utque ferant aequos et caelum et terra calores,
Nec preme, nec summum molire per aethera cursum.
Altius egressus caelestia tecta cremabis,

Inferius terras : medio tutissimus ibis.
Neu te dexterior tortum declinet ad Anguem,
Neve sinisterior pressam rota ducat ad Aram :
Inter utrumque tene. Fortunae cetera mando,. 140
Quae juvet et melius quam tu tibi, consulat opto.
Dum loquor, Hesperio positas in litore metas
Umida nox tetigit ; non est mora libera nobis :
Poscimur : effulget tenebris aurora fugatis.
Corripe lora manu, vel, si mutabile pectus 145
Est tibi, consiliis, non curribus utere nostris,
Dum potes, et solidis etiamnunc sedibus adstas,
Dumque male optatos nondum premis inscius axes.
Quae tutus spectes, sine me dare lumina terris ! "
    Occupat ille levem juvenali corpore currum, 150
Statque super, manibusque datas contingere habenas
Gaudet, et invito grates agit inde parenti.
Interea volucres Pyrois et Eous et Aethon,
Solis equi, quartusque Phlegon, hinnitibus auras
Flammiferis implent, pedibusque repagula pulsant. 155
Quae postquam Tethys, fatorum ignara nepotis,
Reppulit, et facta est immensi copia mundi,
Corripuere viam, pedibusque per aëra motis
Obstantes scindunt nebulas, pennisque levati
Praetereunt ortos isdem de partibus Euros. 160
    Sed leve pondus erat, nec quod cognoscere possent
Solis equi, solitaque jugum gravitate carebat.
Utque labant curvae justo sine pondere naves,
Perque mare instabiles nimia levitate feruntur,
Sic onere assueto vacuus dat in aëra saltus .. 165
Succutiturque alte, similisque est currus inani.
Quod simulac sensere, ruunt tritumque relinquunt
Quadrijugi spatium, nec, quo prius, ordine currunt.

7. PHAETHON.

Ipse pavet, nec qua commissas flectat habenas,
Nec scit, qua sit iter; nec, si sciat, imperet illis.   170
Tum primum radiis gelidi caluere Triones,
Et vetito frustra temptarunt aequore tingui;
Quaeque polo posita est glaciali proxima Serpens,
Frigore pigra prius, nec formidabilis ulli,
Incaluit sumpsitque novas fervoribus iras.   175
Te quoque turbatum memorant fugisse, Boote,
Quamvis tardus eras, et te tua plaustra tenebant.

   Ut vero summo despexit ab aethere terras
Infelix Phaëthon penitus penitusque jacentes,
Palluit, et subito genua intremuere timore,   180
Suntque oculis tenebrae per tantum lumen obortae.
Et jam mallet equos nunquam tetigisse paternos,
Jam cognosse genus piget, et valuisse rogando;
Jam Meropis dici cupiens ita fertur, ut acta
Praecipiti pinus borea, cui victa remisit   185
Frena suus rector, quam dis votisque reliquit.
Quid faciat? multum caeli post terga relictum,
Ante oculos plus est: animo metitur utrumque.
Et modo quos illi fatum contingere non est,
Prospicit occasus, interdum respicit ortus.   190
Quidque agat, ignarus stupet, et nec frena remittit,
Nec retinere valet, nec nomina novit equorum.
Sparsa quoque in vario passim miracula caelo
Vastarumque videt trepidus simulacra ferarum.

   Est locus, in geminos ubi bracchia concavat arcus 195
Scorpius, et cauda flexisque utrimque lacertis
Porrigit in spatium signorum membra duorum.
Hunc puer ut nigri madidum sudore veneni
Vulnera curvata minitantem cuspide vidit,
Mentis inops gelida formidine lora remisit.   200

Quae postquam summo tetigere jacentia tergo,
Exspatiantur equi, nulloque inhibente per auras
Ignotae regionis eunt, quaque impetus egit,
Hac sine lege ruunt, altoque sub aethere fixis
Incursant stellis, rapiuntque per avia currum.   205
Et modo summa petunt, modo per declive viasque
Praecipites spatio terrae propiore feruntur.
Inferiusque suis fraternos currere Luna
Admiratur equos, ambustaque nubila fumant.
   Corripitur flammis, ut quaeque altissima, tellus,   210
Fissaque agit rimas, et sucis aret ademptis.
Pabula canescunt, cum frondibus uritur arbor,
Materiamque suo praebet seges arida damno.
Parva queror: magnae pereunt cum moenibus urbes,
Cumque suis totas populis incendia gentes   215
In cinerem vertunt. Silvae cum montibus ardent,
Ardet Athos Taurusque Cilix et Tmolus et Oete,
Et tum sicca, prius creberrima fontibus, Ide,
Virgineusque Helicon et nondum Oeagrius Haemos.
Ardet in immensum geminatis ignibus Aetne,   220
Parnasusque biceps, et Eryx et Cynthus et Othrys,
Et tandem nivibus Rhodope caritura, Mimasque
Dindymaque et Mycale natusque ad sacra Cithaeron.
Nec prosunt Scythiae sua frigora: Caucasus ardet,
Ossaque cum Pindo majorque ambobus Olympus,   225
Aëriaeque Alpes, et nubifer Appenninus.
   Tum vero Phaëthon cunctis e partibus orbem
Aspicit accensum, nec tantos sustinet aestus,
Ferventesque auras velut e fornace profunda
Ore trahit, currusque suos candescere sentit;   230
Et neque jam cineres ejectatamque favillam
Ferre potest, calidoque involvitur undique fumo,

Quoque eat, aut ubi sit, picea caligine tectus
Nescit, et arbitrio volucrum raptatur equorum.
Sanguine tunc credunt in corpora summa vocato   235
Aethiopum populos nigrum traxisse colorem.
Tum facta est Libye raptis umoribus aestu
Arida, tum nymphae passis fontesque lacusque
Deflevere comis; quaerit Boeotia Dircen,
Argos Amymonen, Ephyre Pirenidas undas.   240
Nec sortita loco distantes flumina ripas
Tuta manent: mediis Tanais fumavit in undis,
Peneosque senex, Teuthranteusque Caicus,
Et celer Ismenos cum Phegiaco Erymantho,
Arsurusque iterum Xanthus, flavusque Lycormas,   245
Quique recurvatis ludit Maeandros in undis,
Mygdoniusque Melas et Taenarius Eurotas.
Arsit et Euphrates Babylonius, arsit Orontes,
Thermodonque citus, Gangesque, et Phasis, et Hister.
Aestuat Alpheus, ripae Sperche*i*des ardent: 250
Quodque suo Tagus amne vehit, fluit ignibus, aurum:
Et quae Maeonias celebrarant carmine ripas
Fluminae volucres medio caluere Caystro.
Nilus in extremum fugit perterritus orbem
Occuluitque caput, quod adhuc latet: ostia septem   255
Pulverulenta vacant, septem sine flumine valles.
Fors eadem Ismarios Hebrum cum Strymone siccat,
Hesperiosque amnes, Rhenum Rhodanumque Padumque,
Cuique fuit rerum promissa potentia, Thybrin.
Dissilit omne solum, penetratque in Tartara rimis   260
Lumen et infernum terret cum conjuge regem.
Et mare contrahitur, siccaeque est campus harenae
Quod modo pontus erat; quosque altum texerat aequor,
Exsistunt montes et sparsas Cycladas augent.

Ima petunt pisces, nec se super aequora curvi 265
Tollere consuetas audent delphines in auras;
Corpora phocarum summo resupina profundo
Exanimata natant. Ipsum quoque Nerea fama est
Doridaque et natas tepidis latuisse sub antris.
Ter Neptunus aquis cum torvo bracchia vultu 270
Exserere ausus erat; ter non tulit aëris ignes.
Alma tamen Tellus, ut erat circumdata ponto,
Inter aquas pelagi contractosque undique fontes,
Qui se condiderant in opacae viscera matris,
Sustulit oppressos collo tenus arida vultus, 275
Opposuitque manum fronti, magnoque tremore
Omnia concutiens paulum subsedit, et infra
Quam solet esse, fuit; siccaque ita voce locuta est:
"Si placet hoc, meruique, quid o tua fulmina cessant,
Summe deum? liceat periturae viribus ignis 280
Igne perire tuo, clademque auctore levare.
Vix equidem fauces haec ipsa in verba resolvo"—
Presserat ora vapor—"tostos en aspice crines,
Inque oculis tantum, tantum super ora favillae.
Hosne mihi fructus, hunc fertilitatis honorem 285
Officiique refers, quod adunci vulnera aratri
Rastrorumque fero totoque exerceor anno,
Quod pecori frondes alimentaque mitia, fruges
Humano generi, vobis quoque tura ministro?
Sed tamen exitium fac me meruisse, quid undae, 290
Quid meruit frater? cur illi tradita sorte
Aequora decrescunt et ab aethere longius absunt?
Quodsi nec fratris, nec te mea gratia tangit,
At caeli miserere tui. Circumspice utrumque,
Fumat uterque polus: quos si vitiaverit ignis, 295
Atria vestra ruent. Atlas en ipse laborat,

Vixque suis umeris candentem sustinet axem.
Si freta, si terrae pereunt, si regia caeli,
In chaos antiquum confundimur. Eripe flammis,
Siquid adhuc superest, et rerum consule summae." 300
   Dixerat haec Tellus: neque enim tolerare vaporem
Ulterius potuit nec dicere plura, suumque
Rettulit os in se propioraque manibus antra.
At pater omnipotens, superos testatus et ipsum,
Qui dederat currus, nisi opem ferat, omnia fato 305
Interitura gravi, summam petit arduus arcem,
Unde solet latis nubes inducere terris,
Unde movet tonitrus vibrataque fulmina jactat.
Sed neque, quas posset terris inducere, nubes
Tunc habuit, nec quos caelo dimitteret, imbres. 310
Intonat, et dextra libratum fulmen ab aure
Misit in aurigam, pariterque animaque rotisque
Expulit, et saevis compescuit ignibus ignes.
Consternantur equi, et saltu in contraria facto
Colla jugo eripiunt abruptaque lora relinquunt. 315
Illic frena jacent, illic temone revulsus
Axis, in hac radii fractarum parte rotarum,
Sparsaque sunt late laceri vestigia currus.
At Phaëthon, rutilos flamma populante capillos,
Volvitur in praeceps, longoque per aëra tractu 320
Fertur, ut interdum de caelo stella sereno
Etsi non cecidit, potuit cecidisse videri.
Quem procul a patria diverso maximus orbe
Excipit Eridanus, fumantiaque abluit ora.
Naides Hesperiae trifida fumantia flamma 325
Corpora dant tumulo, signant quoque carmine saxum:
"Hic situs est Phaëthon, currus auriga paterni;
Quem si non tenuit, magnis tamen excidit ausis."

Nam pater obductos, luctu miserabilis aegro,
Condiderat vultus: et si modo credimus, unum   330
Isse diem sine sole ferunt: incendia lumen
Praebebant, aliquisque malo fuit usus in illo.
  At Clymene, postquam dixit quaecumque fuerunt
In tantis dicenda malis, lugubris et amens
Et laniata sinus totum percensuit orbem: 335
Exanimesque artus primo, mox ossa requirens,
Repperit ossa tamen peregrina condita ripa,
Incubuitque loco, nomenque in marmore lectum
Perfudit lacrimis et aperto pectore fovit.

8. The Heliades.

II. 340-366.

> ".... Where weep
> Even now the sister trees their amber tears
> O'er Phaethon untimely dead."

Nec minus Heliades lugent et, inania morti   340
Munera, dant lacrimas, et caesae pectora palmis
Non auditurum miseras Phaëthonta querellas
Nocte dieque vocant, adsternunturque sepulchro.
Luna quater junctis implerat cornibus orbem:
Illae more suo, nam morem fecerat usus,   345
Plangorem dederant: e quis Phaëthusa, sororum
Maxima, cum vellet terra procumbere, questa est
Deriguisse pedes; ad quam conata venire
Candida Lampetie subita radice retenta est.
Tertia, cum crinem manibus laniare pararet,   350
Avellit frondes; haec stipite crura teneri,
Illa dolet fieri longos sua bracchia ramos.
Dumque ea mirantur, complectitur inguina cortex,

Perque gradus uterum pectusque umerosque manusque
Ambit, et exstabant tantum ora vocantia matrem. 355
Quid faciat mater, nisi, quo trahat impetus illam,
Huc eat atque illuc et, dum licet, oscula jungat?
Non satis est; truncis avellere corpora temptat
Et teneros manibus ramos abrumpit; at inde
Sanguineae manant, tamquam de vulnere, guttae. 360
"Parce, precor, mater," quaecumque est saucia, clamat,
"Parce, precor! nostrum laceratur in arbore corpus.
Jamque vale"—cortex in verba novissima venit.
Inde fluunt lacrimae, stillataque sole rigescunt
De ramis electra novis, quae lucidus amnis 365
Excipit et nuribus mittit gestanda Latinis.

9. Cycnus. Grief of Phoebus.
II. 367–400.

Adfuit huic monstro proles Stheneleïa Cycnus,
Qui tibi materno quamvis a sanguine junctus,
Mente tamen, Phaëthon, propior fuit. Ille relicto—
Nam Ligurum populos et magnas rexerat urbes— 370
Imperio ripas virides amnemque querellis
Eridanum implerat silvamque sororibus auctam:
Cum vox est tenuata viro, canaeque capillos
Dissimulant plumae, collumque a pectore longe
Porrigitur, digitosque ligat junctura rubentes, 375
Penna latus vestit, tenet os sine acumine rostrum.
Fit nova Cycnus avis; nec se caeloque Jovique
Credit, ut injuste missi memor ignis ab illo:
Stagna petit patulosque lacus; ignemque perosus,
Quae colat, elegit contraria flumina flammis. 380
 Squalidus interea genitor Phaëthontis et expers

Ipse sui decoris, qualis cum deficit orbem
Esse solet, lucemque odit seque ipse diemque,
Datque animum in luctus et luctibus adicit iram,
Officiumque negat mundo. "Satis" inquit "ab aevi
Sors mea principiis fuit irrequieta, pigetque
Actorum sine fine mihi, sine honore, laborum.
Quilibet alter agat portantes lumina currus!
Si nemo est, omnesque dei non posse fatentur,
Ipse agat; ut saltem, dum nostras temptat habenas, 390
Orbatura patres aliquando fulmina ponat.
Tum sciet, ignipedum vires expertus equorum,
Non meruisse necem, qui non bene rexerit illos."
Talia dicentem circumstant omnia Solem
Numina, neve velit tenebras inducere rebus,   395
Supplice voce rogant: missos quoque Juppiter ignes
Excusat, precibusque minas regaliter addit.
Colligit amentes et adhuc terrore paventes
Phoebus equos, stimuloque dolens et verbere saevit;
Saevit enim natumque objectat et imputat illis.   400

10. The House of Envy.

II. 760-796.

Minerva purposes to employ the offices of Envy, in punishment of Aglauros, one of the daughters of Cecrops. Thus the poet comes to describe the House of Envy, whither Minerva has come.

Protinus Invidiae nigro squalentia tabo   760
Tecta petit. Domus est imis in vallibus hujus
Abdita, sole carens, non ulli pervia vento,
Tristis et ignavi plenissima frigoris, et quae
Igne vacet semper, caligine semper abundet.

10. THE HOUSE OF ENVY.

Huc ubi pervenit belli metuenda virago, 765
Constitit ante domum, neque enim succedere tectis
Fas habet, et postes extrema cuspide pulsat.
Concussae patuere fores. Videt intus edentem
Vipereas carnes, vitiorum alimenta suorum,
Invidiam, visaque oculos avertit. At illa 770
Surgit humo pigre semesarumque relinquit
Corpora serpentum, passuque incedit inerti;
Utque deam vidit formaque armisque decoram,
Ingemuit, vultumque inita ad suspiria duxit.
Pallor in ore sedet, macies in corpore toto, 775
Nusquam recta acies, livent robigine dentes,
Pectora felle virent, lingua est suffusa veneno.
Risus abest, nisi quem visi movere dolores,
Nec fruitur somno, vigilacibus excita curis,
Sed videt ingratos, intabescitque videndo, 780
Successus hominum, carpitque et carpitur una,
Suppliciumque suum est. Quamvis tamen oderat, illam
Talibus adfata est breviter Tritonia dictis:
"Infice tabe tua natarum Cecropis unam.
Sic opus est. Aglauros ea est." Haud plura locuta 785
Fugit, et impressa tellurem reppulit hasta.
Illa deam obliquo fugientem lumine cernens
Murmura parva dedit, successurumque Minervae
Indoluit; baculumque capit, quod spinea totum
Vincula cingebant; adopertaque nubibus atris 790
Quacumque ingreditur, florentia proterit arva,
Exuritque herbas, et summa cacumina carpit,
Adflatuque suo populos urbesque domosque
Polluit, et tandem Tritonida conspicit arcem
Ingeniis opibusque et festa pace virentem, 795
Vixque tenet lacrimas, quia nil lacrimabile cernit.

11. Cadmus and the Dragon's Teeth.

III. 14-137.

Vix bene Castalio Cadmus descenderat antro,
Incustoditam lente videt ire juvencam   15
Nullum servitii signum cervice gerentem.
Subsequitur pressoque legit vestigia gressu,
Auctoremque viae Phoebum taciturnus adorat.
Jam vada Cephisi Panopesque evaserat arva:
Bos stetit et tollens speciosam cornibus altis   20
Ad caelum frontem mugitibus impulit auras;
Atque ita, respiciens comites sua terga sequentes,
Procubuit teneraque latus summisit in herba.
Cadmus agit grates, peregrinaeque oscula terrae
Figit, et ignotos montes agrosque salutat.   25
Sacra Jovi facturus erat. Jubet ire ministros
Et petere e vivis libandas fontibus undas.
    Silva vetus stabat nulla violata securi,
Et specus in media, virgis ac vimine densus,
Efficiens humilem lapidum compagibus arcum,   30
Uberibus fecundus aquis; ubi conditus antro
Martius anguis erat, cristis praesignis et auro:
Igne micant oculi; corpus tumet omne veneno;
Tresque vibrant linguae; triplici stant ordine dentes.
Quem postquam Tyria lucum de gente profecti   35
Infausto tetigere gradu, demissaque in undas
Urna dedit sonitum, longo caput extulit antro
Caeruleus serpens horrendaque sibila misit.
Effluxere urnae manibus, sanguisque relinquit
Corpus, et attonitos subitus tremor occupat artus.   40
Ille volubilibus squamosos nexibus orbes

11. CADMUS.

Torquet, et immensos saltu sinuatur in arcus,
Ac media plus parte leves erectus in auras
Despicit omne nemus, tantoque est corpore, quanto,
Si totum spectes, geminas qui separat Arctos.   45
Nec mora; Phoenicas, sive illi tela parabant,
Sive fugam, sive ipse timor prohibebat utrumque,
Occupat: hos morsu, longis amplexibus illos,
Hos necat adflati funesta tabe veneni.
    Fecerat exiguas jam sol altissimus umbras: 50
Quae mora sit sociis, miratur Agenore natus,
Vestigatque viros. Tegumen direpta leonis
Pellis erat, telum splendenti lancea ferro
Et jaculum, teloque animus praestantior omni.
    Ut nemus intravit letataque corpora vidit,   55
Victoremque supra spatiosi corporis hostem
Tristia sanguinea lambentem vulnera lingua,
"Aut ultor vestrae, fidissima corpora, mortis,
Aut comes" inquit "ero." Dixit, dextraque molarem
Sustulit, et magnum magno conamine misit.   60
Illius impulsu cum turribus ardua celsis
Moenia mota forent: serpens sine vulnere mansit,
Loricaeque modo squamis defensus et atrae
Duritia pellis validos cute reppulit ictus.
At non duritia jaculum quoque vicit eadem,   65
Quod medio lentae spinae curvamine fixum
Constitit, et totum descendit in ilia ferrum.
Ille dolore ferox caput in sua terga retorsit,
Vulneraque aspexit, fixumque hastile momordit,
Idque ubi vi multa partem labefecit in omnem,   70
Vix tergo eripuit: ferrum tamen ossibus haesit.
Tum vero postquam solitas accessit ad iras
Causa recens, plenis tumuerunt guttura venis,

Spumaque pestiferos circumfluit albida rictus,
Terraque rasa sonat squamis, quique halitus exit 75
Ore niger Stygio, vitiatas inficit auras.
Ipse modo immensum spiris facientibus orbem
Cingitur, interdum longa trabe rectior exstat,
Impete nunc vasto ceu concitus imbribus amnis
Fertur, et obstantes proturbat pectore silvas. 80
Cedit Agenorides paulum, spolioque leonis
Sustinet incursus, instantiaque ora retardat
Cuspide praetenta. Furit ille et inania duro
Vulnera dat ferro, figitque in acumine dentes,
Jamque venenifero sanguis manare palato 85
Coeperat, et virides aspergine tinxerat herbas:
Sed leve vulnus erat, quia se retrahebat ab ictu
Laesaque colla dabat retro, plagamque sedere
Cedendo arcebat, nec longius ire sinebat:
Donec Agenorides conjectum in gutture ferrum 90
Usque sequens pressit, dum retro quercus eunti
Obstitit, et fixa est pariter cum robore cervix.
Pondere serpentis curvata est arbor, et imae
Parte flagellari gemuit sua robora caudae.
  Dum spatium victor victi considerat hostis, 95
Vox subito audita est; neque erat cognoscere promptum,
Unde, sed audita est, "quid, Agenore nate, peremptum
Serpentem spectas? et tu spectabere serpens."
  Ille diu pavidus pariter cum mente colorem
Perdiderat, gelidoque comae terrore rigebant. 100
Ecce viri fautrix superas delapsa per auras
Pallas adest, motaeque jubet supponere terrae
Vipereos dentes, populi incrementa futuri.
Paret, et, ut presso sulcum patefecit aratro,
Spargit humi jussos, mortalia semina, dentes. 105

Inde, fide majus, glaebae coepere moveri,
Primaque de sulcis acies apparuit hastae,
Tegmina mox capitum picto nutantia cono,
Mox umeri pectusque onerataque bracchia telis
Exsistunt, crescitque seges clipeata virorum. 110
Sic ubi tolluntur festis aulaea theatris,
Surgere signa solent, primumque ostendere vultus,
Cetera paulatim, placidoque educta tenore
Tota patent, imoque pedes in margine ponunt.
 Territus hoste novo Cadmus capere arma parabat. 115
"Ne cape," de populo, quem terra creaverat, unus
Exclamat "nec te civilibus insere bellis."
Atque ita terrigenis rigido de fratribus unum
Comminus ense ferit: jaculo cadit eminus ipse.
Hunc quoque qui leto dederat, non longius illo 120
Vivit, et exspirat, modo quas acceperat, auras.
Exemploque pari furit omnis turba, suoque
Marte cadunt subiti per mutua vulnera fratres.
Jamque brevis vitae spatium sortita juventus
Sanguineo tepidam plangebat pectore matrem, 125
Quinque superstitibus: quorum fuit unus Echion.
Is sua jecit humo monitu Tritonidis arma,
Fraternaeque fidem pacis petiitque deditque.
Hos operis comites habuit Sidonius hospes,
Cum posuit jussam Phoebeïs sortibus urbem. 130
 Jam stabant Thebae: poteras jam, Cadme, videri
Exilio felix: soceri tibi Marsque Venusque
Contigerant: huc adde genus de conjuge tanta,
Tot natos natasque et, pignora cara, nepotes,
Hos quoque jam juvenes. Sed scilicet ultima semper 135
Expectanda dies homini, dicique beatus
Ante obitum nemo supremaque funera debet.

12. Pyramus and Thisbe.

IV. 55-166.

Pyramus et Thisbe, juvenum pulcherrimus alter,   55
Altera, quas oriens habuit, praelata puellis,
Contiguas tenuere domos, ubi dicitur altam
Coctilibus muris cinxisse Semiramis urbem.
Notitiam primosque gradus vicinia fecit:
Tempore crevit amor: taedae quoque jure coissent: 60
Sed vetuere patres.   Quod non potuere vetare,
Ex aequo captis ardebant mentibus ambo.
Conscius omnis abest: nutu signisque loquuntur,
Quoque magis tegitur, tectus magis aestuat ignis.
    Fissus erat tenui rima, quam duxerat olim   65
Cum fieret, paries domui communis utrique.
Id vitium nulli per saecula longa notatum—
Quid non sentit amor?—primi vidistis amantes,
Et vocis fecistis iter; tutaeque per illud
Murmure blanditiae minimo transire solebant.   70
Saepe, ubi constiterant, hinc Thisbe, Pyramus illinc,
Inque vices fuerat captatus anhelitus oris,
"Invide" dicebant "paries, quid amantibus obstas?
Quantum erat, ut sineres toto nos corpore jungi,
Aut hoc si nimium, vel ad oscula danda pateres!   75
Nec sumus ingrati: tibi nos debere fatemur,
Quod datus est verbis ad amicas transitus aures."
Talia diversa nequiquam sede locuti
Sub noctem dixere vale, partique dedere
Oscula quisque suae non pervenientia contra.   80
    Postera nocturnos aurora removerat ignes,
Solque pruinosas radiis siccaverat herbas:
Ad solitum coiere locum.   Tum murmure parvo

Multa prius questi, statuunt, ut nocte silenti
Fallere custodes foribusque excedere temptent,   85
Cumque domo exierint, urbis quoque tecta relinquant;
Neve sit errandum lato spatiantibus arvo,
Conveniant ad busta Nini, lateantque sub umbra
Arboris: arbor ibi niveis uberrima pomis
Ardua morus erat, gelido contermina fonti.   90
Pacta placent, et lux, tarde discedere visa,
Praecipitatur aquis, et aquis nox exit ab isdem.
   Callida per tenebras versato cardine Thisbe
Egreditur fallitque suos; adopertaque vultum
Pervenit ad tumulum, dictaque sub arbore sedit.   95
Audacem faciebat amor. Venit ecce recenti
Caede leaena boum spumantes oblita rictus,
Depositura sitim vicini fontis in unda.
Quam procul ad lunae radios Babylonia Thisbe
Vidit, et obscurum trepido pede fugit in antrum,   100
Dumque fugit, tergo velamina lapsa reliquit.
Ut lea saeva sitim multa compescuit unda,
Dum redit in silvas, inventos forte sine ipsa
Ore cruentato tenues laniavit amictus.
   Serius egressus vestigia vidit in alto   105
Pulvere certa ferae, totoque expalluit ore
Pyramus. Ut vero vestem quoque sanguine tinctam
Repperit, "una duos" inquit "nox perdet amantes:
E quibus illa fuit longa dignissima vita,
Nostra nocens anima est: ego te, miseranda, peremi,   110
In loca plena metus qui jussi nocte venires,
Nec prior huc veni. Nostrum divellite corpus,
Et scelerata fero consumite viscera morsu,
O quicumque sub hac habitatis rupe, leones.
Sed timidi est optare necem." Velamina Thisbes   115

Tollit, et ad pactae secum fert arboris umbram.
Utque dedit notae lacrimas, dedit oscula vesti,
"Accipe nunc" inquit "nostri quoque sanguinis haustus!"
Quoque erat accinctus, demisit in ilia ferrum,
Nec mora, ferventi moriens e vulnere traxit. 120
Ut jacuit resupinus humo, cruor emicat alte:
Non aliter, quam cum vitiato fistula plumbo
Scinditur, et tenui stridente foramine longas
Ejaculatur aquas, atque ictibus aëra rumpit.
Arborei fetus aspergine caedis in atram 125
Vertuntur faciem, madefactaque sanguine radix
Puniceo tinguit pendentia mora colore.

  Ecce metu nondum posito, ne fallat amantem,
Illa redit, juvenemque oculis animoque requirit,
Quantaque vitarit narrare pericula gestit. 130
Utque locum et rigua cognoscit in arbore formam,
Sic facit incertam pomi color: haeret, an haec sit.
Dum dubitat, tremebunda videt pulsare cruentum
Membra solum, retroque pedem tulit, oraque buxo
Pallidiora gerens exhorruit, aequoris instar, 135
Quod tremit, exigua cum summum stringitur aura.
Sed postquam remorata suos cognovit amores,
Percutit indignos claro plangore lacertos,
Et laniata comas amplexaque corpus amatum
Vulnera supplevit lacrimis, fletumque cruori 140
Miscuit, et gelidis in vultibus oscula figens,
"Pyrame," clamavit "quis te mihi casus ademit?
Pyrame, responde: tua te carissima Thisbe

Vidit ebur vacuum, "tua te manus" inquit "amorque
Perdidit, infelix. Est et mihi fortis in unum
Hoc manus, est et amor: dabit hic in vulnera vires. 150
Persequar exstinctum, letique miserrima dicar
Causa comesque tui; quique a me morte revelli
Heu sola poteras, poteris nec morte revelli.
Hoc tamen amborum verbis estote rogati,
O multum miseri, meus illiusque parentes, 155
Ut quos certus amor, quos hora novissima junxit,
Componi tumulo non invideatis eodem.
At tu, quae ramis arbor miserabile corpus
Nunc tegis unius, mox es tectura duorum,
Signa tene caedis, pullosque et luctibus aptos 160
Semper habe fetus, gemini monumenta cruoris."
   Dixit, et aptato pectus mucrone sub imum
Incubuit ferro, quod adhuc a caede tepebat.
Vota tamen tetigere deos, tetigere parentes.
Nam color in pomo est, ubi permaturuit, ater: 165
Quodque rogis superest, una requiescit in urna.

13. CADMUS AND HERMIONE.
IV. 563-603.

Nescit Agenorides natam parvumque nepotem
Aequoris esse deos. Luctu serieque malorum
Victus et ostentis, quae plurima viderat, exit 565
Conditor urbe sua, tamquam fortuna locorum,
Non sua se premeret; longisque erratibus actus
Contigit Illyricos profuga cum conjuge fines.
Jamque malis annisque graves, dum prima retractant
Fata domus, releguntque suos sermone labores, 570
"Num sacer ille mea trajectus cuspide serpens"

Cadmus ait "fuerat, tum, cum Sidone profectus
Vipereos sparsi per humum, nova semina, dentes?
Quem si cura deum tam certa vindicat ira,
Ipse precor serpens in longam porrigar alvum."   575
Dixit, et ut serpens in longam tenditur alvum,
Durataeque cuti squamas increscere sentit,
Nigraque caeruleis variari corpora guttis:
In pectusque cadit pronus, commissaque in unum
Paulatim tereti tenuantur acumine crura.   580
Bracchia jam restant: quae restant, bracchia tendit,
Et lacrimis per adhuc humana fluentibus ora
"Accede, o conjunx, accede, miserrima," dixit,
"Dumque aliquid superest de me, me tange, manumque
Accipe, dum manus est, dum non totum occupat anguis."
Ille quidem vult plura loqui, sed lingua repente
In partes est fissa duas: nec verba loquenti
Sufficiunt, quotiensque aliquos parat edere questus,
Sibilat: hanc illi vocem natura reliquit.
Nuda manu feriens exclamat pectora conjunx,   590
"Cadme, mane, teque, infelix, his exue monstris!
Cadme, quid hoc? ubi pes? ubi sunt umerique manusque,
Et color et facies et, dum loquor, omnia? cur non
Me quoque, caelestes, in eandem vertitis anguem?"
Dixerat. Ille suae lambebat conjugis ora,   595
Inque sinus caros, veluti cognosceret, ibat,
Et dabat amplexus, assuetaque colla petebat.
Quisquis adest—aderant comites—terretur: at illa
Lubrica permulcet cristati colla draconis;
Et subito duo sunt junctoque volumine serpunt,   600
Donec in appositi nemoris subiere latebras.
Nunc quoque nec fugiunt hominem, nec vulnere laedunt,
Quidque prius fuerint, placidi meminere dracones.

14. Andromeda's Release.

IV. 663-752.

Perseus, when returning from Libya with the head of the Medusa, finds Andromeda chained to a rock and exposed to a sea-monster, and rescues her. (Read Mr. Kingsley's "Andromeda," and, in Mr. William Morris's "Earthly Paradise," the "Doom of Acrisius.")

    Clauserat Hippotades aeterno carcere ventos,
Admonitorque operum caelo clarissimus alto
Lucifer ortus erat. Pennis ligat ille resumptis   665
Parte ab utraque pedes, teloque accingitur unco,
Et liquidum motis talaribus aëra findit.
Gentibus innumeris circumque infraque relictis
Aethiopum populos, Cepheaque conspicit arva.
Illic immeritam maternae pendere linguae   670
Andromedan poenas immitis jusserat Ammon.
Quam simul ad duras religatam bracchia cautes
Vidit Abantiades—nisi quod levis aura capillos
Moverat, et tepido manabant lumina fletu,
Marmoreum ratus esset opus—trahit inscius ignes   675
Et stupet. Eximiae correptus imagine formae
Paene suas quatere est oblitus in aëre pennas.
Ut stetit, "O" dixit "non istis digna catenis,
Sed quibus inter se cupidi junguntur amantes,
Pande requirenti nomen terraeque tuumque,   680
Et cur vincla geras." Primo silet illa, nec audet
Appellare virum virgo; manibusque modestos
Celasset vultus, si non religata fuisset.
Lumina, quod potuit, lacrimis implevit obortis.
Saepius instanti, sua ne delicta fateri   685

Nolle videretur, nomen terraeque suumque,
Quantaque maternae fuerit fiducia formae,
Indicat.   Et nondum memoratis omnibus unda
Insonuit, veniensque immenso belua ponto
Imminet et latum sub pectore possidet aequor.   690
   Conclamat virgo.   Genitor lugubris et una
Mater adest, ambo miseri, sed justius illa.
Nec secum auxilium, sed dignos tempore fletus
Plangoremque ferunt, vinctoque in corpore adhaerent:
Cum sic hospes ait : " Lacrimarum longa manere   695
Tempora vos poterunt; ad opem brevis hora ferendam est.
Hanc ego si peterem Perseus Jove natus et illa,
Quam clausam implevit fecundo Juppiter auro,
Gorgonis anguicomae Perseus superator, et alis
Aërias ausus jactatis ire per auras,   700
Praeferrer cunctis certe gener.   Addere tantis
Dotibus et meritum, faveant modo numina, tempto.
Ut mea sit servata mea virtute, paciscor."
   Accipiunt legem—quis enim dubitaret?—et orant,
Promittuntque super regnum dotale parentes.   705
Ecce velut navis praefixo concita rostro
Sulcat aquas, juvenum sudantibus acta lacertis,
Sic fera dimotis impulsu pectoris undis
Tantum aberat scopulis, quantum Balearica torto
Funda potest plumbo medii transmittere caeli :   710
Cum subito juvenis pedibus tellure repulsa
Arduus in nubes abiit.   Ut in aequore summo
Umbra viri visa est, visam fera saevit in umbram.
Utque Jovis praepes, vacuo cum vidit in arvo
Praebentem Phoebo liventia terga draconem,   715
Occupat aversum ; neu saeva retorqueat ora,
Squamigeris avidos figit cervicibus ungues :

14. ANDROMEDA'S RELEASE.

Sic celeri missus praeceps per inane volatu
Terga ferae pressit, dextroque frementis in armo
Inachides ferrum curvo tenus abdidit hamo. 720
Vulnere laesa gravi modo se sublimis in auras
Attollit, modo subdit aquis, modo more ferocis
Versat apri, quem turba canum circumsona terret.
Ille avidos morsus velocibus effugit alis:
Quaque patet, nunc terga cavis super obsita conchis, 725
Nunc laterum costas, nunc qua tenuissima cauda
Desinit in piscem, falcato verberat ense.
Belua puniceo mixtos cum sanguine fluctus
Ore vomit. Maduere graves aspergine pennae;
Nec bibulis ultra Perseus talaribus ausus 730
Credere, conspexit scopulum, qui vertice summo
Stantibus exstat aquis, operitur ab aequore moto.
Nixus eo rupisque tenens juga prima sinistra
Ter quater exegit repetita per ilia ferrum.
    Litora cum plausu clamor superasque deorum 735
Implevere domos. Gaudent, generumque salutant,
Auxiliumque domus servatoremque fatentur
Cassiope Cepheusque pater. Resoluta catenis
Incedit virgo, pretiumque et causa laboris.
    Ipse manus hausta victrices abluit unda: 740
Anguiferumque caput dura ne laedat harena,
Mollit humum foliis, natasque sub aequore virgas
Sternit, et imponit Phorcynidos ora Medusae.
Virga recens bibulaque etiamnum viva medulla
Vim rapuit monstri, tactuque induruit hujus, 745
Percepitque novum ramis et fronde rigorem.
At pelagi nymphae factum mirabile temptant
Pluribus in virgis, et idem contingere gaudent,
Seminaque ex illis iterant jactata per undas.

Nunc quoque curaliis eadem natura remansit, 750
Duritiam tacto capiant ut ab aëre, quodque
Vimen in aequore erat, fiat super aequora saxum.

15. Proserpine.

V. 338-571.

The Muse Calliope sings in honor of Ceres, describing her wanderings in quest of Proserpine.

> "Proserpine gathering flowers,
> Herself a fairer flower, by gloomy Dis
> Was gathered, which cost Ceres all that pain
> To seek her through the world."
> Milton, Paradise Lost, iv. 268-272.

Surgit, et immissos hedera collecta capillos
Calliope querulas praetemptat pollice chordas,
Atque haec percussis subjungit carmina nervis.   340
"Prima Ceres unco glaebam dimovit aratro,
Prima dedit fruges alimentaque mitia terris,
Prima dedit leges: Cereris sunt omnia munus.
Illa canenda mihi est.   Utinam modo dicere possem
Carmina digna dea: certe dea carmine digna est.   345
   Vasta Giganteis ingesta est insula membris
Trinacris, et magnis subjectum molibus urguet
Aetherias ausum sperare Typhoëa sedes.
Nititur ille quidem, pugnatque resurgere saepe:
Dextra sed Ausonio manus est subjecta Peloro,   350
Laeva, Pachyne, tibi: Lilybaeo crura premuntur:
Degravat Aetna caput, sub qua resupinus harenas
Ejectat, flammamque ferox vomit ore Typhoeus.
Saepe remoliri luctatur pondera terrae,
Oppidaque et magnos devolvere corpore montes: 355

Inde tremit tellus et rex pavet ipse silentum,
Ne pateat latoque solum retegatur hiatu,
Immissusque dies trepidantes terreat umbras.
   Hanc metuens cladem tenebrosa sede tyrannus
Exierat, curruque atrorum vectus equorum   360
Ambibat Siculae cautus fundamina terrae.
Postquam exploratum satis est loca nulla labare,
Depositique metus, videt hunc Erycina vagantem
Monte suo residens, natumque amplexa volucrem
'Arma manusque meae, mea, nate, potentia,' dixit, 365
'Illa, quibus superas omnes, cape tela, Cupido,
Inque dei pectus celeres molire sagittas,
Cui triplicis cessit fortuna novissima regni.
Tu superos ipsumque Jovem, tu numina ponti
Victa domas ipsumque, regit qui numina ponti.   370
Tartara quid cessant? cur non matrisque tuumque
Imperium profers? agitur pars tertia mundi.
Et tamen in caelo, quae jam patientia nostra est,
Spernimur, ac mecum vires minuuntur Amoris.
Pallada nonne vides jaculatricemque Dianam   375
Abscessisse mihi? Cereris quoque filia virgo,
Si patiemur, erit: nam spes adfectat easdem.
At tu, pro socio, siqua est ea gratia, regno
Junge deam patruo.' Dixit Venus; ille pharetram
Solvit et arbitrio matris de mille sagittis   380
Unam seposuit, sed qua nec acutior ulla
Nec minus incerta est, nec quae magis audiat arcus;
Oppositoque genu curvavit flexile cornum
Inque cor hamata percussit harundine Ditem.
   Haud procul Hennaeis lacus est a moenibus altae, 385
Nomine Pergus, aquae. Non illo plura Caystros
Carmina cycnorum labentibus audit in undis.

Silva coronat aquas cingens latus omne, suisque
Frondibus ut velo Phoebeos summovet ignes.
Frigora dant rami, Tyrios humus umida flores: 390
Perpetuum ver est. Quo dum Proserpina luco
Ludit, et aut violas aut candida lilia carpit,
Dumque puellari studio calathosque sinumque
Implet, et aequales certat superare legendo,
Paene simul visa est dilectaque raptaque Diti: 395
Usque adeo est properatus amor. Dea territa maesto
Et matrem et comites, sed matrem saepius, ore
Clamat; et, ut summa vestem laniarat ab ora,
Collecti flores tunicis cecidere remissis;
Tantaque simplicitas puerilibus adfuit annis, 400
Haec quoque virgineum movit jactura dolorem.
Raptor agit currus, et nomine quemque vocatos
Exhortatur equos, quorum per colla jubasque
Excutit obscura tinctas ferrugine habenas;
Perque lacus sacros et olentia sulphure fertur 405
Stagna Palicorum, rupta ferventia terra,
Et qua Bacchiadae, bimari gens orta Corintho,
Inter inaequales posuerunt moenia portus.
  Est medium Cyanes et Pisaeae Arethusae,
Quod coit angustis inclusum cornibus aequor. 410
Hic fuit, a cujus stagnum quoque nomine dictum est,
Inter Sicelidas Cyane celeberrima nymphas.
Gurgite quae medio summa tenus exstitit alvo,
Agnovitque deam. 'Nec longius ibitis' inquit;
'Non potes invitae Cereris gener esse: roganda, 415
Non rapienda fuit. Quodsi componere magnis
Parva mihi fas est, et me dilexit Anapis;
Exorata tamen, nec, ut haec, exterrita nupsi.'
Dixit, et in partes diversas bracchia tendens

15. PROSERPINE.

Obstitit. Haud ultra tenuit Saturnius iram, 420
Terribilesque hortatus equos in gurgitis ima
Contortum valido sceptrum regale lacerto
Condidit. Icta viam tellus in Tartara fecit
Et pronos currus medio cratere recepit.
 At Cyane, raptamque deam contemptaque fontis 425
Jura sui maerens, inconsolabile vulnus
Mente gerit tacita, lacrimisque absumitur omnis:
Et quarum fuerat magnum modo numen, in illas
Extenuatur aquas. Molliri membra videres,
Ossa pati flexus, ungues posuisse rigorem: 430
Primaque de tota tenuissima quaeque liquescunt,
Caerulei crines digitique et crura pedesque;
Nam brevis in gelidas membris exilibus undas
Transitus est. Post haec umeri tergusque latusque
Pectoraque in tenues abeunt evanida rivos. 435
Denique pro vivo vitiatas sanguine venas
Lympha subit, restatque nihil, quod prendere possis.
 Interea pavidae nequiquam filia matri
Omnibus est terris, omni quaesita profundo.
Illam non udis veniens Aurora capillis 440
Cessantem vidit, non Hesperus; illa duabus
Flammiferas pinus manibus succendit ab Aetna,
Perque pruinosas tulit irrequieta tenebras:
Rursus ubi alma dies hebetarat sidera, natam
Solis ab occasu solis quaerebat ad ortus. 445
Fessa labore sitim collegerat, oraque nulli
Colluerant fontes: cum tectam stramine vidit
Forte casam, parvasque fores pulsavit. At inde
Prodit anus, divamque videt, lymphamque roganti
Dulce dedit, tosta quod texerat ante polenta. 450
Dum bibit illa datum, duri puer oris et audax

Constitit ante deam, risitque, avidamque vocavit.
Offensa est, neque adhuc epota parte, loquentem
Cum liquido mixta perfudit diva polenta.
Combibit os maculas, et quae modo bracchia gessit, 455
Crura gerit; cauda est mutatis addita membris:
Inque brevem formam, ne sit vis magna nocendi,
Contrahitur, parvaque minor mensura lacerta est.
Mirantem flentemque et tangere monstra parantem
Fugit anum, latebramque petit; aptumque colori 460
Nomen habet, variis stellatus corpora guttis.

   Quas dea per terras et quas erraverit undas,
Dicere longa mora est: quaerenti defuit orbis.
Sicaniam repetit: dumque omnia lustrat eundo,
Venit et ad Cyanen. Ea ni mutata fuisset, 465
Omnia narrasset. Sed et os et lingua volenti
Dicere non aderant, nec quo loqueretur, habebat.
Signa tamen manifesta dedit, notamque parenti,
Illo forte loco delapsam in gurgite sacro,
Persephones zonam summis ostendit in undis. 470

   Quam simul agnovit, tamquam tunc denique raptam
Scisset, inornatos laniavit diva capillos,
Et repetita suis percussit pectora palmis.
Nescit adhuc, ubi sit: terras tamen increpat omnes
Ingratasque vocat nec frugum munere dignas, 475
Trinacriam ante alias, in qua vestigia damni
Repperit. Ergo illic saeva vertentia glaebas
Fregit aratra manu, parilique irata colonos
Ruricolasque boves leto dedit, arvaque jussit
Fallere depositum, vitiataque semina fecit. 480
Fertilitas terrae latum vulgata per orbem
Falsa jacet: primis segetes moriuntur in herbis,
Et modo sol nimius, nimius modo corripit imber;

Sideraque ventique nocent, avidaeque volucres
Semina jacta legunt; lolium tribulique fatigant 485
Triticeas messes et inexpugnabile gramen.
　Tum caput Eleis Alpheïas extulit undis,
Rorantesque comas a fronte removit ad aures,
Atque ait: 'o toto quaesitae virginis orbe
Et frugum genetrix, immensos siste labores, 490
Neve tibi fidae violenta irascere terrae.
Terra nihil meruit, patuitque invita rapinae.
Nec sum pro patria supplex: huc hospita veni.
Pisa mihi patria est, et ab Elide ducimus ortus:
Sicaniam peregrina colo, sed gratior omni 495
Haec mihi terra solo est. Hos nunc Arethusa penates,
Hanc habeo sedem: quam tu, mitissima, serva.
Mota loco cur sim tantique per aequoris undas
Advehar Ortygiam, veniet narratibus hora
Tempestiva meis, cum tu curaque levata 500
Et vultus melioris eris. Mihi pervia tellus
Praebet iter, subterque imas ablata cavernas
Illic caput attollo desuetaque sidera cerno.
Ergo dum Stygio sub terris gurgite labor,
Visa tua est oculis illic Proserpina nostris: 505
Illa quidem tristis, neque adhuc interrita vultu,
Sed regina tamen, sed opaci maxima mundi,
Sed tamen inferni pollens matrona tyranni.'
　Mater ad auditas stupuit ceu saxea voces,
Attonitaeque diu similis fuit. Utque dolore 510
Pulsa gravi gravis est amentia, curribus oras
Exit in aetherias. Ibi toto nubila vultu
Ante Jovem passis stetit invidiosa capillis;
'Pro' que 'meo veni supplex tibi, Juppiter,' inquit
'Sanguine, proque tuo. Si nulla est gratia matris, 515

Nata patrem moveat; neu sit tibi cura, precamur,
Vilior illius, quod nostro est edita partu.
En quaesita diu tandem mihi nata reperta est:
Si reperire vocas amittere certius, aut si
Scire, ubi sit, reperire vocas. Quod rapta, feremus, 520
Dummodo reddat eam: neque enim praedone marito
Filia digna tua est, si jam mea filia non est.'
Juppiter excepit: 'commune est pignus onusque
Nata mihi tecum: sed si modo nomina rebus
Addere vera placet, non hoc injuria factum, 525
Verum amor est; neque erit nobis gener ille pudori,
Tu modo, diva, velis. Ut desint cetera, quantum est
Esse Jovis fratrem! quid, quod non cetera desunt
Nec cedit nisi sorte mihi? Sed tanta cupido
Si tibi discidii est, repetet Proserpina caelum, 530
Lege tamen certa, si nullos contigit illic
Ore cibos: nam sic Parcarum foedere cautum est.'
    Dixerat. At Cereri certum est educere natam.
Non ita fata sinunt, quoniam jejunia virgo
Solverat et, cultis dum simplex errat in hortis, 535
Poeniceum curva decerpserat arbore pomum,
Sumptaque callenti septem de cortice grana
Presserat ore suo: solusque ex omnibus illud
Ascalaphus vidit, quem quondam dicitur Orphne,
Inter Avernales haud ignotissima nymphas, 540
Ex Acheronte suo silvis peperisse sub atris;
Vidit, et indicio reditum crudelis ademit.
Ingemuit regina Erebi, testemque profanam
Fecit avem, sparsumque caput Phlegethontide lympha
In rostrum et plumas et grandia lumina vertit. 545
Ille sibi ablatus fulvis amicitur in alis,
Inque caput crescit, longosque reflectitur ungues,

15. PROSERPINE.

Vixque movet natas per inertia bracchia pennas:
Foedaque fit volucris, venturi nuntia luctus,
Ignavus bubo, dirum mortalibus omen. 550
  Hic tamen indicio poenam linguaque videri
Commeruisse potest: vobis, Acheloides, unde
Pluma pedesque avium, cum virginis ora geratis?
An quia, cum legeret vernos Proserpina flores,
In comitum numero, doctae Sirenes, eratis? 555
Quam postquam toto frustra quaesistis in orbe,
Protinus, ut vestram sentirent aequora curam,
Posse super fluctus alarum insistere remis
Optastis, facilesque deos habuistis, et artus
Vidistis vestros subitis flavescere pennis. 560
Ne tamen ille canor mulcendas natus ad aures
Tantaque dos oris linguae deperderet usum,
Virginei vultus et vox humana remansit.
  At medius fratrisque sui maestaeque sororis
Juppiter ex aequo volventem dividit annum: 565
Nunc dea, regnorum numen commune duorum,
Cum matre est totidem, totidem cum conjuge menses.
Vertitur extemplo facies et mentis et oris;
Nam modo quae poterat Diti quoque maesta videri,
Laeta deae frons est, ut sol, qui tectus aquosis 570
Nubibus ante fuit, victis e nubibus exit."

16. ARACHNE, OR THE SPIDER'S WEB.
VI. 1–145.

Arachne, proud of her excellence in weaving, ventures to challenge Pallas herself to a trial of skill in her art. The goddess, indignant at Arachne's success, and also at the scenes which she has wrought into her web, tears the web to pieces, and turns Arachne into a spider.

Praebuerat dictis Tritonia talibus aures,
Carminaque Aonidum justamque probaverat iram.
Tum secum " laudare parum est; laudemur et ipsae,
Numina nec sperni sine poena nostra sinamus";
Maeoniaeque animum fatis intendit Arachnes,   5
Quam sibi lanificae non cedere laudibus artis
Audierat. Non illa loco nec origine gentis
Clara, sed arte fuit. Pater huic Colophonius Idmon
Phocaïco bibulas tingebat murice lanas:
Occiderat mater; sed et haec de plebe suoque   10
Aequa viro fuerat. Lydas tamen illa per urbes
Quaesierat studio nomen memorabile, quamvis
Orta domo parva parvis habitabat Hypaepis.
Hujus ut aspicerent opus admirabile, saepe
Deseruere sui nymphae vincta Timoli,   15
Deseruere suas nymphae Pactolides undas.
Nec factas solum vestes spectare juvabat;
Tum quoque, cum fierent: tantus decor adfuit arti.
Sive rudem primos lanam glomerabat in orbes,
Seu digitis subigebat opus, repetitaque longo   20
Vellera mollibat nebulas aequantia tractu,
Sive levi teretem versabat pollice fusum,
Seu pingebat acu: scires a Pallade doctam.

Quod tamen ipsa negat, tantaque offensa magistra
" Certet" ait " mecum : nihil est, quod victa recusem."
Pallas anum simulat, falsosque in tempora canos
Addit et infirmos, baculum, quod sustinet artus.
Tum sic orsa loqui : " non omnia grandior aetas,
Quae fugiamus, habet ; seris venit usus ab annis.
Consilium ne sperne meum. Tibi fama petatur   30
Inter mortales faciendae maxima lanae ;
Cede deae, veniamque tuis, temeraria, dictis
Supplice voce roga : veniam dabit illa roganti."
Aspicit hanc torvis, inceptaque fila relinquit,
Vixque manum retinens, confessaque vultibus iram 35
Talibus obscuram resecuta est Pallada dictis :
" Mentis inops longaque venis confecta senecta,
Et nimium vixisse diu nocet. Audiat istas,
Siqua tibi nurus est, siqua est tibi filia, voces.
Consilii satis est in me mihi. Neve monendo   40
Profecisse putes, eadem est sententia nobis.
Cur non ipsa venit ? cur haec certamina vitat ?"
Tum dea " venit !" ait, formamque removit anilem,
Palladaque exhibuit. Venerantur numina nymphae
Mygdonidesque nurus. Sola est non territa virgo. 45
Sed tamen erubuit, subitusque invita notavit
Ora rubor, rursusque evanuit : ut solet aër
Purpureus fieri, cum primum aurora movetur,
Et breve post tempus candescere solis ab ortu.
Perstat in incepto, stolidaeque cupidine palmae 50
In sua fata ruit ; neque enim Jove nata recusat,
Nec monet ulterius, nec jam certamina differt.
Haud mora, consistunt diversis partibus ambae
Et gracili geminas intendunt stamine telas.
Tela jugo vincta est, stamen secernit harundo,   55

Inseritur medium radiis subtemen acutis,
Quod digiti expediunt, atque inter stamina ductum
Percusso feriunt insecti pectine dentes.
Utraque festinant cinctaeque ad pectora vestes
Bracchia docta movent, studio fallente laborem.   60
Illic et Tyrium quae purpura sensit aënum
Texitur, et tenues parvi discriminis umbrae;
Qualis ab imbre solet percussis solibus arcus
Inficere ingenti longum curvamine caelum:
In quo diversi niteant cum mille colores,   65
Transitus ipse tamen spectantia lumina fallit:
Usque adeo quod tangit idem est; tamen ultima distant.
Illic et lentum filis immittitur aurum,
Et vetus in tela deducitur argumentum.
Cecropia Pallas scopulum Mavortis in arce   70
Pingit, et antiquam de terrae nomine litem.
Bis sex caelestes medio Jove sedibus altis
Augusta gravitate sedent. Sua quemque deorum
Inscribit facies. Jovis est regalis imago.
Stare deum pelagi longoque ferire tridente   75
Aspera saxa facit, medioque e vulnere saxi
Exsiluisse ferum; quo pignore vindicet urbem.
At sibi dat clipeum, dat acutae cuspidis hastam,
Dat galeam capiti; defenditur aegide pectus:
Percussamque sua simulat de cuspide terram   80
Edere cum bacis fetum canentis olivae:
Mirarique deos: operi victoria finis.
Ut tamen exemplis intellegat aemula laudis,
Quod pretium speret pro tam furialibus ausis,
Quattuor in partes certamina quattuor addit   85
Clara colore suo, brevibus distincta sigillis.
Threïciam Rhodopen habet angulus unus et Haemon,

16. ARACHNE.

Nunc gelidos montes, mortalia corpora quondam,
Nomina summorum sibi qui tribuere deorum.
Altera Pygmaeae fatum miserabile matris 90
Pars habet. Hanc Juno victam certamine jussit
Esse gruem populisque suis indicere bellum.
Pinxit et Antigonen ausam contendere quondam
Cum magni consorte Jovis, quam regia Juno
In volucrem vertit; nec profuit Ilion illi 95
Laomedonve pater, sumptis quin candida pennis
Ipsa sibi plaudat crepitante ciconia rostro.
Qui superest solus, Cinyran habet angulus orbum;
Isque gradus templi, natarum membra suarum,
Amplectens saxoque jacens lacrimare videtur. 100
Circuit extremas oleis pacalibus oras.
Is modus est, operisque sua facit arbore finem.
　Maeonis elusam designat imagine tauri
Europam: verum taurum, freta vera putares;
Ipsa videbatur terras spectare relictas 105
Et comites clamare suas, tactumque vereri
Assilientis aquae timidasque reducere plantas.
Fecit et Asterien aquila luctante teneri:
Fecit olorinis Ledam recubare sub alis:
Addidit, ut Satyri celatus imagine pulchram 110
Juppiter implerit gemino Nycteïda fetu,
Amphitryon fuerit, cum te, Tirynthia, cepit,
Aureus ut Danaën, Asopida luserit ignis,
Mnemosynen pastor, varius Deoïda serpens. 114
Ultima pars telae tenui circumdata limbo 127
Nexilibus flores hederis habet intertextos.
Non illud Pallas, non illud carpere Livor
Possit opus. Doluit successu flava virago, 130
Et rupit pictas, caelestia crimina, vestes.

Utque Cytoriaco radium de monte tenebat,
Ter quater Idmoniae frontem percussit Arachnes.
Non tulit infelix, laqueoque animosa ligavit
Guttura.   Pendentem Pallas miserata levavit,   135
Atque ita " vive quidem, pende tamen, improba," dixit,
" Lexque eadem poenae, ne sis secura futuri,
Dicta tuo generi serisque nepotibus esto."
Post ea discedens sucis Hecateïdos herbae
Sparsit; et extemplo tristi medicamine tactae   140
Defluxere comae, cum quis et naris et aures,
Fitque caput minimum; toto quoque corpore parva est;
In latere exiles digiti pro cruribus haerent,
Cetera venter habet: de quo tamen illa remittit
Stamen, et antiquas exercet aranea telas.

17. Niobe, or Latona's Revenge.

VI. 146-312.

Niobe, daughter of Tantalus, in the pride of her maternity as mother of a numerous and beautiful offspring, claims diviner honors than Latona, the mother of Apollo and Diana. Latona is avenged by her children, who slay all the sons and daughters of Niobe;

> "When in the house her children lay in death,
> Six beauteous daughters and six stalwart sons.
> The youths Apollo with his silver bow,
> The maids the archer-queen, Diana, slew,
> With anger filled that Niobe presumed
> Herself with fair Latona to compare,
> Her many children with her rival's two."
>
> Homer's "Iliad," xxiv. 604-610, Lord Derby's translation.

Lydia tota fremit, Phrygiaeque per oppida facti
Rumor it et magnum sermonibus occupat orbem.
Ante suos Niobe thalamos cognoverat illam,

17. NIOBE.

Tum cum Maeoniam virgo Sipylumque colebat:
Nec tamen admonita est poena popularis Arachnes 150
Cedere caelitibus, verbisque minoribus uti.
Multa dabant animos: sed enim nec conjugis artes
Nec genus amborum magnique potentia regni
Sic placuere illi, quamvis ea cuncta placerent,
Ut sua progenies; et felicissima matrum 155
Dicta foret Niobe, si non sibi visa fuisset.
Nam sata Tiresia venturi praescia Manto
Per medias fuerat, divino concita motu,
Vaticinata vias: "Ismenides, ite frequentes
Et date Latonae Latonigenisque duobus 160
Cum prece tura pia, lauroque innectite crinem:
Ore meo Latona jubet." Paretur, et omnes
Thebaïdes jussis sua tempora frondibus ornant,
Turaque dant sanctis et verba precantia flammis.
Ecce venit comitum Niobe celeberrima turba, 165
Vestibus intexto Phrygiis spectabilis auro,
Et, quantum ira sinit, formosa; movensque decoro
Cum capite immissos umerum per utrumque capillos
Constitit: utque oculos circumtulit alta superbos,
"Quis furor, auditos," inquit, "praeponere visis 170
Caelestes? aut cur colitur Latona per aras,
Numen adhuc sine ture meum est? mihi Tantalus auctor,
Cui licuit soli superorum tangere mensas.
Pleïadum soror est genetrix mea; maximus Atlas
Est avus, aetherium qui fert cervicibus axem; 175
Juppiter alter avus; socero quoque glorior illo.
Me gentes metuunt Phrygiae, me regia Cadmi
Sub domina est, fidibusque mei commissa mariti
Moenia cum populis a meque viroque reguntur.
In quamcumque domus adverti lumina partem, 180

Immensae spectantur opes.   Accedit eodem
Digna dea facies.   Huc natas adice septem
Et totidem juvenes, et mox generosque nurusque.
Quaerite nunc, habeat quam nostra superbia causam,
Nescio quoque audete satam Titanida Coeo   185
Latonam praeferre mihi, cui maxima quondam
Exiguam sedem pariturae terra negavit.
Nec caelo nec humo nec aquis dea vestra recepta est.
Exsul erat mundi, donec miserata vagantem
' Hospita tu terris erras, ego ' dixit ' in undis,'   190
Instabilemque locum Delos dedit.   Illa duorum
Facta parens: uteri pars haec est septima nostri.
Sum felix: quis enim neget hoc? felixque manebo;
Hoc quoque quis dubitet? tutam me copia fecit.
Major sum, quam cui possit Fortuna nocere;   195
Multaque ut eripiat, multo mihi plura relinquet.
Excessere metum mea jam bona.   Fingite demi
Huic aliquid populo natorum posse meorum,
Non tamen ad numerum redigar spoliata duorum,
Latonae turbam: qua quantum distat ab orba?   200
Infectis properate sacris; laurumque capillis
Ponite."   Deponunt, infectaque sacra relinquunt,
Quodque licet, tacito venerantur murmure numen.
Indignata dea est, summoque in vertice Cynthi
Talibus est dictis gemina cum prole locuta: 205
" En ego vestra parens, vobis animosa creatis,
Et, nisi Junoni, nulli cessura dearum,
An dea sim, dubitor, perque omnia saecula cultis
Arceor, o nati, nisi vos succurritis, aris.
Nec dolor hic solus: diro convicia facto   210
Tantalis adjecit, vosque est postponere natis
Ausa suis, et me, quod in ipsam reccidat, orbam

Dixit, et exhibuit linguam scelerata paternam."
Adjectura preces erat his Latona relatis:
"Desine!" Phoebus ait, "poenae mora longa querella est."
Dixit idem Phoebe; celerique per aëra lapsu
Contigerant tecti Cadmeïda nubibus arcem.
Planus erat lateque patens prope moenia campus,
Assiduis pulsatus equis, ubi turba rotarum
Duraque mollierat subjectas ungula glaebas. 220
Pars ibi de septem genitis Amphione fortes
Conscendunt in equos, Tyrioque rubentia suco
Terga premunt, auroque graves moderantur habenas.
E quibus Ismenos, qui matri sarcina quondam
Prima suae fuerat, dum certum flectit in orbem 225
Quadrupedis cursus, spumantiaque ora coërcet,
"Ei mihi!" conclamat, medioque in pectore fixa
Tela gerit, frenisque manu moriente remissis
In latus a dextro paulatim defluit armo.
    Proximus, audito sonitu per inane pharetrae, 230
Frena dabat Sipylus: veluti cum praescius imbris
Nube fugit visa, pendentiaque undique rector
Carbasa deducit, ne qua levis effluat aura.
Frena dabat: dantem non evitabile telum
Consequitur, summaque tremens cervice sagitta 235
Haesit, et exstabat nudum de gutture ferrum.
Ille, ut erat pronus, per colla admissa jubasque
Volvitur, et calido tellurem sanguine foedat.
    Phaedimus infelix et aviti nominis heres
Tantalus, ut solito finem imposuere labori, 240
Transierant ad opus nitidae juvenale palaestrae:
Et jam contulerant arto luctantia nexu
Pectora pectoribus, cum tento concita nervo,
Sicut erant juncti, trajecit utrumque sagitta.

Ingemuere simul, simul incurvata dolore 245
Membra solo posuere ; simul suprema jacentes
Lumina versarunt, animam simul exhalarunt.
   Aspicit Alphenor, laniataque pectora plangens
Advolat, ut gelidos complexibus allevet artus,
Inque pio cadit officio ; nam Delius illi 250
Intima fatifero rupit praecordia ferro.
Quod simul eductum, pars est pulmonis in hamis
Eruta, cumque anima cruor est effusus in auras.
At non intonsum simplex Damasichthona vulnus
Adficit. Ictus erat, qua crus esse incipit, et qua 255
Mollia nervosus facit internodia poples.
Dumque manu temptat trahere exitiabile telum,
Altera per jugulum pennis tenus acta sagitta est.
Expulit hanc sanguis, seque ejaculatus in altum
Emicat, et longe terebrata prosilit aura. 260
Ultimus Ilioneus non profectura precando
Bracchia sustulerat, " di " que " o communiter omnes,"
Dixerat, ignarus non omnes esse rogandos,
" Parcite ! " Motus erat, cum jam revocabile telum
Non fuit, arcitenens ; minimo tamen occidit ille 265
Vulnere, non alte percusso corde sagitta.
   Fama mali populique dolor lacrimaeque suorum
Tam subitae matrem certam fecere ruinae,
Mirantem potuisse, irascentemque, quod ausi
Hoc essent superi, quod tantum juris haberent. 270
Nam pater Amphion ferro per pectus adacto
Finierat moriens pariter cum luce dolorem.
Heu quantum haec Niobe Niobe distabat ab illa,
Quae modo Latois populum summoverat aris,
Et mediam tulerat gressus resupina per urbem, 275
Invidiosa suis ; at nunc miseranda vel hosti.

17. NIOBE.

Corporibus gelidis incumbit, et ordine nullo
Oscula dispensat natos suprema per omnes.
A quibus ad caelum liventia bracchia tollens
"Pascere, crudelis, nostro, Latona, dolore,   280
Pascere" ait, "satiaque meo tua pectora luctu:
Efferor: exsulta, victrixque inimica triumpha.
Cur autem victrix? miserae mihi plura supersunt,
Quam tibi felici: post tot quoque funera vinco." 285
  Dixerat, et sonuit contento nervus ab arcu:
Qui praeter Nioben unam conterruit omnes.
Illa malo est audax. Stabant cum vestibus atris
Ante toros fratrum demisso crine sorores:
E quibus una trahens haerentia viscere tela   290
Imposito fratri moribunda relanguit ore:
Altera solari miseram conata parentem
Conticuit subito, duplicataque vulnere caeco est:
[Oraque compressit, nisi postquam spiritus ibat.]
Haec frustra fugiens collabitur: illa sorori   295
Immoritur: latet haec: illam trepidare videres.
Sexque datis leto diversaque vulnera passis
Ultima restabat: quam toto corpore mater,
Tota veste tegens, "unam minimamque relinque!
De multis minimam posco," clamavit, "et unam." 300
Dumque rogat, pro qua rogat, occidit. Orba resedit
Exanimes inter natos natasque virumque,
Deriguitque malis. Nullos movet aura capillos,
In vultu color est sine sanguine, lumina maestis
Stant immota genis: nihil est in imagine vivum. 305
Ipsa quoque interius cum duro lingua palato
Congelat, et venae desistunt posse moveri;
Nec flecti cervix nec bracchia reddere motus
Nec pes ire potest: intra quoque viscera saxum est.

Flet tamen, et validi circumdata turbine venti 310
In patriam rapta est. Ibi fixa cacumine montis
Liquitur, et lacrimas etiam nunc marmora manant.

18. The Lycians; and Marsyas.

VI. 313–400.

Tum vero cuncti manifestam numinis iram
Femina virque timent, cultuque impensius omnes
Magna gemelliparae venerantur numina divae. 315
Utque fit, a facto propiore priora renarrant.
E quibus unus ait: " Lyciae quoque fertilis agris
Non impune deam veteres sprevere coloni.
Res obscura quidem est ignobilitate virorum,
Mira tamen. Vidi praesens stagnumque locumque 320
Prodigio notum. Nam me jam grandior aevo
Impatiensque viae genitor deducere lectos
Jusserat inde boves, gentisque illius eunti
Ipse ducem dederat. Cum quo dum pascua lustro,
Ecce lacu medio sacrorum nigra favilla 325
Ara vetus stabat, tremulis circumdata cannis.
Restitit, et pavido "faveas mihi" murmure dixit
Dux meus; et simili "faveas" ego murmure dixi.
Naiadum Faunine foret tamen ara rogabam,
Indigenaeve dei: cum talia rettulit hospes: 330
   "Non hac, o juvenis, montanum numen in ara est.
Illa suam vocat hanc, cui quondam regia conjunx
Orbe interdixit; quam vix erratica Delos
Errantem accepit, tum cum levis insula nabat.
Illic incumbens cum Palladis arbore palmae 335
Edidit invita geminos Latona noverca.
Hinc quoque Junonem fugisse puerpera fertur

Inque suo portasse sinu, duo numina, natos.
Jamque Chimaeriferae, cum sol gravis ureret arva,
Finibus in Lyciae longo dea fessa labore   340
Sidereo siccata sitim collegit ab aestu :
Uberaque ebiberant avidi lactantia nati.
Forte lacum mediocris aquae prospexit in imis
Vallibus : agrestes illic fruticosa legebant
Vimina cum juncis gratamque paludibus ulvam.   345
Accessit, positoque genu Titania terram
Pressit, ut hauriret gelidos potura liquores.
Rustica turba vetant.   Dea sic affata vetantes :
'Quid prohibetis aquis ? usus communis aquarum est.
Nec solem proprium natura nec aëra fecit   350
Nec tenues undas : ad publica munera veni,
Quae tamen ut detis, supplex peto.   Non ego nostros
Abluere hic artus lassataque membra parabam,
Sed relevare sitim.   Caret os umore loquentis
Et fauces arent, vixque est via vocis in illis. 355
Haustus aquae mihi nectar erit, vitamque fatebor
Accepisse simul : vitam dederitis in unda.
Hi quoque vos moveant, qui nostro bracchia tendunt
Parva sinu ;' et casu tendebant bracchia nati.

  Quem non blanda deae potuissent verba movere ? 360
Hi tamen orantem perstant prohibere, minasque,
Ni procul abscedat, conviciaque insuper addunt.
Nec satis est ; ipsos etiam pedibusque manuque
Turbavere lacus, imoque e gurgite mollem
Huc illuc limum saltu movere maligno.   365
Distulit ira sitim : neque enim jam filia Coei
Supplicat indignis, nec dicere sustinet ultra
Verba minora dea ; tollensque ad sidera palmas,
'Aeternum stagno' dixit 'vivatis in isto.'

Eveniunt optata deae. Juvat esse sub undis, 370
Et modo tota cava submergere membra palude,
Nunc proferre caput, summo modo gurgite nare,
Saepe super ripam stagni consistere, saepe
In gelidos resilire lacus. Sed nunc quoque turpes
Litibus exercent linguas, pulsoque pudore, 375
Quamvis sint sub aqua, sub aqua maledicere temptant.
Vox quoque jam rauca est, inflataque colla tumescunt,
Ipsaque dilatant patulos convicia rictus.
Terga caput tangunt, colla intercepta videntur;
Spina viret; venter, pars maxima corporis, albet: 380
Limosoque novae saliunt in gurgite ranae."
  Sic ubi nescio quis Lycia de gente virorum
Rettulit exitium, Satyri reminiscitur alter,
Quem Tritoniaca Latous harundine victum
Adfecit poena. "Quid me mihi detrahis?" inquit: 385
"A! piget, a! non est," clamabat, "tibia tanti!"
Clamanti cutis est summos direpta per artus;
Nec quicquam nisi vulnus erat: cruor undique manat,
Detectique patent nervi, trepidaeque sine ulla
Pelle micant venae; salientia viscera possis 390
Et perlucentes numerare in pectore fibras.
Illum ruricolae, silvarum numina, Fauni
Et satyri fratres et tunc quoque carus Olympus
Et nymphae flerunt, et quisquis montibus illis
Lanigerosque greges armentaque bucera pavit. 395
Fertilis immaduit, madefactaque terra caducas
Concepit lacrimas ac venis perbibit imis:
Quas ubi fecit aquam, vacuas emisit in auras.
Inde petens rapidum ripis declivibus aequor
Marsya nomen habet, Phrygiae liquidissimus amnis. 400

19. The Golden Fleece.

VII. 1-158.

Jason goes in quest of the Golden Fleece, and, by Medea's help, triumphs over all obstacles, and afterward carries Medea with him from Iolcos.

There is a good English version of the story in Mr. Morris's "Life and Death of Jason."

Jamque fretum Minyae Pagasaea puppe secabant:
Perpetuaque trahens inopem sub nocte senectam
Phineus visus erat, juvenesque Aquilone creati
Virgineas volucres miseri senis ore fugarant:
Multaque perpessi claro sub Iasone tandem 5
Contigerant rapidas limosi Phasidos undas:
Dumque adeunt regem Phrixeaque vellera poscunt,
Lexque datur Minyis magnorum horrenda laborum,
Concipit interea validos Aeetias ignes:
Et luctata diu, postquam ratione furorem 10
Vincere non poterat, "frustra, Medea, repugnas:
Nescio quis deus obstat," ait; "mirumque, nisi hoc est,
Aut aliquid certe simile huic, quod amare vocatur.
Nam cur jussa patris nimium mihi dura videntur?
Sunt quoque dura nimis. Cur, quem modo denique vidi,
Ne pereat, timeo? quae tanti causa timoris?
Excute virgineo conceptas pectore flammas,
Si potes, infelix! si possem, sanior essem.
Sed gravat invitam nova vis, aliudque cupido,
Mens aliud suadet. Video meliora proboque, 20
Deteriora sequor. Quid in hospite, regia virgo,
Ureris, et thalamos alieni concipis orbis?
Haec quoque terra potest, quod ames, dare. Vivat, an ille
Occidat, in dis est. Vivat tamen: idque precari

Vel sine amore licet. Quid enim commisit Iason? 25
Quem, nisi crudelem, non tangat Iasonis aetas
Et genus et virtus? quem non, ut cetera desint,
Ore movere potest? certe mea pectora movit.
At nisi opem tulero, taurorum adflabitur igne,
Concurretque suae segetis tellure creatis 30
Hostibus, aut avido dabitur fera praeda draconi.
Hoc ego si patiar, tum me de tigride natam,
Tum ferrum et scopulos gestare in corde fatebor.
Cur non et specto pereuntem, oculosque videndo
Conscelero? cur non tauros exhortor in illum 35
Terrigenasque feros insopitumque draconem?
Di meliora velint. Quamquam non ista precanda,
Sed facienda mihi. Prodamne ego regna parentis,
Atque ope nescio quis servabitur advena nostra,
Ut per me sospes sine me det lintea ventis, 40
Virque sit alterius, poenae Medea relinquar?
Si facere hoc, aliamve potest praeponere nobis,
Occidat ingratus. Sed non is vultus in illo,
Non ea nobilitas animo est, ea gratia formae,
Ut timeam fraudem meritique oblivia nostri. 45
Et dabit ante fidem. Cogamque in foedera testes
Esse deos. Quid tuta times? accingere et omnem
Pelle moram: tibi se semper debebit Iason,
Te face sollemni junget sibi, perque Pelasgas
Servatrix urbes matrum celebrabere turba. 50
Ergo ego germanam fratremque patremque deosque
Et natale solum, ventis ablata, relinquam?
Nempe pater saevus, nempe est mea barbara tellus,
Frater adhuc infans, stant mecum vota sororis:
Maximus intra me deus est. Non magna relinquam: 55
Magna sequar: titulum servatae pubis Achivae,

Notitiamque loci melioris, et oppida, quorum
Hic quoque fama viget, cultusque artesque locorum;
Quemque ego cum rebus, quas totus possidet orbis,
Aesoniden mutasse velim, quo conjuge felix 60
Et dis cara ferar et vertice sidera tangam.
Quid, quod nescio qui mediis incurrere in undis
Dicuntur montes, ratibusque inimica Charybdis
Nunc sorbere fretum, nunc reddere, cinctaque saevis
Scylla rapax canibus Siculo latrare profundo? 65
Nempe tenens quod amo, gremioque in Iasonis haerens
Per freta longa ferar. Nihil illum amplexa verebor;
Aut, siquid metuam, metuam de conjuge solo.
Conjugiumne putas, speciosaque nomina culpae
Imponis, Medea, tuae? quin aspice, quantum 70
Aggrediare nefas, et dum licet, effuge crimen."
Dixit: et ante oculos rectum pietasque pudorque
Constiterant, et victa dabat jam terga Cupido.

 Ibat ad antiquas Hecates Perseïdos aras,
Quas nemus umbrosum secretaque silva tegebat. 75
Et jam fortis erat, pulsusque recesserat ardor:
Cum videt Aesoniden, extinctaque flamma revixit.
Erubuere genae, totoque recanduit ore,
Utque solet ventis alimenta assumere, quaeque
Parva sub inducta latuit scintilla favilla, 80
Crescere et in veteres agitata resurgere vires,
Sic jam lentus amor, jam quem languere putares,
Ut vidit juvenem, specie praesentis inarsit.
Et casu solito formosior Aesone natus
Illa luce fuit: posses ignoscere amanti. 85
Spectat, et in vultu veluti tum denique viso
Lumina fixa tenet, nec se mortalia demens
Ora videre putat, nec se declinat ab illo.

Ut vero coepitque loqui dextramque prehendit
Hospes, et auxilium summissa voce rogavit, 90
Promisitque torum, lacrimis ait illa profusis:
"Quid faciam, video: nec me ignorantia veri
Decipiet, sed amor.   Servabere munere nostro:
Servatus promissa dato.'   Per sacra triformis
Ille deae, lucoque foret quod numen in illo, 95
Perque patrem soceri cernentem cuncta futuri,
Eventusque suos et tanta pericula jurat.
Creditus accepit cantatas protinus herbas,
Edidicitque usum, laetusque in tesca recessit.
   Postera depulerat stellas aurora micantes: 100
Conveniunt populi sacrum Mavortis in arvum,
Consistuntque jugis.   Medio rex ipse resedit
Agmine purpureus sceptroque insignis eburno.
Ecce adamanteis vulcanum naribus efflant
Aeripedes tauri, tactaeque vaporibus herbae 105
Ardent; utque solent pleni resonare camini,
Aut ubi terrena silices fornace soluti
Concipiunt ignem liquidarum aspergine aquarum:
Pectora sic intus clausas volventia flammas
Gutturaque usta sonant.   Tamen illis Aesone natus 110
Obvius it.   Vertere truces venientis ad ora
Terribiles vultus praefixaque cornua ferro,
Pulveremque solum pede pulsavere bisulco,
Fumificisque locum mugitibus impleverunt.
Deriguere metu Minyae.   Subit ille, nec ignes 115
Sentit anhelatos—tantum medicamina possunt—
Pendulaque audaci mulcet palearia dextra,
Suppositosque jugo pondus grave cogit aratri
Ducere et insuetum ferro proscindere campum.
Mirantur Colchi: Minyae clamoribus augent 120

19. THE GOLDEN FLEECE.

Adiciuntque animos. Galea tum sumit aëna
Vipereos dentes, et aratos spargit in agros.
Semina mollit humus valido praetincta veneno,
Et crescunt fiuntque sati nova corpora dentes.
Utque hominis speciem materna sumit in alvo, 125
Perque suos intus numeros componitur infans,
Nec nisi maturus communes exit in auras:
Sic ubi visceribus gravidae telluris imago
Effecta est hominis, feto consurgit in arvo;
Quodque magis mirum est, simul edita concutit arma. 130
Quos ubi viderunt praeacutae cuspidis hastas
In caput Haemonii juvenis torquere parantes,
Demisere metu vultumque animumque Pelasgi.
Ipsa quoque extimuit, quae tutum fecerat illum,
Utque peti vidit juvenem tot ab hostibus unum, 135
Palluit et subito sine sanguine frigida sedit;
Neve parum valeant a se data gramina, carmen
Auxiliare canit, secretasque advocat artes.
Ille gravem medios silicem jaculatus in hostes
A se depulsum Martem convertit in ipsos. 140
Terrigenae pereunt per mutua vulnera fratres,
Civilique cadunt acie. Gratantur Achivi,
Victoremque tenent avidisque amplexibus haerent.
Tu quoque victorem complecti, barbara, velles;
Obstitit incepto pudor. At complexa fuisses; 145
Sed te, ne faceres, tenuit reverentia famae.
Quod licet, aspectu tacito laetaris, agisque
Carminibus grates et dis auctoribus horum.

Pervigilem superest herbis sopire draconem.
Qui crista linguisque tribus praesignis et uncis 150
Dentibus horrendus custos erat arboris aureae.
Hunc postquam sparsit Lethaei gramine suci

Verbaque ter dixit placidos facientia somnos,
Quae mare turbatum, quae concita flumina sistunt,
Somnus in ignotos oculos sibi venit, et auro 155
Heros Aesonius potitur, spolioque superbus
Muneris auctorem secum, spolia altera, portans
Victor Iolciacos tetigit cum conjuge portus.

20. The Death of Icarus.

VIII. 183-259.

Daedalus had fled from Athens to Crete, where he built the labyrinth for Minos. Kept now against his will by Minos, he flies across the sea; his son Icarus, who flies with him, falls into the sea.

Daedalus interea Creten longumque perosus
Exilium tactusque loci natalis amore,
Clausus erat pelago. "Terras licet" inquit "et undas 185
Obstruat: at caelum certe patet; ibimus illac.
Omnia possideat, non possidet aëra Minos."
Dixit, et ignotas animum dimittit in artes,
Naturamque novat. Nam ponit in ordine pennas,
A minima coeptas, longam breviore sequenti, 190
Ut clivo crevisse putes: sic rustica quondam
Fistula disparibus paulatim surgit avenis.
Tum lino medias et ceris alligat imas,
Atque ita compositas parvo curvamine flectit,
Ut veras imitetur aves. Puer Icarus una 195
Stabat et, ignarus sua se tractare pericla,
Ore renidenti modo, quas vaga moverat aura,
Captabat plumas, flavam modo pollice ceram
Mollibat, lusuque suo mirabile patris
Impediebat opus. Postquam manus ultima coeptis 200

20. THE DEATH OF ICARUS.

Imposita est, geminas opifex libravit in alas
Ipse suum corpus, motaque pependit in aura.
   Instruit et natum, "medio" que "ut limite curras,
Icare," ait "moneo, ne, si demissior ibis,
Unda gravet pennas, si celsior, ignis adurat.   205
Inter utrumque vola.   Nec te spectare Boöten
Aut Helicen jubeo strictumque Orionis ensem:
Me duce carpe viam."   Pariter praecepta volandi
Tradit et ignotas umeris accommodat alas.
   Inter opus monitusque genae maduere seniles,   210
Et patriae tremuere manus.   Dedit oscula nato
Non iterum repetenda suo, pennisque levatus
Ante volat, comitique timet, velut ales, ab alto
Quae teneram prolem produxit in aëra nido;
Hortaturque sequi, damnosasque erudit artes,   215
Et movet ipse suas et nati respicit alas.
Hos aliquis tremula dum captat harundine pisces,
Aut pastor baculo stivave innixus arator
Vidit et obstipuit, quique aethera carpere possent,
Credidit esse deos.   Et jam Junonia laeva   220
Parte Samos fuerat Delosque Parosque relictae,
Dextra Lebinthus erat fecundaque melle Calymne,
Cum puer audaci coepit gaudere volatu,
Deseruitque ducem caelique cupidine tractus
Altius egit iter.   Rapidi vicinia solis   225
Mollit odoratas, pennarum vincula, ceras.
Tabuerant cerae; nudos quatit ille lacertos,
Remigioque carens non ullas percipit auras,
Oraque caerulea patrium clamantia nomen
Excipiuntur aqua: quae nomen traxit ab illo.   230
At pater infelix, nec jam pater, "Icare," dixit,
"Icare," dixit "ubi es? qua te regione requiram?"

"Icare" dicebat, pennas aspexit in undis,
Devovitque suas artes, corpusque sepulchro
Condidit; et tellus a nomine dicta sepulti. 235
  Hunc miseri tumulo ponentem corpora nati
Garrula ramosa prospexit ab ilice perdix,
Et plausit pennis testataque gaudia cantu est:
Unica tunc volucris, nec visa prioribus annis,
Factaque nuper avis; longum tibi, Daedale, crimen. 240
Namque huic tradiderat, fatorum ignara, docendam
Progeniem germana suam, natalibus actis
Bis puerum senis, animi ad praecepta capacis.
Ille etiam medio spinas in pisce notatas
Traxit in exemplum, ferroque incidit acuto 245
Perpetuos dentes et serrae repperit usum.
Primus et ex uno duo ferrea bracchia nodo
Vinxit, ut aequali spatio distantibus illis
Altera pars staret, pars altera duceret orbem.
Daedalus invidit, sacraque ex arce Minervae 250
Praecipitem misit, lapsum mentitus. At illum
Quae favet ingeniis, excepit Pallas, avemque
Reddidit, et medio velavit in aëre pennis.
Sed vigor ingenii quondam velocis in alas
Inque pedes abiit: nomen quod et ante, remansit. 255
Non tamen haec alte volucris sua corpora tollit,
Nec facit in ramis altoque cacumine nidos;
Propter humum volitat, ponitque in saepibus ova,
Antiquique memor metuit sublimia casus.

21. Philemon and Baucis.

VIII. 616-724.

Philemon and Baucis, an aged couple in Phrygia, entertain Jupiter and Mercury, though they are "strangers" to them; and they find that "they have thereby entertained" gods "unawares."

Obstipuere omnes, nec talia dicta probarunt;
Ante omnesque Lelex, animo maturus et aevo,
Sic ait: " immensa est finemque potentia caeli
Non habet, et quicquid superi voluere, peractum est.
Quoque minus dubites, tiliae contermina quercus   620
Collibus est Phrygiis, modico circumdata muro :
Ipse locum vidi ; nam me Pelopeïa Pittheus
Misit in arva, suo quondam regnata parenti.
Haud procul hinc stagnum est, tellus habitabilis olim,
Nunc celebres mergis fulicisque palustribus undae.   625
Juppiter huc specie mortali, cumque parente
Venit Atlantiades positis caducifer alis.
Mille domos adiere, locum requiemque petentes :
Mille domos clausere serae.   Tamen una recepit,
Parva quidem, stipulis et canna tecta palustri :   630
Sed pia Baucis anus parilique aetate Philemon
Illa sunt annis juncti juvenalibus, illa
Consenuere casa; paupertatemque fatendo
Effecere levem nec iniqua mente ferendo.
Nec refert, dominos illic, famulosne requiras :   635
Tota domus duo sunt, idem parentque jubentque.
  Ergo ubi caelicolae placitos tetigere penates,
Summissoque humiles intrarunt vertice postes,
Membra senex posito jussit relevare sedili,

Quo superinjecit textum rude sedula Baucis. 640
Inde foco tepidum cinerem dimovit et ignes
Suscitat hesternos foliisque et cortice sicco
Nutrit et ad flammas anima producit anili;
Multifidasque faces ramaliaque arida tecto
Detulit et minuit, parvoque admovit aëno. 645
Quodque suus conjunx riguo collegerat horto,
Truncat holus foliis. Furca levat ille bicorni
Sordida terga suis nigro pendentia tigno,
Servatoque diu resecat de tergore partem
Exiguam, sectamque domat ferventibus undis. 650
   Interea medias fallunt sermonibus horas,
Concutiuntque torum de molli fluminis ulva 655
Impositum lecto, sponda pedibusque salignis.
Vestibus hunc velant, quas non nisi tempore festo
Sternere consuerant: sed et haec vilisque vetusque
Vestis erat, lecto non indignanda saligno.
Accubuere dei. Mensam succincta tremensque 660
Ponit anus; mensae sed erat pes tertius inpar:
Testa parem fecit. Quae postquam subdita clivum
Sustulit, aequatam mentae tersere virentes.
Ponitur hic bicolor sincerae baca Minervae,
Conditaque in liquida corna autumnalia faece, 665
Intibaque et radix et lactis massa coacti,
Ovaque non acri leviter versata favilla,
Omnia fictilibus. Post haec caelatus eodem
Sistitur argento crater fabricataque fago
Pocula, qua cava sunt, flaventibus illita ceris. 670
Parva mora est, epulasque foci miscre calentes,
Nec longae rursus referuntur vina senectae,
Dantque locum mensis paulum seducta secundis.
Hic nux, hic mixta est rugosis carica palmis

21. PHILEMON AND BAUCIS.

Prunaque et in patulis redolentia mala canistris 675
Et de purpureis collectae vitibus uvae.
Candidus in medio favus est. Super omnia vultus
Accessere boni nec iners pauperque voluntas.
 Interea totiens haustum cratera repleri
Sponte sua, per seque vident succrescere vina: 680
Attoniti novitate pavent, manibusque supinis
Concipiunt Baucisque preces timidusque Philemon,
Et veniam dapibus nullisque paratibus orant.
Unicus anser erat, minimae custodia villae,
Quem dis hospitibus domini mactare parabant. 685
Ille celer penna tardos aetate fatigat,
Eluditque diu, tandemque est visus ad ipsos
Confugisse deos. Superi vetuere necari:
'Di' que 'sumus, meritasque luet vicinia poenas
Impia' dixerunt; 'vobis immunibus hujus 690
Esse mali dabitur; modo vestra relinquite tecta,
Ac nostros comitate gradus et in ardua montis
Ite simul.' Parent ambo, baculisque levati
Nituntur longo vestigia ponere clivo.
 Tantum aberant summo, quantum semel ire sagitta 695
Missa potest: flexere oculos, et mersa palude
Cetera prospiciunt, tantum sua tecta manere.
Dumque ea mirantur, dum-deflent fata suorum,
Illa vetus, dominis etiam casa parva duobus
Vertitur in templum: furcas subiere columnae, 700
Stramina flavescunt aurataque tecta videntur,
Caelataeque fores, adopertaque marmore tellus.
Talia tum placido Saturnius edidit ore:
'Dicite, juste senex et femina conjuge justo
Digna, quid optetis.' Cum Baucide pauca locutus, 705
Judicium superis aperit commune Philemon:

' Esse sacerdotes delubraque vestra tueri
Poscimus; et quoniam concordes egimus annos,
Auferat hora duos eadem, nec conjugis unquam
Busta meae videam, neu sim tumulandus ab illa.'   710
   Vota fides sequitur.   Templi tutela fuere,
Donec vita data est.   Annis aevoque soluti
Ante gradus sacros cum starent forte, locique
Narrarent casus, frondere Philemona Baucis,
Baucida conspexit senior frondere Philemon.   715
Jamque super geminos crescente cacumine vultus
Mutua, dum licuit, reddebant dicta ' vale ' que
' O conjunx ' dixere simul, simul abdita texit
Ora frutex.   Ostendit adhuc Thymbreius illic
Incola de gemino vicinos corpore truncos.   720
   Haec mihi non vani, neque erat cur fallere vellent,
Narravere senes.   Equidem pendentia vidi
Serta super ramos, ponensque recentia dixi,
' Cura pii dis sunt, et qui coluere, coluntur.' "

22. The Wooing of Deianira.

IX. 1-97.

   The river-god Achelous tells how Hercules contended with him for the hand of Deianira, and how Hercules defeated him and won the prize.

Quae gemitus truncaeque deo Neptunius heros
Causa rogat frontis.   Cum sic Calydonius amnis
Coepit, inornatos redimitus harundine crines:
"Triste petis munus.   Quis enim sua proelia victus
Commemorare velit? Referam tamen ordine. Nec tam   5
Turpe fuit vinci, quam contendisse decorum est;
Magnaque dat nobis tantus solacia victor.

Nomine siqua suo tandem pervenit ad aures
Deïanira tuas—quondam pulcherrima virgo
Multorumque fuit spes invidiosa procorum.   10
Cum quibus ut soceri domus est intrata petiti,
'Accipe me generum,' dixi 'Parthaone nate:'
Dixit et Alcides: alii cessere duobus.
Ille Jovem socerum dare se, famamque laborum,
Et superata suae referebat jussa novercae.   15
Contra ego 'turpe deum mortali cedere:' dixi—
Nondum erat ille deus—'regem me cernis aquarum
Cursibus obliquis inter tua regna fluentum.
Nec gener externis hospes tibi missus ab oris,
Sed popularis ero et rerum pars una tuarum.   20
Tantum ne noceat, quod me nec regia Juno
Odit, et omnis abest jussorum poena laborum.'
   Talia dicentem jamdudum lumine torvo   27
Spectat, et accensae non fortiter imperat irae,
Verbaque tot reddit: 'melior mihi dextera lingua.
Dummodo pugnando superem, tu vince loquendo,'   30
Congrediturque ferox.   Puduit modo magna locutum
Cedere: rejeci viridem de corpore vestem,
Bracchiaque opposui, tenuique a pectore varas
In statione manus et pugnae membra paravi.
Ille cavis hausto spargit me pulvere palmis,   35
Inque vicem fulvae tactu flavescit harenae.
Et modo cervicem, modo crura micantia captat,
Aut captare putes, omnique a parte lacessit.
Me mea defendit gravitas: frustraque petebar;
Haud secus ac moles, magno quam murmure fluctus 40
Oppugnant; manet illa, suoque est pondere tuta.
   Digredimur paulum, rursusque ad bella coimus,
Inque gradu stetimus, certi non cedere; eratque

Cum pede pes junctus, totoque ego pectore pronus
Et digitos digitis et frontem fronte premebam. 45
Non aliter vidi fortes concurrere tauros,
Cum pretium pugnae toto nitidissima saltu
Expetitur conjunx: spectant armenta paventque
Nescia, quem maneat tanti victoria regni.
Ter sine profectu voluit nitentia contra 50
Reicere Alcides a se mea pectora: quarto
Excutit amplexus, adductaque bracchia solvit,
Impulsumque manu—certum est mihi vera fateri—
Protinus avertit, tergoque onerosus inhaesit.
Siqua fides,—neque enim ficta mihi gloria voce 55
Quaeritur—imposito pressus mihi monte videbar.
Vix tamen inserui sudore fluentia multo
Bracchia, vix solvi duros a pectore nexus.
Instat anhelanti, prohibetque resumere vires,
Et cervice mea potitur. Tum denique tellus 60
Pressa genu nostro est, et harenas ore momordi.
Inferior virtute, meas divertor ad artes,
Elaborque viro longum formatus in anguem.
Qui postquam flexos sinuavi corpus in orbes,
Cumque fero movi linguam stridore bisulcam, 65
Risit, et illudens nostras Tirynthius artes
'Cunarum labor est angues superare mearum,'
Dixit ' et ut vincas alios, Acheloe, dracones,
Pars quota Lernaeae serpens eris unus echidnae?
Vulneribus fecunda suis erat illa, nec ullum 70
De centum numero caput est impune recisum,
Quin gemino cervix herede valentior esset.
Hanc ego ramosam natis e caede colubris
Crescentemque malo domui, vetuique renasci.
Quid fore te credas, falsum qui versus in anguem 75

Arma aliena moves? quem forma precaria celat?'
Dixerat, et summo digitorum vincula collo
Inicit: angebar, ceu guttura forcipe pressus,
Pollicibusque meas pugnabam evellere fauces.
   Sic quoque devicto restabat tertia tauri   80
Forma trucis: tauro mutatus membra rebello.
Induit ille toris a laeva parte lacertos,
Admissumque trahens sequitur, depressaque dura
Cornua figit humo, meque alta sternit harena.
Nec satis hoc fuerat: rigidum fera dextera cornu   85
Dum tenet, infregit, truncaque a fronte revellit.
Naides hoc, pomis et odoro flore repletum,
Sacrarunt; divesque meo Bona Copia cornu est."
   Dixerat: et Nymphe ritu succincta Dianae,
Una ministrarum, fusis utrimque capillis,   90
Incessit totumque tulit praedivite cornu
Autumnum et mensas, felicia poma, secundas.
Lux subit; et primo feriente cacumina sole
Discedunt juvenes: neque enim, dum flumina pacem
Et placidos habeant lapsus, totaeque resicant,   95
Opperiuntur, aquae. Vultus Achelous agrestes
Et lacerum cornu mediis caput abdidit undis.

23. The Death of Hercules.
IX. 134-272.

> "As when Alcides, from Oechalia crown'd
>   With conquest, felt the envenom'd robe, and tore
>   Through pain up by the roots Thessalian pines;
>   And Lichas from the top of Oeta threw
> Into the Euboic sea."—"Paradise Lost," II. 542-546.

   Longa fuit medii mora temporis: actaque magni
Herculis implerant terras odiumque novercae.   135

Victor ab Oechalia Cenaeo sacra parabat
Vota Jovi, cum fama loquax praecessit ad aures,
Deianira, tuas, quae veris addere falsa
Gaudet, et e minimo sua per mendacia crescit,
Amphitryoniaden Ioles ardore teneri. 140
Credit amans, venerisque novae perterrita fama
Indulsit primo lacrimis, flendoque dolorem
Diffudit miseranda suum: mox deinde "quid autem
Flemus?" ait "paelex lacrimis laetabitur istis.
Quae quoniam adveniet, properandum aliquidque no-
    vandum est, 145
Dum licet, et nondum thalamos tenet altera nostros.
Conquerar, an sileam? repetam Calydona, morerne?
Excedam tectis? an, si nihil amplius, obstem?
Quid si me, Meleagre, tuam memor esse sororem
Forte paro facinus, quantumque injuria possit 150
Femineusque dolor, jugulata paelice testor?"
Incursus animus varios habet: omnibus illis
Praetulit imbutam Nesseo sanguine vestem
Mittere, quae vires defecto reddat amori.
Ignaroque Lichae, quid tradat, nescia, luctus 155
Ipsa suos tradit, blandisque miserrima verbis,
Dona det illa viro, mandat. Capit inscius heros,
Induiturque umeris Lernaeae virus echidnae.

    Tura dabat primis et verba precantia flammis,
Vinaque marmoreas patera fundebat in aras: 160
Incaluit vis illa mali, resolutaque flammis
Herculeos abiit late diffusa per artus.
Dum potuit, solita gemitum virtute repressit.
Victa malis postquam est patientia, reppulit aras,
Implevitque suis nemorosum vocibus Oeten. 165
Nec mora, letiferam conatur scindere vestem:

23. THE DEATH OF HERCULES.

Qua trahitur, trahit illa cutem, foedumque relatu,
Aut haeret membris frustra temptata revelli,
Aut laceros artus et grandia detegit ossa.
Ipse cruor, gelido ceu quondam lammina candens   170
Tincta lacu, stridit coquiturque ardente veneno.
Nec modus est, sorbent avidae praecordia flammae,
Caeruleusque fluit toto de corpore sudor,
Ambustique sonant nervi; caecaque medullis
Tabe liquefactis tendens ad sidera palmas   175
"Cladibus," exclamat "Saturnia, pascere nostris:
Pascere, et hanc pestem specta, crudelis, ab alto,
Corque ferum satia; vel si miserandus et hosti,
Hoc est, si tibi sum, diris cruciatibus aegram
Invisamque animam natamque laboribus aufer.   180
Mors mihi munus erit: decet haec dare dona novercam.
Ergo ego foedantem peregrino templa cruore
Busirin domui? saevoque alimenta parentis
Antaeo eripui? nec me pastoris Hiberi
Forma triplex, nec forma triplex tua, Cerbere, movit? 185
Vosne, manus, validi pressistis cornua tauri?
Vestrum opus Elis habet, vestrum Stymphalides undae,
Partheniumque nemus? vestra virtute relatus
Thermodontiaco caelatus balteus auro,
Pomaque ab insomni concustodita dracone?   190
Nec mihi Centauri potuere resistere, nec mi
Arcadiae vastator aper? nec profuit hydrae
Crescere per damnum geminasque resumere vires?
Quid, cum Thracis equos humano sanguine pingues
Plenaque corporibus laceris praesepia vidi,   195
Visaque dejeci, dominumque ipsosque peremi?
His elisa jacet moles Nemeaca lacertis:
Hac caelum cervice tuli.   Defessa jubendo est

Saeva Jovis conjunx: ego sum indefessus agendo.
Sed nova pestis adest, cui nec virtute resisti 200
Nec telis armisque potest. Pulmonibus errat
Ignis edax imis, perque omnes pascitur artus.
At valet Eurystheus! et sunt, qui credere possint
Esse deos?" dixit, perque altum saucius Oeten
Haud aliter graditur, quam si venabula taurus 205
Corpore fixa gerat, factique refugerit auctor.
Saepe illum gemitus edentem, saepe frementem,
Saepe retemptantem totas refringere vestes
Sternentemque trabes irascentemque videres
Montibus aut patrio tendentem bracchia caelo. 210
    Ecce Lichan trepidum latitantem rupe cavata
Aspicit, utque dolor rabiem collegerat omnem,
"Tune, Licha," dixit "feralia dona dedisti?
Tune meae necis auctor eris?" tremit ille, pavetque
Pallidus, et timide verba excusantia dicit. 215
Dicentem genibusque manus adhibere parantem
Corripit Alcides, et terque quaterque rotatum
Mittit in Euboicas tormento fortius undas.
Ille per aërias pendens induruit auras:
Utque ferunt imbres gelidis concrescere ventis, 220
Inde nives fieri, nivibus quoque molle rotatis
Astringi et spissa glomerari grandine corpus,
Sic illum validis actum per inane lacertis
Exsanguemque metu nec quicquam umoris habentem
In rigidos versum silices prior edidit aetas. 225
Nunc quoque in Euboico scopulus brevis emicat alto
Gurgite et humanae servat vestigia formae,
Quem, quasi sensurum, nautae calcare verentur,
Appellantque Lichan. At tu, Jovis inclita proles,
Arboribus caesis, quas ardua gesserat Oete, 230

23. THE DEATH OF HERCULES.

Inque pyram structis arcum pharetramque capacem
Regnaque visuras iterum Trojana sagittas
Ferre jubes Poeante satum, quo flamma ministro
Subdita ; dumque avidis comprenditur ignibus agger,
Congeriem silvae Nemeaeo vellere summam   235
Sternis, et imposita clavae cervice recumbis,
Haud alio vultu, quam si conviva jaceres
Inter plena meri redimitus pocula sertis.
 Jamque valens et in omne latus diffusa sonabat,
Securosque artus contemptoremque petebat   240
Flamma suum : timuere dei pro vindice terrae.
Quos ita, sensit enim, laeto Saturnius ore
Juppiter alloquitur : "nostra est timor iste voluptas,
O superi, totoque libens mihi pectore grator,
Quod memoris populi dicor rectorque paterque,   245
Et mea progenies vestro quoque tuta favore est.
Nam quamquam ipsius datur hoc immanibus actis,
Obligor ipse tamen. Sed enim, ne pectora vano
Fida metu paveant, istas despernite flammas !
Omnia qui vicit, vincet, quos cernitis, ignes ; 250
Nec nisi materna vulcanum parte potentem
Sentiet : aeternum est a me quod traxit, et expers
Atque immune necis, nullaque domabile flamma.
Idque ego defunctum terra caelestibus oris
Accipiam, cunctisque meum laetabile factum   255
Dis fore confido. Siquis tamen Hercule, siquis
Forte deo doliturus erit, data praemia nolet,
Sed meruisse dari sciet, invitusque probabit."
 Assensere dei : conjunx quoque regia visa est
Cetera non duro, duro tamen ultima vultu   260
Dicta tulisse Jovis, seque indoluisse notatam.
 Interea, quodcumque fuit populabile flammae,

Mulciber abstulerat: nec cognoscenda remansit
Herculis effigies, nec quicquam ab imagine ductum
Matris habet, tantumque Jovis vestigia servat. 265
Utque novus serpens posita cum pelle senecta
Luxuriare solet, squamaque virere recenti:
Sic ubi mortales Tirynthius exuit artus,
Parte sui meliore viget, majorque videri
Coepit et augusta fieri gravitate verendus. 270
Quem pater omnipotens inter cava nubila raptum
Quadrijugo curru radiantibus intulit astris.

24. Orpheus and Eurydice.

X. 1-77.

> "Such strains as would have won the ear
> Of Pluto, to have quite set free
> The half-regained Eurydice."
>
> Milton's "L'Allegro."

Inde per immensum croceo velatus amictu
Aethera digreditur, Ciconumque Hymenaeus ad oras
Tendit, et Orphea nequiquam voce vocatur.
Adfuit ille quidem, sed nec sollemnia verba
Nec laetos vultus nec felix attulit omen. 5
Fax quoque, quam tenuit, lacrimoso stridula fumo
Usque fuit, nullosque invenit motibus ignes.
Exitus auspicio gravior: nam nupta per herbas
Dum nova naiadum turba comitata vagatur,
Occidit in talum serpentis dente recepto. 10
  Quam satis ad superas postquam Rhodopeïus auras
Deflevit vates, ne non temptaret et umbras,
Ad Styga Taenaria est ausus descendere porta:
Perque leves populos simulacraque functa sepulcro

Persephonen adiit inamoenaque regna tenentem 15
Umbrarum dominum, pulsisque ad carmina nervis
Sic ait: "o positi sub terra numina mundi,
In quem reccidimus, quicquid mortale creamur:
Si licet, et falsi positis ambagibus oris
Vera loqui sinitis, non huc, ut opaca viderem 20
Tartara, descendi; nec uti villosa colubris
Terna Medusaei vincirem guttura monstri:
Causa viae conjunx, in quam calcata venenum
Vipera diffudit, crescentesque abstulit annos.
Posse pati volui, nec me temptasse negabo: 25
Vicit Amor. Supera deus hic bene notus in ora est:
An sit et hic, dubito; sed et hic tamen auguror esse,
Famaque si veteris non est mentita rapinae, [timoris,
Vos quoque junxit Amor. Per ego haec loca plena
Per Chaos hoc ingens vastique silentia regni, 30
Eurydices, oro, properata retexite fata.
Omnia debentur vobis, paulumque morati
Serius aut citius sedem properamus ad unam.
Tendimus huc omnes, haec est domus ultima, vosque
Humani generis longissima regna tenetis. 35
Haec quoque, cum justos matura peregerit annos,
Juris erit vestri: pro munere poscimus usum.
Quod si fata negant veniam pro conjuge, certum est
Nolle redire mihi: leto gaudete duorum."
   Talia dicentem nervosque ad verba moventem 40
Exsangues flebant animae: nec Tantalus undam
Captavit refugam, stupuitque Ixionis orbis,
Nec carpsere jecur volucres, urnisque vacarunt
Belides, inque tuo sedisti, Sisyphe, saxo.
Tunc primum lacrimis victarum carmine fama est 45
Eumenidum maduisse genas. Nec regia conjunx

Sustinet oranti, nec qui regit ima, negare :
Eurydicenque vocant.   Umbras erat illa recentes
Inter, et incessit passu de vulnere tardo.
Hanc simul et legem Rhodopeïus accipit Orpheus,   50
Ne flectat retro sua lumina, donec Avernas
Exierit valles ; aut irrita dona futura.

   Carpitur acclivis per muta silentia trames,
Arduus, obscurus, caligine densus opaca,
Nec procul afuerunt telluris margine summae :   55
Hic, ne deficeret, metuens, avidusque videndi,
Flexit amans oculos : et protinus illa relapsa est,
Bracchiaque intendens prendique et prendere certus
Nil nisi cedentes infelix arripit auras.
Jamque iterum moriens non est de conjuge quicquam
Questa suo : quid enim nisi se quereretur amatam ?
Supremumque vale, quod jam vix auribus ille
Acciperet, dixit, revolutaque rursus eodem est.

   Non aliter stupuit gemina nece conjugis Orpheus,
Quam tria qui timidus, medio portante catenas,   65
Colla canis vidit ; quem non pavor ante reliquit,
Quam natura prior, saxo per corpus oborto :
Quique in se crimen traxit voluitque videri
Olenos esse nocens, tuque, o confisa figurae,
Infelix Lethaea, tuae, junctissima quondam   70
Pectora, nunc lapides, quos umida sustinet Ide.

   Orantem frustraque iterum transire volentem
Portitor arcuerat ; septem tamen ille diebus
Squalidus in ripa Cereris sine munere sedit :
Cura dolorque animi lacrimaeque alimenta fuere.   75
Esse deos Erebi crudeles questus, in altam
Se recipit Rhodopen pulsumque aquilonibus Haemum.

25. HYACINTHUS.

X. 162–219.

... "that sanguine flower, inscribed with woe."
MILTON'S "LYCIDAS."

Te quoque, Amyclide, posuisset in aethere Phoebus,
Tristia si spatium ponendi fata dedissent.
Qua licet, aeternus tamen es: quotiensque repellit
Ver hiemem, Piscique Aries succedit aquoso,　　　165
Tu toties oreris, viridique in caespite flores.
Te meus ante omnes genitor dilexit, et orbe
In medio positi caruerunt praeside Delphi,
Dum deus Eurotan immunitamque frequentat
Sparten: nec citharae nec sunt in honore sagittae: 170
Immemor ipse sui non retia ferre recusat,
Non tenuisse canes, non per juga montis iniqui
Isse comes; longaque alit assuetudine flammas.
　　Jamque fere medius Titan venientis et actae
Noctis erat, spatioque pari distabat utrimque:　　175
Corpora veste levant, et suco pinguis olivi
Splendescunt, latique ineunt certamina disci.
Quem prius aërias libratum Phoebus in auras
Misit, et oppositas disjecit pondere nubes.
Reccidit in solidam longo post tempore terram　　180
Pondus, et exhibuit junctam cum viribus artem.
Protinus imprudens actusque cupidine lusus
Tollere Taenarides orbem properabat; at illum
Dura repercusso subjecit verbere tellus
In vultus, Hyacinthe, tuos. Expalluit aeque　　185
Quam puer, ipse deus, collapsosque excipit artus,
Et modo te refovet, modo tristia vulnera siccat,

Nunc animam admotis fugientem sustinet herbis.
Nil prosunt artes; erat immedicabile vulnus.
Ut siquis violas riguove papaver in horto   190
Liliaque infringat, fulvis haerentia lignis
Marcida demittant subito caput illa gravatum,
Nec se sustineant, spectentque cacumine terram;
Sic vultus moriens jacet, et defecta vigore
Ipsa sibi est oneri cervix umeroque recumbit.   195
  "Laberis, Oebalide, prima fraudate juventa,"
Phoebus ait "videoque tuum, mea crimina, vulnus.
Tu dolor es facinusque meum: mea dextera leto
Inscribenda tuo est! ego sum tibi funeris auctor.
Quae mea culpa tamen? nisi si lusisse vocari   200
Culpa potest, nisi culpa potest et amasse vocari.
Atque utinam merito vitam, tecumque liceret
Reddere! quod quoniam fatali lege tenemur,
Semper eris mecum, memorique haerebis in ore.
Te lyra pulsa manu, te carmina nostra sonabunt: 205
Flosque novus scripto gemitus imitabere nostros.
Tempus et illud erit, quo se fortissimus heros
Addat in hunc florem, folioque legatur eodem."
  Talia dum vero memorantur Apollinis ore,
Ecce cruor, qui fusus humo signaverat herbas,   210
Desinit esse cruor, Tyrioque nitentior ostro
Flos oritur, formamque capit quam lilia, si non
Purpureus color his, argenteus esset in illis.
Non satis hoc Phoebo est—is enim fuit auctor honoris—
Ipse suos gemitus foliis inscribit, et AI AI   215
Flos habet inscriptum, funestaque littera ducta est.
  Nec genuisse pudet Sparten Hyacinthon, honorque
Durat in hoc aevi, celebrandaque more priorum
Annua praelata redeunt Hyacinthia pompa.

26. Atalanta's Race.

X. 560–680.

Venus tells Adonis the story of the beautiful and fleet-footed Atalanta, who would marry no suitor who could not vanquish her in a race. At last Hippomenes outruns her and wins the prize.

This story, too, is told in English verse by Mr. Morris, in his "Earthly Paradise," vol. i.

"Forsitan audieris aliquam certamine cursus   560
Veloces superasse viros. Non fabula rumor
Ille fuit; superabat enim; nec dicere posses,
Laude pedum, formaene bono praestantior esset.
Scitanti deus huic de conjuge 'conjuge' dixit
'Nil opus est, Atalanta, tibi: fuge conjugis usum.   565
Nec tamen effugies, teque ipsa viva carebis.'
Territa sorte dei per opacas innuba silvas
Vivit, et instantem turbam violenta procorum
Condicione fugat, nec 'sum potiunda, nisi' inquit
'Victa prius cursu; pedibus contendite mecum: 570
Praemia veloci conjunx thalamique dabuntur;
Mors pretium tardis. Ea lex certaminis esto.'
Illa quidem immitis: sed tanta potentia formae est,
Venit ad hanc legem temeraria turba procorum.
   Sederat Hippomenes cursus spectator iniqui,   575
Et 'petitur cuiquam per tanta pericula conjunx?'
Dixerat, ac nimios juvenum damnarat amores.
Ut faciem et posito corpus velamine vidit,
Quale meum, vel quale tuum, si femina fias,
Obstipuit, tollensque manus 'ignoscite,' dixit   580
'Quos modo culpavi. Nondum mihi praemia nota,
Quae peteretis, erant.' Laudando concipit ignes,

Et, ne quis juvenum currat velocius, optat
Invidiaque timet. 'Sed cur certaminis hujus
Intemptata mihi fortuna relinquitur?' inquit 585
'Audentes deus ipse juvat.' Dum talia secum
Exigit Hippomenes, passu volat alite virgo.
Quae quamquam Scythica non setius ire sagitta
Aonio visa est juveni, tamen ille decorem
Miratur magis. Et cursus facit ille decorem. 590
Dum notat haec hospes, decursa novissima meta est, 597
Et tegitur festa victrix Atalanta corona.
Dant gemitum victi, penduntque ex foedere poenas.
Non tamen eventu juvenis deterritus horum 600
Constitit in medio, vultuque in virgine fixo
'Quid facilem titulum superando quaeris inertes?
Mecum confer!' ait 'seu me fortuna potentem
Fecerit, a tanto non indignabere vinci.
Namque mihi genitor Megareus Onchestius: illi 605
Est Neptunus avus: pronepos ego regis aquarum.
Nec virtus citra genus est: seu vincar, habebis
Hippomene victo magnum et memorabile nomen.'
Talia dicentem molli Schoeneïa vultu
Aspicit, et dubitat, superari an vincere malit. 610
Atque ita 'quis deus hunc formosis' inquit 'iniquus
Perdere vult, caraeque jubet discrimine vitae
Conjugium petere hoc? non sum, me judice, tanti.
Nec forma tangor,—poteram tamen hac quoque tangi—
Sed quod adhuc puer est. Non me movet ipse, sed aetas.
Quid, quod inest virtus et mens interrita leti?
Quid, quod ab aequorea numeratur origine quartus?
Quid, quod amat, tantique putat conubia nostra,
Ut pereat, si me fors illi dura negarit?
Dum licet, hospes, abi, thalamosque relinque cruentos.

26. ATALANTA'S RACE.

Conjugium crudele meum est.   Tibi nubere nulla
Nolet; et optari potes a sapiente puella.
Cur tamen est mihi cura tui, tot jam ante peremptis?
Viderit! intereat, quoniam tot caede procorum
Admonitus non est, agiturque in taedia vitae.   625
Occidet hic igitur, voluit quia vivere mecum,
Indignamque necem pretium patietur amoris?
Non erit invidiae victoria nostra ferendae.
Sed non culpa mea est.   Utinam desistere velles!
Aut, quoniam es demens, utinam velocior esses!   630
At quam virgineus puerili vultus in ore est!
A! miser Hippomene, nollem tibi visa fuissem!
Vivere dignus eras.   Quod si felicior essem,
Nec mihi conjugium fata importuna negarent,
Unus eras, cum quo sociare cubilia vellem.'   635
  Dixerat: utque rudis, primoque Cupidine tacta,
Quid facit, ignorans, amat et non sentit amorem.
Jam solitos poscunt cursus populusque paterque:
Cum me sollicita proles Neptunia voce
Invocat Hippomenes, 'Cytherea' que 'comprecor, ausis
Adsit' ait 'nostris et quos dedit, adjuvet ignes.'
Detulit aura preces ad me non invida blandas;
Motaque sum, fateor.   Nec opis mora longa dabatur.
Est ager, indigenae Tamasenum nomine dicunt,
Telluris Cypriae pars optima, quam mihi prisci   645
Sacravere senes, templisque accedere dotem
Hanc jussere meis.   Medio nitet arbor in arvo,
Fulva comam, fulvo ramis crepitantibus auro.
Hinc tria forte mea veniens decerpta ferebam
Aurea poma manu: nullique videnda nisi ipsi   650
Hippomenen adii, docuique, quis usus in illis.
Signa tubae dederant, cum carcere pronus uterque

Emicat, et summam celeri pede libat harenam.
Posse putes illos sicco freta radere passu,
Et segetis canae stantes percurrere aristas. 655
Adiciunt animos juveni clamorque favorque,
Verbaque dicentum 'nunc, nunc incumbere tempus,
Hippomene, propera! nunc viribus utere totis.
Pelle moram, vinces:' dubium, Megareïus heros
Gaudeat, an virgo magis his Schoeneïa dictis. 660
O quotiens, cum jam posset transire, morata est,
Spectatosque diu vultus invita reliquit!
Aridus e lasso veniebat anhelitus ore,
Metaque erat longe. Tum denique de tribus unum
Fetibus arboreis proles Neptunia misit. 665
Obstipuit virgo, nitidique cupidine pomi
Declinat cursus, aurumque volubile tollit:
Praeterit Hippomenes: resonant spectacula plausu.
Illa moram celeri cessataque tempora cursu
Corrigit, atque iterum juvenem post terga relinquit. 670
Et rursus pomi jactu remorata secundi,
Consequitur transitque virum. Pars ultima cursus
Restabat. 'Nunc' inquit 'ades, dea muneris auctor!'
Inque latus campi, quo tardius illa rediret,
Jecit ab obliquo nitidum juvenaliter aurum. 675
An peteret, virgo visa est dubitare: coegi
Tollere, et adjeci sublato pondera malo,
Impediique oneris pariter gravitate moraque.
Neve meus sermo cursu sit tardior ipso,
Praeterita est virgo: duxit sua praemia victor." 680

27. The Death of Orpheus.

XI. 1–84.

> "Whom universal Nature did lament,
>   When, by the rout that made the hideous roar,
>   His gory visage down the stream was sent,
>   Down the swift Hebrus to the Lesbian shore."
> Milton's "Lycidas."

Carmine dum tali silvas animosque ferarum
Threïcius vates et saxa sequentia ducit,
Ecce nurus Ciconum, tectae lymphata ferinis
Pectora velleribus, tumuli de vertice cernunt
Orphea percussis sociantem carmina nervis.   5
E quibus una, leves jactato crine per auras,
"En," ait "en hic est nostri contemptor!" et hastam
Vatis Apollinei vocalia misit in ora,
Quae foliis praesuta notam sine vulnere fecit.
Alterius telum lapis est, qui missus in ipso   10
Aëre concentu victus vocisque lyraeque est,
Ac veluti supplex pro tam furialibus ausis
Ante pedes jacuit. Sed enim temeraria crescunt
Bella, modusque abiit, insanaque regnat Erinys.
Cunctaque tela forent cantu mollita: sed ingens   15
Clamor et infracto Berecyntia tibia cornu
Tympanaque et plausus et Bacchei ululatus
Obstrepuere sono citharae. Tum denique saxa
Non exauditi rubuerunt sanguine vatis.
Ac primum attonitas etiamnum voce canentis   20
Innumeras volucres anguesque agmenque ferarum
Maenades Orphei titulum rapuere triumphi.
Inde cruentatis vertuntur in Orphea dextris

Et coeunt ut aves, si quando luce vagantem
Noctis avem cernunt. Structoque utrimque theatro 25
Ceu matutina cervus periturus harena
Praeda canum est, vatemque petunt et fronde virentes
Coniciunt thyrsos, non haec in munera factos.
Hac glaebas, illae direptos arbore ramos,
Pars torquent silices. Neu desint tela furori, 30
Forte boves presso subigebant vomere terram,
Nec procul hinc multo fructum sudore parantes
Dura lacertosi fodiebant arva coloni.
Agmine qui viso fugiunt, operisque relinquunt
Arma sui; vacuosque jacent dispersa per agros 35
Sarculaque rastrique graves longique ligones.
Quae postquam rapuere ferae, cornuque minaces
Divulsere boves, ad vatis fata recurrunt,
Tendentemque manus atque illo tempore primum
Irrita dicentem nec quicquam voce moventem 40
Sacrilegae perimunt; perque os, pro Juppiter! illud
Auditum saxis intellectumque ferarum
Sensibus in ventos anima exhalata recessit.

   Te maestae volucres, Orpheu, te turba ferarum,
Te rigidi silices, te carmina saepe secutae 45
Fleverunt silvae: positis te frondibus arbos
Tonsa comam luxit. Lacrimis quoque flumina dicunt
Increvisse suis: obstrusaque carbasa pullo
Naides et Dryades passosque habuere capillos.
Membra jacent diversa locis. Caput, Hebre, lyramque
Excipis: et — mirum! — medio dum labitur amne,
Flebile nescio quid queritur lyra, flebile lingua
Murmurat exanimis, respondent flebile ripae.
Jamque mare invectae flumen populare relinquunt,
Et Methymnaeae potiuntur litore Lesbi. 55

Hic ferus expositum peregrinis anguis harenis
Os petit et sparsos stillanti rore capillos.
Tandem Phoebus adest, morsusque inferre parantem
Arcet, et in lapidem rictus serpentis apertos
Congelat, et patulos, ut erant, indurat hiatus. 60
    Umbra subit terras, et quae loca viderat ante,
Cuncta recognoscit: quaerensque per arva piorum
Invenit Eurydicen, cupidisque amplectitur ulnis.
Hic modo conjunctis spatiantur passibus ambo,
Nunc praecedentem sequitur, nunc praevius anteit, 65
Eurydicenque suam jam tuto respicit Orpheus.
    Non impune tamen scelus hoc sinit esse Lyaeus:
Amissoque dolens sacrorum vate suorum,
Protinus in silvis matres Edonidas omnes,
Quae videre nefas, torta radice ligavit. 70
Quippe pedum digitos, in quantum quaeque secuta est,
Traxit, et in solidam detrusit acumina terram.
Utque suum laqueis, quos callidus abdidit auceps,
Crus ubi commisit volucris, sensitque teneri,
Plangitur, ac trepidans astringit vincula motu; 75
Sic, ut quaeque solo defixa cohaeserat harum,
Exsternata fugam frustra temptabat: at illam
Lenta tenet radix, exsultantemque coercet.
Dumque ubi sint digiti, dum pes ubi, quaerit, et ungues,
Aspicit in teretes lignum succedere suras. 80
Et conata femur maerenti plangere dextra,
Robora percussit. Pectus quoque robora fiunt:
Robora sunt umeri: longos quoque bracchia veros
Esse putes ramos, et non fallare putando.

28. Midas; or, the King of the Golden Touch.
XI. 85–193.

Nec satis hoc Baccho est : ipsos quoque deserit agros,
Cumque choro meliore sui vineta Timoli
Pactolonque petit ; quamvis non aureus illo
Tempore nec caris erat invidiosus harenis.
Hunc assueta cohors satyri bacchaeque frequentant :
At Silenus abest. Titubantem annisque meroque 90
Ruricolae cepere Phryges, vinctumque coronis
Ad regem duxere Midan, cui Thracius Orpheus
Orgia tradiderat cum Cecropio Eumolpo.
Qui simul agnovit socium comitemque sacrorum,
Hospitis adventu festum genialiter egit 95
Per bis quinque dies et junctas ordine noctes.
Et jam stellarum sublime coegerat agmen
Lucifer undecimus, Lydos cum laetus in agros
Rex venit, et juveni Silenum reddit alumno.
Huic deus optandi gratum, sed inutile, fecit 100
Muneris arbitrium, gaudens altore recepto.
Ille, male usurus donis, ait ' effice, quicquid
Corpore contigero, fulvum vertatur in aurum.'
Adnuit optatis, nocituraque munera solvit
Liber, et indoluit, quod non meliora petisset. 105
    Laetus abit gaudetque malo Berecyntius heros :
Pollicitique fidem tangendo singula temptat.
Vixque sibi credens, non alta fronde virentem
Ilice detraxit virgam : virga aurea facta est.
Tollit humo saxum : saxum quoque palluit auro. 110
Contigit et glaebam : contactu glaeba potenti
Massa fit. Arentes Cereris decerpsit aristas :
Aurea messis erat. Demptum tenet arbore pomum :

Hesperidas donasse putes. Si postibus altis
Admovit digitos, postes radiare videntur. 115
Ille etiam liquidis palmas ubi laverat undis,
Unda fluens palmis Danaën eludere posset.
Vix spes ipse suas animo capit, aurea fingens
Omnia. Gaudenti mensas posuere ministri
Exstructas dapibus nec tostae frugis egentes: 120
Tum vero, sive ille sua Cerealia dextra
Munera contigerat, Cerealia dona rigebant;
Sive dapes avido convellere dente parabat,
Lammina fulva dapes, admoto dente, premebat.
Miscuerat puris auctorem muneris undis: 125
Fusile per rictus aurum fluitare videres.
Attonitus novitate mali, divesque miserque,
Effugere optat opes et quae modo voverat, odit.
Copia nulla famem relevat; sitis arida guttur
Urit, et inviso meritus torquetur ab auro. 130
Ad caelumque manus et splendida bracchia tollens,
'Da veniam, Lenaee pater! peccavimus;' inquit,
'Sed miserere, precor, speciosoque eripe damno.'
Mite deum numen Bacchus peccasse fatentem
Restituit, factique fide data munera solvit. 135
'Neve male optato maneas circumlitus auro,
Vade' ait 'ad magnis vicinum Sardibus amnem,
Perque jugum montis labentibus obvius undis
Carpe viam, donec venias ad fluminis ortus;
Spumigeroque tuum fonti, qua plurimus exit, 140
Subde caput, corpusque simul, simul elue crimen.'
Rex jussae succedit aquae. Vis aurea tinxit
Flumen, et humano de corpore cessit in amnem.
Nunc quoque jam veteris percepto semine venae
Arva rigent auro madidis pallentia glaebis. 145

Ille, perosus opes, silvas et rura colebat,
Panaque montanis habitantem semper in antris.
Pingue sed ingenium mansit; nocituraque, ut ante,
Rursus erant domino stolidae praecordia mentis.
Nam freta prospiciens late riget arduus alto   150
Tmolus in ascensu, clivoque extensus utroque
Sardibus hinc, illinc parvis finitur Hypaepis.
Pan ibi dum teneris jactat sua carmina nymphis
Et leve cerata modulatur harundine carmen,
Ausus Apollineos prae se contemnere cantus,   155
Judice sub Tmolo certamen venit ad impar.
Monte suo senior judex consedit, et aures
Liberat arboribus; quercu coma caerula tantum
Cingitur, et pendent circum cava tempora glandes.
Isque deum pecoris spectans 'in judice' dixit   160
'Nulla mora est.' Calamis agrestibus insonat ille:
Barbaricoque Midan—aderat nam forte canenti—
Carmine delenit. Post hunc sacer ora retorsit
Tmolus ad os Phoebi; vultum sua silva secuta est.
Ille caput flavum lauro Parnaside vinctus   165
Verrit humum Tyrio saturata murice palla:
Instrictamque fidem gemmis et dentibus Indis
Sustinet a laeva: tenuit manus altera plectrum.
Artificis status ipse fuit. Tum stamina docto
Pollice sollicitat, quorum dulcedine captus   170
Pana jubet Tmolus citharae summittere cannas.
Judicium sanctique placet sententia montis
Omnibus: arguitur tamen atque injusta vocatur
Unius sermone Midae. Nec Delius aures
Humanam stolidas patitur retinere figuram: 175
Sed trahit in spatium, villisque albentibus implet,
Instabilesque imas facit et dat posse moveri.

Cetera sunt hominis : partem damnatur in unam,
Induiturque aures lente gradientis aselli.
   Ille quidem celare cupit, turpique pudore   180
Tempora purpureis temptat velare tiaris.
Sed solitus longos ferro resecare capillos
Viderat hoc famulus. Qui cum nec prodere visum
Dedecus auderet, cupiens efferre sub auras,
Nec posset reticere tamen, secedit, humumque   185
Effodit, et, domini quales aspexerit aures,
Voce refert parva, terraeque immurmurat haustae;
Indiciumque suae vocis tellure regesta
Obruit, et scrobibus tacitus discedit opertis.
Creber harundinibus tremulis ibi surgere lucus   190
Coepit, et, ut primum pleno maturuit anno,
Prodidit agricolam : leni nam motus ab austro
Obruta verba refert, dominique coarguit aures.

29. CEYX AND ALCYONE.

XI. 410-748.

   The poet Keats, in his "Endymion," thus alludes to the story of Alcyone :

> "O magic sleep! O comfortable bird,
>   That broodest o'er the troubled sea of the mind,
>   Till it is hushed and smooth."

   Interea fratrisque sui fratremque secutis   410
Anxia prodigiis turbatus pectora Ceyx,
Consulat ut sacras, hominum oblectamina, sortes,
Ad Clarium parat ire deum. Nam templa profanus
Invia cum Phlegyis faciebat Delphica Phorbas.
Consilii tamen ante sui, fidissima, certam   415
Te facit, Alcyone. Cui protinus intima frigus

Ossa receperunt, buxoque simillimus ora
Pallor obit, lacrimisque genae maduere profusis.
Ter conata loqui ter fletibus ora rigavit,
Singultuque pias interrumpente querellas 420
'Quae mea culpa tuam,' dixit 'carissime, mentem
Vertit? ubi est, quae cura mei prior esse solebat?
Jam potes Alcyone securus abesse relicta?
Jam via longa placet? jam sum tibi carior absens?
At, puto, per terras iter est, tantumque dolebo, 425
Non etiam metuam, curaeque timore carebunt.
Aequora me terrent et ponti tristis imago,
Et laceras nuper tabulas in litore vidi,
Et saepe in tumulis sine corpore nomina legi.
Neve tuum fallax animum fiducia tangat, 430
Quod socer Hippotades tibi sit, qui carcere fortes
Contineat ventos, et, cum velit, aequora placet.
Cum semel emissi tenuerunt aequora venti,
Nil illis vetitum est, incommendataque tellus
Omnis, et omne fretum: caeli quoque nubila vexant 435
Excutiuntque feris rutilos concursibus ignes.
Quo magis hos novi,—nam novi et saepe paterna
Parva domo vidi—magis hoc reor esse timendos.
Quod tua si flecti precibus sententia nullis,
Care, potest, conjunx, nimiumque es certus eundi, 440
Me quoque tolle simul. Certe jactabimur una,
Nec nisi quae patiar, metuam; pariterque feremus,
Quicquid erit; pariter super aequora lata feremur.'
 Talibus Aeolidis dictis lacrimisque movetur
Sidereus conjunx: neque enim minor ignis in ipso est. 445
Sed neque propositos pelagi dimittere cursus,
Nec vult Alcyonen in partem adhibere pericli;
Multaque respondit timidum solantia pectus.

29. CEYX AND ALCYONE.

Non tamen idcirco causam probat. Addidit illis
Hoc quoque lenimen, quo solo flexit amantem: 450
'Longa quidem est nobis omnis mora: sed tibi juro
Per patrios ignes, si me modo fata remittent,
Ante reversurum, quam luna bis impleat orbem.'
 His ubi promissis spes est admota recursus,
Protinus eductam navalibus aequore tingui, 455
Aptarique suis pinum jubet armamentis.
Qua rursus visa, veluti praesaga futuri,
Horruit Alcyone lacrimasque emisit obortas,
Amplexusque dedit, tristique miserrima tandem
Ore 'vale' dixit, collapsaque corpore toto est. 460
Ast juvenes, quaerente moras Ceyce, reducunt
Ordinibus geminis ad fortia pectora remos,
Aequalique ictu scindunt freta. Sustulit illa
Umentes oculos, stantemque in puppe recurva
Concussaque manu dantem sibi signa maritum 465
Prima videt redditque notas: ubi terra recessit
Longius, atque oculi nequeunt cognoscere vultus,
Dum licet, insequitur fugientem lumine pinum:
Haec quoque ut haud poterat, spatio summota, videri,
Vela tamen spectat summo fluitantia malo. 470
Ut nec vela videt, vacuum petit anxia lectum,
Seque toro ponit. Renovat lectusque locusque
Alcyonae lacrimas, et quae pars, admonet, absit.
 Portibus exierant, et moverat aura rudentes:
Obvertit lateri pendentes navita remos, 475
Cornuaque in summa locat arbore, totaque malo
Carbasa deducit venientesque accipit auras.
 Aut minus, aut certe medium non amplius aequor
Puppe secabatur, longeque erat utraque tellus,
Cum mare sub noctem tumidis albescere coepit 480

Fluctibus et praeceps spirare valentius eurus.
'Ardua jamdudum demittite cornua,' rector
Clamat 'et antemnis totum subnectite velum.'
Hic jubet: impediunt adversae jussa procellae,
Nec sinit audiri vocem fragor aequoris ullam. 485
Sponte tamen properant alii subducere remos,
Pars munire latus, pars ventis vela negare:
Egerit hic fluctus, aequorque refundit in aequor,
Hic rapit antemnas. Quae dum sine lege geruntur,
Aspera crescit hiems, omnique e parte feroces 490
Bella gerunt venti fretaque indignantia miscent.
Ipse pavet, nec se, qui sit status, ipse fatetur
Scire ratis rector, nec quid jubeatve, vetetve:
Tanta mali moles, tantoque potentior arte est.
Quippe sonant clamore viri, stridore rudentes, 495
Undarum incursu gravis unda, tonitribus aether.
Fluctibus erigitur caelumque aequare videtur
Pontus, et inductas aspergine tangere nubes;
Et modo, cum fulvas ex imo verrit arenas,
Concolor est illis, Stygia modo nigrior unda: 500
Sternitur interdum, spumisque sonantibus albet.
  Ipsa quoque his agitur vicibus Trachinia puppis:
Et nunc sublimis veluti de vertice montis
Despicere in valles imumque Acheronta videtur:
Nunc, ubi demissam curvum circumstetit aequor, 505
Suspicere inferno summum de gurgite caelum.
Saepe dat ingentem fluctu latus icta fragorem,
Nec levius pulsata sonat, quam ferreus olim
Cum laceras aries ballistave concutit arces.
Utque solent sumptis incursu viribus ire 510
Pectore in arma feri protentaque tela leones:
Sic ubi se ventis admiserat unda coortis,

29. CEYX AND ALCYONE.

Ibat in arma ratis, multoque erat altior illis.
Jamque labant cunei, spoliataque tegmine cerae
Rima patet, praebetque viam letalibus undis. 515
 Ecce cadunt largi resolutis nubibus imbres,
Inque fretum credas totum descendere caelum,
Inque plagas caeli tumefactum ascendere pontum.
Vela madent nimbis, et cum caelestibus undis
Aequoreae miscentur aquae. Caret ignibus aether, 520
Caecaque nox premitur tenebris hiemisque suisque.
Discutiunt tamen has praebentque micantia lumen
Fulmina: fulmineis ardescunt ignibus undae.
 Dat quoque jam saltus intra cava texta carinae
Fluctus: et ut miles, numero praestantior omni, 525
Cum saepe assiluit defensae moenibus urbis,
Spe potitur tandem, laudisque accensus amore
Inter mille viros murum tamen occupat unus:
Sic ubi pulsarunt noviens latera ardua fluctus,
Vastius insurgens decimae ruit impetus undae, 530
Nec prius absistit fessam oppugnare carinam,
Quam velut in captae descendat moenia navis.
Pars igitur temptabat adhuc invadere pinum,
Pars maris intus erat. Trepidant haud setius omnes,
Quam solet urbs, aliis murum fodientibus extra 535
Atque aliis murum, trepidare, tenentibus intus.
Deficit ars, animique cadunt: totidemque videntur,
Quot veniant fluctus, ruere atque irrumpere mortes.
 Non tenet hic lacrimas; stupet hic; vocat ille beatos,
Funera quos maneant; hic votis numen adorat, 540
Bracchiaque ad caelum, quod non videt, irrita tollens
Poscit opem: subeunt illi fratresque parensque,
Huic cum pignoribus domus, et quod cuique relictum est.
Alcyone Ceyca movet; Ceycis in ore

Nulla nisi Alcyone est : et cum desideret unam, 545
Gaudet abesse tamen. Patriae quoque vellet ad oras
Respicere, inque domum supremos vertere vultus :
Verum ubi sit, nescit ; tanta vertigine pontus
Fervet, et inducta piceis e nubibus umbra
Omne latet caelum, duplicataque noctis imago est. 550
    Frangitur incursu nimbosi turbinis arbor ;
Frangitur et regimen : spoliisque animosa superstes
Unda, velut victrix, sinuataque despicit undas :
Nec levius, quam siquis Athon Pindumve revulsos
Sede sua totos in apertum everterit aequor, 555
Praecipitata cadit, pariterque et pondere et ictu
Mergit in ima ratem, cum qua pars magna virorum,
Gurgite pressa gravi neque in aëra reddita, fato
Functa suo est. Alii partes et membra carinae
Trunca tenent. Tenet ipse manu, qua sceptra solebat, 560
Fragmina navigii Ceyx, socerumque patremque
Invocat heu! frustra. Sed plurima nantis in ore
Alcyone conjunx. Illam meminitque refertque :
Illius ante oculos ut agant sua corpora fluctus,
Optat, et exanimis manibus tumuletur amicis. 565
Dum natat, absentem, quotiens sinit hiscere fluctus,
Nominat Alcyonen, ipsisque immurmurat undis.
Ecce super medios fluctus niger arcus aquarum
Frangitur, et rupta mersum caput obruit unda.
Lucifer obscurus, nec quem cognoscere posses, 570
Illa nocte fuit : quoniamque excedere caelo
Non licuit, densis texit sua nubibus ora.
    Aeolis interea tantorum ignara malorum
Dinumerat noctes : et jam, quas induat ille,
Festinat vestes, jam quas, ubi venerit ille, 575
Ipsa gerat, reditusque sibi promittit inanes.

Omnibus illa quidem superis pia tura ferebat:
Ante tamen cunctos Junonis templa colebat,
Proque viro, qui nullus erat, veniebat ad aras,
Utque foret sospes conjunx suus, utque rediret, 580
Optabat, nullumque sibi praeferret.   At illi
Hoc de tot votis poterat contingere solum.
   At dea non ultra pro functo morte rogari
Sustinet; utque manus funestas arceat aris,
'Iri, meae' dixit 'fidissima nuntia vocis, 585
Vise soporiferam Somni velociter aulam,
Exstinctique jube Ceycis imagine mittat
Somnia ad Alcyonen veros narrantia casus.'
Dixerat: induitur velamina mille colorum
Iris, et arcuato caelum curvamine signans 590
Tecta petit jussi sub nube latentia regis.
   Est prope Cimmerios longo spelunca recessu,
Mons cavus, ignavi domus et penetralia Somni:
Quo nunquam radiis oriens mediusve cadensve
Phoebus adire potest.   Nebulae caligine mixtae 595
Exhalantur humo dubiaeque crepuscula lucis.
Non vigil ales ibi cristati cantibus oris
Evocat Auroram, nec voce silentia rumpunt
Sollicitive canes canibusve sagacior anser.
Non fera, non pecudes, non moti flamine rami, 600
Humanaeve sonum reddunt convicia linguae.
Muta quies habitat.   Saxo tamen exit ab imo
Rivus aquae Lethes, per quem cum murmure labens
Invitat somnos crepitantibus unda lapillis.
Ante fores antri fecunda papavera florent 605
Innumeraeque herbae, quarum de lacte soporem
Nox legit et spargit per opacas umida terras.
Janua, ne verso stridores cardine reddat,

Nulla domo tota ; custos in limine nullus.
At medio torus est ebeno sublimis in antro, 610
Plumeus, unicolor, pullo velamine tectus ;
Quo cubat ipse deus membris languore solutis.
Hunc circa passim varias imitantia formas
Somnia vana jacent totidem, quot messis aristas,
Silva gerit frondes, ejectas litus harenas. 615
   Quo simul intravit, manibusque obstantia virgo
Somnia dimovit, vestis fulgore reluxit
Sacra domus: tardaque deus gravitate jacentes
Vix oculos tollens, iterumque iterumque relabens
Summaque percutiens nutanti pectora mento, 620
Excussit tandem sibi se, cubitoque levatus,
Quid veniat,—cognovit enim—scitatur. At illa :
' Somne, quies rerum, placidissime, Somne, deorum,
Pax animi, quem cura fugit, qui corpora duris
Fessa ministeriis mulces reparasque labori ! 625
Somnia, quae veras aequent imitamine formas,
Herculea Trachine jube sub imagine regis
Alcyonen adeant, simulacraque naufraga fingant.
Imperat hoc Juno.' Postquam mandata peregit,
Iris abit: neque enim ulterius tolerare vaporis 630
Vim poterat, labique ut somnum sensit in artus,
Effugit, et remeat per quos modo venerat arcus.
   At pater e populo natorum mille suorum
Excitat artificem simulatoremque figurae
Morphea. Non illo jussos sollertius alter 635
Exprimit incessus vultumque sonumque loquendi ;
Adicit et vestes et consuetissima cuique
Verba. Sed hic solos homines imitatur ; at alter
Fit fera, fit volucris, fit longo corpore serpens.
Hunc Icelon superi, mortale Phobetora vulgus 640

Nominat. Est etiam diversae tertius artis
Phantasos; ille in humum saxumque undamque trabem-
Quaeque vacant anima, fallaciter omnia transit.   [que,
Regibus hi ducibusque suos ostendere vultus
Nocte solent, populos alii plebemque pererrant.   645
Praeterit hos senior, cunctisque e fratribus unum
Morphea, qui peragat Thaumantidos edita, Somnus
Eligit: et rursus molli languore solutus
Deposuitque caput, stratoque recondidit alto.
 Ille volat nullos strepitus facientibus alis   650
Per tenebras, intraque morae breve tempus in urbem
Pervenit Haemoniam; positisque e corpore pennis
In faciem Ceycis abit, sumptaque figura
Luridus, exanimi similis, sine vestibus ullis,
Conjugis ante torum miserae stetit: uda videtur 655
Barba viri, madidisque gravis fluere unda capillis.
Tum lecto incumbens, fletu super ora refuso,
Haec ait: 'agnoscis Ceyca, miserrima conjunx?
An mea mutata est facies nece? respice! nosces,
Inveniesque tuo pro conjuge conjugis umbram.   660
Nil opis, Alcyone, nobis tua vota tulerunt:
Occidimus; falso tibi me promittere noli.
Nubilus Aegaeo deprendit in aequore navem
Auster, et ingenti jactatam flamine solvit:
Oraque nostra, tuum frustra clamantia nomen,   665
Implerunt fluctus. Non haec tibi nuntiat auctor
Ambiguus, non ista vagis rumoribus audis:
Ipse ego fata tibi praesens mea naufragus edo.
Surge, age, da lacrimas, lugubriaque induc, nec me
Indeploratum sub inania Tartara mitte.'   670
 Adicit his vocem Morpheus, quam conjugis illa
Crederet esse sui; fletus quoque fundere veros

Visus erat, gestumque manus Ceycis habebat.
Ingemit Alcyone lacrimans, movet atque lacertos
Per somnum, corpusque petens amplectitur auras ; 675
Exclamatque ' mane ! quo te rapis ? ibimus una.'
Voce sua specieque viri turbata soporem
Excutit : et primo, si sit, circumspicit, illic,
Qui modo visus erat : nam moti voce ministri
Intulerant lumen. Postquam non invenit usquam, 680
Percutit ora manu, laniatque a pectore vestes,
Pectoraque ipsa ferit. Nec crines solvere curat ;
Scindit, et altrici, quae luctus causa, roganti
' Nulla est Alcyone, nulla est ' : ait ' occidit una
Cum Ceyce suo ! Solantia tollite verba ! 685
Naufragus interiit. Vidi agnovique, manusque
Ad discedentem, cupiens retinere, tetendi.
Umbra fuit. Sed et umbra tamen manifesta virique
Vera mei. Non ille quidem, si quaeris, habebat
Assuetos vultus, nec quo prius, ore nitebat. 690
Pallentem nudumque et adhuc umente capillo
Infelix vidi. Stetit hoc miserabilis ipso
Ecce loco '—et quaerit, vestigia siqua supersint.
' Hoc erat, hoc, animo quod divinante timebam,
Et ne, me fugiens, ventos sequerere, rogabam. 695
At certe vellem, quoniam periturus abibas,
Me quoque duxisses. Multum fuit utile tecum
Ire mihi : neque enim de vitae tempore quicquam
Non simul egissem, nec mors discreta fuisset.
Nunc absens perii, jactor quoque fluctibus absens, 700
Et sine te me pontus habet. Crudelior ipso
Sit mihi mens pelago, si vitam ducere nitar
Longius, et tanto pugnem superesse dolori.
Sed neque pugnabo, nec te, miserande, relinquam ;

29. CEYX AND ALCYONE.

Et tibi nunc saltem veniam comes. Inque sepulchro 705
Si non urna, tamen junget nos littera: si non
Ossibus ossa meis, at nomen nomine tangam.'
   Plura dolor prohibet, verboque intervenit omni
Plangor, et attonito gemitus e corde trahuntur.
   Mane erat: egreditur tectis ad litus, et illum 710
Maesta locum repetit, de quo spectarat euntem.
Dumque moratur ibi, dumque ' hic retinacula solvit,
Hoc mihi discedens dedit oscula litore' dixit,
Quae dum tota locis reminiscitur acta, fretumque
Prospicit: in liquida, spatio distante, tuetur 715
Nescio quid quasi corpus, aqua. Primoque, quid illud
Esset, erat dubium. Postquam paulum appulit unda,
Et, quamvis aberat, corpus tamen esse liquebat,
Qui foret, ignorans, quia naufragus, omine mota est,
Et, tamquam ignoto lacrimam daret, 'heu! miser,' inquit
'Quisquis es, et siqua est conjunx tibi!' fluctibus actum
Fit propius corpus. Quod quo magis illa tuetur,
Hoc minus et minus est mentis. Jam jamque propinquae
Admotum terrae, jam quod cognoscere posset,
Cernit: erat conjunx. 'Ille est!' exclamat, et una 725
Ora comas vestem lacerat, tendensque trementes
Ad Ceyca manus 'sic, o carissime conjunx,
Sic ad me, miserande, redis?' ait. Adjacet undis
Facta manu moles, quae primas aequoris iras
Frangit et incursus quae praedelassat aquarum. 730
Insilit huc. Mirumque fuit potuisse? volabat,
Percutiensque levem modo natis aëra pennis,
Stringebat summas ales miserabilis undas,
Dumque volat, maesto similem plenumque querellae
Ora dedere sonum tenui crepitantia rostro. 735
Ut vero tetigit mutum et sine sanguine corpus,

Dilectos artus amplexa recentibus alis,
Frigida nequiquam duro dedit oscula rostro.
Senserit hoc Ceyx, an vultum motibus undae
Tollere sit visus, populus dubitabat. At ille   740
Senserat. Et tandem, superis miserantibus, ambo
Alite mutantur. Fatis obnoxius isdem
Tunc quoque mansit amor, nec conjugiale solutum
Foedus in alitibus. Coeunt, fiuntque parentes:
Perque dies placidos hiberno tempore septem   745
Incubat Alcyone pendentibus aequore nidis.
Tunc jacet unda maris: ventos custodit et arcet
Aeolus egressu, praestatque nepotibus aequor.

30. The House of Fame.

XII. 39-63.

Orbe locus medio est inter terrasque fretumque
Caelestesque plagas, triplicis confinia mundi: 40
Unde quod est usquam, quamvis regionibus absit,
Inspicitur, penetratque cavas vox omnis ad aures.
Fama tenet, summaque domum sibi legit in arce,
Innumerosque aditus ac mille foramina tectis
Addidit, et nullis inclusit limina portis.   45
Nocte dieque patet. Tota est ex aere sonanti;
Tota fremit, vocesque refert, iteratque quod audit.
Nulla quies intus, nullaque silentia parte.
Nec tamen est clamor, sed parvae murmura vocis:
Qualia de pelagi, siquis procul audiat, undis   50
Esse solent; qualemve sonum, cum Juppiter atras
Increpuit nubes, extrema tonitrua reddunt.
Atria turba tenet: veniunt leve vulgus euntque;
Mixtaque cum veris passim commenta vagantur

Milia rumorum, confusaque verba volutant. 55
E quibus hi vacuas implent sermonibus aures,
Ili narrata ferunt alio, mensuraque ficti
Crescit, et auditis aliquid novus adicit auctor.
Illic Credulitas, illic temerarius Error
Vanaque Laetitia est consternatique Timores, 60
Seditioque repens dubioque auctore Susurri.
Ipsa, quid in caelo rerum pelagoque geratur
Et tellure, videt, totumque inquirit in orbem.

31. Acis, Galatea, and the Cyclops.

XIII. 750-897.

The Cyclops Polyphemus, jealous of Acis, who is loved by Galatea, hurls a rock at him, and so crushes him to death.

Acis erat Fauno nymphaque Symaethide cretus, 750
Magna quidem patrisque sui matrisque voluptas,
Nostra tamen major, nam me sibi junxerat uni.
Pulcher et octonis iterum natalibus actis
Signarat dubia teneras lanugine malas.
Hunc ego, me Cyclops nulla cum fine petebat : 755
Nec, si quaesieris, odium Cyclopis, amorne
Acidis in nobis fuerit praesentior, edam :
Par utrumque fuit. Pro, quanta potentia regni
Est, Venus alma, tui! nempe ille immitis et ipsis
Horrendus silvis, et visus ab hospite nullo 760
Impune, et magni cum dis contemptor Olympi,
Quid sit amor, sentit, validaque cupidine captus
Uritur, oblitus pecorum antrorumque suorum.
Jamque tibi formae, jamque est tibi cura placendi
Jam rigidos pectis·rastris, Polypheme, capillos ; 765

Jam libet hirsutam tibi falce recidere barbam,
Et spectare feros in aqua, et componere vultus.
Caedis amor feritasque sitisque immensa cruoris
Cessant, et tutae veniuntque abeuntque carinae.
Telemus interea Siculam delatus ad Aetnen,   770
Telemus Eurymides, quem nulla fefellerat ales,
Terribilem Polyphemon adit, 'lumen' que, 'quod unum
Fronte geris media, rapiet tibi' dixit 'Ulixes.'
Risit et 'O vatum stolidissime, falleris,' inquit:
'Altera jam rapuit.' Sic frustra vera monentem   775
Spernit, et aut gradiens ingenti litora passu
Degravat, aut fessus sub opaca revertitur antra.

    Prominet in pontum cuneatus acumine longo
Collis; utrumque latus circumfluit aequoris unda.
Huc ferus ascendit Cyclops, mediusque resedit;   780
Lanigerae pecudes, nullo ducente, secutae.
Cui postquam pinus, baculi quae praebuit usum,
Ante pedes posita est, antemnis apta ferendis,
Sumptaque harundinibus compacta est fistula centum,
Senserunt toti pastoria sibila montes,   785
Senserunt undae. Latitans ego rupe, meique
Acidis in gremio residens, procul auribus hausi
Talia dicta meis auditaque verba notavi:
    "Candidior folio nivei, Galatea, ligustri,
Floridior pratis, longa procerior alno,   790
Splendidior vitro, tenero lascivior haedo,
Levior assiduo detritis aequore conchis,
Solibus hibernis, aestiva gratior umbra,
Nobilior palma ac platano conspectior alta,
Lucidior glacie, matura dulcior uva   795
Mollior et cygni plumis et lacte coacto,
Et, si non fugias, riguo formosior horto:

31. ACIS, GALATEA, AND THE CYCLOPS.

Saevior indomitis cadem Galatea juvencis,
Durior annosa quercu, fallacior undis,
Lentior et salicis virgis et vitibus albis,   800
His immobilior scopulis, violentior amne,
Laudato pavone superbior, acrior igni,
Asperior tribulis, feta truculentior ursa,
Surdior aequoribus, calcato immitior hydro,
Et, quod praecipue vellem tibi demere possem,   805
Non tantum cervo claris latratibus acto,
Verum etiam ventis volucrique fugacior aura!
At bene si noris, pigeat fugisse, morasque
Ipsa tuas damnes et me retinere labores.
Sunt mihi, pars montis, vivo pendentia saxo   810
Antra, quibus nec sol medio sentitur in aestu,
Nec sentitur hiems; sunt poma gravantia ramos;
Sunt auro similes longis in vitibus uvae,
Sunt et purpureae: tibi et has servamus et illas.
Ipsa tuis manibus silvestri nata sub umbra   815
Mollia fraga leges, ipsa autumnalia corna
Prunaque, non solum nigro liventia suco,
Verum etiam generosa novasque imitantia ceras.
Nec tibi castaneae me conjuge, nec tibi deerunt
Arbutei fetus: omnis tibi serviet arbor.   820
Hoc pecus omne meum est; multae quoque vallibus er-
Multas silva tegit, multae stabulantur in antris.   [rant,
Nec, si forte roges, possim tibi dicere, quot sint.
Pauperis est numerare pecus. De laudibus harum
Nil mihi credideris: praesens potes ipsa videre,   825
Ut vix circumeant distentum cruribus uber.
Sunt, fetura minor, tepidis in ovilibus agni;
Sunt quoque, par aetas, aliis in ovilibus haedi.
Lac mihi semper adest niveum. Pars inde bibenda

Servatur, partem liquefacta coagula durant. 830
Nec tibi deliciae faciles, vulgataque tantum
Munera contingent, dammae, leporesque, caperque,
Parve columbarum, demptusve cacumine nidus:
Inveni geminos, qui tecum ludere possint,
Inter se similes, vix ut dignoscere possis, 835
Villosae catulos in summis montibus ursae:
Inveni et dixi " dominae servabimus istos."
Jam modo caeruleo nitidum caput exime ponto,
Jam, Galatea, veni, nec munera despice nostra.
Certe ego me novi, liquidaeque in imagine vidi 840
Nuper aquae; placuitque mihi mea forma videnti.
Aspice, sim quantus. Non est hoc corpore major
Juppiter in caelo: nam vos narrare soletis
Nescio quem regnare Jovem. Coma plurima torvos
Prominet in vultus, umerosque, ut lucus, obumbrat.
Nec mea quod rigidis horrent densissima saetis
Corpora, turpe puta: turpis sine frondibus arbor:
Turpis equus, nisi colla jubae flaventia velent. 848
Barba viros hirtaeque decent in corpore saetae. 850
Unum est in media lumen mihi fronte, sed instar
Ingentis clipei. Quid? non haec omnia magno
Sol videt e caelo? Soli tamen unicus orbis.
Adde, quod in vestro genitor meus aequore regnat.
Hunc tibi do socerum. Tantum miserere, precesque 855
Supplicis exaudi: tibi enim succumbimus uni.
Quique Jovem et caelum sperno et penetrabile fulmen,
Nereï, te vereor: tua fulmine saevior ira est.
Atque ego contemptus essem patientior hujus,
Si fugeres omnes. Sed cur Cyclope repulso 860
Acin amas, praefersque meis amplexibus Acin?
Ille tamen placeatque sibi, placeatque licebit,

81. ACIS, GALATEA, AND THE CYCLOPS.

Quod nollem, Galatea, tibi : modo copia detur !
Sentiet esse mihi tanto pro corpore vires.
Viscera viva traham, divulsaque membra per agros, 865
Perque tuas spargam—sic se tibi misceat !—undas.
Uror enim, laesusque exaestuat acrius ignis,
Cumque suis videor translatam viribus Aetnam
Pectore ferre meo : nec tu, Galatea, moveris."
    Talia nequiquam questus—nam cuncta videbam— 870
Surgit, et ut taurus vacca furibundus adempta,
Stare nequit, silvaque et notis saltibus errat :
Cum ferus ignaros nec quicquam tale timentes
Me videt atque Acin, 'video' que exclamat 'et ista
Ultima sit, faciam, Veneris concordia vestrae.' 875
Tantaque vox, quantam Cyclops iratus habere
Debuit, illa fuit. Clamore perhorruit Aetne.
Ast ego vicino pavefacta sub aequore mergor ;
Terga fugae dederat conversa Symaethius heros :
'Adfer opem, Galatea, precor, mihi ! ferte parentes,' 880
Dixerat, ' et vestris periturum admittite regnis.'
Insequitur Cyclops, partemque e monte revulsam
Mittit, et extremus quamvis pervenit ad illum
Angulus is molis, totum tamen obruit Acin.
At nos, quod solum fieri per fata licebat, 885
Fecimus, ut vires assumeret Acis avitas.
Puniceus de mole cruor manabat, et intra
Temporis exiguum rubor evanescere coepit,
Fitque color primo turbati fluminis imbre,
Purgaturque mora. Tum moles tacta dehiscit, 890
Vivaque per rimas proceraque surgit harundo,
Osque cavum saxi sonat exsultantibus undis :
Miraque res, subito media tenus extitit alvo
Incinctus juvenis flexis nova cornua cannis,

Qui, nisi quod major, quod toto caerulus ore, 895
Acis erat. Sed sic quoque erat tamen Acis, in amnem
Versus; et antiquum tenuerunt flumina nomen.'

32. The Epilogue.
XV. 871-879.

Jamque opus exegi, quod nec Jovis ira nec ignis
Nec poterit ferrum nec edax abolere vetustas.
Cum volet, illa dies, quae nil nisi corporis hujus
Jus habet, incerti spatium mihi finiat aevi:
Parte tamen meliore mei super alta perennis 875
Astra ferar, nomenque erit indelebile nostrum.
Quaque patet domitis Romana potentia terris,
Ore legar populi, perque omnia saecula fama,
Siquid habent veri vatum praesagia, vivam.

AMORES.

1. The Poet's Defense of Himself.
I. 15.

The poet vindicates the noble offices of his art, and predicts the immortality of his own Muse.

Quid mihi, Livor edax, ignavos obicis annos,
    Ingeniique vocas carmen inertis opus?
Non me more patrum, dum strenua sustinet aetas
    Praemia militiae pulverulenta sequi,
Nec me verbosas leges ediscere, nec me   5
    Ingrato vocem prostituisse foro.
Mortale est, quod quaeris, opus. Mihi fama perennis
    Quaeritur, in toto semper ut orbe canar.
Vivet Maeonides, Tenedos dum stabit et Ide,
    Dum rapidas Simois in mare volvet aquas.   10
Vivet et Ascraeus, dum mustis uva tumebit,
    Dum cadet incurva falce reseeta ceres.
Battiades semper toto cantabitur orbe:
    Quamvis ingenio non valet, arte valet.
Nulla Sophocleo veniet jactura cothurno.   15
    Cum sole et luna semper Aratus erit.
Dum fallax servus, durus pater, improba lena
    Vivent et meretrix blanda, Menandros erit.

Ennius arte carens animosique Actius oris
  Casurum nullo tempore nomen habent.   20
Varronem primamque ratem quae nesciet aetas,
  Aureaque Aesonio terga petita duci?
Carmina sublimis tunc sunt peritura Lucreti,
  Exitio terras cum dabit una dies.
Tityrus et fruges Aeneïaque arma legentur,   25
  Roma triumphati dum caput orbis erit.
Donec erunt ignes arcusque Cupidinis arma,
  Discentur numeri, culte Tibulle, tui.
Gallus et hesperiis et Gallus notus cois,
  Et sua cum Gallo nota Lycoris erit.   30
Ergo cum silices, cum dens patientis aratri
  Depereant aevo, carmina morte carent.
Cedant carminibus reges regumque triumphi,
  Cedat et auriferi ripa benigna Tagi.
Vilia miretur vulgus. Mihi flavus Apollo   35
  Pocula Castalia plena ministret aqua,
Sustineamque coma metuentem frigora myrtum:
  Atque ita sollicito multus amante legar.
Pascitur in vivis Livor. Post fata quiescit,
  Cum suus ex merito quemque tuetur honos.   40
Ergo etiam cum me supremus adederit ignis,
  Vivam, parsque mei multa superstes erit.

2. The Death of Tibullus.

III. 9.

Memnona si mater, mater ploravit Achillem,
  Et tangunt magnas tristia fata deas,
Flebilis indignos, Elegeia, solve capillos.
  A, nimis ex vero nunc tibi nomen erit!

2. THE DEATH OF TIBULLUS.

Ille tui vates operis, tua fama, Tibullus 5
    Ardet in exstructo, corpus inane, rogo.
Ecce, puer Veneris fert eversamque pharetram
    Et fractos arcus et sine luce facem.
Aspice, demissis ut eat miserabilis alis,
    Pectoraque infesta tundat aperta manu. 10
Excipiunt lacrimas sparsi per colla capilli,
    Oraque singultu concutiente sonant.
Fratris in Aeneae sic illum funere dicunt
    Egressum tectis, pulcher Iule, tuis.
Nec minus est confusa Venus moriente Tibullo, 15
    Quam juveni rupit cum ferus inguen aper.
At sacri vates et divum cura vocamur!
    Sunt etiam, qui nos numen habere putent!
Scilicet omne sacrum mors importuna profanat.
    Omnibus obscuras inicit illa manus. 20
Quid pater Ismario, quid mater profuit Orpheo?
    Carmine quid victas obstipuisse feras?
Aelinon in silvis idem pater, aelinon, altis
    Dicitur invita concinuisse lyra.
Adice Maeoniden, a quo, ceu fonte perenni, 25
    Vatum Pieriis ora rigantur aquis.
Hunc quoque summa dies nigro submersit Averno:
    Diffugiunt avidos carmina sola rogos.
Durat opus vatum : Trojani fama laboris,
    Tardaque nocturno tela retexta dolo: 30
Sic Nemesis longum, sic Delia nomen habebunt,
    Altera cura recens, altera primus amor.
Quid vos sacra juvant? quid nunc Aegyptia prosunt
    Sistra? quid in vacuo secubuisse toro?
Cum rapiant mala fata bonos, ignoscite fasso, 35
    Sollicitor nullos esse putare deos.

Vive pius, moriere. Pius cole sacra, colentem
    Mors gravis a templis in cava busta trahet.
Carminibus confide bonis: jacet, ecce, Tibullus:
    Vix manet e toto parva quod urna capit.   40
Tene, sacer vates, flammae rapuere rogales,
    Pectoribus pasci nec timuere tuis?
Aurea sanctorum potuissent templa deorum
    Urere, quae tantum sustinuere nefas.
Avertit vultus Erycis quae possidet arces.   45
    Sunt quoque, qui lacrimas continuisse negant.
Sed tamen hoc melius, quam si Phaeacia tellus
    Ignotum vili supposuisset humo.
Hinc certe madidos fugientis pressit ocellos
    Mater, et in cineres ultima dona tulit: 50
Hinc soror in partem misera cum matre doloris
    Venit, inornatas dilaniata comas:
Cumque tuis sua junxerunt Nemesisque priorque
    Oscula, nec solos destituere rogos.
Delia descendens 'felicius' inquit 'amata   55
    Sum tibi: vixisti, dum tuus ignis eram.'
Cui Nemesis 'quid' ait 'tibi sunt mea damna dolori?
    Me tenuit moriens deficiente manu.'
Si tamen e nobis aliquid nisi nomen et umbra
    Restat, in Elysia valle Tibullus erit.   60
Obvius huic venias, hedera juvenalia cinctus
    Tempora, cum Calvo, docte Catulle, tuo.
Tu quoque, si falsum est temerati crimen amici,
    Sanguinis atque animae prodige Galle tuae.
His comes umbra tua est. Siqua est modo corporis umbra,
    Auxisti numeros, culte Tibulle, pios.
Ossa quieta, precor, tuta requiescite in urna,
    Et sit humus cineri non onerosa tuo!

3. Farewell to Love-Songs.

III. 15.

Quaere novum vatem, tenerorum mater **A**morum :
   Raditur hic elegis ultima meta meis :
Quos ego composui, Peligni ruris alumnus :
   Nec me deliciae dedecuere meae.
Siquid id est, usque a proavis vetus ordinis heres,   5
   Non modo militiae turbine factus eques.
Mantua Vergilio gaudet : Verona Catullo.
   Pelignae dicar gloria gentis ego,
Quam sua libertas ad honesta coegerat arma,
   Cum timuit socias anxia Roma manus.   10
Atque aliquis spectans hospes Sulmonis aquosi
   Moenia, quae campi jugera pauca tenent,
'Quae tantum' dicet ' potuistis ferre poetam,
   Quantulacumque estis, vos ego magna voco.'
Culte puer, puerique parens Amathusia culti,   15
   Aurea de campo vellite signa meo.
Corniger increpuit thyrso graviore Lyaeus :
   Pulsanda est magnis area major equis.
Imbelles elegi, genialis musa, valete,
   Post mea mansurum fata superstes opus !   20

FASTI.

1. ROMULUS AND REMUS.
II. 383-422.

Silvia Vestalis caelestia semina partu
  Ediderat, patruo regna tenente suo.
Is jubet auferri parvos et in amne necari.   385
  Quid facis? ex istis Romulus alter erit!
Jussa recusantes peragunt lacrimosa ministri,
  Flent tamen, et geminos in loca jussa ferunt.
Albula, quem Tiberim mersus Tiberinus in undis
  Reddidit, hibernis forte tumebat aquis.   390
Hic, ubi nunc fora sunt, lintres errare videres,
  Quaque jacent valles, Maxime Circe, tuae.
Huc ubi venerunt, neque enim procedere possunt
  Longius, ex illis unus et alter ait:
'At quam sunt similes! at quam formosus uterque! 395
  Plus tamen ex illis iste vigoris habet.
Si genus arguitur voltu, nisi fallit imago,
  Nescio quem vobis suspicer esse deum.'
'At si quis vestrae deus esset originis auctor,
  In tam praecipiti tempore ferret opem.   400
Ferret opem certe, si non ope mater egeret,
  Quae facta est uno mater et orba die.

Nata simul, moritura simul, simul ite sub undas
 Corpora!' desierat, deposuitque sinu.
Vagierunt ambo pariter. Sensisse putares. 405
 Hi redeunt udis in sua tecta genis.
Sustinet impositos summa cavus alveus unda.
 Heu quantum fati parva tabella tulit!
Alveus in limo silvis appulsus opacis
 Paulatim fluvio deficiente sedet. 410
Arbor erat. Remanent vestigia, quaeque vocatur
 Rumina nunc ficus, Romula ficus erat.
Venit ad expositos, mirum! lupa foeta gemellos.
 Quis credat pueris non nocuisse feram?
Non nocuisse parum est, prodest quoque. Quos lupa
 Perdere cognatae sustinuere manus!   [nutrit,
Constitit, et cauda teneris blanditur alumnis,
 Et fingit lingua corpora bina sua.
Marte satos scires. Timor abfuit, ubera ducunt,
 Nec sibi promissi lactis aluntur ope. 420
Illa loco nomen fecit, locus ipse lupercis.
 Magna dati nutrix praemia lactis habet.

2. THE DEIFICATION OF ROMULUS.

II. 475-512.

Proxima lux vacua est. At tertia dicta Quirino. 475
 Qui tenet hoc nomen, Romulus ante fuit:
Sive quod hasta curis priscis est dicta Sabinis,
 Bellicus a telo venit in astra deus:
Sive suo regi nomen posuere Quirites:
 Seu quia Romanis junxerat ille Cures. 480
Nam pater armipotens postquam nova moenia vidit,
 Multaque Romulea bella peracta manu,

'Juppiter,' inquit 'habet Romana potentia vires:
  Sanguinis officio non eget illa mei.
Redde patri natum. Quamvis intercidit alter, 485
  Pro se proque Remo qui mihi restat, erit.
'Unus erit, quem tu tolles in caerula caeli,'
  Tu mihi dixisti. Sint rata dicta Jovis.'
Juppiter annuerat. Nutu tremefactus uterque
  Est polus, et caeli pondera movit Atlas. 490
Est locus, antiqui Capreae dixere paludem:
  Forte tuis illic, Romule, jura dabas.
Sol fugit, et removent subeuntia nubila caelum,
  Et gravis effusis decidit imber aquis.
Hinc tonat, hinc missis abrumpitur ignibus aether. 495
  Fit fuga. Rex patriis astra petebat equis.
Luctus erat, falsaeque patres in crimine caedis:
  Haesissetque animis forsitan illa fides:
Sed Proculus Longa veniebat Julius Alba,
  Lunaque fulgebat, nec facis usus erat, 500
Cum subito motu saepes tremuere sinistrae:
  Rettulit ille gradus, horrueruntque comae.
Pulcher et humano major trabeaque decorus
  Romulus in media visus adesse via,
Et dixisse simul: 'Prohibe lugere Quirites, 505
  Nec violent lacrimis numina nostra suis.
Tura ferant, placentque novum pia turba Quirinum,
  Et patrias artes militiamque colant.'
Jussit, et in tenues oculis evanuit auras.
  Convocat hic populos, jussaque verba refert. 510
Templa deo fiunt. Collis quoque dictus ab illo est,
  Et referunt certi sacra paterna dies.

3. Lucretia.

II. 710-758.

Traduntur ducibus moenia nuda suis. 710
Ecce, nefas visu, mediis altaribus anguis
  Exit, et exstinctis ignibus exta rapit.
Consulitur Phoebus. Sors est ita reddita, 'Matri
  Qui dederit princeps oscula, victor erit.'
Oscula quisque suae matri properata tulerunt, 715
  Non intellecto credula turba deo.
Brutus erat stulti sapiens imitator, ut esset
  Tutus ab insidiis, dire Superbe, tuis.
Ille jacens pronus matri dedit oscula Terrae,
  Creditus offenso procubuisse pede. 720
Cingitur interea Romanis Ardea signis,
  Et patitur lentas obsidione moras.
Dum vacat, et metuunt hostes committere pugnam,
  Luditur in castris, otia miles agit.
Tarquinius juvenis socios dapibusque meroque 725
  Accipit. Ex illis rege creatus ait:
'Dum nos difficilis pigro tenet Ardea bello,
  Nec sinit ad patrios arma referre deos,
Ecquid in officio torus est socialis? et ecquid
  Conjugibus nostris mutua cura sumus?' 730
Quisque suam laudat. Studiis certamina crescunt,
  Et fervent multo linguaque corque mero.
Surgit cui dederat clarum Collatia nomen:
  'Non opus est verbis, credite rebus!' ait.
'Nox superest. Tollamur equis, Urbemque petamus!'
  Dicta placent, frenis impediuntur equi.
Pertulerant dominos. Regalia protinus illi
  Tecta petunt. Custos in fore nullus erat.

Ecce nurum regis fusis per colla coronis
  Inveniunt posito pervigilare mero.   740
Inde cito passu petitur Lucretia. Nebat,
  Ante torum calathi lanaque mollis erat.
Lumen ad exiguum famulae data pensa trahebant:
  Inter quas tenui sic ait ipsa sono:
'Mittenda est domino, nunc, nunc properate, puellae!
  Quamprimum nostra facta lacerna manu.
Quid tamen auditis? nam plura audire potestis:
  Quantum de bello dicitur esse super?
Postmodo victa cades. Melioribus, Ardea, restas,
  Improba, quae nostros cogis abesse viros!   750
Sint tantum reduces! Sed enim temerarius ille
  Est meus, et stricto quolibet ense ruit.
Mens abit, et morior, quotiens pugnantis imago
  Me subit, et gelidum pectora frigus habet.'
Desinit in lacrimas, intentaque fila remittit,   755
  In gremio voltum deposuitque suum.
Hoc ipsum decuit, lacrimae decuere pudicae,
  Et facies animo dignaque parque fuit.
'Pone metum, venio!' conjunx ait. Illa revixit,
  Deque viri collo dulce pependit onus.   760

4. The Building of Rome.

IV. 809-862.

Jam luerat poenas frater Numitoris, et omne
  Pastorum gemino sub duce volgus erat.   810
Contrahere agrestes et moenia ponere utrique
  Convenit. Ambigitur, moenia ponat uter.
'Nil opus est' dixit 'certamine' Romulus 'ullo:
  Magna fides avium est. Experiamur aves.'

Res placet. Alter adit nemorosi saxa Palati :   815
 Alter Aventinum mane cacumen init.
Sex Remus, hic volucres bis sex videt ordine.   Pacto
 Statur, et arbitrium Romulus urbis habet.
Apta dies legitur, qua moenia signet aratro.
 Sacra Palis suberant, inde movetur opus.   820
Fossa fit ad solidum. Fruges jaciuntur in ima,
 Et de vicino terra petita solo.
Fossa repletur humo, plenaeque imponitur ara,
 Et novus accenso fungitur igne focus.
Inde premens stivam designat moenia sulco :   825
 Alba jugum niveo cum bove vacca tulit.
Vox fuit haec regis : 'Condenti, Juppiter, urbem
 Et genitor Mavors Vestaque mater, ades!
Quosque pium est adhibere deos, advertite cuncti!
 Auspicibus vobis hoc mihi surgat opus.   830
Longa sit huic aetas dominaeque potentia terrae,
 Sitque sub hac oriens occiduusque dies.'
Ille precabatur. Tonitru dedit omina laevo
 Juppiter, et laevo fulmina missa polo.
Augurio laeti jaciunt fundamina cives,   835
 Et novus exiguo tempore murus erat.
Hoc Celer urget opus, quem Romulus ipse vocarat,
 'Sint' que, 'Celer, curae' dixerat 'ista tuae.
Neve quis aut muros, aut factam vomere fossam
 Transeat, audentem talia dede neci.'   840
Quod Remus ignorans humiles contemnere muros
 Coepit, et 'His populus' dicere 'tutus erit?'
Nec mora, transiluit. Rutro Celer occupat ausum.
 Ille premit duram sanguinulentus humum.
Haec ubi rex didicit, lacrimas introrsus obortas   845
 Devorat, et clausum pectore volnus habet.

Flere palam non volt, exemplaque fortia servat,
  'Sic' que 'meos muros transeat hostis' ait
Dat tamen exequias. Nec jam suspendere fletum
  Sustinet, et pietas dissimulata patet.   850
Osculaque applicuit posito suprema feretro,
  Atque ait, 'Invito frater adempte, vale!'
Arsurosque artus unxit. Fecere, quod ille,
  Faustulus et maestas Acca soluta comas.
Tum juvenem nondum facti flevere Quirites.   855
  Ultima plorato subdita flamma rogo est.
Urbs oritur—quis tunc hoc ulli credere posset?—
  Victorem terris impositura pedem.
Cuncta regas, et sis magno sub Caesare semper:
  Saepe etiam pluris nominis hujus habe: 860
Et quotiens steteris domito sublimis in orbe,
  Omnia sint umeris inferiora tuis.

TRISTIA.

1. The Poet's Departure from Rome.
I. 3.

Cum subit illius tristissima noctis imago,
   Qua mihi supremum tempus in urbe fuit,
Cum repeto noctem, qua tot mihi cara reliqui,
   Labitur ex oculis nunc quoque gutta meis.
Jam prope lux aderat, qua me discedere Caesar   5
   Finibus extremae jusserat Ausoniae.
Nec spatium fuerat, nec mens satis apta parandi:
   Torpuerant longa pectora nostra mora.
Non mihi servorum, comitis non cura legendi,
   Non aptae profugo vestis opisve fuit.   10
Non aliter stupui, quam qui Jovis ignibus ictus
   Vivit, et est vitae nescius ipse suae.
Ut tamen hanc animi nubem dolor ipse removit,
   Et tandem sensus convaluere mei,
Alloquor extremum maestos abiturus amicos,   15
   Qui modo de multis unus et alter erant.
Uxor amans flentem flens acrius ipsa tenebat,
   Imbre per indignas usque cadente genas.
Nata procul Libycis aberat diversa sub oris,
   Nec poterat fati certior esse mei.   20

Quocumque aspiceres, luctus gemitusque sonabant,
  Formaque non taciti funeris intus erat.
Femina virque meo, pueri quoque, funere maerent:
  Inque domo lacrimas angulus omnis habet.
Si licet exemplis in parvo grandibus uti, 25
  Haec facies Trojae, cum caperetur, erat.
Jamque quiescebant voces hominumque canumque,
  Lunaque nocturnos alta regebat equos.
Hanc ego suspiciens, et ab hac Capitolia cernens,
  Quae nostro frustra juncta fuere lari, 30
'Numina vicinis habitantia sedibus,' inquam,
  Jamque oculis nunquam templa videnda meis,
Dique relinquendi, quos urbs tenet alta Quirini,
  Este salutati tempus in omne mihi!
Et quanquam sero clipeum post vulnera sumo, 35
  Attamen hanc odiis exonerate fugam,
Caelestique viro, quis me deceperit error,
  Dicite. Pro culpa ne scelus esse putet.
Ut quod vos scitis, poenae quoque sentiat auctor,
  Placato possum non miser esse deo.' 40
Hac prece adoravi superos ego. Pluribus uxor,
  Singultu medios impediente sonos.
Illa etiam ante lares passis prostrata capillis
  Contigit extinctos ore tremente focos,
Multaque in adversos effudit verba penates 45
  Pro deplorato non valitura viro.
Jamque morae spatium nox praecipitata negabat,
  Versaque ab axe suo Parrhasis arctos erat.
Quid facerem? blando patriae retinebar amore:
  Ultima sed jussae nox erat illa fugae. 50
A! quotiens aliquo dixi properante, 'Quid urgues!
  Vel quo festines ire, vel unde, vide!'

1. THE POET'S DEPARTURE FROM ROME.

A! quotiens certam me sum mentitus habere
   Horam, propositae quae foret apta viae.
Ter limen tetigi, ter sum revocatus, et ipse   55
   Indulgens animo pes mihi tardus erat.
Saepe vale dicto rursus sum multa locutus,
   Et quasi discedens oscula summa dedi.
Saepe eadem mandata dedi, meque ipse fefelli,
   Respiciens oculis pignora cara meis.   [quam,
Denique, 'Quid propero? Scythia est, quo mittimur,' in-
   'Roma relinquenda est. Utraque justa mora est.'
Uxor in aeternum vivo mihi viva negatur,
   Et domus et fidae dulcia membra domus,
Quosque ego fraterno dilexi more sodales,   65
   O mihi Thesea pectora juncta fide!
Dum licet, amplectar. Nunquam fortasse licebit
   Amplius. In lucro est quae datur hora mihi.'
Nec mora, sermonis verba imperfecta relinquo,
   Complectens animo proxima quaeque meo.   70
Dum loquor et flemus, caelo nitidissimus alto,
   Stella gravis nobis, Lucifer ortus erat.
Dividor haud aliter, quam si mea membra relinquam,
   Et pars abrumpi corpore visa suo est.
Sic doluit Metus tunc, cum in contraria versos   75
   Ultores habuit proditionis equos.
Tum vero exoritur clamor gemitusque meorum,
   Et feriunt maestae pectora nuda manus.
Tum vero conjunx, umeris abeuntis inhaerens,
   Miscuit haec lacrimis tristia dicta suis: 80
'Non potes avelli. Simul, a! simul ibimus,' inquit:
   'Te sequar et conjunx exulis exul ero.
Et mihi facta via est. Et me capit ultima tellus:
   Accedam profugae sarcina parva rati.

Te jubet a patria discedere Caesaris ira, 85
  Me pietas. Pietas haec mihi Caesar erit.
Talia temptabat, sicut temptaverat ante,
  Vixque dedit victas utilitate manus.
Egredior, sive illud erat sine funere ferri,
  Squalidus immissis hirta per ora comis. 90
Illa dolore amens tenebris narratur obortis
  Semianimis media procubuisse domo:
Utque resurrexit foedatis pulvere turpi
  Crinibus, et gelida membra levavit humo,
Se modo, desertos modo complorasse penates, 95
  Nomen et erepti saepe vocasse viri;
Nec gemuisse minus, quam si nataeve meumve
  Vidisset structos corpus habere rogos,
Et voluisse mori, moriendo ponere sensus,
  Respectuque tamen non voluisse mei. 100
Vivat! et absentem, quoniam sic fata tulerunt,
  Vivat ut auxilio sublevet usque suo.

2. To his Daughter Perilla.

III. 7.

Vade salutatum, subito perarata, Perillam,
  Littera, sermonis fida ministra mei!
Aut illam invenies dulci cum matre sedentem,
  Aut inter libros Pieridasque suas.
Quicquid aget, cum te scierit venisse, relinquet, 5
  Nec mora, quid venias quidve, requiret, agam.
Vivere me dices, sed sic, ut vivere nolim,
  Nec mala tam longa nostra levata mora:
Et tamen ad Musas, quamvis nocuere, reverti,
  Aptaque in alternos cogere verba pedes. 10

2. TO HIS DAUGHTER PERILLA.

Tu quoque, dic, studiis communibus ecquid inhaeres,
   Doctaque non patrio carmina more canis?
Nam tibi cum fatis mores natura pudicos
   Et raras dotes ingeniumque dedit.
Hoc ego Pegasidas deduxi primus ad undas,   15
   Ne male fecundae vena periret aquae.
Primus id aspexi teneris in virginis annis,
   Utque pater natae duxque comesque fui.
Ergo si remanent ignes tibi pectoris idem,
   Sola tuum vates Lesbia vincet opus.   20
Sed vereor, ne te mea nunc fortuna retardet,
   Postque meos casus sit tibi pectus iners.
Dum licuit, tua saepe mihi, tibi nostra legebam:
   Saepe tui judex, saepe magister eram:
Aut ego praebebam factis modo versibus aures,   25
   Aut, ubi cessaras, causa ruboris eram.
Forsitan exemplo, quia me laesere libelli,
   Tu quoque sis poenae facta ruina meae.
Pone, Perilla, metum. Tantummodo femina non sit
   Devia, nec scriptis discat amare tuis.   30
Ergo desidiae remove, doctissima, causas,
   Inque bonas artes et tua sacra redi.
Ista decens facies longis vitiabitur annis,
   Rugaque in antiqua fronte senilis erit:
Inicietque manum formae damnosa senectus,   35
   Quae strepitum passu non faciente venit.
Cumque aliquis dicet, 'Fuit haec formosa,' dolebis,
   Et speculum mendax esse querere tuum.
Sunt tibi opes modicae, cum sis dignissima magnis:
   Finge sed immensis censibus esse pares,   40
Nempe dat id cuicumque libet fortuna rapitque,
   Irus et est subito, qui modo Croesus erat.

Singula quid referam? nil non mortale tenemus
    Pectoris exceptis ingeniique bonis.
En ego, cum patria caream vobisque domoque,   45
    Raptaque sint, adimi quae potuere mihi,
Ingenio tamen ipse meo comitorque fruorque:
    Caesar in hoc potuit juris habere nihil.
Quilibet hanc saevo vitam mihi finiat ense,
    Me tamen extincto fama superstes erit,   50
Dumque suis septem victrix de montibus orbem
    Prospiciet domitum Martia Roma, legar.
Tu quoque, quam studii maneat felicior usus,
    Effuge venturos, qua potes, usque rogos!

3. THE POET'S LIFE.

IV. 10.

Ille ego qui fuerim, tenerorum lusor amorum,
    Quem legis ut noris, accipe posteritas.
Sulmo mihi patria est, gelidis uberrimus undis,
    Milia qui novies distat ab Urbe decem.
Editus hinc ego sum, nec non ut tempora noris,   5
    Cum cecidit fato consul uterque pari:
Si quid id est, usque a proavis vetus ordinis heres,
    Non modo fortunae munere factus eques.
Nec stirps prima fui. Genito sum fratre creatus,
    Qui tribus ante quater mensibus ortus erat.   10
Lucifer amborum natalibus adfuit idem:
    Una celebrata est per duo liba dies.
Haec est armiferae festis de quinque Minervae,
    Quae fieri pugna prima cruenta solet.
Protinus excolimur teneri, curaque parentis   15
    Imus ad insignes Urbis ab arte viros.

8. THE POET'S LIFE.

Frater ad eloquium viridi tendebat ab aevo,
   Fortia verbosi natus ad arma fori.
At mihi jam puero caelestia sacra placebant,
   Inque suum furtim Musa trahebat opus.   20
Saepe pater dixit, 'Studium quid inutile temptas?
   Maeonides nullas ipse reliquit opes.'
Motus eram dictis, totoque Helicone relicto
   Scribere conabar verba soluta modis.
Sponte sua carmen numeros veniebat ad aptos,   25
   Et quod temptabam dicere, versus erat.
Interea tacito passu labentibus annis
   Liberior fratri sumpta mihique toga est,
Induiturque umeris cum lato purpura clavo,
   Et studium nobis quod fuit ante, manet.   30
Jamque decem vitae frater geminaverat annos,
   Cum perit, et coepi parte carere mei.
Cepimus et tenerae primos aetatis honores,
   Deque viris quondam pars tribus una fui.
Curia restabat. Clavi mensura coacta est: 35
   Majus erat nostris viribus illud onus.
Nec patiens corpus, nec mens fuit apta labori,
   Sollicitaeque fugax ambitionis eram.
Et petere Aoniae suadebant tuta sorores
   Otia, judicio semper amata meo.   40
Temporis illius colui fovique poetas,
   Quotque aderant vates, rebar adesse deos.
Saepe suas volucres legit mihi grandior aevo,
   Quaeque necet serpens, quae juvet herba, Macer.
Saepe suos solitus recitare Propertius ignes,   45
   Jure sodalicio qui mihi junctus erat.
Ponticus heroo, Bassus quoque clarus iambis
   Dulcia convictus membra fuere mei.

Et tenuit nostras numerosus Horatius aures,
 Dum ferit Ausonia carmina culta lyra. 50
Vergilium vidi tantum. Nec amara Tibullo
 Tempus amicitiae fata dedere meae.
Successor fuit hic tibi, Galle: Propertius illi:
 Quartus ab his serie temporis ipse fui.
Utque ego majores, sic me coluere minores, 55
 Notaque non tarde facta Thalia mea est.
Carmina cum primum populo juvenilia legi,
 Barba resecta mihi bisve semelve fuit.
Moverat ingenium totam cantata per Urbem
 Nomine non vero dicta Corinna mihi. 60
Multa quidem scripsi. Sed quae vitiosa putavi,
 Emendaturis ignibus ipse dedi.
Tunc quoque, cum fugerem, quaedam placitura cremavi,
 Iratus studio carminibusque meis.
Molle Cupidineis nec inexpugnabile telis 65
 Cor mihi, quodque levis causa moveret, erat.
Cum tamen hic essem, minimoque accenderer igne,
 Nomine sub nostro fabula nulla fuit.
Paene mihi puero nec digna nec utilis uxor
 Est data, quae tempus per breve nupta fuit. 70
Illi successit, quamvis sine crimine conjunx,
 Non tamen in nostro firma futura toro.
Ultima, quae mecum seros permansit in annos,
 Sustinuit conjunx exulis esse viri.
Filia me mea bis prima fecunda juventa, 75
 Sed non ex uno conjuge, fecit avum.
Et jam compleverat genitor sua fata, novemque
 Addiderat lustris altera lustra novem.
Non aliter flevi, quam me fleturus ademptum
 Ille fuit. Matri proxima justa tuli. 80

3. THE POET'S LIFE.

Felices ambo tempestiveque sepulti,
    Ante diem poenae quod periere meae!
Me quoque felicem, quod non viventibus illis
    Sum miser, et de me quod doluere nihil.
Si tamen extinctis aliquid nisi nomina restat,   85
    Et gracilis structos effugit umbra rogos:
Fama, parentales, si vos mea contigit, umbrae
    Et sunt in Stygio crimina nostra foro,
Scite, precor, causam, nec vos mihi fallere fas est,
    Errorem jussae, non scelus, esse fugae.   90
Manibus hoc satis est. Ad vos, studiosa, revertor,
    Pectora, qui vitae quaeritis acta meae.
Jam mihi canities pulsis melioribus annis
    Venerat, antiquas miscueratque comas,
Postque meos ortus Pisaea vinctus oliva   95
    Abstulerat decies praemia victor equus,
Cum maris Euxini positos ad laeva Tomitas
    Quaerere me laesi principis ira jubet.
Causa meae cunctis nimium quoque nota ruinae
    Indicio non est testificanda meo.   100
Quid referam comitumque nefas famulosque nocentes?
    Ipsa multa tuli non leviora fuga.
Indignata malis mens est succumbere, seque
    Praestitit invictam viribus usa suis.
Oblitusque mei ductaeque per otia vitae,   105
    Insolita cepi temporis arma manu.
Totque tuli casus pelagoque terraque, quot inter
    Occultum stellae conspicuumque polum.
Tacta mihi tandem longis erroribus acto
    Juncta pharetratis Sarmatis ora Getis.   110
Hic ego finitimis quamvis circumsoner armis,
    Tristia, quo possum, carmine fata levo.

Quod quamvis nemo est, cujus referatur ad aures,
    Sic tamen absumo decipioque diem.
Ergo quod vivo, durisque laboribus obsto,   115
    Nec me sollicitae taedia lucis habent,
Gratia, Musa, tibi. Nam tu solacia praebes,
    Tu curae requies, tu medicina venis.
Tu dux et comes es. Tu nos abducis ab Histro,
    In medioque mihi das Helicone locum.   120
Tu mihi, quod rarum est, vivo sublime dedisti
    Nomen, ab exequiis quod dare fama solet.
Nec qui detrectat praesentia, Livor iniquo
    Ullum de nostris dente momordit opus.
Nam tulerint magnos cum saecula nostra poetas,   125
    Non fuit ingenio fama maligna meo.
Cumque ego praeponam multos mihi, non minor illis
    Dicor et in toto plurimus orbe legor.
Si quid habent igitur vatum praesagia veri,
    Protinus ut moriar, non ero, terra, tuus.   130
Sive favore tuli, sive hanc ego carmine famam
    Jure, tibi grates, candide lector, ago.

NOTES.

NOTES.*

METAMORPHOSES.

I. THE CREATION.

I. 1-88.

1. Fert animus, my mind leads (me), *I purpose*.——**Mūtātas formas**, changed forms, or *changes of forms*. It is a Latin expression for the Greek word *metamorphōses*, transformations. Such changes of form the poet purposes to describe as he finds in the Greek and Roman Mythology: men changed to divine forms, as Hercules or Romulus; or gods changed to human forms; or men changed into beasts, or into trees, and the like.

2. Et illas, *also those*, i. e., as all other things which undergo change.

3. Aspīrāte, used often of winds which are favorable, and so generally in the sense of *favor*.——**Primāque mundi**, *from the very origin of the world*. *Mundus* means first order, κόσμος, and then the orderly *world*.

7. Chāos (from χαίνω), first yawning space, and then used for formless matter; as in the second verse of Genesis, "the earth was without form, and void."

9. Discordia, adjective agreeing with *semina*, which, meaning seeds, expresses what we call *elements*.

10–14. The names Tītan, Phoebe, Amphitrīte, are here personifications for Sun, Moon, and Sea.

13. Ponderibus—suis. The plural in *ponderibus* is used, because the weights of the parts of the whole are thought of, and as equal to one another, i. e., in equilibrium; balanced *by its own weights*, or held in equilibrium; so also in Horace, Ep. i. 6, 51.

14. Amphitrīte; the line is a spondaic hexameter, examples of which are common in this poem.——**Margine**; without the preposition *in*, with the idea of *place*, as often in poetry.

* The grammatical references (H. or Gr.) are to the Latin Grammar of Professor Albert Harkness, revised edition of 1851.

15, 16. Utque—sic, and **as—so**; *though—yet.*

17. Nulli; here neuter; but in prose *nullae rei* is more common.—— **Sua** refers to *nulli;* H. 449, 2.

20. Sine pondere; = eis quae sine pondere sunt.

23. Liquidum—caelum, the clear heavens, in distinction from the denser atmosphere below (*spisso—aere*). It is called *aether* in lines 15 and 67, and *ignea vis* in line 26, as if of the same nature as fire.

24. Quae, i. e., caelum, terras, undas, aer.——**Caeco—acervo;** a circumlocution for chaos, *caeco* being used passively, as no one thing in it could be distinguished from another; *the blind mass.*

26. Join thus: ignea et sine pondere vis—caeli.

27. Summāque—In arce; *arx,* a citadel, is used often for a high place, and for height; here the same as "firmament" in Genesis; *and in the very firmament.*

31. Possēdit, from *possīdo,* and so having an active or causative sense, just as the simple verb *sīdo* is distinguished from *sedeo; took possession of.*

34. Non aequalis, to be taken together.

37. Terrae, dative with acc. *litŏra;* the verb *circumdo* has also the construction of abl. (litoribus) with acc. *terram.*

39. Obliquis, *winding;* **declivia,** *down-running.*

40. Quae, sc. flumina; **ipsā,** sc. terrā.

42. Ripis, the *banks* of rivers, **litora,** the *shores* of the sea; though they are sometimes interchanged by the poets.

43. Subsīdĕre, from *subsīdo.* See above, n. on line 31; literally, to set themselves down, *to sink.*

45-48. Division of the heavens into five zones, to which correspond five zones on the earth's surface.

45. Dextrā, sinistrā, relatively to the equator.

46. Quinta, same as **media** in l. 49.

47. Onus inclusum, i. e., the earth, as encompassed by the heavens.

50. Totĭdem, sc. zonas.——**Utramque,** i. e., on either hemisphere between the torrid and the frigid zone. Haupt reads utrumque.

52. His, i. e., plagis terrestribus.

56. Cum fulminibus; the preposition instead of et fulmina; *and the winds that cause the cold as well as the lightning.* The idea seems to have been that the winds cause the lightning by means of the friction of the clouds.

57. His, sc. ventis. *Habendum* is used in the sense of having under control, and *non passim* implies that only in certain places were the winds allowed such control.

1. THE CREATION. 143

58-60. Nunc with emphasis, and explained by *cum* seqq., *since*, etc.; and *quin lanient* depends upon *obsistitur*, according to H. 504, 4.——**Fratrum**; the Winds were personified as sons of Astraeus and Aurora.

61. The *Nabataei* were an Arabian people.

62. Juga, etc., refers to the range of mountains in India.——**Mātūtīnis**; a spondaic line.

63. Vesper, used in a local sense for *the West*, only by the poets.

64. Septemque trionem, for septemtrionemque; the dactyl of the fifth place makes the division by *que* necessary. The constellation of the Wain or the Great Bear, consisting of seven stars, five for the Wain and two for the steers; the name of it was called, rather irregularly, septem triones, and then in the sing. septemtrio.

66. "The South wind (*aquaticus auster*, 2, 285) brings with it rain in Greece and Italy. Hence the Greek name for it, called by the Romans Notus, cf. *νοτίς*, moisture." Haupt.

67. Haec, i. e., aera, nubes, ventos. *Super* governs *haec*, the preposition coming *after*, as not unfrequently with the poets, especially in dissyllabic words.

72. Animantibus. The ancients ascribed to the stars life and even reason.——**Formae deorum**; the gods were conceived as having bodily forms.

76. Animal; because a *living being;* but *sanctius*, because nobler, as endowed with reason, made in the image of God; *diviner*.

77. Dēĕrat, a dissyllable.——**Quod—posset**, *of such nature that it might be able*, H. 503, i.

80. Nuper, as described in line 22, *terris abscidit undas*.

81. Cognati; because, before the dividing of chaos, the heavens had been mingled with earth.

82. Iăpĕto; four syllables, as the *I* of Greek words is never to be pronounced as *J*. Ovid follows the myth, which represents Prometheus, the son of the Titan Iapetus, as fashioning man from earth and water.

83. Moderantum; the genitive in *um* instead of *ium*, on account of the metre; but see H. 158, 2.——**In effigiem—deorum.** In the same way as the gods were conceived as appearing in human form among men, so, as here, man is made in the image of the gods, reminding us of the words in Genesis 1, 26, "Let us make man in our image."

85. Caelumque videre, sc. cum, referring to *homini*, as the subject of *videre*. Comp. Cic. de Amicitia, c. 21, *caelestium ordinem contemplantes*.

2. THE FOUR AGES.

I. 89-150.

89-150. In Verg. Georg. 1, 125 seqq., and in Tibullus, i. 3, 35 seqq., the golden or good age is that of Saturn, which is followed by that of Jupiter. Hesiod has five ages, the golden, silver, brazen, the fourth without name, and the iron. Aratus has three, the golden, silver, and iron. Ovid has drawn in part from these poets. The designation of the periods by the metals from gold downward manifestly teaches the fall of the race from a golden innocence to successive stages of moral degeneracy. In like manner this idea of four ages is taught in the Zendavesta or sacred books of the ancient Persians, and in those of the Hindoos, both Brahmanic and Buddhistic, and in the Sagas of the ancient Germans; also in the legends of the Aegyptians.

89-112. The Golden Age.

89. Aurea; the first word of the sentence is the emphatic one, as if we should say in English, *with gold was the first age sown*.——**Vindice nullo,** abl. absolute, and may be rendered, *without any to punish*.

91, 92. Poena metusque; penalty and fears, i. e., *fears of penalty*. ——**Verba minacia—aere;** in reference to laws, as of the Twelve Tables, which on brazen tablets were *fixed* on the Capitol and other public places.

93. Erant; an indefinite subject understood, as in English *they*. Another reading is *vindice*, instead of *judice*.

94. Suis, *its own*, in opposition to *peregrinum*.

98. Directi. The *tuba* was straight, and the *cornu* curved. *Aeris*, denoting the material, is in the genitive, after the analogy of the gen. of quality. H. 396, v.

101. Ipsa, in the first place because emphatic, *of itself;* as opposed to what followed, it is = tellus *inarata*.

104. Arbŭteos foetus; *the fruit of the* arbŭtus or wild strawberry, like the *fraga* or common strawberry, but larger.——**Legebant;** the subject indefinite, as above *erant*, l. 93.

105. Corna, the fruit of the wild cornel-tree, a *horn-like* cherry, because so hard.——**Mōra,** *blackberries*, the fruit of the *rubēta* (pl.).

106. Jovis arbore; i. e., the oak, one species of which bears acorns which are edible.

108. Semine; for semente, sowing, i. e., without sowing on the part of any one.

2. THE FOUR AGES.

110. Nec renovatus, i. e., et non renovatus, *and without renewal.*——**Cānebat** (from cānco), *whitened.*

111. Flumina, etc., figurative for abundance; the *nectaris* itself figurative for wine. So of the land of promise in Exodus, 3, 8, "a land flowing with milk and honey."

112. Stillabant; the honey was thought of, as in the golden age distilling like dew from the trees.

113–124. The Silver Age.

113. Saturno. Saturnus, a god of the ancient Italians, was afterward identified with the Greek Kronos.

114. Subiit; the final syllable is long, its original quantity. So also below, iv. 712, *abiīt;* x. 15, *adiīt;* xi. 14, *abiīt.*

116. Contraxit; before, as said on l. 107, the spring was *perpetual.*

117. Another spondaic line.

118. Exēgit. The *ex* in the verb (literally, *out*) gives the verb the meaning of bringing to an end; *brought the year to an end through winters,* etc. Hence it comes to mean *finish.*

121. Sublēre; an indefinite subject again; *they.* The *sub* in the compound verb is well fitted to these primitive homes, as described in the next line.

122. Cortĭce; *bark,* but properly the outer, while *liber* is the word for the inner.

123. Cerealia; because *Ceres* was supposed to have given men the seeds, and to have taught them agriculture; thus we call now the different grains *Cereals.*

125–140. The Brazen and the Iron Age.

128. Vēnae; limits *aevum* as a gen. of characteristic; *an age of a worse vein.* II. 396, v.

133. Quaeque; the antecedent is *carīnae,* which is used figuratively for *naves.*——**Stĕtĕrant—altis;** in reference to the trees, of which the ships were made.

134. Insultavere; with the primary meaning of the word as a compound of *salto; danced upon;* with something, too, of the meaning of our derived word *insult,* as the ships, as it were, despised the danger. So, also, *contemnere* (literally, *not to fear*) is used by Tibullus, i. 3, 37, nondum pinus *contempserat* undas.

135. Prius; limits *communem;—lumina* and *auras,* drawn by attraction in the acc. to *humum;* though regularly it would read, ceu lumina solis et aurae communia sunt.

136. Limite means here *a boundary.*——**Mensor** is *the surveyor.*

137. Segetes, acc. as object of *poscebatur*, as posco in the active governs two accusatives. H. 374.

139. Stygiisque—umbris; the realm of the Shades, where the Styx flows; thought of as in the very depths of the earth. Styx, the Gr. Στύξ, the hateful river. So Milton, in the line ("Paradise Lost," ii. 579) "Abhorred *Styx,* the flood of deadly *hate.*"

140. Malorum is objective genitive. II. 396, III.

142. Utroque, i. e., both iron and gold. In what sense is it true of gold ?

145. Non socer a genero; perhaps, as Haupt suggests, in allusion to Cæsar and Pompeius.

147. Lurĭda; so called from the effect of aconite on the complexion of those who are poisoned by it.

148. Inquirit; i. e., of astrologers, as he is impatient for his father's death, and for the possession of his property.

150. Ultima; in the better times the gods dwelt among men; but one after another left the degenerate earth, Astræa, the goddess of justice, the *Dike* of the Greeks, being the last to take her flight. Astræa, the daughter of Jupiter and Themis, was placed as Virgo among the constellations.

3. The Flood.

I. 244–312.

244–312. Traditions of a flood, similar to the one here given by Ovid, are found among many and very different nations. Buttmann has treated of these traditions in his Mythologus, I. 180 seqq., and also Jacob Grimm in his German Mythology, 541 seqq. The similarity of them all to the Biblical narrative is striking.

244. Dicta Jovis. In the preceding passage Jupiter had declared his purpose, in a council of the gods, to destroy the world.——**Pars;** i. e., of the gods.

245. Partes; here in the sense of their part, or their *duty*, which they *fulfill* as members of the council.

250. Quaerentes; acc. subject of *trepidare.*——**Fore** depends upon a word of saying suggested by *vetat.*

254. Sacer; as the dwelling-place of the gods.

255. Axis; here put for *caelum* itself, as in 6, 64, *longum caelum.*

256. In fatis; it was the opinion of some of the philosophers, especially the Stoics, that the world, having arisen from fire, would also be

3. THE FLOOD. 147

dissolved in fire. Such an opinion Ovid represents as an utterance of the fates. What is the derivation of *fatum?*

259. Cӱclōpum; the fabled sons of Urănus and the Earth, hurled to Tartarus by Saturn, and then rescued by Jupiter, for whom they afterward forged thunderbolts. Homer represents them in the Odyssey as a giant race in Sicily. Later they were fancied as Vulcan's workmen in his smithy in Aetna, or in Lipara.

262. Aeoliis; from Acŏlus, the god of the winds, fabled, as in Vergil, Aen. i, 52, to hold them in *caves* in the *Aeolian* or Liparaean islands, near Sicily.——**Aquilonem;** this wind is shut up as it brings clear and dry weather. On *Notum* see n. 1. 66.

264. Alis; the winds, from their swiftness, often are winged with the poets; so, also, in Hebrew poetry, Psalm xviii. 10, *upon the wings of the wind.*

265. Vultum acc. of the part., Gr. § 378.

266. Barbă, sc. est; *canis—capillis;* preposition omitted; see n. 1. 14.

267. Sinus; the personification is thus kept up, as the wind is cloud-clad, as it were, and the *sinus* are the folds of his dress, as so often used of the toga.

269. Aethĕre, the upper air, and so = caelo.

271. Concĭpit, *draws to itself,* as the Iris, or rainbow, was thought to draw up the moisture from the earth; as in Verg. Georg. i. 38, *bibit ingens arcus.* So Homer often represents Iris as the messenger of Juno, and, as such, forming the rainbow for her bright path through the heavens.

273. Vota, put for the crops, as the object of his hopes; the whole may be rendered, *and the farmer mourns over his prostrate hopes.*——**Pĕrit.—Irrĭtus,** *comes to naught.*

274. Suo, i. e., as *his own* peculiar abode; not content with what is furnished by the heavens, he avails himself, too, of the resources of the sea.

275. Frater; Neptune, represented, like all sea-deities, as of the color of the sea itself.

276. Tecta, the depths of the sea as Neptune's *abode.*

279. Dŏmōs, the caves and clefts of the earth, where the waters arise.——**Mōlĕ,** the rocky mass which, like a *dam* or a *dike,* confines the waters.

280. In this line, and the two next ones, the image is drawn from horses, the *reins flung loose upon the streams* (*immittite habenas*), the bits *let go from the mouths of the springs* (*fontibus ora relaxant*), and then the rivers (*amnes* to be supplied with *hi*) rolling down *in unbridled course* (*defrenato—cursu*).

283. Tridente; here, and below 330, tricuspide telo, the trident, the three-pronged spear of Neptune, is the symbol of his power. So, too, in Homer, with whom also he is the earth-shaker, ἐννοσίγαιος.

286, 287. Cum sātis, together *with the crops* = et sata. So, also, *cum —sacris*. *Sacra* for the images of the gods, which are kept in the *pĕnĕtralia*, or innermost part of the house.

289. Hujus refers to *domus*, and limits *culmen*.

290. Turres, towers, here used for high, tower-like buildings.

292. Dēĕrant, as in l. 77.

296. Summā—in ulmo, *on the top of the elm.* So Horace, O. i. 2, 9, *summa—ulmo*, also in describing the flood.

299. Mŏdŏ quā, *where just now;* observe the contrasts in the corresponding places of the two lines, *graciles* and *deformes, capellae* and *phocae*.

302. Nereīdes, the daughters of the sea-god Nereus.

303. Ăgĭtātăque, i. e., by the swaying waves.

305. Nec vires fulminis, i. e., the wild boar, strong as he is, unequal to contend with the lightning.

306. Ablāto, *carried away* by the flood.

307, 308. Quaesitisque, etc. *And having long sought for places on the* (*solid*) *earth, where it may be given* (*her*) *to stand.* Compare the description in Genesis, viii. 9, "But the dove found no rest for the sole of her foot."

309, 310. Observe the climax from *tumulos, the hills*, to *montana cacumina, the tops of the mountains.*——**Novi,** *strange*, because never before there.

4. DEUCALION AND PYRRHA.

I. 313–415.

313. Ăŏnĭŏs, etc. Phocis, a district between Mount Oeta, in Thessaly, and Boeotia, was also called Aonia, from the Āŏnes who formerly inhabited it.

316. Verticibus—duobus, the two spurs of Mount Parnassus, so famous in ancient story, between which flowed the fountain of Castalia. At the foot of the mount was Delphi, the seat of the oracle.

318. Deucalion was the son of Prometheus, and his wife Pyrrha the daughter of Epimetheus. Deucalion had been the ruler of Phthia, in

4. DEUCALION AND PYRRHA. 149

Thessaly, and by his son Hellen was the founder of the race of the Hellenes.

320. Cōrўcĭdās. Behind the above-mentioned heights of Parnassus was a cave called Corycus, which was sacred to the nymphs and to Bacchus.

321. Thĕmĭn. Themis, the goddess of justice, was also a prophetess. The Delphic oracle was presided over first by Gaea, the mother of Themis, then by Themis, afterward by Phoebe, and finally by Phoebus Apollo.

330. Posĭtoque; in the sense of *deposito, and having laid aside.*—— **Trĭcuspĭde;** see n. on *tridente*, 283.

331. Mulcet, soothes, *quiets* the waters.——**Profundum,** for *mare, the deep.*

332. Ŭmĕrōs; acc. of part, as above 265, *vultum.*——**Murĭce,** properly the shell-fish from which the purple dye was obtained, is here used for *concha,* or any sea-shell.

333. Trĭtōnă. Triton, a sea-god subordinate to Neptune, and, with some of the poets, son of Neptune and Amphitrite.——**Conchae sonanti.** The use of spiral shells for horns is not uncommon now on the Mediterranean coasts.

336. Turbĭne—imo; the lowest bend of the *winding (tortilis)* horn is narrowest and serves for the *mouthpiece,* and from this the horn grows larger with the other bends.

337. Āĕrā; used of the Triton's breath as he blows the horn.

338. Ŭtrōquĕ, i. e., oriente et occidente, *in the East and the West.*

340. Contĭgĭt; the subject is a pronoun referring to *bucina.*——**Receptus,** the expression in prose for *sounding a retreat* is *receptui canere.*

344. Plēnōs cāpĭt. The rivers are still full, as they flow, but are kept within their beds.

346. Dĭem longam. *Dies* here feminine, as it means *time.*——**Nūdātā,** i. e., undis, as the next line shows that they are still clothed with leaves.

349. Terras is the subject, and is used with *agere silentia* after the analogy of *agere vitam, aetatem,* and the like; *lying in profound silence.*

352. Patrŭēlĭs; Prometheus and Epimetheus, the fathers respectively of Deucalion and Pyrrha, were brothers.

353. Deinde; a dissyllable.

355. Turba; peculiarly, and not without a turn of wit in the expression, is *turba* here used of two persons; so, also, in vi. 200, *Latonae turbam; we two make up the crowd of all the lands.*——**Possedit,** as above, l. 31.

356. Haec—fīdūcia, *even this pledge,* i. e., that we alone survive.—— **Adhuc non**=nondum, *not yet,* and followed in next line by *etiam nunc, now also.*

358. Quid—fŏret; *animi* limits *quid; what courage would you have?* ——**Fatis,** *by the fates,* i. e., if fate had rescued you alone.

360. Quo consōlante dŏlēres;=quis te dolentem consolaretur.

363. Paternis; i. e., of Prometheus.

365. Nunc; i. e., as things now are.

367. Plăcuit, it pleased them, *they determined.*

369. Cēphīsĭdas, *of the Cephisus,* which has its sources in the range of Parnassus, in Phocis, and flows into the lake Copāis.

370. Ut—sic; *though—yet.*

371. Irrōrāvēre, bedewed; render *sprinkled upon; when they had drawn (libatos) water, and sprinkled it upon,* etc. It was necessary to purify themselves by washing in the running water, before coming to the shrine.

374. Pallebant; used to express the contrast to the before bright and cheerful aspect of the temple; now it wears a *dull* look, and is overgrown with moss.

376. Hŭmi, for the construction, Gr. § 426, 2.——**Oscŭla;** the derivation and primary meaning of the word? Also of *numina* in the next line?

380. With *res* and an adj., as *secundae, adversae,* and here *mersae,* the condition of things is described as fortunate or unfortunate, and so= fortune or misfortune; *come to our help in our misfortunes* from the flood.

382. Velāte, etc. The head was to be veiled in sacred transactions, to avoid all distraction; and the ungirding the dress was a token of the unloosing of all bonds, and so signified entire submission.

386. Detque, etc. *Det* depends upon rogat, Gr. § 498, II., and 499, 2. ——**Pāvetque.** It was deemed sacrilegious to disturb the remains of the buried dead; and the poet fitly represents the woman as yet more sensitive to the impiety than the man.

388. Caecis—lătēbris; the sense of the words was hidden, as in a riddle; the whole may be rendered: *hidden in blind riddles.*

390. The patronymics here are adroitly used to indicate that the cunning of the parents is inherited by the children.

391. Sollertia, from sollers, sollus=totus, and ars; all art, *sagacity.* ——**Nobis,** in the sense of the singular, *my sagacity;* but what is the construction of the dative?

395. Augŭrio; as an augury is a sign by which something is to be known, it comes to mean, as here, *interpretation.*

5. PYTHON.

400. Credat—sit; the subj. is potential; *who could believe this, unless the old tradition* (oldness) *were the witness?*

401. Pōnere, for deponere, as above, l. 330, *posito*.

404. The *ut* is concessive, as above, 370; *though a certain form of man may be seen, yet it is not clear to the sight.*

406. Exacta; see n. on exigere, i. 118.

408. Corpŏris, *of flesh*.

410. Vēna; the word is used of stone also, as is our word *vein*.

413. Femĭna, collectively for the sex.

414. Dūrum. So, also, in Verg. Georg. 1, 61, unde homines nati, durum genus.

5. PYTHON.

I. 434-451.

434. Ergo. The poet has been describing the *discordant harmony* (*discors concordia*) of the forces of nature, and especially of moisture and heat, in producing different species of animals. The *ergo, therefore*, now takes up and carries forward the narrative.

435. Sōlĭbus, *sun's rays.*

438. Nollet, sc. te genuisse. The imperf. represents the wish as impossible of fulfillment.——**Python** (the Gr. Πύθων), according to olden legend the dragon that guarded the Delphic shrine; also called son of earth. Ovid seems to have added the fiction of the creature as a growth of the slimy earth, simply to make a transition to his next story.

440. De monte, i. e., Parnassus.

441. Arcĭtĕnens, one of the many names of Apollo, as in Gr. ἀργυρότοξος, god of the silver bow, and many others.

444. Nigra, *black*, from *the poisonous blood, vĕnēno.*

446. Cĕlĕbri certāmine, abl. of characteristic.——**Ludos.** The Pythian games were *celebrated*, in historic times, every four years at Delphi.

447. Pȳthia, sc. certamina; but, as here, the noun is generally omitted.

448. Mănu—rŏtāve, referring respectively to contests in boxing, running, and chariot-racing.

450. Longo—crine. As the god of youthful beauty, Apollo is thus generally figured with long, flowing locks. So the epithet *intonsus*, and others like it.

6. Daphne.

I. 452–567.

452. Pēnēïa. So, too, it was a legend that the oldest Delphic shrine of Apollo was a hut of laurel-branches, brought from Tempe, the valley of the Peneus.

454. Dēlĭŭs, from the island of Delos, the place of his fabled birth and worship.

455. Cornua, Cupid's bow, tipped with horn, or as made of two horns put together; called also sometimes in the sing., *cornu*.

456. Tĭbĭ, sc. est. *What have you* to do?

457. Ista, *those of yours,* which *you* are carrying.

460. Innŭmĕris, as above, 443, *mille*.

461. Făce, torch; in poetry, as in sculpture and in painting, Cupido or Amor often carries a torch, with which he kindles love.——**Nescĭŏ quos,** here, as usual, with something of contempt, as loves which Apollo cares not for.

462. Laudes, i. e., his bow and quiver, as above, 441, *arcitenens*.

463. Fīgat, potential *may,* but in the concessive sense of *though it may;* with the *meus arcus* in next line supply *fīget*.

465. Observe the quantities in tuā glorĭă nostrā, and the consequent case for each.

466. Ēliso; from *e* and *laedo,* whence elide, elision, and many other cognate English words; *having parted the air with the beating of his wings*.

467. Impĭger, *with swiftness* of flight; the adj. at the beginning of the line goes straight to *constitit arce,* whither the winged god is flying.

469. Operum, *effects;* this *duplicity* of the arrows seems to be the invention of Ovid.

473. Mĕdullas (from *mĕdius*), the marrows; i. e., *the very heart* of Apollo.

474. Nōmen ămantis; i. e., the very name of lover is hateful; she will not have it.

476. Exŭvĭis; i. e., as a huntress; a rival of Phoebe or Diana in this, as well as in being *innupta*.

477. On *sine lege,* Haupt compares the expression, which occurs in Ovid II. 413, vitta coercuerat neglecta alba capillos.

479. Nĕmōrum ăvĭă; Gr. 397, 3, Note 4; *the pathless woods*.

480. Hȳmen, or Hymenaeus, the god of marriage. The word, the

6. DAPHNE.

Gr. ὑμήν, was originally the name of the song at bridals; hence Hymen is made by the poets the son of Calliope.

483. Taedas jūgāles, *bridal torches,* by which the bride was brought home on the wedding-day.

484. Ōrǎ; acc. of part; *is suffused in face.*

485. Patris, etc., *and clinging to her father's neck with coaxing arms.*

487. Pătĕr, i. e., Jupiter, the father of Diana; *her father.*

488. Iste, *that grace of yours;* the poet, by a sudden turn, addresses the maiden herself, as if she were present.——**Quod optas** is the subject of *esse.*

491. Sua, *his own; sua* referring to illum.

492. Ădŏlentur. The Romans were wont to burn the stubble, in order thereby to improve the soil.——**Adolere** is often used of the burning of incense, but here in the general sense.

494. Jam sub lūce, i. e., at daybreak.

498. Quid, etc.; that is, how beautiful they must be, *if they are dressed,* if so attractive now?

499. Oscula, here in the literal sense of the diminutive of *os; lips;* but seldom so used.——**Non—sătis,** *is not enough;* he longs to kiss them.

501. Mĕdĭā—parte; abl. after the compar. *plus.*

502. Observe the quantities, *si quă* and fŭgit, and consequently the case of the one, and the tense of the other, word.

507. Quaeque, by apposition to the preceding nominatives; but in prose the order would be *suos quaeque;* why?

513. Armenta, *herds,* as oxen; *greges, flocks,* as sheep; "*I am not an unkempt* (*horridus*) *shepherd,*" *I do not tend here herds and flocks.*

516. Clărŏs, in Ionia, where were a temple and oracle of Apollo; hence the name *Clarius deus.*——**Tĕnĕdos,** an island in the Aegean, off the coast of Troas, where also was a temple of Apollo.——**Pătăra,** a city in Lycia, was also celebrated for Apollo's worship.

517–524. Apollo proclaims himself the god of prophecy (*per me—patet*), of music (*concordant—nervis*), of the bow (*certa—fecit*), and of medicine (*inventum—artes*).

518. Concordant expresses the harmonious accompaniment of the song and the strings (*nervos*) of the instrument.

520. Văcuo, i. e., free hitherto from love.

523. Ămŏr, (*my*) *love,* as appears from the next line.

526. Cumque ipso verba, i. e., *both himself and his words.*

530. Sĕd ĕnim. The *sed* belongs to *sequitur* in l. 532, and *enim* to *sustinet.* But the god follows, etc., for he bears (it) *no longer to lose,* etc.

532. Admisso passu. *Admittere* or *immittere* is often used with *habenas*, to give (a horse) the rein; and so figuratively here, *with quickened pace*.

533. Gallĭcus. The Gallic hounds were much valued for the chase.

535. Inhaesuro, in the dat., limits *similis*, like to; i. e., *as if about to fasten upon* the hare.——**Jam jamque** expresses the creature's eagerness of expectation.

536. Vestigia, here means *the feet*.——**Stringit**, grazes, *is close upon*.

541. Tergŏque—immĭnet, *and is close upon the back*.

547. I have followed Haupt in the reading, though most MSS. have another line (546), thus: *Qua nimium placui, tellus, ait hisce, vel istam, Quae facit ut laedar, mutando perde figuram*.

548. Vix—finita may be rendered like our nom. independent, *her prayer hardly finished;* and so *occŭpat* has its proper sense of being beforehand with a person or thing. Before the prayer was fairly finished the transformation begins.

551. The juxtaposition of the words *vēlox, pĭgris*, helps very much the expression of contrast, the *swift foot*, and the *dull roots*.

552. Rĕmănet, only the beauty of the maiden remains in the brightness of the laurel-leaf. Haupt compares Ovid, 14, 720, *nitida lauru*.

556. Rĕfŭgit, etc., "It loves the shade, and so shuns the sun's kisses."

560. Ducĭbus. The Roman general, when triumphing, was adorned with the laurel.——**Triumphum**, i. e., *Io triumphe*, as in Hor., O. iv. 2, 49; also Ovid, Tristia, 4, 2, 51. The Triumphus was personified, and thus addressed with the shout.

562. Postĭbus Augustis; of the Palace of Augustus, on the Palatine, on each side of which stood a laurel-tree.

565. Semper, i. e., as an evergreen.

566. Paean; fr. the Gr. Παιών or Παιάν, which was a name of Apollo; also of Aesculapius. In the Iliad it is the name of the physician of Jupiter.

7. PHAËTHON.

I. 748–779. II. 1–339.

748. Huic; refers to Io, the story of whom had just been told by the poet: how she was changed into a heifer, and was driven by the jealousy of Juno over the earth; how finally she ended her wanderings in Egypt, where, together with her son Epăphus, she was worshiped. The Greeks identified Io and Epaphus with the Aegyptian Isis and Serapis.——Tandem; i. e., after all that had been suffered by his mother and himself, *at last*.

750. **Animis**, the plural expresses the fullness of spirit, as we also say, in good *spirits;* here, *in proud feelings*.

752. **Sibi**; i. e., to him, as the son of Jupiter.——**Phoebōque**. The sun-god, in Gr. Helios, though by some Greek writers distinguished from Apollo, yet is generally one and the same with him.

753. **Ĭnăchĭdes**. Inăchus, king of Argos, was the father of Io.

754. **Īmāgĭne** means here *the notion*, and *falsi* expresses the idea that his descent from Phoebus is only an invention of his mother. So in ii. 37, *falsa—sub imagine;* render, *with the false notion of* (*Phoebus being*) *your sire*.

757. **Ille**; the pronoun in the sense of "that one" points to a person as one well known; and so = *I, who am usually free of speech and impetuous, was* (in this case) *silent*.

761. **Assĕre caelo**; in imitation of the Roman legal phrase *asserere in libertatem*, to assert or maintain one's liberty; so here, *and vindicate my heavenly descent*.

763. **Mĕrops** was the husband of Clȳmĕnē.——**Taedas** (see n. on l. 483) stands here for the fortunate marriages *of the sisters* of Phaethon, the Heliades.

764. **Trāderet**; the subj. in dependence upon *oravit*, with the omission of *ut;* Gr. 493, 2.

765. **Clȳmĕnē**, subject of *porrexit*, and the clause *ambiguum*, etc. (with est omitted), is thrown in. *Clymene, it is uncertain whether moved the more by the entreaties, or,* etc.

766. **Dicti—crimĭnis**, *at the charge uttered against her*, i. e., that she had made up the story of Phaëthon's birth.

771. **Nĕget**, etc., *deny me the sight of him*, which is equivalent to denying one the light of life, as appears from the next line.

774. Construe *domus unde oritur*, etc. The subject of *oritur* is *pater*, to be supplied from the adj. *patrios*.

777. **Concĭpit—mente**. *Aethĕră*, the upper air, or *the heavens*, the abode of the gods. With *concipite* the meaning is that he conceives of, has the thought of, the heavens in his mind as if he were there already; and, *with the thought of the heavens in his mind, he passes his own Aethiopians,* etc.

II. 1-339.

2. Pȳrōpo; πυρωπός, a mixture of gold and copper.

3. Cujus, to be construed with *fastigia* and with *ebur* in the sense of decorations sculptured in *ivory*.

5. Mulciber, an epithet of Vulcan; derived, perhaps, from *mulcere*, as the god of fire, *qui aes mulcet*.——**Ille,** i. e., on the *valvae*, which were *embossed*, as described in the next following lines.

8. Habet, i. e., as represented by the artist.

9. Ambiguum, *dubious;* Proteus was a sea-god, who had the power of taking on various forms; hence our word *Protean*.

10. Aegeōna, called also Briareus, a fabulous sea-god, having an hundred arms, and represented as borne on the backs of whales.

11. Dōris was the daughter of Oceanus and Tethys, and wife of the sea-god Nereus; their daughters (*natas*) were called hence Nereides.

12. Mōle, meaning primarily any solid mass, may here be used of the shore, or some huge rock in the sea.

13. Una, etc., they have not *one and the same face, and yet not different;* they have a family likeness.

18. Signa, the signs of the Zodiac.

19. Clȳmĕnëia—prōles; so used of the mother, as his descent from Phoebus was *in question (dubitati)*.

26. Hōrae, here the *Hours* (not, as usual, the seasons), and subject to the god of day (*Dies*). So also below, 118. All these—*Dies, Mensis*, etc.—are conceived by the poet as persons, and attendant upon the sun-god.

28. Nūdă, *lightly clad*, as expressive of the heat of summer.

29. Ūvis, in allusion to the vintage of the autumn season.

30. Cānos—capillos; for the acc., II. 378.

31. Inde, i. e., ex solio.——**Loco,** abl. of specification with *medius*.

32. Oculis, *with* those *eyes*.

37. Imagine; see n. i. 754.

39. Animis—nostris, *from my mind, nostris* being used for *meis*, and *animi* in the plural, because the *uncertainty* (*errorem*) touches all his feelings and thoughts, his whole mind.

43. Veros—ortus, *has declared your real origin;* for a similar reason as 29, *animis, ortus* here in the plural, as his brother is thought of in reference to his father, and also his mother; and their ancestry also.

46. Pălūs; the Styx, called *palus* because of the sluggishness of its current; so, also, in iv. 434, Styx—iners. For the long *ūs* in *palus*, Gr.

7. PHAETHON.

581, IX. 1.——**Juranda,** *by which the gods have to swear.* The passive *juranda* is used, as the accusative is sometimes used in the active, instead of *per* with the acc.; so below, 101, Stygias juravimus undas.

——**Incognĭtă,** because the sun's light does not reach the lower world.

——**Ŏcŭlis,** figuratively of the sun's rays.

48. Ālĭpĕdum. Also in Greek poetry and art, the steeds of the sun's chariot are *winged;* but Ovid uses *alipedum* only as poetic for *swift-footed,* So also below, 153, 159.

51. Meă—tuă; *Rash did my word* (promise) *become through yours* (your request).

53. Non—vŏluntas; *what you will have is not safe.*

54, 55. Et quae—convĕnĭant; *and of such sort as are not suited,* etc.; the relative=talia munera ut non, etc.; Gr. 503, I.——**Istis,** *those powers of yours.*

57. Ētĭam, *even.*——**Superis** limits *fas,* and *fas* expresses what is allowed by divine law; *right.*

58. Plăcĕat, in the subjunctive depends upon *licebit,* with *ut* omitted; Gr. 499, 2.

59. Axe, used here for *curru.*

62. Nōn ăgat, *may not drive,* with the force of the potential in the subj.

63. Primă, *the first of* the way.——**Qua,** with the subj. *enitantur,* as above, *quae,* 54.

65, 66. Mĭhi ipsi limits *fit,* and *videre* is the subject of *fit; I, myself, often become alarmed to see,* etc.

68. Etiam, to be construed with *Tethys solet. Then, also, Tethys herself is wont to fear.*

70. Vertigine caelum. *Vertigo,* from *vertere.* to turn, means a turning or whirl (hence our word vertigo). The heavens constantly revolving from west to east, and carrying with them the fixed stars; the sun, with the planets, in the opposite direction: hence below, of the sun, *nitor in adversum.*

73. Răpĭdo; from the nearness here of *rapitur* caelum the primary meaning of the adj. is more readily noticed.——**Orbi,** i. e., of the heavens; the word limits *contrarius.*

74, 75. Finge—currus; *fancy the chariot given* (to you).——**Rŏtātis —pŏlis,** *the wheeling poles; poli,* taken for the heavens, as the extremities of the *axis* of the heavens, in the same way as *axis* itself, *citus axis* (*the swift-revolving axis*). *Ne* seems to be here=ita ut non.

76-78. Forsĭtăn, etc. Perhaps you are expecting to see many fine things on your way, as groves and cities and shrines rich in gifts (*donis* limits *ditia*); no, your way is beset with snares and perils.──**Animo** limits *concipias*.──**Formas ferarum,** *the shapes of wild beasts ;* referring, in illustration of the dangers of the way, to the signs of the Zodiac, five of which are then mentioned, the Taurus, Sagittarius or Archer, Leo, Scorpio, and Cancer.

80. The position of *per*, as parted from the noun which it governs, is not unusual in poetry.

81. Haemŏnĭosque arcus ; in allusion to the sign of Sagittarius or the Archer, who was figured as a Centaur. The Centaurs lived in Thessaly, which was called also Haemonia, from a king Haemon, father of Thessalus.

83. Scorpĭŏn, Greek acc. from the Gr. Scorpios.──**Aliter,** *in a different direction.*

84–86. Tibi limits *in promptu*, in readiness, which has here the force of an adj. *promptum*, ready, *easy ; nor for you is it easy to govern*, etc. *Promptus*, from *promo*, which is a compound of *emo*, and means, literally, to bring out. Thus, *promptus*, brought out, prompt, *easy*.──**Ignĭbus,** the abl. of cause, limits *animosos*.

89. Căvē ; Gr. 581, IV. 3. The *que* in *resque* connects *corrige* with *cave*.

91. Timendo, *by fearing* (for you).──**Posses ;** the force of the *Imperfect* (in the subj.) with *utinam ?* See Gr. 483, 2.

101. Undas, for the acc. see n. above on 46.

104. Prĕmit, *insists upon his purpose.*

105. Qua licŭit, *so far as he might ;* limiting *cunctatus*.

107. Summae—rŏtae, of the *extremity* of the wheel, its *rim*.

109. Jŭga, *the yoke*.──**Chrȳsŏlĭthi,** literally (from the Greek) gold stone, *topaz*.──**Gemmae,** *and the* (other) *jewels*, *aliae* being omitted.

110. Phoebo, figurative for *sole ; by the reflection of Sol threw back bright lights.*

111. Magnanimus, *high-spirited.*

113. Plēna rosarum, *full of rosy light.*

114. Agmina cōgit ; *chases the troops.*

115. Nŏvissimus ; *last* (of all) *leaves his post in the heavens.*

116. Quem, referring to *Lucifer*.──**Vidit** agrees with a pronoun which refers to *Titan*. On *Titan* see n. i. 10.

117. Extrēmae, *waning,* in its last quarter.

118. On **Hōris** see n. above on 26.

120. Ambrŏsĭae suco. They are the horses of a god, and so in a sense divine, and fed with a divine food. Ovid fancies the ambrosia as a plant, and its juice as the food of the gods. So in Metam. iv. 215, where also the poet is speaking of the horses of the sun; *Ambrosiam pro gramine habent.*

123. Patientia, *able to bear;* with the gen. for which see Gr. 399, ii.——**Rapidae,** *swift-consuming.*

127. Fortius; i. e., the *bits* (*loris*) more than the *spurs* (*stimulis*).

128. Volentes, sc. properare.

129. Directos, etc., *straight across the five zones.*

130. Sectus, etc. The order of the words (and especially the word itself *obliquum*) is in contrast with *directos,* etc. Cut obliquely with a broad bend is the path; render, *the path cuts obliquely with a wide curve.* The poet describes the sun's path, or the Ecliptic, as *bounded* by three zones, the torrid zone and the two temperate zones.

132. Arcton, the constellation of the Bear, which is near the North Pole.

133. Hac, sc. via.

133. Manifesta; the poet fancies a plain path through the heavens, marked by the *track of the wheels.* So also below, 167, *tritum—spatium.*

135. Nec preme, *neither drive too low,* i. e., near the horizon, *nor force the chariot upwards through the heights of the sky. Cursum* is the object of both verbs. On the expressions for the two extremes, and also the safe mean, compare Horace, O. ii. 10.

136, 137. Altius, *too high;* **Inferius,** *too low.* The preposition in *egressus* implies the getting *out of* the right track into one too high or too low.

138, 139. Here, too, the extremes are to be shunned; and now, of *too far to the right,* and *too far to the left,* the former toward the Serpent, which *winds* (*tortum*) through the heavens, between the Great and Little Bear in the north (as in Metam. iii. 45, geminas qui separat Arctos), the latter toward the Altar, which *lies low* (*pressam*), near the South Pole.

141. Juvet, consulat, in the subj. depending upon *opto, ut* being omitted.——**Tibi.** What is the difference in the meaning between the dat. (tibi) with *consulo,* and the acc. ?

142. Hesperio litore; ἕσπερος, Hesperus, vesper; and so the evening, *western.*——**Metae** means primarily the cones of a fir-tree, and then the three conical posts set up at either end of the spina of a race-course, around which the chariots ran. Here the word (*metas*) is figurative for the bounds of the course of the Night across the sky, at the extreme west, the *shore of the western ocean*. Now that Night has run her course, the Sun *must* begin his (*poscimur*).

147. Dum belongs to *adstas* as well as to *potes*.

149. Quae has *lumina* for its antecedent, and with *species* expresses purpose.——**Sine**, imperative.

150. Ille, referring to Phaethon. The chariot is *light* (*lĕvem*), as it bears now only a youth's body, and not that of Phoebus.

153. The names, from the Greek, are all significant. *Pўrŏis*, πυρόεις, the Fiery; *Ēŏus*, 'Ηῷος (but the Roman poets, as here, shorten the first syllable), the Early (of the dawn); *Aethon*, Αἴθων, the Burning; *Phlĕgon*, Φλέγων, the Flaming.

155. Repagula; *the barriers*, the sun's course being thought of as a race. Comp. in Hebrew poetry, as said of the sun, "And rejoiceth, as a strong man, to run a race." Ps. xix. 5.

156. Tethys, the goddess of the ocean. Since the sun is seen arising from the ocean in the morning, and sinking into it at evening, the poet naturally represents Tethys as *letting go the barriers* (*quae reppulit*) for the sun's *free course* (*copia*) over the world.

160. Praetereunt, *pass.* The poet has still in mind the image of a race. They are swifter than the winds, and leave them behind.

161. Lĕve, the emphatic place at the beginning gives the adj. the stronger meaning of *too light.*——**Quod** with the subj. *posset* is=tale ut id; *and not such as the horses of the Sun could recognize*, i. e., as their usual weight. Gr. 503, i.

163. Juste—pondere, *regular weight*, in the same sense as *justus* is used with *triumphus* and *exercitus*.

165. Dat—saltus, gives leaps,=*salit,* leaps.——**Onere,** abl. with *vacuus* by Gr. 414, iii.

168. Quo prius; the antecedent is *ordine ; as before.*

169, 170. The **qua—flectat** depends upon *scit*, as well as *qua sit iter.* ——**Nec—illis,** *nor if he knew, could he master them.* We should expect the imperfect sciret—imperaret; but the poet, either because of the preceding present tenses, or because he chooses to represent the *scire* as possible, uses the present.

171. Triōnes; see n. i. 64.

172. Vetito; because the constellation of the Wagon or the Wain (the septem triones, the seven stars in the Great Bear) is always above the horizon.

173. Glaciali, *icy*, as *junctam—Arcton*, in l. 132, for the North Pole. ——**Serpens,** same as *Anguis*, in l. 138, where see note.

7. PHAETHON.

176. Boote. Böŏtes, Gr. βοώτης, the ox-driver, the constellation just behind the Wagon. He is called *tardus*, from his slow and late setting. This constellation is also called Arctophylax, when the Wagon is thought of as the Bear.

179. Penitus penitusque, *deep and yet deeper;* like Milton's "In the depths a lower deep."

181. Per tantum lumen, *in the midst of so much light darkness arose before his eyes;* "dark with excess of light."

182. Mallet. Comp. n. on *nollet*, i. 438.

184. Merŏpis, sc. filius. Merops was the husband of Clymene. Phaethon would now gladly claim an humbler birth.

185. Pinus, for *navis*, as the ships were so often made of pine.——**Victa,** i. e., by the storm on sea.

186. Frena—rector. The expressions are transferred from a chariot to a ship, from driving to sailing.

187. Quid—faciat; *what is he to do?* a rhetorical question. See Gr. 486, II.

189. Fātum—est, *for him it is not fated.* What is the primary meaning of *fari*, and how is it connected in meaning with our word *fate?*

192. Nec nomina; not knowing their names, he can not call to them.

193. Vario; used in reference to the many stars and constellations; *the spangled heavens.* For *miracula*, and in the next line *simulacra ferarum,* see n. on 78.

195. Concăvat; an unusual word for *curvat;* curves his claws into *two bows.*

197. Duorum; according to the earlier view, which Ovid follows, the Scorpion filled the space of two twelfths of the Zodiac; but later his claws were fashioned into the sign of the Libra.

198. Sudore venēni; *veneni,* because from the Scorpion; *sudore,* on account of the heat; he sweats poison.

199. Curvatā cuspide, the curved (pointed) *sting,* at the end of the Scorpion's tail.

202. Exspătiantur, *stray from the track,* from *ex* and *spatium,* whence our word *expatiate.*

204. Hāc corresponds to *quā*, with *viā* understood.——**Sine lege,** *lawlessly.*

207. Spatio, *in a track;* the abl. with the omission of *in*, as often in poetry.

208. Suis, abl. with comparative *inferius;* *lower down than her own.*

—— **Fraternos,** i. e., of the Sun, as Artemis or Diana and her brother Apollo were synonymous with Luna and Sol.

210. Quaeque subject of *est* understood; but *ut—altissima* may be rendered *according to its height.* The usual construction would require *ita maxime* with *corripitur.*

211. Agit rimas; an expression not uncommon with Ovid; so in Metam. x. 512, Arbor agit rimas; but in iv. 65, the noun is used with *duco ; it splits and gets cracks* in it.

213. Suo damno, *to its own damage.*

214. Parva, i. e., the things he has already mentioned are *small matters* for complaint; but he goes on to say that *great cities* and *entire races* are consumed.

217. In the enumeration which here follows, alike of mountains and rivers, the poet seems to follow no particular order, but only illustrates the universal conflagration. *Athos,* in Macedonia; *Tmōlus,* in Lydia; *Oete,* in Thessaly.

218, 219. Ide (or Ida) in Phrygia, *Helicon* in Boeotia, and *Haemos* in Thrace.

221. Eryx, in Sicily, *Cynthus,* on the island of Delos, and *Othrys,* in Thessaly, as also (below) *Ossa, Pindus,* and *Olympus.*

222. Rhŏdŏpē, in Thrace, and *Mimas,* in Ionia.

223, 224. Dindўma, also Dindymus, in Phrygia, *Mycălē,* in Ionia; *Cithaeron,* in Boeotia, was the seat of the worship of Bacchus (*natus ad sacra*); Caucăsus (with *ardet*) illustrates the allusion to the cold climate of *Scythia.*

226. Appenninus in the spondaic line makes a fitting rhythmic ending to the long catalogue of names.

230. Ore trăhit, *inhales.*

233. Eat, sit, subjunctives of *indirect question,* in dependence upon *nescit.*

235. Tunc limits *vocato. Credunt* has an indefinite subject understood, as in English, *they believe.*—— **In corpora summa,** i. e., to the surface; the belief was, that from the blood thus drawn to the surface and becoming black from the heat the people got their dark complexion.

237. As in l. 123 *rapidae flammae* meant the *swift-consuming flame,* so here *raptis umoribus,* the *swift-consumed moisture.*

238-240. Nymphae—deflevere, *the nymphs with disheveled hair bewailed the loss of the springs and lakes. Passis* from pando. *Dirce,* a fountain near Thebes; *Amymŏne,* a fountain and river flowing into

7. PHAETHON.

Lake Lerna, in Argolis (Argos); and Pirēnē in Corinth, the old name of which was Ephy̆rē.

242. Tanais, the Don. This river and the other rivers here are personified as river-gods. Hence *mediis in undis.*

243. Pēnēos, which rises on Pindus in Thessaly; a river which forms the valley of Tempe.——**Caïcus,** in Mysia, in the district of Teuthrania (*Teuthrantēus*), which got its name from a mythical king, Teuthras.

244. Ismēnos, near Thebes in Boeotia.——**Erymanthus,** in Arcadia, and the epithet comes from the city of Phēgia, by which it flows. Observe the hiatus in the fifth foot, the *o* in Phēgĭăcŏ being preserved from elision; this is common with Ovid in using Greek words.

245. Xanthos, or Scamander, the famous Trojan river. *Iterum*, because Homer, in Il. 21, 342, represents it as set on fire by order of Juno. ——**Lycormas,** in Aetolia.

246. Maeandros, in Phrygia. The syllable *re* in *recurvatis* expresses the many-winding course of the river; whence our word *meander.*

247. Melas, in Thrace, from μέλας, the black river. The Mygdones were emigrants from Thrace into Phrygia.——**Taenărĭūs,** from Taenarus, the southern promontory of Laconia; and so the *Eurotas* is here called Taenarian instead of Laconian. The *ūs* in Taenarius is long, because from the Gr. word which ends long. Gr. 581, IX. 3. The line is spondaic.

249. Thermōdon, in Pontus; *Ganges*, the well-known river of India. *Phāsis*, in Colchis, and *Hister* (so better spelled than Ister),·the modern Danube.

250. Alphēos, in Elis.——**Sperchēĭdēs,** from the river Sperchēos, in Thessaly; for the short quantity *ĕs*, Gr. 581, VI. 3.

252, 253. Maeŏnĭa was the old name for Lydia, the home of the river Cayster. *Celebrārant,* here in the primary sense of *celebro*, which has in it the idea of great numbers, and so of filling a place with anything; *had filled with their song;* so in Lucretius, i. 4.

The word *volŭcres* refers to the swans, which so early as Homer's time (in Iliad, 2, 461) gave *celebrity* to the banks of the Cayster.

255. Adhuc lătet. It is a playful fancy of the poet, that the Nile *hides its head* (*caput* for the *head*-waters of the river) *from terror;* but the fact of the sources of the Nile being unknown is one that is often mentioned by ancient writers. The discovery of these sources was reserved for these modern days.

257. Ismărĭos, from Ismărus, a mountain in Thrace. Supply *amnes* from the next line.

258. Hespĕrĭosque, literally of the evening (vespers), and so western; and here in relation to Greece, *the rivers of the West.*——**Thybrin,** the Grecian, and also the poetic, form for *Tiberim.*

261. Regem, i. e., Pluto with Proserpine.——**Terret,** the *light* (*lumen*) *terrifies,* as something never before seen in the lower world.

262. The subject of *est* is *id,* which is to be supplied as the antecedent of *quod.*

264. Augent. The *mountains* which *arise* form new islands, thus *increasing* the number of the Cyclădes in the Aegean Sea. For the short final syllable in Cycladăs see Gr. 581, V. 2.

265. Curvi describes the curve of their backs, as they just project above the surface of the water.

267. Rĕsŭpīna, *stretched out on their backs upon the surface of the deep,* as is the habit of seals.

269. Dorĭdaque, etc. See n. above, l. 11.

272-274. Ut erat circumdăta, *surrounded, as she was;* in accordance with the ancient idea that the earth was encompassed by the sea.

276. Opposuitque, etc.; to shield her eyes from the heat.

277. Infra quam. *Infra* has in it a comparative sense, *lower than,* a use of the word not unknown in prose. But *fuit,* following *esse,* seems to be a very tame expression for Ovid to use.

278. Siccā is well applied to *vōce,* because when the throat is dry we notice it directly in the voice. But Merkel has the reading *sacra.*

279. Si placet hoc, *if this is your pleasure.*

280. Peritūrae, sc. mihi; *let me, if destined to perish by the forces of fire, perish by your fire.*

281. Clademque—lĕvare; as if the thought that Jove himself were the author of her destruction would be an alleviation; *and to lighten my calamity by the thought* (of thee) *as its author.*

282. Vix, etc.; *scarcely indeed for these very words do I open my mouth;* so also in i. 181, *ora—solvit.*——The preposition *in* expresses purpose.

283. Presserat, *the heat had closed her mouth.*

285. Fructus, figurative for praemia; *such rewards as these, such thanks* (*honorem*) *as this do you give in return* (*refers*) *for my fruitfulness, and for the service I render?*

288. Alimenta is in apposition to *fruges.*

290. Fac in the sense of put the case, *suppose.*——With **undae** supply from the next line *meruerunt.*

291. Frater; Neptune, Jupiter's brother.——**Sorte;** in allusion to

7. PHAETHON.

the myth, that after the fall of Saturn, his three sons, Jupiter, Neptune, and Pluto, drew lots for their respective shares in their father's dominion, and to Neptune fell, as his share, the sea.

293. Meā is used objectively, as if *mei* (gen.); *if you are touched by good-will neither towards your brother nor towards me.*

294. At, *yet at least.*——**Utrumque,** sc. polum.

296. Atlas; the poet follows the ancient fancy of Atlas, the son of the Titan Iapetus, supporting the arch of the heavens upon his shoulders.

300. Rerum—summae, i. e., *for the welfare of the world.*

301. Haec; it is implied that *she had spoken only these* things, and no more, *for*, etc., *neque enim,* etc.

303. Rettŭlit—in se. The poet, departing from the personification of *tellus,* mingles here the plain with the figurative.——**Mănibus;** if the word were *mănibus,* with the first syllable short, what would be the meaning? Compare the meaning of this line with that in i. 139.

304. Ipsum, i. e., Phoebus.

306. Interitura, sc. esse, depends upon *testatus.*

311. Libratum, etc. The image is that of poising a spear or other weapon before hurling it (*librare*); and *dextra—ab aure,* because in such poising the uplifted hand would of course be on the *right* and near *the ear.* So Vergil, ix. 417, summā telum *librabat ab aure,* where the spear was poised from the *tip of the ear.*

313. Expŭlit. By the figure called zeugma the verb is made to do double duty, first with *rotis,* to which alone it properly applies, and then with *anima;* we should expect with *anima* such a word as *privavit.*

318. Vestigia, *the fragments,* which are *traces* that once they belonged to a chariot; so sometimes *vestigia urbis,* of a ruined city.

322. Potuit is used in an aoristic sense, as not unfrequently of things which are wont to take place.

323. Diverso; in the western world, far off from the original home of Phaethon.

324. Eridănus, a mythical river, mentioned by Hesiod, and also by Herodotus, the latter placing it in the extreme west of Europe, and describing it as a river where amber was found. Aeschylus and Euripides also have it in their tragedies, connecting it sometimes with the Rhone, and sometimes with the Po.——**Fumantiăque—ora.**

326. Corpŏra; used instead of the singular.

328. Excĭdit. The word is skillfully chosen to express both his fall and his failure; and *magnis tamen* comes in with like skill; *yet great was the venture in which he failed.*

329. Nam, etc., as a reason for the father's not doing this last office to his son.

331. Unum, etc., *that one day went without the sun.*

333. Quaecumque—dicenda, the prayers and other services usual at a burial.

335. Sĭnus, acc. of the part, with *laniata. Sinus* primarily means the *folds* of the dress. Such tearing of the dress, also of the hair, is often mentioned as a token of grief.——**Percensuit,** *wandered over.*

336. Artus, the limbs; here put for the *body.*

337. Peregrīnā. The being buried in a *foreign* land is mentioned as an aggravation of the misfortune.

8. The Heliädes.

II. 340–360.

341. Munera, in apposition to *lacrĭmas.*——**Pectŏra,** acc. of the part.

343. Adsternuntur, used in a middle or reflexive sense; *throw themselves upon his tomb.*

346. Phaëthūsa; the name of Phaëthon's sister, the *Shining bright.* A similar name of another sister in 349, *Lampĕtĭe,* from λάμπειν, *the Flaming.* Other poets mention other sisters, in number (in all) sometimes five, sometimes seven.

351. Haec, subject of *dolet* in the next line.

352. Fĭĕri, are becoming, *are turning into.*

356. Nĭsi limits *eat; except to go,* etc.——**Huc** makes the antecedent to *quo.*

363. Cortex—vēnit. Ere she has said the last words, the bark closes her mouth.

364. Stillata, the fact, well known to the ancients, that amber was an exudation from trees, undoubtedly gave rise to this fancy of Ovid's. Comp. Tacitus, Germania, c. 45.

365. Lūcĭdus amnis, the *Erĭdănus.* See n. above, 324.

366. Gestanda, *to wear,* i. e., in the form of ornaments.——**Nurus,** often used in poetry, as here, for young women.

9. CYCNUS. GRIEF OF PHOEBUS.

II. 367–400.

367. Monstro, used of anything unusual in nature, and here of the *strange transformation,* which has just been described.——**Stheneleïa,** *the offspring of Sthenĕlus;* related, as mentioned in next line, to *Clymene* (*materno*).

369. Propior, *yet nearer in mind* (by friendship), i. e., than in blood.

370. The *Ligŭres* inhabited that part of the Italian coast which now comprises Nice, the southern part of Piedmont, Genoa, and the western parts of Parma and Piacenza.

372. Sororĭbus, i. e., of Phaethon, who, now turned to poplar-trees, made the forest larger.

373. Vĭro, dat. limiting *est tenuata;* Gr. 384, 4, Note 2. This is a regular Latin construction, as the dative expresses the relation to *viro* of the verb's action.

375. Junctura, i. e., of skin.

376. Tĕnet os, *holds the place of the mouth ; rostrum* is, of course, the subject.

377. Jŏvique seems to be added in its original sense of *Juppiter,* as the father of day or of light (*Dies-piter*). The root is *div* (brightness, bright light), also djav—djov—djuv ; and thus (D)jov-is, Jup-pater, Juppiter. So Dies-piter=Di(v)es-(old gen.) păter.

380. Quae cŏlat; subjunctive of purpose, to dwell in, *chooses the rivers—for his dwelling.*

381. Squalĭdus; from the custom of the Romans to wear squalid dress as a token of grief, *squalidus* comes to mean *in mourning.* The word is here transferred from human relations to divine.

382. Dēfĭcit orbem, when he fails, i. e., *when he withdraws himself from—the world,* as in an eclipse.

385. Satis limits *irrequieta,* and *aevi* limits *principiis.*

387. Mihi with *actorum* as dat. of the agent.

388. Quilĭbet alter, *let another, whoever you please.*

390. Ipse, *let himself;* the supremacy of Jove making the mention of the name unnecessary.——**Ut saltem—ponat,** *that at least he may lay aside;* i. e., that while thus occupied he may give over the sending of thunderbolts that bereave fathers of their sons.

400. Objectat; *and reproaches them with the death of his son,* literally, casts at—as *illis* limits both verbs in the line. *Impŭtat,* imputes, *charges it to them.*

10. THE HOUSE OF ENVY.

II. 760-796.

760. Haupt mentions the personification of Envy by the Greek poet Callimachus, in his Hymn to Apollo. But in this passage the conception of Envy and her house is original with Ovid.

761. Petit agrees with a pronoun referring to Minerva.——**Hujus** limits *domus*.

764. The subjunctives in the line with *quae*, which has the force of *talis ut ea; of such sort that it*, etc., Gr. 503, I.

765. Belli, with *metuenda*, a poetic genitive, which, however, sometimes occurs also in Tacitus. Gr. 399, III.——**Virāgo.** See n. vi. 130; but here the word is used in a good sense; *heroine*.

767. Extrēma cuspide, *with the point of her spear*.

769. Alīmenta; her own poisonous nature is fed by this poisonous food.

770. Visāque, ablative; *from the sight of her*.

771. Pigre, used adverbially; *slowly*.

774. Ingemuit, etc.; from envy at the superiority of the goddess.

776. Ācies; with the negative *nusquam* = obliquus (as below, 787, obliquo lumine; and as in Horace, Epp. i, 14, 37, *obliquo oculo;* and Verg. Aen. xi, 337, *Invidia obliqua*. *Acies* (acer, ak), sharpness (edge), and then sharp vision. Envy always looks askance.

778. Nisi quem, *except (that) which*.

780. Ingratos, etc., *unwelcome* (to her); *and pines at seeing them*.

781. Carpit; *carps* (at others), and (in so doing) *wears herself away*. So Thomson (Seasons, Spring, 283): "Base envy withers at another's joy."

782. Ōdĕrat agrees with a pronoun referring to *Trītōnia; quamvis* qualifies *oderat*, and *tamen* qualifies *adfata est*. The goddess has the epithet from the brook *Triton* in Boeotia, near which she was worshiped. A later myth connects it with the Libyan river Triton.

786. Reppulit; the goddess bounds upward in her flight, as behind her she strikes her spear into the ground.

788. Successurum governs *Minervae*, dative; that it is to succeed or go well for Minerva; *that Minerva is to succeed*, i. e., in her plan against Aglauros.

794. Arcem; the citadel or Acropolis of Athens for the city itself; as so often *Arx* is used for Capitolium, and for *Roma*. For *Tritonida*, see n. above, line 782.

11. CADMUS AND THE DRAGON'S TEETH.

795. Ingeniis, *with men of genius.* The poet transfers back to the mythic days the historic glories of Athens.

796. A striking passage, in illustration of an envious nature. She can scarce help weeping at the sight of prosperity.

11. CADMUS AND THE DRAGON'S TEETH.
III. 14–137.

14. Vix bene; see above, n. ii. 47.——**Castalio—antro,** the cave at Delphi, where was the shrine of Apollo; called *Castalian,* from the neighboring stream of Castalia, in the waters of which all who came to consult the oracle had first to bathe. Cadmus had asked the oracle where and how he was to find his sister Europa, who had been carried away by Jupiter. The oracle directs him to Boeotia, where he finds and slays the dragon of Mars.

17. Subsĕquĭtur, *follows close. Legit* is used in the same sense as *carpit; tracks her steps;* and *presso—gradu* expresses the *slow pace* with which he follows.

19. Cephisi; see n. i. 369.——**Panŏpe,** a town on the Cephisus.

21. Impŭlit auras, *shook the air.*

25. Figit, *imprints kisses.*

27. Libandas, here used simply in the sense of drawing water; *to fetch waters* to be drawn, *which they were to draw from the living springs.*

30. Lapĭdum compāgibus, by the joinings of its stones, i. e., *by its stones, which were compactly fastened together.* They thus formed a *low arch.*

31. Fecundus agrees with *specus. Specus* represents the place simply as a cavity in the ground; but *antrum* adds the idea of a place to live in, like our word *grotto.*

32. Martius, so called because fable made the creature the offspring of Mars.——**Cristis et auro,** by hendiadys for *golden scales.*

35. Quem, to be construed with *lucum.*——**Tyriā—profecti,** a circumlocution for Tyrians, *those who came of Tyrian descent.*

43. Mediā plus parte= plus quam parte, more than by the half, *more than half.* Gr. 417, 1, note 2. For the abl., Gr. 423.

44. Tanto corpore, abl. of characteristic. So also *quanto,* sc. corpore. For the antecedent of *qui,* in next line, supply ille serpens. The poet makes a comparison between the size of this dragon and that of the constellation of the Anguis, *which lies between the Two Bears,* the Greater and the Lesser.

46. Nec mŏrā, sc. est; and = sine mora.
49. Adflāti—venēni may be rendered *of its poisonous breath.*
50. Sol altissimus, *the sun at high noon.*
52. Tegŭmen—erat, *he had for his covering.*
56. Spatiosi corporis; gen. of characteristic, § 396, IV. Render *huge-bodied.*
59. Mŏlārem, from *mola,* a mill, means first a stone for a mill, and then, as here, *a stone as big as a mill-stone.*
61. Illĭus, i. e., molaris.——**Ardŭa celsis.** Here may be observed the difference in meaning of these two adjectives, *arduus,* high in the sense of steep and difficult of access; *celsus* (excelsus) (from cell-, the stem of *cello*) high, in the sense of being thrust up, and so of something that is prominent.——Is *cum* in this line a preposition or conjunction?
63. Loricae, in gen. limiting *modo,* after the manner of a shield, *as with a shield.*
66. Lentae means here *pliant.*
70. Idque refers to the *hastile,* and is the object of *labefecit. Hastile,* from *hasta,* is the shaft of the spear.
71. Vix—eripuit, *with difficulty got it out of his back.*——**Ferrum tamen,** *yet the iron point,* etc. With great exertion the creature loosened the spear, *yet* the point *stuck fast in his bones.*
76. Vitiatas really expresses the result of *inficit,* and *eo* is to be supplied as antecedent to *qui*=ita inficit ut eo vitientur; render, *infects the air with the poisonous breath which,* etc.
78. Cingitur has a reflexive sense, *encircles itself in the folds (spiris).*
78. Exstat; the preposition expresses his standing out from the ground.
79. Impĕte, an old abl. form from the obsolete *impes;* has the same meaning as the common form *impetu. Impetis* (gen.) also occurs.
81. Spolio, i. e., the *lion's* hide, which serves Cadmus as a shield.
83. Praetenta (from *tendo*), *stretched out in front of him.*——**Furit,** etc. The dragon seeks, but to no purpose (*inania*), *to bite the hard iron;* the sharp point, fastening in his jaws, brings out the poisonous blood.
87, 88. Se retrahebat, *retreated.*——**Dabat retro,** *drew back.*——**Sedere,** *to sit, to sink deep;* an unusual construction of the infinitive with *arcere;* but it is=non sinebat, *and by retiring prevented the blow from sinking deep.*
90, 91. Donec, etc. *Until the son of Agēnor hurled his spear into his throat, and following him up close (usque) pressed him hard.*——**Dum,**

11. CADMUS AND THE DRAGON'S TEETH. 171

until; following *donec,* and having the same meaning, *dum* is rather carelessly used by the poet.——**Eunti,** sc. *ei,* referring to *serpens.*

92. Robŏre; this word, which means *strength,* as in l. 94, is applied, as here, to the *quercus,* because of the strength of the trunk of the oak.

93. Imae, *the end* of the tail, because the dragon is hanging from the tree.

94. The tree is represented as *groaning at the strength of its trunk (sua robora) being lashed by the end of the serpent's tail.* The object of *gemuit* is the expression *flagellari robora.*

98. Et tu, *you also,* an allusion to the fabled transformation of Cadmus to a serpent. To this Milton alludes: "Never since of serpent-kind lovelier, not those that in Illyria changed Hermione and Cadmus." Paradise Lost, ix. 505.

100. Rigebant, *stood on end.*

102. Motaeque—terrae; translate the *motae* as a verb; *and bids him turn up the soil, and to plant in it the teeth of the viper.*

105. Jussos—dentes, *the teeth which he was ordered to sow.*——**Semina,** by apposition to *dentes.*

106. Fide majus, by apposition to *glaebae—moveri; a thing beyond belief.*

107. Primăque is followed by *mox—mox,* in the next two lines. The *sharp* points of the spears make the sharp edge or line, *acies,* that first appears above the soil. The root of *acies* is ak, which means sharpness. Thus it comes to be used for battle-line, and then for battle, and for army in battle-line.

108. Cono. Conus, whence our word cone, means first a fir-cone, then the cone-like top of the helmet, and then, as here, the *crest* of horse-hair which waved from it. It was painted, *colored (picto),* as in Verg. Aen. 9, 50, crista rubra.

111. Tolluntur. In the ancient theatres the curtain (*aulaea*) was fastened to a roller below the stage, and so was *raised* at the closing of a play.

112. Signa, the figures on the curtain, which *are wont* first to *show the face,* and *then the rest by degrees.*

114. Ponunt; the subject is still *signa.*——**Imo in margine,** *at the lowest border.*

117. Civilibus—bellis, *our civil wars;* the men were brothers, as it were, having sprung from the same sowing.

120. Leto dĕdĕrat. Here is an instance of the original meaning of *do,* dĕre, to place, to put, as distinct from *do,* dăre, to give; thus it means, with *leto*, the same as our expression, *to put to death;* had put to death.

121. Exspirat, in its literal meaning of breathe out; *auras=animam;* modo, *just now,* as the men had just come into life.

122. Suo, their own, in distinction from any other than themselves. *Marte*=pugna, *in their fight with one another.*

123. Subiti, *who had suddenly sprung into being.*

124. Brevis—sortita; *spatium* is the object of *sortita;* but, as the English idiom is different, render, *to whom was allotted only a brief space of life.*

126. Quinque superstitibus, abl. absolute.

127. Tritōnĭdis; see n. ii. 783.

129. *Sidonian* is the same as Phoenician, as Sidon was a chief town of Phoenicia, and Agenor was the Phoenician king.

132. Sŏcĕri. Harmonia or Hermiŏne, the wife of Cadmus, was the fabled daughter of Mars and Venus.

135. Hos refers to *nepotes;* i. e., Cadmus lived to see his grandchildren quite grown up.

136, 137. The sentiment of these lines, that no man may be pronounced happy till his whole course of life is run, is ascribed to Solon by Herodotus, i, 32. It occurs also in a fine passage in Sophocles, the last words of the *Oedipus Tyrannus,* which describe the end of the ill-fated Oedipus. The sentiment finds its significance here in the disasters which afterward befell Cadmus and his race.

12. PYRAMUS AND THISBE.

IV. 55–166.

Read Shakespeare's version of this story in his "Midsummer Night's Dream," Act V.

58. Coctilibus muris, *with walls of burnt brick; coctilibus* from *coquo.*——**Urbem,** Babylon.

59. Notitiam, *acquaintance.*——**Gradus,** sc. amoris, *steps of love.*

60. Taedae; see n. i. 483. As *taeda* is equivalent to *taeda jugalis,* a marriage torch, the poet will say: *they would have been duly joined in marriage, but*—

61. The antecedent of *quod* is the following line.

62. Captis, as in English, taken with a person; *they were taken with one another in equally ardent love.*

65. Olim; we may see here the original force of this word. It is

12. PYRAMUS AND THISBE.

archaic for the locative of *ille*, and=illo tempore; *olim cum, at that* (former) *time, when it was made* (or *making*). At the time the wall was made, it had got *split* in some way, and there was *a little crack* still in it. See note on ii. 211.

69. Et fecistis, *and made it a passage for the voice.*——**Illud** refers to *iter;* and *safe through that were wont to pass in slightest whisper* (your) *caressing words.*

74. Quantum erat, *what great thing would it have been for you to let us*, etc. In Latin the indic. imp. is used where we should have expected the subjunctive pluperfect.——**Sineres** with *ut* is the subj. of result.

75. With *pateres, ut* is to be supplied from *ut sineres*. *Vel* is felt here in its full force, as coming from *velle—or if you would;* and so coming to mean *at least.*

78. Diversa, agreeing with *sede.*

79. Parti, i. e., of the wall.

80. Non—contra, *that did not reach through to the other side.*

84, 85. Ut—temptent; used here in the primary sense, to try, like our word *attempt; to attempt. Fallere, to escape the notice of.*

87. Neve; the negative *ne* belongs only to *sit errandum;* and, *that they may not have to go wrong* (so as to miss one another) while *walking* (*spatiantibus*), etc. With what does *spatiantibus* agree, and in what construction?

88. Ninus was the husband of Semirămis. *Busta*, primarily the place where a corpse was *burned*, here means *the tomb*. As Shakespeare has it, " To meet *at Ninus' tomb,* there, there, to woo."

92. Aquis (*praecipitatur*); dative=in oceanum.

93. Versato—cardine; here the same as *having opened the door*, as the door in opening and shutting *turns on its hinges.*

95. Pervĕnit—sēdit; a change from present to perfect.

97. Oblita, from oblīno, not *oblīta* (see below, iv. 677), from *obliviscor*. What is the construction of *rictus?*

101. Fŭgit—reliquit; again a change of tense.

103, 104. Rĕdit—laniāvit; here, too, a change of tense. *Dum* in prose, also, is joined with the present, even when the principal verb is in the past tense.——**Sine ipsā;** i. e., Thisbe; *without their* (*owner*) *herself.*

110. Nostrā, in opposition to *illa* (Thisbe), and refers to Pyramus.

111. Jussi—venires; unusual, for jussi te venire. See II. 535, II. note, and 499, 2.

115. Optare nĕcem, *to long for death;* i. e., not to be willing to put one's self to death.

117. Notae agrees with *vesti;* and, having shed tears over the well-known garment, kissed it.

118. Accipe, etc.; *drink now my blood also.*

121. Humo is a poetical construction for *humi.*

122. Fistula means here a *water-pipe.*

124. Ejaculatur, in its proper sense, as derived from *jacio.* How is our word *ejaculate* derived from it?

131, 132. Utque—sic, *though—yet.* She recognizes the *form* of the tree, but is perplexed by *the color of the fruit.*

134. Buxo, etc.; in allusion to the yellowish pale color of the box-tree. The same simile occurs in xi. 417.

138. Indignos; = immeritos, *innocent.*——**Claro,** clear, means here *loud.*

139. Cŏmas, accusative; II. 378.

141. Vultĭbus; here, and 144, *vultus,* why the plural?

146. Visāque—illā. Observe the quantity; *at the sight of her closed them again.*

148. Ebur; by metonymy for the *scabbard,* which was made of ivory.

153. Solā agrees with *morte;* and the subject of *poteris* is the antecedent of *qui.*

155. Meus, vocative; but if *parens* had been expressed, the form would have been *mi.*——**Parentes,** i. e., the *patres.*

157. Non invideatis, sc. mihi, or nobis, the direct object being *componi;* the two words make one thought—not grudge, i. e., *grant;* hence *ut non,* instead of *ne,* after *rogati.*

159. Unīus; for the quantity of the penult, Gr. § 577, 3.

160. Pullos; *pullatus* is the common expression for "in mourning." See below, line 165, *ater.*

164. Tamen; sad as was the fate of these lovers, *yet,* etc.

166. Urnā. The ashes of the departed were collected in an *urn* after the body had been burned.

13. CADMUS AND HERMIONE.

IV. 563–603.

Cadmus and Hermione depart from Thebes to Illyria, and there are changed into serpents.

563. Nātam—nepotem; i. e., Ino and her son Melicertes. As Ino, in madness, threw herself and her son into the sea, they were said to have become sea-deities; Ino as Leucŏthŏe, and Melicertes as Palaemon.

14. ANDROMEDA'S RELEASE.

564. Mālōrum; the deaths of his grandsons, Actaeon and Pentheus, and of his daughters, Autŏnŏë, Agāve, Semĕle, and Ino.

566. Locorum; he ascribes his misfortunes to the *place*, not to *himself* (*suā*, in line 567).

572. Fuerat, pluperfect, because the slaying of the dragon had preceded the sowing of the dragon's teeth.

574. Sī—certā īrā. Ovid makes him pray, that if the gods are to *avenge* the dragon by an *anger so sure* in its punishment, he may himself be changed to a serpent, that thus the miseries which pursue him may come to an end.

575, 576. Serpens, appositive to *ipse; as a serpent.* So, also, in the next line *serpens* is appositive to the subject of *tenditur*.

590. Nudā agrees with what, and why?

596. Sinus, *folds* or bosom of a dress; and then, as perhaps here, used for the bosom itself.

600. Juncto volumine, i. e., together, or by the side of one another.

603. Quidque; the *que* connects *meminēre* with *laedunt*.

14. ANDROMEDA'S RELEASE.
IV. 663–752.

663. Hippŏtădes, Aeŏlus, the mythical son or grandson of Hippŏtes.

666. Parte—pedes, i. e., *both his feet.*——**Telo—unco,** a crooked, sickle-shaped sword, which had been given him by Mercury, called below, 727, *falcato ense.*——**Accingitur** is reflexive: girds himself with, *girds on.*

667. Talaribus, the winged sandals, also the gift of Mercury.

669. Cephēaque—arva, *the fields of Cepheus;* he was king of Aethiopia.

670. Linguae. Cassiŏpe had boasted that her daughter Andromeda surpassed the Nereids in beauty.

671. Poenas; the *penalty* of her mother's rash speech was the exposure of Andromĕda to the sea-monster, sent up by Neptune to ravage the land.——**Ammon,** the Libyan oracle, had given Cepheus the *cruel* response, that the land could be delivered only by his giving up his daughter as a prey to the monster.

672. Bracchia, acc. of part with *religatam.*

673. Abantiădes. Perseus was the son of Danae, the daughter of Acrisius, and Acrisius was the son of Abas.

675. Trăhit inscius ignes, *without knowing it,* (he) *is on fire* with love.

678. Istis—catenis, *of those chains of yours.*

685. Instanti, sc. ei, referring to Perseus.——**Suā** is emphatic; it was not *faults of her own*, but her mother's, that had to be told.

686. Videretur, imperfect and in dependence upon *indicat;* but *indicat* is historic present. Gr. 495, II.

687. Māternae in sense belongs to *fiducia ; her mother's confidence in her* (i. e., Andromeda's) *beauty*.

695. Lacrimarum—est. Observe the emphatic place of *lacrimarum ; for tears a long time will possibly await you ; for bearing aid,* etc.

697. Si pĕtĕrem, *if I were to woo her ;* but with that he is not content, but he will win her by desert (*addere meritum,* 701, 702). Observe, too, the emphatic pronoun *ego ; if I, Perseus, the son of Jove,* etc.; then he would be preferred to all others; but he will do more.

698. Clausam—auro. Acrisius had shut up his daughter Danae in a brazen chamber, as he had been told by oracle that he would be slain by the son of his daughter; but Jupiter gained access to her chamber in the form of a golden shower. Comp. Horace (on the power of gold), O. iii. 16, 7, 8.

699. Gorgŏnis; Medusa, one of the three Gorgons, who was slain by Perseus, as related by Ovid in this book, 770 seqq. Her locks of hair had been turned by Minerva into snakes.

702. Dōtibus. *Dos,* primarily dowry, used, as here, for endowments, gifts.

703. Meă—meā. With what does the first agree?

706. Rostro, in the abl. limits *sulcat.*

709, 710. Quantum—caeli. *Caeli* limits *quantum* as a partitive genitive; the meaning is, that he was as far off from the rocks as a Balearic sling's throw.——**Plumbo,** the bullet of *lead,* hurled by the sling. The people of the *Balearic* islands in the Mediterranean were famous *slingers.*

715. Praebentem Phoebo; as *Phoebo*=soli, the whole means in English *sunning.*

716. Āversum, sc. cum, referring to *draconem,* "*comes down upon him from behind.*"

718. Per ināne, through the void, i. e., the air, as *inane* is used for *aër.*

719. Frĕmentis, sc. *ejus,* referring to *draconem.*

720. Ināchĭdes; Perseus was descended from Ināchus, an ancient king of Argos.

725. Pătet, sc. ea, referring to fera; *wherever it is exposed.*——**Terga** is the object of *verberat,* and *conchis* in the abl. limits *obsĭta ;* and *super* is used adverbially.

727. Dēsĭnit in piscem; as in Horace, A. P., 4, desinat in piscem.

730. Ausus; he did not *venture longer to trust his sandals*, as they *soaked in* the water and the blood.

732. The rock *stands out* from the *waters* when they are *quiet* (*stantibus*), and is *covered by it when they are in motion* (*operītur—moto*).

733. Sinistrā, sc. manu.

734. Exēgit—ferrum, *drove his sword through his vitals with repeated blows.*

736. Implevēre; plural because *cum plausu clamor* = plausus et clamor.

739. Prĕtiumque et—laboris, *at once the price* (prize) *and the cause of his labor.*

741. Anguiférum; see n. above, on l. 699.

742. Natasque—virgas, *sea-plants.*

743. Phorcȳnĭdos; from Phorcȳnis (gen. Ĭdos), as the Medusa was the fabled daughter of Phorcys or Phorcus, Homer's old man of the sea, in Od. i. 72.

744. Rĕcens, *fresh-plucked*, and hence *the pith still full of sap* (*bibulā —medullā*).

745. Vim rapuit monstri. *Rapuit* is a strong word, expressing the suddenness of the change, *straightway took into itself the power of the monster.* It may be noticed here that, as the Medusa's head was said to turn to stone whatever person looked upon it, Ovid represents whatever *thing* (as here *virga*) that the head looked upon as undergoing the change.

747. Temptant, i. e., by bringing them in sight of the Medusa's head.

749. Illis refers to *virgis; and repeatedly throw out over the waves the seeds of these.* The poet seems to be trying to explain the continuance of the corals, as though the sea-nymphs get continually new plants by sowing the seeds.

750. Eādem is explained by the next two lines; *the same, that they take on hardness from contact with the air.* But this theory of the hardening of coral from contact with the air is hardly more scientific than the myth of its formation by the look of the Medusa's head.

15. PROSERPINE.

V. 338–571.

338. Immissos, *flowing.* The ivy (*hederā*), conceived as the source of inspiration, is constantly used of poets and poetry. So in Verg. Ecl. vii. 25, hedera crescentem ornate poetam. Also Ecl. viii. 13; and in Hor. Od.

i. 1, 29. Thus here Calliope is represented as *having gathered up with ivy her flowing hair.*

343. Dĕdit—lēges ; so by Vergil Ceres is called *legifera* (Aen. iv. 58), because agriculture, which Ceres promoted, leads to a well-ordered life, to the origin of property and legislation.

346. The Muse begins with the fate of Typhōëus, because the song of the Pierides, which she is answering, had celebrated him as the terror of the gods.

347. Trĭnăcrĭs ; the Greek name of Sicily, from its having three promontories, which are named in lines 350, 351. The giant is conceived as imprisoned under the island, and his struggles produce the volcanic action of Aetna; see lines 352–355.

356. Silentum ; gen. plural; *of the silent (dead).*

361. Ambibat ; the old form of *ambiebat ;* Gr. 240, 1.

363. Ĕrycīna, *the goddess of Eryx ;* Venus, so called from Eryx in Sicily, where she was worshiped.

364. Natum—volŭcrem ; i. e., Cupido or Amor, *her winged son.*

365. Arma, etc. So Verg. Aen. i. 664: Nate, meae vires, mea magna potentia solus; because it is through his hand and arms that Venus exerts her power.

368. Trĭplĭcĭs ; see n. on ii, 291.

371. Cessant, *hold back,* i. e., from submission to your power.

372. Ăgĭtur, *is at stake ;* i. e., whether you are to win or lose it.

377. Easdem ; i. e., *the same* as Pallas and Diana; viz., to continue ever virgin goddesses.

378. Pro socio regno, *for the sake of our common dominion.*—— **Ea,** by attraction to *gratia,* instead of ejus (rei); *if you have any regard for that,* i. e., for our common dominion.

379. Patrŭo, *her uncle,* i. e., Pluto, as Proserpine was the daughter of Jupiter, Pluto's brother.

382. Audiat, for *ob-audiat* or *obediat, more obedient to the bow ;* the arrow is personified, as though it heard and obeyed; the verb is in the subj. expressing result.

385. Hennaeis, of Henna or Enna, in Sicily.

387. Cycnorum ; the Caÿster, in Lydia, was famous for its swans; see n. on ii. 253.

389. Ut vēlo, *as with a veil ;* in allusion to the awning spread over the theatres (which had no roof) to protect the spectators from the sun and rain.

395. The verse marks well, in its rhythm, the rapidity of the ac-

15. PROSERPINE.

tion it describes; Ovid reminds us here of Caesar's words, Veni, vidi, vici.

398. Lāniarat. The act expresses her terror and grief.

401. Obscūrā—ferrūgĭne; as above, l. 360, the horses were dark, *atri*, so the reins (as everything in the infernal regions) have *a dusky hue*.

406. Pălĭcorum; the Palīci were thought to be sons of Jupiter and Thalia. Their name was given to the city of Palīca, not far from Enna, and also to the lake, here referred to, in which were *boiling* sulphurous springs.

407. Bacchlădae, the descendants of the Heracleid Bacchis, a race of rulers in Corinth, who afterwards settled Syracuse in Sicily.

409. Cyānes—Arethūsae, gen. for the more common construction inter Cyanem et—Arethusam. The last syllable of *Pisacae* is preserved from elision before the initial vowel of the following word. Cyane and Arethusa are here described as nymphs of the fountains which bear their names, the former on the western, the latter on the eastern side of the great *harbor* (*aequor*) of Syracuse. The Cyane springs from a marsh and flows into the Anāpus, and this flows into the harbor. On the east of the harbor is the peninsula Ortygia, on which was the fountain of Arethusa. Arethusa is here called Pisacan, from Pisa in Elis, as it was a poetic fancy that the nymph Arethusa was pursued by the river-god Alpheus from Elis to Sicily; or that the Alpheus, after having flowed into the Ionian Sea, re-appeared in Sicily as the fountain Arethusa. Shelley's poem, "Arethusa," should be read in comparison with Ovid.

413. Summā—alvo, *as high as the waist.*

416. So Vergil, Georg. iv. 476, si parva licet componere magnis.

417. Anāpis; the usual form is of the o-decl. Anāpus.

420. Sāturnius, *the Saturnian,* name of Pluto, as son of Saturn.

421. In gurgĭtĭs ĭmā, poetic for In gurgitem imum, *into the depths of the lake.*

422. Contortum—condidit, *swung—and plunged—his scepter,* etc.; in English we thus use two verbs, where the Latin has a participle and a verb.

429. Extĕnuatur; a strong expression for the nymph's *pining away* and being absorbed into the stream, as is described in the next following lines. What is the primary meaning of *extenuatur?*

431. De totā, sc. illā, of the whole of her; i. e., *of her whole body.*

439. Profundo, for mari, *in every sea.*

440. Illam, i. e., Cererem. Preserve the Latin order in translating.

Her, not Aurora, as she comes, etc.——**Udis,** because she is thought of as coming up out of the sea.

441. Dŭābus; thus holding one of the *pine torches* (*pinus*) in each hand.

444. Alma; in poetry the gender of *dies*, as here, is often feminine when the word has its ordinary meaning; but in prose, only when it means an indefinite period.

450. Dulce, used as a substantive, *a sweet drink.*

453. Parte, *the half.*

454. Mixtā, agrees with *polenta*, and is to be joined with *cum liquido.*

455. Quae—gessit, *and what just now he carried as arms, he carries as legs.*

458. Parvā—lacertā, *than a small lizard.*

461. Stellatus, i. e., the *stellio* (as if from *stella*), the spotted lizard.

463. Quaerenti, etc.; i. e., in her search she wanted another world; this world she had searched through and through.

465. Mutata, as described above, 429 seqq.

466. Vŏlenti, sc. ei, depending upon *aderant.*

468. Notam, agrees with *zonam.* *Parenti*, i. e., to Ceres.

470. Persĕphŏnes; the poet here chooses the Greek name for Proserpĭna, perhaps because the latter was less easy in verse.

473. Rĕpĕtita, though a participle and agreeing with *pectora*, may be translated *repeatedly.*

478. Părĭli, in dat. agreeing with *leto.* *Parĭlis* is poetic for *par.*

480. Fallere depositum; the full and more common expression would be, fallere cum qui deposuit, sc. semina. The seed put in the ground is something intrusted to it, like a *deposit* in a bank; thus the words may be rendered, "*to betray their trust.*" Hanson and Rolfe.

481. Terrae, i. e., Sicily, well known for the fruitfulness of its soil.

482. Falsa follows up *fallere*, and so is a better reading than *cassa; lies there betrayed.*

484. Sidĕrăquĕ; the quĕ is lengthened by the arsis.——**Volūcres—legunt;** as in the parable of the sower, "the *fowls of the air* came and devoured them up"; and *volucres* means radically the same as the Saxon word *fowls.*

485. Lŏlium tribŭlique, *the tares and the thorns.*——**Gramen** in the next line is also one of the subjects of *fatigant.*

487. Alpheïas; this patronymic is given to Arethusa, from the fancied relation to the river-god Alphĕus. See n. on 409.

491. Tĭbĭ, dat. limiting *fidae; terrae*, dat. limiting *irascĕre.*

15. PROSERPINE.   181

492. Meruit, here in a bad sense, no *ill*-desert.

494. Pisă; see n. on *Pisaeae*, 409.

499. Věniet, etc.; *there shall come a seasonable time for my narrative (about this), when,* etc.

504. Lābor, not lăbor, and so is the verb, not the noun. *While I was gliding.* The pres. with *dum*, as a kind of historical present, occurs also in prose, especially in Livy.

505. Visa tuă, etc. *Your Proserpine was seen there by these eyes of mine.*

507. Sed—tămen follows up Illa *quidem. She was indeed sad—but yet queen.* So also with the following *sed*, and *sed tamen*.

509. Ceu—saxĕa, as if turned to stone, *petrified.* Then the following *attonitae* has here its full meaning from *tono; was for a long time like one thunderstruck.*

512. Nubĭlă; an adj.; *lowering.* In the next line *invidiosa, full of hate.*

517. Illius, *for her.*——**Nostro,** i. e., non *Junonis; because she was born of me.*

519. Sĭ rĕpĕrire, etc. *If you call it finding, to lose with the more certainty.*

521. Praedōne—non est; these words, and especially *praedone marito,* follow closely *reddat;* and then the pronouns tuă and meă are emphatic. The sense is: *my daughter does not deserve to have a robber for her husband, and, of course, yours does not.*

523. Excepit, took up her words, i. e., *immediately answered her thus.*

525. Injuriă is the predicate, as well as *amor; this act is not a wrong, it is love.*

528. Quid, quod, as usual, introduces here something stronger than what has been said before. He has just said, *even though the other things be wanting;* but now he says, the other things are *not* wanting. *What* (say you to this), *that the other things are not wanting, nor does he give way to me, except by lot.* Jupiter will persuade the mother that it is a pre-eminently good match for her daughter.

531. Lēgĕ—certă, *on the fixed condition.*

532. Foedere. *Foedus,* as a thing fixed by agreement, is here used in the sense of *a law.*

534. Jējūnia—solverat, *had broken her fast.*

535. Dum—errat. See n. on *dum—labor,* 504. Of these *cultivated gardens (cultis—hortis)* in the lower world, Haupt quietly remarks, that they seem to be a discovery of Ovid's.

536. Poenĭcĕum—pomum, purple-red fruit, i. e., a pomegranate. The color gives the name *Punica* to the kind of fruit to which it belongs.—— **Curvā,** bent, i. e., under the weight of the fruit.

540. Ăvernales ; from Avernus, which is used for the waters of the lower world, and then, as here, for the lower world itself. It is supposed to be the same as the Gr. ″Αορνος, without birds, as the name was applied to places whose poisonous air was fatal to birds, and especially to the lacus Avernus in Campania, which Vergil, Aen. vi. 237, represents as the entrance to the lower world.

541. Ăchĕronte, name of a river, and then of a river-god in Hades. The word is Gr. 'Αχέρων, the stream of woe, or as Milton describes it in a passage in Paradise Lost, B. ii. 579, "Sad Acheron, of sorrow, black and deep." See the passage for like descriptions of the Styx, Cocytus, Phlegethon, and Lethe.

544. Ăvem ; the bird was the owl, in Latin, *bubo,* as below, 550.

546. Sĭbĭ ablatus, i. e., robbed of his former self.

552. Ăchĕlōides, daughters of Achelous (an Aetolian river-god) and the Muse Melpomene, the Sirenes. The fable was that these were the companions of Proserpine, when she was carried away by Pluto. In seeking her all in vain, they wished they might have wings, and thereafter they had, with the faces and voices of maidens, the plumage and wings and feet of birds, as described in succeeding lines.

555. Doctae, *skilled* (in *song*).

557. Curam, *careful search.*

559. Făcĭles, *compliant.*

563. Remansit, agrees with *vox,* the nearer noun ; and the verb in plural understood with the other nom. *vultus.*

564. Medius, *mediating between his brother,* etc.

565. Volventem—annum, *the rolling year ;* as in Thomson's line in his "Seasons," "The rolling year is full of Thee."

566. Duorum, i. e., the upper world, and the lower.

16. ARACHNE, OR THE SPIDER'S WEB.

VI. 1–145.

1. Tritonia ; a name of Pallas, from Triton, a stream in Boeotia, the fabled place of her birth. Some writers take the name from Tritōnis, a lake in Africa, and for a similar reason.

2. Aŏnĭdum ; the Muses were so named from the Boeotian hill Helicon. Aonia was a district in Boeotia ; see n. i. 313.

16. ARACHNE, OR THE SPIDER'S WEB.

3. Laudare; she had praised the Muses, but that was *too little* (*parum*); her own merits (*ipsae*) needed to be vindicated against the pretensions of Arachne.

5. Maeŏniae. See n. ii. 253.

6. Sibi. Pallas was conceived as the inventress of weaving and embroidery.

9. Mūrĭce; the *murex* was a shell-fish from which an extract was gotten for a purple dye; it was taken at different places, here at *Phocaea*, a town of Ionia, on the Mediterranean.

11. Aequa, i. e., in origin and rank.——**Illa,** i. e., Arachne.

12. Studio, *by diligence in her art.*

13. Hӯpaepis. Ὑπαεπα (neuter) was a town in Lydia.

15. Tīmōli. Timolus or Tmolus was a mountain in Lydia, famous for its vineyards. The river Pactōlus had its rise on one of the heights of Tmolus.

18. Cum fierent, *when they were making.* They took delight in watching the weaving through all its processes, as Arachne handled all with such grace (*decor*). The poet's own touch of description in the succeeding lines may well yield an equal delight.

19. Rudem; as we say, in its *raw* state. The *orbes* are the *balls* of wool, made ready for the *colus,* distaff.

20-23. Here the poet briefly alludes to the drawing out with the fingers (*digitis subigebat*) of the fibres of wool from the distaff, then the softening them and making them finer by the fingers or the carding-comb (*repetitaque—tractu*), then the twisting them into threads by the spindle (*lĕvi—fusum*), and finally the embroidering of the fabric with the needle (*pingebat acu*).

20. Subigebat is more special than *tractabat* would be: *plied the work.*

21. Vellĕra, *the flocks of wool.* By *nebulas aequantia* he compares the flocks with clouds, as we say in English, the *fleecy* clouds; they vied with such fleecy clouds in softness and fineness.

22. Tĕrĕtem—fusum, *twirled the smooth-worn spindle.* The distaff, loaded with the wool, was held with the left hand, and then the fibres were drawn down with the right to the spindle, which was set twirling with the thumb and finger, and so twisted the fibres into a thread. See the illustration in Smith's "Dictionary of Antiquities," under *Fusus.*

24. Tantāque; she took it as an offense that she was thought a pupil of Pallas, and yet Pallas was *so great a teacher* in the art.

29. Quae fŭgiamus, *for us to shun;* the subj. expresses purpose.—— **Usus** means *experience.*

31. Maxima; in translation to be taken with *inter mortales*.
34. Torvis, sc. oculis, as is clear from *aspĭcit*.
36. Obscuram refers to the disguise of the goddess.
38. Istas—voces, those words *of yours*.
41. Prōfēcisse, *that you have gained* anything.——**Eădem,** i. e., the same that I had before you gave your advice.
45. Nurus, used here in the sense of *puellae*.
53. Consistunt. The earliest looms were upright ones, and so the posture was a *standing* one. Thus in iv. 275, *stantis telae*.
54. Tēlas; *tela*, contracted from tex-la (from *texo*), means first the *web* itself; then, as in 55, the *warp*, and, in this sense, hardly differing from *stamen*, from *stare;* then, as here, the *loom*.
55–58. The *jugum* (literally yoke, as it joined the two uprights of the loom) was the *beam* from which hung the *warp* (*tela* in this line), and substantially the same as *stamen*, the fibres being thought of as *standing*, or as the material for *weaving*. The *harundo, the reed*, is a rod which separates (*secernit*) the threads of the warp, passing in and out, before and behind each alternate thread, thus separating the whole into two parcels, and forming a passage for the *shuttle, radius*, 56. The *subtēmen* is *the woof*, the threads of which are passed in by the shuttle, and then driven home by the *pecten*, or *comb*, the *teeth* of which, *insecti—dentes*, inserted between the threads of the warp, drive the woof-threads close together. Properly it is the *pecten* which is *insectus*, but here the *teeth* are said to be *cut into* the comb.
60. Studio—laborem, *their interest beguiling the toil*.
61. Tyrium—aēnum, *the Tyrian vat*, as the best purple dye was made at Tyre. The *purpura* here expresses the wool, which has thus *felt* the Tyrian dye, and is now wrought into the woof of the texture. The dye was yielded by a fish called *murex*. See note, vi. 9.
62. Tenues—umbrae; *the fine shades* of the colors, their *difference so slight*, suggest the simile of the *rainbow*.
63. Solibus; *when the sun's rays are struck by the rain-drops* (*ab imbre percussis*).
66. Transitus, *the transition* from one color to another.——**Fallit,** *escapes the notice of*.
67. Usque, etc.; *so is* (*that*), *which touches, the same;* every color is so like the one next it; yet the remotest, the first and the last, are quite unlike.
68. Lentum, *flexible*.——**Immittitur,** *is let in*.
69. Telā here means all that has been woven, the *web*. See above,

16. ARACHNE, OR THE SPIDER'S WEB.

n. l. 54.——**Argumentum**, as of a poem, is here the *subject* of the work.

70. Scopulum Mavortis, *the hill of Mars*, or the Areopagus, which was near the Acropolis of Athens; though the poet rather loosely says *in* arce.

71. Litem. The *contention* was between Neptune and Pallas, which was to give a name to the city when it was built. The agreement was that whichever should make the more useful present to mankind should be the victor in the contest. While Neptune created the horse, Pallas created the olive, and won the prize.

72. Bis sex; the twelve celestial gods, or Dii Superni; as given in two verses from Ennius (quoted by Haupt), Juno, Vesta, Minerva, Ceres, Diana, Venus, Mars, Mercurius, Jovi' (Jovis = Juppiter), Neptunus, Vulcanus, Apollo.

74. Inscribit, makes the inscription; the face so perfectly wrought into the texture, that no name needs to be inscribed.

77. Ferum, sc. equum. See n. 71.

79. Aegide, the famous *aegis*, having on it the Medusa's head, originally forged by Vulcan for Jove (Homer, Il. 15, 310), and afterward worn as a coat of mail by Pallas.

80. Simulat, *represents*.

82. Victoria, here put for that which won the victory (see n. on 71), the olive; compare below l. 101.

84. Ausis. As a lesson to Arachne, the goddess weaves into the four corners of the work illustrations of presumptuous mortals who *ventured* (like Arachne) to compare themselves with the gods.

86. Distincta, *set off*. The *sigilla*, diminutive of *signa*, are little pictures.

89. Nōmĭna. Rhodope and Haemon, sister and brother, were wont to call one another Zeus and Hera, Jupiter and Juno; afterwards changed, as the poets fabled, into mountains.

90. Pygmaeae. It is a story as old as Homer (Il. 3, 5) that the Pygmies (Πυγμαῖοι, πυγμή, *Tom Thumbs*) and the cranes were at war with one another. Ovid here touches a story of a Pygmaean woman, Gerana (the Gr. for *crane*), or Oenoë, as sometimes called, who for presumption was changed by Juno into a crane, and also made an enemy to the Pygmies (*suis*—populis). Juvenal has a passage on these ancient Liliputians in Satire xiii. 167-170.

93. Antigŏnen; daughter of Laomedon, who in conceit of her long flowing hair compared herself with Juno, and was turned by the goddess into a stork (*ciconia*).

98. Cĭnўran. The daughters of Cinyras, an Assyrian king, were turned into the steps of a temple of Juno.

101. Pācālĭbus; *peaceful*, as the olive was a symbol of peace.

103. In this line, and the following ones to 114, the poet describes the subjects of Arachne's work. They all illustrated, in dishonor of the gods, transformations, by means of which Europa, Asterie, Leda, and others were abducted by Zeus.

111. Nycteĭda, Antiŏpe, daughter of Nycteus, king of Bocotia.——**Gemino—fetu;** i. e., Amphīon and Zethus.

112. Amphĭtrўon was king of Tirynth; and *Tirynthia* refers to Alkmēna, his wife.

113. Āsōpĭda; Aegina, the daughter of the river-god Asopus.

114. Dēōĭda; Persephone, the daughter of Δηώ, a name for Demeter.

129. Carpere, *carp at.*

130. Vĭrāgo; from *vir*, used of Pallas, from her masculine appearance and qualities. Here Minerva's feeling of resentment, and its results in action in the next line, seems to make a transition to the bad sense of the word in the English, *virago*.

131. Crimĭna. The excellence of the work seemed to *criminate*, or cast a reproach upon the goddess.

132. Cўtōrĭăci, from Cytōrus, in Paphlagonia, which abounded in boxtrees; the *radii, shuttles*, were made of box-wood.

137. Ne sis secura, i. e., to keep her anxious about the future; otherwise there might be a hope of being changed back again.

138. Dicta—generi; the penalty was to act upon her posterity just the same as upon herself. The poet uses *nepotibus*, as he is thinking of the transformation from a human being.

139. Hĕcătēĭdos, *of Hecăte*, because with the ancients she was the mistress of all magical charms and spells. So also Shakspeare, in " Macbeth," makes Hecate preside over the witch-scenes.

145. Telas. See n. on *telas*, 54. *Antiquas* and *remittit* are playfully used, as the *aranea* now spins and weaves, even as before Arachne.

17. NIOBE, OR LATONA'S REVENGE.

VI. 146–312.

147. Rumor, i. e., of the fate of Arachne.

148. Illam refers to Arachne. *Thalamos* is here=*nuptias*.

149. Maeonĭam; the Homeric name for Lydia and Phrygia.——**Sĭpўlum;** the name of a hill and town in Phrygia.

17. NIOBE, OR LATONA'S REVENGE. 187

150. Pŏpŭlāris, *her countrywoman,* as they both lived in Phrygia.

152. Sed enim. The *sed* qualifies the idea contained in *multa dabant animus,* i. e., *but* nothing gave her such *proud feelings* (*animos*) as her children; the *enim* qualifies *sic placuere,* etc.; *for neither her husband's arts, nor the race—and the power—pleased her so much,* etc.——**Artes** refers to Amphion's skill in music and song.

153. Genus amborum. Amphīon and Tantalus were both sons of Jupiter.

156. Si—fuisset, *if she had not seemed such to herself;* in allusion to her pride. The sentence reminds one of Tacitus's words concerning Galba: omnium consensu capax imperii, *nisi imperasset,* Hist. i. 49.

157. Manto was a famous prophetess. The word is Greek, from μαντεύεσθαι, *vaticinari.*

159. Ismēnĭdes, for Thebaides, from Ismēnus, a river near Thebes.

160. Duobus, her two children, Phoebus and Artemis, or Apollo and Diana.

161. Lauro; because the *laurel* was sacred to Phoebus.

165. Cĕlĕberrĭmă carries the idea of great numbers; *encompassed with a crowd of attendants.*

166. Vestībus, dat., limiting *intexto.*

167. Mōvensque—capillos, in expression of haughty anger; *and shaking, together with her head, her hair, which flowed down on either shoulder.*

169. Alta, to be translated adverbially, *loftily.*

170. Audĭtos—visis; the gods were only *heard of,* but others, as herself, *seen.*

173. Mensas; the story was, that Tantalus was a guest at the table of the gods.

174. Gĕnĕtrix; Dione, one of the Hyădes, who, with the Pleĭădes, were daughters of Atlas.

176. Sŏcĕro; see n. above, on l. 152.

177. Regia Cadmi, i. e., the *arx* or citadel of Thebes, of which Cadmus was the founder; see below, l. 217, *Cadmeïda arcem.* Of the city itself Amphion was the reputed founder.

178. Commissa=*exstructa, built up.* It was fabled that the walls of Thebes rose up under the magic influence of Amphion's song and lyre.

182. Septem. Homer, Il. 24, 603 seqq., puts the number at *six.*

185. Nescĭŏ quōque=et nescio quo; and *quo* agrees with *Coco. Nescio quis,* literally, I know not who, is used contemptuously for an obscure, unknown person.

186, 187. Maxĭmă—exiguam; *great as it was, the earth refused her a* *small place.* Juno, in her jealousy of Latona, bound every spot on earth by an oath, not to give Latona a place for the delivery of her children; but Neptune provided her a place on the island of Delos.

191. Instābĭlem. The island had before floated about in the Aegean, but it was now made stationary.

195. Possit. The cui=ut mihi, greater than that Fortune can hurt me; i. e., *too great for Fortune to hurt.* See Gr. 503, II. 3.

196. Ut is concessive; *though she may take away.* Gr. 515, III.

198. Huic—populo; a proud expression for her family, as though they made a *people, this people of mine*, in comparison with the two children of Latona. *Populo* is in the dative, by Gr. 385, 4.

200. Quā refers to turbam; as though with only two children she was hardly better than with none at all, *orba*.

201. Infectis properate sacris. This reading I prefer, with Siebelis, to the many conjectural readings adopted instead of the MSS. reading, ite satis propere sacris. Merkel reads, ite, satis pro prole sacri est, and Haupt, ite, satis, propere ite, sacri est. *Infectis* agrees well with *infecta* in the next line, and *ponite* with *deponunt.*

203. Quodque licet; their worship is *silent*, as that alone is *allowed them* (*licet*) by their queen.

204. Cynthi; Cynthus, a mountain in Delos, where Apollo and Diana were worshiped.

206. Animosa expresses her maternal pride; *proud of having borne you.*

208. An dea sim, in allusion to Niobe's words in lines 170, 171. *An*, as used here in a simple question, is poetic, and so is *dubitor* instead of dubitatur.

212. Quod—recĕĭdat, *may it fall back upon herself;* i. e., that she calls me *childless* (*orbam*).

213. Paternam, like her *father's*, Tantalus.

215. Mora is the predicate nom., and *longa* agrees with *querella. Poenae* limits *mora.*

217. Nūbĭbus, in the abl. and limits *tecti; cloud-clad.*

219. Assĭdŭis, used adverbially.

222, 223. Tyrioque suco; see n. above on l. 61. The trappings of the horses were purple. *Terga premere*, in the sense of *sit* or *ride*, is not uncommon. So in Ov. viii. 34, 35: Stratis insignia pictis *Terga premebat;* where also compare the *stratis—pictis* with the expression here, *rubentia suco.*

224. Sarcĭna is here nom. pred.; but the words may be rendered, *whom first his mother had borne.*

17. NIOBE, OR LATONA'S REVENGE.

229. Dēfluit is more special than *decidit* would be, *sinks down;* it expresses the weakness of the dying men. So in Livy, ii. 20, *moribundus* (eques)—ad terram *defluxit*.——**In latus**, on the side, or *sideways*.

230. Per ĭnāne; see n. iv. 718.

232. Rector, sc. navis; *the master of the ship.*

233. Dēdūcit, lets down, i. e., *unfurls.*

233. Quā, sc. parte, *anywhere. Lēvis,* light; observe the quantity; *that not anywhere* (even) *a light breeze be lost.*

234. Dantem; with this reading, *cum* must here be supplied.

235. Cervīce, used here with chief reference to the *back* of the neck; but *gutture,* in next line, the *front.*

237. Prōnus, *leaning forward;* as he was riding fast.——**Admissa** in form agrees with *colla,* but in sense refers to the horse itself; *over the neck of the horse who was let go;* admittere equum is like *immittere habenas.* The rider had to lose hold of the reins, and so the horse was *let go at full speed.*

241. Nitĭdae; i. e., with the oil, with which in the palaestra their bodies were anointed.

247. A spondaic line.

254. Intōnsum, sc. comas, as the Grecian youth wore their hair long till they reached manhood.

258. Pennis, abl. with *tenus, up to the feathers;* i. e., to the very extremity of the arrow.

263. Non omnes; i. e., only Apollo.

265. Mĭnĭmo; the wound was lessened by the pity of the archer.

269. Pŏtuisse. Supply *superos* for the subject, and *hoc* for the object.

271. Nam explains why only Niobe is now mentioned; *for* the father had already killed himself in despair.

276. Invidiosa, on account of her fortunes an object of envy even to her own friends.

280. Pascere; passive imperative, in reflexive sense; *feast yourself.*

282. Effĕror; *I am carried out* to burial.

286. Ab arcu; i. e., of Diana, who now slays the daughters of Niobe.

289. Dēmisso, in token of mourning, as also *atris* in the preceding line.

293. Duplicataque, *bent double;* by the *unseen* (caeco) *wound.*

296. Trepidare opposed to *latet;* you might see one *hiding herself,* another *hurrying about in tremulous fear.*

301. Orba, etc. These lines Byron has in mind in his picture of fallen Rome:

> "The Niobe of nations! there she stands,
> Childless and crownless, in her voiceless woe."

311. In patriam; Phrygia, as above in line 149. In the time of Pausanias, people still fancied they could see the petrified figure of Niobe on Mount Sipylus.

18. THE LYCIANS; MARSYAS.
VI. 313–400.

313. Cuncti, here in its full force of *conjuncti* from which it is contracted; *all together*.

315. Nūmĭna, in the plural, because referring to various manifestations (by *nod*, as it were) of the power of the goddess.

319. Ignobilitate; because it was only country people who were punished.

322. Impatiens, *not able to bear,* because *very aged, grandior aevo.*

323. Illius; i. e., of the Lycians; *ducem, a guide.*

325. Nĭgră; and so agrees with *ară.*

327. Făvĕas, a common form of prayer.

329. Tamen limits *rogabam; I asked, however.*

332. Rēgĭa conjunx; Juno, who in her jealous anger against Latona denied her any spot of earth whereon to rear her twin children.

333. Errātĭca. Delos was then a *floating* island; the word as put with *errantem* seems to represent the fate of the island and of Latona as alike.

336. Noverca; Juno, as the wife of Jupiter, is *the stepmother* of Latona's twins.

339. Chĭmaerĭfĕrae. It was said that the fire-breathing monster Chimaera was native to Lycia. It was slain by Bellerophon.

346. Pŏsĭtoque—pressĭt; i. e., *kneeled upon.*

354. Loquentis, sc. mei; *as I speak.*

357. Dederĭtis. The long *i* of the penult is here, and elsewhere in classic Latin, a return to the quantity of *i* in the early Latin.

366. Coei; Latona was the daughter of the Titan Coeus.

367. Sustĭnet ultra, *does she endure longer.*

368. Minora, less than became her as a goddess, *too humbling words.*

370. Juvat, sc. rusticos; these rustic Lycians, who are now turned into frogs.

19. THE GOLDEN FLEECE. 191

372. Summo, *on the surface of.*

376. The line seems in its sound to imitate the croaking of the frogs.

384. Tritoniaca, of Tritonia, or Minerva (s. note ii. 782), who invented the flute.

385. Mē, humorously said for *cutem meam;* as if, in being flayed alive, he was *pulled off* from himself.

386. Non—tanti; i. e., *so much*, that I should thus suffer for its sake.

393. Tunc quoque, *even then;* i. e., when in the agony of death. Olympus is here the name of a youth whom Marsyas taught to play on the flute.

398. Ēmisit, sc. aquam, *sent it forth*, like a spring.

399. Petens; *aqua* to be supplied, as subject, from the preceding line.

400. Marsya, the Latin form, instead of Marsyas; but the nominative in apposition to *nomen* is unusual. So also i. 169, *lactea nomen* habet; and xv. 96, cui fecimus *aurea nomen.*

19. THE GOLDEN FLEECE.
VII. 1–158.

1. Minyae; the Argonauts were called *Minyans*, from their ancestor Minyas, a king of Thessaly; and the ship Argo was called *Pagasaean*, from the Thessalian town Pagăsa, where it was built.

3. Visus erat, from *viso; had been visited*. The Argonauts stopped at Salmydessus, a Thracian town, to consult Phineus as to the way of getting through the Symplēgădes, two rocks at the mouth of the Euxine. Phineus was blind, hence *perpetua sub nocte;* and the Harpies (*volŭcres*) snatched the food from his mouth whenever he sat down to eat. Milton mentions him in Paradise Lost, iii. 35:

"Blind Thamyris and blind Mæonides,
And Tiresias and Phineus, prophets old."

3. Juvenes; Călăis and Zētes, sons of Aquilo, or Boreas.

6. Phāsĭdos. The *Phasis* was a river in Colchis.

7. Phrixēa, *of Phrixus*, son of Athamas, who, in escaping from his stepmother Ino, was carried through the air, as it was fabled, on the back of a ram that had a golden fleece.

8. Lēxque—horrenda; *the condition* was to tame to the yoke two fire-breathing bulls, to sow a field with serpents' teeth, and to elude the dragon which guarded the fleece.

9. Aeētĭas, *the daughter of Aeetes;* i. e., Medea.

11. This whole passage, to the 70th line, gives us in very skillful touches the conflict between the heart and the reason of Medea. At first, 13–16, she confesses the sway of love, but then, 17–21, strives by force of reason to overcome it.

18. Possem, *if I were able.* The imperfect gives the sure answer to *excute—flammas;* she knows she is *not* able.

20. Video meliora, etc. An expression famous in antiquity, as also in modern literature. Horace has a similar one in Epp. i. 8, 11, Quae nocuere, sequar; fugiam quae profore credam. It is found, too, in the Greek of Euripides, Hippol. 380.

21, 22. She blames herself for loving a stranger and a *foreigner* (*alieni*).

23. Potest—dare, *can give* (something—some one) for me *to love.*

25. Sine amore; she will convince herself that it is only humanity, not love, that makes her wish to save him.

28. Ōrĕ; i. e., by his beautiful countenance.

30. Suae precedes *segetis* for emphasis' sake; *his own,* because the serpent's teeth were sown by his own hand.

32, 33. Hoc ego, etc. She condemns herself as brutally cruel not to save him from such a fate.

34–41. Yet why should she save him, and imperil herself, that he then may wed another?

37. Non—prĕcanda. The words *di—velint* were a prayer, *and yet* it is not praying (*precanda*) which is necessary, but *action* (*facienda*).

41. Poenae, dative; *for* (*the*) *punishment* which her father would inflict for her unfaithfulness to him.

43–50. But he can not be so ungrateful as to wed another; his looks give the lie to that. All must be safe with him.

47. Tūtă, feminine, agreeing with subject of *times.*

51, 52. Yet ought she to abandon home and country?

53–68. Yes, she will gain a better home, a better country. With Jason she will be happy and honored and secure.

54. Stant mecum, *are on my side;* perhaps because her *sister* Chalciŏpe had married Phrixus, who was a Greek.

55. Deus, i. e., Amor.

59. Quemque—velim. The relative precedes the antecedent *Aesŏnĭden;* and son of Aeson, for whom I would be willing to exchange.

61. Ferār=efferar, *I shall be extolled.* The final syllable in *ferar* is lengthened in the arsis of the foot. So above, ii. 247, *Taenărĭŭs.*

61. Sidera tangam. So in Horace, O. i. 1, 36, sublimi feriam sidera vertice.

63. Montes; see note above, on line 3. Charybdis and Scylla, in the

19. THE GOLDEN FLEECE. 193

Sicilian Straits, the former a whirlpool on the Sicilian, and the latter a rock on the Italian side.

69. Conjugiumne, etc. The mention of *conjuge* in the preceding line awakens the doubt whether she would really be the wife of Jason, and so she arouses herself at last to resist the temptation before her.

74. Persēidos. Hecate was the daughter of the Oceanid Perse.

80. Scintillă is the subject of *solet*. The order is: *utque scintilla solet ventis alimenta assumere, et quae—latuit, crescere,* etc.

84. Solĭto, ablative after the comparative *formosior*.

85. Luce=*dic.*

94. Promissa dato, *you shall fulfill your promises;* the future form of the imperative corresponds to *servabere.*——**Triformis;** Hecate was also called *triceps,* as below, vii. 194.

95. Quod numen; i. e., per *numen quod—foret.*

96. Patrem soceri; i. e., Helios, the sun-god, the father of Acētes.

98. Cantatas, *charmed,* over which some formula of *incantation* had been pronounced. Observe that our word *charm* and the Latin *canto* are of the same origin. Thus Milton (in "Comus"): "How *charming* is divine philosophy!—Musical as is Apollo's lute."

101. Mavortis. Mavors is an old name for Mars, as also Marmar, Marmor, and the Oscan Mamers.

104. Ădămantēis, from adamas, Gr. a priv. and δμαω, unconquerable, *adamantine.*

107. Aut ŭbi, etc.; i. e., *aut ut silices—terrena* resonare *solent, ubi concipiunt,* etc.——**Solŭti,** loosened of their hardness, *made brittle.*

111. Trŭces agrees with the subject of *vertere;* venientis, sc. ejus, and limiting *ora.*

116. Mĕdĭcāmĭnă; i. e., the *cantatas herbas* of line 96.

122. Dentes; the teeth of the dragon, which Cadmus slew, and which Minerva had given to Acetes. The *veneno,* in line 123, is the *poison* of the dragon.

126. Nŭmerŏs; i. e., *members,* as these are parts of the whole body.

132. Haemŏnĭi; i. e., Jason, as Haemonia is an old name for Thessaly, from King Haemon, father of Thessalus.

137. Grāmĭnă; the *herbae* of line 96, and the *medicamina,* 116; *carmen auxiliare,* some magic formula, *a charm* to come in aid of the *charmed plants.*

151. Arbŏrĭs aurĕae; i. e., the tree on which hung the golden fleece. *Aureae* is here a dissyllable. This is the reading of Merkel from the MSS., though others read *arietis aurei.*

152. Lēthaeī. The juice of the plants is *Lethaean*, or like the waters of the river Lethe of the lower world, in that both induce sleep and forgetfulness.

155. Sibi; i. e., Somno; these eyes were till now unknown to him, had never been closed in sleep.

20. The Death of Icarus.
VIII. 183–259.

186. Obstrŭăt, sc. Minos.

190. Longam brĕvĭore sĕquentī. If he began *with the smallest (a minimā coeptas)*, it would seem that a long one would follow the shorter every time. Haupt suggests that it should perhaps read *a summā coeptas*.

206. Bŏŏten; see note ii. 176; for *Helice*=Arctos, see note ii. 132. The name Helice was taken from the town Helice, the birth-place of Callisto, who was changed into the constellation.

207. Oriŏnis; also in the northern heavens, and in the form of a man with a *drawn sword*.

215. Ērŭdīt; sc. *eum;* erudire, like *docere*, is followed by two accusatives.

219. Quīque; the *que* connects *credidit* and *obstipuit;* and *believed that* those *who could*, etc.

220. Jūnōnia; *of Juno*, because Samos was a sanctuary of Juno.

222. Dextrā; nominative with Lĕbinthus, though laevā occurred just before.

227. Nudos, sc. *alis, bereft of the wings.*

230. Ăquā: nomen. The water got from him the name of Icarian Sea, between Chios and Cos.

233. Dicebat, *kept saying.*

234. Devovitque, and *cursed* his arts.

235. Tellus; i. e., the island Icaria.

236. With this line begins the story of Perdix, the nephew of Daedalus, whom Daedalus had destroyed in jealousy of his skill in art. He was changed by Minerva into a bird, *Perdix*, the *partridge.* The Perdix has now his revenge.

239. Ūnĭcā; *the only one of its kind.*

243. Bis, etc. *Bis* qualifies *senis, twice six, senis* agreeing with *natalibus. Puerum,* by apposition to *progeniem.*

246. Serrae, *of a saw;* i. e., he used the spine of a fish as a pattern, and invented the saw.

21. PHILEMON AND BAUCIS.

247. Primus et, etc.; *he was also the first* to invent the compasses.
249. Duceret orbem, *drew a circle.*
255. Quod et ante, sc. fuerat.

21. PHILEMON AND BAUCIS.
VIII. 616–724.

616. Tālĭă dĭctă. Pirithŏus had just said that the gods had not the power to change persons and things from one form to another.

621. Phrygiis. This *Phrygian* story reminds one of the incident related of the Lycaonians in the Acts, xiv., who called Barnabas, Jupiter, and Paul, Mercurius, saying, "The gods are come down to us in the likeness of men."

622. Pĕlŏpēïă Pittheus. Pittheus was son of Pelops, and Lelex had once been a guest of Pittheus in Troezen.

627. Atlăntĭădēs. Mercury, the son of Maia, who was the daughter of Atlas. The syllable *ant* is long, but the vowel *a* before *nt* is naturally short.

636. Īdem, nominative plural for *iidem.*

639. Pŏsĭtŏ—jussit. Translate by two verbs, *set a chair and bade,* etc.

640. Textum, from *texĕre,* to weave; and so *textum* with *rude*=*a cloth of coarse texture.*

642. Hesternos; i. e., *the embers of yesterday's fire.*

646. Suus. We might expect *ejus;* but the possessive expresses better the near relation.

648. Sordĭdă; i. e., with the smoke.——**Suĭs,** not the pronoun, but the genitive of *sus.*

655. Tŏrum, *the mattress,* and *lecto,* the couch, or *bedstead. Spondā* and *pedibus* modify *lecto* as ablatives of characteristic, the former the *frame* as part of the *lectus.*

662. Clivum, the *slope,* which was taken away by the *testa.*

664. Bĭcŏlor, *dark green.* The olive, however, was black when it was quite ripe, but was eaten *green.*

665. Condĭtă, put away; i. e., *preserved.* But observe that it is *condĭta* from *condo,* not *condīta* from *condio;* from *con* and *do,* dĕre, *to put.*

666. Lactis—coactĭ, *curdled milk.*

668. Eodem, humorously said; the same sort of silver as the *omnia;* i. e., all earthenware. The word *caelatus* also in jest, as it is properly used of highly artistic work on metals.

671. Ĕpŭlas. So far the poet has been describing the first course of the meal; now comes what the Romans called the *caput cēnae* (the French *pièce de resistance*), the *suis* mentioned above, in line 648.

672. Nec longae=*et non l., the wine of not long age;* i. e., the new wine, as that only might be had at a poor man's table. The *referuntur* means, are set back, or *put aside*, to make room (*locum* in next line) for the *mensae secundae, the dessert.*

675. Māla; observe the quantity of the penultimate. How is it with *malus, evil; malo, I had rather; malus,* a mast?

677. Vultus—bŏni, *kindly looks;* as in Proverbs, xv. 17: "Better is a *dinner of herbs, where love is,* than a stalled ox and hatred therewith."

678. The *nec* belongs to both adjectives; *neither niggardly nor poor.*

680. Succrescĕre; observe the force of the preposition; the wine kept growing up from below; it sprang up, as from a hidden perennial source. The poet's words make us think of the prophet Elijah and the poor widow of Zarephath, I Kings, xvii. 16: "And the barrel of meal wasted not; neither did the cruse of oil fail." The pious old people might well believe that they had gods at their table.

684. Custōdia, for *custos,* as with the Romans the goose was a proverb for vigilance. Comp. Ovid, Met. ii. 538, and xi. 599. The poet has, perhaps, in mind the good service done by the cackling of the watchful geese of the capitol, as told by Livy, B. v. 47.

689. Poenas; i. e., for their want of hospitality, as above, in lines 628, 629.

690. Immūnĭbus, the predicate adj. in the dative. See Gr. 536, 2, 3).

699. Dŏmĭnis limits *parva; small even for its two owners.*

700. Furcas, the forks, or *fork-like props* which supported the gables; these become pillars.

711. Fĭdes means here *fulfillment,* because it carries with it faithfulness to the promise.

719. Thymbrēĭus comes from Thymbris, the name of a river in Phrygia.

724. Cura, etc. "Them that honor me, I will honor." I Samuel, ii. 30.

22. THE WOOING OF DEÏANIRA.

IX. 1-97.

1. Deo, Achelous. *Deo* depends upon *sit* understood, which has *causa* for its subject. *Neptunius heros* refers to Theseus, the fabled son of Neptune.

2. Calȳdōnĭus, Aetolian, as Calȳdon was an Aetolian town.

22. THE WOOING OF DEÏANIRA.

3. Hărŭndĭne. It was usual in art to represent river-gods with horns, and their heads crowned with sedge and reed. The vowel *u* is short here, though the syllable is long. Gr. 651, VII.

8. Si qua, and **also** *tandem, ever,* are enviously said in disparagement, as if Deianira were a prize of no account.

11. Intrāta est, sc. a me; was entered by me; *when I entered.*

12. Parthăŏne nāte; Oeneus, king of Calydon.

14. Dăre se, that he would give; i. e., *would bring (to her)* as a kind of dowry.

15. Referebat, *declared. Novercae* refers to Juno, and *jussa* to the labors imposed upon Hercules through the agency of Juno, and *overcome* (*superata*) by him.

19. Hospes, appositive to *gener;* this is said in depreciation of Hercules, who was not Aetolian. It thus means *stranger,* though originally *host.* It is formed of hos=(Ghas), the root of *hos-tis,* and *pes,* from pa, the root also of *pasco,* to feed; and as *hostis* originally means a *stranger,* hospes=qui hostem pascit, means first a host, then a guest (Ghas, German Gast), and so a stranger, in distinction from a native. From what does our word host=multitude, come, and also *host*=victim?

28. Spectat, sc. Hercules.

29. Tot; i. e., *just so many,* and no more; meaning that Hercules would not contend in words, but only in deeds. Observe that it is *dextĕră* and *linguā;* in what case each?

32. Vĭrĭdem; because he is a river-god; so of the Nereids in ii. 12, virides—capillos. The wrestlers contended with bodies naked and rubbed with oil. Hence the throwing of dust (as in 31) in order to get a hold of the otherwise slippery body.

33. Tĕnŭĭ; verb; *and held. Varas, bent,* and *in statione, in* (firm) *posture.*

43. Certi, *determined.*

49. Quem. We should expect *utrum.* Why?

51. Relcere. The wrestlers keep close to one another, each striving to keep his adversary from a free use of his limbs. This *embrace* (*amplexus*) Hercules *strikes off* (*excŭtit*), and then loosens the *close-drawn arms* of Achelōus, and so turns him sideways, and clasps him from behind, hanging upon him with *mountain pressure* (*pressus—monte*).

57. Insĕrŭĭ. Achelous manages, by inserting his arms between his chest and the arms of Hercules, to loosen his adversary's grip; but *hardly* (*vix*) has he done this when Hercules is *on him again* (*instat*).

61. Hărēnas, etc. So Horace O. ii. 6, 12. Solum tetigere mento.

66. Tīrynthĭus; Hercules, from Tiryns, in Argŏlis, where he was brought up.

67. Cūnarum, etc. The first achievement of Hercules was to strangle two serpents in his *cradle*.

69. Unus is emphatic, as the Lernaean hydra was hundred-headed.

71. Centum, sc. capitum.

72. Gĕmĭno; in reference to the two heads, which every time grew up from the one head, which was cut off.

74. Vĕtuĭque. Hercules seared every new wound with a red-hot iron, and so prevented any new growth.

81. Tauro, abl. of price. H. 422, note 2.

82. Tŏris means *the dew-lap*, or brawn of the animal, which hangs down from the throat. This Hercules wraps round his arms (literally, with the dew-lap clothes his arms), and then *drags* (*trahens*) him with it as he *comes on at full speed* (*admissum*), and thus pulls his head down and *buries his horns in the ground* (*cornua—humo*). On *admissum* see n. vi. 237.

88. The horn of Achelous, as a symbol of blessing, is used in art with Bona Copia as the goddess of abundance; hence *cornucopia*. The Naïdes are *water-nymphs*, from *νάω*, Latin *no*, *nare*, literally the swimmers.

89. Succincta. Diana, as a huntress, is represented in art and in poetry with tunic *girt up* to the knees.

93. Lux sŭbĭt. So the night had been passed in feasting and discourse.

94. Jŭvĕnes; i. e., Theseus and his companions, as mentioned earlier, viii. 566.

96. Oppĕriuntur agrees with a pronoun referring to *juvenes*.

97. Cornu, in abl. and limiting *lacerum*.

23. The Death of Hercules.

IX. 134–272.

While Hercules and Deianira, on their way to Tiryns, are crossing the river Evēnus, the centaur Nessus attempts to carry off Deianira. Hercules shoots the centaur, who gives to Deianira a blood-stained robe, telling her that it will revive Hercules' love if it should ever grow cool.

135. Ŏdĭum, also object of *implerant*.

136. Hercules had captured *Oechălĭa* (with *ab*), a city in Euboea, and was on his way to the *Cenaean* promontory, to offer sacrifices to Jove.

23. THE DEATH OF HERCULES. 199

140. Iŏles. Iole was the daughter of Eurў̆tus, king of Oechalia.
157. Det depends upon *mandat, ut* omitted.
161. Vis—mali ; i. e., that powerful poison.
165. Oeten ; here masculine, but usually feminine.
167. Illa, subject both of *trahitur* and of *trahit.*
169. Dĕtĕgit ; because the skin and the flesh cleave to it.
171. Lăcu. *Lacus* here is for a *tank* of water, in which heated metals were cooled, as here *lammina candens, the plate of metal at white heat.* Ovid has the same figure in Met. xii. 276, ut dare *ferrum Igne rubens,* quod forcipe curva cum faber eduxit, *lacubus* demittit. *Strĭdit,* in third conjugation ; *hisses.*
174. Caecā, blind, in the sense of *unseen,* as in Met. vi. 293.
176. Saturnia, Juno, *the daughter of Saturn,* on whom he calls, because it was she through whose agency he is made thus to suffer.—— **Pascĕre,** passive imperative, with reflexive sense ; *feast yourself on my sufferings ;* so the word was used above in Met. vi. 280, where also (281) the same word *satia* is used as here ; *glut thy cruel heart,* bitterly expressing Juno's delight in his pains.
179. Tibi is emphatic, as in *hosti* Juno herself was meant.
180. Lăbōrĭbus, dative ; for labors.
183–197. In these lines Hercules recounts some of these famous labors of his : the slaying of *Busiris,* the Egyptian king ; his victory over *Antaeus,* the giant wrestler ; the carrying off of the oxen of Gerў̆on (*pastoris,* 184), the king in Spain ; bringing of the monster dog *Cerberus* (185) up from Hades ; the capture of the Cretan bull (*tauri,* 186) ; cleansing the stables of king Augēas, in *Elis* (187) ; the destruction of the birds on the lake Stymphālis, in Arcadia ; fetching the golden *apples* of the Hesperides ; his victorious fight with the *centaurs* in Arcadia ; the capture of the Arcadian stag on Mount Parthenius (188) ; the seizure of the *gold-embossed girdle* of the Amazonian queen, on the river *Thermōdon,* in Cappadocia (189) ; the destruction of the Erymanthian *boar,* in Arcadia (192), and of the Lernaean *hydra ;* the capture of the horses of the Thracian Diomēdes (194), and the strangling of the *huge Nemaean lion* (197).

183. Părentis ; i. e., his mother Earth, from whom by every contact he gained new strength.
198. Caelum tuli ; in place of Atlas, while the latter was getting for him the golden apples.
203. Et sunt, etc. ; *and* (yet) *there are some who can believe that there are gods !* In his despair at the idea of Eurystheus prevailing in bringing upon him all these labors, he denies for a moment the existence of the gods.

204. Oeten, here also masculine (*altum*), as in l. 165.

205. Haud aliter, not otherwise; i. e., as swiftly as (*quam si*). He compares the swift pace of Hercules with that of some hunter who has wounded a bull, and then fled from the beast when he has turned upon him in the rage of his pain. The bull *is carrying* (*gerat*) the spear, the hunter *has fled* (*refugerit*). For the subjunctive in both verbs, Gr. 513, II.

209. Vĭdēres; potential subjunctive; *you might have seen.* Gr. 485, note 3.

210. Montĭbus, in dative, limiting *irascentem*.

216. Gĕnĭbus—adhĭbere, *to clasp his* (Hercules's) *knees,* the usual attitude of a suppliant.

218. Tormento, ablative after the comp. *fortius.* The *tormentum* (in this sense) was an engine for hurling missiles, so called (from *torqueo*) because they were worked by the force of *twisted* ropes, or horse-hairs, or other fibres. Lichas was projected from Hercules's hands *with more force* than he could have been from one of these engines.

220. Imbres—corpus. *Concrescere* with gelidis (*gelu*) expresses our word *congeal.* In the simile he describes the rain congealing into snow, and then the *snow-flakes* (*nivibus*) as they *whirl about* in the air are contracted by the *astringent* cold, and so condense into the ball-like hailstones. *Nivibus* is in the dative, and limits *astringi*.

225. Prior—aetas; i. e., the afore-time, or *antiquity.*

232. Săgittas. The oracle had declared that without the arrows of Hercules Troy could never be destroyed; and so Ulysses was sent to Lemnos to bring *Philoctetes* (*Poeante satum*), the son of Poeas, with them; this is the subject of the *Philoctetes* of Sophocles.

232. Iterum. Once Hercules himself had used them in conquering Troy, when it was under the rule of Laomedon.

233. Quo—ministro, abl. abs., and = cujus ministerio.

234. Subdĭtă, sc. pyrae est.

235. Congĕriem—summam, *the top of the pile. Congeries s.* and *agger,* from the same root in *gero,* mean here the same thing.

237. Convīva, etc. Horace has a similar comparison in Sat. i. 1, 119 —uti *conviva* satur; and also Lucretius, iii. 951, ut plenus vitae *conviva*.

241. Vindĭce. Hercules is so called because he freed the earth from so many evils.

245. Mĕmŏris; i. e., of the many beneficent acts done by Hercules.

248. Sed enim. See n. i. 530. *But* do not fear, *for* he will come off conqueror.

251. Māternā; i. e., so far as he is mortal, as born of a human mother (Alcmēna).

257. Deo; i. e., *shall take offense at his being made a god. Nolet,* with what follows, makes the apodosis of the sentence.

261. Nŏtatam, marked for censure; i. e., by the preceding words of Jupiter.

265. Jovis vestigia; i. e., *traces of* (likeness to) *Jove.*

24. ORPHEUS AND EURYDICE.

X. 1-77.

1. Inde; i. e., from the wedding, just before related, of Iphis and Ianthe.

3. Orphĕī. Hymenaeus comes from Ianthe's wedding to that of Orpheus, but *to no purpose* (*nequiquam*), as the marriage is to have a sad end in the loss of Eurydĭce.

7. Mōtibus; move about the torch as he might, it would not burn bright; a bad omen for the marriage.

11. Ad—auras deflevit. We say praised to the skies; but here, in Latin, it is wept to the skies; i. e., raised to the skies his mourning voice.

14. Lĕves, because disembodied, and so only *umbrae.* So Horace, O. i. 16, 18, uses *levem turbam* of the shades.

14. Simulacra—sepulcro; so also iv. 435, simulacra functa sepulcris. It is = *simulacra functorum sepulcro,* the ghosts of the buried.

22. Terna—monstri, in allusion to Cerberus and his three heads. Also allusion is made in *vincirem* to the feat of Hercules in *binding* and carrying away Cerberus.

28. Răpinae; i. e., of Proserpine by Pluto.

31. Retexĭte, in allusion to the spinning (or *weaving*) by the Parcae of the thread of human destiny. Here it is *to unweave,* and so reverse the destiny of Eurydĭce.

33. Serius—citius. So Horace, O. ii. 3, 25, versatur—*serius ocius;* and in the Ars Poetica, 63, Debemur morti nos.

36. Haec; i. e., Eurydice.——**Justos,** due her, *allotted.*

37. Pro mūnere, *instead of a gift;* opposed to *usum,* which is a law-term for something only used, in usufruct, and not one's own in fee simple.

42, 43. Refūgam; an unusual word. It expresses, with *undam,* a part of the punishment of *Tantălus,* that while he was always suffering from a raging thirst, and was always in the middle of a lake, the water was always *escaping* from him (in a fearfully *tantalizing* way) when he would fain drink. "Water, water, everywhere, Nor any drop to drink."

——**Ixion** was punished by being tied to an ever-revolving *wheel*. The word *jecur* refers to Tityus, whose punishment it was to have vultures (*volŭcres*) ever preying on his *liver*.——The **Bĕlĭdĕs**, granddaughters of Belus, daughters of Danaus (and therefore called Danaïdes), were condemned, in Tartarus, to be always drawing water from perforated, sieve-like *urns*. For the quantity of the last two syllables in Belĭdĕs, Gr. 587, II. 1, and foot-note; and 581, VI. 3.——**Sisўphus** was doomed to roll a huge stone up a hill, which always rolled down again the moment it touched the top. These are some of the ancient images of endless punishment; but the poet represents these sufferers as having a respite from their toils when Orpheus sang. Horace has a similar passage in O. ii. 14, 33–40.

46. Eumĕnĭdum. *Eumenides* is the Greek euphemistic name for the Furies, the Avenging Deities of crime and sin. Even these are now *overcome by the song* of Orpheus; they feel compassion, and their *cheeks* are *wet with tears*.

47. Neither the *queen* (*regia conjunx*) nor the king of Hades can *hold out* (*sustinet*) *in saying No* (*negare*) *to his prayer* (*oranti*); *and they call Eurydice*.

50. Rhodopēïus, from Rhodŏpe, a mountain in Thrace.

51. Ne flectat retro, etc. Forward, not backward; a confident going straight on, not a timid looking back, was the inexorable *condition* (*lex*) for Orpheus' success; as always in achieving any good, or shunning any evil. The tenses, present in *flectat* and perfect in *exierit*, because in dependence upon *accipit*; the direct prohibition would be *ne flectas donec exieris*.

55. Afuĕrunt, from *absum*; the penult here short, though it is usually long.

56. Illic is here an adverb of place, referring to the preceding line. *Deficeret* agrees with a pronoun referring to Eurydice, and it depends upon *metuens*; *lest she should fail* in strength (sc. *viribus*), and so be lost to him. So in Met. xii. 518, *deficit*, and ib. xiv. 484, *deficiunt* (sc. *animo*); and Tacitus, Agric. 43, *deficientis*, and 45, *deficientem*.

63. Acciperet, subj. with *quod* after an indefinite antecedent. Compare note on *possent*, ii. 161.

64. Stŭpuit. The poet compares the amazed Orpheus first with some one petrified at the sight of Hercules carrying off Cerberus, and then to Lethaea and her husband Olenus, who (for some crime) were both turned to stone.

73. Portitor, from the root por, per, as also the word portus, and the Gr. πορθμεύς; *ferryman* of the Styx; Charon.

25. Hyacinthus.
X. 162-219.

The story of Hyacinthus the poet represents as told by Orpheus.

162. Te quoque; *you also,* as the poet has been singing of the translation of Ganymede to Olympus.——**Amyclīdē,** the fabled son or grandson of Amỹclas, the Laconian king.——**In aethere** is = here to *in caelum.*

167. Genitor; Apollo.

169. Immunītam. Sparta was not a walled city till 206 b. c.

175. Noctis, limiting, in the genitive, *medius;* usually it would be inter—*noctem;* so above, v. 409.

177. Disci; *quoit,* circular, and made of metal or stone, or of wood.

184. Repercusso—verbere, *by the rebound.*

186. Aeque quam=*aeque ac, as much as.*

191. Liguis. Another reading is *virgis,* which, though a more special word than *lignis,* yet refers, as does *lignis,* to *the stalks* of the flower; these have a *pale-yellow* color in contrast with the whiteness of the leaves. Other readings are *linguis* and *liguis.*

192. Demittant, with *ut,* is potential subjunctive, and makes the conclusion to the condition *si quis—infringat.*

196. Oebālīde. Hyacinthus was the son of Oebalus, king of Sparta.

198. Dŏlŏr—fācĭnusque meum; i. e., the object of *my grief and crime.*——**Dexterā,** etc.; *my right hand* must be inscribed upon = *designated as the cause of—your death;* i. e., inscribed on the tombstone.

206. Scripto, *in writing;* by the letters written, as it were inscribed on the leaves of the flower, as explained below, in line 215.

207. Heros; that is, Ajax, from whose blood, as related in xiii. 196, sprang the same flower as from that of Hyacinthus.

213. His—illis, *these;* i. e., hyacinths are nearer to the present thought of the speaker, *illis, those,* in reference to the lilies.

215. AI AI, the Gr. αἰαῖ, as seeming to be inscribed on the leaves of the flower ΑΙΑΙ; not, however, our hyacinth, but perhaps the larkspur, *Delphinium Ajacis.*

26. Atalanta's Race.
X. 560-680.

564. Scitanti, sc. oraculum. She consulted the oracle.——**By deus,** Apollo is meant.

566. Ipsā vīvă; join ipsā with *te*, but vīvă with the subject of *carebis*. In genuine oracular tone she is told that though she will live, yet it will be without herself; whether in allusion to the loss of independence by marriage (?), or to the transformation by and by to be undergone, in being changed into a lioness, as related in x. 698 seqq.

567. Sorte, by the response, as *sors* is always the word (literally, lot) for an oracular response.

578. Vēlāmĭne; i. e., her outer garment, the *palla*, or ἱμάτιον, as she would run in her *tunica*, or χιτών.

579. Tuum; i. e., Adonis, as the poet represents Venus (meum) as telling this story to Adonis.

583. Ne follows both *optat* and *timet*. He desires that none of the runners may outrun Atalanta, and in his jealousy he is afraid some one may.

588. Sētĭus, derived from *sĕcĭtus*, and more correct than *sēcĭus*; in either form, from seq or sec of *sequor*; not otherwise than, i. e., *as swiftly as a Scythian arrow*. The Scythians excelled with the bow and arrow.

589. Āŏnĭo; see n. i. 313.

597. Metă. See note on ii. 142.

605. Onchestĭus, *of Onchestus*. The Bœotian town Onchestus was so called from the so-named son of Neptune, and father of Měgăreus.

609. Schœnēĭa; she was the daughter of the Bœotian king Schœneus.

611. Formosĭs, dative, and limits *iniquus*.

618. Cōnūbia; the antepenultimate (*ū*) long here, and also xi. 226; but it is short in vi. 428.

619. Ut pereat, following *tanti*, expresses result.

623. Tamen. She now changes her tone, and tries to get rid of what seems weakness; and hence the change to the third person in *viderit*; but the weakness is back again directly in utinam—*velles*.

624. Viderit, in perf. subj., *let him look to that!* The perf. subj. gains in such instances an imperative force, as especially in *videris*, *look you* to that!

628. Non must be joined with *ferendae*, and *invidiae ferendae* expresses a characteristic or quality of the *victoria*, and also with *erit* makes the predicate; will be of an odium not to be borne; i. e., *will bring me an intolerable odium*.

633. Ĕras; we might expect the subjunctive, *esses*, but the indicative is more emphatic; *you were the one*.

637. Fäcit; the indicative here is so strange a construction that it is hard to explain it. Does Ovid mean so to sympathize with Atalanta as *not to know what* he is saying?

639. Sollĭcĭtā used in all its original meaning of sollus-cita (fr. cico), *thoroughly aroused.* On *proles N.*, see above, lines 599, 600.

652. Carcĕre limits *emĭcat; darts out from the barrier.*

668. Spectacula, here the place of the show, *the theatre.*

27. The Death of Orpheus.

XI. 1–84.

1. Carmĭne; i. e., the narratives sung by Orpheus, as those of Hyacinthus, Atalanta, and others, in x. 148–680.

2. Saxa. Compare Horace, O. i. 12, 7, Unde vocalem temere insecutae Orphea silvae, etc.

4. Pectora; adverbial acc. The *Bacchae* were wont at the Bacchic festivals to clothe themselves with doe-skins.

8. Apollĭnĕi. Orpheus was the fabled son of Apollo and the Muse Calliŏpe.

9. Follis. The thyrsus-staff (*hastam*) was twined at the top with ivy and vine-shoots; these protect Orpheus, and though the thyrsus makes a *spot* (*nota*) there is no contusion.

11. Victus. There was "music in the air," and it quite *vanquished* the stone, which, falling at the feet of the musician, seemed to ask pardon (*veluti supplex*) for its rudeness.

13. Sed enim. Comp. i. 530; *but* in vain, *for,* etc.

14. Abĭit. See n. on *subiit,* i. 114. *Erinys* here not in the sense of the avenging deity, but of one who excites to crime and frenzy.

15. Cunctăque, etc.; i. e., all the missiles had been subdued but for "the barbarous dissonance of Bacchus and his revelers." Compare Milton, "Paradise Lost," vii. 32.

17. Bacchēi. Observe the hiatus in the fifth foot, and see note ii. 244.

20. Primum prepares the way for *inde* in l. 23.——**Etiamnum,** *even now;* i. e., during the clamor of the Bacchic rout.

22. Titulum, *the honor;* appositive to *volŭcrēs angues, agmen;* and all these are thought of as making a triumphal *procession* for Orpheus.

25. Noctis avem; the owl is meant. The words *structo—theatro* make the Latin for the Greek amphi-theatre.

26. Mātūtīnā, because the combats with wild beasts were wont to take place in the *morning,* and with these the games began.

37. Fĕrae; i. e., the Maenādes, *frenzied women.*

41. Sacrilĕgae, so called because they are assailing the priest and bard of Apollo.

54. Invectae agrees with *lyra* and *lingua.* *Populare,* because Thracian, as it were the countryman of Orpheus.

55. Lesbi. Lesbos was the home of the poets Alcaeus and Sappho; and also of Arīon, who was a native of the Lesbian town Methymna.

62. Arva piorum; one of the expressions in the Latin writers for the abodes of the good after death, like *sedes—piorum* in Horace, O. ii. 13, 23; *sedes beatas* in Vergil, Aen. vi. 639; *Elysium,* Verg. v. 735, and many others. It is conceived as a part of the lower world, and opposed to *sedes scelerata,* Ovid, iv. 456.

65. Anteit; a word of two syllables, as usual in verse, the *e* not being pronounced.

67–84. The poet tells in these lines the story of the change of Orpheus's murderers into trees.

68. Sacrorum; see below, xi. 92, 93.

71. In—secuta est, *so far as each* (i. e., they severally) *followed* Orpheus. The poet says that just at the place to which they had followed Orpheus they were *thrust* by Bacchus (*detrusit*) into the ground.

72. Traxit, to be joined with *in terram,* as well as *detrusit ;* and the subject of both verbs, as of *ligavit,* is a pronoun understood, referring to Bacchus.——**Acumina,** appositive to *digitos.* But both these lines, 71, 72, seem to be a gloss rather than Ovid's words.

73. Suum, reflexive to *volŭcris,* and *volŭcris* is the subject of *commisit* and *sensit.*

75. Plangitur, *beats itself* with its wings.

76. Harum refers back to *matres.*

78. Exsultantem expresses the effort *to spring up.*

79. Digiti—pes—ungues. The poet represents the change as beginning with the feet, at the roots, as it were, of the trees.

82. Fiunt agrees in number with the nearer and the predicate noun.

28. MIDAS.

XI. 85–193.

Finely has Hawthorne told this story in English in his "Wonder-Book."

85. Hoc; i. e., the punishment of the Thracian *Bacchae.* Not content with this, Bacchus now leaves their *country* (*agros*), and goes to

28. MIDAS.

Lydia, and to the *vineyards of his Timolus* there (or Tmolus, a mountain in Lydia), and to the river *Pactolus*.

87. Aureus; see below, line 142.

88. Invidiosus, *envied for its precious sands; harēnis,* ablative.

93. Cum to be joined with Orpheus in translation; *Orpheus together with—Eumolpus;* as Eumolpus was a pupil of Orpheus, and afterwards settled in Attica (*Cecropio,* from Cecrops, the mythic founder of Athens), and was the founder of the Attic family of the Eumolpidae.

97. Coēgĕrat; *cogo* is here used from its military meaning, to bring up the rear. The stars are thought of as an army marching off the field of the heavens, and Lucifer, as the morning star, *brings up the rear.* So also in Ovid, ii. 114.

100. Optandi is to be joined with *muneris,* and the two words limit *arbitrium.* Midas is to have his choice of a gift; that is agreeable, but *useless,* as the sequel will show.

103. Vertatur; subjunctive after *effice,* with omission of *ut.*

104. Solvit; this verb is used in like manner with *dona,* ix. 794. The expression is like *pecuniam solvere,* because the gift as fulfillment of a promise is like paying a debt.

105. Petisset. Why is the subjunctive used?

107. Polliciti fidem, *the trustworthiness of the promise. Fidem* limits *temptat,* and *singula* limits *tangendo.*

112. Massa; i. e., of gold; a nugget.

117. Dănăën; in allusion to the story of Danae being *deceived* by Jupiter in the form of a shower of gold.

125. Auctorem muneris; Bacchus, by metonymy for *vinum.*

133. Spĕcioso (from *specio*), used like *splendida* (line 131), of the glitter of the gold; *from* (this) *splendid curse.* Why not our word *specious?*

134. Numen, appositive to *Bacchus.*

135. Rēstĭtuit; i. e., to his human touch.

135. Facti que, etc. The reading *facti fide* is doubtful; but it may mean *in confirmation of the act, facti* referring to *restituit. Data munera solvit;* (dissolved, i. e.) *took back the gifts he had bestowed;* changed them back to what they were before. But this meaning of *solvo* with *munera* is unusual; and especially as *solvit munera,* in one of its ordinary uses, has been given above, in line 104. Harper's Dict. (Andrews's, revised by Lewis and Short) translates thus: *freed the gift from the obligation of an accomplished fact;* i. e., *revoked the gifts.*

137. Amnem; the Pactolus.

144. Venae means *the vein* of gold, and *semine* the seed or golden sand brought down by the river into the surrounding fields.

146–193. Midas and Apollo. Midas ventures to declare Pan's music to be better than Apollo's; and, to punish his *stupid ears* (175), the god of song changes them into the ears of an ass.

148. Mānsit; i. e., just as *dull* as in the wish for the golden touch.

150. Nam, etc. The poet goes on to explain what he has just said of the *pingue ingenium* of Midas.

152. Sardis, in Lydia, was on the northern slope of Mount Tmolus, and *Hypaepa* on the southern.

154. Observe that the *first e* in *leve* is short, *lĕve;* what then is its meaning? Also *cerata* has the last syllable long, *ceratā;* in what case then?

156. Judice; Tmolus is conceived here as the god of the mountain, and so is to be the umpire in the musical contest. So, too, in the next line the poet, by a singular fancy, transfers the *trees* (*arboribus*) that crown the mountain to the mountain-god.

162. Barbarico; Phrygian, and so not Greek, *foreign*.

163. Post hunc; i. e., after *his* singing the god turns his *face* (*ora*) to the face of Phoebus; *os* used as part for the whole.

164. Sua refers to *vultum;* see II. 449, 2.

165. Caput; accusative, as in II. 378. In these lines, 165–168, the poet describes Phoebus as in the dress of the *citharoedus*, or cithern-player, as he was represented in ancient statues, one of which is extant in the gallery of the Vatican. It was the costume, too, in which performers appeared in Rome in the poet's time.

165. On Parnāside, see note i. 316; on *murice*, note on vi. 61.

167. Fidem, from *fides*, meaning a string, and then a *lyre; Indis*, of India; i. e., of ivory from the tusks of Indian elephants.

169. Stāmina (from *stare*), originally for what *stands* in the loom, the warp, thread, and here the *strings* of the lyre.

174. Dēlius; Apollo, so called from Delos, his birthplace. *Aures* is the subject, and *figuram* the object of *retinere*. So, in the next line, a pronoun referring to *aures* is the obj. of *trahit*.

178. In unam partem, in reference to *cetera* means *on* (*this*) *one part*.

179. Aures; in acc. by II. 378.

180–193. The servant who dressed King Midas's hair, not daring to tell men of the strange ears of his master, whispers the secret in the earth; by-and-by reeds spring up from the spot, and these, as they sway in the wind, murmur the story to all the air.

181. The *tiara* was a Phrygian head-dress, pointed at the top, and covering the ears, and fastened under the chin.

184. Cupiens is equivalent to a concessive clause; *though he wanted* (to bring it out into the air, i. e.) to utter it, *to make it known*, yet (*tamen*), etc.

192. Agrĭcŏlam; the *famulus* is thought of as a farmer, who has intrusted the secret to the earth, just as he would sow seed in it.

29. CEYX AND ALCYŎNE.
XI. 410–748.

Ceyx, king of Trachis in Thessaly, is drowned while on a voyage to Claros. His body is washed ashore, and is discovered by his wife Alcyone, who is anxiously awaiting his return. As she throws herself into the sea to reach her husband, she is changed into a king-fisher or halcyon; and Ceyx is changed in like manner. So they mate and live together. They build their nest, as the fable has it, on the sea; and the seven winter days, when Alcyone broods over her nest, are "Halcyon days," when a calm broods over the

> "Ocean,
> Who now hath quite forgot to rave,
> While birds of calm sit brooding on the charmed wave."
> MILTON'S "HYMN TO THE NATIVITY."

410–143. Alcyone endeavors, but all in vain, to dissuade her husband from the voyage.

410, 411. Pectora, in the acc. limits *turbatus* by II. 378. *Fratris* limits *prodigiis*, and *secutis* agrees with *prodigiis*. Daedalion, the brother of Ceyx, had been changed into a hawk; and after his death a wolf, which had attacked the flocks of Peleus, had been turned to stone.

413. Clarium, *of Claros*, near Colophon, in Asia Minor, where was a celebrated oracle of Apollo.

414. Phlĕgȳis; the *Phlegyae* were a Boeotian people, and *Phorbas* was their king.

417. Buxo; see note iv. 134.

425. At puto, etc. She thinks to herself, that if it were a journey by land, then she should only suffer from the *grief* of parting; but *the sea* is what she *fears*.

428, 429. Tabulas; i. e., planks from shipwrecks; and *sine corpore* refers to empty tombs, cenotaphs, when people have been lost at sea.

431. Hippotădes; i. e., Aeŏlus, the god of the winds, whose daughter Alcyone was. See note iv. 663.

432. Plăcet; the long *a* points to what verb? and what would *plăcet* mean?

436. Concursibus; see note i. 56.

442. Nisi—patiar. If she were not with him, her fears might be greater, because imaginary; but if she is with him, then she will *fear* only what she really *suffers*.

444–477. The departure.

445. Sidereus, in reference to his descent, as the son of *Lucifer*.

449. Non tamen, etc. *Causam* refers to the whole thing of which he is talking to her; and with *probat* (sc. Ceyx) *ei* is understood, referring to Alcyone; literally, he does not approve the thing to her; i. e., with all that he says, *yet he does not convince her of the thing*.

452. Patrios, in allusion to Lucifer.

455. Navalibus, in connection with the poetic *aequore tingui*, seems to mean what we call *a dry dock;* indeed, in iii. 661, Ovid uses the expression *siccum navale*.

462. Geminis; they sat on both sides of the ship, where the banks of oars were arranged, so as to be opposite each other. The *pinus*, or ship, was thus a *biremis*.

475. Pendentes; this would be the position of the oars during the rowing; *hanging down* into the sea; but now, with a breeze filling the sails, the sailor lays the oars across the side of the ship. The vowel *e* is by nature short before *nt* and *nd;* but the syllable is long by position.

476. Cornua means, first, the (horn-like) extremities to the *yard* of the ship (*antenna*); then, as here, the ropes which passed from these extremities to the *top of the mast* (*summa—arbore*).

478–573. The shipwreck, and the death of Ceyx.

478. Amplius; *quam* is omitted. H. 417, 1, note 2.

481. Eurus, a contrary wind for a voyage from Greece to Asia Minor.

487. Ventis—negare; *to reef the sails*.

495. Clamore, etc. So Vergil, i. 87, Insequitur *clamorque virum stridorque rudentum*.

496. Undarum—unda. The words are purposely repeated, as in xv. 181, unda impellitur unda.

506. Suspicere, *to look up*, as contrasted with *despicere* in l. 404. The ship, when on the crest of a sea, seems to look down into its very depths (*Acheronta*, the lower world), and when it has gone down into the troughs (*valles*) of the sea, it seems thence to look up to the heights of the

29. CEYX AND ALCYONE.

sky. *Acheron* is first the name of a river in the Lower World, meaning, as a Greek word, the stream of woe, and then the name of the Lower World itself.

507. Lătus. H. 378.

508. Quam, etc. The order of the words as follows: quam cum olim ferreus aries ballistave concutit laceras arces. The battering-ram *aries*, and the *ballist* (a machine for *throwing* projectiles) were used in the sieges of cities.

512. Sē admīserat; *admittere* with *equum* means to *let a horse run*, as in vi. 237, where see note; so, too, *admisso passu*, i. 532; and here it is used figuratively of *unda ; when it had given itself free course.* Thus the *se admiscrat* corresponds in the simile to *incursu*. As the lion is wont *by running* to gather up its strength for the assault, *ire in arma*, etc., so the wave, after having given itself full course, *ibat in arma*, etc.

514. The **cunei** were the wedge-like plugs by which the planks of the keel were held together; *cera, wax,* was used as well as pitch in protecting the joinings of the ship.

525. Omni numero, all the number; i. e., *all the rest* (of his fellow-soldiers).

530. Decĭmae—undae; i. e., the *fluctus decumanus*, as the Romans called it, every *tenth wave*, which they thought to be the strongest and most perilous.

536. Trepĭdare depends upon *solet*. *Tencntibus intus*, said of such of the enemy as are already *inside* (*intus*), corresponds to *pars maris intus*, in l. 534.

539. Vocat—maneant; because it was supposed that the spirits of the unburied wandered restless on this side the Styx.

542. Subeunt illi, *occur to his mind.* So in vii. 170.

543. Pignŏrĭbus; i. e., the children.

550. Dŭplĭcata; explained by line 521, the darkness of the night, and of the storm.

552. Regĭmen, guiding, something that guides, and so means, as here, *the rudder*. *Spoliis ;* i. e., the mast, and the rudder, which are, as it were, *the spoils of the wave ; proud of her spoils, like a conqueror, rising up* (*superstes*) *and high-arched, looks down upon* (the other) *waves*.

554. Ăthon, a mountainous peninsula in Macedonia; *Pindum*, the mountain-range which parts Thessaly from Epirus.

558. Fāto functă; the abl. in *fato* by II. 421, I.; *reached their destined end.*

561. Sŏcĕrumque pătremque; i. e., Aeolus and Lucifer.

562. Plūrĭmă; an adjective agreeing with *Alcyone*, but here adverbial in meaning; Alcyone's name is *very much* (i. e., *saepissime*) on his lips.

563. Rĕfert; again and again he utters her name.

564. Illĭŭs; the penultimate here short. The word, as the first in the line, is emphatic; before *her eyes he longs that the waves may bear his body.* It is she, above all others, by whose *friendly hands* he would fain be buried.

568. Nĭgĕr—ăquārum. *Arcus* seems to express the arched, bow-like shape of the wave; the expression *arcus aquarum* is thus much like our word *billow*.

570. Posses; the subjunctive by H. 503, I.

571. Excēdĕre caelo. See note ii. 115. *Lucifer*, though the father of Ceyx, yet as leader of the stars, may not leave his post in the sky.

573–709. At the bidding of Juno, through her messenger Iris, Morpheus is dispatched by Somnus to make known to Alcyone in a vision the death of Ceyx.

573. Aeŏlĭs. Alcyone, the daughter of Aeolus.

574–576. Indŭăt—gĕrat. Subj. of purpose, H. 497.

578. Jūno was worshiped as the goddess of marriage, and the guardian deity of married women.

579. Nullus, a strong expression for no longer among the living; *who was no more.*

583. Morte, abl. as above, 559, by H. 421, I., and *functo morte*, another euphemistic expression for *mortuo*.

583. Rogari, used as the object of *sustinet;* does not endure being asked.

584. Mănus fūnestās, *unclean hands;* i. e., ceremonially; in accordance with the idea that a house and family were unclean so long as a member of it who had died still lay unburied.

585. Īrĭ. See note, i. 271.

587. Mittat, in subjunctive with *jube*, and *ut* omitted. See H. 535, II., note, and 499, 2.

587. Ĭmāgĭne seems to limit *somnia*, as a descriptive abl. or abl. of quality. H. 419, II.

589. Vĕlāmĭna; acc. by H. 378.

590. Arcuāto, in two syllables, as when written *arquato*.

591. Jussi; i. e., to whom she was *ordered* to go. So above, xi. 142.

592. Cimmerios, a word meaning, perhaps, as Haupt suggests, "the Dark," and the name of a mythical people, mentioned also by Homer (as in Od. xi. 14), as living in the remote West, by the ocean. Here, then, it is that the poet fancies the abode of Somnus to be, in a region enveloped by perpetual mists and darkness.

593. Penetrālĭa, a word of the same origin as *penātes, pĕnĭtus, penetro,* and expressing the idea of somewhat inner, and so secret and sacred. Through the word *penus,* an inner chamber for a *store-house,* it is thought to be allied to *pasco* and kindred words, and to come from a root *pa.*

594. Ŏrĭēns—cādēnsve; i. e., *at his rising, mid-course, or setting.*

596. Dŭbĭaeque—lūcis, *and the dimness of twilight.* Indeed, twilight, as a compound, is just the same as *dubiae lucis,* as *twi* is the Saxon tweon, doubt, and *light* the Saxon leoht. As *dubius* comes from *duo,* may not tweon be allied to twi, or twa, the Saxon for two?

597. Vĭgĭl ālĕs, etc. It is worth while to compare other passages in Ovid, which give expression to the *wakefulness* of the cock, and to the early hour of cock-crowing, Horace's *Sub galli cantum,* Sat. i. 1, 10, which is here poetically given in *Evocat Auroram.* Thus, in the Fasti, i. 455, *cristatus ales,* quod tepidum *vigili provocet ore diem;* also Fasti, ii. 767, Iam dederat *cantus lucis praenuntius ales.* These Latin passages are matched in English in Milton's "Allegro," "While the cock with lively din Scatters the rear of darkness thin."

599. Sāgācĭŏr ānser. On the *sagacity* of the goose, Ovid has also a passage, Met. ii. 538, *servaturis vigili Capitolia voce—anseribus,* in allusion to the preservation of the capitol through the cackling of the geese when the city was taken by the Gauls; Livy, v. 47.

603. Rīvus—Lēthes, etc. Comp. n. vii. 152. The river is similarly described by Milton in "Paradise Lost," ii. 584: "A slow and silent stream, Lethe, the river of oblivion, rolls her watery labyrinth."

610. Mĕdĭo agrees with *antro,* and *ĕbĕno* limits *sublimis; ebeno* for the bedstead made of *ivory,* and so = *spondā ebeninā.* *In the middle of the cave is a bolster, raised high (sublimis) on an ivory bedstead.*

616. Vĭrgo; Iris.

618. Sācrā, because the dwelling of a god.

619. Relābens; he will, on raising his heavy eyes, raise himself up, but again and again *slips back,* and his *nodding chin* strikes the *top of his breast.*

621. Sĭbĭ se; he *shakes himself* out of himself; i. e., *out of sleep.*

625. Mulces reminds us of Young's familiar line: "Tired nature's sweet restorer, balmy sleep!"

626. Quae—aequent; subjunctive of result, Gr. 500; such as may resemble; i. e, *representing real forms.*

627. Trāchīnē; we should expect the acc. of place instead of the abl. (Herculeam Trachina) after *adeant*. *Hercŭlĕă*, so called because in Trachis, a town in Thessaly, Hercules was said to have lived in the last part of his life.

630. Vaporis, in allusion to the *poppies* and other plants mentioned in line 605.

632. Arcus; i. e., *the rainbows*, as described vi. 63.

633–635. Pater, Somnus.——**Morphea,** from Morpheus, from μορφή, the god of dreams; so called from the *forms* which he calls up before the sleeper. The words *artificem—figurae* thus explain the Greek word.

638. Alter; i. e., *a second one*, whose names are given in the next line.

640. Icĕlon—Phobētŏra, Greek words, meaning, the former, *similis*, like; the latter, one who terrifies.

642. Phantăsos, the god of appearances or apparitions, from the same Greek root as our words fancy, phantasm, fantastic, and the like.

647. Thaumantĭdos; i. e., of Iris, the daughter of Thaumas, son of Pontus and Gaea.

652. Haemŏnĭam. Trachis was a city of Thessaly, which was called Haemonia, from Haemon, father of Thessalus.

662. Me; i. e., meum reditum, as above, in l. 576. *Falso* is an adverb, qualifying *promittere*, the two words expressing a false expectation; *do not cherish a false expectation of my return.*

669. Lūgūbria, used substantively for *lugubria vestimenta; put on mourning.*

678. Illīc, join with *sit, if he is there, who seemed just now to be* (there).

697. Fuit; *it would have been.* See II. 476, 5.

698. De—quicquam, *any of my life-time.*

699. Non simul, not with you; i. e., *without you.*

700. In her sense of one-ness with him, she feels that in his dying she has died herself, and that parted from him (since te) it is the same as if she too had been drowned in the sea.

706. Littĕra, meaning the inscription on the tomb.

710–748. On awaking from sleep Alcyone hastens to the shore, whence she sees the form of her husband, and, in springing forward to meet him, is changed, together with him, into a bird.

713. Hoc—litŏre, *at this* spot on the *shore*.

719. Ōmine; she looks at it as a new omen of the death of her husband, that just here and now she sees this body of a *shipwrecked man* (*naufrăgus*).

30. THE HOUSE OF FAME. 215

722, 723. Quo—mentis, *the more she looks upon it,* the less and less has she of her senses; i. e., *the more and more is she beside herself.* The repetition of the comparative *minus* expresses the gradual loss of consciousness; compare the repetition, in the next two lines, of *jam.*

724. Quod—posset, the subjunctive expresses result; *now so near that she could—*

729. Facta manu, *made by* man's *hand;* hence our word manufacture, and its cognates.

734, 735. Maesto—rostro; *maesto,* sc. sono. *Tenui* describes the *slender* shape of the halcyon's beak. The *mournful* notes of the bird are mentioned by other writers, as Homer, Iliad, 9, 561; Propertius, iii. 10, 9.

741, 742. Superis; Vergil makes the bird the favorite of Thetis, as in Georg. i. 399, Dilectae Thetidi alcyones. For the construction in abl. *alite,* see II. 422, note 2.

742—744. Fatis isdem; i. e., in both of them being changed into birds.——**Obnoxius,** *subject.*——**Coeunt,** *they mate.*

745. Hiberno, etc. So Pliny, Hist. Nat. 10, 99—*bruma,* qui dies halcyonides vocantur, placido mari per eos. The tenacity of the story is illustrated by our own expression, "halcyon days," as used in literature as well as in life. So Denham says of Augustus, "His *halcyon days* brought forth the arts of peace." As to the *nests,* the halcyons or kingfishers build on cliffs or in holes in the rocks; but, from these nests being often washed off by the waves, there probably arose the story of their building on the *surface of the sea, pendentibus aequore; sea-hanging nests.*

30. THE HOUSE OF FAME.

XII. 39–63.

This description, by the poet, of the House of Fame, is incidental to his mention of the intelligence having reached the Trojans that the Greeks were nearing their shores. From this house it is, as the poet fancies it, that the intelligence has issued. For a description of *Fama* herself, see Vergil, Aen. iv. 173.

39. Orbe, here and in line 63, for the circle of the universe; like the Scripture expression of the earth, "It is He that sitteth upon the circle of the earth." Isa. xl. 22. The same idea is in the next line, *mundi;* so, too, the *orbis* includes earth, sea, and sky—*terras, fretum, caelestes plagas.*

41. Regionibus is an abl. of specification.

42. Penetrat depends also upon *unde.*

46. Tota agrees with *domus*, to be supplied.

49. Murmŭra, in connection with *fremit*, line 47, seems to express a kind of *hum*, like Thomson's "ceaseless hum" in the "woods at noon," or, as the poet has it here himself, of the far-off waves, or the distant thunder.

53, 54. Lĕve, *a light crowd*, appositive to *milia rumorum*. *Commenta* agreeing with *milia* instead of *rumorum;* he might have written milia commentorum rumorum.

57, 58. Mensūraque, etc. Like Vergil's description in Aen. iv. 195, Mobilitate viget, *viresque acquirit eundo*. Comp. also Ovid himself, in ix. 137.

61. Dubioque auctore, abl. of characteristic.

31. ACIS AND GALATEA.
XIII. 750–897.

750–777. Gălătēa tells the story of her love for Acis, and her hatred of the Cyclops, and of the love of the Cyclops for herself.

750. Fauno; the name of an old king of Latium, who, after his death, was worshiped as the god of fields and flocks: afterward identified with the Greek god Pan.——**Sȳmaethĭde;** Symaethis, the daughter of the river-god Symaethus; the river was on the east coast of Sicily, near Mt. Aetna. For the ablative with *cretus*, Gr. 415, II.

752. Me, i. e., Galatea, who is speaking.

753. Nātālibus, ablative of quality, Gr. 419, II.; and the whole expression *octonis—actis* is a circumlocution for age; he had passed twice eight *birthdays*.

754. Mālas; observe the long penult. The word, meaning *cheek*, is allied to the verb *mando*, to chew.

755. Cȳclops, from the Greek word meaning round-eyed; Polyphemus, like all the Cyclopes, was represented as having but one eye, and that in the middle of the forehead.

755. Finĕ is here feminine, though generally masculine; Gr. 107, I.

758. Prŏ, interjection with *Venus*.

759. Almă, from *alo*, and a constant epithet for Venus as the source of life and growth in nature; *nourishing*.

760. Silvis, dative limiting *horrendus;* the rude Cyclops was *a terror even to the woods*. *Horrendus* is a common epithet with *silva* or *nemus*. So also *Sylvanus*, the god of the woods, is called *horridus* or *horrendus*, from *horreo* in its primary meaning.

31. ACIS AND GALATEA.

761. Join *cum dis* with *Olympi, of Olympus and its gods*. Compare below, lines 843 and 857.

765. Rastris. Such a monster needed a *rake* for a comb, and a *scythe* (*falce*) for a razor.

770. Tĕlĕmus ; *Telemus, the son of Eurymus*, the soothsayer of the Cyclops, and one *whom no bird had deceived*, i. e., who always read aright the omens.

773. Ŭlĭxes ; in allusion to Homer's story in the Odyssey, that Ulysses put out the one eye of Polyphemus.

775. Altĕră—răpŭit. Love makes the rude Cyclops quite fine in his wit. He says, *the other* (meaning Galatea, as the other of the two) *has already robbed me* of my sight, thus confessing how love has blinded him.

776. Grădiēns—passu. Hoping to see his love, who is a Nereid, and so a sea-nymph, *he stalks along the shore with huge step ; litora* the object alike of *gradiens* and *degrăvat*.

778-809. Galatea goes on to tell how Polyphemus turns minstrel, through the influence of his love, and how he lauds her charms in song, and also bewails her coldness to him.

778. The poet describes here a *wedge-like* (*cuneatus*) promontory stretching far out into the sea.

780. Mĕdius ; he sat *sat down* on *the middle of the hill*, so as to command a view of the sea on both sides.

783. Antemnis, etc. The *pine-wood staff* was *big enough to carry a sail-yard*.

784. Centum ; the *shepherd's pipe* (*fistula*), usually *made of* (*composita*) seven reeds, is made of a *hundred* for the Cyclops.

785. Sibĭlă, *pipings*.

789. Ligustri, a white plant, *the privet*, Vergil's *album ligustrum*, Ecl. 2, 18.

791. Lascivior, *more playful*. The line is imitated in the English song: "O nymph more bright Than moonshine night, Like *kidlings*, blithe and merry."

792. Lēvior, *smoother*. What would *lĕvior* mean?

795. Ūvā ; in the English song, "Ripe as the melting cluster."

798. Ĕădem ; *yet the same Galatea is also*, etc.; in the English song again: "Yet *hard to tame* As raging flame, And fierce as storms that bluster."

800. Lentior—sălĭcis, etc. The willow, because so pliant and flexible, is hard to break; and so when used of character, as here of a coy maiden, comes to mean *inflexible.* The *vitis alba* is a creeping vine, called (from the Greek) *bryony.*

803. The **trĭbŭlus** is a prickly plant, *the caltrop. Fēta, with young,* from the root fu, fe (as in fu-i, fe-lix); the bear is then most *fierce.*

810—837. In illustration of *si—noris* (*if you* only *knew* me *well*) he goes on to tell how much he has to offer her.

810. Pars montis expresses how great his *cave* is, and *vivo—saxo,* hanging with living stone, describes the cave as arched with *living stone.*

816. Frāgă lĕges ; see note i. 104, and for *corna,* ib. 105.

819. Dēĕrunt, dissyllable, as in i. 77.

821. Multae, sc. pecudes, as suggested by the generic word *pecus.*

826. Ut means here *how ; you yourself can see how.* Then *uber* is the object of *circumeant,* and the preposition (*circum*) is quite in place to describe the movement of the legs around the amply filled udders ; *how on both sides of the distended udder they can scarcely move their legs.* But Siebelis makes *ut—circumeant* the result after *distentum* sc. ita, and *uber* the object of *videre,* a forced and unnatural construction.

830. Partem is the object of *durant,* and *coagula* the subject. *Coagulum* (from *cogo*) means, first, something that coagulates or curdles, as here, and then (passively) something which is coagulated, as curdled milk. Thus it is like our Saxon word rennet or runnet, which is also used in the passive sense as well as in the active. The *coagulum, rennet* (which is prepared from the stomachs of calves), when *softened in water* (*liquefacta*), *hardens* or curdles the milk, so as to make cheese.

833. Parvĕ ; i. e., *par* and *vĕ, or a pair.*

838-858. The Cyclops goes on to describe his own personal attractions.

844. Torvos, here in a good sense, *earnest.*

853. Orbis, in the sense of *oculus ; yet the sun has* but *a single* (round) *eye.*

854. Gĕnĭtor ; i. e., Vulcan, the father of Galatea.

859-869. He would not take it so hard of Galatea, if she were just as indifferent to all others.

859. Contemptūs, genitive (of fourth decl.), limits *patientior.*

863. Quod nollem refers only to *tibi ;* it is the pleasing Galatea (*tibi*) that he *wouldn't like ;* he may please himself as much as he likes.

864. Sentiet, etc., is the conclusion to the condition to *placeat licebit ;* but *modo—detur* is interposed. Only let the chance be given me, or *let me only get the chance ! Pro* means here *in proportion to.*

868. Cumque—Aetnam. It seems to him as if he were carrying in his breast all the raging violence of Aetna's fires. It was fabled that Vulcan's forge was under Aetna.

870-884. All at once the Cyclops catches sight of Galatea and her lover, and forthwith hurls at Acis a huge rock.

874. The *que* really belongs to *exclamat, and shouts*.

875. Sit depends upon *faciam, ut* omitted. *I will make that the last,* etc.

876. Tantăque, etc.; *and such a voice as the Cyclops ought to have had, that he had;* he had just such a voice as you would fancy such a creature to have.

884. Angŭlus is only another expression (the corner) for *partem e monte;* though it was only the very edge of the piece of rock that *reached him,* yet it dashed Acis quite to pieces.

885-897. Galatea does her utmost for her poor lover; she turns him into a stream, which flows from under the rock.

886. Ăvītas, *of his grandfather,* the river-god Symaethus.

887. Intra—exĭguum; *temporis* limits *exiguum; in a short time.*

890. Mŏrā, with delay; i. e., *gradually.*

894. Cornua cannis; as in ix. 3, so here, horns wreathed with the reed that grows by the river-side are with the poets characteristic of the river-gods.

895. Caerŭlus, because the color of the sea; so also, with the poets, of the sea-gods; as in i. 275, of Neptune.

32. THE EPILOGUE.

XV. 871-879.

In these concluding lines of the poem, Ovid proudly predicts his own immortality as a poet. He has given expression to the same sentiments in his "Amores," iii. 15, 7; ib. 20; and also in his "Ars Amatoria," iii. 339, 340. Compare with these passages of Ovid, the celebrated ode of Horace, iii. 30, *Exegi monumentum aere perennius*, with the introduction and notes to it in my edition of Horace.

871. Jŏvĭs Ira, by metonymy for *fulmen,* lightning. Compare in xv. 811, *fulminis iram.*

872. Ĕdax, *devouring,* as in xv. 234, *tempus ĕdax rerum.* From what verb is *ĕdax* (observe the short *ĕ*) derived ? Horace has Od. iii. 30, 3, *imber edax.*

873. Corpŏris—jus. *Jus* with the genitive, as in ii. 48, *power over.*

875. Partĕ tămen, etc. So in Horace, *multaque pars mei.* Od. iii. 30, 6. The *better part* he counts to be his poetic genius and fame.

876. Indēlēbĭlĕ; a briefer expression for Horace's *crescam laude recens.*

878. Ōrĕ lĕgar, etc. Compare the poet's words in his "Tristia," iv. 10, 127; iii. 7, 50; iii. 14, 19.

AMORES.

1. The Poet's Defense.

I. 15.

The poet celebrates the praises of the great bards, Greek and Roman, and the noble offices they have discharged—in answer to the carpings of envious dullards. Horace has a parallel passage in his "Ars Poetica," 391–407. Wordsworth expresses a similar sentiment in his "Personal Talk": "Blessings be with them, and eternal praise, Who gave us nobler loves, and nobler cares, The poets, who on earth have made us heirs Of truth and pure delight by heavenly lays!"

1. Quid. *Why?* See Gr. 454, 2.——On **ĕdax** see note, Met. xv. 872. ——**Livor,** which literally means a bluish color, is figuratively used, as here, for *envy;* perhaps because the face takes on a bluish complexion when the heart is suffering from envy or malice.

3. Me, with *sĕqui,* dependent upon *ŏbicĭs.* Indeed, these three accusatives with their infinitives seem to be used appositively, to illustrate *obicĭs annos* and *vŏcas carmĕn.* The poet resents the inference, that because he has not, like most Romans, given himself to *arms (mĭlĭtiae),* or to legal learning *(leges),* or to public life *(foro),* therefore his years are *inactive,* and his poetry the *work of an idle mind.*

6. Prōstĭtŭĭsse; not in so bad a sense as our derived word to prostitute, though it is used disparagingly; from its literal meaning, to put a thing forward *(pro* and *statuo),* it comes to mean, to make a show of anything, and so to offer it for sale or for hire. So Juvenal, Sat. vii. 149, *mercedem ponere linguae.*

7. Mortăle—perennis; the contrast of the two words is well expressed by their being put, the one in the first place in the line, the other in the last.

9. Maeŏnĭdes; of Maeonia, or Lydia, of which Homer, who is here referred to, was supposed to be a native. Of the seven cities, which

1. THE POET'S DEFENSE. 221

claimed the honor of giving Homer birth, two were in Maeonia, viz., Smyrna and Colophon.

9, 10. Tĕnĕdos—Ide—aquas. Tenedos, an island off the Trojan coast. To this Vergil refers in Aen. ii. 21, Est in conspectu Tenedos, etc. Ida is the name of the mountain range around Troy, and the Simöis and the Scamander were the two famous Trojan rivers.

11. Ascraeus, *the Ascraean,* i. e., the poet Hesiod, so called from Ascra, in Boeotia, where he lived. See Epist. ex Ponto, iv. 14, 31. He wrote a didactic poem called Ἔργα καὶ Ἡμέραι, "Works and Days," to which Vergil alludes in his Georgics, ii. 176, Ascraeumque cano Romana per oppida carmen. It treated, among other subjects, of the vintage (*uva*), and of farming (*Ceres*).

13. Battĭădes, *the son of Battus,* i. e., Callimachus. It may be, however, that the patronymic means that he was a native of Cyrene, a city founded by Battus. He was a writer of elegies.

14. Quamvis—non valet. The corresponding clause is, *arte valet; though not in genius,* yet *in art.*

15. The *cothurnus,* the thick-soled, high-heeled shoe, *the buskin,* worn by tragic actors to help give them the heroic stature, befitting the characters in tragedy. It is here, as often, used for *tragoedia,* as *buskin* in English for *tragedy.* So *soccus,* the name of the low shoe worn by comic actors, is used for *comedy.* Sŏphocles was the greatest of the three great Greek tragic writers.

16. Ărātus; a Greek poet who had lived at Soli, in Cilicia (circa 260 B. C.), author of a poem called "Phaenomena." Cicero translated it into Latin verse. The Apostle Paul quoted from this poem in his Mars-Hill address to the Athenians, in Acts, xvii. 28, "For we are also his offspring."

18. Mĕnandros. The first in merit of the writers of the so-called New Comedy in Greek literature; he was born at Athens 321 B. C., and died there 291 B. C. Terence made free use of his plays in his Latin comedies. The *tricky slave,* the *harsh father,* the *base procuress,* and the *flattering harlot* always were found among Menander's *dramatis personae.*

19. Ennius, called "noster Ennius" by Lucretius, i. 119, was the founder of Roman literature, and the author of a celebrated epic, called "Annales," the history of Rome in verse. We have extant fragments of his poetry, which have been collected from quotations from Cicero and other writers. Cicero called him *Summus poeta noster* (Pro Balbo, 22). The expression *arte carens* is illustrated by Ovid in another passage (Tristia, ii. 259), Ennius ingenio maximus, arte rudis. Horace alludes to him in several passages, Ars Poetica, 58, 258, and Sat. i. 10, 53.

19. Accius, a Latin writer of tragedies, born 170 B. C., died 103 B. C. The epithet *animosi, spirited,* is well illustrated by Horace, Ep. ii. 1, 55, famam senis Accius *alti.*

21, 22. Varrōnem—dŭci. Publius Terentius Varro, called Ătăcī-nus, from the river Atax, on the banks of which he was born, wrote a poem on the voyage of the Argo (*ratem*), and on the fortunes of Jason, the son of Aeson (*Aesonio*), and the *leader* (*duci*) of the Argonauts. *Aurea* of course refers to the *golden* fleece, that the expedition went in quest of. But Varro's poetry was far inferior to his learning. St. Augustin well calls him "doctissimus Romanorum Varro;" "Civitas Dei," vii.

23. Carmĭnă—Lŭcrētĭ; the celebrated poem, "De Rerum Natura," of Lucretius, who died 55 B. C. Ovid's praise of him is amply deserved; and it is significant of his judgment of his poetic merits that, while he conceives of the fame of the Aeneid (just below, in lines 25, 26) as co-eval with the duration of Rome's supremacy, he predicts here that the Lucretian poetry will perish only when the world itself perishes. In the words exitio—una dies, he evidently has in mind the lines of Lucretius, v. 93 seqq., and especially (96) Una dies dabit exitio, etc.

28. Tĭbullĕ. Albius Tibullus, a contemporary and friend of Ovid, wrote elegies, and also love-poetry (*ignes—Cupidinis*). It is his death which is the subject of the next selection from the "Amores."

29. Gallus; another Roman elegiac poet of Ovid's times. *Lȳcŏris* was the name of his love, who was celebrated in his elegies. Gallus was a friend of Vergil, who celebrates him in his Tenth Eclogue.

31. Ergo, etc. From this brilliant list of poets Ovid now argues, in his defense, the *undying* nature of poetry (*morte carent*).

34. Tagi; the river in Spain, celebrated also by Vergil, Aen. x. 141, Juvenal (xiv. 299), and other poets, on account of its golden sands.

36. Castālĭă plēnă. Castalia, the name of the famous spring on Parnassus, and associated ever with Apollo and the Muses.

2. THE DEATH OF TIBULLUS.

III. 9.

1. Memnŏnă. Memnon was the son of *Eos* or *Aurora* (*mater*) and Tithonus. He was the nephew of Priam, whom he assisted in the Trojan war. He was killed by Achilles.

1. Achillem; the son of Thetis. He was killed by Paris, the son of Priam.

2. THE DEATH OF TIBULLUS.

3, 4. Flēbĭlĭs—ĕrĭt. Elegeia, here personified for elegiac verse; the word itself is probably derived from Greek words expressive of the cry of grief. Hence *ex vero*, as by the death of the elegiac poet Tibullus the name proves quite too *true*.

5. Tŭi—tŭā, of *thy* work—*thy* fame, because the *work* is elegy, and the *fame* is elegiac. For a mention of Tibullus, see note, Amores, i. 15, 28.

7. Puer Vĕnĕris ; Cupido, the son of Venus. As Tibullus wrote love-poetry also, Cupido is here represented as present at the funeral with *quiver reversed*, his *bows broken*, his *torch unlighted*, his *wings drooping* (*demissis alis*), and himself *sobbing loudly* (*singultu sonant*), and *beating his breast* for grief.

13. Fratris. As Aeneas was fabled to be the son of Venus, he was the *brother* of Cupido. Iulus, the son of Aeneas, from whose *dwelling* the funeral procession of his father *went out*.

16. Jŭvĕnĭ, in allusion to Adonis, beloved of Venus, who was killed by a wound from the tusks of a *wild boar* (*ferus aper*). The word *juveni* is in the dative, limiting *rupit*, and *inguen* is the direct object.

17. At, etc. *But,* the poet exclaims, *we are called sacred poets and the care of the gods ;* and yet, he implies, Tibullus, the sacred poet, is dead.

19. Săcrum is here well opposed to *profānat*. *Sacrum*, from the root sa, as also the English word safe, save, and hence something in the care of a divinity, and so sacred. Prŏfănat, from *pro* and *fanum* (fa), before the fane; i. e., outside of it, profane. Thus *death* puts *everything sacred*, as it were, outside the fane or *consecrated* place; *profanes* it.

20. Obscūrās, perhaps = *nigras*, as the darkness of the lower world (Hades) was associated with death. *Obscurus* is derived from the root sku, scu, meaning to cover. So with the preposition ob, the *hands* of *death* cover over; covering over, or *darkening*.

21. Ismărĭo ; i. e., Thracian, from Ismarus, a mountain and city in Thrace. Orpheus was a poet of Thrace, the fabled son of Apollo and the Muse Callīŏpe; according to other poets, however, his father was Oeăgrus.

22. Victas—feras. As in Metam. x. 41, seqq., Ovid sings of the wondrous influence of Orpheus's music as bringing a respite to the condemned in the lower world, so here, as often among the poets, he *conquers wild beasts* with his lyre. So also Horace, in describing the civilizing influence of Orphean music, says: Dictus ob hoc lenire tigres rabidosque leones.

23. Idem păter; i. e., Apollo, the *father* also of Linus, the other Thracian bard; Aclĭnŏn, the Greek word (ἂι Λίνος), "woe is me for Linos," Apollo's lamentation for his son.

25. Maeŏnĭden. See note, Amores, i. 15, 9.

26. Pĭĕrĭis. Pieria, a country between Macedonia and Thessaly, was the fabled haunt of the Muses; hence *Pierian waters* is a figurative expression for poetry.

27. Averno; here figurative for death, as lake Avernus, in Campania, was thought of as an entrance to the lower world. So also in Metam. v. 540; x. 51.

29, 30. Only the poets' work endures, as the Aeneid of Vergil, *Trojani —lābōris*, and the Odyssey of Homer (*tĕlă rĕtexta*). The last expression refers to the story in the Odyssey of Penelope's robe or *web woven over and over again*. In Ulysses's long absence, she was beset by suitors, whom she put off by saying that she could not marry till she had finished the robe she was weaving. By an ingenious *device* (*dolo*) she unwove by night (*nocturno*) what she had woven by day. Odyssey, ii. 93–110.

31. Nĕmĕsis—Dēlĭa; names familiar alike to the poetry and to the heart (*cura, amor*) of Tibullus.

34. Sistra; the *sistrum* was a kind of *rattle* used in the worship of the Egyptian Isis, during the praying and singing. Isis had many worshipers also in Rome.

35. Fasso, from fătĕor, sc. mihi. He would fain be pardoned for confessing to his temptation to skepticism, when he sees that ill fates befall the good as well as the bad.

39. Jăcĕt; here in the sense of *lying* dead.——**Ecce,** *see!* A good illustration of the view, that *ecce* has the same root, ok, ac, as *oculus*, the root meaning *to see*.

41. Rŏgāles. See note on *rogo*, line 6; also note, Metam. iv. 166. The *urna* in the preceding line refers to the same rite of burning the bodies of the dead, as the ashes of the dead were collected in an urn and deposited in the sepulchre. English poetry is full of allusions to this ancient rite; as in that fine word of "the great of old," in Byron's Manfred: "The dead but sceptred sovereigns, who still rule our spirits from their urns."

44. Quae, referring to *flammae*. *Sustinuere*, from meaning bore up, comes to mean here *ventured* (*to do*).

45. Quae; i. e., Venus, who was worshiped in a celebrated temple on the top of Mount Eryx, in Sicily.

46. Nĕgant; for the indicative, see Gr. 503, I., note 3.

8. FAREWELL TO LOVE-SONGS. 225

47. Phaeācĭă. Corcyra, the fancied abode of Alcinous and the Phaeacians of the Odyssey. Tibullus had gone to Corcyra for his health. The *soil* (*solo*) is called *vile* (*vili*) because Homer represents the Phaeacians as lovers of sensual pleasures.

49. Hinc; i. e., from Rome (and not Corcyra), and from his dying at Rome.——**Ocellos,** poetic for *oculos.*——**Pressit,** *closed;* and **fūgĭentĭs** (acc. plural, Gr. 62), *dying.*

52. Cŏmas, the acc. of specification; Gr. 378.

53. Prior; i. e., Delia, as above, 32, *primus amor.* The first que = *both.*

57. Tibi—dolori. Gr. 390.

62. Calvo, a poet who wrote elegies and love poems, none of which, however, have come down to us. Cicero speaks of him as an orator, in "Brutus," 81, 82; Horace, as Ovid here, in connection with Catullus, as a poet, Sat. i. 10, 19. Catullus (87–54 B. C.) excelled in lyrics and other kinds of poetry; many of his poems are preserved to us. He is called *doctus* from his familiar acquaintance with Greek literature.

64. Galle; see note, Amores, i. 15, 29. The clause *si falsum,* etc., modifies *prodige.* Gallus lost the favor of Augustus because suspected of treason (*temerati—amici*), and therefore committed suicide in his fortieth year.

65. Si quă est modo, etc., *if only there is any shadow of the body;* i. e., if you live at all; in allusion to the ordinary belief that the departed still existed, but in quite unsubstantial forms, *umbrae* or *imagines.*

68. Nōn ŏnĕrōsă. The peace of the dead is often prayed for in such words as these. It was a common form of sepulchral inscription, *sit tibi terra levis.*

3. FAREWELL TO LOVE-SONGS.

III. 15.

2. Rādĭtŭr. *Rado,* literally to scrape, or scratch, is often used of the race-course in the sense of just touching, grazing, the *metae,* or turning-posts. On *Meta* see note, Metam. ii. 142.

3. Peligni. Sulmo, the poet's birthplace, was in the country of the Peligni, in Central Italy.

5. A prŏăvis. He claims that he is of equestrian rank by ancestry, not by the *whirling round* (*turbine*) of military promotion. And that, perhaps, is worth boasting of, *si quid id est.*

10. Sŏcĭas—arma, the so-called Social war (90, 89 B. C.), sometimes called Italian, of the allied Italian nations against Rome. The Peligni were one of these nations. *Libertas,* because the allies were contending for the Roman franchise.

11. Ăquōsī ; so called because the neighborhood abounded in springs and streams.

15. Ămăthūsĭa ; Venus, who was so called from Amathus, a town in Cyprus, where she was worshiped.

16. Aurea—signa ; figurative for breaking with love-poetry, as the Roman soldiers *pulled up the standards* from the ground when they broke up the camp and left a place.

17. Lўaeus, a Greek epithet of Bacchus, corresponding to the Latin Liber, the deliverer from care. Bacchus was often represented as a bull (*corniger*).

17. Incrĕpŭlt, sc. me, *has chided me ; thyrso graviore ;* the thyrsus was the ivy-twined Bacchic staff, which by its stroke was thought to incite the "fine frenzy" of the poet. Here the word, with *graviore*, means a *more dignified style of poetry.* He should turn from love-poems to tragedies ; perhaps he at that time turned to the writing of his tragic poem *Medea.*

FASTI.

1. ROMULUS AND REMUS.

II. 383-422.

In the context Ovid has been treating of those holy-days of the Roman Calendar which were called the Lupercalia. The inquiry into their origin and the etymology of the word brings him here to the story of the birth of Romulus and Remus.

383. Silvia, the mother of Romulus and Remus ; known also by the name of Ilia, and of Rhea, and of Rhea Silvia. She was a *Vestal,* or priestess of Vesta. *Caelestia,* because the fabled offspring of Mars.

384. Pătrŭo ; i. e., Amulius, the brother of Numitor.

385. In amne. Livy tells the story (Book i. 4) of the children's exposure, and its result.

387. Rĕcūsantes. The obsolete simple verb *cuso* has the same root (skav) as the verb *caveo,* and so, in all its forms, carries the notion of a *cautious,* deliberate procedure. Here the compound word implies that the servants go through with the orders *reluctantly.*

389. Albŭlă. Livy also (i. 3) gives this name for the river, and in the

1. ROMULUS AND REMUS. 227

same chapter mentions Tiberinus as an Alban king, who was drowned in the Albula, and so gave the name Tiber to the river.

391. Vĭdērēs; *you might have seen.* See Gr. 485, note 1.

392. Valles. The valley between the Palatine and the Aventine; in the olden time, the *Vallis Murtia* (or *Murcia*); in Ovid's day, the Circus Maximus.

395. The *At* expresses their admiration.

398. Suspīcer, potential; *I should* (or may) *suspect;* but some MSS. read *suspicor*. *Vobis* dat with *esse*. It seems, he means, as if they may be of a divine origin. And yet (as in lines 399, 400) if *a god were their father*, then *would he lend aid in so perilous a time*.

405. Vāglĕrunt. For the quantity of the penult, see Gr. 586, II. 4. On *putares*, see note above on l. 391.——**Sensisse,** *that they were aware* of their peril; i. e., from their wailing cry.

407. Alveus is the vessel in which they were put. Meaning first hollowness, it next means the hollow of the body, the *alvus;* then the channel of a river, as hollowed out by the stream; then the hollow or hold of a ship; and finally, as here, a hollow vessel, whatever it was, which served the children for a cradle. From its being called, in the next line, *tabella*, *a little board* or *plank*, we may fancy it a rude piece of wood, hollowed out for the purpose.

412. Rūmīna—Rōmŭlă. These words, as well as Roma itself, are probably all from rūma, rūmis, rūmen, and these from the root sru, to flow, break forth. *Ruma* means the breast that gives suck; hence *Rūmīna*, the goddess of nursing mothers; also *Ruminalis*, of the fig-tree, as fruitful. So Rumon is an old name for the river Tiber, and then Roma (= Srouma, Rouma), the city of the river, and *Romulus*, the child of the city. See Vanicek, Lat. Etym. Wörterbuch. Livy, i. 4, gives the same account as Ovid of the names of the fig-tree, Ruminal and Romular.

416. Sustĭnĕre. See note, Amores, iii. 9, 44.

417. Caudā; i. e., *by* (wagging) *her tail*.

418. Fingit linguā—suā; fashions with her tongue; i. e., by licking them; she licks them into shape! So, too, Vergil, Aen. viii. 635, Mulcere alternos et *corpora fingere lingua*.

420. Nec = et non; *Et*—aluntur ope lactis *non* sibi promissi.

421. Now the poet comes to the origin of the words Lupercal and Luperci. *Illa* refers to *lupa*.

2. THE DEIFICATION OF ROMULUS.

II. 475-512.

475. Proxĭmă. He has been treating of the Lupercalia, which fell on the 15th of February; *the next day* (*lux*) *is free;* i. e., no holy-day. But *the third* (*at tertia*), i. e., the 17th of February, is consecrated to Quirinus.

477. Sive, etc. The poet now gives the various derivations of the word *Quirinus:* 1, from *cŭris* or *quiris,* the Sabine spear; 2, from *Quirītes;* 3, from the town *Cures.*

481. Păter; Mars, the father of Romulus.

484. Sanguinis mei; i. e., my son Romulus.

485. Intercĭdit alter; i. e., Remus, who had been killed. He would thus have Romulus (*erit qui—restat*) to represent both himself and the lost Remus.

487. Unus, etc.; a line quoted from Ennius, both here and in Metam. xiv. 814, and prophetic of the deification of Romulus.——**In caerula caeli,** "to the blue of the heavens," poetic for caerulum caelum, as in English the *azure heavens.*

491. Capreae pălūdem; a place in the Campus Martius. So also Livy, i. 16, ad Caprae paludem; a chapter in which Livy, in a vein no less poetic than Ovid's, narrates the translation of Romulus to the skies.

496. Astra—equis. So Horace, O. iii. 3, 15: Quirinus, *Martis equis* Acheronta fugit.

497. Falsaeque, etc.; for falso in crimine caedis; *were falsely charged with murder.* Livy, in B. i. 16, refers to this as a report on the part of some; *discerptum regem patrum manibus.*

501. Sinistrae. As the Roman augurs faced the south, the omens from the east were on their *left,* and so the word *sinister* (unlike our English word sinister), and also *laevus,* came to be used for favorable. With the Greeks, the augur's position was just the reverse; and that made the omens on the right the favorable ones.

502. Horruĕrunt. On the quantity of the penult, see note on Fasti, ii. 405. On the meaning of *horreo,* see note on *horrendus,* Metam. xiii. 760; here render *stood on end.*

508. Militiamque cŏlant. So Livy, i. 16, with more force, and with a diction no less poetic: *rem militarem colant,* sciantque et ita posteris tradere, nullas opes humanas armis Romanis resistere posse.

510. Pŏpŭlos; i. e., the Romans and the Sabines.

3. LUCRETIA.

II. 710-758.

710. Moenia; of Gabii, the conquest of which the poet has just narrated. *Suis* agrees with *ducibus*, and *ducibus*, abl., limits *nuda*. Gr. 414, III.

713. Phoebus; i. e., the oracle at Delphi, which king Tarquin sent his two sons, with Brutus, to consult. So Livy, i. 56.

714. Dĕdĕrit. Why in the future perfect here? Livy says, in like manner, imperium Romae habebit, qui vestrum primus osculum matri *tulerit*. Ovid's *victor erit* is explained by Livy's *imperium habebit;* the question of supremacy, as well as of the prodigy, had been submitted to the oracle.

717. Stulti—Ĭmĭtator; so in Livy, *ad imitationem stultitiae*. *Sapiens*, because he had put on the semblance of being under-witted, in order to escape Tarquin's *plots* (*insidiis*). Hence the word Brutus, the Dullard.

720. Offenso—pede. The participle is here used in the literal sense. *Offendo*, ob and fendo, means to *strike against* something, and so to *stumble*.

721. Ardĕă; a town of the Rutuli in Latium.

726. Rege, in ablative by Gr. 415, II.; *the king's son*.

729. Ecquid, fom *ecquis*, used here, as often, simply as an interrogative particle. *Socialis* is used by Ovid for *conjugalis*, and the whole expression for *conjugium*, and then as here for *conjunx*.

731. Quisque, as an enclitic, usually follows *suus*.

733. Cui—nomen; i. e., Tarquinius Collatinus, the nephew of the king.

738. Nullus. The absence of the janitor from the door is the first indication of something wrong indoors.

740. Posito, in the sense of *apposito*. As Livy has it, they found the princesses *in convivio luxuque cum aequalibus*, but Lucretia, as here in lines 741, 742, deditam lanae inter lucubrantes ancillas.

744. Tenui—sono; the expression reminds one of Shakespeare's words: "Her voice was ever soft, gentle, and low; an excellent thing in woman."

746. Lacerna; a cloak usually worn over the toga; sometimes, as here, used as an army cloak.

749. Restas, in the sense of *resistis, you are withstanding those superior to yourself*.

751. Tantum, etc.; *only let them come back.* *Sed, but* (they may not come back) *enim, for rash is that* (husband) *of mine.*

758. Facies animo digna—par; *her face was in keeping* (*digna—par*) *with the feelings of her heart;* i. e., her sorrow was real, and it showed itself in her tears.

4. THE BUILDING OF ROME.

IV. 809–862.

810. Gĕmĭno; i. e., Romulus and Remus.

815, 816. So Livy, i. 6, *Palatium Romulus, Remus Aventinum*, ad inaugurandum templa capiunt.

818. Stătŭr, sc. iis in the dative; *they stand by the agreement.*

819. Signet, sc. ille. Subjunctive of purpose; *on which to mark* the line of *the walls with the plow.* The ground was to be plowed, according to usage, with *a snow-white* ox and *a white cow, yoked together* (*jugum tulit*), (826) and then earth from the neighborhood and the fruits of the country were thrown into the furrow (821).

820. Pălis, the name of the divinity (Pales) that presided over flocks and herds.

824. Fungĭtur, sc. officio, or some such word; *does its duty.*

825. Stīvam, *the plow-handle,* probably derived from sto, stāre, sta-iva, stīva.

827. Condenti, sc. mihi, limiting *ades.*

833. Laevo. See note on *sinistrae*, Fasti, ii. 501.

838. Ista, i. e., fundamina. *Curae,* sc. tibi.

841. Quod, relative pronoun, and the object of *ignorans.*

842. Iliis, sc. muris, in abl. *With these — ?*

843. Mŏră, sc. est.——**Rŭtro;** from the same root as *ruo;* a *spade* or like farming instrument.

850. Pietas, *his affection for his brother.*

852. Invito, sc. mihi, limiting *adempte.*

854. Cŏmas, acc. of specification.

856. Ultĭmă, used adverbially; *at last.*

860. Pluris, acc. plural.

TRISTIA.

1. THE POET'S DEPARTURE FROM ROME.

I. 3.

The poet describes the misery which befell himself and his family, when ordered suddenly by the emperor to quit Rome, and live in exile at Tomi, a place on the shore of the Euxine.

1. Illius; for the quantity of the penult, see Gr. 577, I. 3.

5. Lux; following *noctem* (3), this word seems to show that it was at daybreak that he was to set out from Rome.

6. Finibus, *dative,* though with *discedere* we might have expected *in fines.* *Ausŏnia* came to be used for Italia, and, as here, for the whole empire, though it applied originally to the country near Beneventum, where lived the Ausŏnes, one of the oldest tribes of Italy.

9. Servorum; legendorum to be supplied, as *legendi* agrees with *comitis.*

16. Mŏdŏ, etc. Before, his friends were *many; now, one or two.*

19. Nata; *his daughter* Perilla, to whom the next elegy (iii. 7) is addressed. She was at this time *far away* in Africa (*Libya*), and so in an *opposite direction* (*diversa*) from that in which his journey lay.

22. Intus. *Indoors,* he means to say, was all the seeming of a noisy (*non taciti*) funeral; *men, women,* and *boys, too,* all as the hired mourners at a funeral wailed over his departure.

29. Suspiciens, *looking up to.* *Ab hac,* from this = (post hanc) *and then looking to the capitol.*

30. Frustrā. He lived near the capitol, where were the temples of Jupiter, Juno, and Minerva, the very sanctuary of Roman religion; but all *in vain* for him was such a sacred vicinity.

34. Este salutati = salvete. Both *salve* and *vale* originally mean "be well," though usually the former is the salutation at meeting, and the latter at parting. Here the poet with *este salutati* says his last *farewells* to the temples and the gods of Rome.

35. Sēro, etc. To take the shield after being wounded came to mean to do a thing too late; and so the poet would say that he would gladly defend his conduct from odium, too late though it is, as his banishment is already ordered.

37. Caelesti viro, i. e., Augusto. The expression illustrates the exalted conception the Romans of the time had of Augustus, or, if one must take that view, the language of adulation which the poets used in all their allusions to him. *Error* used here and elsewhere by Ovid, in explanation of his banishment, to show that it was owing to some *mistake*, and if to a wrong, at least not an intentional one; in next line it was a *culpa* not a *scelus*.

40. Deo, still in allusion to Augustus. If only he be *pacified*, the poet can not be *wretched*.

41. Pluribus, sc. precibus.

44. Extinctos—focos. The extinction of the fire on the family hearth was thought of as the desertion of the home, the going out of the family's life.

45. Adversos, literally turned toward her; *in front of her*.

48. Parrhăsĭs, the Greek form, and poetic in Greek, for *Parrhasia*, and then, as the Parrhasii were an Arcadian tribe, for Arcadian. Arcas, whose mother Callisto was the daughter of Lycaon, king of Arcadia, was changed into a bear (*Arctos*), and then, as the fable has it, was transferred to the skies, and became the constellation of that name. *Versāque ab axe*, turned away from the axis; only a circumlocution for turned toward its setting, which is toward the morning. It seems to be turned to the side opposite to that on which it was at the beginning of the night. The *axis* here is the north star, which seems to be fixed, while the stars turn round it.

53. Sum mentitus; he means that he *often* (*oh, how often !*), in excuse for his delaying, *pretended* that he had a *certain hour* as the *fitting* one for his departure.

62. Utrăque, *both a just* cause for *delay*; in reference to the place he was to leave, and the place to which he was to go.

66. Thēsēā. In allusion to the *fidelity* of Theseus, of Athens, for his friend Pirithŏus; *with a Thesean fidelity*.

72. Lucifer, the name for Venus when it appears as the morning star; a compound Latin word, like the Greek Phosphorus.

75. Metus, also written Mettus; the name of the Alban general who was torn asunder by horses, in punishment for his bad faith to the Romans. See Livy, i. 28.

86. Pietas. From its generic meaning of dutiful disposition, this word means here affection for a husband; as in Fasti, iv. 850, it meant affection for a brother; also, as often, filial affection.

86. Caesar erit, *shall be a Caesar* to me; her affection as a wife just as imperial a rule for her as Caesar's to her husband for his exile.

88. Dĕdit—mănus; a familiar figurative expression in Latin for giving up, or submitting, to a victor or a captor. It is originally used for a captive, when he gives up his hands to be fettered.

89. Sive, etc.; as if he had said, Sive *efferor*, which is the regular word for being carried out to burial; only now he was living and not dead.

92. Sēmĭanĭmĭs ; to be pronounced as a word of four syllables here.

2. To his Daughter Perilla.
III. 7.

This is one of the most touching of all these elegies, one of the *Tristissima* of all the Tristia of Ovid's elegiac Muse. And now it is not so much the capital itself, rich and gay Rome, with its cherished associations of place, delicious climate, and literary and social companionships, of which the poet plaintively sings; but it is his own home, that lost home near by the capitol, and under the shadow of its august and venerable temples (Tristia, i. 3, 29–34), and his wife and daughter there, from whom he is hopelessly parted—all this it is, to which, from his forlorn exile on the Euxine, he casts back his longing eyes and heart; and it is the expression of this "home-sick passion" which gives its singular pathos to the poem. There is, however, another source of interest to this elegy. We learn from it that it was Ovid's good fortune to have a daughter who inherited her father's poetic gifts, and who elicited from him glad words of praise for her own efforts in verse (11–32). There is also a calm dignity imparted to the closing lines, in the exiled poet's expression of his sense of the exalted worth of "the good things of heart and mind," and of the inalienable possessions of poetic gifts and fame. It was a great lesson which he taught his daughter in those words (43, 44):

> Nil non mortale tenemus
> Pectoris exceptis ingeniique bonis.

1. Pĕrărătă. This figure of plowing (*arare*) is derived from the action of the *stilus* on a waxen tablet. So Cicero uses the word *exaro* in Ad Att. xii. 1, Hoc litterarium *exaravi*.

6. Nec mŏră, sc. est; a common expression with Ovid, having the force of an adverb like *statim*.

8. Nec mălă—mŏră ; *lĕvāta*, sc. esse, in the same construction as *vivere*.

11. Ecquid inhaeres, a strong expression for devotion to literary pursuits; *whether you cling to ;* or our word from the Latin, *adhere*, may express it.

12. Non pătrio; *not according to your father's custom.* The meaning is not obvious; perhaps he will say that her poetry is less free and more serious in tone than her father's.

15. Hoc refers to *ingĕnium.*——**Pēgăsĭdas;** Pegasides, from the name of the winged horse Pegăsus, is a name for the Muses, because the fountain Hippocrene, the Greek word for horse's well, was said to have sprung forth where the hoof of Pegasus struck the earth. The fountain was on Mount Helicon, in Boeotia, and was sacred to the Muses.

16. Măle qualifies *pĕrīrĕt.*

19. Ignes—Idem; i. e., of poetic inspiration; the *same fires* of genius.

20. Lesbĭa; i. e., Sappho, the celebrated *poetess of Lesbos.*

25, 26. Aut—aut, *either—or.* The father *either lent his ears to the verses* his daughter had *just composed;* or, if she *had been inactive* in her art, then he would chide her, and so bring *the blush* of shame to her cheek.

27. Exemplo—meae. Instead of *facta ruina,* another reading is *fata secuta,* and there are also conjectural readings. The idea of the poet is probably substantially the same as in line 21, only more fully expressed. He thinks that perhaps from the precedent of her father's suffering such a penalty on account of the books he has written, the daughter may be fatally deterred from continuing her poetical career. The *me laesere libelli* evidently refers to the poet's exile; *exemplo,* too, with *poenae—meae,* has in it the same reference.

29. Tantummŏdŏ—non. We might have expected *ne* instead of *non.* See Gr. 483, 3.

30. Discat ămare; in allusion to his own poems on love, which had done mischief to others as well as to himself.

36. Strĕpĭtum—făciente; i. e., *with an* imperceptible, because *noiseless, step.*

37. Fuit, *was,* with its full aoristic force; her beauty was a thing only of the past.

38. Quĕrĕrĕ; from the quantity of the penult, in what tense?

40. Cēnsĭbus, *riches.* Census from *censeo,* registered property, census, then property in general, possessions.

42. Irus—Croesus; proverbial for a poor, and for a rich, man.

45. Cum; concessive; *though.*

46. Raptă—ădĭmī; *rapio* expresses the *taking away (adimi)* as a sudden, violent act; *have been snatched away* (sc. *ea,* those things), which it *was possible to take away.*

48. In hoc, i. e., *ingenio*. The poet has a proud assurance that his genius was a possession beyond even Caesar's *rapacious* power. See the introduction to the notes on this piece, toward the end.

3. THE POET'S LIFE.
IV. 10.

1. Qui fuĕrim ; dependent upon *ut nōris* in the next line. *Lūsor*, like *lūdo*, is often used of poems of a light, sportive nature ; and *ămorum* is meant for his love-poems.

6. Cōnsŭl ŭterque. The *o* in consul is naturally long. He refers here to the consuls Hirtius and Pansa, who *both fell* at the battle of Mutīna, now Modena, in the year 43 B. C.

7. Si quid, etc. The same line as above, in Amores, iii. 15, 5 ; and the next line is nearly the same as in Amores, iii. 15, 6. See notes on these lines.

10. Quăter qualifies **tribŭs ;** *four times three months before*.

13. Festis—Minervae ; the Quinquatria, the *five days* festival, 19th–23d of March.

14. Pugnā prīmā cruentā. Observe, for the construction, the quantity of the final syllables. There were gladiatorial combats on the second, third, fourth, and fifth days, but none on the first day. Thus *the first which* (*prima quae*, etc.) *is wont to be made bloody* is the second of the five days, and the first of the last four ; and the whole expression is only a circumlocution for the 20th of March as his birthday.

15. Prōtĭnŭs, *forthwith ; tĕnĕrī*, in nom. plural.

16. Ab arte. *Ars* here in the general sense of knowledge, learning ; and *ab* shows from what the distinction (*insignes*) comes ; *distinguished for their learning*.

19. Caelestia, heavenly ; used, as so often *divina*, for *the exalted* pursuits of poetry and letters.

24. Sŏlūtā mŏdis, freed from measures ; i. e., prose.

25. Spontĕ suā. So Pope says of himself, in imitation of these words: "I lisped in numbers, for the numbers came."

28. Libĕrior, only another expression for *virīlis*, the robe of manhood, which brought more freedom with it.

29. The *latus clavus*, or *broad stripe of purple* on the tunic, was properly the distinction of senators ; then it was allowed by Augustus to the sons of senators, and finally to the sons of *equites*, or knights, who possessed the fortunes of senators.

34. Vĭris—trĭbŭs. He means that he was sometimes one of the *triumviri*. There were different offices which had this name, as Triumviri *Capitales, Nocturni, Monetales*, commissions of three, which had charge respectively of capital punishments, of the night police, and of the Mint.

35. Curia, i. e., the senate-house, used here, as often, for the senate itself. The poet means that it only *remained* for him to be a senator; but, as he goes on to say, he waived that, and so assumed the *angustus clavus, the narrow stripe* of purple, the usual equestrian badge. This was customary with those sons of wealthy knights who did not aspire to public office. *Coacta est* here means *narrowed*.

38. Ambĭtĭonis; for the genitive, see Gr. 399, II.

39. Ăŏnĭae. Aonia was another name for Boeotia, where was Mt. Helicon; the Muses thus were *Aonian sisters*.

43, 44. Suas vŏlŭcres, *his birds*. Aemilius Macer wrote a poem on *birds, serpents*, and *plants*.

45. Propertius. Sextus Aurelius Propertius, an elegiac poet, older than Ovid, younger than Tibullus; his poems have come down to us in four books of elegies.

47. Hērŏō, sc. versu. Ponticus is mentioned by Propertius, i, 7, 1, as an epic poet. *Bassus* is also mentioned by Propertius, but nothing more is known of him as a poet.

50. Ausŏnĭā, for Italica or Latina, as in Tristia, i. 3, 6, where see note. It was the boast of Horace that he was the lyric poet of Rome, especially that he was the first to illustrate in Latin the Greek lyric measures. See the last ode of Horace in the third book.

51. Tantum qualifies *vīdī*. Vergil died B. c. 19, when Ovid was at the age of twenty-four. Vergil lived mostly at Naples the last years of his life, which is probably the reason that Ovid *only saw* him, and was not well acquainted with him.

51. Tĭbullo. See note, Amores, i. 15, 28. Tibullus died the same year as Vergil.

53. Galle. See note, Amores, iii. 9, 64, and on *Propertius*, above, l. 45.

56. Thălĭă, properly the muse of comedy; here used generally for poetry, and with *mea*, his own muse.

57. Lēgi; referring to public readings of his poetry, or *recitationes* as they were called (above, l. 45, *recitare*). These readings were common at Rome, not only for poets, but for prose writers. It was in this way that writers became known to the public.

66. Quod—mŏvērĕt. Subjunctive of result, with *quod* after an indefinite antecedent.

3. THE POET'S LIFE.

67, 68. Hic, in the sense of *talis, such a person as this;* i. e., so very susceptible; yet there was *no town-talk (fabula)* of scandal about his name.

75. Filia; *the daughter,* to whom the elegy, Tristia, iii. 7, was addressed.

78. Lustra; here in the sense of a period of five years. But, as derived from *luo,* it originally meant the expiatory sacrifice, or lustration, made by the censors for the Roman people, on the completion of the census, at the end of every five years. The addition (*addiderat*) of a second (*altera*) period of *nine lustra* thus makes the age of Ovid's father, at his death, to be ninety.

79. Me flēturus—fuit, *would have wept for me.*

80. Justa, in the sense of regular or lawful, means here, with *tuli, performed the last duties.*

88. Stȳgio, from the river Styx, the fabled river of the lower world, *Stygian* comes to mean *of the lower world.* The word (from the Greek) means originally hateful; as Milton expresses it, "Abhorrèd Styx, the flood of deadly hate." By *crimina* Ovid means the *offense* for which he was banished; and he would have the *shades of his parents know* that it was a *mistake* (*errorem*), *not* a crime (*scelus*), *that was the cause of his exile.*

91. Stŭdĭōsă, sc. mei, with *pectora,* means *the hearts of* those who were *fond of* him; and it would appear from *qui—quaeritis,* in the next line, that this poem was written at the instance of his friends at Rome.

95. Pisaeā—ōlĭvā; in allusion to the Olympic games at Olympia, near Pisa, in Elis; these took place every four years. With *dĕcies,* the simple meaning is that ten periods of four years, or ten Olympiads, had gone by in his life when he was exiled. But he is only using a round number, as he was fifty-one years old at the time of his exile. Perhaps he uses the Olympiad, like a Roman *lustrum,* for five years.

96. Ĕquus. Horace has two passages illustrative of the *crowning* of the victorious *horse* at the Olympia. In O. iv. 2, 18, *pugilemve equumve;* and Ars Poetica, 85, *equum certamine primum.*

97. Tŏmitas; the accusative of Tomitae, the name of the inhabitants of Tomi, or Tomis, the town on the western shore of the Euxine, to which Ovid was banished.

102. Ipsā multā—lĕvĭŏrā fŭgā. The quantity shows the construction?

103. Indignata—est; here used in the literal sense of *dignor* with the negative *in, deigned not,* or *disdained.*

106. Temporis arma. The meaning of *temporis* is not clear; perhaps the time or *the situation* in which he now found himself. *The arms* seem, from the three preceding lines, to mean figuratively his submission and resignation to his misfortune. *Insŏlītā*, of course, agrees with *manu*.

110. Sarmatĭs (gen. ĭdis), an adjective agreeing with *ōrā*. The country called Sarmatia was bounded on the south by the Euxine; and the land of the Gētae was on the east, bounded by the Euxine.

113. Quod has its antecedent in *carmine*.

119, 120. Ab Histro—Hĕlĭcŏnĕ. The poet's genius thus withdraws him *from the Ister*, and its barbarous surroundings, and *gives him place on the center of Helicon*, and amid all its chosen haunts of Apollo and the Muses.

124. Nostris, sc. operibus, *any one of my works.*

128. In toto orbe. It was a lofty prediction of the poet, that he should be *very much read in the whole world* of the Roman Empire; but when we think of the extent of that *whole world* in which he has since been read, and is still read, how much loftier the prediction becomes!

VOCABULARY

ABBREVIATIONS IN THE VOCABULARY.

‾. Only this sign is used in marking quantity, and it marks the vowels which are *long by nature*, all vowels not marked being considered as *naturally short*. If the *naturally long* vowels are followed by two consonants (except a mute and liquid), or a double consonant, the long mark is still retained for the vowels, and there the *syllable* is *long by nature;* but where the *naturally short* vowels are so followed, the *syllable* is *long only by position*.

R. stands for the Indo-European Root, and, generally, as given in Vanicek's (Alois) "Griechisch-Lateinisches Etymologisches Wörterbuch," 2 vols., 8vo, Leipzig, 1877. To the **R.** are added the successive growths out of which issues the given Latin word ; as, for example, audeō, **R.** AV, *to be eager for*, av-ē-re, avi-du-s, *eager*, av-d, au-d, au-d-e-ō, aud-ē-re, *to dare*.

---

adj., adjective.	m., masculine.	pass., passive.
adv., adverb.	f., feminine.	subst., substantive.
conj., conjunction.	n., neuter.	acc., accusative.
comp., comparative.	pl., plural.	abl., ablative.
superl., superlative.	fr., from.	interj., interjection.
pron., pronoun.	dep., deponent.	part., participle.
prep., preposition.	def., defective.	unc., uncertain.

VOCABULARY.

A

AB

ab, ā, abs, prep. with abl. (Gr., ἀπό; Eng., *of, off*), *from, away from, on, by, on account of.*

ā, āh, interj., *ah! ah me!*

Abantiadēs, ae, son or descendant of Abas, king of Argos; Perseus, great-grandson of Abas.

ab-dō, didī, ditum, 3 (fr. do, *to put*), *to put away, hide, conceal.*

ab-dūcō, xī, ctum, 3, *to lead away.*

ab-eō, iī, itum, īre, *to go away, disappear, pass over* (by change), *be changed, go forth.*

ab-luō, luī, lūtum, 3, *to wash away* or *off, to wash.*

ab-oleō, ēvī, itum, 2, ab *and* oleō, o!escō, *to grow* (to grow away from); then v. a., *to stop the growth of, abolish.*

ab-rumpō, rūpī, ruptum, 3, *to break off.*

abs-cēdō, cessī, cessum, 3, *to go away, withdraw.*

ab-scindō, cidī, cissum, 3, *to tear away, separate.*

absēns, entis, part. of absum, *absent.*

ab-sum, āfuī, abesse, *to be away from, be absent, be not at hand, be wanting, be removed from.*

ab-sūmō, mpsī, mptum, 3 (ab, sumo, sub-im-(em)ere), *to take away, exhaust, consume.*

ab-undō, 1 (ab, und-, unda), *to flow over* (as a wave), *abound* (**R.** UD, UND, *wet,* ὕδωρ, *wave*).

Acca (Larentia), wife of the shep-

ACHILLES

herd Faustulus, and nurse of Romulus and Remus.

ac-cēdō, cessī, cessum, 3 (ad-cedō), *to come to, approach, be added.*

ac-cendō, cendī, cēnsum, 3 (ad *and* candeo, candō), *to be white, glisten;* then transitive, as here, *to make shine, kindle, light.*

ac-cingō, nxī, nctum, 3 (ad-cingō), *form a circle; to gird, gird around, gird up.*

ac-ciō, ivī, ītum, 4 (ad-ciō), *to move, call; to call to, summon.*

ac-cipiō, cēpī, ceptum, 3 (ad *and* capiō), *to take, receive, perceive, hear.*

ac-clīvis, e, adj. (ad *and* clīvus), *gradually ascending, sloping.*

ac-commodō, 1, (mod-u-s), (ad-commodō), *to fit, to measure; to adjust, fit.*

ac-cumbō, cubuī, cubitum, 3 (ad-cumbō), *to recline* (at table).

ācer, ācris, ācre, adj., *sharp, hot, fierce, impetuous* (**R.** same as in aciēs).

acervus, i, m., *a heap.*

Achelōidēs, um, the daughters of Achelous: *the Sirens.*

Achelōus, a river separating Aetolia from Acarnania; *the god of the river.*

Acherōn, ntis (Ἀχέρων, *stream of woe*), a river in the lower world; by meton., *the lower world.*

Achillēs, son of Peleus, king of Phthia in Thessaly, and the Nereid Thetis.

12

Achīvus (fr. Achaeus), *Achaean, Grecian.*
aciēs, ēi, f. (R. AK, *to be sharp*), *sharpness, sharp point, point ; sharpness of sight, keen glance ;* (sharp edge of army in line), *line of battle, army in battle-line, battle of army in line ; general engagement, pitched battle.*
Ācis, idis, m., son of Faunus and the nymph Symaethis.
aconītum, I, n., a poisonous plant, *aconite.*
ācrius, adv. comp. of acriter, *more fiercely.*
Actius, I, a Latin tragic writer.
actum, I, n. (ago), that which is done ; *act, deed, event.*
acūmen, inis, n. (R. AK), *point, pointed end.*
acus, ūs, f. (R. AK), *a needle.*
acūtus, a, um, adj. (R. AK), *sharp, pointed, shrill.*
ad, prep. with acc., *to, up to, for, at.*
adāctus, a, um, part., *driven.*
adamantēus, a, um, adj. (adamas), *of hard steel, adamantine.*
ad-dō, didī, ditum, 3 (dō, *to put*), *to put near to or by the side of, to add to.*
ad-dūcō, xī, ctum, 3, *to lead to, draw to.*
ad-edō, ēdī, ēsum, 3, *to eat at, to begin to eat,* (then by consequence) *to eat up, consume.*
ad-eō, adv., *up to this, to such a degree, so much.*
ad-fectō, 1 (factō, faciō), to make for ; *to strive after, aspire to.*
ad-ferō, attulī, allātum, 3, *to bring to, bring, bring with, afford.*
ad-ficiō (faciō), fēcī, fectum, 3, *to affect with, inflict* (punishment) *upon.*
ad-fīgō, fixī, fixum, 3, *to fix to, fasten to.*
ad-flātus, ūs, m., *a blowing on, breathing upon, breath.*
ad-flō, 1, *to blow upon, breathe upon.*
ad-for, fātus, 1, *to speak to, address.*
ad-haereō, haesī, haesum, 2, *to hang to, cleave to.*
ad-hibeō (habeō), uī, itum, *to hold towards, bring to, apply to, invite, employ,*
ad-hūc, adv., *till now, as yet, still.*
aditus, ūs, m., *an entrance.*

ad-iciō (adjiciō, jaciō), 3, jēcī, jectum, *to throw to, apply to, add to, direct to.*
ad-imō (emō), ēmī, emptum, 3, *to take away, deprive of.*
ad-juvō, jūvī, jūtum, 1, *to help, support.*
admīrābilis, e, adj., *worthy of admiration, admirable.*
ad-mīror, ātus, 1, v. dep., *to wonder at, admire.*
ad-mittō, mīsī, missum, 3, *to send to, let go, give loose reins to.*
ad-moneō, uī, ītum, 2, *to remind of, admonish.* **admonitor,** ōris, m.
ad-moveō, mōvī, mōtum, 2, *to move to, bring near.*
ad-nuō, nuī, nūtum, 3, *to nod to, give assent to, grant.*
ad-oleō, oluī, ultum, 2, *to burn* (in sacrifice), *consume.*
ad-operiō, operuī, opertum, 4, *to cover, cover over.*
ad-ōrō, 1, *to speak to, pray to, worship.*
ad-sternō, ere, *to throw one's self down by, to lie prostrate by.*
ad-stō, stitī, 1, *to stand by.*
ad-sum, ad-fuī, ad-esse, *to be present, be at hand, aid, help.*
adulter-ium, 2, n. (ad-ulter, alter, R. ALJA, *another*), *adultery.*
ad-uncus, a, um, adj., *bent to, curved, hooked.*
ad-ūrō, ussī, ustum, 3, *to set fire to, burn.*
ad-vehō, xī, ctum, 3, *carry to, bear.*
ad-veniō, vēnī, ventum, 4, *to come to, arrive.*
ad-ventus (veniō), ūs, m., *arrival.*
ad-versus, a, um, adj., vertō, turned to, *turned against, opposite, in front, adverse.*
ad-vertō, tī, sum, 3, *to turn to.*
ad-vocō, 1, voc-ō, *to call to, call to one's aid.*
ad-volō, 1, vol-ō, *to fly to.*
Aeēta, Aeētēs, king of Colchis, son of Sol and Persa, the daughter of Oceanus.
Aeētiās, daughter of Aeētes, Mēdēa.
Aegaeōn, ōnis, m., a sea-god, son of Pontus and Terra.
Aegaeus, a, um, adj., Aegean, name

of the sea between Greece and Asia Minor.

aeger, gra, grum, adj. (R. ig, *tremble*), *sick, ill, troubled, sad.*

Aegīna, ae, f., daughter of the river-god Asopus.

aegis, idis, f. (αἰγίς, aegis), the shield of Minerva ; n. Met. VI, 79.

Aegyptius, a, um, adj., *Egyptian.*

aelinos, I, m., *a dirge ;* see n. Am. III, 9, 23.

aemulus, I, m. (R. ik, aik, aik-ma, ac-mu, *like*), one who will do the like, *emulous, a rival.*

Aenēius, a, um, adj., *of Aeneas.*

aēneus, a, um, adj. (aes), (R. ajas, *metal*), *of brass.*

Aeolis, idis, f., the daughter of Aeolus, Alcyone.

Aeolius, a, um, adj., belonging to Aeolus, the god of winds, *Aeolian.*

Aeolus, I, m. son of Hippotes ; the god of winds.

aequālis, e, adj. (R. ik, aik, aik-a, *like*), *equal, like.*

aequō, adv., *equally, alike ;* for R. see aequalis.

aequō, 1 (for R. see aequalis), *to make equal, equal.*

aequor, oris, n. (same R. as aequalis), *an even surface, the level* (of the sea), *the sea.*

aequoreus, a, um, adj., *belonging to the sea.*

aequus, a, um, adj. (R. ik, aik, aik-a), *even, equal, favorable, equitable, just.*

āēr, eris, m., ἀήρ, *the air ;* R. av, *to blow,* av-er, ā-ēr.

aerātus (aes), a, um, adj., *covered with bronze or copper ; of bronze.*

aeripēs (aes, pēs), pedis, *bronze-footed.*

āerius, a, um, adj. (āēr), pertaining to the air, *aërial, airy.*

aes, aeris, n. (R. ajas, *metal*), *bronze, copper, brass.*

aesculeus, a, um, adj., *of oak.*

Aesonidēs, ae, the son of Aeson ; Jason.

Aesonius, a, um, adj., *Aesonian.*

aestās, ātis, f. (R. idh, *burn,* aid, aid-tat-i, aes-ta-s), *summer.*

aestivus, a, um, adj. (aestas), *of summer.*

aestuō, 1 (aes-tu-s, same R. as aesta-s), *to boil up, rage with heat, grow hot, glow.*

aestus, ūs, m. (same R. as aestas), *boiling, swell of the sea, heat of fire, glow, ardor.*

aetās, ātis, f. (R. I, ai, ai-va (Eng. *ever, aye*), ac-vu-m, aevi-tas, aetas), *time, age of life, generation, age.*

aeternus, a, um, adj. (aevi-ternu-s), *eternal, endless, perpetual.*

aethēr, eris, m., *ether, heaven.*

āgna, ae, f., *a lamb.*

āgnōscō, nōvi, nitum, 3, *to know.*

agō, ēgi, āctum, 3, *to drive, lead ;* agito, 1, *to agitate ;* agitābilis, e, adj., *light.*

agrestis, e, adj. (ager), *of the country, rustic, rude ;* subst., *a farmer, peasant.*

agricola, ae, m. (ager, colō), a cultivator of land, *farmer,* in Met. 8, 192 ; fig. of one who, as it were, sowed words in the soil.

ai (ăi), interj., *ah ! alas !*

āiō, v. defect., *to say,* Gr. 297, II (R. agh, *to say,* ag, a-j-o, ag-i-o).

āla, ae, f. (R. ag, ag+s=ax=*turn ;* ax-u-la, ax-la, as-la, ā-la), *a wing.*

Alba, ae, f., *a city in Latium,* Alba Longa.

albeō, ēre (R. albha, albu-s, *white*), *to be white.*

albēscō, ere, *to grow white.*

albidus, a, um, adj., *white.*

Albula, ae, f., river in Latium.

albus, a, um, adj. (R. albha, *white*), *white.*

Alcīdēs, ae, m., *son* (or descendant) *of Alcaeus ;* Hercules.

Alcyonē, ēs, f., daughter of Aeolus

ālēs, itis, adj. and subst. (ala), *winged, bird, birds.*

aliēnus, a, um, adj. (alius, R. alja, ali, *other,* ali-ēnu-s), *belonging to another, another's, strange, foreign.*

alimentum, I, n. (alō), *means of nourishment, food.*

aliō, adv. (alius), *else-whither, elsewhere.*

ālipēs, pedis, adj. (āla, pēs), *wing-footed.*

aliquandō, adv., *at some time, finally* (ali, *some,* quando, *when*).

aliquis, indef. pron. adj. and subst., (ali-quis), *some one, some, somebody* or *something or other.*

aliter, adv., other-way, *otherwise.*

alius, a, um, adj. (alja, *another,* aliu-s), *another, other, some, the others.*

alligō, 1, ad, ligō, *to bind to, fasten.*

alloquor, locutus sum, 3, v. dep., ad-loquor (**R. RA,** ra-k, lak, loqu-i), *to speak to, address.*

almus, a, um, adj. (alō), *nourishing.*

alnus, I, f., *alder.*

alō, uī, itum and altum, 3 (**R.** AR, al, *make grow, nourish*), *to nourish, bring up.*

Alōīdae, 1, m., the Aloidae, sons of Iphimedia, the wife of Aloeus.

Alpēs, ium, f., *the Alps.*

Alphēīas, adis, f., the nymph of the fountain Arethusa, which unites its waters with the river Alpheus.

Alphēnor, oris, m., son of Niobe.

Alphēus (os), I, m., a river in the Peloponnesus ; *the river-god* Alphēus.

altāria, ium, n. (altus), something put upon the *ara,* on which the offerings were burned, then *the altar* itself.

altē, adv. (altus), *high, on high ; deep.*

alter, tera, teram, adj. (**R.** ALJA, al, al-tero), *the other, one of two.*

alternus, a, um, adj. (alter), one after the other, *alternate.*

altrīx, īcis, f., *a nurse.*

altus, a, um, adj. (**R.** AR, al, *to raise*), *high, exalted, deep ;* subst., *the high, height ; the deep, depth.*

alumnus, I, m. (alō), *foster-son.*

alveus (alvus), I, m., a hollow (like that of the *alvus*), *the bed of a river.*

alvus, I, f. (**R.** AR, al, *to nourish,* al-o, al-vu-s), *the body, womb.*

amārus, a, um, adj. (**R.** AM, *raw*), *bitter.*

Amathūs, untis, f., a town on the south coast of Cyprus.

Amathūsia, ae, f., see n. Am. 3, 13.

ambāgēs, um, f. pl., *evasions.*

ambīgō, 3, amb-ago, (**RR.** AMBII, (amb) and AG), to go about ; impers., ambigitur, it is uncertain (ambiguous).

ambīguus, a, um, adj. (amb-igō, agō), *ambiguous, doubtful.*

ambīō, īvī and iī, ītum, 4, amb, eō (**RR.** AMBH, amb, *round,* and I, *to go*), *to go around, compass, solicit, pray.*

ambītīō, ōnis, f. (ambiō), a going around, canvassing, *ambition.*

ambō, ae, ō, *both* (**R.** AMBH, amb).

ambrosia, 1, f., *ambrosia.*

ambūrō, ussī, ustum, 3, amb-uro, (**RR.** AMBII, amb, *around,* and VAS, aus, ōs, ūs, *to burn,* ur-ere, us-si), *to burn around, consume.*

āmēns, mentis, adj. (a, mēns), *out of mind, beside one's self, distracted.*

āmentia, ae, f. (amēns). *madness.*

am-iciō, icuī and ixī, ictum, 4, am (**R.** AMBII) *and* jaciō, *to throw around, enwrap.*

amictus, ūs, m. (amiciō), *clothing, garment, veil.*

amīcus, a, um, adj. and subst., I, m. (amō), *friendly, a friend.*

ā-mittō, mīsī, missum, 3, *to lose.*

amnis, is, m., *a stream, river.*

amō, 1 (**R.** KAM (k), am, *to love*), *to love ;* amāns, tis, m., *a lover.*

amor (amō), ōris, m., *love.*

Amor, ōris, m., god of love.

Amphīōn, onis, m., son of Jupiter and Antiope, husband of Niobe.

Amphītrītē, ēs, f., daughter of Nereus, wife of Neptune ; by meton., *the sea.*

Amphītryōn, ōnis, m., son of Alcaeus, and husband of Alcmene.

Amphītryōnīadēs, ae, m., Hercules, as stepson of Amphitryon.

am-plector, plexus, 3, v. dep. (plecto), *to twine round, compass, embrace.*

am-plexus (amplector), ūs, m., a surrounding, *embracing.*

amplius, adv. (amplē), *further, longer, besides.*

Amyclīdēs, ae, m., son of Amyclus, king of Laconia ; Hyacinthus.

an, R. AN, ana, interrog. particle, *or, whether not.*

ancora, ae, f. (**R.** AK, ANK, *crook*), *anchor.*

Andromēda, ae, f., daughter of Cepheus and Cassiope, rescued by Perseus, and then married to him. Met. 4, 671.

angō, anxī, anctum and anxum, 3 (**R.** ANGH, ang, *to straiten*), *to strangle, distress, make anxious,*

angui-comus, a, um, adj. (anguis, coma), *with snaky hair, snake-haired*.

angui-fer, a, um, adj. (ferō), *serpent-bearing*.

angui-pēs, edis, adj., *snake-footed*.

anguis, is, m. (R. ANGH, ang, *to straiten*), *a serpent, snake*.

Anguis, is, m., constellation of the Dragon.

angulus, ī, m. (same R. as angō), *a corner, angle*.

angustus, a, um, adj. (angō), *narrow*.

anhēlitus, ī, m. (anhēlō), *panting breath, breath*.

an-hēlō, 1 (hēlō), *to breathe with difficulty, pant*.

anīlis, e, adj. (anus), *of an old woman*.

anima, ae, f. (R. AN, *to breathe*), an-i-ma), *breath, air, life, the soul*.

animal, ālis, n. (anima), *a living being, animal*.

animāns, antis, part. and adj., *a living being, living*.

animōsus, a, um, adj. (anima), full of spirit, *spirited, eager*.

animus, ī, m. (R. AN, *to breathe*), the rational soul, *spirit, heart, sense, mind; pride, anger, purpose*.

annus, ī, m. (R. AK, ANK, *to bend*), ā-nu-s (for ac-nu-s), an-nus, *year*.

annōsus, a, um, adj., *aged*.

Annus, ī, m. (as person), *the year*.

annuus, a, um, adj. (annus), *yearly, annual*.

ānser, eris, m. (R. GHAN, *to grate, hiss*, ghans-a; Ger., Gans), *a goose*.

Antaeus, ī, m., name of a Libyan giant, son of Earth.

ante, R. AN (an-ta, abl. anti-d, anti, ante), 1, adv. of place and of time, *before, sooner than—, earlier;* 2, prep. with acc., *before* (of place, time, or rank).

ante-eō, iī, itum, 4 (eō), *to go before*.

antemna, ae, f., *sail-yard* (akin to ἀνατείνω?).

Anthēdōn, onis, f., a city in Boeotia, opposite to Euboea.

Antigonē, ēs, f., daughter of Laomedon. Met. 6, 93.

antīquus, a, um, adj. (ante), of the *afore*-time, *ancient, old, antique*.

antrum, ī, n. (R. AN, ana, *ἐν-ί, in*, an-tara, antru-m), *a cave, den, grotto*.

anus, us, f. (R. AN (same as of ante), anā, originally an *a*-stem noun, then an-u-s; so Ger., Ahn, *ancestor*), *an old woman, matron*.

anxius, a, um, adj. (angō), *anxious*.

Aonis, idis, f., of Aonia, Aonides, the Muses, as dwellers in Aonia.

Aonius, a, um, adj., *Aonian*.

aper, aprī, m. (R. AP, *to breed*, ap-ro, ap-e-r), *a wild boar*.

a-periō, peruī, pertum, 4 (ab *and* pariō), (R. PAR, *to bring*, par, par-i), to bring from, *uncover, open, disclose*.

Apollineus, a, um, adj., *of Apollo*.

Apollō, inis, m., son of Jupiter and Latona.

ap-pārēō, uī, itum, 2 (ad-pareō), *to be visible, appear*.

ap-pellō, pulī, pulsum, 3 (ad-pellō), *to drive to, drive forward*.

ap-pellō, 1 (ad-pellō), *to go to or drive to for the purpose of addressing, to speak to, address, accost, name*.

Appennīnus, a, um, adj. (the radical syllable *penn* probably Celtic, *mountain-top*), *Apennine, the Apennines*.

ap-plicō, āvī and uī, ātum and itum (ad-plicō) (to fold to), 1, *apply, put to*.

ap-pōnō, posuī, positum, 3 (ad-pōnō), *to place near, near to*.

aptō, 1 (freq. fr. apō), *to fit to, place upon, furnish*.

aptus, a, um, adj. (apō), *fitted, fitting, suitable*.

aqua, ae, f. (R. AK, *swift*), *water*, pl. *waters, streams*.

aquila, ae, f. (R. AK, ANK, *dark*), (aquilus, *dark color*), dark bird, *the eagle*.

aquilō, ōnis, m. (same R. as aquila), bringing dark, lowering weather, *north wind*.

aquōsus, a, um, adj. (aqua), full of water, *full of rain*.

āra, ae, f. (R. AS, *to sit*, ās-a, ār-a), *altar*.

Āra, ae, f., the constellation of the Altar.

Arachnē, ēs, f., the Lydian maiden in the story of Met. 6, 5, seqq.

arānea, ae, f., *the spider* (R. AR, *fit, spin*).

arātor, ōris, m. (arō), *plower.*
arātrum, ī, n. (arō), *plow.*
Arātus, ī, m., a Greek poet of Soli; see n. Am. 1, 15, 16.
ar-bi-ter, trī, m. (ar = ad, *and* bi, fr. R. GA, gua, BA, *to go*), one that goes to; i. e., *witness, observer, arbiter.*
arbitr-iu-m, ī, m. (arbiter-ium), *decision, choice, will.*
arbor (arbōs), oris, f. (R. ARDH, arf-, arb-, *to raise, lift*), *tree, mast.*
arboreus, a, um, adj. (arbor), *of a tree.*
arbustum, ī, n. (arbōs), (arbos-ō-tum, arbus-tu-m), *a plantation of trees, trees.*
arbut-eus, a, um, adj. (arbutum), *of the strawberry-tree, of the arbute.*
arb-u-tum, ī, n. (arbor), *the wild strawberry-tree,* arbute, arbutus.
Arcadia, ae, f., *a province of the Peloponnesus.*
arceō, uī, ctum, 2 (R. ARK, *to keep strong, keep off*), *to keep off, hinder, keep back, keep away.*
arci-tenēns, entis, adj. (arcus), *bow-holding,* epithet of Apollo.
Arctos, ī, f., the constellation of the Great and the Lesser Bear (R. ARK, *to attack, injure*).
arcuātus, a, um, adj. (arcuō), *bow-formed, arched.*
arcus, ūs, m. (R. AR, *to bend*), *a bow ; bow* (as half-circle), *rainbow.*
Ardea, ae, f., chief city of the Rutuli in Latium.
ardeō, arsī, arsum, 2 (R. AR, *to burn, dry,* ārē-re, āri-du-s, āridi-tās, ārid-ēre ; ard-ēre), *to burn, be afire, burn up, glow.*
ardēscō, arsī, 3 (ardeō), *to take fire, glitter.*
ardor, ōris, m. (ardeō), *heat, glow, ardor.*
arduus, a, um, adj. (R. ARDH, ardh-va, ard-uu-s, *to raise high*), *steep, high ; hard to reach, arduous.*
ārea, ae, f. (R. AR, *dry*), *a* (dry) *free place, open field, area.*
āreō, ēre (see R. of ardeō), *to be dry, arid.*
Arethūsa, ae, f., name of a nymph in Elis, and of the celebrated fountain in Sicily ; see note Met. 5, 409.

argenteus, a, um, adj. (argentum), *of silver, silver-bright, silver.*
argentum, ī, n. (R. ARG, *to shine,* arge-nt-u-m), *silver.*
Argos, n. (Lat., Argi, orum, m.), a city in Argolis, Peloponnesus.
argūmentum, ī, n. (arguō), *subject-matter, subject* (for representation in art), *argument.*
arguō, uī, ūtum, 3 (R. ARG, argu, *to shine, be clear*), to make clear, *argue, prove, reprove, censure.*
āridus, a, um, adj. (arcō), *dry, arid.*
ariēs, etis, m. (R. unc., V. gives AR, *to hurt,* ari, ari-ē-s), 1, *a ram ;* 2, the constellation of the Ram.
arista, ae, f. (R. AK, *sharp,* acr-ista, ar-ista, ista superlative), *a beard of grain, ear, harvest* (of ears).
arma, ōrum, n. (R. AR, *to fit,* cf. armu-s, *joint*), *shoulder, arm,* something fitted to the body, *arms, armor ;* (for the field), *tools, utensils.* **armipo-tēns,** tis, *valiant.*
armāmenta, ōrum, n. (arma), (for a ship), *tackle, armament.*
armentum, ī, n. (arma, AR-men-tum, in the sense of being *put together ;* but perh. fr. ar, *to plow*), *herds, cattle* (as oxen, horned cattle, or horses).
armi-fer, fera, ferum, adj., *arms-bearing, armed.*
armi-ger, gera, gerum, adj., *arms-carrying, armor-bearer.*
armus, ī, m. (R. AR, *to fit*), joint, *shoulder, arm.*
arō, 1 (R. AR, *to plow*), *to plow.*
arripiō (ad-rapiō), uī, reptum, 3, *to lay hold of.*
ars, artis, f. (R. AR, *to fit*), *art.*
arti-fex, icis, m. (faciō), *artist, artisan, maker, author, contriver.*
artus, a, um, adj. (arceō), *narrow, close ;* as subst., *a strait.*
artus, ūs, m. (R. AR, *to fit*), a joint of the body, pl. *joints, limbs ; body, bodies.*
arvum, ī, n. (arō), plowed or arable land, *field, fields.*
arx, cis, f. (R. ARK, *to make strong*), a stronghold, *castle, citadel,* a high place, *height, summit.*
Ascalaphus, ī, m., son of Acheron and Orphne, changed to an owl.
ascendō (ad *and* scandō), scendī,

scēnsum, 3, *to climb up, ascend, go up into.*

ascēnsus, ūs, m. (ascendō), *an ascent.*

Ascraeus, I, m., of Ascra, a village in Boeotia; *the Ascraean* (used of Hesiod).

asellus, I, m., dim. (asinus), *a little ass, an ass's colt.*

Āsōpis, idis, f., daughter of Asōpus; Aegīna.

asper, era, erum, adj., *rough, uneven.*

aspergō, inis, f. (ad-spargō), *a sprinkling, besprinkling, spray.*

a-spiciō, spexI, spectum, 3 (ad, speciō), *to look to, look upon, behold, consider.*

a-spīrō, 1 (ad, spīrō), to breathe to, favor.

assēnsus, ūs, m. (assentiō), *agreement, assent.*

as-sentiō, sēnsī, sēnsum, 4 (ad, sentiō), *to agree with, assent.*

as-serō, seruI, sertum, 3 (ad, serō), *to join to, claim, appoint to.*

assiduus, a, um, adj. (ad, sedeō), *unremitting.*

as-siliō, siluI, sultum, 4 (ad, saliō), *to leap to, spring upon.*

as-suēscō, suēvI, suētum, 3 (ad, suescō), *to accustom one's self to;* part., assuētus, *accustomed to, wonted.*

assuētūdō, inis, f., *custom, habit, intercourse.*

as-sum, s. ad-sum.

as-sūmō, sumpsI, sumptum, 3 (ad, sumō), *to take to, receive.*

Assyrius, a, um, adj., *Assyrian.*

Asteriē, ēs, f., daughter of Coeus; Met. 6, 108.

Astraea, ae, f. (Ἀστραία, goddess of stars), goddess of justice. Met. 1, 150.

a-stringō, strinxI, strictum, 3 (ad, stringō), *to bind to, bind fast.*

astrum, I, n. (R. STAR, *to strew* (sternō), ster, ster-u-la, stel-la (ἄστρον, ἀστήρ, στερ), a-stru-m), *a star, constellation;* by meton., *the heavens.*

at, conj. (ast), (R. A, pron. stem, 1st and 2d pers., ĕ-τι, a-t), *but, yet, yet at least.*

Atalanta, ae, f., d. of king Schoeneus, of Boeotia; Met. 10, 565, seqq.

āter, ātra, um, adj. (R. IDH, *to burn,* aid, aid-tro (?), ā-tro, ā-ter, *burnt black*), *black, dark, gloomy.*

Athōs (ōnis), (Ἄθων), mountain in Macedonia; Met. 2, 217.

Atlantiadēs, ae, m., son or descendant of Atlas; n. of Mercury as son of Maia, Atlas's d.; Met. 8, 627.

Atlās, antis, m., s. of Iapetus, father of the Plēiades, and grandf. of Niobe; Met. 2, 296; 6, 174.

at-que (āc), conj. (ad-que), *and-too, and also, and even, and; as.*

ātrium, I, n. (āter), (R. IDH, *to burn*), the room in which was the hearth ("atrum ex fumo"?), the entrance-room in the house, *family-room, reception-room; hall;* by meton., *the house, home.*

at-tamen, *and yet, yet.*

at-tollō, ere (ad-tollō), *to lift up.*

at-tonō, uI, itum, 1 (ad, tonō), *to thunder at* or *upon, stun, amaze, charm.*

au-ceps, cupis, comm. (avi-ceps, fr. avis, capiō), *a bird-catcher, fowler.*

auctōr, ōris, m. (augeō), the author, promoter, doer; cause, occasion; *giver, lender;* producer, father; founder; relater; *authority.*

audax, ācis, adj. (audeō), *daring, bold,* spirited, *audacious, rash.*

audeō, ausI (ausim), ausus sum, 2 (R. AV, *to like, be eager for,* av-ēre, avi-du-s, av-d, au-d, au-d-ē-re), *to dare, be bold, venture.*

audiō, ivI or iI, Itum, 4 (same R. as au-d-ē-re), *to hear, perceive, to know by hearing, to give heed to.*

au-ferō, abstulI, ablātum, 3 (ab (abs), ferō), *to carry away, take away,* rob of, *destroy.*

augeō, xI, ctum, 2 (R. VAG, UG, *to be strong, wax,* aug), *to increase, enlarge, heighten.*

augurium, I, n. (au-gur, fr. avi-gur, R. AV, *to blow, wave,* avi-s + R. GAR, *to call*), interpreting of the flight of birds, interpretation, *augury.*

au-guror, 1, v. dep. (augur), to interpret omens, *surmise, augur.*

augustus, a, um, adj. (augeō), *exalted, august.*

Augustus, I, m., 1, the August, Majestic, *Majesty, Imperial Majesty,* title of honor of Octavian on his attainment of sovereign power; 2, adj., *of Augustus, Augustan, imperial.*

aula, ae, f. (Gr., αὐλή, free, airy, place, fr. **R.** AV, *to blow*), *court* (of a building), *hall* (of a palace).

aulaeum, I, n. (aula), pl. aulaea, hall-hangings, *curtain* (of a theatre).

aura, ae, f. (**R.** AV, *to blow,* av-ra, au-ra), *air, draught of air;* pl. *breezes, breath of life.*

aurātus, a, um, adj. (aurum), *gilded, adorned with gold.*

aureus, a, um, adj. (aurum), *of gold, golden.*

auri-fer, fera, ferum, adj., *gold-bearing.*

aurīga, ae, comm. (aurī-ga, fr. auri-jug-a; auri- fr. **R.** AR, *to run,* αὖρο-ς, arvu-s, *a horse;* and jug fr. **R.** JU, ju-g, *to bind,* cf. jug-u-m), *a charioteer.*

auris, is, f. (**R.** AV, *to be eager for,* av-s, au-s-i-s, au-r-i-s), *the ear.*

Aurōra, ae, f. (**R.** VAS, AVS, aus, *to burn, shine,* αὐσ-ος), aus-os, aus-os-a, Aur-ōr-a), goddess of the rosy morn, dawn, *Aurora;* by meton., *the East.*

aurum, I, n. (**R.** same as Aurora, VAS, aus, aus-o, aur-u-m), the (shining) *gold.*

Ausonia, ae, f., poetic name for Italy, fr. the Ausones.

Ausonius, a, um, adj. (Ausonia), *Ausonian.*

auspex, spicis, comm., fr. avi-spex, avis, speciō (see augurium for avis), speciō fr. **R.** SPAK, *to see,* spec, spec-s), one who observes the birds, *augur, diviner.*

auspicium, I, n. (avi-spicium), (auspex), observation of the birds, *auspice.*

auster, strī, m. (**R.** VAS, aus, *to burn,* aus-ter), *the* (hot) *south-wind, Auster.*

austrālis, e, adj. (auster), in the direction of the south-wind, *southerly.*

ausum, I, n. (audeō), *a daring attempt,* venture, design.

aut, conj. (fr. au-te-m, au-t, the t repr. tem, the demon. pron. stem of 3d pers., au repr. pron. st. as adv. and = Gr. ἄν, αὖτε, and aut = ἠέ, ἤ), *or, or rather, or even, either—or.*

autem (au-te-m), conj. (see aut), *but, however.*

autumnālis, e, adj. (autumnus), *of the autumn, autumnal.*

autumnus, I, m. (**R.** AV, *to satisfy, be full,* au-tn, au-t-u-mnu-s), the season that brings fullness, *the autumn;* by meton., *the fruits of the autumn;* personified Met. 2, 29, *Autumn.*

auxiliāris, e, adj. (auxilium), *bringing help, helping.*

auxilium, I, n. (augeō, q. d., aug-to, aug-tu-lo, aug-su-lo, aug-sul-io, aux-il-io), *help, aid;* by meton., *helper.*

a-vellō (vellī), vulsī, vulsum, 3, *to tear away, rend from.*

avēna, ae, f. (**R.** same as autumnus, AV, av-as, avasa, av-as-na, av-es-na, av-ē-na), *a stalk of grain, of straw, a reed.*

Aventīnus, a, um, adj. and subst., *Aventine* (hill), *the Aventine.*

Avernālis, e, adj., *of* (lake) *Avernus;* see note Met. 5, 540.

Avernus, a, um, adj., same as Avernālis.

āversor, 1, v. dep. (avertō), *to turn away.*

a-vertō, tī, sum, 3. *to turn from, away, avert.*

avidus, a, um, adj. (aveō), *desirous, eager, greedy.*

avis, is, f. (**R.** AV, *to blow,* avi-s), *bird,* as bird of omen, by meton. for *omen.*

avītus, a, um, adj. (avus), *of a grandfather, grandfather's, ancestral.*

āvius, a, um, adj. (a or ab, via), *out of the way, remote;* subst. pl., *out-of-the-way places, by-ways.*

avus, I, m. (**R.** AV, *to like, protect*), *grandfather;* in pl., *ancestors.*

axis, is, m. (**R.** AG, *to drive,* ag+s= ax, axi-s), *axle;* by meton., *carriage, chariot; the axis, of the earth, of the heavens;* by meton., *the heavens.*

B

Babylōnĭus, a, um, adj., *of Babylon, Babylonian.*

bāca, ae, f. (BABKA), *a berry, berry of Minerva;* i. e., the olive.

Bacchae, ārum, pl., *female attendants of Bacchus.*

Bacchēus, a, um, adj., *belonging to Bacchus; Bacchic.*

Bacchĭadae, pl. m., the *Bacchiads,* an ancient princely family of Corinth, descended from Bacchis.

Bacchus, I, m., s. of Jupiter and Semele, foster-son of Silenus, Met. 11, 99.

baculum, I, n., and **bacŭlus,** I, m. (R. GA, *to go,* ba, ba-k, ba-c-ulu-m), something used for *going; a staff.*

Baleārĭcus, a, um, adj., *Balearic, of the Baleāres,* islands in the Mediterranean (βάλλω).

ballaena, ae, f., *a whale.*

ballista, ae, f. (βάλλω), a machine for *throwing* missiles, *ballist.*

balteus, I, m., *a belt, girdle.*

barba, ae, f. (R. BARDHA), *beard.*

barbarĭcus, a, um, adj., *foreign,* not Greek or Roman, *barbarian.*

barbarus, a, um, adj., *foreign, barbarous;* subst., *foreigner, barbarian.*

Bassus, I, m., name of an epic poet, Tr. 4, 10, 47.

Baucis, idis, f., wife of Philemon, Met. 8, 631, seqq.

beātus, a, um, adj. (beō), *made happy. happy.*

Bēlīdes, nm, pl. f., granddaughters of Belus, usually called Danaides, fr. their f. Danaus.

bellĭcus, a, um, adj. (bellum), *of war, warlike.*

bellum, I, n. (R. DVA, DVI, *two,* duc-llu-m, bellu-m), *war, contest, duel.*

bēlua, ae, f. (R. BARGH, *to break, tear,* balgh, balh̄, belh, bel-), *a (tearing, fierce) beast, a monster.*

bene, adv. (R. DVI, du, *to honor,* bonc, bene), *well, exactly, right.*

benignus, a, um, adj. (bene-gīgnō, beni-n-gnu-s, gnu fr. R. GAN, gen, gna, gnu), *kindly* by nature, *benignant.*

Berĕcyntĭus, a, um, adj., *of* (Mt.) *Berecyntus, Berecynthian.*

bĭbō, bibī, itum, 3, *to drink.*

bibulus, a, um, adj., *bibulous.*

bĭceps, cipitis, adj. (bis, caput), *two-headed.*

bi-color, ōris, adj. (bis, color), *two-colored.*

bĭcornis, e, adj. (bis, cornu), *two-horned.*

bi-foris, e, adj. (bis, foris), *having two doors.*

bĭ-maris, e, adj. (bis, mare), lying on two seas, *two-seaed.*

bīnī, ae, a, distrib. pronom. adj. (bis), *two by two, two each.*

bis, adv. (R. DVA, DVI, dvi-ies, dbi-ies, bi-ies, bis), *two times, twice.*

bi-sulcus, a, um, adj. (bis, sulcus), *two-furrowed, two-cleft, cloven.*

blandior, v. dep., 4 (blandus), to say or do *bland* (soft) things, *flatter, fondle.*

blanditia, ae, f. (blandus), *bland* (soft) speeches, *flattery.*

blandus, a, um, adj. (R. MAR, mal (*rub, make soft*), mal-d, mlad, mla-n-d, bla-n-d-), *bland, flattering.*

Boeōtĭa, ae, f., a country in central Greece, Met. 2, 239.

bŏnus, a, um, adj., melior, optimus (R. DVI, du, *honor*), good, *good-natured, kindly; of better kind, best;* subst., bonum, i, n., *a good, a blessing;* pl., *goods, excellences, blessings.*

Boōtēs, ae, m., the constellation Bootes (Βοώτης, *ox-driver*).

Borĕās, ae, m., 1, the N. wind; 2, the god of the N. wind.

bōs, bovis, comm. (R. GU, *to sound,* gnov, vov, bov), *an ox, a bull, a cow.*

bracchium, I, n. (R. BARGH, βραχ, βραχ-ίων), *the arm, the fore-* or *lower arm; claw,* pl. *the claws.*

brevis, e, adj. (R. BARGH (*break, tear*), bragh, bregh-u-i, breh-u-i, bre-v-i-s), broken off, *brief, short, small.*

brĕvĭter (brevis), *briefly, shortly.*

Brūtus, I, m. (R. GAR, *heavy,* garu (gravis), gur, gru, bru-), L. Junius (who feigned *dullness*), the deliverer of Rome fr. the Tarquins, and fr. regal government; Fasti, 2, 717.

bŭbo, ōnis, m. (R. BU, *scream*), *an owl.*
bŭcerus, a, um, adj. (βούκερως, *ox-horned, horned* (cattle).
bŭcina, ae, f. (R. BU, *sound*), bu-k, buc-a, buc-ina), *a horn* or *trumpet, signal-trumpet.*

Busīris, idis, m., mythical king of Egypt, Met. 9, 183.
bustum, I, n. (burō = urō), place of burial (burning), *tomb.*
buxum, I, n., *box-tree, wood of the box-tree.*

C

cacūmen, inis, n. (R. KUAD, KUD, *to drive* (shoot) *forth,* by redupl. ka + kud, ca-cu-men), *peak, summit, top; point.*
Cadmēis, idis, f., *of Cadmus, Cadmean.*
Cadmus, I, m., s. of Phoenician king Agenor.
cadō, cecidī, cāsum, 3 (R. KAD, *to fall*), *sink, set.*
cādūci-fer, fera, ferum, adj. (caduceus), *bearing a herald's staff.*
cadūcus, I, adj. (cadō), (something) that falls, *falling, fallen, liable, ready, to fall.*
caecus, a, um, adj. (R. SKA, *cover, hide,* sca, sca-i-co, ca-i-co, cacco), *dark, hidden, blind.*
caedes, is, f. (caedō), *a cutting down, killing, murder, carnage, bloodshed.*
caedō, cecīdī, caesum, 3 (R. SAK, SKA, *to cut, cleave,* ska-d, ski-d, scae-d, caed-), *to make fall, to fell, slay, kill.*
caeles, itis (caelum), adj., *in heaven,* pl. masc., the heavenly (ones), *the gods.*
caelestis, e, adj. (caelum), *belonging to heaven, heavenly, divine;* subst. pl., the heavenly (ones), *celestial* (beings).
caelicola, ae, comm. (caelum), *dweller in heaven.*
caelō, 1 (same R. as caedō, SKA, *to cut,* caed-, cael-, cael-u-m, *burin* or *chisel*), *to represent in relief, to engrave, to adorn with reliefs.*
caelum, I, n. and m. (R. KU, KUA-N, *to be hollow,* kau, kav, cavi-lu-m, cai-lu-m, caelum), the (hollow) vault of heaven, *heaven, the heavens.*
caeruleus, a, um, adj., caerulus (same R. as caelum, caelu-lu-s), *heaven-blue, blue, dark-blue, dark.*
Caesar, aris, m., C. Julius, assassinated B. C. 44.
caespes, itis, m. (caedō), *sod, turf.*

Caïcus, I, m., river in Teuthrania, Mysia.
Calais, idis, m., one of the winged sons of Boreas.
calamus, I, m. (κάλαμος, R. kar, *to project*), *a reed.*
calathus, I, m. (κάλαθος, R. karatho, *basket*), *a wicker-basket, flower-basket.*
calcō, 1 (calx, *heel*), *to tread with the heel, stamp.*
caleō, uī, 2 (R. SKAL, *to glow,* cal), *to be warm, glow.*
calēscō, uī, 3 (caleō), *to grow warm.*
calidus, a, um, adj. (caleō), *warm.*
cālīgō, inis, f. (R. SKAL, kal, *cover*), *misty darkness, gloom.*
callēns, ntis, part. (fr. calleō, R. KAR, *to swell*) (of bark), *callous, hard.*
callidus, a um, adj., *cunning.*
Calliopē, ēs, f. (Καλλιόπη, *the fine-voiced*), the Muse of epic song.
calor, ōris, m. (caleō), *warmth.*
Calvus, I, m., see n. Am. 3, 9, 62.
Calydōnius, a, um, adj., *of Calydon,* a town in Aetolia; *Calydonian.*
Calymnē, ēs, f., an island in the Aegean.
Camēnae, ārum, f., pl. (R. KAS, *sing,* cas, cas-mena, goddess of song), *the Camenae, Muses.*
camīnus, I, m. (R. AK, *sharp,* ἀκμινος, Sansc. aç-manta, κάμινος, camīnu-s, Vanicek, p. 5), *a smelting furnace, forge, stove* (Eng., *chimney*).
campus, I, m. (R. SKAP, *dig,* sca-m-p, ca-m-p), *a level ground, an open field, a plain, a battle-field.*
cancer, crī, m. (R. KAN, *hard,* kar, ka-n + kar, ca-n-cer), *a crab,* the sign of Cancer in the zodiac.
candeō, uī, 2 (R. SKAND, *to light, shine,* kand, cand), *to shine, glisten.*
candēscō, uī, 3 (candeō), *to grow shining (white), begin to glow.*

candĭdus, a, um, adj. (candeo), shining, shining-white, *brilliant*.

candor, ōris, m., a shining whiteness, *brightness, candor*.

cānĕō, uī, 2 (cānus), to be grayish white, *hoary, gray*.

cānēscō, uī, 3 (cānus), *to grow hoary, gray*.

canis, is, comm. (R. KU, KVI, KVAN, *to be strong*, can-is, κύων; Fr., *chien*; Eng., *hound*), *a dog*; the dog (Cerberus), *the Gallic = hunting dog*.

canistra, ae, f. (canna), a basket made of *reeds, a fruit-basket*.

cānĭtĭēs, em, ē, f. (cānus), *gray hairs*.

canna, ae, f., *a reed*.

canō, cĕcĭnī, cantum, 3 (R. KAN, *to sound, tone*), to produce a melodious tone, *sing, sing* (in prophecy), *to predict, sound* (a signal).

canor, ōris, m. (canō), *song*.

canōrus, a, um, adj., *tuneful*.

cantō, 1 (canō), *to sing, sing of, celebrate in song*.

cantus, ūs, m., *song, singing*.

cānus, a, um, adj. (R. KAS, *to be white, gray*), *gray-white, gray*, in pl. cani (sc. capilli), *gray hairs*.

capāx, ācis, adj. (capio), that can take, *capacious, susceptible for, apt for*.

capella, ae, f., *a she-goat, the Capella.* **caper**, prī, m., *a goat*.

capillus, ī, m., dim. (caput), hair of the *head* (in distinction from the beard), *hair*.

capĭō, cēpī, captum, 3 (R. KAP, *take*), *to seize, take, comprehend, understand (take), win, gain*.

Capitōlium, ī, n. (caput), *the Capitol*.

caprea, ae, f. (capra, R. KVAR, KUAP, *to smell*, çap, Van., but Curtius fr. KARP, KRAP, *to spring*, capr), *a wild goat*.

Caprea, ae, f. (capra), (the marsh) *of Caprea*.

captīvus, a, um, adj. (capio), *taken, captive*.

captō, 1 (capio), to take (eagerly), *to strive to take*.

caput, itis, n. (R. KAP, *take, comprise*, cap), *the head*, (of a river) *the head, source*.

carbăsus, ī, f., pl. carbasa, a texture of fine Spanish flax, *fine linen* (robes).

carcer, cris, m. (R. SKAR, *to keep*, skar(s), kar, car-cer), *a prison, barrier* (of the race-course).

cardō, inis, m. (R. SKARD, *to swing*, kard, card), *the hinge (of a door)*.

căreō, uī, 2 (R. SKAR, *to cut off*, car-ĕre, *to be cut off*), *to be without, be free from, want, lose*.

cărica, ae, f. (sc. ficus), *a Carian* (fig), *a dried fig, dried figs*.

carīna, ae, f. (R. KAR, *to be hard*, car), *the keel* (of a ship); by meton., *a ship*.

carmen, inis, n. (R. KAS, *sing*, kasman, car-men), *a song, song, a poem*.

carō, carnis, f. (R. KRU, *to become rough, raw*, car), *flesh, piece of flesh, meat*.

carpō, psī, ptum, 3 (R. SKARP, *to cut, tear*, scarp, carp-ō), *to pluck, break off, browse, eat, enjoy, carp at*; (with viam), *to go*; (with aethera), *to cleave, to fly through*.

cărus, a, um, adj. (R. KA, *to love*), *dear, precious, loved by*.

căsa, ae, f. (R. SKAD, *cover*, scad, cad, cad-ta, cas-ta, cas-sa, casa), *a hut*.

Cassiopē, ēs, f., wife of Cepheus and Andromeda's mother.

cassus, a, um, adj., *empty, worthless*.

Castalius, a, um, adj., *Castalian*.

castanea, ae, f., *chestnut-tree*.

castra, ōrum, n. (R. SKAD, *to cover*, cad, cad-tro, cas-tru-m), *a camp*.

cāsus, ūs, m. (cado), *fall, accident, fortune, misfortune*.

catēna, ae, f. (R. KAT, *make to fall*), *a fetter, chain*.

Catullus, ī, m., a poet; s. Am. 3, 15, 7. **cătŭlus**, ī, m., *a cub*.

cauda, ae, f. (R. SKUD, *to spring forth*), *tail of an animal*.

causa, ae, f. (R. SKAV, *be on one's guard*, guard, kav, cav, cav-es, cav-es-ta, cau-s-ta, cau-s-sa, causa), a matter guarded, *a cause, reason, ground, occasion, an affair*.

cautēs, is, f. (R. KA, KAN, *to sharpen*), *a pointed rock*.

căveō, cāvī, cautum, 2 (R. SKAV, *guard*), *to take care, to make provision*.

caverna, ae, f. (cavus), *a hollow, a cavern.*

cavō, 1 (cavus), *to hollow out.*

cavus, a, um, adj. (R. KU, kvi, kvan, *to be hollow*, cav), *hollow, hollowed out.*

Cĕcrops, opis, m., mythical king of Athens.

Cĕcropius, a, um, adj., *of Cecrops, Cecropian.*

cĕdō, cessī, cessum, 3 (R. same as cad-ō, cad, ce-cid, ce-id, cēd-), *to go forth, yield, give way, go over.*

celeber, celebris, e, adj. (R. kar, *to go, go to*, kal, cel, cele-ber, *gone to*), (much gone to), *frequented, numerous, celebrated.*

celebrō, 1 (celeber), *to frequent, to fill with one's presence, to solemnize, celebrate, praise.*

celer, cris, adj. (same R. as celebrō, *go swiftly*), *quick, swift.*

celer, prop. name (R. KAR, *be prominent*, cer, cel), one of the king's body-guard; cf. Celsi.

cēlō, 1 (R. SKAL, cel, *to cover*), *to conceal, hide.*

celsus, a, um, adj. (cellō), (R. KAR, kal, cel, *to be prominent*), *raised high, lofty.*

Cĕnaeus, a, um, adj., *of Cēnaeum, Cenaean.*

cēnsus, us, m. (cēnseō), (R. KAS, *sing, formally declare;* but Harpers' Dict. derives it fr. centum, centere, to hundred, number), the registering and taxing of the R. people, *census, property.*

Centaurus, I, m., *Centaur*, pl. *Centaurs*, a Thessalian people; Met. 2, 636; 9, 191.

centum, num. adj. (R. DAKAN, *ten*, dakan × da, kanta), *hundred.*

Cēpheus, eī, m., s. of Belus, and father of Andromeda; Met. 4, 738.

Cēphĕus, a, um, adj., *of Cepheus, Cephean.*

Cēphīsis, idis, fem. adj., *of Cephisus.*

Cēphīsus, I, m., a river in Phocis; Met. 3, 19.

cēra, ae, f. (R. SKAR, kar, *to separate*), *wax.*

cērātus, a, um, adj. (cēra), *of wax, waxed, waxen.*

Cerberus, I, m., the three-headed dog of the lower world, offspring of Echidna, *Echidnea canis*, also monstrum *Medusaeum*, as Echidna was descended fr. Medusa.

Cereālis, e, adj. (Ceres), *of Ceres, cereal* (cereals).

Cerēs, eris, f., daughter of Saturn and Rhea, mother of Proserpine; Met. 5, 338-571.

cernō, crēvī, crētum, 3 (R. SKAR, kar, *separate*, cer, cre-), *to separate, divide, distinguish, see clearly, discern.*

certāmen, inis, n. (certō, cernō), *a contest, a prize-fight.*

certē, adv. (certus), *certainly, surely, at any rate, at least.*

certō, 1 (cernō), *to contend, decide by a contest, vie with, struggle.*

certus, a, um, adj. (cernō), *determined, fixed, sure, unerring, resolved, assured of.*

cerva, ae, f. (R. KAR, *hard*, cer), *a hind.*

cervix, Icis, f. (R. kar + R. vi, KAR, *prominent*, and vi, vi-k, vi-N-K, *bind*), *the neck.*

cervus, I, m. (same R. as cerva), *the* (horned) *stag, deer.*

cessō, 1 (cedō), *to fall back, delay, linger.*

cēterus, a, um, adj. (R. KI, kai, demon. pronom. stem, kai-tara), *the other* (that which is over), *the others, the rest.*

ceu, adv., ceve (fr. R. KI, as in ceterus, + R. ve, fr. VAR, val, vol (vol-o), *to will*), *or this* (this if you will); (in comparison) *just as, like as.*

Cēyx (dissyl.), ȳcis, s. of Lucifer, husband of Alcyone.

chaos, nom. and acc. n., abl. chaō, *chaos;* see n. Met. 1, 7; for *the* (vast) *lower world.*

Charybdis, is, f., a whirlpool in the strait of Sicily.

Chimaerifera, ae, adj., f., epithet of Lycia, as the *Chimaera-* or *monster-bearing.*

Chīrōn, ōnis, m., the Centaur, son of Saturn and Philyra.

chorda, ae, f., *a string, chord* (R. GHAR, *to be flexible*, χορ, χορδή, chorda).

chorus, I, m., *a dance in a ring, a band of dancers and singers, a chorus.*

chrysolith- us or os, I, m. and f., *chrysolite or topaz.*

cibus, I, m. (**R.** RAP, *to take,* cip, cib, cib-u-s), *food.*

Cibyrēius, a, um, adj., *of Cibyra,* a city in Phrygia, *Cibyreian.*

Cicones, um, m., a people in Thrace; Met. 10, 2; 11, 3.

icōnia, ae, f., *a stork* (**R.** KAN, *to bend,* con-).

Cilix, icis, adj., *of Cilicia, Cilician.*

Cimmeriī, ōrum, m., see note, Met. 11, 592.

cingō, nxī, ctum, 3 (**R.** KAN, *to be bent,* ka-n + k(ar), c-i-n-g-cre), *to compass in a circle, surround, gird, gird about, wreathe.*

cinis, eris, m. (**R.** KNU, cnu, cun-, *to scratch, to scrape*), *ashes.*

Cinyrās, ae, m., 1, name of an Assyrian king, Met. 6, 98 ; 2, of a Cyprian prince, s. of Pygmalion.

circā, adv. and prep. (**R.** KAN, *to be bent,* kar + k(ar), cir-ca), *around, round about.* circu-eō, 4. *to go around.*

circuitus, ūs, m. (circueō), *circuit.*

circum, adv. and prep. (same **R.** as circa), *around, round about.*

circum-dō (dō), dedī, datum, dare, *to surround, encompass.*

circum-ferō, tulī, lātum, 3 (ferō), *to carry around, cast around.*

circum-fluō, fluxī, 3, *to flow around.*

circum-fluus, a, um, adj., *flowing around, surrounded by water.*

circum-fundō, fūdī, fūsum, 3, *to pour around, press around.*

circum-linō (linō), litum, 3 (linō), *to smear around, besmear, embellish.*

circum-sonō, āre, *to sound about.*

circumsonus, a, um, adj., *barking.*

circum-spiciō (speciō), spexī, spectum, 3, *to look about, to look about one's self.*

circum-stō, stetī, 1, *to stand around, surround.*

Circus, I, m. (same **R.** as circa), *the* Circus Maximus, in the valley between the Palatine and Aventine.

cithara, ae, f., *the cithern. guitar.*

citius, adv. comp. (cito), *more quickly, sooner.*

citrā, adv. and prep. (**R.** KI, dem. pron. stem, ci-ter-tra, ci-trā, abl. fem., *on this side*), *on this side,* nec virtus *citra genus, nor is* (my) *merit this side of*—i. e., *lower than*—(my) *birth.*

citus, a, um, adj. (cieō), *quick, swift.*

cīvīlis, e, adj. (civis), *of a citizen, civil.*

cīvis, is, m. (**R.** KI, *lie down* (*abide*), κεῖ-μαι, kei, kei-va, *a house,* cei-vi-s, ci-vi-s, one in the house, at home, in opp. to a foreigner), *a citizen, a fellow-citizen.*

clādes, is, f. (**R.** KAR, *to thrust, slay,* kal, cal, cla-), *a throwing down, overthrow, defeat, disaster.*

clāmo, 1 (**R.** KAR, *to sound, call,* kal, cal, cla-), *to shout, cry aloud, to call by name.*

clāmor, ōris, m. (clamō), *a shout, a shout of applause, a shout of joy.*

Clarius, a, um, adj., *of Claros, Clarian.*

Claros, I, a city in Ionia, celebrated for its temple of Apollo.

clārus, a, um, adj. (**R.** same as clāmō), (loud), *clear, bright, illustrious.*

classis, is, f. (**R.** same as clāmō, cla + t), *a calling together,* 1, of citizens to vote), (*classis*) ; 2, to arms ; then 3 (to naval warfare), *a fleet.*

claudō (dsi), sī, sum, 3 (**R.** SKLU, *to shut,* klu, clau-), *to close, shut in, shut, inclose, shut up.*

clāva, ae, f. (**R.** KAR, *to thrust,* kal, cal, cla-), *a stick, club.*

clāvus, I, m. (**R.** SKLU, *shut,* klu, clan-, clav-), *a nail.*

clipeātus, a, um, adj. (clipeus). (**R.** KLA-p), *steal, hide,* cle-p, clip-), *shield-armed ;* **clipeus,** I, m., *a shield.*

clīvus, I, m. (**R.** KRI, *to lean*), *an acclivity, a slope, declivity.*

Clymenē, ēs, f., d. of Tethys, Met. 1, 756.

Clymenēius, a, um, adj., *of Clymene.*

co-arguō, uī (con, arguō), *to convict, expose.*

coctilis, e, adj. (coquō), *burned, of brick.*

co-eō, iī, itum, 4 (con, eō), *to go together, assemble, unite.*

coepī, perf., coeptum, coepisse (fr.

R. AP, *bind*, ap-e-re (aptus), co-ap-e-re, coep-ere), *to fit, together, on all sides, begin, undertake.*
coeptum, I, n. (coepī), *something begun, undertaking.*
co-erceō, ercuī, ercitum, 3 (arceō), *to keep together, inclose, restrain, confine.*
Coeus, I, m., father of Latona.
co - (con)gnātus (nātus, nāscor), (born with), *related, kindred.*
co - (con)gnōscō, nōvī, nitum, 3 (gnōscō, nōscō), *to come to know, to become acquainted with, to know, recognize, perceive.*
cōgō, coegī, coactum, 3 (con, agō), *to drive together, bring up* (mil. with agmen), *force, compel.*
co-haereō, haesī, haesum, 2, *to hang together, cohere.*
co-hors, hortis, f. (hors, fr. **R.** GHAR, *seize, inclose,* har, hor-tu-s (an inclosure), then (of men) co-hor-ti, cohors), *a cohort, troop, multitude, retinue.*
Colchus, a, um, adj., *of Colchis, Colchian.*
col-lābor, lapsus, v. dep., 3 (con, labor), *to fall together, sink in, fall in ruins (collapse).*
col-ligō, lēgī, lectum, 3 (con, legō), *to gather together, assemble, collect, gather up.*
collis, is, m. (**R.** KAR, kal, cel, *be prominent, high*), *a hill.*
col-luō, luī, lūtum, 3, *to moisten.*
collum, I, n. (**R.** KAR, *bend,* kal, cal), *the neck.*
colō, uī, cultum, 3 (**R.** KAR, *go, move*), *to till, cultivate, dwell in, inhabit, honor, worship.*
colōnus, I, m. (colō), *a tiller of the ground, farmer, peasant, tenant, inhabitant.*
Colophōnius, a. um, adj., *of Colophon,* a city in Ionia.
color, ōris, m. (**R.** SKAL, kal, *cover,* col-), *color, complexion.*
colubra, ae, f. (same **R.** as color, (*dark*) *color*), *a female serpent, snake.*
columba, ae, f. (of same **R.** as color), *a dove.*
columna, ae, f. (**R.** KAR, *prominent,* kal, cal), *a column.*
coma, ae, f. (**R.** KAS, *rub* (cār-ere, *to comb*), co-ma, *hair* (considered as an ornament).
com-bibō, bibī, 3 (con, bibō), *to drink together, to drink in, absorb.*
comes, itis, m. (con, cō), (one who goes with), *a companion, partner, attendant.*
comitō, 1 (comes), *to accompany, attend.*
comitor, ātus, v. dep., 1, *to accompany, attend.*
com-memorō, 1 (con, memorō), *to make mention of, commemorate.*
commentus, part. pass. of comminiscor, *contrived, invented.*
com-mereō, uī, itum, 2, *to merit, deserve.*
comminus, adv. (con, manus), *hand to hand, in close contest.*
com-mittō, mīsī, missum, 3, *to bring together, join, begin, put together, commit, give up to.*
commūnis, e, adj. (con, mūnus), *common, in common.*
cōmō, compsi, comptum, 3 (**R.** AM, *take,* co-am, co-em, com-, *to put together*), *to arrange, dress, comb, adorn.*
compāgēs, is. f. (compingō, con, pangō), *a joining together, union.*
compescō, pescuī, 3 (**R.** PARK, *to bind*), *to hold in check, confine.*
com-plector, plexus sum, v. dep. (con, plector), *to twine around, clasp, embrace.*
com-pleō, ēvī, ētum, 2 (con *and* pleō), *to make full, fill full, fill, fulfill, complete.*
complexus, ūs, m. (complector), *a clinging about, surrounding, embrace.*
com-pōnō, posuī, positum, 3 (con *and* pōnō), *to put together, arrange in order, put to rest, compose, compare.*
com-precor, 1, v. dep., *pray earnestly* (con *and* precor).
com-prendō (con *and* prehendō), prendī, prēnsum, 3, *to seize together, on all sides, grasp; comprehend.*
com-primō (con, premō), pressī, pressum, 3, *to press together, compress, suppress.*
cōnāmen, inis, n. (conor), *an exertion, struggle, effort.*
con-cavō, 1, *to make hollow, bend, curve.*

concentus, ūs, m. (concinō), *a harmony, symphony.*

concha, ae, f., *a bivalve, shell-fish, mussel.*

con-cinō, cinuī, 3 (con, canō), *to sing or play together, sing harmoniously, sing of.*

con-cipiō, cepī, ceptum, 3 (capiō), *to lay hold of, catch, to receive into one's self, conceive, compose, utter.*

concitus, part. fr. concieō, *aroused, stormy, stirred.*

con-clāmō, 1 (clamō), *to shout, call together.*

concolor, ōris, adj., *of like color.*

concordō, 1 (concors), *to agree together, harmonize.*

concors, cordis, adj. (cor), *concordant, harmonious.*

con-crēscō, crēvī, crētum, 3, *to grow together, cleave together, thicken, harden, congeal.*

con-currō, currī, cursum, 3, *to run together, engage in combat, to fight.*

con-cursus, ūs, m., *a running together, concourse, an encounter* (in battle).

con-custōdiō, 4, *to guard together, to guard carefully.*

con-cutiō (quatiō), cussī, cussum, 3, *to strike together (to bring into concussion), shake violently, shatter.*

condiciō, ōnis, f. (condicō), *an agreement, a condition.*

con-dō, didī, ditum (dō, dere, *to put), to put together, build, put away, put in,* put in (the grave), *bury.*

conditor, ōris, m., *a builder.*

con-dūcō, xī, ctum, 3, *to draw together, unite, bind.*

cōn-ferō, tulī, lātum, 3, *to bring together, try one's strength with, in fight, try with.*

cōn-ficiō, fēcī, fectum, 3 (faciō), *to finish;* part., confectus, a, um, *exhausted.*

cōnfīdō, fīsus sum, 3, *to trust, confide in.*

cōnfīnium, ī, n. (confīnis), in pl. confinia, the common boundary, *confine.*

cōnfiteor, fessus sum, 2 (fateor), *to confess, to make known.*

cōn-fugiō, fūgī, 3, *to flee for refuge.*

con-fundō, fūdī, fūsum, 3, *to pour together, mix together.*

con-gelō, 1, trans. and intrans., *to thicken, harden, stiffen.*

con-geriēs, ēi, f. (congerō), *what is brought together, a heap, mass, pile.*

con-gerō, gessī, gestum, 3, *to bring together, heap up, unite.*

con-gredior (gradior), 3, *to meet together, engage together, in fight, attack.*

cōniciō (coniiciō, conjiciō), jēcī, jectum, 3, *to throw together, hurl.*

conjugiālis, e, adj. (conjugium), relating to marriage, *conjugal.*

conjugium, ī, n., *union, marriage.*

con-jungō, junxī, junctum, 3, *to join together, unite.*

conjunx (conjux), jugis, comm. (conjungō), *a spouse, wife, husband.*

conor, v. dep., 1 (**R.** perhaps KAM, *trouble one's self,* con), *to undertake, endeavor.*

con-queror, questus sum, v. dep., *to complain, bewail.*

cōn-scelerō, 1, *to cause to share a crime, to dishonor.*

cōn-scendō, dī, sum, 3 (scandō), *to mount, go on board of, together.*

cōn-scius, a, um, adj. (sciō), *one who knows together with, privy to, conscious.*

cōn-senēscō, senuī, 3, *to grow old together.*

cōnsēnsus, ūs, m. (consentiō), *an agreement, consent.*

cōn-sequor, cūtus sum, v. dep., *to follow up, come up with, overtake.*

cōn-sīderō, 1 (fr. sīdus, **R.** SUID, *to be smooth, bright,* sīd-us, *a* (bright) *constellation,* considerāre, *to observe the stars), to consider, observe.*

cōn-sīdō, sēdī, sessum, 3, *to set one's self down, to be seated.*

cōnsilium, ī, n. (consulō), *counsel, purpose, wisdom.*

cōn-sistō, stitī, 3, *to cause to stand, to place one's self, to put in position, to take, have, a place.*

cōnsōlor, v. dep., 1, *to console.*

cōnsors, tis, adj. (con, sors), *sharing lot with, consort, wife.*

cōnspiciō (speciō), spexī, spectum, 3, *to look at, behold.*

cŏnspĭcuus, a, um, adj. (conspicio), *conspicuous, stately.*

cŏn-sternō, āvi, ātum (strengthened form of consterno, 3), *to throw into confusion, consternation.*

cŏn-stō, stĭtī, stātum, 1, *to stand, to remain standing.*

cŏn-suēscō, suēvī, suētum, 3, *to accustom one's self, be accustomed.*

cōnsŭlō, sŭluī, sultum, 3 (saliō), (R. SAR, *go, spring, sal, sol, sul,* con-sul-ō, *to come together*), to meet in consultation, *to consult, deliberate, to consult* (an oracle).

cŏn-sūmō, sumpsī, sumptum, 3 (sumo, fr. sub and emo, sub-im-ere, sū-mere, R. AM, *to take*), *to consume, exhaust, devour, destroy.*

cŏn-surgō, surrexī, surrectum, 3, *to raise one's self, rise.*

contactus, ūs, m. (contingo), *contact.*

con-temnō, tempsī, temptum, 3, *to contemn, despise.*

contemptor, ōris, m. (contemno), *a despiser.*

contemptrix, icis, f., a woman who despises, *a despiser.*

con-tendō, tendī, tentum, 3 (tendo, *to stretch*), *to stretch, strain, to compare one's self with.*

conterminus, a, um, adj. (con, terminus), *bordering on, near by.*

con-terreō, terruī, territum, 2, *to terrify.*

con-ticēsco, ticuī (taceo), 3, *to be silent, keep silent.*

contĭguus, a, um, adj. (contingo), *touching upon, contiguous.*

con-tĭneō, tinuī, tentum (teneo), 2, *to hold together, hold fast, to contain;* part., contentus, *limited, bounded; content.*

con-tingō, tigi, tactum, 3 (tango), *to come in contact with, touch, reach, to happen to one, to fall to one's (good) fortune.*

con-torqueō, torsī, tortum, 2, *to hurl violently, hurl, brandish.*

contrā, adv., cum, con (R. SAK, sakam, skvom, skom (*follow, be with*), con, con-ter-trā, contrā, abl. fem., *over against, on the contrary.*

con-trahō, xī, ctum, 3, *to draw together, contract.*

contrārius, a, um, adj. (contrā), set over against, lying opposite, *opposite, contrary.*

conubium, i, n. (the u before b - (u) in Met. 1, 480, but short (ŭ) in 6, 428, also pronŭba in same line; short ŭ in Verg. seven times, and once in Lucret. 3, 777); (con, nūbo), *intermarriage, marriage.*

cōnus, i, m. (κῶνος, R. KAN, *sharpen*), *a cone, the* (cone-like) *top,* or *apex, of a helmet, crest.*

con-valēsco, valuī, 3, *to get well, convalesce, gain strength.*

con-vellō, vulsī, vulsum, 3, *to pull violently, tear up, grind.*

con-veniō, vēnī, ventum, 4, *to come together, assemble.*

con-vertō, vertī, versum, 3, *to turn round, turn against, convert, change.*

convexus, a, um, adj. (conveho), *arched, convex.*

convīcium, i, n., con, vīcium (R. VAK, *cry out,* vōc (vox), vīc, *a crying out together*), *a loud noise, wrangling, quarreling, abusive speech.*

convictus, ūs, m. (vivo), *a living together, intimacy, social life.*

convīva, ae, comm. (vivo), one who lives with, *a guest.*

con-vocō, 1, *to call together, convoke.*

co-orior, ortus sum, 4, *to rise together, break forth together.*

cōpĭa, ae, f. (co-ops, is), abundant means, *abundance, wealth, riches, supplies.*

Cōpia, ae, f., personif., the goddess of plenty.

coquō, coxī, coctum, 3 (R. PAK (*bake*), (or R. kak, Corssen), *cook,* kap, pok, coc, coqu-), *to cook.*

cor, dis, n. (R. SKARD, *spring, swing,* skard (καρδία), kard, cord, cord-i), *the heart.*

Corinna, ae, f., a feigned name of the object of Ovid's love (fr. the name of the celebrated Gr. poetess).

Corinthus, ī, f., a city on the isthmus between Peloponnesus and Hellas, *Corinth.*

corniger, era, erum, adj. (cornu, gero), *horn-bearing, horned.*

cornū, ūs, n. (R. KAR, *hard,* car,

cor), *a horn, horn ; wing* (of an army) ; (used of) *a point of land;* also cornum, n.

cornum, I, n., *the cornel-cherry.*

corōna, ae, f. (**R.** KAR, *to be bent,* kor, κορώνη, cor, corōna), *a wreath, garland, crown.*

corporeus, a, um, adj. (corpus), *of body, flesh, meat.*

corpus, oris, n. (**R.** KAR, *to make,* kar-p, cor-p, cor-p-us), *what is made, body, substance, a body, flesh, corpse.*

cor-rigō, rexī, rectum, 3 (regō), *to set right, correct.*

cor-ripiō, ripuī, reptum, 3 (rapiō), *to seize violently, lay hold of, hasten over, ruin, destroy, attack.*

cortex, icis, m. (**R.** SKAR, *rub*, skor, cor-), *the bark of a tree, shell* (of fruit).

coruscus, a, um, adj. (coruscō), (**R.** SKAR, *to spring, leap,* move tremulously, coruscate), *vibrating, glittering.*

Cōrycides, um, f. (sc. Nymphae), of the promontory Cōrycus, in Cilicia.

costa, ae, f., *a rib.*

cothurnus, I, m. (κόθορνος), a high Grecian shoe ; the high-heeled, thick-soled shoe of Gr. tragic actors), *buskin ;* see note, Am. 1, 15, 15.

crātēr, ēris, m. (κρατήρ, κρητήρ, a *mixing-vessel* (for the mixing of wine with water, *bowl ;* a (bowl-like) *opening, abyss, crater.*

creber, bra, brum, adj. (**R.** KAR, *make, create,* kra, cre, creo, cresc-ō ; + varah fr. **R.** kvar, var, ber, *bent, stretched*), outspread, *numerous, frequent, abounding in.*

crē-dō, didī, ditum, 3 (fr. **R.** KRAT, *confidence,* cret, cred-, + **R.** DHA, *put* (dō, dere), cred-dere, crē-dere, *put confidence), to trust, believe, think.*

crēdulitas, ātis, f. (crēdō), *credulity.*

crēdulus, a, um, adj. (crēdō), *credulous.*

cremō, 1 (**R.** KAR, *cook, seethe,* kar, cre-), *to burn.*

creō, 1 (**R.** KAR, *make,* kra, crejā, creā-), *to produce, create.*

crepitō, 1 (crepō. **R.** KRAP, *make a noise,* crep-), *to rattle, clatter, clash, gnash.*

crepusculum, ī, n. (dimin. of creper, creperus, **R.** SKAR, *cover, dark-*en, c-nep, c-rep), *dusk, evening, twilight.*

crēscō, crēvī, crētum, 3 (creō, crē-scere), *to grow, increase ;* part. crētus, a, um, *sprung from, born of.*

crīmen, inis, n. (**R.** SKAR, kar, *distinguish,* cer, cer-nō, cer-ni-men, crī-men), *a judgment, charge, reproach, guilt, crime.*

crīnis, is, m. (**R.** KAR, *jut out,* kri, cri-), *hair.*

crīnītus, a, um, adj. (crīnis), *haired,* with *angue, snake-haired,* Met. 10, 349.

crista, ae, f. (same **R.** as crīnis), *crest.*

cristatus, a, um, adj. (crista), *crested.*

croceus, a, um, adj. (crocus), *of saffron, saffron-colored.*

Croesus, I, m., see note, Trist. 3, 7, 42.

cruciātus, ūs, m. (cruciō, crux), *torture.*

crūdēlis, e, adj. (crūdus), *rough in character, cruel.*

crūdus, a, um, adj. (cruor, cruidus), *raw, crude, unfeeling.*

cruentō, 1 (cruor), *to stain, cover with blood.*

cruentus, a, um, adj. (cruor), *bloody, blood-stained.*

cruor, ōris, m. (**R.** KRU, *to become rough, raw*), *blood.*

crūs, crūris, n. (**R.** KAR, *go, move*), *the leg, shank, shank-bone, foot.*

cubīle, is, n. (cumbō, cubi), *a couch.*

cubitus, ī, m., cubitum, ī, n. (cubō), *the elbow,* for lying or leaning upon; (as a measure), *a cubit.*

cubō, uī, itum, 1 (cumbō, 3), (**R.** KUP, *go up and down,* kub, cub-), *to lie down.*

culmen, inis, n. (**R.** same as crinis, skar, kar, cel, cul-), *top, point ;* (of a building), *gable.*

culpa, ae, f. (**R.** skarp, *scratch,* skalp, sculp, culp-), *injury, guilt, fault, blame.*

culpō, 1 (culpa), *to blame, censure.*

cultor, ōris, m. (colō), *tiller, cultivator,* of the soil ; *a worshiper.*

cultus, ūs, m. (colō) *worship.*

cum, prep. (**R.** SAK, *follow, be with,*

sakam, skom, com, cum), *with, together with, at same time with.*

cum, conj. (R. pronom. stem KA, *which*, kva, qua, quo abl., quo-m acc., cu-m, *when, as, while, as often as, as soon as; since, inasmuch as* (causal), *though, although, while* (concessive).

cumba, ae, f. (R. KUBH, *hollow*), *a boat, skiff.*

cūnae, ārum, f. pl., *a cradle.*

cunctor, v. dep., 1 (R. KAK, kank, *to be anxious*, canc-, cunc-ta-ri), *to delay* (wisely), *hesitate.*

cunctus, a, um, adj. (conjunctus), joined together, *all together, all.*

cuneus, I, m. (R. KAN, *sharpen*), *a wedge.*

cupīdŏ, inis, f. (R. KAP, *swell up*, cup-, cup-ere), *a desire, wish, for.*

Cupīdŏ, inis, m., the god of love, Amor, s. of Venus.

cupidus, a, um, adj. (cupio), *desirous, eager for.*

cupĭō, īvī or iī, ītum, 3 (R. as cupido), *to wish, desire.*

cūr, adv. (R. pron. stem KA, quā, interrog. abl. quā-re, qua-r, quo-r, co-r, cūr), *wherefore, why.*

cūra, ae, f. (R. SKAV, *beware*, kav, cav, cov, cov-i-ra, co-i-ra, coe-ra), *care.*

cūrālium, I, n., *coral.*

cūria, ae, f. (R. SKU, *cover*, skav, cav-ro, cov-os-ia, cov-s-ia, cu-s-ia, cūria, *house;* but perh. fr. VAS, *dwell*), *the curia, senate-house.*

cūrō, 1 (cūra), *to care for, be anxious for.*

currŏ, cucurrī, cursum, 3 (R. KAR, *go*, cur, cur-jere, cur-r-), (of hasty motion), *to run, fly, sail, flow.*

currus, ūs, m. (currō), *a chariot.*

cursus, ūs, m. (currō), *a running, course, prize-race, flight, sail, journey.*

curvāmen, inis, n. (curvus), *a bend, curve.*

curvātūra, ae, f. (curvus), *a rounding, rim.*

curvō, 1 (curvus), *to crook, bend, curve.*

curvus, a, um, adj. (R. KAR (*to be bent*), kvar, cur, cur-vu-s), *crooked, bent, curved.*

cuspis, idis, f., etym. unc., *a point, pointed end;* by meton., *a lance, spear.*

custōdia, ae, f. (custōs), a watching, guard; by meton., *guardian.*

custōs, ōdis, m., comm. (R. KUDH, *guard*, cud-to, cus-to-s), *a guard, protector, protectress;* by meton., *a safe, a* (safe) *quiver.*

cutis, is, f. (R. SKU, *cover*, scu, cu), *the skin.*

Cyanē, ēs, f., a fountain near Syracuse.

Cybelē, ēs, f., a goddess worshiped in Phrygia and in Rome; mother of Midas.

Cyclades, um, f., islands in the Aegean, *the Cyclades.*

Cyclōps, ōpis, m., see note, Met. 13, 755.

cycnus, I, m. (R. KAN, *sound* (canō), cinu-s, cycnu-s, κύκνο-ς), *the swan;* for its dying *song*, Cic. Tusc. I, 30, 73.

Cycnus, I, m., s. of Sthenelus, turned into a swan; Met. 2, 367.

Cynthus, I, m., a mountain in Delos, birthplace of Apollo and Diana.

Cyprius, a, um, adj., *of Cyprus, Cyprian.*

Cytherēa, ae, f., name of Venus, fr. Cythera, an island where she was worshiped; *Cytherea.*

Cytōriacus, a, um, adj., *of Cytorus*, a mountain in Paphlagonia, *Cytorian.*

D

Daedalus, I, m., δαίδαλος (R. DAR, *hew, work in art*, δαλ, by redupl., δαιδαλ-), worker in art, *Daedalus.*

damma (dāma), ae, f. (etym. unc., perh. fr. DAM, *tame*), *a deer, buck, doe, antelope, gazelle, chamois.*

damnō, 1 (damnum), *to occasion loss to, damage; to condemn, censure.*

damnātus, a, um, adj., *injurious, hurtful, damaging.*

damnum, I, n. (R. DA, *share*, da-p, dap-s, dap-no, dam-nu-m), *a sharing* (giving) in vain, *a loss, damage, injury.*

damnōsus, a, um, adj., *ruinous.*

Danaē, ēs, f., d. of Acrisius, mother of Perseus.

Daphnē, ēs, f., d. of the river-god Peneus; changed into a laurel-tree, δάφνη.

daps, apis, f. (R. DA, see damnum), *a feast, banquet, food, meat.*

dē, prep. with abl. (fr. pronom. stem DA, de), *from, down from, up from, out of* (made); from (causal); *about, in accordance with.*

dea, ae, f. (R. same as deus, which see), *a goddess.*

dē-beō, uī, itum, 2 (de-habeō), to have something f. some one, *to owe,* be in debt, *be bound, be under obligation, be under the necessity.*

decem, num. (R. dakam), *ten.*

dē-cerpō, cerpsī, cerptum, 3 (carpō), *to pluck off, pluck.*

decet, uit, 2 (R. DAK, *honor,* dec), (*it*) *is seemly, becoming.*

dē-cidō, cidī, 3 (cadō), *to fall down.*

decies, num. adv. (DAKAM), *ten times.*

decimus, a, um, num. adj. (decem), *tenth.*

dē-cipiō, cepī, ceptum (capiō), *to deceive.* **dē-clīnō,** 1, *to turn.*

dēclīvis, e, adj. (clīvus), *inclining downwards, sloping.*

decor, ōris, m. (decet), *comeliness, grace; ornament.*

decōrus, a, um, adj. (decor), *becoming, fitting, decorous, beautiful, stately.*

dē-crēscō, crēvī, crētum, 3 (crēscō), *to decrease, grow less, shorter, smaller.*

decus, oris, n. (decet), *ornament, grace, honor, glory, rank.*

dē-decet, uit, 3 (decet), *it is unbecoming.*

dēdecus, oris, n., *dishonor, disgrace, shame.*

dē-dūcō, duxī, ductum, 3, *to bring down, draw down, carry away, to weave* (in tela).

dē-fendō, dī, sum, 3, *to ward off, defend, protect.*

dē-ferō, tulī, lātum, 3, *to carry away, bring.*

dē-ficiō, fēcī, fectum, 3 (faciō), *to fail, be wanting, leave, desert.*

dē-fīgō, fixī, fixum, 3, *to fasten, fix, down.*

dē-fleō, flevī, flētum, 2, *to weep over, lament.*

dē-fluō, fluxī, fluxum, 3, *to flow down, fall down.*

dē-formis, e, adj., *ill-formed, ugly.*

dē-frēnātus, a, um, adj. (frenō), *unbridled.*

dē-fungor, functus sum, v. dep., 3, *to bring to an end, to finish* (with *terra*) *one's earthly course.*

dē-gravō, 1, *to weigh down.*

Dēianīra, ae, f., d. of Oeneus, sister of Meleager.

dēiciō (jaciō), jēcī, jectum, 3, *to hurl down;* part. fig., *dejected.*

deinde, adv., pron. stem DA, de, inde, *from there, afterwards, then.*

dē-lābor, lapsus sum, v. dep., 3, *to glide down, fall down.*

dē-lēniō, ivī, itum, 4, to soften down, *soothe, charm.*

dē-leō, lēvī, lētum, 2, etym. unc., *to destroy.*

Dēlia, ae, f., see note, Am. 3, 9, 31.

deliciae, ārum, f. (R. LAK, *lac, entice,* lic-ere, de-lic-ia, iae), *enticing things, delights.*

dē-lictum, ī, n. (delinquō, *to fail*), *a failing, fault.*

Dēlius, a, um, adj., *of Delos, the Delian;* name of Apollo, as born in Delos.

Dēlos, ī, f., an island in the Aegean, *Delos.*

Delphī, ōrum, m., city of Apollo's oracle, in Phocis, *Delphi.*

Delphicus, a, um, adj., *of Delphi, Delphian, the Delphian.*

delphīn, inis, m, *a dolphin.*

dēlūbrum, ī, n. (lu-e-re, R. LU, *lou, lō, lī, wash, cleanse,* lu-e-re, lū-bru-m, de-lū-bru-m, place for cleansing), *a temple, shrine.*

dē-mēns, tis, adj., *out of one's mind, demented, foolish.*

dē-mittō, mīsī, missum, 3, *to let, send, down, drop, plunge, sink.*

dēmō (de, emō), dempsi, demptum, 3, *to take from, remove, take off, away.*

dēnique, adv. (pron. stem DA, de, de-no-que), *and then, finally, at length.*

dēns, tis, m. (R. AD, *eat,* ed-ere, ed-e-nt, dēn-s), *a tooth* (elephant's tusk), *ivory.*

dēnsus, a, um, adj. (R. DASA, *thick*), *dense, thick, thick-set, surrounded.*

Deŏis, idis, f., d. of Deo (Δηώ, Demeter); Persephone, Proserpine.
dē-pellō, pulī, pulsum, 3, *to drive, chase, away.*
de-pendeō, ēre, *to hang down, from.*
dē-perdō, didī, ditum, 3, *to destroy, ruin, utterly ruin.*
dē-pereō, iī, itum, 4, de, per, eō, *to perish utterly, go to ruin.*
dē-plōrō, 1, *to deplore, lament.*
dē-pōnō, posuī, positum, de, po-, sinō. 3. *to lay down, away, lay aside,* subst., dēpositum, a thing laid down, *deposit, trust.*
dē-precor, v. dep., 1, to pray away, *turn away by prayers, deprecate.*
dē-prendō (prehendō), prendī, prēnsum, 3, *to snatch away, seize, catch, perceive.*
dē-primō, pressī, pressum, 3 (premō), *to press down, depress.*
dē-rigēscō, riguī, 3, only the perf. in use, *to become stiff, fixed.*
dē-scendō, dī, sum, 3 (scandō), *to descend.*
dē-serō, uī, sertum, 3, *to desert.*
dē-sīderō (see consīderō), 1, *to desire, long for, miss, regret.*
dēsidia, ae, f. (de-sīdō), *a sitting down, idleness.*
dē-sīgnō, 1, *to mark out, design, depict.*
dē-sinō, īvī, iī, itum, 3, *to leave off, cease, end.*
dē-sistō, stitī, stitum, 3, *to desist, cease.*
dēsōlātus, a, um, adj. (dēsōlō), *left alone, desolate.*
dē-spernō, ere, *to despise.*
dē-spiciō, spexī, spectum, 3 (speciō), *to look down upon, disdain, despise.*
dē-stituō, uī, ūtum, 3 (statuō), to set down, *leave alone, forsake.*
dē-suētus, a, um, adj., *unaccustomed.*
dē-sum, fuī, esse, *to fail, be wanting.*
dĕtĕgō, xī, ctum, 3, *to uncover, lay bare, detect.*
dētĕrior, ius, adj. comp. (fr. pronom. stem DA, de, *down, downwards,* obs. de-ter), *lower, inferior, worse.*
dē-terō, trīvī, trītum, 3, *to wear away.*

dē-terreō, uī, itum, 3, *to frighten from, keep from, deter.*
dē-trahō, xī, ctum, 3, *to draw from* or *down, draw off.*
dē-trectō, 1 (tractō, trahō), *to draw down, to lower, detract, decline.*
dē-trūdō, sī, sum, 3, *to thrust from, drive down.*
Deucaliōn, ōnis, m., s. of Prometheus; Met. 1, 318, seqq.
Deus, I, m. (R. same as div-us, DI, DIV, *to be bright, bright heavens,* dju, djau, djav, djō, daiva, divu-s, dīus, dius, deus), *God, deity.*
dēvius (via), a, um, adj., *out of the way, retired, devious.*
dē-volvō, volvī, volūtum, 3, *to roll down, roll off from.*
dē-vorō, 1, *to swallow, check.*
dē-voveō, vōvī, vōtum, 2, *to curse.*
dexter, tra and tera, trum, adj. (R. DAK, *to seize, take,* dak-s, dex, dex-ter), *to the right, right;* subst., *the right hand,* sc. manus.
Diāna, ae, f. (same R. as deus, DIV, div-, deiv-ana, Diāna, Diăna), Gr. Artemis, d. of Jupiter and Latona; *Diana;* also as goddess of the moon, Luna.
dīcō, xī, ctum, 3 (R. DA, *show, teach,* da-k, doc, di-k, dic, deic, dīco), *to say, speak, relate, determine, be called.*
diēs, ēi, m. and f. (same R. as deus, div, diva-s, diā-s, die-s), *day, daylight, day* (in sense of time).
Diēs, *day,* personified, *Day.*
dif-ferō, dis-tulī, dī-lātum, 3 (to put apart), (of time) to put off, *defer, make forget,* Met. 8, 366.
difficilis, e, adj. (facilis), *difficult, hard.*
dif-fīdō, fīsus sum, 3, *to distrust.*
dif-fugiō, fūgī, 3, to flee apart, *to scatter.*
dif-fundō, fūdī, fūsum, 3, to pour forth, *to spread, diffuse.*
digitōsus, a, um, adj. (digitus), *many-fingered.*
digitus, I, m., *a finger, a toe.*
dī-gnōscō, gnōvī, 3, *to know apart.*
dignus, a, um, adj. (R. DAK, to honor, dic, dic-nu-s, dig-nu-s), *worthy, deserving, worth.*
dī-gredior (gradior), 3, gressus sum, v. dep., *to go apart, separate, go away.*

dī-laniō, 1, to tear apart, *rend.*
di-ligō, lexī, lectum, 3 (lego), to choose out, *esteem, value, love.*
dī-luvium, ī, n. (luo), (a washing away), *a flood, deluge.*
dī-mittō, mīsī, missum, 3, to send away, *send down, let go, give up.*
di-moveō, mōvī, mōtum, 2, to move apart, *put aside, dispel.*
Dindyma, ōrum, n., a mountain in Mysia.
Dircē, ēs, f., a fountain near Thebes.
dīreptus, a, um, part. (di-ripiō), *torn off.*
dī-rigō, rexī, rectum, 3 (rego), to set straight, *direct;* part. adj., dīrectus, *straight.*
dīrimō (dis, emo), ēmī, emptum, 3, to take apart; *decide.*
dīrus, a, um, adj. (R. DVI, *to fear,* dī-), fearful, *cruel, dire.*
Dis, Ditis, m. (dives, fr. R. DIV), name of the ruler of the lower world, of Pluto.
dis-cēdō, cessī, cessum, 3, to go apart, *part from, go away, disappear.*
dis-cernō, crēvī, crētum, 3, *to distinguish, set apart, divide, separate.*
discidium, ī, n. (scindo), a rending apart, *a separation.*
discō, didicī, 3 (R. DA, da-k, *to show, point out,* di-k, dīc, dic, di-sc-ere, *to begin to show = to learn*), *to learn.*
discordia, ae, f. (dis, cor), *discord.*
discors, dis, adj., *discordant.*
discrīmen, inis, n. (discerno), *a distinction, test.*
discus, ī, m. (δίσκος), *a quoit.*
dis-cutiō, ssī, ssum, 3, *to strike asunder, scatter.*
dis-iciō, jēcī, jectum, 3 (jacio), *to throw apart, scatter.*
dispar, aris, adj., *unequal.*
di-spergō (spargo), spersī, spersum, 3, *to scatter about, disperse.*
di-spiciō (specio), xī, ctum, 3, *to see distinctly, distinguish.*
dis-pōnō (po-sino, pōnō), uī, itum, 3, *to set apart, dispose.*
dis-saepiō, psī, ptum, 4, *to part off by a hedge, separate, divide.*
dis-sideō (sedeo), sēdī, sessum, 2, *to sit apart, be at variance.*
dis-siliō (salio), uī, 4, *to leap apart.*

dis-similis, e, adj., *dissimilar, unlike.*
dis-simulō, 1, *to dissemble, disguise.*
dis-sociō, 1, *to disjoin, to part.*
dis-suadeō, suāsī, suāsum, 2, *dissuade.*
di-stinguō, nxī, nctum 3 (stinguo, R. STIG, stig, *to prick,* mark by pricking, sti-n-gu-ere), *to distinguish.*
di-stō, āre, 1, to stand apart, *be distant, remote, different.*
diū, adv. (dies, wh. see for R.), *a long time, long.*
diurnus, a, um, adj. (dies, dius-nus), *of the day, daily.*
di-vellō, vulsī, vellī, vulsum, 3, *to tear apart, rend.*
dīversus, a, um, adj. (diverto), turned a different way, *opposite, diverse, separate, different.*
dī-vertor, dep., *to turn aside, turn.*
dīves, itis, adj. (same R. as deus, dīvus), *rich.*
dī-vidō, vīsī, vīsum (R. VID, *see, know,* di-vid-ere, *to see one thing from another*), *to distinguish, divide.*
dīvīnus, a, um, adj. (dīvus), *divine.*
dīvus, a, um, adj. (same R. as deus), *divine, godlike;* also subst., *a god.*
dō, dedī, datum, 1 (R. DA, Skr. dā, da, *give*), *to give, grant, give over.*
doceō, uī, ctum, 2 (same R. as disco, wh. see), *to teach, show;* part., doctus, *taught, clever, practiced.*
documentum, ī, n. (doceo), *proof, lesson, example.*
doleō, uī, 2 (dolor), *to feel pain, to grieve, mourn.*
dolor, ōris, m. (R. DAR, *to cleave, break,* dal, dol), *pain, grief, sorrow.*
dolus, ī, m. (R. DAR, have an eye to, aim at, dal, dol), *deceit, cunning, fraud.*
domina, ae, f. (domus), *mistress* (of the house), *lady.*
dominor, āri, v. dep. (dominus), *to lord it, to rule, govern.*
domō, uī, itum, 1 (R. DAM, *to tame,* subdue, dom), *to tame, overcome, subdue, conquer.*
domus, us, f. (same R. as domo, Vaniçek; but Curtius, fr. DAM, *to build*), *a house* (as dwelling), *dwelling, home, family, household.*

dōnec, conj. (same R. as dies, DIV, divu-s, diū-s, dic-s ; then fr. dju, diu-s, dio ; abl., do, *on the day,* do-ni-cum ; literally, on the day not when, marking the time of ceasing, *until ;* then (fr. the falling away of um) doni-c-, done-c-, donec; Vaniçek, p. 359 ; Corssen, Beitr., p. 435), *until, so long as, while.*

dōnō, 1 (donum), *to present, bestow.*

dōnum, I, n. (R. DA, *give,* dō), a thing given, *a gift, present, offering.*

dōs, dōtis, f. (dō, dō-s), a marriage gift, *a dowry ; a gift ;* pl., *gifts* (of mind).

dōtālis, e, adj. (dōs), belonging to a dowry ; *dotal.*

dōtō, 1 (dōs), *to endow, portion.*

dracō, ōnis, m., *a serpent, dragon.*

Dryades, um, f. (Δρυάδες), *wood-nymphs, Dryads.*

dubitō, 1 (R. DVA, *two,* duo, du-b-iu-s (dubi-tus), dubito), (to be *two*-ing), turn in *two* directions, *doubt, waver, be undecided, hesitate.*

dubius, a, um, adj. (duo, see dubitō), moving in two directions, *dubious, doubtful, uncertain.*

dūcō, xī, ctum, 3 (R. DU, *go,* du-k, dou-k, dū-c, dūc-o), *to lead, draw, bring forward, induce, allure, take on, deduce, derive, hold, consider.*

dulcēdō, inis (dulcis), *sweetness, charm.*

dulcis, e, adj. (R. GAR, *swallow,* gul, glu, gul-c-is, dul-ci-s), *sweet, lovely, charming.*

dum, conj. (fr. dies, wh. see, dju, diu, diu-s, diu-m ; acc., du-m, *the day long, all day,* dum), *while, so long as ; until.*

dummodo, conj. (dum, modo), *if only, provided that.*

duo, ae, o (R. dva, *two*), *two ; both.*

duplicō, 1 (duplex), *to double, enlarge.*

dūritia, ae, f. (dūrus), *hardness.*

dūrō, 1 (dūrus), *to make hard, harden ;* intrans., *endure, continue.*

dūrus, a, um, adj. (R. DHVAR, dhur, *to hurt,* dūr), *rough, hard, harsh, hardened, insensible, oppressive.*

dux, ducis, comm. (R. DU, *go,* du-k, duc), *a leader, guide,* army-leader, general (Eng., duke).

E

ē, see ex.

ebenus, I, f., the ebony-tree, *ebony.*

ē-bibō, bibī, bibitum, 3, *to drink out, exhaust.*

ebur, oris, n., *ivory.*

eburnus, a, um, adj. (ebur), *of ivory.*

ecce, interj. (perhaps a strengthened form for e-ce, of which e is the pronom. stem i in locative, and ce the demonst. pron. particle ; the meaning being, there ! see there !), *lo! see there!*

Echīon, onis, a Theban, husband of Agave ; Met. 3, 126.

ec-quis, quid, pron. interr. adj. and subst. (formed fr. ec-ce, e-ce, as *hic* fr. hi-ce, see ecce), *is there any one who,* or *thing which ?*—ecquid, interr. particle, *whether.*

ē-discō, didicī, 3, *to learn by heart.*

edō, ēdī, ēsum, 3 (R. AD, *eat,* ed-ere), *to eat.* **edāx,** ācis, adj., *devouring.*

ē-dō, didī, ditum, 3 (e, dō, *dare*), *to give out, bring forth, produce ; to give out, declare.*

Edōnis, idis, adj. f., *Edonian,* belonging to the Thracian people Edōni.

ē-dūcō, xī, ctum, 3, *to draw out, lead forth, bring up.*

ef-ferō, extulī, ēlātum, 3 (e, ferō), *to carry out, raise up, lift up, bring forth.*

ef-fervēscō, buī, 3, e, ferveō (of the stars), *to shine out.*

ef-ficiō, fēcī, fectum, 3 (e, faciō), *to bring to pass, accomplish, bring forth.*

effigiēs, ēī, f. (fingō), *an image.*

ef-flō, 1, *to breathe out.*

ef-fluō, xī, 3, *to escape.*

ef-fodiō, fōdī, fossum, 3 (e, fodiō), *to dig out, dig up.*

ef-fugiō, fūgī, 3 (e, fugiō), *to flee away, escape, shun.*

effulgeō, fulsī, 2 (e, fulgeō), *to shine forth,* or *upon.*

ef-fundō, fūdī, fūsum, 3, *to pour out,* or *forth ;* part., effusus (of comae), *loosened, disheveled.*

egeō, uī, 2 (R. AGH, *to need,* eg-), *to need, be in want of, be without.*

ē-gerō, gessī, gestum, 3, *to get out, throw out, pour forth, exhaust.*
ego, pers. pron. (R. GHA, a pron. stem ho), *I;* pl., *nos, we.*
ē-gredior, gressus sum, 3 (gradior), *to go forth, go up.*
ēgressus, ūs, m., *a going forth, egress.*
ēheu, interj., *alas! ah!*
ei (hei), interj., *ah* (me)*!*
ē-jaculor, 1, v. dep., *to hurl forth, shout out (ejaculate).*
ē-iciō, jēcī, jectum, 3 (e, jaciō), *to cast out or forth, eject.*
ejectō, 1 (ciciō), *to throw out violently.*
ē-lābor, lapsus sum, 3, v. dep., *to glide forth, slip out, escape.*
ēlectrum, I, n. (ἤλεκτρον, fr. R. ARK, *to flash), amber;* in pl., *amber-drops.*
elegus, I, m. (ἐ-λεγ-ος, fr. R. RA, *to sound,* ra-k, la-k, λεγ-, e-leg-), *an elegy.*
elegēius, a, um, adj.; see note, Am. 3, 9, 3.
elementa, ōrum, n., *the elements.*
Elēus, a, um, adj., *of Elis,* Elēan.
ē-līdō, sī, sum, 3 (laedō), *to strike out, shatter, strangle.*
ē-ligō, lēgī, lectum, 3 (legō), *to choose out, elect.*
Elis, idis, f., *a district of the Peloponnesus.*
ēloquium, I, n., *eloquence.*
ē-lūdō, lūdī, lūsum, 3, *to win fr. in play; to elude, parry; to delude, deceive.*
ē-luō, luī, lūtum, *to wash out, or away.*
Elysius, a, um, adj., *of Elysium, Elysian.*
ēmendō, 1 (menda), (R. MA, *fail*), *to clear of failure, to improve, amend, purify.*
ē-micō, uī, ātum, 1, *to dart forth, mount up, project.*
ēminus (e, manus), adv., *from a distance.*
ē-mittō, mīsī, missum, 3, *to send out or forth, give loose to.*
ēn, interj. (etym. unc.), lo! there! (see! there!).
enim, conj. (e, nam, e fr. pron. stem i, and *nam* fr. R. GNA, na, *know,* na-m, acc. sing. fem.), *(namely), for, indeed.*
Enīpeus, I, m., *river in Thessaly;* also a river-god.
ē-nītor, nixus, nisus, sum, 3, v. dep., *to work one's way out, struggle, strive.*
Ennius, I, m., name of the earliest Roman epic poet; Am. I, 15, 19.
ēnsis, is, m. (R. AS, *throw,* as-i), *a sword.*
eō, īvī, iī, itum, 4 (R. I, *go), to go, go away, go against, pass away.*
eōdem (idem), adv., *to the same (place), to that, thereto.*
Eōus, a, um, adj., *of ἠώς, Eos, the dawn, eastern.*
Epaphus, I, m., s. of Jupiter and Io.
Ephyrē, ēs, an old name for Corinth; fr. a nymph of the name.
Epimēthis, idis, f., d. of Epimetheus.
ē-pōtō, avī, pōtum, 1, *to drink out, swallow up.*
epulae, ārum, f. (etym. unc.), *costly food, a banquet.*
eques, itis (equus), *a horseman, knight.*
equidem, adv. (comp. of interj. e, qui (abl.) and dem fr. R. DA, 3d pers. pron. stem, de, de-m, acc.), *indeed, by all means.*
equus, I, m. (R. AK, *to be sharp, swift,* ac, cc, equ-), *a horse, steed.*
Erebus, I, m., Ἔρεβος (R. RAG, *to color), the dark, darkness,* (the dark) *lower world, Erebus.*
ergō, adv. (fr. e and regō), (R. RAG, *reach, extend,* e-reg-o, e-rg-ō), from the direction, *on account of,* consequently, *therefore.*
Eridanus, I, m., the legendary name of the river Po; Met. 2, 324.
ē-rigō, rexī, rectum, 3 (regō), *to raise up, rise up.*
erīlis (herīlis), e, adj. (erus), belonging to the *master* or the *mistress* of a family, *the master's, the mistress's.*
Erīnys, yos, f., Greek name for the goddess of vengeance, corresponding to the Latin *Furia.*
ē-ripiō, ripuī, reptum, 3 (rapiō), *to snatch out or away, tear off, take away.*
errāticus, a, um, adj. (errō), *wandering.* errātus, ūs, m., *a wandering.*

errō, 1 (R. AR-S, *wander*), *to wander, go astray, err.*
error, ōris, m., *wandering, going astray, error.*
Error, ōris, m. (personified), *Error.*
ĕrŭbēscō, uī, 3 (ruber), *to turn red, blush.*
ĕrŭdĭō, 4 (rudis), *to instruct, teach.*
ē-rŭō, ruī, rutum, 3, *to pluck out.*
erus, I, m. (improp. herus), (R. AS, *to be*, es, es-u-s, es-a ; Ger., Herr), (the one that is ?), *master, lord, owner.*
Ĕrycīna, ae, f., *of Eryx,* name of Venus, worshiped at Eryx.
Ĕrymanthus, I, a river in Arcadia.
Ĕryx, cis, m., a mountain in Sicily, on which was a temple of Venus.
et, conj. (R. A, pron. stem of 1st and 3d pers., a+ta, a+ti, ἔτι, a-t, e-t), *and, and indeed, and so, also, both—and.*
ĕtĕnim, conj. (et, enim), (and—for), *for.*
ĕtiam, conj. (et, iam = jam, jam fr. ja, pron. stem of 3d pers., ja-smin, locative, ja-m), also, *and also, and even.*
etsī, conj. (et and si fr. reflex pron. SAV, SVA, sva-i, εἰ), *and if, if also, though.*
Euboĭcus, a, um, adj., *of Euboea, Euboean.*
Eumĕnĭdes, um, f. (Εὐμενίδες), the euphemistic word for the Erīnyes (wh. see), the well-minded, well-disposed, gentle.
Eumolpus, I, m., a Thracian singer, pupil of Orpheus.
Euphrātes, is, m., river in Babylonia.
Eurōpa, ae, f., d. of Agēnor ; Met. 6, 104.
Eurōtas, ae, m., a river in Laconia.
Eurus, I, m., *S. E. wind, E. wind.*
Eurystheus, eī, m., s. of Sthenelus; Met. 9, 203.
Eurytus, I, m., king of Oechalia, father of Iole.
Euxīnus, a, um, adj., the Euxine (sea).
ē-vādō, vāsī, vāsum, 3, *to go out, pass out of, over.*
ē-vānēscō, vānuī, 3, *to disappear.*
ēvānĭdus, a, um, adj., *vanishing.*

ē-vĕhō, vexī, vectum, 3, *to carry out, to be borne on or up.*
ē-vellō, vulsī, vulsum, 3, *to pull, tear, out or up.*
ēventus, ūs, m. (evenio), *issue, event, consequence.*
ēvertō, vertī, versum, 3, *to turn about, overturn, throw down ;* part. pass., *inverted.*
ēvītābĭlis, e, adj., *avoidable.*
ēvŏcō, 1, *to call out, bring in, evoke.*
ē-vŏlō, 1, *to fly out, fly away.*
ē-volvō, volvī, volūtum, 3, *to roll out, unroll.*
ex, or **ē,** prep. with abl. (R. AG, eg, *out*), *out of* or *from, from, in consequence of, according to.*
ex-anĭmis, e, adj., *lifeless.*
ex-anĭmō, 1, *to deprive of life;* part. perf., *lifeless.*
ex-audĭō, 4, *to hear* (distinctly).
ex-cēdō, cessī, cessum, 3, *to go out from, retire, depart, exceed, be beyond.*
ex-cĭdō, cidī, 3 (cado), *to fall out, to fail.*
ex-cĭō, cīvī, cītum, 4, *to call forth, to frighten, start from.*
ex-cĭpĭō, cēpī, ceptum, 3 (capio), *to take out, except, receive, catch, take up the word.*
ex-clāmō, 1, *to cry out, exclaim.*
ex-clūdō, clūsī, clūsum, 3 (claudo), *to shut out, exclude.*
ex-cŏlō, coluī, cultum, 3, *to improve, educate.*
ex-cūsō, 1 (causor, fr. R. SKAV, kav, cav, caves, cav-es-ta, cau-s-ta, cau-s-sa, causa, causa-ri, *to bring causes, grounds for*), *to excuse.*
ex-cŭtĭō, cussī, cussum, 3 (quatio), *to strike, shake out, to shake violently, drive out.*
exemplum, I, n. (eximo), something taken out, *an instance, example, proof, manner.*
ex-ĕō, iī, itum, 4 (eo), *to go out, come out, go away, leave, mount up.*
exequĭae, ārum, f. (ex, sequor), *following out, a funeral procession, obsequies.*
ex-erceō, uī, itum, 2 (arceo), *to set in motion, employ, exercise, vex, trouble.*
ex-hālō, 1, *to breathe out, exhale.*

ex-haurĭō, hausī, haustum, 4, *to draw out, exhaust.*
ex-hĭbĕō, uī, ĭtum, 2 (habeō), *to hold forth, exhibit, show.*
ex-horrēscō, uī, 3 (horreō), *to shudder.*
ex-hortor, 1, v. dep., *to exhort, encourage, spur.*
ex-ĭgō, ēgī, actum, 3 (agō), *to drive forth, drive, exact, to finish.*
exiguus, a, um, adj. (exigō), *small, short, weak.*
exīlis, e, adj. (exigo, ex-ĭg-ili, ex-ĭg-li, exīlis), *thin, lean, weakly.*
eximius, a, um, adj. (eximō, *take out*), taken out from the crowd, *select, distinguished.*
ex-ĭmō, ēmī, emptum, 3 (emō, *to take, buy*), *to take out.*
exĭtĭābĭlis, e, adj. (exitium), *destructive.*
exĭtĭum, ī, n. (exeō), *destruction, ruin.*
exĭtus, ūs, m. (exeō), (out-go), *issue, end.*
exonĕrō, 1 (onus), *exonerate, free from the burden of, free.*
ex-ōrō, 1 (to beg out), *to move by entreaties, prevail upon.*
exōsus, part. (odī), *filled with hate, detesting.*
ex-pallēscō, uī, 3, *to grow pale at, pale.*
expĕdĭō, 4 (pēs), (to get one's feet from), *to set free, let loose, disengage.*
ex-pellō, pulī, pulsum, 3, *to drive out, expel.*
experior, pertus sum, 4 (fr. ex and R. PAR, *pass through, try*, par, per), (put to a pass through), *to try, put to the test.*
expers, tis, adj. (ex priv. and pars), *without share in, destitute, not having experience.*
ex-petō, īvī, ītum, 3, *to seek out, seek after, desire.*
ex-plōrō, 1 (plōrō, R. PRU, *to flow*, plav, plov-, plor-, *make to flow*), (to make flow out), *to bring out, search, explore, discover.*
ex-pōnō, posuī, positum, 3 (pōnō = po-sinō), *to set out or forth, to land, expose.*

ex-prĭmō, pressī, pressum, 3 (premo), *to press out, express, give expression to.*
ex-sanguis, e, adj. (ex priv.), *without blood, bloodless, pale.*
ex-sĕrō, seruī, sertum, 3, *to thrust forth, put forth.*
ex-sĭlĭō, uī, 4 (saliō), *to leap forth, spring out or up.*
exsĭlĭum, ī, n. (exsul), *banishment, exile.*
ex-sistō, stitī, stitum, 3, *to stand forth, come forth, appear.*
ex-spătĭor, 1, v. dep., *to go out of the track, wander.*
ex-spectō, 1, *to look out, wait for, expect.*
ex-spīrō, 1, *to breathe out, expire.*
ex-sternō, strāvī, strātum, 1, to drive (out of) beside one's self, *to affright.*
ex-stinguō, stinxī, stinctum, 3, *to put out, extinguish, destroy.*
ex-stō, āre, 1, *to stand forth, be conspicuous, extant.*
ex-strŭō, struxī, structum, 3, *to heap up, pile up.*
exsul, ulis, comm. (R. SAR, *go*, sal, sal-o, sul), one who has gone out, *is banished, an exile.*
ex-sultō, 1 (ex-siliō), *to leap forth, exult.*
exta, ōrum, pl. n. (R. (Europ.) anksta, enksta, eksta, exta, ἔγκατα (ἐν)), what is *within*, the inwards (the nobler, as heart, lungs), *entrails.*
extemplō, adv. (ex, tempulo, templo, tempus), *in a moment, instantly.*
ex-tendō, tendī, tēnsum, tentum, 3, to stretch out, *extend.*
ex-tĕnŭō, 1 (tenuis), *to thin out, make thin, reduce, absorb, extenuate.*
externus, a, um, adj. (R. AG, EG, ec, ecs, ex, ex-ter(us); comp., out, outer, exter-nu-s), on the outside, *outward, foreign, strange.*
ex-terrĕō, uī, ĭtum, 2, *to frighten, terrify.*
ex-tĭmēscō, tĭmuī, 3 (timeō), *to fear greatly.*
extĭmus, a, um, adj. (superl. to ex-ter, see externus), *outermost.*
extrā, adv. (fr. ex-ter, extrā; abl., extrā-d, S. C. de Bacch. 16), *without,*

ex-trahŏ, traxī, tractum, 3, *to draw out, extract*.
extrĕmus, a, um, adj. (superl. of ex-ter, see externus), *outermost, extreme, last*.
ex-uŏ, uī, ūtum, 3 (R. AV, *put on*, ex-uv- (as in ex-uv-iae), ex-u-ere, *to put off*), *to draw out, put off, unclothe, divest*.
ex-ūrŏ, ussī, ustum, 3, *to burn out, burn up, destroy*.
exuviae, arum, f. pl. (see exuŏ), what is *taken off, clothing; equipments, arms; skin; spoils*.

F

fabricŏ, 1 (faber, fr. R. DHABH, dhab, *to fit*, fab-, faber, fabri, fabri-ca, fabricā-re), *to frame, fashion, fabricate*.
fābula, ae, f. (fāri, fr. R. BHA, *appear, show*, fa, fā-ri, *show, reveal* (by the voice), *speak*), *tale, narrative, fable*.
facies, ēī, f. (R. BHA, *appear*, bha-k, fac), *the face, figure, beautiful form, look*.
facilis, e, adj. (faciŏ), *to be done, easy to do, easy*.
facinus, oris, n. (faciŏ), *a deed, a bold or evil deed, a crime*.
faciŏ, fēcī, factum, 3 (R. DHA, *put, do*, fa, fa-c-ere, fe-fac-ī, fe-fic-ī, fe-ic-ī =fēcī), *to make, do, build, create, give, occasion;* pass., fīo, fieri, factus sum, *to be made, become*.
factum, ī, n. (faciŏ), *a deed*.
faex, cis, f. (etym. unc.), *the dregs*.
fāgus, ī, f., *a beech-tree*.
falcātus, a, um, adj. (falx), *sickle-shaped, hooked*.
fallāx, ācis, adj. (fallō), *deceitful, fallacious*.
fallŏ, fefellī, falsum, 3 (R. SPAL, *waver*, Skr. sphal, fal-), *to deceive;* in pass., *deceive one's self, beguile*.
falsus, a, um, adj. (fallō), *false, deceitful, unreal, fictitious*.
falx, cis, f. (R. PARK, *to crook*), *a sickle, pruning-hook*.
fāma, ae, f. (same R. as fābula), what is said, *fame, report, renown, good name*.
fames, is, f. (R. GHA, *be empty, want*), *hunger, famine*.
famula, ae, f. (R. BHAG, *take possession of*, fag-ma, fa-ma, *house, property*, famulus, familia), *a maid-servant, female attendant*.
famulus, ī, m. (same R. as famula, allied to Oscan famel), *a house-servant, attendant*.

fās, indecl. n. (R. as in fābula, BHA, fa, fā-ri), *the divine word, right, justice*.
fastidium, ī, n. (R. DHARS, *be bold*, fars, fās-tu-s, fastu-taedium, fastu-tīdium, fāstīdium), *disdain, disgust*.
fastīgium, ī, n. (R. BHARS, *be stiff*, bhars-ti, *a point, top*, fast + igium, fr. ag-ere), something carried upward, *a gable, roof, top*.
fātālis, e, adj. (fātum), determined by fate, *fatal, fated*.
fateor, fassus sum, 2, v. dep. (same R. as fābula), *to confess, allow*.
fātidicus, a, um, adj. (fātum, dīco), *prophetic*. **fātifer**, *death-dealing*.
fatīgŏ, 1 (R. same as fames, GHA, fa, *to be empty, want*, fa-ti, *want, weariness*, fa-ti-sce-re, *grow weary*, then fatig-āre, ig fr. agere), *to make weary, to fatigue*.
fātum, ī, n. (fāri, see fābula), what is uttered, *fate, destiny, ruin, death*.
Faunus, ī, m., ancient king of Latium, then honored as god of fields and woods; like the Greek *Pan*.
Faustulus, ī, m., see Fasti, 4, 854.
fautrīx, īcis, f. (faveō), *one that favors, protectress*.
faucēs, f. plural (faux), (R. BHŪKA, *an opening*), *throat, mouth*.
faveŏ, fāvī, fautum, 2 (R. BHA, *shine, appear*, bha-v, fav-), orig., *to shine upon, to favor, stand by*.
favilla, ae, f. (faveō), *glowing ashes, ashes*.
favor, oris, m. (faveō), *favor, applause*.
favus, ī, m. (R. BHU, *to grow*, fu, fau, fav), *a honey-comb*.
fax, facis, f. (same R. as faveō, bha-k, fac-, fac-s), *a fire-brand, torch-light, torch*.
fēcundus, a, um, adj. (same R. as

favus, fau, fav, feu, fev-ūre, *to bear*), *fruitful.* fel, fellis, n., *gall.*

fēlix, īcis, adj. (same **R.** as fēcundus), fruitful, *fortunate, happy, lucky, promising.*

fēmina, ae, f. (**R.** DHA, *suck, give suck,* fē), *female, a woman, woman.*

fēmineus, a, um, adj. (fēmina), *of a woman, womanly.*

femur, oris, n., *a thigh.*

fĕrālis, e, adj. (ferō), pertaining to the dead, *death-bringing, deadly.*

ferāx, ācis, adj. (ferō), *fruitful.*

ferē, adv. (**R.** DHAR, *hold, hold firm,* far, fer, fere, *firmly*), close upon, nearly, *about, almost.*

feretrum, ī, n. (ferō), *a bier.*

ferīnus, a, um (ferus), *of wild animals.*

feriō, īre (**R.** DHVAR, dhur), *to strike.*

feritās, ātis, f., *fierceness.*

ferō, ferre, tulī, lātum, 3 (**R.** BHAR, carry, fer, fer-o), *to carry, bear, bring, carry away, bring forth, relate, praise.*

ferōx, ōcis, adj. (ferus), *wild, fierce, ferocious, raging.*

ferreus, a, um, adj. (ferrum), *of iron, hard-hearted.*

ferrūgō, inis, f. (ferrum), *iron-rust.*

ferrum, ī, n. (**R.** BHARS, *stiffen*, fers, fers-u-m, ferrum), *iron;* by metōn., an iron instrument, *knife, weapon.*

fertīlis, e, adj. (ferō), *fruitful, fertile.*

fertilitas, ātis, f., *fertility.*

ferus, a, um, adj. (**R.** DHVAR, dhur, *disturb,* fer-), *wild;* fera, *a wild animal;* cruel.

ferveō, ferbuī, fervī, 2 (**R.** BHAR, bhur, *swell, brew, boil,* bhru, fru, frev, ferv), *to rage* (for heat), *be hot, foam.*

fervor, ōris, m. (ferveō), *heat, rage, fervor.*

fessus, a, um, adj. (same **R.** as fatīgō, gha, fa, fe), *weary.*

festīnō, 1, **R.** (DHAN, *strike, storm,* dhan-d, -fend, -fend-tu-s, in-fes-tu-s, fed-tī-no, festīno), *to hasten, hastily get ready, prepare.*

festus, a, um, adj. (same **R.** as faveō, bha, bha-s, fes-), *festive;* subst., festum, *a feast, festival.*

fētus, a, um, adj. (**R.** same as fēcundus), *fruitful.*

fētus, ūs, m., *the bringing forth, the offspring;* also **fētūra**, ae, f.

fībra, ae, f. (**R.** BHID, *cleave,* fid, fidbra, fībra), *a fiber, filament.*

fictīlis, e, adj. (fingō), *earthen.*

ficus, ī, ūs, f., *a fig-tree.*

fidēlis, e, adj. (fidēs), *faithful, true.*

fidēs, eī, f. (**R.** BHADH, *bind,* bhidh, fid, fid-c-s), *faith, truth, credit, confirmation, warrant.*

fidēs, fidis, f. (**R.** SPA, SPA-N, *span, stretch,* spi, spi-d, sfi-d, fid-), *a string, chord,* a stringed instrument, *cithern, lyre, lute.*

fidūcia, ae, f. (fidus), *confidence, a pledge, security.*

fidus, a, um, adj. (same **R.** as fides, feid, fīd, fīdus), *faithful, true.*

fīgō, fixī, fixum, 3 (**R.** DHAGH, DHIGH, *to touch, mold, to fix,* fig, fi-n-g, fig), *to fix in* or *upon, fasten, strike in, pierce.*

figūra, ae, f. (fingō), *a figure, form, beautiful form, beauty.*

fīlia, ae, f. (**R.** perhaps same as fēmina, fē, fī, *a suckling*), *a daughter.*

fīlius, ī, m. (**R.** as fīlia), *a son.*

fīlum, ī, n. (**R.** GHAR, *to wind, twist,* har, hir, hīlu-m, fīlu-m), *a thread, string.*

findō, fidī, fissum, 3 (**R.** BHID, *to cleave,* fid, fi-n-d), *to cleave, split, rend.*

fingō, finxī, fictum, 3 (**R.** same as fīgō), *to form, mold, form to one's self, imagine, invent.*

fīniō, 4 (fīnis), *to limit, bound, end, finish, bring to an end.*

fīnis, is, m. (**R.** same as findō, fidnī, fīnis), something that divides off, *a boundary, limit, end.*

fīnitimus, a, um, adj. (fīnis), *bounding, adjoining, bordering upon, neighboring.*

firmus, a, um, adj. (**R.** same as fere, DHAR, *hold firm,* far, fir), *firm, strong.*

fistula, ae, f. (**R.** SPU, *blow, breathe,* spu + s(pu), pu-s, fus-ta, fus-tu-la, fistula), something to blow through, *a reed, shepherd's pipe, pipe.*

flagellō, 1 (flagellum), *to scourge.*

flagellum, ī, n. (**R.** BHLAGH, *to strike,* flag, flag-ru-m, flagel-lu-m, dimin.), *a whip, scourge.*

flagrō, 1 (R. BHARG, *to light, burn,* bhlag, flag), *to burn, glow, burn with passion.*

flāmen, inis, n. (R. BHAL, BHLA, *to blow, flow,* fla, flā-rc, flo), blowing of the wind, *a blast.*

flamma, ae, f. (R. same as flagrō, flag, flag-ma, flam-ma), *a flame, blazing light, blaze, flash of lightning, flame of love.*

flammifer, fera, ferum, adj. (flamma), *flame-bearing, flaming.*

flātus, ūs, m. (flō, R. same as flāmen), *blowing, breath, breeze.*

flăvēns, ntis, part. adj. (flāveō), *golden-yellow, gold-colored.*

flăvēscō, ere, 3 (flaveō), *to become yellow or gold-colored.*

flāvus, a, um, adj. (R. GHAR, *to be green or yellow,* ghal, fla-), *yellowish, yellow, blond, fair.*

flēbilis, e, adj. (fleō), to be wept over, *lamented, lamentable, tearful.*

flectō, flexī, flexum, 3 (R. PARK, *to bend,* falc, flec, flec-t-), *to bend, curve, turn.*

fleō, 2 (R. same as flō, flāmen), to shed tears, weep, cry, *lament.*

flētus, ūs, m., *weeping, tears, stream of tears.*

flexilis, e, adj. (flectō), *flexible.*

flōreō, uī, 2 (flōs), *to bloom, blossom.*

flōridus, a, um, adj., *flowery.*

flōs, flōris, m. (R. same as flātus, fla, flu, flou, flo, flo-s), that which is *blown, blossom, flower.*

fluctus, ūs, m. (fluō), flowing, streaming. *flood, wave.*

fluitō, 1 (fluō), *to float, flow.*

flūmen, inis, n. (fluo), flowing water, *a stream, flood, river,* god of a river, *river-god.*

flūmineus, a, um, adj. (flūmen), *of a river.*

fluō, fluxī, fluxum, 3 (R. same as flō, flātus, flu, flu-ere), *to flow.*

fluviālis, e, adj., *of a river.*

fluvius, I, m. (fluō), *a river.*

focus, I, m. (R. same as fax, BHA, *shine,* bha-k, fac, foc-), *fire-side, hearth.*

fodiō, fōdī, fossum, 3 (R. BHADH, *dig,* fod-), *to dig, dig up or through.*

foedō, 1 (foedus), *to make foul, defile, pollute, deform.*

foedus, a, um, adj. (R. DHU, *to blow, kindle, smoke,* fu, fou, fov, foe-du-s, *smoked), foul, base, ugly, loathsome.*

foedus, eris, n. (R. BHADH, BHIDH, *to bind,* fid, foid, foed, foed-u-s), something that *binds, a compact, league, treaty, bargain, law.*

folium, I, n. (R. same as flos, BHAL, *blow, swell,* fol-), *a leaf, foliage.*

fōns, fontis, m. (R. GHU, *pour,* fu, fou, fov, fov-ont, font), *a spring.*

forāmen, inis, n., *an opening.*

for-ceps, ipis, m. (RR. for, fr. GHAR, *glow, far,* for, for-mu-s, adj., *warm,* forma, things that are warm, ceps fr. kap, *seize, take,* cap (as in capere), formu-cape-s, forcipes), that wh. *takes* what is *warm,* glowing, *tongs, fire-tongs, pincers.*

forem, = essem, fr. v. sum ; fore = futurum esse ; *I would be, were ; will be, about to be ;* R. of both, BHU, *become,* fu, fu-re, fo-re, fu-rem, fo-rem.

foris, is, f. (R. DHU (as in foedus), *blow,* dhva-ra), *a door ;* in pl., *the leaves or folds of a door, folding-doors ; entrance.*

forma, ae, f. (R. DHAR, *hold, make firm,* far, fer, for, for-ma), *a form, shape, figure. beautiful form. beauty.*

formīdābilis, e, adj. (formīdāre, formīdo. inis), *formidable, fearful.*

formīdō, inis, f. (R. MAR, *frighten,* mor, mov + m(or), mor-mi, mor-mī-re, for-mī-re), *fear, horror, fright.*

formō, 1 (see forma for R.), *to form, fashion, represent.*

formōsus, a, um, adj. (forma), *well-formed, handsome, beautiful.*

forn-āx, ācis, f. (R. GHAR, *glow),* (see forceps), *a furnace, oven.*

fors, tis, f. (R. BHAR, *carry, bring,* fer, for-ti, for-s, that wh. *brings itself about,* happens, comp.fors, fert), *chance, hap, fortune.*

forsitan = fors sit an, adv. (chance-maybe-whether). *perchance, perhaps.*

fortis, e, adj. (R. DHARGH, *to hold out,* forgh, for-tis), one that *holds out ; firm, strong, brave, courageous.*

fortiter, adv. (fortis), *bravely, vigorously.*

fortūna, ae, f. (fors), fortune, *decision, prosperity ;* goddess of Fortune.

forum, i, n. (**R.** same as foris, DHU, to blow, dhva-ra, prop., a place where *it blows,* an open place), *the Forum* at Rome.

fossa, ae, f. (fodiō), *a ditch, pit.*

foveō, fōvī, fōtum, 2 (**R.** DHU, *kindle, warm,* fu, fou, fov, foveo), *to warm, cherish.*

fragilis, e, adj. (frangō), easily broken, *fragile, frail.*

fragmen, inis, n. (frangō), *a fragment, ruin.*

fragor, ōris, m. (frangō), *a breaking, crackling, rustling.*

frāgum, i, n. (**R.** GHRA, *to smell,* fra; the word fragra-re fr. ghra + ghra = fra-gra-, *to be fragrant), strawberries.*

frangō, frēgī, fractum, 3 (**R.** var, *draw, bend, break,* var-k, vrag, fra-n-g-ō), *to break,* break to pieces, *fracture.*

frāter, frātris, m. (**R.** BHAR, *carry, support* (fer-, fer-ō), bhra-tar, φρή-τηρ, fra-ter, one that *supports;* i. e., in relation to the sister), *a brother.*

frāternus, a, um, adj., *of a brother, fraternal, brotherly.*

fraudō, 1 (fraus), *to defraud, cheat.*

fraus, fraudis, f. (**R.** DHVAR, DHUR, *hurt, break,* dur (durus), fru, fru-d, frau-s), *fraud, deceit, deception.*

fremō, uī, itum, 3 (**R.** BHAR, *sound,* bhra-m, frem-ere), *to roar, rage, murmur, hum.*

frendō, frēsum, fressum, 3 (**R.** GHAR, *rub,* ghar-dh, fre-n-d-ere), *to bruise, crush, gnash.*

frēnō, 1 (frēnum), *to bridle, curb.*

frēnum, i, n. (**R.** DHAR, DHRA, *hold firm,* far, fre-nu-m), *a bridle, curb, bit.*

frequēns, ntis, adj. (**R.** BHARK, *press,* farc, frac, frcc, frequ-erc, frequēn-s), *frequent, numerous, rich in, full of.*

frequentō, 1, *to frequent, to visit in numbers, to celebrate.*

fretum, i, n. (**R.** BHAR, *move quick, swell, rage,* bhra, fre-t-u-m), *a strait, a channel.*

frigidus, a, um, adj. (frīgus), *cold, frigid, stiff.*

frīgus, oris, n. (**R.** DHARS, *stiffen, be stiff,* bhars-k, firk, frik, frīk, frīg), *cold, frost, coolness, coldness of death, shudder.*

frondeō, ēre (frōns), *to be in leaf, to have leaves.*

frōns, dis, f. (etym. unc.), *a leaf, leafage, foliage, a garland of leaves.*

frōns, tis, f. (**R.** BHAR, BHUR, of quick movement, *quiver,* bhru (φρυ), fru (Eng., brow, eyebrow), fru-ont, front, frōns), *the brow, forehead, front.*

fructus, ūs, m. (fruor), *fruit, proceeds, profit.*

fruor, fructus, fruitus sum, 3 (**R.** BHUG, *enjoy,* fug, frug, frugv-i, fru-i), *to enjoy, rejoice in.*

frustrā, adv. (**R.** same as fraus, DHUR, fru, fru-d, fru-d-tru-s, fru-s-tru-s, abl. fem., frustrā, prop., *erroneously), in vain, to no purpose.*

frutex, icis, m. (**R.** BHAR, BHUR, fru, *to swell), a shrub, bush, shrubbery.*

fruticōsus, a, um, adj., *bushy.*

frux, frugis, f. (**R.** same as fruor, BHUG, bhrug, *enjoy, use,* fug, frug, frug-i-s), *fruit, fruits of the earth.*

fuga, ae, f. (**R.** BRUGH, *bend, turn, flee,* fug), *flight, exile.*

fugāx, ācis, adj. (fuga), *inclined to flee, fleeing, swift.*

fugiō, fūgī, fugitum, 3 (fuga), *to flee, shun, disappear.*

fugō, 1 (fugiō), *to put to flight.*

fulgeō, fulsī, 2 (**R.** BHARG, *to light, shine,* bhalg, falg, fulg-ēre), *to shine, lighten, glitter.*

fulgor, ōris, m. (fulgeō), *effulgence.*

fulica, ae, f., *a coot.*

fulmen, inis, n. (fulgeō), *lightning.*

fulmineus, a, um, adj., *of lightning, brilliant, splendid.*

fulvus, a, um, adj. (**R.** GHAR, *green* or *yellow,* ghal, ful-vu-s), *deep yellow, reddish yellow, gold-colored.*

fūmō, 1 (fūmus), *to smoke, fume.*

fūmus, i, m. (**R.** DHU), *smoke.*

funda, ae, f., *a sling.*

fundāmen, inis, n. (fundō), 1 (fundus, **R.** BHU, *grow, make grow,* fu, fu-d, fu-d-no, fundō), *a foundation.*

fundō, fūdī, fūsum, 3 (**R.** GHU, *pour,* fu, fu-d, fu-n-d-ere), *to pour, pour out, scatter, extend.*

fūnestus, a, um, adj. (fūnus), *death-bringing, deadly, fatal.*

fungor, functus sum, 3 (**R.** BHUG, *use, enjoy,* fug, fu-n-g-i, *have use of),* *to discharge, perform, fulfill,* end (with morte), *die.*

fūnus, eris, n. (**R.** same as fumus, DHU, *to smoke,* fu, fu-n-us, *smoke from burning a body), funeral procession, burial, funeral, death.*

furca, ae, f. (**R.** BHAR, *to cleave, split,* for, fur), *a fork.*

furiālis, e, adj. (furiae, **R.** same as furō), *of the Furies, raging, mad.*

furō, uī, 3 (**R.** BHAR, BHUR, *to swell, rage, quiver,* fur), *to rage, be mad.*

furor, ōris, m. (furo), *rage, madness, fury.*

furtim, adv. (fūr, fr. **R.** BHAR, *carry, carry away), stealthily.*

furvus, a, um, adj., BHAR, BHUR (as in furō), the idea of rapid motion (e. g., quivering) being mingled with that of color), *dark-colored, dusky, gloomy.*

fūsilis, e, adj. (fundō), *fluid, molten.*

fūsus, ī, m. (**R.** SPAD, SPAND, *move violently, swing,* fund-to, fū-su-s), *a spindle.*

G

galea, ae, f. (**R.** SKAL, KAL, *cover,* cal, gal, gal-ea), (*a covering* for the head), *a helmet* (of leather).

Gallicus, a, um, adj., *of Gaul, Gallic.*

Gallus, I, m., see n. Trist. 4, 10, 53.

garrulus, a, um, adj. (**R.** GAR, *to sound,* gur + s, gar-s-u-s, gar-r-u-s, gar-r-u-lus), *garrulous, talkative.*

gaudeō, gāvīsus sum, 2 (**R.** GAV, *to rejoice,* gau-), *to rejoice, enjoy.*

gelidus, a, um, adj. (gelū), *cold, icy;* gelu fr. **R.** GAR, *be bright, shine,* gal, gel.

gemellipara, ae, f. (gemellus), *twin-bearing.*

gemellus, ī, m. (geminus), *twin-born, twin.*

geminō, 1 (geminus, ī, m.), *to double, repeat.*

geminus, ī, m. (**R.** GA, GAN, *produce, beget,* gam, gem), *twin-born, double, two-fold.*

gemitus, ūs, m. (gemō), *a sighing, groan, complaint.*

gemma, ae, f. (gemō) *a bud, the eye* (of the grape); figuratively, fr. resemblance in shape, *a gem, precious stone.*

gemō, uī, itum, 3 (**R.** GAM, *press, be full, sigh,* gem), *to sigh, groan, cry, lament.*

gena, ae, f. (**R.** GANU, *cheek,* gen), *the cheek.*

gener, erī, m. (gīgnō, gen-uī), *a son-in-law.* **generōsus,** a, um, adj., *fine.*

genetrīx, īcis, f. (gīgnō), she that produces, *a mother, producer.*

geniālis, e, adj. (genius, gīgnō, gen-), what belongs to the Genius, *genial, glad, delightful.*

geniāliter, adv. (genialis), *genially, gladly.*

genitor, ōris, m. (gīgnō, gen-), one that produces or begets, *parent, father, sire.*

gēns, tis, f. (gīgnō, gen), that which is united by birth, *a race, clan, people.*

genū, ūs, n. (**R.** GA, *to bend, curve,* ga-nu, ge-nu), *the knee.*

genuālia, um, n. (genū), *knee-bands, garters.*

genus, eris, n. (gīgnō, gen-), *birth, offspring, race, kind.*

germānus, a, um, adj. (germen, fr. **R.** KAR, *make, create,* car, cer, gar, ger, ger-men, and so Eng., germ, germ-ane), *full, own, true* (of birth), *real, genuine, germane.*

gerō, gessī, gestum, 3 (**R.** GAS, *go, come, make go* or *come, carry,* ges, ger-ere), *to carry, bring, bear, carry out, execute, wage.*

gestāmen, inis (gerō), something carried, *a burden.*

gestiō, 4 (gerō, ges-tu-m), *to use gestures, to desire* (demonstratively) *eagerly, long for.*

gestō, 1 (gerō), *to bear, carry, wear.*

gestus, ūs, m. (gerō), *carriage* (of the body), *gesture.*

Getae, ārum, pl. m., see note, Tristia, 4, 10, 110.

gigantēus, a, um, adj. (gigas), *of the giants, gigantic.*

gīgnō, genuī, genitum, 3 (**R.** GA, GA-N, *produce, beget,* gen, gi-gen, gi-gn-ere), *to give birth to, beget, bear.*

glaciālis, e, adj. (glaciēs), *icy.*

glaciēs, ēī, f., *ice.*

glaeba, ae, f. (**R.** GAR, GUR, *to*

round, gar-g, glo-g, gle-(glac)b-a), *a clod or lump of earth, land, soil, mass.*
glāns, dis, f. (**R.** GAR, *fall*, gal, galan = βάλ-αν-ο-ς, glan-s), *an acorn.*
glomerō, 1 (glomus, fr. same **R.** as glaeba, glo-b-mo, glo-m-us), *to form into a ball, press together, thicken.*
glōria, ae, f. (**R.** KRU, *hear, sound,* klu, clou-os, glov-os, glo-os, glōs), *renown, glory.*
glōrior, 1, v. dep. (glōria), *to boast one's self, glory in.*
glūbō, cre (**R.** SKALBU, calbh, clabh, GLAB, *scratch, peel*, glūb-cre), *to shell, peel.*
Gorgō, ōnis, Medusa, d. of Phorcys ; Met. 4, 743.
gracilis, e, adj. (**R.** KARK, *to be lean,* kur + kar, kra + kal, gra-cil-i-s), *slender, thin, fine.*
gradior, gressus sum, 3, v. dep. (**R.** GARDH, *strive after, stride*, grad), *to step, walk, go.*
gradus, ūs, m. (gradior), *step, pace, course, position, step* (of a temple).
grāmen, inis, n. (**R.** GAR, *swallow, eat*, gra-s, grā-men), *grass, turf, plant, herb.*
grāmineus, a, um, adj. (grāmen), of grass, *grassy.*
grandis, e, adj. (**R.** GAR, *be heavy, strong*, gra, gra-ndi-s), *great, grown up, advanced* (in age).
grandō, inis, f. (**R.** GHRAD, *to sound, rattle*, grad, gra-n-d-o), *hail.*

grānum, I, n. (**R.** GAR, *wear away,* grā-), *a grain, kernel.*
grātēs, pl. f. (**R.** GHAR, *glow, desire,* ghra, gra), *thanks.*
grātia, ae, f. (same **R.** as grātēs), *favor, friendship, grace, thanks.*
grātor, 1, v. dep. (same **R.** us grātēs), *to wish* (one) *joy.*
grātus, a, um, adj. (same **R.** as grātēs), *dear, agreeable, gracious, thankful.*
gravidus, a, um, adj. (gravis), *loaded, great with child, pregnant.*
gravis, e, adj. (same **R.** as grandis), *heavy, dull, covered with, heavy* (to bear), *sad.*
gravitās, ātis, f. (gravis), *weight, gravity, weariness, dignity, worth.*
gravō, 1 (gravis), *to make heavy, load, oppress.*
gremium, I, n. (**R.** GARBH, GRABH, *to seize, hold*, grab-mo, greb-mo, gremo), *the lap.*
gressus, ūs, m. gradior), *a step, course.*
grex, egis, m. (**R.** GAR, *come together*, gar + g(ar), gre-g), *a herd, flock, swarm, crowd.*
grūs, uis, comm. (**R.** GAR, *sound*, garu, gru-s), *a crane.*
gurges, itis, m. (**R.** GAR, *swallow*, gar + gar, gur-g-e-s), *a whirlpool, abyss, depth.*
gutta, ae, f. (**R.** SKJU, SKU, *flow out, fall*, sku-t, gutt-a), *a drop.*
guttur, uris, n. (**R.** same as gutta), *throat.*

H

habēna, ae, f. (habeō), *thong, rein, reins.*
habeō, uī, itum, 2 (etym. unc., but in Corssen, Krit. Beitr. 100, fr. **R.** GHA, gha-p, ha-p, *hold fast*), *to have, hold, possess, show, hold for, consider.*
habitābilis, e, adj. (habitō, habeō), *habitable.*
habitō, 1 (habeō), *to have, possess, inhabit.*
hāc, adv. (hic), abl., *here.*
haedus, I, m., *a kid.*
Haemonius, a, um, adj., *Haemonian.*
Haemus, I, m., a mountain in Thrace.
haereō, haesī, haesum, 2 (**R.** GHAIS,

haes, haer-ēre, *hang, cling*), *to cling to, stick fast in, to keep firm, adhere, hesitate.*
hālitus, ūs, m. (halō, 1, halitō, 1), *breath.*
hāmātus, a, um, part. adj., *hooked.*
hāmus, I, m. (**R.** GHAM, *bent*), *a hook.*
harēna, ae, f. (**R.** BHAS, *bruise, crush*, has, har-ena), *sand, sand-floor, arena* (of the amphitheatre).
harundō, inis, f. (**R.** AR, *grow*, arund-o), *a reed, sedge ;* by meton., *a wreath of reeds, shaft of an arrow, arrow ; fishing-rod, a comb of reed* (in weaving).

hasta, ae, f. (R. GHAS, *strike*, has-), a *spear, lance*, thyrsus-*staff*.

hastīle, is, n. (hasta), *the shaft of a spear*.

haud, adv. comp. of ho + au (as in au-fero) + d = de (as in unde), *not, not at all*.

hauriō, hansī, haustum, 4 (R. GHU, *pour*, ghu-s, hau-s, hau-r-īre), *to draw up* or *out, drain, drink up*.

haustus, ūs, m. (hauriō), *a draught, drink*.

hebetō, 1 (hebes), *to dull, weaken*.

Hĕbrus, I, m., river in Thrace.

hedera, ae, f. (R. GHAD, *seize*, had, hed), *ivy*.

Hĕliades, um, f., the three daughters of Helios, who were changed into poplars, Met. 2, 340, *amber*.

Helicē, ēs, f., the constellation of the Great Bear, Met. 8, 207.

Helicōn, ōnis, m., a mountain in Boeotia, sacred to the Muses.

Hennaeus, a, um, adj., *of Henna* or Enna, a city in Sicily.

herba, ae, f. (R. BHAR, *carry, support*, bhar-bh, her-b-a), *green stalk* or *blade, grass, plant*.

Hercules, is, m., son of Jupiter and Alcmene.

Herculeus, a, um, adj. (Hercules), *of Hercules, Herculean*.

hērēs, ēdis, m. (R. GHAR, *take, seize*, har, her, her-ē-re, hērē-s), *an heir, successor*.

hērōs, ōis, m. (ἥρως fr. R. VIRA, man, Fηρο), *hero*.

hērōus, a, um, adj. (herōs), *heroic*.

Hesperides, um, f., daughters of Night, or of Atlas, and Hesperis ; Met. 11, 114.

Hesperius, a, um, adj. (Hesperus), *Hesperian, western*.

Hesperus, I, m., *the evening, evening-star*.

hesternus, a, um, adj. (heri fr. R. GHJAS, *yesterday*, hies, hes, hes-i, her-i), *of yesterday, yesterday's*.

heu, interj., alas ! ah ! oh !

hiātus, ūs, m. (R. GHA, *be empty, yawn*, ghi, ghi-a, hia-sc-ere, hiā-re), *a yawning, opening, cleft, mouth*.

hībernus, a, um, adj. (hiems), *wintry*.

Hibĕrus, a, um, adj., *Iberian, of Iberia*.

hīc, adv., *here, in this thing, on this occasion*.

hīc, haec, hōc, pron. demonst. (R. GHA, ho, ho-ka (ka = pron. stem interrog. indef.), hi-ce, hic), *this, the latter* (in reference to the nearer, or the last mentioned).

hiemps, hiems, emis, f. (R. GHI, *throw* (χι-ών, *snow*, as *thrown* fr. the heavens), ghj-am, hj-am, hiem)), *winter, storm, stormy weather*.

hinc, adv. (hin-ce, hic), *from here, hence, hereupon, in consequence of*.

hinnītus, ūs, m. (hinniō fr. R. GHAR, *sound*, ghir, hir-ni-s, hin-ni), *a neighing*.

Hippomenes, is, m., son of Megareus ; Met. 10, 575.

Hippotades, is, m., son of Hippotes, i. e., Aeolus ; Met. 4, 663.

hirsūtus, a, um, adj. (R. GHAR, GHAR-S, *make rough*, hirs, hirs-u), *rough, shaggy, hirsute*.

hirtus, a, um, adj. (R. same as hirsūtus), *rough*.

hiscō, cre (R. GHA, *be empty, yawn*, ghi, ghi-a, hi-sc-cref, *to open, yawn, gape*.

Hister, strī, m., *the Hister, the Danube*.

holus, eris, n. (R. GHAR, *be green*, ghal-as, hol-us), *vegetables*.

homŏ, inis, n. (R. GHAMA, *earth*, gham-an, *the earthly, son of earth*, hom-o-n), *man, human being*.

honestus, a, um, adj. (honor), *honored, honorable*.

honor (honōs), ōris, m. (R. GHVA, *praise*, ho + suffix nas), *honor, place of honor, honorary gift, prize*.

honōrō, 1 (honor), *to honor*.

hōra, ae, f. (borrowed fr. ὥρα, R. JA, *go*, comp. Lat. I), *hour, time*; pl., *Hōrae, the Hours*.

Horātius, Q. Flaccus ; see n. Trist. 4, 10, 50.

horrendus, a, um, adj. (horreō), *dreadful, fearful, horrible*.

horreō, uī. 2 (R. GHAR, GHAR-S, *to be rough, stiff*, hors, hors-ē-re, horr-ē-re), *to bristle ; shudder, be afraid of*.

horridus, a, um, adj. (horreō), *rough, bristling, dread*.

horrifer, fera, ferum, adj. (horreō, fero), horror-bringing, *dreadful.*
hortāmen, inis, n. (hortor), an encouragement, *incitement.*
hortor, 1, v. dep. (**R.** DHARGH, *to hold to,* forgh, forcta-ri, hortā-ri), *to encourage, urge on.*
hortus, ī, m. (**R.** GHAR, *take,* har, hor, hor-tu-s), *a garden.*
hospes, itis, comm. (fr. hosti-pet-s, hosti fr. **R.** GHAS, *to injure,* hos, hosti-s, and pet- fr. **R.** PA, *protect,* pa-t, pe-t), one who protects a stranger, or is protected by a stranger, *a guest, a host, stranger.*
hospita, ae, f., see hospes.
hostis, is, comm. (**R.** GHAS, *injure*), one that injures, a stranger, enemy, *enemy* (to the state).

hūc, adv. (h|c), *hither.*
hūmānus, a, um, adj. (homō), *of man, human.*
humilis, e, adj. (humus), what lies on the *ground, low, humble.*
humus, ī, f. (**R.** GHAMA, *earth*), *earth, ground, soil.*
Hyacinthia, ōrum, n., festival in honor of Hyacinthus ; Met. 10, 219.
Hyacinthus, ī, m., son of Amyclas ; Met. 10, 162.
hȳdra, (ὕδρα), ae, f., *water-serpent, hydra.*
hȳdrus, ī, m. (ὕδρος), *a water-serpent, snake.*
Hymēn, enis (ὑμήν), or Hymenaeus, *god of marriage, Hymen.*
Hypaepa, ōrum, n., a city in Lydia.

I

Iambus, ī, m. (ἴαμβος) ; Trist. 4, 10, 47.
Iapetus, ī, m., father of Prometheus.
Iāsōn, onis, son of Aeson, the king of Iolcos.
ibī, adv., **R.** I (pron. stem 3d pers.) + bi (local ending), i-bī, *in that place, there.*
Icarus, ī, m., son of Daedalus.
Icelos, ī, m., a god of dreams, son of Somnus.
Icō, Icī, ictum, 3 (**R.** IK, *strike*), *to strike, hit.*
ictus, ūs, m. (Icō), *a stroke, blow.*
Ida, ae, Idē, ēs, f., Mt. Ida in Phrygia.
idcircō, adv. (id-circa), *on that account.*
idem, eadem, idem (i + idem, the former a pronom. stem, the latter the demonstr. suffix dem from da), *the same.*
ideō, adv. (id *and* eo), *for that reason, therefore.*
Idmōn, ōnis, m., the father of Arachne.
Idmōnius, a, um, adj., belonging to Idmon, *Idmonian.*
igitur, adv. (the pron. stem i + (the particle) ge, = je, + (the suffix), tus, i-ge-tus, i-gi-tur), *therefore, accordingly.*
Ignārus, a, um, adj. (in *and* gnārus), *not knowing, ignorant, unacquainted with.*

Ignāvus (in *and* gnāvus), a, um, adj., *not active, inactive, lazy.*
Ignis, is, m. (**R.** AG, *drive,* ig-), *fire, flash, glow, heat, splendor.*
Ignifer, a, um, adj., *fire-bearing.*
Ignōbilitās, ātis, f. (in *and* nōbilitās), *low birth.*
Ignōrantia, ae, f. (ignōrāns), *ignorance.*
Ignōrō, 1 (i(n)gnōrā-re), (**R.** GNA, *know,* gnā-ru-s (gnō-ru-s), gnōrā-re), *not to know, be ignorant of.*
Ignōscō, nōvi, nōtum, 3 (in-gnōscō, same **R.** as ignōrō), to take no knowledge of, *to pardon.*
Ignōtus, a, um, adj., *unknown.*
Ilex, icis, f., *the holm-oak, scarlet-oak, ilex.*
Ilia, ium, n. pl., the lower part of the abdomen, *the groin.*
Ilion, ī, n., and Ilios, ī, f., poetic name of Troy, *Ilium.*
Ilioneus, ei, m., son of Niobe.
illāc, adv. (ille, wh. see, and -ce, fr. pron. stem KI, cei, -ci, -ce, ille-ce), *in that way, on that side, there.*
ille, a, ud, pron. dem. 3d pers. (fr. pron. stem ANA, ANA-LA, ono-lo, on-lo, ol-lo, ollu-s, illu-s, ille), *that, that* (one) *there, that* well-known ; *he, she, it.*
illīc, adv. (see illac and ille), *in that place, there.*

illinō (in, lino), illēvī, illitum, 3, *to smear, spread, over.*
illūdō, in, lūdō, illūsī, illūsum, 3, *to play at, make sport of, jeer at.*
illustris, e, adj. (lux, il-lus-tri-s), *light, lustrous, illustrious.*
Illyricus, a, um, adj., *of Illyria, Illyrian.*
imāgō, inis, f. (R. IK, *be like* (ima-re), imi-ta-ri, imā-gō), *an image, copy, form, conception, thought.*
imbellis, e, adj. (in, bellum), *unwarlike.*
imber, bris, m. (R. ABH, AMBH, *to swell, break forth*, imb-, imb-e-r), *pouring forth, rain, rain-storm.*
imbuō, uī, ūtum, 3 (in, *and* R. PA, *drink*, po, pu, bu (bu-a, *a drink*), imbu-cre), *to wet, moisten ; imbue.*
imitāmen, inis, n. (imitor), *imitation, resemblance.*
imitātor, ōris, m. (imitor), *imitator.*
imitor, āri, v. dep. (see imāgō), *to imitate, resemble.*
im-madēscō, maduī, 3 (in, madēscō), *to grow moist* or *wet.*
immānis, e, adj. (in *and* mānis, fr. mānus, old Latin for *bonus*, and fr. R. MA, *to measure*), (measureless), *immense, monstrous, violent, fierce.*
immedicābilis, e, adj. (in, medicabilis), *incurable.*
immemor, oris, adj. (in, memor), *unmindful.*
immēnsus, a, um, adj. (in, metior), unmeasured, *immense, boundless.*
immeritus, a, um, adj. (in meritus), undeserving, *innocent ;* undeserved.
im-mineō, ēre (in *and* mineō, fr. R. MAN, *jut out*, min, min-ēre), *to project over, lean toward, hang over, to be close to, to strive for.*
im-mītis, e, adj. (in, mītis), not mild, *unmerciful, cruel.*
im-mittō, mīsī, missum, 3 (in, mittō), *to send in, let loose upon* or *in, let loose, hasten ;* part., immissus, *hanging down, loose.*
im-mō, adv. (fr. pron. stem ANA, en, in, in-mo, im-mo, superl. abl.), in inmost, *by no means, no indeed.*
immōbilis, e, adj., *immovable.*
im-morior, mori, mortuus sum, 3,

v. dep., *to die in*, or *upon*, or *over*, *die away.*
im-mōtus, a, um, adj. (in, moveō), *unmoved, immovable, calm.*
immūnis, e, adj. (in *and* mūnis, fr. R. MU, *bind*), not bound, *free from service, exempt from.*
im-mūnītus, a, um, adj. (in, mūniō, 4), *unfortified.*
im-murmurō, 1, *to murmur*, or *whisper in* or *upon.*
impār, paris, adj. (in, pār), *unequal.*
im-patiēns, ntis, adj. (in, patiēns), *not able to bear*, or *suffer, impatient.*
impediō, 4 (in *and* pēs), (in-foot, get the foot in), *impede, hinder, obstruct, stop.*
im-pellō, pulī, pulsum, 3 (in, pellō), *to set in motion, drive on* or *in, impell, strike.*
impēnsē, adv. (in *and* pendō), *at* or *with expense, richly ; eagerly.*
im-perfectus, a, um, adj. (in, perficiō), *incomplete, imperfect, undeveloped.*
imperium, ī, n. (im-perō, -parō), *command, dominion, dominions, empire.*
im-perō, 1 (in, parō, prop. *to bring* or *get into ;* c. g.. *terrae seges imperatur*, Tac. Germ. 26), *to enjoin, command, govern.*
impetus, ūs, m. (in, petō), *a pressing*, or *falling, upon, attack, assault, press ; impulse ; impete*, old abl.
impiger, gra, grum, adj. (in, piger), *not indolent, active.*
impius, a, um, adj. (in, pius), without a sense of duty, *undutiful, ungodly, ruthless.*
im-pleō, plēvī, plētum, 2 (in, pleō), *to fill in* or *up, fill full, fill, make full, fulfill.*
im-plicō, uī, itum, or āvi, ātum, 1 (in, plicō), *to infold, embrace, clasp, twine about.*
im - pōnō, posuī, positum, 3 (in, pōnō), *to place upon*, or *into*, or *in*, *set in, lay upon, impose, ascribe to.*
importūnus, a, um, adj. (in *and* -portu-nu-s, fr. same R. (POR) as portu-s, not op-portune, *inopportune, unfit, grievous, impudent, importunate.*

im-primō, pressī, prĕssum, 3 (in, premō), *to press upon, impress, strike into.*
improbus, a, um, adj. (in, probus), *not good, bad, mischievous, wicked.*
im-prūdēns, ntis, adj. (in, prūdēns, not foreseeing), *improvident, imprudent.*
impulsus, ūs, m. (impellō), *a pushing against, thrust, impulse.*
impūne, adv. (impūnis), *without punishment, with impunity, safely.*
impūnis, e, adj. (in *and* poena), *unpunished.*
im-putō, 1 (in, putō), *to reckon, to impute, ascribe.*
in, prep. (fr. ANA, pron. stem, 3d pers., en, in), with acc. = *into, to, toward, till, for, according to ;* with abl., *in, among, on, under, within.*
Inachides, ae, m., *descendant of Inachus, Inachide ;* used of Epaphus, Met. 1. 753 ; of Perseus, ib. 4, 720.
in-aequālis, e, adj., *unequal.*
in-amoenus, a, um, adj., *unlovely, disagreeable.*
inānis, e, adj. (R. AK, *to reach to,* ac-na, acn-ua, *a measure of land,* in-acni-s, in-āni-s), *empty, void ; lifeless, vain, useless.*
in-arātus, a, um, adj., *unplowed.*
in-ardēscō, arsī, 3, *to burn, kindle, glow.*
in-calēscō, caluī, 3, *to grow warm, to glow, kindle.*
in-cēdō, cessī, cessum, 3, *to step, march.*
incendium, ī, n. (incendō), *a fire, conflagration.*
in-certus, a, um, adj., *uncertain, untrustworthy ; undecided, doubtful.*
incessus, ūs, m. (incēdō), *a step, gait, walk, manner of walking.*
in-cīdo, cīdī, cīsum, 3 (caedō), *to cut into, inscribe, carve on* or *in.*
in-cipiō, cēpī, ceptum, 3 (capiō), *to take in hand, to begin ;* subst., *inceptum, beginning, undertaking.*
inclitus, or inclutus, a, um, adj. (cluō), *in* intensive, *very much heard of, renowned.*
in-clūdō, clūsī, clūsum, 3 (claudō), *to shut in, inclose, shut, close.*

in-cognitus, a, um, adj. (cognōscō), *unknown.*
incola, ae, m. (colō), *an inhabitant, dweller.*
in-commendātus, a, um, adj., *unrecommended, given up, abandoned.*
in-cōnsōlābilis, e, adj. (consōlor), inconsolable, *incurable.*
incrēmentum, ī, adj. (crēscō), *increment, increase.*
in-crepō, uī, itum, 1 (crepō), *to let sound, sound ; chide, reprove.*
in-crēscō, crēvī, crētum, 3, *to grow upon, increase.*
in-cubō, uī, itum, 1, *to lie upon* or *in.*
in-culpātus, a, um, adj. (culpō), *unblamed, blameless.*
in-cumbō, cubuī, cubitum, 3 (cumbō), *to lay one's self upon* or *in, lean upon, bend to.*
in-cūnābula, ōrum, pl. n. (cūna), swaddling-clothes, hence *cradle ; birthplace ; childhood.*
in-currō, currī, cursum, 3, *to run into.* incursō, 1, *to run against.*
incursus, ūs, m. (currō), *an incursion, assault.*
in-curvō, 1, *to bend, crook, curve.*
incurvus, a, um, adj., *crooked, bent.*
in-custōdītus, a, um, adj. (custodiō), *unwatched.*
indāgō, 1 (indāges), (to drive in, of game), *to trace out, search for.*
indāgō, inis, f. (R. AG, *drive,* ind-ag-o), (an in-driving as of game in hunting), *an incircling, inclosing.*
inde, adv. (fr. RR. ANA (pron. stem of 3d pers.), *an, in,* and pron. stem DA, *the, that one), from there, from that place, there ; from that time ; thence, in consequence of that.*
in-dēfessus, a, um, adj., *unwearied.*
in-dējectus, a, um, adj., *not cast down.*
in-dēplōrātus, a, um, adj., *undeplored, unwept.*
indicium, ī, n. (dico, R. DA, da-k, *show, teach), a showing, discovery, evidence, proof.* indicō, 1, *to show.*
in-dīcō, dixī, dictum, 3 (dīco, fr. da, da-k, dik, deic, dīc), *to declare.*
indigena, ae, comm. (indu = in *and* gigno), *one born in a country, native,* indigenous ; *a native.*

in-dĭgestus, a, um, adj. (dĭgero), *undigested, unarranged.*

in-dīgnō, 1, v. dep., *to consider as unworthy, to be indignant at, to be angry.*

in-dīgnus, a, um, adj., *unworthy, undeserving, undeserved.*

in-dŏlēscō, dolŭī, 3 (doleo), *to feel pain, be grieved.*

in-dūcō, duxī, ductum, 3, *to lead or bring in, draw over;* part. perf., *spread over.*

indulgeō, sī, tum, 2, etym. unc., *to indulge, be indulgent to, yield to.*

induō, uī, ūtum, 3 (inde and u (ind-u), fr. R. AV, *clothe*), *to put on, assume, clothe with, invest.*

in-dūrēscō, uī (dūrus), *to grow hard, harden.*

in-dūrō, 1 (dūrus), *to make hard, harden.*

Indus, I, *Indian, of India.*

in-eō, īī, itum, 4, *to go into, enter; begin, enter upon.*

inermis, e, adj. (arma), *unarmed.*

iners, ertis, adj. (ars), *unskilled, inactive, idle, dull.*

in-expugnābilis, e, adj. (expugno), *impregnable; (of gramen) that can not be rooted out.*

Infāns, ntis, adj. and subst. (in-for, fārī), *one that can not talk, infant, young; an infant.*

Infaustus, a, um, adj., *unfortunate, unpropitious, unlucky.*

Infectus, a, um, adj. (facio), *not done, unfinished.*

In-fēlīx, īcis, *not happy, unfortunate, unlucky.*

Infernus, a, um, adj. (inferus), *that which is below, of the lower world, infernal.*

In-ferō, tulī, illātum, 3, *to carry, bring, into or to.*

Inferus, a, um, adj. (pron. stem a + dha; adha + ra (compar. suffix), a-n-dhara, i-n-feru-s), *the lower, that which is below, of the lower world;* comp., Inferior, *lower (in place) than, inferior;* superl., Imus, or Infimus, *lowest, deepest, innermost.*

In-festus, a, um, adj. (fr. in-fend-tu-s, fend the same root as in de-fend-o, fr. DHAN-D, *to strike*), *hostile.*

In-ficiō, fēcī, fectum, 3 (facio), *to put upon, to stain, dye, color; to infect, taint.*

In-fĭtior, 1 (fateor), *not to confess, to deny, disown.*

In-flectō, exī, exum, 3, *to bend, curve.*

In-flō, 1, *to blow into or upon, to inflate.*

Infrā, adv. (inferus), abl. sc. parte or viā, *in the lower part, below;* comp., Inferius, *lower.*

In-fringō, frēgī, fractum, 3 (frango), *to break in or off, bruise.*

In-fundō, fūdī, fūsum, 3, *to pour in or upon, infuse.*

In-gemō, uī, 3, *to groan, sigh over.*

Ingenium (gigno, gen), *what is inborn, natural quality of mind or heart.*

ingēns, tis, adj., *great.*

in-gerō, gessī, gestum, 3, *to put into or upon, throw or heap upon.*

in-grātus, a, um, adj., *unpleasant, unthankful, ungrateful.*

in-gredior, gressus sum, 3, *to go into, enter, enter upon.*

inguen, inis, n. (R. AGH, ANGH, *to narrow*), (narrowing), *the groin.*

in-haereō, haesī, haesum, 2, *to hang to or upon, cleave, adhere, inhere.*

in-hĭbeō, uī, itum, 2 (habeo), *to have in, restrain, check, hinder.*

In-iciō, jēcī, jectum, 3 (jacio), *to throw upon or into, to lay upon.*

inimīcus, a, um, adj. (amicus), *unfriendly, inimical;* subst., *an enemy, a foe.*

inīquus, a, um, adj. (aequus), *not even, uneven; unfair, unjust, unfavorable; hostile.*

injūria, ae, f. (injūrius, in-jūs), *injury, wrong, injustice.*

injustē, adv., *unjustly, unfairly, wrongly.*

in-justus, a, um, adj., *unjust, wrongful, unjustly gained.*

innābilis, e, adj. (in-no), *that can not be swum in.*

in-nātus, a, um, adj. (in-nascor), *born in, inborn, innate.*

in-nectō, xuī, xum, 3, *to tie to or upon, to bind, encircle.*

innocuus, a, um, adj. (noceo), *harmless, innocent.*

innubus, a, um, adj. (in-nūbō), *unmarried.*
in-numerus, a, um, adj., *unnumbered, numberless.*
in-nuptus, a, um, adj. (nūbō), *unmarried.*
in-ops, opis, adj. (in-(ops), opis), without help, *helpless, poor, needy, scanty, weak.*
in-ornātus, a, um, adj., *unadorned.*
inquam, v. defective, (R. syllable qua (in-qua-m), cognate to Sansc. khjā, *to view,* Vanicck), *I say, say I* (always used after one or more words in a direct quotation).
inquīrō, quīsīvī, quīsītum, 3 (quaerō), to seek after or into; *to inquire, examine, into.*
In-sānus, a, um, adj., *not sound, unsound in mind, insane, mad.*
Inscius, a, um, adj., *not knowing, ignorant of.*
In-scrībō, psī, ptum, 3, *to write in or upon, inscribe, ascribe, designate.*
In-secō, uī, ctum, 1, *to cut into or in;* insecti, *notched.*
In-sequor, secūtus sum, 3, *to follow after or upon, follow, pursue.*
In-serō, uī, rtum, 3, *to put into, insert, involve, mingle.*
Insidiae, f. plural (insideō), (a sitting in), *lying in wait, ambush, ambuscade, deceit, plot, snare.*
Insīgnis, e, adj. (sīgnum), distinguished by a mark, *remarkable, signal;* subst., insigne, *a sign, badge;* (in plural), *costume, attire.*
In-siliō, siluī, 4 (saliō), *to leap into* or *upon, spring upon.*
In-sistō, stitī, 3, *to step upon, tread;* in Met. v, 558, with *alarum-remis, to hover, poise,* the *oar-like wings* keeping them from sinking.
In-solitus, a, um, adj. (soleō), *unwonted.*
In-somnis, e, adj. (somnus), *sleepless.*
In-sonō, uī, itum, 1, to sound in, *sound loudly, resound.*
In-sōpītus, a, um, adj., *not lulled to sleep, sleepless.*
In-spiciō, exī, ctum, 3 (speciō), to look into, *inspect, examine.*

In-spīrō, 1, *to breathe into, blow into, inspire.*
In-stābilis, e, adj. (stō, sta), that does not stand firm, *unsteady, unstable.*
Instar, indecl. (etym. unc.), *image, form;* ad instar, or simply instar with gen. after the image of, *like, as, as good as.*
Instīgō, 1 (stig, stīg; stigō, not used, *to be sharp, sharpen), to incite, urge, instigate.*
In-stituō, uī, ūtum, 3 (statuō), *to establish, institute.*
In-stō, stitī, 1, to stand upon, *press upon; draw nigh, impend; press, insist upon, urge.*
In-stringō, nxī, ctum, 3, *to bind upon* or *around;* part., instrictus, *set* (sc. gemmis).
In-struō, xī, ctum, 3, *to furnish, provide; instruct.*
In-suētus, a, um, adj., *unaccustomed, unused.*
Insula, ae, f., *island.*
Insultō, 1 (Insiliō), *to spring at* or *upon, dance.*
In-sum, fui, esse, *to be in* or *on,* or *upon.*
In-super, adv., *over and above, besides.*
In-surgō, surrexī, surrectum, 3, *to rise upon* or *up to.*
In-tābēscō, buī, 3, *to waste away, pine, melt, dissolve.*
In-tactus, a, um, adj. (tāngō), *untouched, intact.*
intellegō (inter-legō), exī, ectum, 3, *to see into, understand.*
in-temptātus, a, um, adj., *untried.*
in-tendō, dī, tum, 3, *to stretch upon* or *out, extend, stretch out, cover.*
inter, prep. with acc., pron. stem AN + TARA, comp. suffix, an-tara, in-ter), *between, among, in the midst of, during.*
inter-cidō (cadō), idī, 3, *to fall between, perish, die.*
inter-cipiō (capiō), cēpī, ceptum, 3, *to take away between, seize upon, intercept, carry away, rob.*
inter-dīcō, xī, ctum, 3, *to speak between, interpose, forbid, interdict.*
inter-dum, adv., *now and then, at times, sometimes.*

inter-eā, adv., *meanwhile, in the mean while.*
inter-eō, iī, itum, īre, *to perish, go to ruin, die.*
interior, ius, ōris, adj. comp., *inner, interior;* superl., intimus, a, um, *innermost.*
interius, adv., *within.*
inter-mittō, mīsī, missum, 3, *to leave off, intermit, omit.*
inter-nōdium, ii, n. (nōdus), the space between two knots or joints, *an internode* or *joint.*
in-territus, a, um, adj., *unterrified.*
inter-rumpō, rūpī, ruptum, 3, *to interrupt.*
inter-serō, uī, rtum, 3, *to put in between, interpose.*
inter-texō, uī, xtum, 3, *to weave in between, interweave.*
inter-veniō, vēnī, ventum, 4, *to come in between, intervene, interrupt.*
in-texō, uī, xtum, 3, *to weave into* or *in, inweave, interweave.*
intībum, i, n., *endive.*
in-tonō, uī, 1, *to thunder.*
in-tōnsus, a, um, adj. (tondeō), *unshorn.*
intrā, prep. with acc. (for **R,** see inter), abl. intrā-(d) = interā parte, *within.*
in-tremō, uī, 3, *to tremble, quake.*
in-trō, avī, atum (**R.** TAR, TRA, *to move,* trā-re, tra-n-s, part. pres., intrāre), *to enter, go into, tread.*
introrsum, adv. (intrōversus), *toward the inside, inward.*
intus, adv. (in, tus), *within, into.*
in-ūtilis, e, adj., *useless, injurious.*
in-vādō, sī, sum, 3, *to go into, fall upon, invade.*
in-vehō, xī, ctum, 3, *to carry into* or *to, to ride, drive, sail, fly.*
in-veniō, vēnī, ventum, 4, *to come upon, find, meet with, find out, invent.*
in-vergō, ere, *to turn, incline to, pour upon.*
in-victus, a, um, adj. (vincō), *unconquered, unconquerable.*
in-video, vīdī, vīsum, 2, *to look askance at, to envy, be envious, refuse, grudge.*
invidia, ae, f., *envy, hate, dislike, odium.*

invidiōsus, a, um, adj., *envious, invidious, envied, hated.*
invidus, a, um, adj., *envious, unfavorable.*
invīsus, a, um, adj. (invideō), *hated.*
invītō, 1 (**R.** VAK, VOC, VOCŌ, vocitāre, invoci-tāre, invici-tāre, in-vic-tāre, in-vi-tare, *to call*), *to invite, entertain.*
invītus, a, um, adj. (**R.** VAK, *to will,* vic, in-vic-(i)tu-s, in-vī-tus), *unwilling, reluctant, contrary to one's will.*
invius, a, um, adj. (in-via), *impassable, impenetrable.*
in-vocō, 1, *to call upon, invoke, call to one's assistance.*
Iolciacus, a, um, adj., *of Iolchos, Iolchian.*
Iolē, ēs, f., d. of Eurytus, king of Oechalia.
ipse, a, um, pron. (**RB.** I, pron. stem 3d pers. + PSE, *self,* fr. PA-T, po-t, poti-s, *one who is able, master*), *he himself, in person, the very one;* then with pronouns of other persons, and all genders, *herself, itself, myself, thyself.*
Ira, ae, f. (**R.** IR, *to be angry, injure*), *anger, wrath, angry feeling, assault of anger.*
īrāscor, i, 3 (for **R.** see ira, ira-sc-i), *to be angry, get angry.*
īrātus, a, um, adj. (ira, ira-tu-s), *angry, enraged.*
Iris, is, f., goddess of the rainbow, d. of Thaumas, messenger of Juno.
ir-requiētus, a, um, adj. (in, re, qnies, quietus), *unquiet, restless.*
ir-rīdeō, sī, sum, 2, *to laugh at, ridicule, laugh to scorn.*
irrītāmentum, i, n. (irrītō), *an incitement.*
irrītō, 1 (**R.** RA, rai, *to sound,* ir-rī-re, ir-rī-tā-re), *to move to passion, to excite, incite, provoke, irritate.*
irritus, a, um, adj. (in, ratus), *not determined, invalid, void, in vain, ineffectual.*
irrōrō, 1 (rōrō), *to bedew, moisten, sprinkle.*
irrumpō, rupī, ruptum, 3 (in, rumpō), *to break in* or *into,* or *upon.*
Irus, I, m., name of a beggar in Ithaca.
is, ea, id, demons. pron. (pron. stem I), *he, she, it, that, this; such an one.*

Ismarius, a, um, adj., *of Ismaros*, a mountain in Thrace, *Ismarian ; Thracian.*

Ismēnos, I, m., 1, a river in Boeotia, near Thebes ; 2, son of Niobe.

Issē, ēs, f., d. of the Lesbian Macareus.

Iste, a, ud, fr. I, pron. stem + TA pron. stem i-s (is-tu-s), is-te, is-ta, is-tu-d, demonstr. pron., *this, that* (pointing to the 2d pers.), *that one of yours, that one near you.*

ita, adv., fr. I + TA, ita, *so, thus, in this way.*

iter, itineris, n. (fr. I, R. of eo, i-tu-m, it-es, it-in-es, it-er, it-in-er-is), *a going, a way, journey, march, road, street.*

iterō, 1 (for R. see iterum), *to do a second time, repeat, reach again.*

iterum, adv. (fr. pron. stem I (is), with comparative as adv., acc. sing. n., i-teru-m), the other, *a second time, once more, again.*

Iūlus, I, m., son of Aeneas, also called Ascanius.

Ixīōn, onis, m., king of the Lapithae in Thessaly, punished in Tartarus by being bound fast to an ever-revolving wheel.

J

Jaceō, uī, itum, 2 (for R. see jaciō), (intrans. of jaciō, *to be thrown,* hence), *to lie down, recline, rest, lie in the grave, lie in ruins.*

jaciō, jēcī, jactum, 3 (R. JA, ja-k, *to go, cause to go*), *to throw, lay, throw out* (in speaking).

jactō, 1 (jaciō), freq., *to throw, hurl, shake, throw out, fling out, boast.*

jactūra, ae, f., *a throwing away, a loss, damage.*

jactus, ūs, m. (jaciō), *a throw, cast, throw* (of dice).

jaculātrīx, Icis, f., she that throws, shoots (of Diana), *the huntress.*

jaculor, dep., 1 (jaciō), *to throw.*

jaculum, I, n., *a javelin.*

jam, adv. (R. JA, pron. stem 3d pers., ja-smin, ja-m, locative), *now, just now, already ; only now.*

jam-dūdum, adv. (jam, du-dum, fr. diu-dum, see dum), *now for some time, some time ago, long since.*

jānua, ae, f. (R. JA, jā, *to go*), a passage-way, *entrance, door, house-door.*

jecur (jocur), jecoris, jecinoris, jocinoris, n. (fr. jak-an), *the liver.*

jējūnium, I, n. (jejūnus, etym. unc.). *fasting, hunger.*

juba, ae, f. (etym. unc.), *the mane* of a horse, Met. v, 403.

jubar, aris, n. (R. DIV, dju, *to shine,* ju-bar), *brightness, radiance,* of the sun, of a star.

jubeō, jussī, jussum, 2 (R. JU, JU-G, ju-dh, ju-b, *to bind, make binding*), *to order, bid, command.*

jūdex, icis, m. (jūs-dex, jūs same R. as jubeo, dex same as dīcō, which see), *a judge ; an umpire.*

jūdicium, I, n. (judex), *a judgment, judicial sentence, decision.*

jugālis, e, adj. (jugum, wh. see), of a yoke ; *of a marriage-union ; nuptial, matrimonial.*

jūgerum, I (is), n. (same R. as jugum), a piece of land, 240 feet long by 120 wide, *a juger; acre* (though much smaller than the English acre).

jugulō, 1 (fr. jugulum, which has same R. as jugum), *to cut the throat, slay, murder.*

jugulum, I, n., *the throat.*

jugum, I, n. (same R. as jubeo, wh. see), *a yoke, collar ; a team ; span ; the beam of a weaver's loom ; a mountain-ridge* (or yoke), *height.*

junctūra, ae; f., *a ligament.*

juncus, I, m., *a rush, a bulrush.*

jungō, nxī, nctum, 3 (R. JU, ju-g, ju-n-g, *to bind*), *to join, unite, yoke ; unite in marriage, wed, marry.*

Jūnōnius, a, um, adj. (Junō), *of Juno, Junonian.*

Jūppiter, jovis, m. (R. DIV, dju, djau, djav, *to shine ;* djov, Jov-i-s ; Jupiter (pater), then with doubling of consonant, Ju-ppiter, *father of light ;* but Cic. in De Nat. D. II, 25, 64, derives from juvo, "juvans pater" ; juva-re, however, is fr. same R. DIV) ; Jupiter, or Jove, Gr. Ζεύς, son of Saturn and Rhea, chief god of the Romans.

jūrō, 1 (R. JU, *to bind,* ju-s, ju-r-is,

jūrā-re), *to swear, take an oath, swear by some person or thing.*
jūs, jūris, n. (**R.** JU, *to bind,* ju-s, *that which binds*), *right, law, justice ; duty ; justness; power, authority.*
justē (justus), *justly, with right.*
justus, a, um, adj. (jūs), *just, righteous, rightful, true, lawful, equitable, legitimate.*
juvenālis, e, adj. (juvenis, and fr. same **R.** as juvō), *youthful, juvenile.*
juvenāliter, adv. (juvenālis), *youthfully, after manner of youth.*
juvenca, ae, f. (juvencus, contr. fr. juvenicus, fr. juvenis), *a young cow, heifer.*
juvencus, ī, m. (juvenis), *a young bullock, bullock.*
juvenis, is, adj. and subst. (fr. same **R.** as juvō), *youthful, young, a youth, a young man.*
juventa, ae, f. (juvenis), *youth, the goddess of youth.*
juventus, ūtis, f. (juvenis), *age of youth ; youth, young persons.*
juvō, jūvī, jūtum, 1 (**R.** DIV, dju, juv-), *to help, aid, assist ; to delight, please, rejoice.*

L

labefaciō, fēcī, factum, 3 (labō, faciō), *to cause to fall, shake, weaken.*
labō, 1 (**R.** RAB, *to hang down, fall,* lāb (lābi), lab, labā-re), *waver, totter, give way.*
lābor, lapsus sum, dep., 3 (see labō), *to slide, slip, glide, fall, sink.*
labor, ōris, m. (labos), (**R.** RABH, rab, lab, *to seize, undertake*), *effort to reach anything, labor, exertion, trouble.*
labōrō, 1 (labor), *to labor, take pains, be in trouble.*
lac, ctis, n. (**R.** GALAKT, GLAKT, lac), *milk ; milk of plants.*
lacer, era, erum, adj. (**R.** VAR, *to draw, tear,* var-k, vlak, lac-), *torn, lacerated, lacerating.*
lacerna, ae, f. (see lacer ; fr. lacinia, *a piece of cloth*), *a mantle worn over the toga, as a dress-robe, or worn on journeys, or in wet or cold weather.*
lacerō, 1 (lacer), *to lacerate, mangle ; to distress, trouble.*
lacerta, ae, f., *a lizard.*
lacertōsus, a, um, adj. (lacertus), *muscular, powerful.*
lacertus, ī, m. (**R.** LAK, *to bend*), *the upper arm,* from the elbow to the shoulder ; *the arm ;* lacerti, *the claws* of the scorpion ; *the arm* of a river.
lacessō, īvī, ītum, 3 (laciō, **R.** LAC, *to allure*), *to excite, provoke, attack.*
lacrima, ae, f. (**R.** DAK = lac, *to bite,* Gr. δάκρυ), *a tear.*
lacrimō, 1 (lacrima), *to shed tears, weep.*
lacrimōsus, a, um, adj. (lacrima), *tearful, full of tears ; lamentable.*

lactō, 1 (lac), *to give milk.*
lacus, ūs, m. (**R.** LAC, *to bend ; hollow*), a hollowing out, deepening ; *a basin, vessel, tank ; a cooling-trough,* Met. ix, 171 ; *a lake ; pool.*
laedō, sī, sum, 3 (**R.** SRIDH, *to injure,* slidh, lid, laid, laed-ere), *to hurt, injure, wound ; to trouble, annoy, grieve.*
laetābilis, e, adj. (laetus), *joyful, glad.*
laetor, dep., 1 (laetus), *to rejoice, be glad.*
laetus, a, um, adj. (**R.** PRI, *to rejoice,* prai, plai, plac, lac-), *joyful, glad, pleasing, delightful.* **laetitia,** ae, f., *joy.*
laevus, a, um, adj., LAIVA, laivo, *left;* subst. (manus *understood*), *left hand.*
lambō, mbī, bitum, 3 (**R.** LAP, *to lick,* lab, la-m-b-), *to lap, lick ; reach.*
lāmina, ae, f., *a thin plate,* especially of metal ; also of wood or marble.
Lampetiē, ēs, f., one of the Heliades ; Met. ii, 349.
lāna, ae, f. (**R.** LAC, *to bend,* lac-na, lā-na), *wool.*
lancea, ae, f. (**R.** lanka), *a lance.*
langueō, ēre (**R.** LAG, *to be soft,* la-n-g). *to be faint, inactive, languid.*
languor, ōris, m. (langueō), *faintness, languor.*
lānificus, a, um, adj. (lana-faciō), *that works in wool, of wool-working.*
lāniger, gera, gerum, adj. (lanagerō), *wool-bearing, fleecy.*
laniō, 1 (**R.** same as lacer), *to rend in pieces, lacerate, to tear.*
lānūgō, inis (lāna), f., *down of the beard.*

Lăomedon, ontis, m., king of Troy, son of Ilus, father of Priam.
lapĭdōsus, a, um, adj. (lapis), *stony.*
lapillus, ī, m. (lapis), *a little stone.*
lapis, ĭdis, m. (**R.** LAP, *to peel*), *a* (bare) *rock.*
lapsus, ūs, m. (lābor), *a falling, fall.*
laqueus, ī, m. (**R.** same as lacĭō, LAC, *to allure*), *a noose, snare.*
lar, laris, m. (**R.** RA, la-la-s, la-r, *to stop, rest*), originally a place of rest, *house, home;* then *the deity of the household, tutelary deity.*
largus, a, um, adj. (etym. unc., perhaps from same **R.** as lascīvus), *abundant, rich, large.*
lascīvus, a, um, adj. (**R.** same as lar), *playful, sportive.*
lassō, 1 (lassus), *to weary, fatigue, tire.*
lassus, a, um, adj. (etym. unc.), *weary, tired.*
lātē, adv. (lātus), widely, *broadly, to a great extent.*
latĕbra, ae, f. (lateō), *a hiding-place, retreat.*
lateō, uī, 2 (**R.** RADH, *to forsake,* ladh, lat-), *to be hidden, hide one's self.*
latĭtō, 1, reg., *to hide.*
Latīnus, a, um, adj., *Latin.*
Latius, a, um, adj., *of Latium, Latin.*
Lātōna, ae, f., d. of the Titan Coeus and Phebe, mother of Apollo and Diana.
Lātōnĭgena, ae, comm. in pl., children of Latona, Apollo and Diana.
Lātōus, ī, m., son of Latona, Apollo.
latrō, 1 (**R.** RA, *to sound*, ra-t, lat, latrā-re), *to bark.*
latrō, ōnis, m. (**R.** LU, *to win, plunder,* lau, lav, la-tr-o), *a robber.*
lātus, a, um, adj. (**R.** STAR, *to strew, spread*, strā, stlā, lā-tu-s), outspread, *broad, wide, extended.*
latus, eris, n. (**R.** PRAT, *to broaden,* plat, lat-), breadth, *the side, flank,* of animals, men, things.
laudō, 1 (laus), *to praise, count happy.*
laurea, ae, f. (laurus), *laurel-tree.*
laurus, ūs, m. (**R.** DU, *to burn*, dau-, lau-ro), *laurel-tree, laurel, crown, victory.*

laus, dis, f. (**R.** KRU, *to hear, sound,* klu, clu- (clu-ere), lau-s), praise, renown, fame; *words, deeds, of fame.*
lavō, lāvī, lōtum, lautum, lavātum, 1 (**R.** LU, *to wash,* luv, lau, lav), *to wash, bathe.*
lea, ae, f. (leō), *a lioness.*
leaena, ae, f. (λέαινα), *a lioness.*
Lebinthus, or os, ī, f., one of the Sporadic isles, S. W. of Asia Minor.
lectus, ī, m. (**R.** LAGH, *to lie down,* leg, lec-tu-s), *a couch, bed; a bier;* by meton., *marriage.*
Lĕda, ae, f., d. of Thestius, wife of Tyndareus, mother of Castor and Pollux.
legō, legī, lectum, 3 (**R.** RAG, *to gather, read,* lag, leg), *to gather, collect, read; choose.*
Lelex, egis, m., one of the Calydonian hunters of Naryx, in Locris.
lēna, ae, f. (lēnō, **R.** LAG, *to be soft,* leg, leg-na, lēna), *a bawd, procuress.*
Lēnaeus, a, um, adj. (ληνός), a name of Bacchus.
lēnīmen, inis, n. (leniō), *a soothing remedy, a solace.*
lēnis, e, adj. (**R.** LANA, *soft*, lēni-s), *mild, soft, gentle.*
lentē, adv., *slowly.*
lentus, a, um, adj. (same **R.** as lēnis; lan-ta, len-tu-s), *pliant, soft, tough; insensible. sluggish, slow.*
Leō, ōnis, m. (**R.** LIV, *to be grayish-yellow,* laiv-an, le-o(n)), *a lion;* the Lion in the zodiac.
lepus, oris, m. (**R.** LAP, *to be bright, light,* lep-us, *the light, the gray*), *a hare.*
Lerna, ae, f., a marsh in Argolis.
Lesbos, or ūs, ī, f., an island in the Aegean.
Lesbius, a, um, adj., *of Lesbos, Lesbian.*
lētālis, e, adj. (lētum), *deadly.*
Lēthaea, ae, f., wife of Olenos; changed into stone on Mt. Ida.
Lēthaeus, a, um, adj. (Lēthē), *of Lethe, Lethean.*
Lēthē, ēs, f. (same **R.** as lateō, Gr. λήθη), *forgetfulness, oblivion;* name of a river in the lower world.
lētĭfer, era, erum, adj., *death-bringing, deadly.*

lētŏ, 1 (lētum), *to put to death.*
lētum, ī, n. (R. RI, *to let run, dissolve*, li, lē-tu-m), *death, ruin.*
levis, e, adj. (R. RAGH, *to run,* lagu-i, legu-i, legv-i, levi-s), *light.*
lēvis, e, adj., *smooth.*
levitās, ātis, f. (levis), *lightness.*
leviter, adv., *lightly.*
levŏ, 1 (same R. as levis), *to make light, lighten, relieve, lift up, soften, moderate.*
lēx, lēgis, f. (same R. as lectus, leg, leg-s, lĕx, *what is laid down*), *a law, rule, order, decision, condition.*
liber, lĭbrī, m. (R. LAP, *to peel*, lib, lib-ro, lib-er), *the bark* of a tree.
līber, era, erum, adj. (R. LUBH, *to desire, please*, libh, lib, loub, loib, loeb, lib-er), *free, frank, open.*
Līber, erī, m. (R. RI, *to let run, pour*, lib, lib-er), originally an Italian deity, who presided over all that is fruitful ; then the name transferred to the Gr. Bacchus.
līberŏ, 1 (līber, *free*), *to free, liberate.*
lībertās, ātis, f. (līber), *liberty, freedom.*
libet, nit, impers. v. (fr. same R. as līber, *free*), *it pleases, is agreeable* ; with mihi, *I like.*
lībŏ, 1 (same R. as Līber, Bacchus), *to draw, pour out, to make a libation ;* figuratively, *to touch lightly, skim.*
lībrŏ, 1 (R. KRI, *to lean, bend*, cli, cle-bra, li-bra, libra-re), *to balance, weigh, poise, swing.*
lībum, ī, n. (R. KAR, *to cook, mix*, kri, cli-, cli-bu-m, li-bu-m), *a cake, pancake.*
Libycus, a, um, adj., *Libyan.*
Libyē, ēs, f., *Libya ; Africa.*
licentia, ae, f. (fr. licēre), *freedom, license.*
licet, uit, licitum est, 2, imp. v. (R. RIK, *to let, let go*, ric, lic, lic-ēre), *it is for sale, it is free), it is allowed, permitted, one may* (or) *can.*
Lichās, ae, m., servant of Hercules.
līgnōsus, a, um, adj. (lignum), *woody, of wood.*
līgnum, ī, n. (R. RAG, *to gather*, leg, lig, lig-nu-m, *what is gathered*), *wood, timber.*

lĭgŏ, 1 (R. VARG, *to press, confine*, valg, vilg, vlig, lig, liga-re), *to bind, bind fast.*
lĭgŏ, ōnis, m. (R. LAGHAN, ligon), *a spade.*
Ligures, um, the Ligurians, a people in northern Italy.
līlium, ī, n. (Gr. λείριον). *a lily.*
Lilybaeŏn, ī, n., the western promontory of Sicily.
limbus, ī, m. (R. RAB, *to hang down*, lamb, limb-), *a border, edge, fringe.*
līmen, inis, n. (same R. as limes), *a threshold ; entrance, door, house.*
līmes, itis, m.(R. LAK, *to bend, turn*, lic, lic-mit, līmes), *a cross-path, path, limit, boundary.*
līmōsus, a, um, adj. (limus), *slimy, muddy.*
līmus, ī, m. (R. RI, *to let run, pour*, li, li-mu-s), *slime, mud.*
lingua, ae, f. (R. DANGUA, dingua, lingua, *tongue*), *speech, language,* utterance ; *tongue* of land ; *anther of a lily,* Met. X, 191.
linter, tris, f. (R. PRU, *to swim, float*, plu, plun, lun-, lin-ter), *a trough, vat ; a boat, skiff.*
linteum, ī, n. (linum), *a linen cloth ; a sail.*
līnum, ī, n. (R. LINUM, *flax*), *linen.*
liquefacĭŏ, fecī, factum, 3, *to make liquid, to dissolve, melt.*
liqueŏ, liquī, 2 (R. RI, *to pour out*, li, lic, liqu-), *to be liquid* or *fluid ; to be clear, distinct.*
liquēscŏ, licnī, 3 (liqueŏ), *to become liquid.*
liquidus, a, um, adj. (liqueo), *fluid, liquid ; bright, clear.*
liquor, oris, m. (liqueŏ), *fluidity ; a fluid, liquid* (clear) *water.*
liquor, liquī (liqueŏ), *to be fluid, liquid ; to dissolve, disappear.*
līs, lītis, f. (R. STAR, *to disturb*, stir, stri, strei-ti, stlei-ti, stli-ti, li-s), *a dispute, quarrel ; lawsuit.*
līttera, ae, f. (R. RI, *to pour, spread over*, li, li-ttera), (what is spread over, marked), *a letter* (of the alphabet), *a mark* or *sign ;* collect., *writing ; an inscription* (as writing on a tomb).
lītus, oris, n. (fr. same R. as littera),

something marked out, *a shore, beach, strand.*

līveō, ēre (fr. same R. as leo), *to be lead-colored, bluish, livid ; to envy.*

līvor, ōris, m. (liveō), *a leaden color, taint, spot ; envy.*

locō, 1 (locus), *to place, put, set.*

locus, ī, m. (R. STAR, *to strew, cover,* stark, stra-k, stlo-c, lo-c-u-s), *a place, spot, situation ; space ;* room ; *social position.*

lolium, ī, n., *darnel, tares.*

longē, adv. (longus), *long, in length, far ; for a long period.*

longus, a, um, adj. (etym. unc.), *long ; tall ; vast ; long-continuing.*

loquāx, ācis, adj. (loquor), *loquacious, talkative.*

loquor, locūtus sum, dep. v., 3 (R. RA, *to sound,* ra-k, lak, loqu-), *to talk, speak, say, mention. relate, declare.*

lōrīca, ae, f. (lorum), *a leather cuirass, coat of mail.*

lōrum, i, n. (R. VAR, *to wind, turn,* val, vol, vlo, lo-ru-m), *a thong, strap, reins, bridle.*

lōtos, ī, f., *lotus-tree.*

lūbricus, a, um, adj. (R. GLA, *to be slippery,* glu, glu-b, lu-br-o, lu-bri-cu-s), *slippery.*

lūceō, x, 2 (for R. see lūx), *to shine, gleam.*

lūcidus, a, um, adj. (lūx), *bright, shining, clear.*

Lūcifer, erī, m. (lūx, fero), *light-bringing, the morning-star.*

Lūcrētia, ae, f., the wife of Callatinus ; Fasti, II, 741.

Lūcrētius, ī, m., the poet, T. Lucretius Carus, author of the poem "De rerum natura"; Am. I, 15, 23.

lucrum, ī, n. (R. LU, *to win, gain,* lou, lu, lu-cru-m), *gain, lucre.*

luctor, ārī, 1, v. d. (R. RU, ru-g, *to break, bend,* lug, luc-tāri), *to wrestle, struggle, take pains.*

luctus, ūs, m. (lūgeō), *mourning, sorrow, distress, grief.*

lūcus, ī, m. (lūx), the shining as in an open place in a wood, *a grove,* sacred to some deity, *a wood.*

lūdō, sī, sum, 3 (R. KRID, *to play,* crid, croid, cloid, loid, lūd), *to play, sport,* mock, play off, *foil, parry.*

lūdus, ī, m. (lūdo), *a game, sport,* play ; in pl., *public games, sports.*

lūgeō, xī, 2 (from same R. as luctor), *to mourn, grieve, bewail ; be in mourning.*

lūgŭbris, e, adj. (lugeō, ferō, luge-ferō, lugu-ferō, lug-u-bri-s), *belonging to mourning, mournful, sad.*

lūmen, inis, n. (lūx), *a light,* light, *ray of light, light of the eyes ;* by meton., *the eye ; light of life.*

Lūna, ae, f. (R. RUK, *to shine,* luc, louc, lūc, luc-na, luna), *the moon ; the goddess of the moon, Diana.*

luō, luī, lūtum, 3 (R. LU, *to loose,* lu, lu-e-re), *to wash, loose ; atone for, expiate.*

lupa, ae, f. (lupus). *a she-wolf.*

Lupercus, ī, m. (RR. ARK (and see lupus), *to keep off* (arc-e-re)), (one that keeps off wolves), the Roman name of Pan, a priest of Pan.

lupus, ī, m. (R. VAR, *to tear,* var-k, vlak, vluk, lup-u-s), *a wolf.*

lūridus, a, um, adj. (R. GHAR, *to be green* or *yellow,* ghvar, var, lū-ri-dus), *pale yellow, pale, lurid.*

lūsor, ōris, m. (lūdō), *one who plays, a player ; a playful* writer, Trist. IV, 10, 1.

lūstrō, 1 (lūstrum), *to purify* by an offering ; *to go around* (as the priest, in sacrifice, went around the object sacrificed), *to traverse ; to review* (military).

lūstrum, ī, n. (R. LU, *to wash), a marsh, morass, bog.*

lūsus, ūs, m. (lūdō), *playing, sport.*

lutulentus, a, um, adj. (lutum, fr. LU, *to wash), muddy, slimy.*

lūx, lūcis, f. (R. RUK, *to shine,* lnk, luc, louk, lūc, luc-s, lūx), *light, daylight, day, light of the eye ; life.*

luxurio, 1 (R. RIK, *to let go, give up,* lūc, luc-tu-s, luxus, luxur-ia, luxuriare), *to be rank, luxuriant, to swell, shine.*

Lyaeus, a, um, adj. (Λυαῖος), one that loosens, frees ; epithet of Bacchus.

Lycia, ae, f., a district in southern Asia Minor.

Lycius, a, um, adj. (Lycia), *a Lycian.*

Lycormas, ae, m., a river in Aetolia.
Lycōris, idis, f. (also called Cythere), a freedwoman, mistress of Cornelius Gallus, Am. I, 15, 30.
Lȳdia, ae, f., a district in western Asia Minor.
Lȳdus, a, um (Lydia), *Lydian.*

lympha, ae, f. (**R.** LAP, *to shine,* lamp, lump, limp, lymph-a), *clear water, spring-water.*
lymphātus, a, um, adj. (lymphō, lympha), *frenzied.*
lyra, ae, f. (λύρα), *a lute, lyre; a strain, tune.*

M

Macarēis, idis, f., daughter of the Lesbian Macareus.
Macer, Aemilius, name of a poet; Tr. IV, 10, 44.
maciēs, ēi, f. (**R.** SMAK, SMIK, *to be small,* mac, maciā-re, maciē-s), *leanness, meagerness.*
macula, ae, f. (**R.** SMA, *to rub, smear,* ma, mac-), *a stain, spot.*
madefaciō, fēcī, factum, 3 (madeō, facio), *to make wet, moisten.*
madeō, uī, 2 (**R.** MAD, *to swell, drop, drip,* mad-ēre), *to be wet, moist.*
madēscō, uī, 3 (madeō), *to grow wet, moist.*
madĭdus, a, um, adj. (madeō), *wet, moist.*
Maeandros, ī, m., river in western Asia Minor.
Maeonia, ae, f., an old name of Lydia.
Maeonis, idis, f., the Maeonian, Arachne.
Maeonius, a, um, adj., *Maeonian.*
maereō, ēre (**R.** MI, *to injure, disturb,* mi-s, mais, maer-ēre), *to mourn, lament, be sad.*
maestus, a, um, adj. (same **R.** as maereō), *mournful, full of sorrow.*
magis, adv. (**R.** MAK, MAG, *to be great;* comp. (mag-ius), mag-is), *more, rather, in greater degree.*
magister, trī (same **R.** as magis); double comp., magis-ter, the higher, greater, *master, teacher.*
magistra, ae, f. (magis), *a directress, school-mistress.*
magnanimus, a, um, adj. (magnus, animus), *great-souled, magnanimous.*
magnus, a, um, adj. (same **R.** as magis), *great;* major, *greater (in age),* older, maximus, greatest (in age), *oldest; great (of persons), powerful, famous.*
male, adv. (malus), *ill, badly.*

maledīcō, xī, ctum, 3 (male, dīco), *to speak ill, slander.*
malignus, a, um, adj. (maligenus, fr. male *and* g(e)n-o, fr. gen, GAN, see gignō), *of an evil disposition, ill-disposed, malignant.*
mālō, māluī, malle (magis-volō), *to have rather, prefer.*
mālum, ī, n. (**R.** MALO), *an apple.*
malus, a, um, adj. (**R.** "MAR, mal, *to rub, rub to pieces, grind* = soil, blacken," Vanicek), *hateful, ugly, destructive, bad, evil; unfortunate;* subst., malum, ī, n., anything *evil* or *hurtful, evil, mischief, harm, suffering, misfortune.*
mandō, 1 (manus, dō, both wh. see), *to give in hand, charge, commend, enjoy, instruct;* subst., mandātum, ī, n., *direction, commission, instruction, order.*
mandō, dī, sum, 3 (**R.** MAD. *to swell, drip, moisten,* man-d-ō), *to chew, eat, bite.*
māne, adv. (**R.** MA, *to measure,* mā, mā-tu, *time,* mātu-ru-s, *timely,* māne), *early, in good season, at early morning.*
maneō, nsī, nsum, 2 (**R.** MA, MA-N, *to think,* man-ēre (like Gr. μέν-ω), *to bethink one's self, to stop,* wait, stay, remain; *await, wait for.*
mānēs, ium, m. (same **R.** as māne, MA, *to measure, form,* mānus, an (old) adj., *conformable, good;* mānes, the souls of the good), the souls of the departed, the *manes; the deities of the lower world; the lower world.*
manifēstus, a, um, adj. (manus *and* festus, fr. **R.** DHAN-D, *to strike, seize,* fend-, fend-tu-s, fēnsu-s, manu- = manifestus, *seized with the hand), manifest, palpable, plain, evident.*
mānō, 1 (same **R.** as madeō, MAD, *to*

drip, mad-ĕre (mad-nu-e), mā-nā-re), *to flow, run, drop, trickle.*

Mantō, ūs, f., a Theban prophetess, d. of Tiresias.

manus, ūs, f. (**R.** MA, *to measure, form*, ma, ma-nus, that which measures, forms), *the hand;* (hand-fight), *boxing;* ultima manus, *the last touch.*

marcĭdus, a, um, adj., *withered.*

mare, is, n. (**R.** MAR, *to rub, grind, ruin, die*, mar-e, Vaniçek, II, 708; but others, as Curtius and Corssen, refer it, and better, in meaning, to **R.** MAR, *to shine, sparkle*), *the sea* (as opposed to the land), *a sea; sea-water.*

margō, ĭnis, m. (**R.** MARG, *to touch, graze*), *a brink, edge, border, margin.*

marītus, ī, m. (for **R.** see mās, male), *a married man, husband.*

marmor, oris, n. (same **R.** as mare, MAR, *to shine*, mar + mar, mar-mor), *marble, a marble, marble statue.*

marmŏreus, a, um, adj. (marmor), *of marble*, like *marble, marble-white.*

Mars, rtis, m. (same **R.** as marmor; the splendor-bringing god; also Mar-mar, Mamers), son of Jupiter and Juno, god of war; by meton., *war, battle.*

Marsya (or -as), ae, m. (fr. the Gr.), the name of a Satyr; Metam. VI, 382–400.

Martius, a, um, adj. (Mars), *of Mars, warlike, martial.*

mās, maris, m. (**R.** MA, ma-n, *to think*, man-s, ma-s, Eng. *man*), *male, masculine, manly, man.*

massa, ae, f. (**R.** MAK, *to knead*, māc, fr. Gr. μάζα, *dough*), *a lump, mass, mass of gold, of marble, of milk;* used of Chaos, Metam .I. 70,

māter, tris, f. (**R.** MA, *to measure, to form*, ma-ter, like genetrix in meaning), *a mother*, of men, of animals; also used of the earth, as producing all things; of fountains, as the *source* of waters; of Cybele, as the mother of the gods.

mātěria, ae, and **mātěriēs**, ēi, f. (fr. same **R.** as māter, as that of which anything is *formed*), *matter*, materials, *stuff; object.*

māternus, a, um, adj. (māter), *of a mother, maternal, motherly.*

mātrōna, ae, f. (māter), *a married woman, wife, matron.*

mātūrescō, tūruī (mātūrus), v. inch., *to grow ripe, ripen.*

mātūrus, a, um, adj., *ripe.*

mātūtīnus, a, um, adj. (fr. same **R.** as mātūrus, māne, *and* Mātū-ta, the goddess of the morning), *of the morning, morning.*

Māvors, ortis, m. (**RR.** MAGH, MAH, *to cut* (Gr. μάχ-η), and vor-t-ere, vertere, the battle-turner), an old name of Mars; by meton., *war, battle.*

Mēdēa, ae, f. (Μήδεια, wise woman, fr. **R.** MA), *Medea.*

medeor, ēri, v. dep. (**R.** MA, *to think*, ma-dh, *to learn, to be wise*, Gr. μαθε, medē-ri), *to help, heal, cure.*

medĭcāmen, ĭnis, n. (medicor, medeor), *a remedy, a drug, means of sorcery.*

medĭcīna, ae, f. (medicor), *medicine; art of healing.*

medĭŏcris, e, adj. (medius), *middling, moderate, ordinary.*

meditor, 1 (v. dep., fr. same **R.** as medeor, which see), *to think of, reflect upon, meditate.*

medĭus, a, um, adj. (**R.** MADHJA, *the middle*), *that is in the midst* or *the middle, middle;* subst., *medium, the middle; the midst of all, the public.*

medulla, ae, f. (medius), *the* (middle) or interior of bones, or of plants, *marrow, pith.*

Medūsaeus, a, um, adj., *of Medusa* (one of the Gorgons), *Medusan.*

Megarēius, a, um, adj., *of Megareus* (Hippomenes), *Megareian.*

mel, mellis, n., 1 (**R.** MAR, *to rub*, mal, *to be soft*), *honey.*

Melanthō, ūs, d. of Deucalion.

Melās, anis, m., a river in Thrace.

membrum, i, n. (**R.** MA, MI, *to lessen*, mi-n, mi-nu, min-bro, mem-bru-m), (a small thing), *a limb, member, part*, of animals, then of things generally.

meminī, isse (same **R.** as mēns, wh. see), *to bear in mind, remember.*

Memnōn, onis, m., son of Tithonus and Aurora.

memor, oris, adj. (**R.** SMAR, *to mark, think*, mar, mor, me-mor-ia, memor), *mindful, remembering.*

memorŏ, 1 (same **R.** as memor), *to bring to remembrance, commemorate, to speak, remark.*

Menandros, *or*-cr, ĭ, m. ; see note on Amorcs, I, 15, 18.

mendācium, ĭ, n. (mendāx), *a lie.*

mendāx, ācis, adj. (same **R.** as mēns, men-ti-ri, mendāx), *lying, mendacious, false, hypocritical.*

mĕns, ntis, f. (**R.** MA, *to think,* ma-n, men, men-ti, mēns), *the mind, disposition, soul, heart, feeling, sentiment; thought, reason, presence of mind; purpose.*

mĕnsa, ae, f. (**R.** MA, *to measure, form,* mā, ma-n, men-sa), something measured off, *a table;* by meton., *a meal, feast, course.*

mēnsis, is, m. (same **R.** as mēnsa), me-n-s-ĭ-s, measure of time, *a month.*

mēnsor, ōris, m., *a measurer.*

mēnsūra, ae, f. (same **R.** as mēnsa), *a measure.*

menta, ae, f. (**R.** MAT, *to turn*), *mint* (the plant so called).

mentior, 4, v. dep. (see mendāx), *to lie, deceive, impose upon.*

mentum, ĭ, n. (**R.** MAN, *to jut, project,* men, men-tu-m), *the chin.*

Mercurius, ĭ, m. (merx, fr. **R.** SMAR, mer, mer-ēre), Gr. *Hermes,* son of Jupiter and Maia, *Mercury.*

mereŏ, 2 (**R.** SMAR, mer, *to mark, share*), *to merit, deserve, earn, get.*

meretrīx, īcis, f. (mereō), one that earns money, *a harlot.*

mergŏ, sī, sum, 3 (**R.** MASG, merg-, *to sink*), *to dip, plunge, sink, immerse.*

mergus, ĭ, m. (mergō), *a diver,* name of a water-fowl.

meritum, ĭ, n. (mereō), *a service, benefit; reward.*

meritŏ, adv. (mereō), *deservedly, justly.*

Merops, opis, m., king of Aethiopia.

merus, a, um, adj. (**R.** MAR, *to shine*), mer, mer-u-s, *bright, clear, pure, unmixed, mere.*

merum, ĭ, n. (merus), *unmixed wine; wine.*

messis, is, f. (metō), *the harvest.*

mēta, ae, f. (**R.** MI, *to sink in the earth, set up*), mai-ta, mēta, the conical pillar set up at either end of the *spina* of the race-course, *the mark, goal; limit, boundary.*

Mĕthymnaeus, a, um, adj., *of Methymna, Methymnean.*

mĕtior, mēnsus sum, 4, v. dep. (**R.** MA, *to measure,* me, mē-ti, me-tī-rĭ), *to measure, to pass over, traverse.*

metuŏ, uī, 3 (metus), *to fear, be in fear of, revere;* part., metuendus, a, um, *fearful;* metuēns, *fearing.*

metus, ūs, m. (**R.** MA, *to think,* me, me-tu-s), *fear, dread, apprehension;* by meton., what creates fear, *a terror.*

meus, a, um, adj. (pron. stem, 1st pers., MA, me), *mine, my own.*

micŏ, uī, 1 (etym. unc.), *to quiver, glitter, flash forth.*

Midās, ae, m., a Phrygian king, son of Cybele.

mīles, itis, m. (**R.** MIL, *to join, come together,* meile-t, meile-s, mīles), *soldier, warrior;* (collective) *soldiery.*

mīlitia, ae, f. (mīles), *military service, war.*

mīlle, num. adj. (**R.** MIL, as of mīles), *a thousand;* subs. plural, milia, *thousands.*

Mimās, antis, m., a promontory in Ionia.

minae, arum, f. (**R.** MAN, *to put forth, project,* min), *threats, menaces.*

mināx, ācis, adj. (minae), *threatening, menacing.*

Minerva, ae, f. (**R.** MA, *to think,* men, min, Min-er-va), *the goddess of wisdom,* d. of Jupiter, *Minerva.*

minister, strī, m. (**R.** MA, MI, *to minish, diminish,* mi-n, mi-nu, (minor, min-us, *less*), min-ius-tro, double comp. suff., min-is-ter), the lesser, *servant, subordinate, minister.*

ministerium, ĭ, n. (minister), *service, ministry.*

ministra, ae, f. (minister), *a servant.*

ministrŏ, 1, *to serve, wait upon, hand.*

minitor, 1, v. dep. (minac), *to threaten.*

minor, 1, v. dep. (minac), *to threaten.*

Mīnōs, ōis, m., son of Jupiter and Europa.

minuŏ, uī, 3 (same **R.** as minister), *to diminish, impair, weaken.*

minus, adv. (see minister for R.), *less*.

Minyae, ārum, m., *the Minyans*, so called from Minyas, a king in Thessaly.

mīrābilis, e, adj. (mīror), *wonderful, admirable*.

mīrāculum, ī, n. (mīror), *a wonderful thing, marvel, miracle*.

mīror, 1, v. dep. (for R. see mīrus), *to wonder at, admire*.

mīrus, a, um, adj. (R. SMI, *to laugh, wonder*, smai-ro, smi-ro, mi-ru-s), *wonderful, strange, marvellous*.

misceō, uī, mixtum, mistum, 2 (R. MIK, *to mix*, mic-sc-, mi-sc-ĕre), *to mix, mingle, unite*.

miser, era, um, adj. (R. MI, *to disturb*, mis, mis-er), *miserable, wretched, unhappy*.

miserābilis, e, adj. (miser), *miserable, pitiable*.

misereor, itus, sum, v. dep., 1 (miser), *to pity*.

miseror, v. dep., 1 (miser), *to lament, bewail*.

mītis, e, adj. (etym. unc.), *mild, gentle, friendly*.

mittō, mīsī, missum, 3 (R. MAT, *to turn, set in motion*, mit, mīt-t-ere), *to send, let go, throw, hurl*.

Mnēmosynē, ēs, f., mother of the nine Muses.

moderāmen, inis, n. (modus), *a means, of ruling, of guiding ; direction, management*.

moderātē, adv. (modus), *with moderation, moderately*.

moderātor, ōris, m. (modus), *one who directs, manager, ruler, governor*.

moderātus, a, um, part. and adj. (modus), *moderated, governed ; moderate*.

moderor, 1, v. dep. (modus), *to moderate, direct, govern, rule*.

modestus, a, um, adj. (modus), *modest, kind*.

modicus, a, um, adj. (modus), *moderate, measured*.

modo, adv. (modus), *only, if only ; just now ; now—now*.

modulor, 1, v. dep. (modus), *to sing and play with due measure, to modulate, tune*.

modus, ī, m. (R. MA, *to measure*, mo, mo-d-), *measure ; melody, harmony, tune ; way, manner*.

moenia, ium, n. pl. (R. MU, *to bind, make firm*, mun-, moe-ni, old sing., moe-ne, moe-ni-a), *walls, defenses, fortifications ;* by meton., *a city, town*.

molāris, e, m. (fr. mola, R. MAR, *to rub, crush*, mal, mol, mol-a), *of a mill, a millstone, stone*.

mōlēs, is, m. (R. MAK, MAKH, MAG, MAGH, mah, *to be great*, mah-li, mo-li, mo-le-s), *a great mass, weight ; a massive building*, pile ; *a dam, pier, mole ;* fig., *labor, trouble*.

mōlīmen, inis, n. (molior), *a great effort, exertion*.

mōlior, 4, v. dep. (R. same as mōlēs), *to set in motion something heavy, to hurl, to exert one's self, strive, toil*.

molliō, 4 (mollis), *to make soft, soften, tame, check*.

mollis, e, adj. (R. MAR, *to rub, make soft*, mal, mal-d, moll-), *soft, mild ; weak*.

moneō, uī, itum, 2 (R. MA, ma-n, men, mon-, mon-ēre, causal of men), *to remind, admonish, advise, warn*.

monimentum, ī, n. (moneō), *a monument, memorial*.

monitum, ī, n., *an admonition, advice, counsel*.

monitus, ūs, m., *a reminding, warning, admonition*.

mōns, tis, m. (R. MAN, *to project, jut out*, men, min, mon, mon-s), *a mountain, range of mountains ;* by meton., *the god of a mountain*.

mōnstrum, ī, n. (same R. as moneō, mōn-s-tru-m = quod nos monet), *an evil omen, portent ; a wonder, marvel ; a monster*.

montānus, a, um, adj. (mōns), *of a mountain, mountainous*.

monticola, ae, m. (mōns, colō), *inhabitant of a mountain*.

mora, ae, f. (R. smar, *to mark, bethink*, mar, mor, mor-a), *bethinking, stopping, a delay, hindrance*.

morātus, a, um, adj. (mōs), *of manners, mannered, constituted, conditioned*.

mordeō, momordī, morsum, 2 (R. SMARD, *to hurt*, mard, mord, mord-ĕre), *to bite*. **morsus**, ūs, m., *a bite*.

moribundus, a, um, adj. (morior), *dying.*

morior, morī, mortuus sum, 3 (**R.** MAR, *to rub,* mor, *vex one's self,* mor-i), *to die.* **moror,** 1, dep., *to delay.*

mors, tis, f. (morior), *death;* by meton., *the dead.*

mortālis, e, adj. (mors), *mortal, liable to die; human;* subst., *mortal, a man.*

mōrum, I, n. (μῶρον), *a mulberry.*

mōrus, I, f., *a mulberry-tree.*

mōs, mōris, m. (**R.** MA, *measure, form,* mo, mō-s), *a custom, manner, usage, habit;* in pl., *manners, habits, character.*

mōtus, ūs, m. (moveō), *a moving, movement; emotion.*

moveō, mōvī, mōtum, 2 (**R.** MU, *to push, move,* mav, mov, mov-ēre), *to set in motion, move, remove; break up; excite, cause; arouse.*

mox, adv. (**R.** probably same as of māgnus), *soon, presently, soon after, then.*

mūcrō, ōnis, m. (**R.** MUK, *to prick,* muc-r-o), *the point of a sword;* by meton., *sword.*

mūgītus, ūs, m. (mūgiō), (**R.** MA, MI, *to sound), a lowing, bellowing.*

mulceō, mulsī, mulsum, 2 (**R.** MARK, *to touch,* mulc-), *to touch lightly, stroke; soften, soothe, quiet.*

mulciber, eris *or* erī, m. (mulceō, and perhaps ferrum (a molliendo ferro, Paul D., p. 144 ; or fr. BHAR, fer, fer-o), *a name of Vulcan;* by meton., *fire.*

multifidus, a, um, adj. (multus, findō), *cleft into many parts, many-cleft.*

multō, adv. (multus), *by much, much.*

multum, adv. (multus), *much, very.*

multus, a, um, adj. (**R.** MANAGHA, *much,* monogo-s, mologo-s, molgo-s, mulgu-s, mulgī-re, then the part. pass. perf., mulgī-tus, mul-tu-s), *much, many, great, wide;* comp. plus, *more;* superl., plurimus, *most, very many.*

mundus, I, m. (**R.** MAND, *to adorn,* mund), *order* (cf. κοσμος), *beauty; the universe, world.*

mūniō, 4 (mūnus), *to make firm, strong, to fortify.*

mūnus, eris, n. (**R.** MU, *to bind, strengthen,* mū, moi, moe), *something which binds, service, office, function; favor, gift, reward, offering.*

mūrex, icis, m. (**R.** SMA, *to wipe, smear,* sma-r, mur, mur-o, muri-co, muri-c), *the purple (shell-) fish, purple dye, purple.*

murmur, uris, n. (**R.** marmara, *murmur, murmuring, whispering ; roaring, growling ; rushing sound.*

murmurō, 1 (murmur), *to murmur, rustle.*

murra, ae, f. (perhaps fr. same **R.** as mūrex), *myrrh-tree, myrrh.*

mūrus, ī, m. (same **R.** as mūnus), *a wall;* by meton., *city, town.*

mūsa, ae, f. (fr. the Gr.), *a, the, Muse;* pl., *the* (nine) *Muses.*

muscus, I, m. (**R.** MUSA, mus-cu-s), *moss.*

mustum, I. n. (**R.** MUD, *fresh, young,* mud-to, mus-tu-s), *new wine, must;* by meton., *vintage.*

mūtābilis, e, adj. (mutō), *mutable, changeable.*

mūtō, 1 (**R.** MU, *to set in motion,* mav, mov, mov-ta-re, mu-ta-re), *to move away from, change, alter; exchange.*

mūtus, a, um, adj. (**R.** MU, as of mūnus, *to bind, close* (the mouth)), *mute, dumb, silent.*

mūtuus, a, um, adj. (mutō), *changed, borrowed, lent; mutual, reciprocal.*

Mycalē, ēs. f., 1, name of a promontory in Ionia ; 2, name of a Thessalian sorceress.

Mygdonis, idis, adj., *of Mygdonia = Lydia; Mygdonian, Lydian.*

myrtus, ī and ūs, f., *a myrtle, myrtle-tree.*

N

Nāias, adis, f. = Nāis, idis (from nō, *to swim), a Naiad;* in pl., *the Naiads.*

nam, conj. (**R.** GAN, GNA, *to know,* na-man, na-ma, na-me (nomen), acc. sing. fem., na-m ; or (Corssen) fr. pron. stem, na), *namely, for, indeed, certainly.*

namque, conj. (nam, a strengthened nam), *for, verily, indeed.*

nanciscor, v. dep., nactus sum, 3 (R. NAK, *to reach, get*, nac-ni-sc-i, na-nci-sc-i), *to reach, attain, get, find.*

nāris, is, f. (R. SNA, SNU, *to flow, swim*, na-s, na-s-i, na-r-i-s), *a nostril; the nose;* in pl., *the nostrils.*

narrātus, ūs, m. (narrō), *narration, relation.*

narrō, 1 (R. GNA, *to know*, gnā-ru-s, narrā-re), *to make known, narrate, relate.*

nāscor, nātus sum, v. dep., 3 (R. GA, GA-N, *to beget, produce*, gna, na-sc-o-r), *to be born, begotten; to spring forth, arise, grow;* part., nātus, *born;* and subst., one born, *a son;* and nāta, *a daughter.*

nātālis, e, adj. (nāscor), relating to birth, *natal, native;* sc. dies, *birthday.*

natō, 1 (fr. nō, nāre), *to swim.*

natūra, ae, f. (nāscor), *nature; being, creature; element; natural quality* or *disposition.*

naufragus, a, um, adj. (nāvis, frangō), *shipwrecked; wrecked, ruined;* subst., *a shipwrecked person.*

nāvigium, i, n. (nāvis, -agium, fr. ago, nav-ig-iu-m), *a sailing, navigation; a ship, boat, vessel.*

nāvigō, 1 (nāvis, agō), *to sail, go by sea; sail over, navigate.*

nāvis, is, f. (R. SNA, *to flow, swim*, na-vi-s), *a ship.*

nāvita, nauta, ae, m. (nāvis), *a sailor, seaman.*

nāvō, 1 (R. GAN, GNA, *to know*, gnā, nā (g-)na-vu-s, navā-re), *to perform intelligently, accomplish.*

ne, encl. interrog. particle (R. NA, negative particle), (but weaker than nē); enclitic to other interrogatives for emphasis.

nē, neg. adv. (R. same as ne), *that not, in order that not; not*, with imper.; *only not, in order not to.*

nē, interj. (R. NA, pron. stem, nac, nō), *truly, verily, indeed.*

nebula, ae, f. (R. NABH, *to swell, break forth*, neb, neb-ula), *mist-cloud, mist, fog, vapor.*

nec, see neque.

necō, 1 (nex), *to put to death, kill.*

nectar, aris, n., drink of the gods, nectar; by meton., *wine, milk.*

nefās, n, indecl. (ne *and* fās, wh. see), *not right, wrong, sin, crime, a wicked deed.*

negō, 1 (RR. nc, neg. part., and AGH, ag, a-j-o = ag-i-o, aio, *to say*), to say no, *to deny, refuse, decline.*

Nemeaeus, a, um, adj., *of Nemea in Argolis; Nemean.*

Nemesis, is and ios, f. (Νέμεσις), the avenging goddess of justice, *Nemesis.*

nēmō, neminjs, comm. (nē-homo), *no man, no one, nobody.*

nemorōsus, a, um, adj. (nemus), *woody, full of woods.*

nempe, conj. (nam, wh. see, nem + pe = que, wh. see), *namely, truly, surely, certainly.*

nemus, oris, n. (R. NAM, *to allot, possess; to pasture*, nem, nem-us), a wood with places in it for pasture-land, *a wood, grove.*

neō, 2, nēvi, nōtum (R. SAN, SNA, *to spin*, (s)ne-), *to spin; to weave.*

nepōs, ōtis, m. (R. NAPAT, *son, grandson*, nepōt-), *grandson; nephew; descendant.*

Neptūnius, a, um, adj., *of Neptune, Neptunian.*

Neptūnus, i, m. (R. same as of nebula, neb, Nep-), the god of water, the sea, the clouds, son of Saturn, *Neptune.*

neque, and nec, conj. (ne, que), *and not, also not*, neque (nec)—neque (nec), *neither—nor, not only not—but also, and besides, and indeed.*

nequeō, 4 (ne, queō), *not to be able, to be unable, I can not.*

nēquiquam, nōquicquam, nōquidquam, adv., *to no purpose, in vain.*

nervus, i, m. (R. SNAR, *to turn, weave*, ner-, ner-vu-s), *a sinew, nerve; bow-string; string of the lyre* or similar musical instrument; in pl., *the strings.*

nescio, 4 (ne, scio), *not to know, to be ignorant of;* nescio quis, *I know not who, somebody* or *other.*

nescius, a, um, adj. (nescio), *not knowing, ignorant of, unable.*

neu, see neve.

nē-ve, conj. = et ne, *and not, nor, and that not, and lest.*

nex, necis, f. (R. NAK, *to disappear,*

destroy, nec, nec-is), *a violent death, murder ; death.*

nexilis, e, adj. (necto), *tied together.*

nexus, ūs, m. (necto), *a fastening, clasping ;* in pl., *coils, folds.*

nī, conj. and adv. (same **R.** as ne, nō), *unless, if not.*

nīdus, ī, m. (**R.** NAS, *to go, dwell,* nis, nis-do, nī-du-s), *a nest.*

niger, nigra, nigrum, adj. (same **R.** as nex, nox, nic-ro), *of night, dark, black.*

nihil, nihilum, nīlum, nīl, n. indecl. (ne, hilum ; hilum (fr. **R.** GHAR, *to bend*), a thread, something of no consequence), *not a thread, nothing, not the least thing.*

Nīlus, ī, m., *the Nile*, a river in Egypt.

nimbus, ī, m. (same **R.** as nebula, ne-m-b, ni-m-bu-s), *a violent rain, rainstorm ; rain-cloud, storm-cloud, cloud.*

nimis, adv., *too much, very* (fr. nimius).

nimium, adv. (nimius), *by far, too much, exceedingly.*

nimius, a, um, adj. (**R.R.** ne, ni, *and* MA, *to measure*), *not in measure, beyond measure, too great, too much.*

Ninus, ī, name of an Assyrian king, *Ninus.*

Niobē, ēs, f., d. of Tantalus and Dione, *Niobe.*

nisi, conj. (nī, sī), *if not, unless ; except, only, save, except that.*

niteō, 2 (**R.** SKI, *to shine,* skint, knit, cnit, nit-ēre), *to shine, glitter, glisten.*

nitidus, a, um, adj. (niteō), *shening, glittering, brilliant.*

nitor, ōris, m. (niteō), *splendor.*

nītor, nīsus, nīxus, 3, *to strive ; lean.*

niveus, a, um, adj. (nix), *snowy, snow-white.*

nix, nivis, f. (**R.** SNIG, SNIGH, *to wash, rinse,* nigh-v, nigh-s, nih-s, nix), *snow, snowflake.*

nō, 1 (**R.** same as navis), *to swim.*

nōbilis, e, adj. (nōscō), *known, well known, famous ; of noble origin ; noble.*

nōbilitās, ātis, f. (nōbilis), *noble origin, nobility. noble rank ; nobleness.*

noceō, uī, 2 (**R.** same as nex, nak,

nec, noc), *to injure, do harm to, be a hindrance to ;* part., nocēns, *hurtful, guilty.*

nocturnus, a, um, adj. (nox), *nightly, by night, nocturnal.*

nōdus, ī, m. (**R.** GHADH, *to seize, hold,* hed, he-n-d ; ghand, ghnad, gnōd-o, nōd-u-s), *a knot, girdle ; circle* (of the equator) ; *knob, fold ; a knotty point.*

nōlō, nolle, nōluī (nōn, volo), *not to will, to be unwilling.*

nōmen, inis, n. (nōscō), *a name ; title, fame.*

nōminō, 1 (nōmen), *to name, call by name.*

nōn, adv. (fr. NA, neg. part. ne, and pron. st. 3d pers., I, ai, ai-na, oi-no-s, u-nu-s, ne oenu-m, noenum, nōn), *not.*

nōndum, adv. (non, dum), *not yet.*

nōnne, non, ne (interr. part.), *not ?* (expecting the answer, yes).

nōscō, nōvī, nōtum, 3 (**R.** GAN, GNA, *to know,* gnō, nō-sc-ō), *to come to know, to become acquainted with, get a knowledge of* (so the perf., nōvi, *I have come to know = I know*) *; to recognize, understand.*

noster, stra, strum, pron. poss. (nōs), *our, our own, of us.*

nota, ae, f. (nōscō), *something which makes known, a mark, sign, character.*

nōtitia, ae, f., *acquaintance.*

notō, 1 (nōscō), *to make known, a mark, indicate, note, censure, brand.*

notus, ī, m. (νότος), (same **R.** as nō, nāre), *the rain-bringing wind, the south wind.*

novem, num. adj. (**R.** NAVAN), *nine.*

noverca, ae, f. (same **R.** as novus), *a step-mother.*

noviēs (noviēns), num. adv. (novem), *nine times.*

novitās, ātis, f. (novus), *newness, novelty, news.*

novō, 1 (novus), *to make new, renew, find out anew, change, alter.*

novus, a, um, adj. (**R.** pron. st. NU, nom, nu-n-c, nava, novu-s), *new, fresh, recent, strange, unusual ;* superl., novissimus, *the newest, the last ; the lowest.*

nox, ctis, f. (**R.** same as nex), nak, nec, noc, noc-ti, nocti-s, nox), *night ; darkness, blindness.*

nūbēs, is, f. (R. NABH, *to swell,* nūb, nub-c-s), *a cloud.*

nūbĭfer, fera, ferum, adj. (nūbēs, fero), *cloud-bearing.*

nūbĭlus, a, um, adj. (nūbēs), *cloudy, lowering, clouded, darkened.*

nūbĭlum, I, n. (nūbēs), *a cloud.*

nūbō, nupsi, nuptum, 3 (same R. as nūbēs), *to cover, veil ; to marry* (of the bride, *to veil herself*), *be married;* part., nupta (*veiled*), *a married woman, bride.*

nūdō, 1 (nūdus), *to make naked or bare ; strip, uncover.*

nūdus, a, um, adj. (R. NAG, *naked,* nug, nug-du-s, nūdus), *naked, bare, uncovered, exposed.*

nullus, a, um, adj.; gen., īus ; dat., ī (ne, ullus), *not any, no one, none, nobody.*

num, an interr. part. (fr. pron. stem NU, *now,* nu-m, originally of time, *now*), expecting the answer, *no ;* in ind. question, *whether.*

nūmen, inis, n. (nuō), *a nodding, nod ; will, divine will ;* by meton., *deity, divinity.*

numĕrō, 1 (numerus), *to number, count ; reckon.*

numĕrōsus, a, um, adj. (numerus), *numerous ; harmonious, melodious.*

numerus, I, m. (R. NAM, *to allot, count,* num, nam-e-ru-s), *a counting, count, number ;* multitude, *crowd ; numbers* (of song).

Numĭtŏr, ōris, m. (Numa, R. NAM, as of numerus), son of the Alban king Proca ; *Numitor.*

nunquam, adv. (ne, unquam), *not ever. never.*

nunc, adv. (fr. pron. stem NU, nu + demonst. ce, nu-n-ce, nu-nc), *now, at present.*

nuntia, ae, f. (same R. as nunc, novus, nove-nt-io, nov-nt-io, nou-nt-iu-s, nūntius), one that brings news, *messenger, reporter.*

nūper, adv. (fr. NU (pron. stem as in novus)+per, fr. PAR, πάρα), *newly, lately, recently, in recent times.*

nurus, ūs, f. (R. SU, *to beget, bear,* sunu-sa, snu-sa, snu-ra, then by transition to the *u* decl., nu-ru-s), *a daughter-in-law ; a young woman, married woman.*

nusquam, adv. (ne, usquam), *not anywhere, nowhere.*

nūtō, 1 (nuō), *to nod with the head, command with a nod ; waver, hesitate.*

nūtrĭō, 4 (same R. as nō, nāre, SNA, SNU, *to flow,* nu, nu-t-rī-re (fr. the flow of milk)), to suckle, *nourish, feed, bring up.*

nūtrix, Icis, f. (nūtriō), *a* (wet) *nurse, nurse.*

nūtus, us, m. (nuō), *a nodding, nod, sign.*

nux, nucis, f. (R. KNU, KNUK, *to scrape*), *a nut.*

Nyctēis, idis, f., daughter of Nycteus ; Antiope.

Nympha, ae, f., -e, es, *a nymph, Nymph.*

O

O, interj., O ! oh !

ob, prep. with acc. (R. apa, prep., op, ob), *to, toward ; on account of.*

ob-dūcō, xī, ctum, 3, *to draw,* or *cover over ;* part., obductus, *clouded, darkened ; contracted.*

ob-eō, iī, itum, 4, *to go to ; go around, draw around, spread over.*

ŏb-ĭcĭō, jēcī, jectum, 3 (jaciō), *to throw before* or *toward, bring before ; throw out against, to reproach with ; lay to one's charge ; object.*

obitus, ūs, m. (obeō), *a going down, setting ; death.*

ob-jectō, 1 (jactō), *to reproach with* or *for.*

oblectāmĭna, um, n. pl. (oblectō), *delights ; sources of consolation.*

oblēnĭmĭna, um, n. pl. (lēniō), *means of soothing, remedies.*

ob-lĭgō, 1, *to bind to, oblige.*

ob-lĭnō, lēvī, litum, 3, *to smear over, besmear.*

oblīquus, a, um, adj. (ob and liquus, fr. R. LAK, *to bend,* lic, lic-n-us), *sidelong, slanting, oblique ; crooked, curved.*

ob-lĭviscor, oblītus sum, 3 (ob *and* R. LIV, *to be grayish-yellow,* lai-va, liva (lividus), ob-liv-i-sc-i), to grow pale ; *to forget, be forgetful.*

oblĭvium, I, n. (same R. as obliviscor), *forgetfulness, oblivion.*

ob-noxius, a, um, adj., *subject to, liable to, obnoxious.*

ob-orior, ortus sum, 4, v. dep., *to arise, spring up, break forth.*

ob-ruŏ, ruī, rutum, 3, *to overthrow, cover over, bury, sink.*

obscūrus, a, um, adj. (fr. ob and **R.** sku, *to cover,* scū, ob-scū-ru-s), *covered, dark, gloomy, obscure.*

ob-sequor, seccūtus sum, 3, *to comply.*

ob-servŏ, 1, *to observe, give attention to, watch, tend.*

[**obsidiŏ**, ōnis, f. (obsideō), *a siege.*

ob-sistŏ, stitī, stitum, 3, *to set one's self before or against, oppose.*

ob-situs, a, um, part., *sown, covered.*

ob-stipēscō, stipuī, 3, *to be stupefied, amazed, astonished, confused.*

ob-stŏ, stitī, stātum, 1, *to stand against or in the way of ; oppose, hinder, withstand.*

ob-strepŏ, uī, itum, 3, *to make a noise at, shout against or at.*

ob-strūsus, a, um, adj. (obstrudō, obtrudō), *veiled, bordered.*

obtūsus, a, um, adj. (tundō), *blunt, dull, obtuse.*

ob-vertŏ, vertī, versum, 3, *to turn toward or against, to direct.*

obvius, a, um, adj. (via), *in the way of, meeting ;* with irc or venire, *go or come to meet ; obvious.*

occāsus, ūs, m. (ob, cadō), *the going down or setting of the sun ; the land of the setting sun, the west.*

oc-cidŏ, cidī, cāsum, 3, *to fall or go down, sink* in death ; *fall, die, perish.*

occiduus, a, um, adj. (cadō), *going down, failing, decaying.*

occulŏ, uī, tum, 3 (ob and culō, fr. **R.** skal, kal, *to cover, hide,* cal, ob-calcre, oc-cul-cre), *to hide, conceal.*

occupŏ, 1 (ob, capiō), *to take possession of, lay hold of, occupy ; fall upon ; surprise ; get the start of, anticipate* in doing a thing.

oc-currŏ, currī, cursum, 3, *to run to meet, meet.*

ocellus, ī, m. (oculus), *a little eye, eyelet ;* (dear) *eyes.*

ōcior, us, adj. comp. (**R.** ak, *to be sharp, swift,* oc, oc-ior), *swifter, quicker, sooner.*

ōcius, adv. (ocior), *quicker, sooner, swifter.*

oculus, ī, m. (**R.** ak, *to be sharp, to see,* oc-u-lu-s), *an eye ; sight ; a luminary, world-eye, god of the sun, an eye* (of a plant).

ōdī, isse, praet. def. v. (**R.** vadh, *to strike, thrust,* vad, od-, od-io ; perf., ōd-ī), *to be vexed at, not like, hate.*

odium, ī, n. (ōdī), *hate, odium.*

odor, ōris, m. (**R.** ad, *to smell,* od-, od-or), *smell, odor, fragrant odor ; a bad smell.*

odōrŏ, 1 (odor), *to fill with fragrance ;* part., odōrātus, *sweet-smelling, fragrant.*

odōrus, a, um. adj. (odor), *sweet-smelling, odorous.*

Oeăgrius, a, um, adj., *of* (the Thracian king) *Oeagrus.*

Oechalia, ae, f., *a city in Euboea.*

Oetaeus, a, um, adj., *of Oeta, Oetean.*

Oetē, ēs, f., a range of mountains in Thessaly.

of-fendŏ, dī, sum, 3, *to strike against ; to hit upon ; to stumble ; to offend, injure.*

officium, ī, n. (opificium, fr. opus and facio), (a work-making), *a service, favor, a service of love ; ceremony, office ; obligation, duty.*

olea, ae, f., *an olive ; olive-tree.*

Ōlenos, ī, m., Met. X, 69.

olēns, ntis, part., fr. oleō, *smelling, fragrant ; foul, rank.*

ōlim, adv. (fr. pron. stem ana, 3d pers., ana-la, ono-lo, on-lo, ol-lo ; illu-s, ille ; oll-m), *at that time, once, formerly ; at times, sometimes.*

olīva, ae, f., *the olive, olive-tree ; olive-berry.*

olīvum, ī, n., poetic = oleum, oil.

olōrīnus, a, um, adj., *of the swan, swanlike.*

Olympus, ī, m., 1, mountain in northern Thessaly, *the seat of the gods, Olympus ;* by meton., *heaven ;* 2, a pupil and friend of Marsyas.

ōmen, inis, n. (**R.** av, *to observe, mark,* au, au-d, aus, os-men, ō-men), *a sign, token, omen.*

omnipotēns, ntis, adj. (omnis, potens), *all-powerful, omnipotent.*

omnis, e, adj. (**R.** AMBII, *to hold together*, ambi, umb-, an, om-ni-s), *all, every;* omnes, *all men;* omnia, *all things.*

Onchestius, a, um, adj., *of Onchestus*, a city in Bocotia.

onerō, 1 (onus), *to load, lade, burden.*

onerōsus, a, um, adj. (onus), *burdensome, heavy, onerous.*

onus, eris, n. (**R.** AN, *to breathe, sigh*, on-, on-us (whereby one sighs)), *a burden, weight; trouble, pains.*

opācus, a, um, adj. (ctym. unc.), *shady, shaded; dark, darkened.*

operiō, uī, pertum, 4 (**R.** PAR, *to fill, share, prepare*, par-i, ob-par-i, o-per-i-re), (*to prepare for*), *cover, shut.*

operōsus, a, um, adj. (opus), *full of work, pains-taking, laborious, difficult; effective.*

opifer, era, erum, adj. (ops-ferō), *aid-bringing, helpful.*

opifex, icis, m. (opus, faciō), *workmaker, worker, maker, artisan, artist.*

opperior, ītus and pertus sum, 4, v. dep. (ob and -perior), *to wait, wait for, await.*

oppidum, ī, n. (**R.** PAD, *to tread*, ped (pes, pedis), pedu-m, *what is trodden, the soil*, op-pedum, oppidum, *what lies on the soil), town, city.*

op-pōnō, posuī, positum, 3 (ob, pono), *to set* or *place before* or *against, oppose, hold before.*

op-primō, pressī, pressum, 3 (ob, premo), *to press under* or *down, oppress, overcome.*

opprobrium, i, n. (ob, probrum), *a reproach, scandal, opprobrium; shame, disgrace.*

op-pūgnō, 1 (ob, pūgnō), *to fight against, storm.*

ops (in sing. only, opis, opem, ope, pl. entire), f. (**R.** AP, *to bind, possess*), op, op-s, *help*, might, power; *means* of any kind, *property; helper.*

optō, 1 (**R.** same as ops), *to choose, wish, desire.*

opus, eris, n. (**R.** AP, *to work*, op-, op-us), *a work, labor, work of art, workmanship; deed.*

opus, indecl., adj. (same **R.** as opus, *work*), *need, necessity, needful, wanting; it is* (est) *needful, there is need of.*

ōra, ae, f. (**R.** AS, *to breathe, live, be*, ōs, ōs-ōris, ōra), *the lip, edge, brim, border, margin, coast, land, district.*

ōrāculum, ī, n., orāclum (ōrō), *oracle.*

orbis, is, m. (etym. unc.), *a circle, disk, orbit, ring, circle of the world, orb, the earth; wheel.*

orbō, 1 (orbus), *to deprive, bereave.*

orbus, a, um, adj. (**R.** ARBII, *to give over, deprive*, orb-u-s), *bereft, deprived, fatherless, childless; orphaned.*

ordior, orsus sum, 4 (**R.** AR, *to lift up, arise, begin*, or, ol, ord-i-ri), *to begin.*

ōrdō, inis, m. (same **R.** as ordior), *a beginning, row, order, line, regular order, regularity.*

orgia, ōrum, n., noisy feasts of Bacchus, *orgies.*

orīgō, inis, f. (same **R.** as ordō, AR, ol, or, or-ig-o), *a beginning, origin, descent;* by meton., *author, ancestor.*

orior, ortus sum, 4 (same **R.** as ordior), *to rise, go up, go forth, descend from; originate;* oriēns, sc. sol, *the rising sun, the east, Orient.*

ōrnō, 1 (**R.** VAR, *to cover, surround*, ornā-re), *to fit out, furnish; adorn, deck.*

ōrō, 1 (ōs), *to speak, beg, entreat, plead, pray.*

Orontēs, is and ae, m., a river in Syria.

Orpheus, eī, m., a Thracian singer, son of Apollo and the Muse Calliope.

Orphēus, a, um, adj., *of Orpheus, Orphean.*

Orphnē, ēs, f. (ὄρφνη, *darkness*), a nymph of the lower world.

ortus, ūs, m. (orior), *a rising, sunrise, east; origin, beginning.*

ōs, ōris, n. (**R.** AS, *to breathe, live, be*, ōs), *the mouth, the lips; bits; jaws; beak;* by meton., *speech; face, countenance; head.*

os, ossis, n. (**R.** AS, *to throw away*, os, *something thrown away*, *a bone;* in pl., *bones, body; bones of the dead.*

osculum, ī, n. (ōs), *a little mouth, a kiss.*

Ossa, ae, f., a mountain in Thessaly.

ostendō, dī, sum, and tum, 3 (ob, tendo), *to show, stretch out.*

ostentum, ī, n., *a sign, prodigy.*

ostium, I, n. (ōs), *mouth of a river.*
ostrum, I, n., *the juice, blood of the sea-snail, purple.*
Ōthrys, yos, m., a mountain in Thessaly.
ōtium, I, n. (R. AV, *to be glad, to protect,* au, au-tio, o-tio, o-tiu-m), *protection, security, peace, leisure.*

păbulum, I, n. (pāsco), *food, nourishment, fodder; grass.*
pūcālis, e, adj. (pāx), *peaceful.*
paciscor, pactus, sum, v. dep., 3 (R. PAK, *to make strong, put together,* pac, pac-i-sc-i), *to make a contract, agree, stipulate;* part., pactus, *agreed upon, settled.*
pācō, 1 (pāx), *to bring to quietness, to peace, pacify.*
Pactōlis, idis, adj., *of Pactolus, Pactolian.*
Pactōlos, or us, I, m., a river in Lydia.
pactum, I, n. (paciscor), *an agreement, covenant, compact.*
Padus, I, m., *the Po,* a river in Upper Italy.
Paeān, ănis, m., *Paean,* a name of Apollo; the song to his honor, *paean.*
paelex, pelex, icis, (R. PALAVAKA, *a maiden,* pellex, paelex), *a mistress, concubine; rival.*
paene, adv. (etym. unc.), *almost, nearly.*
paenitet, uit, 2, v. impers. (R. KI, *to seek, pay, punish,* kvi, pi, poi, pae, paenit-ěre, *to repent = feel pain, punishment*), *it repents one;* (I, you, etc.) *repent, grieve, rue; one is discontented, dissatisfied.*
Paeones, um, m., *the Paeonians;* a people in Macedonia.
Paeonis, idis, *a woman of Paeonia.*
palam, adv. (R. PAR, *to pass through, bring forward,* para, *before,* pala-m, adverb. acc.), *before the people, openly, publicly.*
Palātium, I (iī), n. (R. PA, *to nourish, guard,* pa-l, pal-at-iu-m), the first, in time, of the seven hills of Rome, the site of the earliest Rome; then, as Augustus had there his residence, *the imperial residence, palace.*

ovīle, is, n. (ovis), *a sheepfold.*
ovis, is, f. (R. same as otium, AV, ov, ov-i-s, prop., one that is protected), *a sheep.*
ōvum, I, n. (R. AV, *to blow,* au; aura, av-er, a-er, *air;* av-i, avi-s, *a bird;* ōvu-m (as coming from a bird)), *an egg.*

P

palātum, I, n. (etym. unc., perhaps fr. same R. as palatium, pāsco, pater), *the palate.*
palear, āris, n. (etym. unc.), the skin that hangs from the neck of an ox, *the dew-lap.*
Palĭcī, orum, m., twin sons of Jupiter and Thalia.
Palēs, is, f. (R. PA, *to feed,* pa-l, pali), the guardian deity of shepherds and flocks, *Pales.*
palla, ae, f. (R. SPA, SPA-N, *to spin, weave,* pann-, pann-u-s, pānn-la, palla), the long upper garment of Roman women, *the palla, robe, mantle.*
Pallas, adis, f., the Greek name of *Minerva, Pallas.*
palleō, uī, 2 (R. PALA, gray, pal-va, pal-lu-s, pal-lē-re), *to be pale, sallow;* part., pallēns, *pale; dark-colored; discolored.*
pallēscō, uī, 3 (palleō), *to grow pale, pale.*
pallĭdus, a, um, adj., *pale, sallow.*
pallor, ōris, m. (palleō), *paleness, pallor.*
palma, ae, f. (R. PALMA, the open hand), 1, *palm of the hand; hand;* 2, *a palm-tree, palm; a palm-wreath;* by meton., *victory, palm; a date, dates.*
palmes, itis, m. (palma, 2), *a palm-shoot, vine-shoot.*
palūs, ūdis, f., *a marsh.*
paluster, stris, *marshy.*
Pān, Pānis, m., the god of shepherds and woods; of nature; *Pan.*
pandō, ndī, passum, 3 (R. PAT, *to spread out,* pa-n-t, pa-n-d, pand-e-re), *to spread out, expand, unfold;* passae comae, *disheveled hair.*
Panopē, ēs, f., an ancient city in Phocis, *Panope.*
papāver, eris, n. (R. PAP, PAMP, *to swell up,* pap-ā-ver), *the poppy.*

pār, paris, adj. (**R. PAR,** *to come to, be like,* pari, par), *equal ;* substantively, a match for ; *a pair.*

Parcae, ārum, f. (**R. PARK,** *to weave, spin,* Parc-a, Parc-ac, *spinner, spinners* (spinsters ?) of the thread of fate), *the Fates* (three), Clotho, Lachesis, and Atropos.

parcō, peperci, parcitum, and parsum, 3 (parcus, *to spare, be sparing of ; refrain from ; guard.*

parcus, a, um, adj. (**R. SPAR,** *to refuse, shrink from,* spar-u-s, paru-m ; acc. as adv., *too little,* parcu-s), *sparing, frugal, thrifty.*

parēns, ntis, comm. (pariō), *a father* or *mother, parent.*

parentālis, e, adj. (parēns), *of parents, parental.*

pareō, uī, itum, 2 (**R. PAR,** *to allot, fill, prepare, be ready,* parē-re), to be at hand or appear, *to obey, submit to, comply with.*

paries, etis, m. (**R. I,** *to go,* and **PAR,** per, *around* or *through,* something that goes around), *a wall, partition-wall.*

parilis, e, adj. (pār), (*poetic*), *equal, like.*

pariō, peperi, partum, 3 (**R. PAR,** *to bring, bring forth,* par-i-ō), *to bear, bring forth, beget ; produce.*

pariter, adv. (pār), *equally, in like manner, alike, together, at the same time.*

Parnāses, idis, adj., *Parnassian, of Parnassus.*

Parnāsus, ī, m., *Parnassus,* a mountain in Phocis, sacred to the Muses and Apollo.

parō, 1 (**R. PAR,** *to allot, prepare*), *to get ready, prepare, provide.*

Paros, I, f., one of the Cyclades in the Aegean ; *Paros.*

Parrhasis, idis, f., *Parrhasis, Parrhasia ; Arcadia.*

pars, rtis, f. (**R. PAR,** *to allot, share,* par-ti, par-s), *a part of* a whole, *portion, share ; a party, faction ; a place, region, part ; a task, duty, part.*

Parthāōn, onis, m., king of Calydon, *Parthaon.*

Parthenium nemus, Parthenius, I, m., a mountain between Arcadia and Argolis.

partim, adv., acc. of pars, *in part, partly.*

partus, ūs, m. (pariō), *a bringing forth, birth ; offspring, child.*

parum, adv. (**R. SPAR,** *to refuse,* spar-u-s, paru-m), *too little, not.*

parvus, a, um, adj. (**R. PAVA,** *little, small,* pau, pau-ru-s, par-vu-s), (minor, minimus), *small, young ; little, low, mean, weak.*

pāscō, pāvī, pāstum, 3 (**R. PA,** *to feed,* pa-sc-ere), *to feed, pasture, nourish ; maintain ; feast ; gratify, feast one's self.*

pascuum, ī, n., *a pasture.*

passim, adv. (pandō), *everywhere.*

passus, ūs, m. (pandō), *a step, pace, foot-step, track.*

pāstor, ōris, m. (pāscō), *a shepherd.*

Patarēus, a, um, adj., *of Patara.*

patefaciō, fēcī, factum, 3 (pateō, faciō), *to make* or *lay open, open.*

pateō, uī, 2 (**R. PAT,** *widen*), *to be open.*

pater, pātris, m. (**R. PA,** *to feed, support*), *father ;* pl., *fathers* of the state, *patricians, senators ; elders.*

patera, ae, f. (pateō), *an open dish* or *saucer,* used in libations ; *a patera.*

paternus, a, um, adj. (pater), *of a father, paternal.*

patientia, ae, f. (patior), *patience, endurance.*

patior, passus sum, v. dep. (**R. SPA,** SPA-N, *to strain, exert one's self,* spa-ti, pa-ti, pa-ti-o-r), *to suffer, endure, bear, hold out ; allow, permit.*

patria, ae, f. (pater), *fatherland, country, home.*

patrius, a, um, adj., *of a father, fatherly, of the fathers ; of the fatherland, of home ; old, ancient.*

patruēlis, e, adj. (patruus), *of* or *from a father's brother ;* subst., *son of a father's brother, cousin.*

patruus, ī, m. (pater), *a father's brother, paternal uncle.*

patulus, a, um, adj. (pateō), *standing open, open ; broad, wide, widespread.*

paucus, a, um, adj. (same **R.** as parvus, PAVA), *little, few ;* in pl., *a few, few, few things, little.*

paulātim, adv. (same **R.** as paulum), *by degrees, gradually.*
paulum, adv. (**R.** PAVA, *little,* pau, pau-l-lu-s), *a little, a short time.*
pauper, eris, adj. (**RR.** PAVA, *little,* and PAR, *to bring, get,* pava-par(o), pav-per, pau-per, *one that brings, gets little), poor;* subst, *a poor man, a pauper.*
pavĕō, pāvī, 2 (**R.** PU, *to strike,* pav, pavĕ-re, *to be struck down, be anxious), to be struck with fear, to tremble, quake, be afraid.*
pavidus, a, um, adj., *fearful.*
pāvō, ōnis, m., *a peacock.*
pavor, ōris, m. (pavĕō), *a trembling, anxiety, fear, panic.*
pāx, pācis, f. (**R.** same as pacīscor, pak, pāc, pāx), *reconciliation, tranquillity, peace, quiet.*
peccō, 1 (**R.** PAD, *to step, tread,* ped, pes, *foot,* pedi-cus, pec-cu-s, peccā-re), *to step over, transgress, to do amiss, to commit a fault, to sin.*
pecten, inis, m. (**R.** PAK, *to comb,* pec, pec-t-en), *a comb.*
pectō, pexī, pexum, 3, *to comb.*
pectŭs, oris, n. (Vaniček gives **R.** same as pecus), *the breast, heart, feelings, spirit, soul, sense.*
pecus, oris, n. (same **R.** as pacīscor; Vaniček), *cattle, herd, flock.*
pecus, udis, f., *a single head of cattle, one of a herd* or *flock.*
pedes, itis, m. (pēs), *one that goes on foot; a foot-soldier.*
Pēgasides, um, f. pl., *of Pegasus; the Muses.*
pelagus, ī, n. (πέλαγος, fr. **R.** PAR, *to strike,* πλα-γ), *the sea, the open sea.*
Pelasgī, ōrum, m., *a people, living in early times in Greece;* so, poetic for *the Greeks;* adj., Pelasgus, a, um, *Pelasgian.*
Pēlignus, a, um, adj., *of the Peligni, Pelignian.*
pellis, is, m. (**R.** PAR, *to fill, cover,* pel, pel-ni, pellis), *a skin, hide.*
pellō, pepulī, pulsum, 3 (**R.** SPAR, *to hinder, drive,* spal, pel (pol, pul), pel-je-re, pel-le-re), *to beat, strike, thrust, drive, drive away, expel.*
penātēs, ium, m. (**R.** PA, *to nourish,* pa-n, pen, pen-u-s, *pantry,* Pen-at-ēs), *the guardian deities of the household;*
of the state; by meton., *house, dwelling.*
pendĕō, pependī, 2 (**R.** SPAD, SPAND, *to move one's self violently,* pend, pend-e, intrans. to pendo), *to hang, hang down, be hung* or *suspended; to hover, float,* in the air; *to waver, be uncertain.*
pendō, pependī, pēnsum, 3 (transitive to pendĕō, wh. see), *to cause* or *make to hang, to weigh; to pay.*
pendulus, a, um, adj. (pendĕō), *hanging down, pendent.*
Pēnēis, idis, f. adj., 1, *of Peneus, Penean;* 2, *a nymph,* daughter of the river-god Peneus.
Pēnēius, a, um, adj., *Penean.*
penetrālis, e (penetrō), *penetrating; inward, interior;* pl., penetrālia, *the inner rooms,* penetralia; *a sanctuary.*
penetrō, 1 (**R.** PA, pa-n, pen-u-s, *pantry,* penes, *within,* + **R.** TRA, *to move), to press,* trū-re (in-trū-re), *to press within, penetrate, enter, reach.*
Pēnēus (os), ī, m., a river in Thessaly.
penitus, adv. (same **R.** as penus), *within, deep within, inwardly.*
penna, ae, f. (**R.** PAT, *to move quickly,* pet, pet-na, pes-na, pen-na), *a feather; wing.*
pēnsō, 1 (pendō), *to weigh, weigh carefully; make good, compensate.*
pēnsum, ī, n. (pendō), *something weighed out* for spinning or weaving; *a task;* a *work; lesson.*
per, prep. with acc. (**R.** PAR, *to press through* or *over,* para, per), *through, over, throughout, during, by means of.*
per-agō, ēgī, actum, 3, *to carry through, to finish, complete, go through with.*
per-arō, 1, *to plow through; to scratch over; to write carefully,* fr. *scratching* with the *stilus* on the waxen tablets.
per-bibō, bibī, 3, *to drink up.*
per-cēnseō, uī, 2, *to count up, enumerate; survey, travel over, traverse.*
per-cipiō, cēpī, ceptum, 3, *to take up* or *through; to receive, obtain, get; receive, feel, perceive.*
per-currō, cucurrī and currī, cursum, 3, *to run through* or *over, hasten over.*

percutio, cussi, cussum, 3 (quatio), to strike through, thrust through, pierce.

Perdix, Icis, comm., 1, a bird, (perhaps) partridge; 2, the nephew of Daedalus, turned into a bird, Perdix.

per-do, didi, ditum, 3 (to put through), to ruin, destroy, throw away, waste, lose.

per-domo, ui, itum, 1, to subdue thoroughly, overcome.

peregrinus, a, um, adj. (per, ager, peregre), that comes from abroad, foreign, strange; subst., a foreigner, stranger.

perennis, e, adj. (per, annus), that continues through the year, perpetual, perennial.

per-eo, ii, itum, 4, to go or run through, perish, go to ruin; die.

per-erro, 1, to wander or roam through.

per-fero, tuli, lātum, 3, to carry through, bring, bear, suffer, endure, to the end.

per-fundo, fūdi, fūsum, 3, to pour over; drench; scatter over; flood.

Pergus, i, m., a lake in Sicily.

per-horresco, rui, 3, to tremble.

periculum, i, n. (R. PAR, to go through, per, peri-ri, πειράω, peri-tus, peri-cu-lum), a trial, test; peril, danger.

Perilla, ae, f., name of Ovid's daughter.

perimo, 3, ēmi, emptum (per, emo), to take away, destroy, put to death.

per-luceo, luxi, 2, to shine through, illumine; to be transparent.

per-maneo, nsi, nsum, 2, to stay through, hold out, to remain.

per-māturesco, tūrui, 3, to become fully ripe, mature.

per-mitto, misi, missum, 3, to let go, cast, hurl; allow, permit.

per-mulceo, si, sum, 2, to stroke gently; soften; charm.

perosus (per-ōdi), a, um, adj. and part., hating greatly, full of hate; tired of; hateful.

per-petior, pessus sum, 3, v. dep. (patior), to bear steadfastly, endure, suffer, allow.

perpetuus, a, um, adj. (R. PAT, to go, pat, per-pe-s, per-pet-is), going through, continuous, perpetual.

Perseis, idis, daughter of the Titan Perses.

Persephone, ēs, f., the Greek name for Proserpine.

per-sequor, secūtus sum, 3, to follow through or after, to follow further, pursue; to report fully.

Persis, idis, f., Persia.

per-spicio, spexi, spectum, 3, to see through, look into, examine; observe carefully.

per-sto, stiti, stātum, 1, to continue standing, to remain unchanged, hold out, endure.

per-terreo, ui, itum, 2, to frighten, terrify, very much or thoroughly.

per-ūro, ussi, ustum, 3, to burn through and through, consume.

per-venio, vēni, ventum, 4, to come (through) to, arrive at, reach.

per-vigilo, 1, to watch, or be awake, all night; keep watch.

pervigil, ilis, adj., ever watching, watching through the night.

pervius, a, um, adj., having a passage through, passable.

pes, pedis, m. (R. PAD, to tread, step, ped, ped-is), a foot, of man or of beast.

pestifer, era, erum, adj., bringing ruin, baneful, pestiferous.

pestis, is, f. (fr. per-de-re, per-d-ti, per-s-ti, pes-ti-s, something that destroys), a plague, pest, pestilence.

peto, ivi and ii, ītum, 3 (R. PAT, to move swiftly, fall upon, pet, pet-ere), to fall upon, attack, strive for; go to, reach; desire, request, ask for.

Phaeacius, a, um, adj., belonging to Phaeacia, the island of Scheria, in the Aegean; a Phaeacian.

Phaethon, ontis, m., son of Phoebus and Clymene, Phaethon.

Phaethūsa, ae, f., one of the Heliades, sister of Phaethon.

Phantasos, i, m., the dream-god, Phantasus.

pharētra, ae, f., φαρέτρα (R. BHAR, to carry), something that carries, a quiver.

pharētrātus, a, um, adj., quivered.

Phāsis, idis and idos, m., a river in Colchis.

Philoctētēs, ae, m., son of Poeas, Met. IX, 243.

Phīneus, eī, m., 1, brother of Cepheus, king of Aethiopia ; 2, king of Salmydessus in Thrace.

Phlegethontis, idis, adj. f., *of Phlegethon.*

Phlegyae, ārum, m., a people of Thessaly or Thrace, who plundered the temple of Delphi.

Phobětor, oris, m. (φοβήτωρ), the frightener, the dream-god, son of Morpheus.

phōca, ae, and **phocē,** ēs, f., *a seal, sea-calf.*

Phōcaicus, a, um, adj., *of Phocis, Phocaean.*

Phōcis, idis, f., a country in Central Greece.

Phoebē, ēs, f., sister of Phoebus ; Diana ; also goddess of the moon, Luna.

Phoebēus, a, um, adj., *of Phoebus, Phoebean.*

Phoebus, i, m. (φοῖβος, the brightshining), Gr. name of Apollo.

Phoenīx, īcis, m., *Phoenīcas,* acc. pl., *a Phoenician.*

Phrixěus, a, um, adj., *of Phrixus, Phrixean.*

Phrygēs, um, m. pl., the inhabitants of Phrygia ; *Phrygians.*

Phrygia, ae, f., a country in Asia Minor.

Phrygius, a, um, adj., *of Phrygia, Phrygian.*

piceus, a, um, adj. (pix, fr. PI, *to swell,* pik, pix), *of pitch, pitch-black.*

Pĭerĭdēs, um, the daughters of Pierus ; the Muses ; *the Pierides.*

Pĭerius, a, um, adj., *of Pieria, Pierian.* See n. Am. III, 926.

piĕtās, ātis, f. (pius). *dutifulness, dutiful conduct ; sense of duty ; piety ; filial piety ; truth, mercy.*

piger, ra, rum, adj. (R. PAK, *to make firm, hinder,* pig, pig-er, hindered), *heavy, dull, sluggish ; unwilling.*

piget, uit, 2, v. impers. (R. PI, pi-k, *to grieve), it grieves, is irksome.*

pignus, oris and eris (R. PAK, *to make firm,* pig, pign-u-s, *what is made firm), a security, pledge ; token, proof.*

pĭgrē, adv. (piger), *slowly, reluctantly.*

Pindus, ī, m., a mountain in Thessaly.

pingō, pīnxī, pictum, 3 (R. PIK, *to pierce, adorn,* pi-n-g-ere), *to represent in art, to paint, embroider, embellish.*

pinguis, e, adj. (R. same as paciscor, παχύς, *fat), fat, rich, heavy, coarse.*

pinna, ae, f. (R. SPA-N, *to draw, sharpen,* spi, pi-t-na, pi-n-na), *a feather, wing, pinion ; point.*

pīnus, ūs and ī, f. (R. PI, *to swell,* pi-nu-s), *a pine, pine-tree ; anything made of pine, a ship.*

Pīsa, ae, f., a city in Elis.

Pīrēnis, idis, adj., *of Pirene.*

Pīsaeus, a, um, adj., *of Pisa, Pisaean.*

piscis, is, m. (R. PASKA, *a fish), a fish ;* in pl., pisces, the name of a constellation.

Pittheus, eī, m., son of Pelops, grandfather of Theseus.

pius, a, um, adj. (R. KI, *to seek, honor,* kvi, pi, pai, paio, pio, piu-s), *dutiful in sentiment and conduct, pious, affectionate, loyal.*

placĕō, uī, itum, 3 (R. PARK, *to ask, seek, beg,* plak, plac-ēre), *to please ;* placet, impers., *it is agreeable, seems good.*

placidus, a, um, adj. (placeō), *pleasing, gentle, mild, agreeable, peaceful, quiet.*

plācō, 1 (R. same as placeō), *to quiet, soften, reconcile, appease.*

plaga, ae, f. (R. PARK, *to weave, fold,* plak, plag), *a net, toil, snare ; a tract, region, quarter.*

plāga, ae, f. (R. PAR, *to strike,* pra-k, pla-g, plāg-a), *a blow, stroke, cut, thrust.*

plangō, nxī, nctum, 3 (R. same as plāga, pla, pla-n-g-ere), *to strike, beat ; to beat* one's *head, breast, in grief ; to lament, bewail.*

plangor, ōris, m. (plangō), *a noisy striking, beating, loud mourning, wailing.*

planta, ae, f. (R. PRAT, *to spread out,* plat, pla-n-t-a), *anything spread out, a plant, sprout, shoot, sucker ; sole of the foot.*

plānus, a, um, adj. (same R. as plāga, pla-k, *flat), level, plane.*

platanus, ī, f., *a plane-tree.*

plaudō, sī, sum, 3 (etym. unc.), *to*

clap, strike; to clap the hands, to applaud, approve.

plaustrum, I, n. (R. PRU, PLU, *to swim, sail, flow ; rain,* plav, plov, plos-tru-m, plau-s-tru-m, fr. the idea of traveling by water (sail), to the more general one of conveyance in any way by land), *a vehicle,* carriage, wagon ; the name of a constellation, *the Wagon, Charles's Wain.*

Plausus, ûs, m. (plaudō), *clapping of hands, applause.*

plĕbs, plēbis, f. (R. PAR, *to fill,* pal, pla, plū, ple-b-s *or* ple-be-s, *a multitude*), a crowd of people, *the common people, the commons, the plebeians.*

plectrum, I, n. (R. PAR, *to strike,* pra, pra-k, πλα-γ, πλῆκ-, plec-tru-m, *something to strike with*), *a quill, bow,* plectrum (to strike the strings of a musical instrument).

Plēias, adis, a daughter of Atlas and Pleione, *a Pleiad.*

plēnus, a, um, adj. (same R. as plĕbs), *full, filled, complete.*

plōrō, 1 (R. PRU, PLU, *to swim, rain, flow,* plav, plov, plov-ero, plōrō, *to cause to flow* (tears)), *to weep, cry, cry out, wail, lament, deplore.*

plūma, ae, f. (same R. as ploro, plov-ma, plou-ma, plū-ma), *a soft feather, down, feathers, plumage.*

plumbum, I, n. (R. MLUVA, *lead,* mlu-m-vo, plu-m-vo, plu-m-bo, plumbu-m), *lead, a bullet of lead.*

plūmeus, a, um, adj. (plūma), *full of down, downy.*

pluvius, a, um, adj. (fr. pluō, R. PRU, PLU, *to rain*), *of rain, rainy, rainbringing.*

poculum, I, n. (R. PA, PI, *to drink,* po, po-to, po-culu-m), *a drinking-vessel, cup, goblet.*

Poeās, antis, m., father of Philoctetes.

poena, ae, f. (R. KI, *to seek, pay, punish,* kvi, pi, poi, poe-na), *penalty, punishment, vengeance.*

Poeniceus, a, um, adj. (Pūnicus), *Punic; red, purple-colored.*

polenta, ae, f., *barley, peeled barley.*

pollens, ntis (part. fr. pollĕō, fr. R. PA, *to protect, guard,* pa-l, polle-re), *powerful.*

pollex, icis, m. (polliceor), *the thumb.*

polliceor, pollicitus sum, v. dep., 2 (RR. PAR, PRATI, PORTI, por-, pol-, *toward, forth,* and RIK, *to give over, allow,* lik, lic (lic-ēre), pol-liceor), *to hold forth, promise, offer.*

polluō, ui, ūtum, 3 (1st pt. of the R. same as in polliceor, pol-, 2d pt. LU, *to wash,* pol-luō), *to pollute, soil, defile; desecrate, violate.*

polus, I, m., πόλος (fr. R. KAR, *to move, turn,* that about wh. something turns), *the pole, axis; the globe, earth, the heavens.*

Polyphēmus, I, m., a Cyclops.

pompa, ae, f., πομπή, *a procession.*

pōmum, I, n. (R. PU, *to produce,* pau, pav, pov, pov-mo, pō-mō), *fruit* (of trees), apples, nuts, berries, etc.

pondus, eris, n. (R. SPAD, SPAND, *to move violently, swing,* pand, pend-ere, pond-us), *a weight, weight, heaviness, a burden; weight, importance.*

pōnō, posui, positum, 3 (fr. PORTI, por-t, por-, pol-, po (prep.), *before, toward,* and R. SA, *to plant, set, lay,* si, si-n-ere, po-sino, pos-no, pōnō), *to put, place,* set, *lay, arrange, build,* plant; *set away, put aside.*

Ponticus, I, m., name of a poet; Trist. IV, 10, 47.

Pontus, I, m. (πόντος, fr. R. PAT, *to go,* originally *a path,* then *the open sea*), 1, *the sea, the deep; a wave;* 2, *the Black Sea;* 3, a country in Asia Minor, *Pontus.*

pōples, itis, m. (R. SPAR, *to move tremulously, move,* spal + spol, po-pol, po-pol-o, pō-pl-o, pō-pli-to, po-pli-t, poples, *a part of the body* much *moved*), *the ham of the knee, ham-string; the knee.*

populābilis, e, adj. (populor), *that may be laid waste, destructible.*

populāris, e, adj. (populus), *of the people, of the same people, belonging to the people, for the people; popular;* subst., *a fellow-countryman; a popular man, a people's man; a democrat, demagogue.*

pōpulifer, era, erum (pōpulus, f., fr. same R. as poples), *poplar-bearing.*

populor, 1, v. dep. (R. SKAR, *to cut,*

hurt, skal, spal, spol, spo-spul, po-pul-ari), *to lay waste, destroy.*

populus, I, m. (**R.** PAR, *to fill*, pal, pol, pul, po-polo, po-pulu-s), *a multitude, people, crowd, population ; the people ; populace.*

porrĭgŏ, rexī, rectum, 3 (fr. portī, pro, por, po, *and* regō, pro-regō), *to stretch forth* or *out, extend, spread out, reach, offer, lengthen.*

porta, ae, f. (**R.** PAR, *to go through*, por, por-ta), *a gate, door, a city-gate, entrance.*

portŏ, 1 (**R.** PAR, *to fill, bring, produce*, por, por-ta-re), *to carry, bring, convey, bear.*

portus, ūs, m. (**R.** same as portō), a place to bring to, *a harbor, haven, port.*

poscō, poposcī, 3 (**R.** PARK, PARSK, *to ask, demand*, porsc-, posc-), *to demand, request, beg, challenge.*

Possĭdĕō, sēdī, sessum, 2 (fr. portī, por-t, pro, por, pol, pos- (as in porrigō), and sedeō, *to sit*), *to be in possession, possess, have.*

possĭdŏ, sēdī, sessum, 3 (fr. pos- (as in possideo) *and* sīdō, *to set*), *to take in possession, possess one's self of.*

possum, potuī, posse, v. irreg. (fr. potis *and* sum, potis-sum, pos-sum), *to be able, have power, influence, capacity ; to be powerful ;* possum, I can, and so in the other persons.

post (**R.** PAS, *behind*, pos, pos-t), 1, prep. with acc., *behind, after*, of place, and of time ; also of rank, *next after, inferior to ;* 2, adv., *back, backwards ; after, afterward.*

posterĭtās, ātis, f. (posterus), *aftercomers, posterity.*

posterus, a, um, adj. (post), *coming after, following, future.*

postis, is, m. (etym. unc., but perhaps fr. post), *a post, door-post ;* by meton., *door.*

post-modo, adv., *afterward, soon after.*

post-pōnō, posuī, positum, 3, *to put after, place after.*

postquam, conj., *after that, after, as soon as.*

potēns, adj. and part. (**R.** PA, *to protect*, pa-t, po-t, pote-ns), *having power over, ruling over, master of ; powerful, mighty.*

potentĭa, ae, f. (potēns), *power, might, authority, dominion ; effect.*

potĭor, 4 (same **R.** as potēns), *to have power over, to become master of ; to get, obtain ; possess, be in possession of.*

pōtŏ, avī, atum and potum, 1 (**R.** PA, PI, *to drink*, po, po-to), *to drink.*

prae, prep. with abl. (**R.** PAR, para, pra, pro, prae, *before*), *before, in front of, in comparison with.*

praeacūtus, a, um, adj. (acuō), *sharpened before*, at the end, *sharpened, pointed.*

praebĕō, uī, itum, 2 (prae-habeō), *to reach out, offer, afford ; grant, give, render.*

prae-cēdō, cessī, cessum, 3, *to go before, precede.*

praeceps, cipitis, adj. (prae *and* caput), *head first, headlong ; steep.*

praeceptum, I, n., *a rule.*

praecĭpĭtō, 1 (praeceps), *to throw headlong, precipitate ; to fall headlong, destroy one's self.*

praecordĭa, ōrum, n. pl. (prae-cor), *the breast, heart.*

praeda, ae, f. (**R.** GHADH, *to seize*, hed, he-n-d, prae-hed-a, praed-a), *plunder, booty, spoils.*

prae-dē-lassō, 1, *to weary out beforehand.*

prae-dīves, itis, adj., *very rich.*

praedō, ōnis (praeda), *a robber, plunderer.*

prae-ferō, tulī, lātum, 3, *to carry before, to prefer.*

prae-fīgō, xī, xum, 3, *to fix* or *set up in front ; to point, tip.*

praemĭum, I, n. (**R.** AM, *to take*, em-e-re, prae-im-iu-m, praem-iu-m), *something taken away from, profit, advantage, reward, prize, premium.*

praepes, etis, adj. and subst. (**R.** PAT, *to move swiftly, fly*, pet, pet-is, prae-pe-s). *very swift, swift of flight, fleet ;* a bird.

prae-pōnō, posuī, positum, 3, *to place before, prefer.*

praesaepe, praesēpe, is, n. (**R.** SAK, SAG, *to make strong, stop*, suak, sēk-i, sēp-i, sacp-e-s, prae-saep-e), *an inclosure, stall, fold, hut, hovel.*

praesāgium, I, n. (R. same as praesaepe, SAK, SAG, *to seek after*, sag-ire, sagium, praesagium), *a presentiment, foreboding, presage.*

praesāgus, a, um, adj. (praesāgium), *foretelling, divining, prophetic.*

praescius, a, um, adj. (sciō), *knowing beforehand, foreknowing, prescient.*

praesēns, ntis (part. fr. praesum), *one who is before or at hand, present, at hand, in person; efficient, able.*

praeses, idis, adj. and subst. (prae, sedeō, *one who sits before*), *presiding, protecting; a protector, defender, ruler, chief, president.*

praesignis, e, adj. (signum), *distinguished before others, excellent.*

prae-stō, stiti, stāturus, 1, *to stand before or in front, be superior, excel; to answer for, be good for;* part., praestāns, antis, *superior, distinguished.*

prae-suō, uī, ūtum, 3, *to sew in front, to sew over or up; cover over.*

prae-temptō, 1, *to try beforehand.*

prae-tendō, dī, tum, 3, *to stretch before or forth; to pretend.*

praeter, prep. with acc. (comparative of prae, prae-ter), *past, beyond, above, more; except, save.*

praeter, eō, iī, itum, 4, *to go by or beyond, or past;* in trans. sense, *to overtake; pass by, omit, mention of.*

praetinctus, a, um, part. of praetingō, *dipped in or moistened beforehand.*

prae-ūrō, ussī, ustum, 3, *to burn at the edge or end, singe, scorch.*

prae-vius, a, um, adj., *going before, leading the way.*

prātum, I, n. (R. PRAT, *to become wet*, prat-u-m, *the wet*), *meadow, meadow-land.*

precārius, a, um, adj. (prex, precis), *gained by prayers or entreaties, precarious.*

precor, v. dep., 1 (prex), *to pray, beg, entreat, implore.*

pre-hendō, prendō, dī, sum, 3 (R. GHADII, *to seize*, hed, he-n-d, pre(prae)-he-n-d-ere, prehendere, prendere), *to seize, lay hold of, catch.*

premō, pressī, pressum, 3 (R. PRAM, *to press*, prem-), *to press, press down; burden, oppress, press together or to, or into; impress; to stop; pursue, press close, insist upon.*

pretiōsus, a, um, adj. (pretium), *precious, costly.*

pretium, I, n. (R. PAR, *to exchange, buy, trade*, per, pre, pre-tiu-m), *worth, price, value; wages, reward.*

prex, precis, f., nom. and gen. not in use (R. PARK, PARSK, prak, prec-s, prex), *a prayer, entreaty, request, good wish.*

prīmō, adv. (primus), *at first, at the beginning.*

prīmum, adv. (primus), *at first, at the first time, in the first place.*

prīmus, a, um, adj. superl. (for R. see prior), *the first, first, foremost, earliest, chief.*

princeps, cipis, adj. and subst. (primus *and* capiō), *first, in order or in time; the first, chief;* as subst., *the first man, the chief, the head; prince.*

principium, I, n. (princeps), *the beginning, origin.*

prior, us, adj. comp. (R. PAR, para, pra, pro, prae, *before*, pra-ior, pr-ior), *former, prior; first;* subst., priores, *predecessors, forefathers, ancestors.*

prīscus, a, um, adj. (same R. as prior, pra-ius, prius-, pris-, pris-cu-s), *olden, ancient, of former or ancient times.*

prīstinus, a, um, adj. (same R. as prior and priscus, pris-tinus), *former, original, pristine.*

prius, adv. (prior), *before, earlier, sooner, previously.*

prō, prep. with abl. (R. par, para, pra, pro, *before*), *before, in front of, for, instead of, in behalf of, according to, in proportion to.*

prō (proh), interj., *O! ah! alas! alas for!*

proavus, I, m. (pro, avus), *forefather, ancestor.*

probō, 1 (etym. unc.), *to prove, judge of, approve, praise, recommend, make acceptable or credible, show, represent, demonstrate, accredit.*

prō-cēdō, cessī, cessum, 3, *to go forth or forward, proceed.*

procella, ae, f. (fr. prō, *before*, and cellō, fr. R. KAR, *to move quickly*, cal, cel, cello, pro-cella, *as storm-wind, as* *one driving forward*), *a violent wind, storm, tempest.*

procer, cris, m., chiefly in pl., proceres, um (fr. pro and R. KAR, *to jut forth, be prominent*, cer, pro-cer-es), those who are prominent, *chiefs, princes, leaders, heads of the state.*

prōcērus, a, um, adj. (from pro and R. KAR, *to make, create*, cer, procēru-s, *made, grown up*), *high, tall, slender.*

procul, adv. (same RR. as procella, cel, cul), pro-cul (forward driven), *far, at a distance, at some distance, far away, from afar.*

Proculus, i, m., a Roman, to whom Romulus is said to have appeared; Fasti, II, 499.

prō-cumbō, cubui, cubitum, 3, *to fall forward, fall down, sink down.*

procus, i, m. (R. PARK, PARSK, *to ask*, prak, proc-u-s), one who asks, *a wooer, suitor.*

prōd-eō, ii, itum, 4 (pro-eo), *to go forth, come forth, appear.*

prōdigium, i, n. (fr. pro and R. AGH, *to say*, ag, ag-i-o, ā-j-o, aio, agiu-m, prod-ig-iu-m, *something said beforehand, foretold*), *a prophetic token, omen, wonder, prodigy.*

prōdigus, a, um, adj. (fr. pro and AG, *to lead, drive*, ag-a, ag-o, prod-igu-s, *driving away*), *wasteful, lavish, prodigal.*

prōditio, ōnis, f. (prodo), *betrayal, treason.*

prō-dō, didi, ditum, 3, *to put forth* or *out, disclose, betray, surrender.*

prō-dūcō, xi, ctum, 3, *to bring* or *lead forward, bring to; produce.*

profānō, 1 (profanus), *to profane.*

profānus, a, um, adj. (pro and fanum, *that which is before* or *outside the fane or temple*), *profane, unholy, not sacred; unconsecrated; impious, godless; ill-omened, of ill omen.*

prōfectus, ūs, m. (proficio), *advance, progress, gain, success.*

prō-ferō, tuli, latum, 3, *to bring forward, carry forth* or *out, stretch out, extend, widen.*

prō-ficiō, fēci, fectum, 3 (pro, facio), *to go* or *come forward, advance, make progress; to profit.*

proficiscor, fectus sum, v. dep. (proficio), *to make forward or forth, set out, depart.*

prōfugus, a, um, adj. (profugio), one that flees or has fled, *fugitive, escaped from, banished, exiled.*

prō-fundō, fūdi, fūsum, 3, *to pour forth* or *out, shed profusely.*

prōfundus, a, um, adj. (fundus), *deep, profound;* subst., *the deep, the deep sea.*

prōgeniēs, ēi, f. (pro-gigno), *race, family, offspring, progeny; a descendant.*

prōhibeō, ui, itum, 2 (pro, habeo), *to hold before, to hold* or *keep back, prohibit, hinder, prevent.*

prō-iciō, jēci, jectum, 3, *to cast* or *throw forth, throw away, drive away.*

prōlēs, is, f. (fr. pro and olesco), *that which grows forth, progeny, offspring, child; son, daughter; race; generation, age.*

Promēthiades, and Promēthīdes, ae, m., son of Prometheus; Deucalion.

prō-mittō, misi, missum, 3, *to send forth, let grow, grow, spread forth; promise.*

prōmō, mpsi, mptum, 3 (pro-emo), *to take* or *draw forth, produce;* part. and adj., promptus, a, um, *drawn forth, ready, at hand, prompt, evident, clear.*

promptus, ūs, m. (promo), *the being visible, in readiness;* in promptu est, *it is clear, plain, easy.*

pronepōs, ōtis, m., *a great-grandson.*

prōnus, a, um, adj. (R. PAR, para, pra, pro, *before*, pra-va-na, pro-vo-no, pro-v-no, pro-nu-s), *inclined forward* or *downward, leaning down, running forward; easy, prone.*

propāgō, inis, f. (R. PAK, *to make firm, join*, pag, pag-o, pro-pag-o), *a layer* of a plant, *slip, shoot;* then generally, *a descendant,* child; *offspring.*

prope, adv. (R. PARK, *to braid, bind*, proc-, prop-, prope), *near, near by, nearly, almost;* prep. with acc., *near to, near by, hard by, near.*

properē, adv. (propero), *hastily, in haste.*

properō, 1 (R. PAR, POR, *to bring, make, get*, per, peru-s, pro-peru-s, get-

ting forward), *to hasten, get ready quick, make haste.*
Propertius, I, m., Sextus Aurelius, name of a Roman elegiac poet.
propinquus, a, um, adj. (same R. as prope, propi-n-co, propi-n-quu-s), *near, neighboring.*
propior, us, adj. compar. (prope), *nearer;* later ; more like ; *more intimate;* prŏximus, a, um, superl., *nearest, next.*
prō-pŏnō, posuī, positum, 3, *to put forth, set out or forth, exhibit; propose to one's self, undertake, propose.*
proprius, a, um, adj. (etym. unc., perhaps fr. prope), *one's own, special, peculiar; proper.*
propter, prep. with acc. (prope, propi-ter, propter), *near by, at hand, close by;* also adv. with same meaning.
prō-scindō, scidī, scissum, 3, *to tear up, cleave.*
Prōserpinā, ae, f., daughter of Jupiter and Ceres ; *Proserpine.*
prō-siliō, uī, 4 (saliō), *to leap forth, spring up.*
prō-spiciō, spexī, spectum, 3 (speciō), *to look forth or forward, to look at, look, survey.*
prō-sternō, strāvī, strātum, 3, *to cast or strew in front of, to throw down, prostrate.*
prōstĭtuō, stituī, stitūtum, 3 (statuō), *to place before, expose publicly, prostitute.*
prō-sum, prō-fuī, prod-esse, v. n., *to be of use or profit, do good, benefit, profit.*
prō-tendō, tendī, tentum, 3, *to stretch forth or forward.*
prō-terō, trīvī, trītum, 3, *to drive forth, tread down.*
Prōteus, eī, m., a sea-god, who changed readily his form ; *Proteus.*
prōtinus, adv. (pro, tenus), *before one's self, forward, forthwith, on the spot.*
prō-turbō, 1, *to drive forward, to thrust away.*
pruīnōsus, a, um (pruīna, of unc. etym., perhaps fr. R. PAR, *to sprinkle,* pru, pru-s, prus-ina, pru-īna, prop. *cold sprinkling*), full of *hoar-frost, frosty.*
prūnum, ī, n., *a plum;* fr. the Gr.

pūbēs, is, f. (R. PU, *to beget,* pu-be-s), signs of manhood, *puberty; grown-up males, youth, young men ; men.*
pūblicus, a, um, adj. (fr. populus ; populicus, poplicus, publicus), *belonging to the people,* or *state,* or *community; common to all, public.*
pudet, uit, 2, v. impers. (R. PU, *to strike, strike down, be dejected), it strikes down, makes ashamed, is or feels ashamed, shames; one is ashamed of.*
pudīcus, a, um, adj. (pudet), *bashful, modest, chaste.*
pudor, ōris, m. (pudet), *shame, sense of shame, modesty, chastity, innocence ; shame, disgrace.*
puella, ae, f. (puer, puerula, puella), *a girl, maiden.*
puellāris, e, adj. (puella), *of a maiden, maidenly.*
puer, erī, m. (R. PU, *to beget), a child; a male child, boy, lad, youth.*
puerīlis, e, adj. (puer), *of a child or boy, childish, boyish ; youthful.*
puerpera, ae, f. (puer, pariō), a woman that brings forth ; *a woman in child-bed.*
pūgna, ae, f. (R. PAK, *to strengthen, join,* puk, pug, pug-nu-s, *a fist,* pug-na, prop., *a fist-fight), a fight, battle.*
pūgnō, 1 (pūgna *and* pūgnus), *to fight with the fist, to fight, contend, do battle ; to strive, struggle.*
pulcher, pulchra, pulchrum, adj. (R. SPARK, *to sprinkle, scatter,* sparg, palk, polc-ro, pulch-er), *bright, fair, beautiful; noble, fine, glorious.*
pullus, a, um, adj. (R. PALA, *gray, dark gray,* pal-va, pul-vu-s, pul-lu-s), *dark-colored.*
pulmō, ōnis, m. (R. PU, *to purify, to blow,* plea, plu, pul-mo), *the lungs.*
pulsō, 1 (pellō), *to strike violently, beat, stamp ; knock ; drive.*
pulvereus, a, um, adj. (pulvis), *dusty.*
pulverulentus, a, um, adj. (pulvis), *full of dust.*
pulvis, eris, m. (R. SPAR, spal, pel, pul, *to swing, to shake,* pul-vi-s), *dust;* by meton., *the race-course.*

304 PUMEX   -QUE

pūmex, icis, m. (**R.** spju, *to spit, foam,* spu (spu-ma, *foam*), pu, pu-me-x), *a pumice-stone.*

pūnĭceus, a, um, adj. (Pūnicus), *red, purple-red.*

puppis, is, f. (etym. unc.), *the hinder part of a ship, the stern.*

purgō, 1 (**R.** pu × ag, pur-ig-o), *to clean.*

purpura, ae, f. (πορ-φύρ-α), *the purple-fish; purple color; purple;* by meton., *purple wool.*

purpureus, a, um, adj. (purpura), *of purple, red; shining; clad in purple.*

pūrus, a, um, adj. (**R.** ru, *to cleanse, purify*), *clean, pure, unstained, stainless; free.*

putō, 1 (**R.** ru, *to cleanse, make right*), *to reckon, consider, value; believe, think.*

Pygmacus, a, um, adj. (πυγμή), *Pygmaean;* Pygmaei (*Fistlings, Tom Thumbs*), *the Pygmies.*

pyra, ae, f., *a funeral-pile, pyre.*

Pyramus, I, m., *Pyramus.*

Pyroīs, entis, m. (Πυρόεις), *the fiery; Pyrois.*

pyrōpus, I, m., *a mixture of bronze and gold, gold-bronze, gold.*

Pyrrha, ae, f., daughter of Epimetheus, and wife of Deucalion.

Pȳthia, ōrum, n., pl., the games in honor of the Pythian Apollo; *the Pythian games.*

Pȳthōn, ōnis, m., a dragon killed by Apollo on Parnassus; *Python.*

Q

quā (abl. fem. of qui, wh. see), sc. parte, viā, *where, by which way; so far as, anywhere,*

quădrĭjugus, a, um, adj., quadru-s, jugum (**RR.** quadro, ju, ju-g, quadri-jug-u-s), *of or belonging to a team of four; with four horses,* sc. currus; quādrĭjugi, sc. equi, *a team of four horses.*

quădrŭpēs, edis, adj., quadru-s, pēs (**RR.** quadro and pad, *to tread,* ped, pe-s), *four-footed.*

quaerō, quaesīvī, quaesītum, 3 (**R.** ki, *to seek,* kvi, kvai, kvai-s, quae-s, quaer-erc), *to seek, miss, desire, reach, attain, strive after, inquire.*

quālis, e, pron. relative (**R.** ka, as of quī, wh. see, ka-li, qua-li-s), *how made, of what quality, kind, what.*

quālis-cumque, pron. rel., *of what quality soever, of whatever kind.*

quam, adv. (acc. fem. of quī, wh. see), *how, how much, than, as.*

quam-libet, adv., *as it pleases, how much soever, ever so much.*

quam-prīmum, adv., *as soon as possible.*

quam-quam, adv., *though, although.*

quam-vīs, 1, adv., *as you will, ever so much, very much;* 2, conj. concessive, *although.*

quandō, adv., indef. (fr. qua-m and **R.** di, div, fr. wh. dies; thus: dju, djau, djav, dio, abl. = do, quan-do, *on what day), when, at any time;* also adv. interr., *when?*

quandō-cumque, adv. indef., *at some time or other.*

quantus, a, um, adj. (fr. quī, **R.** ka, ka-nta, qua-ntu-s), *how great;* with tantus, tantus-quantus, *so great—as;* neut., quantum, *how much, as much, as much—as;* adv., *as much as, so much as;* abl., quantō, *by how much as, according as.*

quantulus-cumque, a, um, adj. (quantus), *however small.*

quārē (quā rē), adv. relat. and of indirect question, *wherefore, on what account, why.*

quartus, a, um, num. adj. (**R.** katvar, katur, *four,* quatur-tu-s, quatr-tu-s, qnar-tu-s), *the fourth.*

quasi (quā, sī), *as if, as it were.*

quater, adv. (same **R.** as quartus, quatur-iens, quatr-iens, quatr-ies, quatr-is, quatr-s, quater-s, quater), *four times.*

quatiō, quassī, quassum (**R.** skju, sku, sku-t, quat-io, *to cause to move, stir*), *to shake, shatter, swing.*

quattuor, adv. (**R.** katvar, katur), *four.*

-que, conj. enclitic (fr. quī, **R.** ka, = τέ), joining things in themselves closely connected, *and, and indeed, and in general, and yet, yet ;* que—que, *partly—partly, not only—but also, and at the same time.*

queō, quīvī, quītum, 4 (**R.** KU, KVI, KVA-N, *to be strong,* qui-o, queō), *to be able.*

quercus, ūs, f. (**R.** KAR, *to be hard*), *an oak, oak-tree ;* by meton., *wreath of oak.*

querēla (-ella), (queror), ae, f., *a plaint, complaint.*

queror, questus sum, 3, v. dep. (**R.** KVAS, KUS, *to sigh*, ques-tu-s), *to complain, bewail ;* with tālia, *to make such complaints.*

querulus, a, um, adj. (queror), *complaining, plaintive.*

questus, ūs, m. (queror), *a complaint, plaint.*

qui, quae, quod, 1, pron. rel. (**R.** KA, pronom. stem, fr. the indef. meaning *all, every ;* originally demonst., kva, qua, quo, quo-i, qua-i, quī), *who, which, that, what ;* after idem,=*as ;* in joining sentences,= a demonstr. with *and, but, now, then ;* also demonstratively used in clauses of *purpose* or of *result ;* 2, interrogative, both as substantive and as adjective, *who ? which ? what ? what kind of ?*

quia, conj. (unc., but perhaps from quī, abl. sing. + jam, as explained by Corssen, II, 850 ; B. 503), *because.*

quī-cumque, quae-cumque, quodcumque, pron. indef. rel., *whoever, whatever, every one who, all who.*

quīdam, quaedam, quoddam (and subst. quiddam), (**RR.** KA (quī) *and* DA, pronom. stem, 3d pers., de, da-m, acc., qui-da-m), pron. indef., *a certain one, some one, somebody, something.*

quidem, adv. (quī *and* DA, de, de-m, sec quīdam), *indeed, truly, too, also ;* used concessively, e. g., ille quidem, *to be sure, it is true.*

quiēs, ētis, f. (**R.** KI, *to lie down,* kia, quic-sc-cre, quic-s), *rest, quiet, repose ; sleep ; place of repose.*

quiescō, ēvī, ētum, 3 (for **R.** see quiēs), *to rest, repose, keep quiet.*

quiētus, a, um, adj. (quiescō), *quiet, calm, at rest.*

quī-libet, quae-libet, quod-libet, and subst., quid-libet, *every one you please, who you please, every one, whoever, whatever.*

quīn, conj. (same **R.** as quī, KA, quī-n, fr. quī + ne, *how not*), 1, interrog., *how not ? why not ? nay, nay even ;* 2, rel., *so that not, but that, that ; from*—after verbs of hindering.

quīnī, ae, a, num. adj., distrib. (for **R.** see quinque, quinc-nī, quī-nī), *five each.*

quinque, num. adj. (**R.** ΓANKA-N, penque, quenque, quinque), *five.*

quintus, a, um, adj. (see quinque, quin(c)tu-s, quin-tu-s), *the fifth.*

quippe, adv. (qui-ppe, pe=que, then quippe instead of quīpe), *indeed, truly, doubtless ; forsooth, for.*

Quirīnus (Curītis, Curēs), name of Romulus, as deified.

Quirīs, ītis, m. (Curēs), *of Cures,* usually in pl. *the Quirites.*

quis (quī), quae, quid, pron. (**R.** KI, weaker form for KA, **R.** of quī, ki, kvi, qui-s), 1, interrog., *who ? what ? what sort of ?* neut., quid, *what ? why ?* 2, indef., *any one, anything, some one, something.*

quisquam, quaequam, quicquam or quidquam, pron. indef., *any one, anything.*

quisque, quaeque, quidque or quodque, pron. indef., *each one, every one, every, everything ;* used of several, while uterque is used of only two.

quisquis, quidquid (quicquid), pron. rel. indef., *whoever, whatever.*

quī-vīs, quae-vīs, quod-vīs, quid-vīs, pron. indef., *who you please, any one you please, any one.*

quō (quī), adv., old dat. for quo-i, *whither ; for what purpose, to what end.*

quod (quī), (fr. acc.), 1, adv., *as to which, as to that, that, and so if, and so ;* 2, conj., *because, that, in that.*

quondam, adv. (fr. quī, quo-m, quon, *and* dam, old acc. fr. de, da, a pronom. stem), *(at a certain time), once, formerly ; one day, by and by, sometimes.*

quoniam, fr. quom,=cum, *and* jam (iam), conj., *when now, now that, since, inasmuch as.*

quoque (quī, que), conj., *also, as well, even.*
quot, num. adj. (R. KA, ka-ti, quo-t), *how many.*
quotiēns, num. adv. (same R. as quot, ēns), *how many times, how often.*
quotus, a, um, adj. (same R. as quot, kati-ta, quoti-to, quotu-s), *of what number, how many.*

R

rabidus, a, um, adj. (rabiōs), *raving, raging, furious.*
rabiēs, em, ō, f. (R. RABH, *to seize, rage*, rab, rab-ere, rab-ie-s), *rage, madness, fury, savageness.*
radiō, 1 (see radius), *to shine, be radiant.*
radius, ī, m. (R. VARDH, vard, vrad, rad, *to heighten, grow*), *a staff, rod; spoke* (of a wheel); *a shuttle* (in weaving); *a ray, beam*, in pl. *the rays.*
rādīx, īcis, f. (same R. as radius), *a root; the lowest*, as *the foundation, the foot* (of a mountain); *radish.*
rādō, rāsī, rāsum, 3 (R. RAD, *to scratch*, rad-ere, rad-si, rāsī), *to scrape, scratch; to graze* (rādere frēta).
rāmāle, is, n. (rāmus), *a branch, shoot;* gen. pl. *shoots, brushwood.*
rāmōsus, a, um, adj. (rāmus), *full of branches, branching.*
rāmus, ī, m. (same R. as radius, rad, rad-mo, rāmo), *a branch, bough, twig.*
rāna, ae, f. (R. RA, *to sound*, ra-k, rac-na, rāna), *a frog.*
rapāx, ācis, adj. (rapiō), *grasping, greedy of plunder, rapacious, tearing.*
rapidus, a, um, adj. (rapiō), *seizing, tearing, fierce; rapid, swift.*
rapīna, ae, f. (rapiō), *plunder, rapine.*
rapiō, rapuī, raptum, 3 (R. RAP, *to seize, rob*), *to seize, snatch, tear away, hurry off, rob, tear to pieces.*
raptō, 1 (rapiō), *to seize with violence, drag away, carry off.*
raptor, ōris, m. (rapiō), *a plunderer, plundering.*
rārus, a, um, adj. (etym. unc.), *loose, thin, scattered; rare* (of endowments); *rarely.*
rāstrum, ī, n. (same R. as rādō, rad-tru-m, ras-tru-m), *a heavy hoe, mattock;* pl., rastri.
ratiō, ōnis, f. (R. RA, *to reckon, think*, ra-tu-s, ra-ti-ō), *a reckoning; relation, account, method, plan, means; intelligence, reason.*
ratis, is, f. (R. AR, *to plow* (of the sea), *to row*, by metathesis, ra, ra-ti-s), *a float, raft; a boat, ship.*
raucus, a, um, adj. (R. RU, *to sound*, rau, rau-cu-s), *deep-sounding, hoarse, harsh, roaring.*
re-bellō, 1 (same R. as bellum, dvi, duī, duē, dbellu-m, bellu-m), *to make war again; to rebel.*
re-candēscō, duī, 3 (candeō), *to grow white again;* (with unda), *to grow white with foam; to grow hot again, glow.*
re-cēdō, cessī, cessum, 3, *to move back, retire, withdraw, recede, retreat.*
recēns, tis, adj. (R. KAN, *to begin*, participial form, *beginning*), *new, fresh, recent, newly arisen, just made.*
receptus, ūs, m. (capiō), *a retreat.*
recessus, ūs, m. (cēdō), *a withdrawing, retreat; a retired spot, a retreat, recess.*
re-cidō, reccidī, recāsurus, 3 (cadō), *to fall back, retire, relapse; to fall upon, reach.*
re-cīdō, cīdī, cīsum, 3 (caedō), *to cut off, cut away, cut down.*
re-cingō, cinctum (no perfect), *to ungird, unbind, loosen.*
re-cipiō (capiō), cēpī, ceptum, 3, *to take back, take again, receive, recover, retake;* with se, *to retire, withdraw.*
recitō, 1 (R. KI, *to sharpen, arouse, excite*, ci-jo, ci-e-re, citus, re-citō), *to read in public, read out; recite.*
re-clūdō (claudō), sī, sum, *to unclose, open, lay bare, disclose; pierce.*
re-cognōscō, nōvī, nitum, 3 (nōscō), *to review, examine; recognize.*
re-condō, didī, ditum, 3, *to put away, hide, hide away; of the eyes, to close again; to conceal.*
rector, ōris, m. (regō), *a leader, ruler, director; a pilot, steersman.*

rectus, a, um, adj. (rego), *direct, straight;* subst., *right.*
re-cubō, 1, no perf. or supine, *to fall back, lie down, lie on the back.*
re-cumbō, cubui, cubitum, 3, *to lie down, sink down, recline.*
re-currō, currī, cursum, 3, *to run back, hasten back.*
recursus, ūs, m. (re-currō), *a return.*
re-curvō, 1, *to bend back;* part. with undae, *many-winding.*
recurvus, a, um, adj. (re-curvō), *bent backward, curved backward.*
recūsō, 1 (causa, causor), *to make objection, excuse one's self, refuse, decline.*
red-dō, dere, didī, ditum, 3, *to give back, restore, return, render, give in return; bestow.*
red-eō, iī, itum, 4, *to go back, return, come back, come again.*
red-igō, ēgī, actum, 3 (re, agō), *to bring back, reduce.*
redimiō, iī, ītum, 4 (etym. unc.), *to bind around, encircle, wreathe.*
red-imō, ēmī, emptum, 3, *to buy back, redeem, ransom, rescue.*
reditus, ūs, m. (redeō), *a return.*
red-oleō, oluī (no supine), *to be fragrant, redolent.*
re-dūcō, xī, ctum, 3, *to bring, lead, back, draw back, reduce.*
redux, ucis, adj., *returning; returned.*
re-fellō, fellī (no supine), (re-fallō), *to refute, answer.*
re-ferō, tulī (rettulī), lātum, 3, *to bear back, carry back, turn again, restore, repeat; give in return; answer; relate.*
rē-fert, rētulit, rōferre (rēs and fert), *it concerns, it matters, it is important.*
re-flectō, flexī, flectum, 3, *to bend back, turn back; reflexive, bend itself back;* longos reflectitur ungues, bends itself back into long claws, i. e., *gets its nails lengthened into claws.*
re-foveō, fōvī, fōtum, 3, *to warm again, revive, restore.*
refringō (re and frangō), frēgī, fractum, 3, *to break open; tear open.*
re-fugiō, fūgī (no supine), *to flee back, withdraw, give way; avoid, shun.*
re-fundō, fūdī, fūsum, 3, *to pour back, pour out.*

rēgālis, e, adj. (rēx, rego), *kingly, regal, royal, princely.*
regāliter (rēgālis), adv., *like a king, regally; tyrannically.*
re-gerō, gessī, gestum, 3, *to bring back, throw back.*
regimen, inis, n., *the rule, direction, guidance; a rudder.*
rēgīna, ae, f., *a queen, princess.*
regiō, ōnis, f. (regō), *a direction; region, district.*
rēgius, a, um, adj. (reg, rēg, rēx), *regal, royal, princely, queenly.*
rēgnō, 1 (rēg, rēg-s (rēx), regn-āre), *to reign;* part., regnātus, *reigned over, ruled.*
rēgnum, ī, n. (rēgnō), *regal rule, reign; power, might; kingdom, realm.*
regō, rexī, rectum, 3 (R. ʀᴀɢ, *to direct,* reg, reg-ere), *to lead, direct, rule, govern.*
rē-iciō (reiicio), jecī, jectum, 3 (jacio), *to throw or hurl back, throw off; reject, despise.*
re-lābor, lapsus sum, 3, v. dep., *to glide back, sink back.*
re-languēscō, languī, 3, *to grow weary, sink fainting.*
re-laxō, 1, *to stretch out* or *widen again; to loosen, open.*
re-legō, lēgī, lectum, 3, *to run through again, review, repeat.*
re-levō, 1, *to lift up again, relieve, lessen.*
re-ligō, 1, *to bind to, fasten; moor.*
re-linquō, līquī, lictum, 3, *to leave behind, leave, abandon, forsake, give up, relinquish.*
re-lūceō, luxī, 2, *to shine again, blaze up.*
re-lūcēscō, luxī, *to flame up again, shine again.*
re-māneō, mānsī, mānsum, 2, *to remain behind, stay, be left.*
re-meō, 1, *to go* or *turn, back.*
rēmex, igis, m. (rēmus and agō), *an oarsman, a rower.*
rēmigium, ī, n. (rēmex), *oars, oarage; rowing;* poetically, *for wings.*
reminiscor, 3, v. dep. (R. ᴍᴀ, ᴍᴀɴ, *to think,* men, me-min-i, re-min-i-sci), *to call to mind again, recall, remember.*
re-mittō, misī, missum, 3, *to send back, let go* (back); *send forth, give*

out ; (of the spider), *to spin* the threads (of its web) ; remit, allow.

re-molior, 4, v. dep., *to press* or *push back,* or *away*.

re-mollescō, 3, *to become soft again, be softened, yield.*

re-moror, 1, v. dep., *to linger* or *stay behind ;* transitive, in remorata, *delayed,* Met. X, 671.

re-moveō, mōvī, mōtum, 2, *to move back, remove, separate ; stroke back, put aside.*

Remus, ī, m., the brother of Romulus.

rēmus, ī, m. (**R.** AR, *to plow* (plow the sea), *to row,* cret-mos, ret-mo-s, rē-mu-s), *an oar ;* figuratively, with alarum, *oarlike wings.*

re-nārrō, 1, *to tell* or *narrate again.*

re-nāscor, nāscī, 3, v. dep., *to be born again, spring up* or *grow again.*

rē-nīdeō, 2, to shine forth, *shine.*

re-novō, 1, *to renew.*

reor, ratus, 2 (**R.** RA, *to join, reckon*), *to think, believe.*

repāgula, ōrum, n. pl., *barriers.*

re-parō, 1, *to repair, renew.*

re-pellō, -ppulī, pulsum, 3, *to let go.*

repēns, tis, *sudden.*

repercussus, part. (re-per-quatiō), *reflected, rebounding.*

re-periō, perī, pertum, 4, to *discover.*

re-petō, īvī, iī, ītum, 3, *to seek again, repeat ; heave.*

re-pleō, plēvī, plētum, 2, *to fill again, fill, satisfy.*

re-pōnō, posuī, positum, 3, *to put back* or *away, lay aside, lay down ; restore, replace.*

re-primō, pressī, pressum, 3, *to press back, repress, suppress.*

re-pūgnō, 1, *to fight against, resist, struggle ; to be repugnant to, oppose.*

repulsa, ae, f. (repellō), *a repulse, refusal, denial.*

requiēs, ētis, f., acc. requiem, abl. requiē (quiēs fr. **R.** KI, *to lie down*), *rest, repose, quiet.*

requiescō, quiēvī, quiētum, 3, *to rest, repose.*

re-quīrō (quaerō), quīsīvī, quīsītum, 3, *to seek out, search for, seek, call for, ask for, desire, require.*

rēs, reī or reī, f. (**R.** RA, *to lend, give,* ra-I, rā-I, rā-s, rē-s), *a thing, matter, object, affair, circumstance, event ;* in pl., *realm, state, the world, nature, universal dominion ; a fact, a deed.*

re-secō, secuī, sectum, 1, *to cut off* or *away, cut.*

re-sequor, resecūtus sum, v. dep., *to follow. in discourse, answer.*

re-sideō, sēdī, sessum, 2 (sedeō), *to remain sitting, sit down, sit ; reside.*

re-sīdō, sēdī, 3, *to seat one's self ; subside. settle down.*

re-siliō (saliō), uī, 4, *to leap* or *spring back.*

re-sistō, stitī, 3, *to remain standing, stand ; to resist.*

re-solvō, solvī, solūtum, 3, *to unloose, loosen, break through, relax, dissolve.*

re-sonō, 1, *to sound again, resound.*

respectus, ūs, m. (respiciō), *a looking back ; a refuge, retreat ; respect, regard.*

re-spiciō (speciō), spexī, spectum, 3, *to look back* or *about, look at* or *toward ; have regard for, respect.*

re-spondeō, spondī, spōnsum, 2, *to reply, answer, respond ; to correspond* or *answer to ; to be fitting.*

re-stituō (statuō), stituī, stitūtum, 3, *to restore ; to put in* (his) *former condition,* Met. XI, 135.

re-stō, stitī, 1, *to remain, be left ; be wanting to.*

re-sūmō, sumpsī, sumptum (re, sub, emō), 3, *to take again, win,* or *gain again ; resume.*

resupīnus, a, um, adj., *bent back, lying on the back, on the back.*

re-surgō, surrexī, surrectum, 3, *to rise,* or *raise one's self, again ; to arise, rise again, return.*

re-tardō, 1, *to hinder, retard.*

rēte, is, n. (**R.** SVAR, *to bind, join,* scr, sre, rē, rē-te), *a net.*

re-tegō, texī, tectum, 3, *to uncover, lay bare, open ; take away ; disclose.*

re-temptō (tentō), 1, *to try again, try anew.*

re-texō, texuī, textum, 3, *to unweave ; lessen,* or *diminish, again,* to *alter, change, annul ; weave again, renew, repeat.*

re-tíceō (tacco), *to be silent, keep silent, refrain from answering, be reticent.*
retināculum (retinco, re, tenco, ten-āx, tenāc-u-lu-m), something that *holds back, a cable, rope, fastening.*
retíneō (tenco), retinui, retentum, 2, *to hold back, stop, detain, retain, restrain ; keep.*
re-torqueō, torsi, tortum, 2, *to twist,* or *turn, back,* or *around.*
re-tractō, 1, *to review.*
re-trahō, traxi, tractum, 3, *to draw back, withdraw ; draw again.*
retrō, adv. (see intro), *backward, back.*
re-vellō, vulsi, vulsum, 3, *to tear,* or *pull, away, drag from.*
reverentia (re, vereor), timidity, shyness ; reverence ; *shame.*
re-vertor, verti, versus sum, v. dep., *to turn back, return.*
re-vīvisco, vixi, 3, *to come to life again, live again, revive.*
revocābilis, e, adj. (revoco), *that may be recalled* or *revoked, revocable.*
re-volvō, volvi, volūtum, 3, *to roll back, sink back ; renew, repeat.*
rēx, rēgis (R. REG, RĒG, rĕg-s, *to rule*), *a king, prince, leader.*
Rhēnus, i, m., *the Rhine*, the river parting Gaul from Germany.
Rhodanus, i, m., *the Rhone*, river in Gaul.
Rhodopē, ēs, f., 1, a mountain in Thrace ; 2, a Thracian woman, who was changed into a mountain of this name.
Rhodopēius, a, nm, adj., *of Rhodope, Rhodopeian ; Thracian*, used of Orpheus, Met. VI, 87.
rictus, ūs, m. (R. RIK, *to cleave, tear apart,* ric, rig, ri-n-gi (inin. pass.), rictu-s, part., then rictus, subst., *cleft, opening, the opening of the mouth, the mouth wide open* ; in pl., *mouth, jaws.*
rīdeō, risi, risum, 2, etym. unc., *to laugh, smile ; to laugh at ; to ridicule.*
rigeō, 2 (same R. as rēx, rectus, RAG, *to direct, make straight,* reg, rig, rig-ēre), *to be stiff, to stand stiff* or *upright ; to harden.*
rigēscō (rigeo), 3, to grow stiff, *stiffen.*

rigidus, a, um, adj. (rigeo), *stiff, hard, rigid, rough.*
rigor, ōris, m., *stiffness, hardness, rigor ; rigid cold.*
riguus, a, um, adj. (rigo), *watered, irrigated.*
rīma, ae, f. (same R. as rictus, RIK, ric, ric-ma, rīma), *a cleft, crack, fissure.*
rīpa, ae, f. (R., according to Vanicek, same as rīma, rik, rig, rip-a ; but according to Corssen, fr. R. RI, *to flow,* same as rīvus), *a bank* (of a river).
rīsus, ūs, m. (rideo), *laughter, laugh.*
rītus, ūs, m. (R. same as ratus, RA, re, ri-tu-s), something established, *a religious usage, rite, ceremony, form.*
rīvus, i, m. (R. RI, *to flow,* ri, ri-vu-s), *a stream, brook, river, rivulet.*
rōbīgō (rūbīgo), inis, f. (R. RUDH, *to be red,* rud, rub, roub, rūb, rōb-i-go), *rust* (on metals) ; *mold* or *deposit* on the teeth.
rōbur, oris, n. (R. RABH (same as rabiēs), *to seize*), rab, rōb-ur), trunk-wood, *hard wood ;* in pl., *trunks of trees ;* especially *oak-wood, oak ;* figuratively, *strength, hardness, force, courage, military might.*
rogālis, e, adj. (rogus), *belonging to,* or *of, a funeral pile.*
rogō, 1 (R. same as rectus, RAG, *to set straight,* reg, rog, rogā-re, *to put straight, to reach after,* as in legem rogāre, *to try for, to try to get by asking, ask*), *to ask, beg, sue for.*
rogus, i, m. (same R. as rectus, RAG, reg, rog, rogu-s, *something set up*), *a funeral pile, a pyre.*
Rōma, ae, f. (R. SRU, *to flow,* srou, srō, rū, rō, Rō-ma, *the stream-city*), *Rome.*
Rōmulus, a, um, adj., *of Romulus.*
Rōmulus, i, m. (Rŏma), *Romulus,* son of Mars and Rhea Silvia or Ilia.
rōrō, 1 (ros), *to bedew ; to drop* or *distill dew ; to trickle, drip.*
rōs, roris, m. (R. RAS, *to trickle, to besprinkle,* ros), *dew ; trickling water, spring-water, moisture, spray ;* ros marinus, *rosemary.*
rosa, ae, f. (etym. unc.), *a rose.*
rostrum, i, n. (rodo, wh. is fr. R. RAD, *to scratch, gnaw,* rād, rōd, rōd-ere, *to gnaw, corrode,* rod-tru-m, ros-tru-m,

something that scratches), *a beak, bill; snout, muzzle; beak* of a ship.

rota, ae, f. (R. same as rŏmus, AR, ra, re, ro, ro-ta), *a wheel;* by meton., *a chariot, wagon, cart.*

rotō, 1 (rota), to turn as a wheel, *to whirl, whirl about.*

rubefaciō, fecī, factum, 3 (rubeō, faciō), *to make red or ruddy, to redden.*

rubeō, uī, 2 (R. RUDH, *to be red,* rud, rub, rub-ēre), *to be red.*

rubēns, tis, part. and adj. (rubeō), *red, ruddy; blushing.*

rubēscō, rubuī, 3, *to grow red.*

rubēta, ōrum, n., *bramble-thickets.*

rubor, ōris, m. (rubeō), *redness.*

rudēns, tis, m. (R. RU, *to sound,* ru-d, rud-ere, rud-ē-ns, *whistling sound,* clamor sibilus (rudentum)), *a* (ship's) *rope, hawser, line, sheet, cordage.*

rudis, e, adj. (R. VARDH, *to rise up, to grow,* vrad, vrud, rud, rud-i-s, *grown, overgrown), rough, rude; uncultivated, inexperienced, unknown, a stranger to.*

rūga, ae, f. (R. VARG, *to turn,* vurg, vrūg, rūg-a), *a wrinkle.*

rūgōsus, a, um, adj. (rūga), *full of wrinkles, wrinkled; dried.*

ruīna, ae, f. (ruō), *a fall, crash; ruin, destruction; ruins.*

Rūmina, sc. fīcus; see n. Fasti, II, 412; *of Rumina.*

Rūmor, ōris, m. (R. RU, *to sound,* rū, rūm-or), *a rumor, report, common talk;* personified, Rūmōrēs, *Rumors.*

rumpō, rūpī, ruptum, 3 (R. RAP, RUP, *to break,* ru-m-p-ere), to break, burst, break down, burst through; *to split, bore or cut through, cleave, tear apart; destroy.*

ruō, ruī, rutum, 3 (R. DAR, *to cleave, burst,* dru, ru, ru-ere), *to rush, run, rush in, fall in, fall in ruins.*

rūpēs, is, f. (R. same as rumpō, rūp-e-s, *something broken off or cleft), a cliff, a precipitous rock.*

rūricola, ae, m., adj. and subst. (rūs and colō), *one that tills the field, or that lives in the country; rustic; peasant.*

rūrsus, adv. (re-vorsu-m, fr. re *and* vertō, vort, vors, fr. R. VART), (turned backward), *back, again, anew.*

rūs, rūris, n. (R. RAV-AS, *the wide, the free,* rov-os, rūs, *the free, open, land), the country; land; field, fields.*

rūsticus, a, um, adj. and subst. (rūs), rustic, rural; *boorish; a rustic; a boor.*

rutilus, a, um, adj. (same R. as rubeō, RUDH, rud, rud-tu-lo (Ru-tu-li), ru-ti-lu-s), *red, bright-red, flaming-red.*

Rutulī, ōrum, m. pl. (R. same as rutilus), a people in Latium; *the Rutuli or Rutulians.*

S

Sabīnī, ōrum, m., a people in Central Italy; *the Sabines.*

Sabīnus, a, um, adj., *Sabine.*

sacer, sacra, sacrum, adj. (R. SAK, SAG, *to make firm, ordain,* sac-er), consecrated to a deity, *sacred, holy.*

săcrum, i, n. (sacer), *something sacred, a sanctuary;* in pl., *sacred rites; sacrifices, offerings.*

săcrilegus, a, um, adj. (sacer *and* lego), plunderer of things sacred, *sacrilegious, impious.*

săcrō, 1 (same R. as sacer), *to consecrate, make sacred.*

saeculum, i, n. (R. SA, *to strew, sow,* se, se-r-ere, sē-vī, sē-men, se-(sac)-culu-m, *sowing, increase), (saeclum), a generation, race of men, men; an age, century, lifetime;* in pl., Saecula, *the Ages.*

saepe, adv. (same R. as sacer, sak, suak, saep-e-s, saep-i-s, saepe, acc. n.), *often, oftentimes, frequently.*

saepēs (sepes), is, f. (see saepe), *a hedge, inclosure, fence.*

saeta (sēta), ae, f. (etym. unc.), the short, coarse hair of an animal, *a bristle, bristling or shaggy hair.*

saeviō, īvī (iī), ītum, 4 (saevus), *to rage, be angry, be furious.*

saevus, a, um, adj. (R. SAVJA, SKAV-JA, *left, unlucky* (scaevus, laevus), saiva, saevu-s), *fierce, wild, raging, furious; cruel, savage.*

sagāx, ācis, adj. (R. sāgiō, fr. R. SAK, sag (same as sacer), *to seek after,*

be of keen perception), of keen perception, acute, sagacious; sharp-sighted, keen-scented; quick of hearing.
sagitta, ae, f. (same R. as sagiō), *an arrow.*
sagittifer, -era, erum, adj. (sagitta, ferō), *arrow-bearing, armed with arrows.*
salignus, a, um, adj. (salix), *of willow.*
saliō, uī (iī), tum, 4 (R. SAR, *to go, to flow,* sal, sal-īre), *to spring, leap, hop, dance.*
salix, icis, f. (same R. as saliō), *a willow-tree, willow.*
saltem, adv. (same R. as salvus (salti-m), sal-te-m), *at least, at any rate.*
saltus, ūs, m. (saliō), 1, *a leaping, leap, spring;* 2, *an uprising place, a narrow pass;* an opening, *a forest-pasture, woodland, wood.*
salūs, ūtis, f. (same R. as salvus), *welfare, health, safety, rescue;* by meton., *a greeting.*
salūtō, 1 (salvus), *to wish one's welfare, to salute, greet.*
salvē, imper., fr. salveō, *be well, hail!*
salvus, a, um, adj. (R. SAR, *to protect, heal,* sal, sal-vu-s, healed, safe), *unharmed, safe, well.*
Samos, ī (-us), f., 1, *an island on the W. coast of Asia Minor;* 2, *an island in the Ionian sea; Samos.*
sānābilis, e, adj. (sānō), *curable.*
sanctus, a, um, adj. (same R. as sacer, SAK, sac, sa-n-c-īre), part. fr. sanciō, *sacred, holy, inviolate; pure; unsullied.*
sanguineus, a, um, adj. (sanguis), *of blood, bloody.*
sanguinulentus, a, um, adj. (sanguis), *bloody, sanguinary.*
sanguis, inis, m. (R. SAK, SAG, *to drop, drip, taste,* sa-n-gu-i-s), *blood* (in the body); *bloodshed;* by meton., *race, blood, family.*
sānus, a, um, adj. (R. SAVA, *sound, well,* sav, sav-no, sā-nu-s), *sound, healthy; of sound understanding, rational, sane.*
sapiēns, tis (sapiō), part. adj., *having taste, sensible; wise, discerning, shrewd.*

sapienter (sapiēns), adv., *wisely, sensibly.*
sapiō, īvī, iī, 3 (R. same as sanguis, SAK, *to taste), to taste, to have taste or sense; to be wise, intelligent.*
sarcina, ae, f., *a burden;* see note, Met. VI, 224.
sarculum, I, n. (fr. sar-(sarr)īre, R. SAR, *to weed), a light hoe.*
Sardes, ium (Sardīs), f. pl., *capital of Lydia.*
Sarmatis, idis, adj., *of Sarmatia, Sarmatian;* see note, Trist. IV, 10, 110.
satiō, 1 (see satis for R.), *to satisfy, satiate, glut.*
satis and **sat,** adv. (R. SA, *to satisfy,* sa-t, sat-i-s), *enough, sufficiently.*
satur, ra, rum, adj. (satis), *full, satiated; rich.*
Sāturnius, a, um, adj. (Sāturnus), *of Saturn, Saturnian;* subst., *the Saturnian,* Jupiter; *Saturnia,* the daughter of Saturnus, Juno.
Sāturnus, ī, m. (R. SA, *to sow,* satur, Sa-tur-nu-s, god of sowing, of Agriculture), son of Uranus and Gaea, and father of Jupiter and Juno. His reign was the golden age, and his dethronement by Jupiter was followed by the silver age; Met. I, 113.
saturō, 1 (satis), *to satiate, saturate.*
Satyrus, ī, m., *a Satyr.*
saucius, a, um, adj. (etym. unc.), *injured, wounded, smitten, struck.*
saxeus, a, um, adj. (saxum), *of stone, stony.*
saxum, ī, n. (R. SAK, SKA, *to cut,* sac, sac-so, saxu-m), *something cut or split, a detached fragment of rock, a rock, a stone, a crag, a broken rock; a cave, cavern.*
scelerātus, a, um, adj. (scelus), *wicked, guilty, infamous, accursed, impious.*
scelus, eris, n. (R. SKAR, *to turn quickly, sway, err,* skal, scel-us), *an error, crime, evil deed; evil word.*
sceptrum, ī, n. (R. SKAP, *to support* (σκῆπτρον)), *a sceptre, royal staff;* by meton., *regal rule, dominion.*
Schoenēius, a, um, adj., *of Schoeneus,* king of Boeotia; *Schoeneian.*
scīlicet (sci, imper. of sciō *and* licet),

312 SCINDO SENATUS

adv., *no doubt, certainly, forsooth, indeed, namely.*

scindō, scidī, scissum, 3 (R. same as saxum, SAK, *to cut*, ska, sci, skid, scid, sci-n-d-ere), *to cleave, split, cut, tear apart, tear off.*

sciō, scīvī, scītum, 4 (same R. as scindō, sak, ska, sci, *to cut, part, decide), to know, experience.*

scitor, v. dep., 1 (scīscō, sciō), *to seek to know, to search into, inquire.*

scītus, a, um (part. adj. fr. scīscō), *experienced, skilled, versed in.*

scopulus, ī, m. (Gr. σκόπελος), *a projecting rock, a cliff, a crag.*

Scorpius (-os), ī, m. (σκορπίος), the constellation *Scorpion.*

scrībō, scripsī, scriptum, 3 (R. SKARP, SKARBH, *to cut, engrave*, scrabh, scriύh, scrīb-ere), *to write;* subst., scriptum, *the writing, writing.*

scrobis, is, m., scrobs, bis (same R. as scrībō), *a pit, trench, ditch, hole.*

Scylla, ae, f., a rock in the Strait of Sicily or Messina, opposite the whirlpool of Charybdis ; originally fabled as a sea-monster ; or, in another myth, as a nymph.

Scythia, ae, f., the land of the Scythians, a general name for the northern lands of Europe and Asia from the lower Danube to the Caspian Sea ; *Scythia.*

Scythicus, a, um, adj. (Scythia), *Scythian.*

sē-cēdō, cessī, cessum, *to withdraw, go aside, retire.*

sē-cernō, crēvī, crētum, 3, *to set apart, separate ;* part., sēcrētus, *separate, retired, remote ; secret, hidden.*

secō, secuī, sectum, 1 (R. SAK, sec, *to cut*), *to cut, cut off, cleave, separate, part, cut through.*

sē-cumbō, cubuī, cubitum, 3, *to lie apart, lie alone.*

secundus, a, um, adj. (sequor, *following), the second, next following,* in time, rank, or degree ; *favorable, seconding.*

secūris, is, f. (same R. as secō, sec, *to cut*, sec-ū-ri-s), *an axe, a battle-axe.*

sē-cūru-s, a, um, adj. (sē, *apart, without*, and cūra, cūra fr. R. skav,

kav, cav, cov, cov-i-ra, cū-ra), *without care, secure ; free from care.*

secus, adv. (R. SAK, *to follow*, sek (sequ), sec, comparative sectius (sak-ta-jans), sētius, secus, originally, *following*, secus fluvios, Plin. 23, 15), *otherwise ;* generally with negatives (nōn), *not otherwise, no less.*

sed, conj. (R. SAVA, SVA, reflex pronom., sovo, svo, suu-s, sua-d, sva-d, sed, *of itself, for itself apart*), *but, but yet, yet.*

sedeō, sedī, sessum, 2 (R. SAD, *to sit*, sed, sed-ēre), *to sit, sit down ; settle.*

sēdēs, is, f. (sedeō), *a seat, dwelling, residence ; a place, spot, foundation, soil, ground.*

sēditiō, ōnis, f. (R. I, *to go*, e-ō, i-tu-m, sēd-itiō, *a going apart*), *a sedition, uprising, faction, mutiny.*

sēdō, 1 (same R. as sedeō, sēd-es, sēdā-re), *to cause to sit, settle ; to still, quiet, calm, allay.*

sē-dūcō, xī, ctum, 3, *to draw aside, to separate, part.*

sēdulus, a, um, adj. (R. SAD, *to go*, sēd, sēd-ulu-s, *inclined to going hither and thither*), *active, busy; sedulous.*

seges, etis, f. (R. SAK, SAG, *to make firm, nourish* (same R. as sacer), sagina, seg-e-s, *the nourishing crop*), the seed or grain from the planting to the harvest, grain, growing grain, crop ; grain-field ; *seed, growth.*

segnis, e, adj., same R. as seges, seg-ni-s.

semel, adv. (R. SA, insep. particle, meaning *union* or *likeness ; with, together with, at once*, sama, semo, semo-l, seme-l), *once, at a single time, the first time.*

semen, inis, n. (R. same as serō, SA, sū, sō, *to sow*), *a seed, seed* (of grain) ; (*of* men and beasts), *seed, young; principles.*

sēmēsus, a, um, adj. (sēmi-edō), *half eaten.*

semper, adv. (sem-per, sem fr. same R. as simul, SA, sama, semo, *the whole, all*, per fr. R. PAR, para, per, *through* (to pass through) ; *through the whole, ever), always, at every time, ever.*

senātus, ūs, m. (R. SANA, *old*, sen, sen-e-c, sen-e-x, senec-tu-s, sen-u-s,

SENECTA   SICULUS   313

senā-re, senā-tu-s), *council of elders, the senate.*
senecta, ae, f. (for **R.** see senātus), *age, old age.*
senectus, ūtis, f. (same **R.** as senātus), *age, old age.*
senex, senis (see senātus for **R.**), adj. and subst., *old, aged; an old man.*
sōnī, ae, adj., plural distrib. (same **R.** as sex, svaks, saks, sechs, seks, sex, secs-ni, ses-ni, sŏnī), *six each, six at a time.*
senīlis, e, adj. (senex). *of or belonging to old people, aged, senile.*
sēnsus, ūs, m. (sentīō), *feeling, sensation, perception, sense, taste;* in pl., *the senses, feelings; mind.*
sententia, ae, f. (sentiō), *a feeling, opinion, thought, sentiment; determination, decision, view.*
sentīō, sēnsī, sēnsum, 4 (**R.** SANT, *to take a direction* or *tendency*, sent-īre), *to feel, perceive,* by any one of the senses; *to trace, experience, observe, have intelligence of.*
sentis, is, m. (etym. unc.), *a thorn, thorn-bush, brier.*
sē-parō, 1, *to separate, part.*
sepeliō, īvī, pultum, 4 (**R.** SAK, *to follow,* sap, *to strive for, be dependent upon,* Vedic saparj, *to honor,* sepelī-re), *to bury* (honor by burying), *to inter;* part., sepultus, *buried.*
sē-pōnō, posuī, positum, 3, *to put aside, withdraw, put away, separate.*
septem, adv. num. (**R.** SAPTAN, *seven*), *seven.*
sepulcrum, ī, n. (sepeliō), *place of burial, grave, sepulchre.*
sequor, sequī, secutus sum, 3, verb dep. (**R.** SAK, sec-, sequ-or, *to follow*), *to follow, follow after;* pursue; *go after* or *behind; accompany.*
sera, ae, f. (**R.** SVAR, *to bind, join,* ser, ser-ere (serul), ser-a, something to bind or make fast with), *a bolt.*
serēnus, a, um, adj., *clear.*
seriēs, ēī, f. (same **R.** as sera), *a row, line, train, series.*
sermō, ōnis, m. (same **R.** as sera, serō), *discourse, conversation, talk, speech.*
sērō, adv. (serus), *late, too late;* serius, *later.*

scrō, sēvī, satum, 3 (**R.** SA, *to sow,* si-s-ere, si-r-cre, se-r-cre), *to sow, plant; produce, bring forth, beget;* part., satus, *sown, planted; sprung from, born, descended;* subst., *son of, descendant of.*
Serpēns, ntis (fr. serpō, **R.** SARP, *to creep,* serp), (a creeping thing), *a serpent, snake, dragon;* the constellation *Dragon.* **serpō,** psī, ptum, 3, *to creep.*
serra, ae, f. (**R.** SAK, SKA, *to cut,* sec, sec-ra, serra), *a saw.*
serta, ōrum, n. pl., fr. serō, serui, sertum, *garlands, wreaths.*
sērus, a, um, adj. (**R.** SA, *to bring to an end,* sō-se-rus), *late, too late.*
servātōr, ōris, m., *a preserver, deliverer.*
servātrīx, īcis, f., *a protectress, preserver.*
serviō, īvī, iī, ītum, 4 (servus), *to be a servant or slave, to serve, to be in service; to be enslaved to, be serviceable to.*
servitium, ī, n. (servus), *service, servitude, slavery.*
servō, 1 (serviō, servus), *to watch over, preserve, keep; preserve, spare.*
servus, ī, m. (**R.** SAR, *to protect,* servu-s, *one that is protected* or *kept*), *a servant, slave.*
sētius (secius, see secus for **R.**), *otherwise.*
sex, num. adj. (**R.** svaks, *six,* saks, sechs, sex), *six.*
sī, conj. (**R.** SA, pronom. demons., 3d pers., sā, sī, cf. sī-c). *in that case, in case, if, if indeed; since, seeing that; when, whether.*
sībilō, 1 (sībilus), *to hiss.*
sībilus, ī, m. (**R.** SIP, SIF, *to be hollow, to whistle,* sib, sīb-ilus), *hissing, whistling; piping;* also n., sibila.
sīc, adv. (**R.** same as sī, sa, sā, sī-ce, sī-c), *in this way, thus, so; in like manner, even so; in such a degree, so very.*
Sicānia, ae, f., poetical for Sicilia; *Sicily.*
siccō, 1 (siccus), *to dry, dry up, drain; stanch.*
siccus, a, um, adj. (**R.** SIK, sic, *to dry*). *dry; dried up, parched.*
Sicelis, idis, adj. f., *Sicilian.*
Siculus, a, um, adj. (Sicilia), *Sicilitan; Sicvlian.*

15

sic-ut, comp. adv., *so as, as, just as.*

sidereus, a, um, adj. (sidus), *belonging to the stars, starry, star-like; belonging to the sun.*

sido, sidi, 3 (R. same as sedeō, sad, sed, sid, *to sit*), *to seat one's self, to sit down.*

Sidōn, ōnis, f., a city in Phoenicia.

Sidōnius, a, um, adj., *Sidonian.*

sidus, eris, n. (R. svid, *to sweat, to smelt* (of metals), sid, *to be molten, smooth, bright*), *a constellation, star;* in pl. mostly, *the stars;* by meton., *the heavens.*

sigillum, i, n. (dimin. fr. signum), a little sign, *an image, a little figure, picture.*

signō, 1 (signum), *to set a mark or sign upon, to mark, designate; to trace; to color.*

signum, i, n. (R. sak, *to show*, sec, sig-nu-m), *a sign*, mark, trace, indication; *a* (memorial) *sign; a statue, picture; a sign in the heavens, sign* (of the zodiac).

silentium, i (ii), n. (sileō), *silence, stillness.*

Silēnus, i, name of a Satyr; *Silenus.*

sileō, ui, 2 (R. sil, *to be silent*), *to be silent, still, quiet;* part., silentes, *the silent* (shades of the lower world).

silex, icis, m. (R. sar, *to protect, make whole,* sal (sal-vu-s), sol (solidu-s), sile-x), *a hard stone, flint, stone.*

silva, ae, f. (R. svar, *to shine,* sval, sil, sil-va), *a wood, forest; woodland, wood;* by meton., *forest-trees.*

silvestris, e, adj. (silva), *of a wood, woody, wild.*

Silvia, ae, f., the mother of Romulus and Remus; *Silvia.*

similis, e, adj. (R. same as semel, wh. see, sa, sama, semo, semo-li, similis). *similar, like, resembling, the same.*

Simois, entis, m., a river near Troy; *the Simois.*

simplex, icis, adj. (R. sa, same as of semel, similis, sama, semo, simo, sin-guli, *single, one,* and R. park, *to fold,* plak, plec, = sem-plic, sim-plex, *one-fold), single, simple, pure, plain.*

simplicitās, ātis, f. (simplex), *simplicity; naturalness.*

simul, adv. (same R. as semel,

simul, *at the same time;* simul ac (atque), *as soon as*), *at once, together; immediately.*

simulācrum, i, n. (simulō), *a likeness, image; a ghost, phantom; imitation.*

simulāmen, inis, n. (simulō), *imitation.*

simulātor, ōris, m., *imitator.*

simulō, 1 (see similis for R.), *to make similar, imitate;* to counterfeit; *to pretend, feign.*

sincērus, a, um, adj. (R. same as the first part of simplex, sa, sama, sam, sin, *whole, all,* and R. skar, kar, *to part, divide,* cer, sin-cer-u-s, *all separated, quite pure*), *unmixed, pure, genuine, sincere; sound, unhurt.*

sine (si and ne, *if not, since not, separated from*), prep. with abl., *without.*

singuli, ae, a, adj. (see semel, similis for R.), *single, one by one, singly.*

singultus, ūs, m. (R. sa, sama, sam, sin- (as in singuli) + R. gar, *to swallow, hiccup,* gal, gul; = sin-gul-tu-s), *a sobbing,* speech interrupted by sobbing; *hiccup; rattling* in the throat.

sinister, sinistra, sinistrum, adj. (R. sana, *old,* sin, sin-is, then with repeated compar suffix, sin-is-ter, properly *older, worthier,* with the Romans, *lucky,* as the augur faced the south, and so had the east on his *left;* with the Greeks, *unlucky* (sinister), as the Greek in observing auspices faced the north), *left, on the left side* or *hand; perverse, awkward;* (with manus understood), subst., sinistra, *the left hand.*

sinō, sivi, situm, 3 (R. sa, *to sow,* si, *to plant, set, to lay, lie*), *to let take place, allow, permit;* part., situs, *laid away, buried; situated.*

sinuō, 1 (sinus), *to bend* like a bow, *fold, twist, curve, arch.*

sinus, ūs, m. (R. sanu, *ridge of a mountain,* sinu-s, *a rounding, bending*), *a fold* of the dress on the breast, *a bend, curve, coil* of a serpent; by meton., *the breast, bosom; lap;* also fr. the bend of a shore, *a bay, a gulf.*

Sipylus, i, m., 1, a mountain in Lydia; 2. son of Niobe.

Sirēnes, um, sing. Sirēn, ēnis, f.,

the Sirens, a Siren, daughters, daughter, of the river-god Achelōus; fabled to have women's heads and bodies of birds, and to entice by their song the mariners who passed their islands off the bay of Naples.

sisto, stitī, statum, 3 (**R.** STA, *to stand,* si-sta-re, si-ste-re, *to cause to stand*), *to place, set, put ; to bring to a stand-still, to stop, stay ; to bring to rest, to quiet ; to put one's self, to stand, remain, stay.*

sistrum, ī, n. (Gr., σεῖστρον), the metallic *rattle* used in the service of Isis.

Sīsyphus, ī, m., son of Aeolus, and notorious for his cruel robberies, and punished in the lower world by ever rolling a huge stone up hill, which ever rolled down again.

sitis, is, f. (**R.** SATI, *to desire,* siti-s), *thirst ; drought.*

sīve, sī-ve (seu), conj. (see **R.** for sī; ve fr. **R.** VAL, vol, vol-ō, *to will*), if you will, *or if ; either—or, whether—or.*

smaragdus, ī, m. and f., a precious stone of a bright-green color ; *smaragdus.*

socer, socerī, m. (fr. **R.** SAVA, sva (sa + va), sovo, suo, sua, *one's own,* + **R.** KU, KVI, kva-n, *to be strong, to lord it,* ku, ku-ra ; = sva-kura, so-cerō (Gr., ἑ-κυρό-ς), *one's own lord*), father-in-law; pl., *parents-in-law.*

sociālis, e, adj. (socius), *companionable, sociable, social ; conjugal, nuptial.*

sociō, 1 (socius), *to associate,* make in common, *unite, join, share with.*

socius, ī, m. (**R.** SAK, *to follow,* sec, soc, soc-iu-s, *a follower*), adj. and subst., *associated, joined, social, united, in common ; companion, ally, associate, comrade ; shipmate.*

sodālis, is, comm. (**R.** SVA, sua, *one's own,* + DHA, *to make ;* = sva-dha, *making one's own, custom, habit,* so-dā-li-s), a companion, comrade.

sodālicius, a, um, adj. (sodālis), *of* or *belonging to a comrade* or *friend.*

sōl, sōlis, m. (**R.** SVAR, *to shine,* sval, sōl), *the sun, sunlight, heat of the sun ;* in pl., *rays of the sun, sunbeams ;* personified, Sōl, *the Sun-god, the Sun.*

solācium (solātium), ī, n. (sōlor), *solace, comfort, consolation.*

soleō, 2 (etym. unc.), *to be wont, be accustomed ;* solitus, part. and adj., *wonted, customary, usual.*

solidus, a, um, adj. (**R.** SAR, *to protect, make whole,* sal (solu-s), soli-du-s, properly, *whole, complete*), *firm, solid, strong, entire ;* subst., solidum, ī, n., *the solid ground.*

solium, ī, n. (**R.** same as sedeō, sad, sed, then with (l instead of d, cf. odor, olēre), sol-iu-m, *a seat*), *a throne.*

sollemnis, e, adj. (sollennis), (**R.** same as solidus, sar, sal, sol, sollu-s, *whole, all,* + **R.** of an-nu-s, AK, ank, *to bend, round,* ac, ac-nu-s, an-nu-s, *around, circle ;* = soll-emnis), *all-yearly, annual ; stated ;* then, fr. sacred rites occurring annually, *solemn, festal, sacred.*

sollers, rtis, adj. (**R.** SAR, soll (see sollemnis), + **R.** AR, *to join, fit,* ar-s ;= soll-ers, *all-art*), *skillful, well skilled, expert, inventive.*

sollerter, adv., *skillfully* (sollers).

sollertia, ae, f. (sollers), *skill, inventiveness.*

sollicitō, 1 (**R.** soll, as in sollers, + **R.** KI, *to call, move,* ci, ci-jo, ci-ē-re, ci-tu-s, citā-re ; solli-citus, solli-citō, *to wholly move), to move strongly, stir up, agitate ; to disturb, harass, make solicitous.*

sollicitus, a, um, adj. (for **R.** see sollicitō), *strongly moved, troubled, solicitous, anxious.*

sōlor, 1, v. dep. (**R.** same as salvus, solidus, SAR, *to make whole, heal,* sal, sol, sōlā-rī), *to console, comfort.*

sōlum, adv. (sōlus), *only, alone.*

solum, ī, n. (**R.** SAD, *to go,* sod, then (d changed to l) sol, sol-u-m ; but Corssen takes it fr. **R.** sar, same as solidus, wh. see), *the ground, foundation ; the soil ; land.*

sōlus, a, um, adj. (**R.** same as solidus), *whole ; alone, only, single, the only ; unattended, solitary.*

solvō, solvī, solūtum, 3 (**R.** LU, *to loose,* se-lu-ere, so-lv-ere), *to loose* anything wh. is bound ; *to open ;* to pay, *fulfill ; to discharge ; to dissolve,* see note. Met. XI, 135 ; *to free from.*

somnium, ī (iī), n. (for **R.** see somnus), *a dream ;* Somnia (by personification, *Dreams, dream-gods.*

somnus, I, m. (**R.** SVAP, *to sleep,* svop, sop, sop-nu-s, som-nu-s), *sleep, slumber; a dream;* Somnus, the god of sleep, *Sleep.*

sonitus, ūs, m. (sonō), *sound, noise, roar, din.*

sonō, uī, sonitum, 1 (sonus), *to sound, resound, make a noise ; to rattle, ring, twang, whiz.*

sonus, I, m. (**R.** SVAR, *to sound,* son, son-u-s), *a sound, tone, noise ; a ring ; a din, a crash, a roar.*

Sophŏclēus, a, um, adj., *of Sophocles,* Sophoclean.

sōpĭŏ, īvī (iī), ītum, 4 (sopor), *to lull to sleep.*

sopor, ōris, m. (**R.** same as somnus, sop, sop-or), *deep sleep.*

sopōrĭfer, fera, ferum, adj. (sopor), *sleep-bringing, drowsy.*

sorbĕō, uī, rptum, 2 (**R.** SVARBH, *to swallow,* sorb, sorb-ēre), *to swallow, suck in ; swallow up ; absorb.*

sordĭdus, a, um, adj. (from sordes, wh. is fr. **R.** SVAR, *to be foul ; dark,* svar-dn, sorde-s, i-s), *foul, filthy; sordid.*

soror, ōris, f. (**R.** VAS, *to dwell,* sa-vas-tar, *dwelling with,* sa-s-tar, sa-s-sar, sa-sar, so-ror, originally *one who dwells with her brother), a sister ; a near relation* (wife), as in Met. I, 351 ; *sister-nymph.*

sors, sortis, f. (**R.** SVAR, *to join, bind,* ser (ser-ere), sor-s), *a lot, a part ; an allotment, oracle ; oracular saying, fate ; destiny.*

sortĭor, 4, v. dep., sortītus, *to gain by lot, gain, reach, obtain.*

sospes, itis (**R.** SAVA, *whole, well,* sov-os, sos-+PA, *to protect, keep,* pu-t, pat, pet-s, pe-s :=sos-pe-s, *well protecting; pass., well protected), unhurt, safe, saved, sound.*

spargō, sparsī, sparsum, 3 (**R.** SPARK, *to sprinkle,* sparg (k to g), spargere), to sprinkle, *scatter, strew, spread, bespread, diffuse.*

Spartē, ēs, Sparta, ae, f., the city of *Sparta* in Laconia.

spatior, 1, v. dep. (spatium), (*to space it), to go back and forth, wander; spread one's self, spread.*

spatĭōsus, a, um, adj. (spatium), *wide, great, roomy, spacious ; far extended, long continuing,*

spatium, I (iī), n. (**R.** SPA, spa-n, *to span, extend,* spa-ti-iu-m), *span, reach, space, room ; extent, greatness; interval of space* or *of time ; time.*

spĕcĭēs, ēī, f. (**R.** SPAK, *to see,* spec (spec-ere), spec-iē-s), *an appearance, a look* or *sight, form ; vision.*

spĕcĭōsus, a, um, adj. (spcciēs), *fine-looking, beautiful, shining, brilliant.*

spectābĭlis, e, adj. (spectō), *visible; splendid ; fine.*

spectāculum, ī, n. (spectō), *a spectacle, sight, an exhibition.*

spectātor, ōris, m. (spectō), *a spectator.*

spectō, 1 (**R.** same as spcciēs, SPAK, *to see,* spec (spec-ere), spec-tā-re), *to behold, gaze upon, look at* or *on ; to consider, view ;* part., spectātus, *looked upon, tried, approved.*

speculum, ī, n. (same **R.** as spcciēs, wh. see, spec-u-lu-m), *a looking-glass, mirror.*

specus, ūs (**R.** same as speculum, wh. is a dimin. of specus), m. f. n., *a cave, cavern, hollow, den.*

spēlunca, ae, f. (fr. Gr. σπῆλυγξ), *a cavern, cleft ; grotto.*

Sperchēĭs, idis, adj. f., *belonging to the Sperchĭus,* a river in Thessaly ; Met. II, 250, *ripae Sp.*

spernō, sprevī, sprētum, 3 (**R.** SPAR, *to keep off* (spur ?), *separate,* sper-n-ere), *to spurn, disdain, despise.*

spēro, 1 (fr. spē-s, wh. is fr. **R.** SPA, *to stretch, span,* spē-rāre), *to hope.*

spēs, ēī, f. (see spērō), *hope, expectation ; a hope* (the thing hoped for).

spīceus, a, um, adj., fr. spīca, wh. is fr. same **R.** as spes, SPAN, *to span, stretch,* spī, spī-ca, *a point,* then *an ear* (of grain), *a spike, a beard), of ears* or *blades of grain, bearded.*

spīna, ae, f. (**R.** same as spīca, spīna, *something pointed), a thorn ; the spine.*

spīneus, a, um, adj. (spīna), *of thorns, thorny.*

spīra, ae, f. (**R.** SPAR, *to wind,* spīr-a, *a winding), the coil* of a snake.

spiritus, ūs, m. (spīrō), *breath* (of air), *breath, breathing ; life ; spirit.*
spīrō, 1 (**R.** spas, *to breathe, blow,* spīsā, spīsā, spīrā-re), *to breathe, blow ; breathe forth ; live.*
spissus, a, um, adj. (**R.** spi, *to unite, press,* spi-t-tu-s, spi-s-tu-s, spi-s-su-s), *thick, close-pressed, close, dense.*
splendeō, 2 (**R.** skard, *to shine,* skrad, splad, spled, sple-n-d-ēre), *to shine, glisten, be bright.*
splendēscō, splenduī, splendēscere, *to grow splendid, to shine.*
splendidus, a, um (splendeō), *bright, glistening, splendid.*
spoliō, 1 (**R.** skar, *to cut, strip off,* skal, spal, spol-iu-m, *skin stripped off, enemy stripped of armor,* spoliā-re), *to rob,* of clothing, armor, *to despoil ; to plunder.*
spolium, ī (iī), n. (for **R.**, see spoliō); *the skin of an animal stripped off; spoil, spoils, booty.*
sponda, ae, f. (**R.** spa, spa-n, *to stretch,* span, span-d, spond-a), *a bedstead ; a bed, couch.*
spondeō, spopondī, spōnsum, 2 (**R.** skad, skand, *to please, to offer,* spond-ēre), *to agree, promise in marriage, betroth ; promise.*
sponte, abl. f., fr. lost nom. spon-s (**R.** same as spolium and spatium, spa-, spa-n, *to stretch, make effort, of one's own effort), voluntarily, of one's own accord, spontaneously ; of one's self.*
spūma, ae, f. (**R.** spju, spu, spu-ere, *to spit, spew), foam, froth ; scum.*
spūmāns, tis (part. v., spumō, fr. spuō, see spūma), *foaming, foamy, frothy.*
spūmiger, era, erum, adj. (spūma and gerō), foam-carrying, *or* -making, *foaming.*
squāleō, uī, 2 (**R.** skar, *to cover, clothe,* skal, squāl-ēre), *to be rough or stiff ; to be rough fr. dirt, or fr. slovenliness ; to be dirty or slovenly.*
squālidus, a, um, adj. (squāleō), *stiff, rough* fr. dirt, *dirty, foul, squalid ; in mourning* (as persons in mourning were dressed in *squalid* garments).
squāma, ae, f. (**R.** skad, *to cover,* scad, squā-ma), *a scale,* of a fish or serpent, *scaly covering ;* in pl., *scales* or *plates* in armor.
squāmiger, era, erum, adj. (squāma and gerō), *scale-bearing, scaly.*
squāmōsus, a, um, adj. (squāma), *full of scales, scaly.*
stabulor, 1, v. dep. (stabulum, fr. stō), *to be in stall or stable, to stable, kennel, be stalled.*
stabulum, ī, n. (stō), a standing-place, *stable, stall, fold.*
stāgnō, 1 (stāgnum), *to be covered with standing water, to be stagnant, to stagnate.*
stāgnum, ī, n. (fr. stō, wh. see, sta, sta-k, sta-g), *standing water, a pool, pond, marsh ; lake.*
stāmen, inis, n., fr. stō, sta, stā-re, stā-men, the *standing* threads or fibres of the warp, in weaving; *the warp ; the thread, threads* (in spinning); see note, Met. VI, 55; then *the threads of fate* (as spun by the Parcae); the threads or *strings* of the lyre or other *stringed* musical instrument, as in Met. XI, 169, where see note.
statiō, ōnis, f. (fr. stō), a standing, standing-place, *a station, position ; post, watch.*
statuō, statuī, statūtum, 3 (sta-tu, fr. stō, sta, statu-ere), *to cause to stand, to set in position, to set, set up ; to set firm, determine, ordain.*
status, ūs, m. (statuō), a standing, *a position, condition, state, status.*
stella, ae, f. (**R.** star, *to cover, strew,* ster (ster-n-ere), ster-u-la, stel-la (cf. astrum)), *a star* (single one in distinction fr. sīdus, *a constellation*).
stellātus, a, um, adj. (stella), *covered or studded with stars ; starred, starry.*
sterilis, e, adj. (**R.** same as stō, sta-r, ster, ster-ili-s), *sterile, barren, unfruitful.*
sternō, strāvī, strātum, 3 (for **R.** see stella), *to spread, spread out, strew, cover over, throw down.*
Sthenelēius, a, um, adj., *of Sthenelus,* king of Liguria ; *Sthenelēian.*
stillō, 1 (fr. same **R.** as stō, sta-r, stir, stir-ia, stil-la, *standing, firm, a drop,* stillā-re, *to drop), to drop, drip, trickle, distill ; to let drop.*

stimulus, ī, m. (**R.** stig, *to prick, goad,* stig-mo, sti-mu-lu-s), *a goad, a spur; an incentive, incitement; a spur, stimulus.*

stīpes, itis, m. (same **R.** as stŏ, sta, stip, stĭp, stīpe-s), *the trunk of a tree, a post, stock, log.*

stipula, ae, f. (same **R.** as stīpes, stip-a, stip-u-la), *a stalk; straw; a blade.*

stirps, stirpis, f. (same **R.** as sternō, star, star-p, stirp-e-s, stirp-s), *a stock, stem, root;* figuratively, *stock, race, family.*

stīva, ae, f. (same **R.** as stŏ, sta, stai-vu, stī-vu), *a plow-handle.*

stŏ, stetī, statum, 1 (**R.** sta, *to stand, make to stand,* stā, stā-re), *to stand, stand by, stand fast, remain standing, to stay quiet; to stand by, come to one's aid.*

stolidus, a, um, adj. (same **R.** as stŏ, sta, sta-l, sto-l, stoli-du-s, *standing, unmovable*); *dull, slow, coarse; stolid.*

strā-men, inis, n. (fr. sternō, star, stra), *straw.*

strātum, ī, n. (sternō), *something spread out or upon a couch, bed, bedding, blanket; a covering* (for a table), *cover.*

strĕnuus, a, um, adj. (same **R.** as sterilis, sto, sta, sta-r, ster, stre, strĕ-nuu-s), *quick, busy, active, strenuous.*

strepitus, ūs, m. (strepō, ctym. unc.), *a noise.* rushing sound; *din, roar.*

strīdeō, stridī, 2, and strīdō, strīdī, 3 (**R.** star, *to sound,* star-g, star-dh, stra-dh, stri-dh, strīd-ēre, ere), to make a harsh sound, *to hiss, whiz, creak, rush, roar, rattle, buzz.*

strīdor, ōris, m. (strīdeō), *a harsh sound or noise,* a hissing, *whizzing, creaking, rattling, roaring.*

strīdulus, a, um. adj. (strīdeō), *hissing, whizzing, rattling.*

stringō, strinxī, strictum, 3 (**R.** same as sternō, star, stra-g, strig, string, stri-n-g-ere), *to touch lightly, graze; to wound slightly; to draw* (of weapons), as *to draw a sword.*

struŏ, xī, ctum, 3 (**R.** same as stringō, star, stra, stri, stru, stru-ere), *to pile, heap up; to join or fit together; to build, construct.*

Strymōn, onis, m., a river in Thrace; *the Strymon.*

studiōsus, a, um, adj. (studium), *full of zeal or desire; zealous, eager, desirous.*

studium, ī (ii), n. (**R.** spa, spa-n, *to make effort,* spa-d, spu-d, stu-dĕ-re, stud-iu-m), *intense effort, zeal, eagerness, earnestness, studious fondness, study; an occupation, a pursuit.*

stultus, a, um, adj. (same **R.** as stolidus, wh. see, sta-l, sto-l, stul-tus), *stupid, dull, foolish, fool.*

stupeō, uī, 2 (same **R.** as stultus, stu-p, stŭp-ere), (to be stupid), *to be dazed, amazed, dazzled,* from terror or other strong emotion.

Stygius, a, um. adj. (Styx), *Stygian; hateful, abhorred.*

Stymphālis, idis, adj., *Stymphalian,* of the river or lake Stymphalus, in Arcadia.

Styx, ygis, f. (Στύξ), the river of hate, "abhorred Styx," name of a river in the lower world, *the Styx.*

suādeō, suāsī, suāsum, 2 (**R.** svad, *to please, taste,* suad, suad-u-s, suad-ēre, *to make pleasing*), *to persuade; to advise, counsel, encourage.*

sub, prep. (**R.** upa, *under* (ὑπό), sub), 1, with the abl., *under, underneath, below, beneath, close under, under in or within, close by, under the rule of, under the influence of, in consequence or by occasion of;* 2, with the acc., *upon, up to, toward, under, against, close by, about, forth.*

sub-dŏ, didī, ditum, dere, 3, *to put* or *lay under, bring under.*

sub-dūcō, xī, ctum, 3, *to draw under or away, draw up; to draw in; to withdraw.*

sub-eō, īvī, iī, itum, 4, *to go under or beneath, to go into, undergo, take upon one's self; to go toward; to take the place of, to follow; to occur to, come into the mind of.*

sub-igō, ēgī, actum, 3, *to drive or force under,* to compel, force, subdue; *to work through, plow.*

sŭb-iciō, jēcī, jectum. 3, *to throw or cast under, to subject;* part., subjectus, *cast under, lying under; to throw* (from under), *on high* (into the air).

subitus, a, um, adj. (subeō), *that comes unexpectedly* or *stealthily ; sudden, unexpected.*

sub-jungō, junxī, junctum, 3, *to attach* or *join to ; add to* or *unite with.*

sub-levō, 1, *to lift up from beneath, hold up, support.*

sublīmis, e, adj. (fr. sub *and* līmis, fr. **R.** LAK, *to bend,* lac, lic, līć, lic-mu-s, līc-men, lī-men, *head-piece* or *top of a door-way,* sub-līmis, *under the top of a door, high*), *lifted up, high, lofty, uplifted, on high ; sublime, noble ;* subst., sublīmia, *the lofty, the sublime.*

sub-mergō, mersī, mersum, 3, *to sink under, submerge.*

sub-mittō (summ-), mīsī, missum, 3, *to send* or *sink under, sink, let down ; to submit, lower ; to yield to, give up to.*

sub-moveō (summ-), mōvī, mōtum, 2 (to move from under), *to move away, remove, carry* or *drive away.*

sub-nectō, nexuī, nexum, 3 (to bind from beneath), *to bind under, bind around, fasten under.*

subolēs, is (sub-olēscō), something that grows after, an after-growth, *a new race, offspring, progeny ; a descendant ; descendants.*

sub-sequor, sequī, secūtus sum, v. dep., *to follow upon* or *after.*

sub-sīdō, sedī, sessum, *to set one's self down, sink down ; to sink, settle ; subside.*

sub-sum, fuī, esse, *to be under, lie under, underlie ; to be near by.*

subtēmen, inis, n. (fr. sub *and* texo, fr. **R.** TAK, *to order, arrange,* tak-s, tax, tex, tex-ere, sub-tex-men, sub-tē-men), *the woof ;* see note, Met. VI, 55.

subter (fr. sub), prep. with acc. or abl., *under, beneath.*

succēdō (sub, cēdō), cessī, cessum, 3, *to go* or *pass under,* or *into, step in one's place, succeed, follow after, follow ; to succeed, be successful.*

suc-cendō (sub, candō, candeō, fr. **R.** SKAND, kand, *to shine, burn,* cand-ūre), cendī, cēnsum, 3, *to set on fire from under, to inflame, burn.*

successor, ōris, m. (succēdō), a successor ; *an heir.*

successus, ūs, m. (succēdō), fortunate result, *success.*

succingō, cinxī, cinctum (sub *and* cingō), *to bind under* or *about, to gird about, gird up ; to bind up ;* part., succinctus, *girt.*

succumbō (sub *and* cumbō), cubuī, cubitum, 3, *to fall under ; to give way to, succumb.*

suc-currō (sub *and* currō), currī, cursum, 3, *to run to the aid of, help, succor.*

succutiō (subc-), (sub *and* quatiō), cussī, cussum, 3, *to throw* or *fling up, fling on high, toss up.*

sūcus, I, m. (**R.** SAK, sag, *to drop, flow,* svak, sūc-u-s), *juice, moisture, sap ; flavor ; vigor.*

sūdō, 1 (**R.** SVID, *to sweat,* sūd, sudā-re), *to sweat ; to be wet with.*

sūdor, ōris, m. (sūdō), *sweat ; poison.*

sufficiō (sub *and* faciō), fecī, fectum, 3, *to suffice, be enough for ; to be at one's service, be ready.*

suffundō (sub *and* fundō), fūdī, fū-sum, 3, *to pour in* or *upon ; to suffuse.*

suī, reflex. pron. 3d pers. (**R.** suva, sva, sovo, svo, sovo-s, suu-s, suī), *one's self, himself, herself, itself, themselves, each other, one another.*

sulcō, 1, etym. unc., *to furrow ; to plow.*

sulcus, I, m., *a furrow.*

sulphur (sulpur), uris, n., ctym. unc., *sulphur.*

sum, fuī, esse (**R.** AS, *to be,* es, es-u-m, s-u-m), *to be, exist, live ; to stand, find one's self, to be really ;* with dat., *to have, possess ;* with gen., *to be of, to belong to, to pass for ;* with dat. of end, *to serve for, be for, to cause ;* part., futūrus, futūrum, *about to be, the future.*

summa, ae, f. (fr. summus, fr. **R.** UPA, upa-ma, up-mu-s, s-up-mu-s, sum-mu-s, summa), the uppermost thing, *the chief thing, the conclusion of the whole, the sum, the whole.*

summus (**R.** as in summa ; for meaning, see superus).

sūmō, sumpsī, sumptum, 3 (sub-emō), *to take, take up, bear, wear, put on, lay hold of, receive, choose.*

super (**R.** same as sub, upa, upari, *above, over* (ὑπέρ), super), adv. and prep., *above, over, upon, over above, in addi-*

tion to, besides ; furthermore ; from above ; concerning, about, of.

superātor, ōris, m. (superō, super), (an overcomer), *a conqueror.*

superbia, ae, f. (super), *pride, haughtiness.*

superbus, a, um, adj. (super), one that raises himself *above* another, *haughty, high-spirited, proud;* Superbus, epithet of the younger Tarquin.

super-in-iciō, jēcī, jectum, 3, *to throw* or *cast over* or *above* or *upon.*

superō (same **R.** as super, upa, *above*, supe-ru-s, superā (sc. parte, supra), superā-re), *to be above, rise above ; to get the better of, overcome, surpass; to exceed, rise above, project beyond ; to conquer.*

superstes, stitis, adj. (super and stō), *standing over, projecting over; surviving, outliving ; a survivor.*

super-sum, fuī, esse, *to be over, remain over ; to survive, abound.*

superus, a, um, adj. (for **R.** sec superō), *being above, on high, high ; heavenly;* in pl., superī, *the heavenly ones, the gods, the gods above ;* superl., 1, suprēmus, a, um (probably also fr. superō, super), *the highest, extreme, last ;* 2, summus, a, um (see summa), *the highest, top of, uppermost, head of; supreme, most distinguished, chief, greatest ;* subst., summum, n., *the chief thing, chief point, the end.*

supīnus, a, um, adj. (fr. sub, wh. sec. sup, sup-īnus), *bent back, laid on the back ;* (of the hands), *turned back, upturned, in supplication.*

suppleō (sub *and* pleō), plēvī, plētum, 2, *to fill out* or *up, to supply.*

supplex, icis, adj. (sub *and* plex fr. **R.** PARK, PARSK, *to ask, demand, plak, plic ;* = sup-plicāre, sup-plex, sup-plic-is), *asking humbly, begging, entreating, suppliant, as a suppliant, in supplication.*

supplicium, ī (iī), n. (see supplex, supplic-iu-m), *the bending* or *kneeling down, in punishment ; supplication ;*

punishment ; heavy penalty ; capital punishment ; torture.

supplicō, 1 (see supplex for **R.**), *to ask humbly, supplicate.*

suppōnō (sub *and* pōnō), posuī, positum, 3, *to put* or *place under; to put in place of, substitute.*

suprā (superā, sc. parte, see superō), *above, over.*

sūra, ae, f., *the calf of the leg.*

surdus, a, um, adj., *deaf.*

surgō (sub *and* regō), surrexī, surrectum, 3, *to raise on high, lift up ; to raise one's self ; to arise, rise ; to join on, fit to.*

sūs, suis, comm. (**R.** su, *to produce, beget*, su-s, *a sow*), *a boar, pig, sow, swine.*

suscitō (fr. sub *and* citō), 1, *to stir up, arouse.*

suspendō (sub *and* pendō), *to hang up, hang, suspend; to leave in suspense.*

suspiciō (sub *and* speciō), *to look up* (from under), *to observe, notice ;* part., suspectus, *suspected.*

suspicor, 1, v. dep. (sub *and* speciō, spicāri), *to suspect, conjecture.*

suspīrium (sub *and* -spīrium fr. spīrō), *to breathe up from below*), *a sigh, sighing.*

sustineō (sub *and* teneō), *to hold up, support, sustain ; to bear, carry, hold ; to withstand, hold out.*

susurrus, ī, m. (**R.** SVAR, *to sound, sar,* sar-sar, sur-sur, su-surr-u-s), *a whisper, whispering ; a murmur;* personified, Susurrī, *the Whispers.*

suus, a, um, reflex. pron. possessive, 3d pers. (for **R.** sec suī), *one's own, his own, her own, its own, their own ; favorable, propitious ;* pl., suī, substantively used, *his* (her, their) *friends, companions.*

Symaethius, a, um, adj., *of* or descended from Symaethus ; *Symaethian.*

Symplēgades, um, f. pl (fr. Gr.), *the Symplegades*, two islands in the Euxine, that *dash against* (συμπλήσσω), one another.

T

tabella, ae, f. (**R.** TA, *to extend, broaden*, ta-bola, tabula), *a plank, board, a little board ; a tablet* (covered with wax, to write upon with a stilus) ; *a votive tablet ;* by meton., *a letter.*

tābēs, is, f. (**R.** TAK, *to run, flow*, tābes), a flowing away, *wasting, pining, consumption;* a corrupting *moisture, corruption; poison.*

tābēscō (tābēs), tābuī, 3, *to waste away; to dissolve, waste away, melt.*

tabula, ae, f. (for **R.** see tabella), *a tablet, a painting.*

tābum, ī, n. (tābēs), *wasting, moisture, corruption; wasting disease, consumption.*

taceō, uī (**R.** TAK, *to be silent,* tacēre), *to be silent* (not to speak), *keep silent, be still.*

taciturnus, a, um, adj. (taceō), *silent, still; taciturn.*

tacitus, a, um, adj. (taceō), *silent, quiet, still.*

tactus, ūs, m. (tangō), *touch, contact.*

taeda, ae, f. (**R.** TU, *to swell, grow,* tau, tav, tav-i-da, ta-i-da, tae-da), *a pine-tree, pine-wood, a pitch-pine, a pine-torch, torch;* (from torches being used at marriages), *a wedding-torch, a wedding, marriage, marriage union.*

taedium, ī (iī), n. (**R.** same as taeda, tu, tau, tav, ta-vido, taedo, taede-t, *it swells, over-swells), it disgusts, wearies, is irksome, one is weary of.*

Taenaridēs, ae, one from Taenarus, a promontory in Laconia; *a Laconian,* Hyacinthus, in Met. X, 183.

Taenarius, a, um, adj., *of Taenarus.*

taeter, tra, trum, adj., *foul.*

Tagus, ī, m., a river in Spain; *the Tagus.*

tālaria, um, adj., n. pl. (tālus), *of the heel,* the talaria, the winged sandals of Mercury.

tālis, e, adj. (**R.** TA (?) as in tantus, pron. stem, 3d pers., ta-lis), *such, of such kind or sort;* subst., tālia, *such things, things of that kind.*

tālus, ī, m. (**R.** TAK, *to cut, hew, arrange,* tak-s, tax-lu-s, tas-lu-s, tā-lu-s), *the ankle-bone, ankle.*

tam, adv. (**R.** TA, pron. stem, 3d pers., ta+me; loc. fem., ta-m, originally referring to *time,* then to *manner), so, so much, so very, so far;* with quam, *so—as, as well—as.*

Tamasēnus, a, um, adj. (-sēnus), *of* the city of *Tamasus,* in Cyprus; *Tamasean.*

tamen, conj. (**R.** same as tam, ta-m, ta+pron. sma ; locat., ta+smin,= ta-me-n), *for all that; yet, nevertheless, still, however, after all, at least.*

tamquam (tanq-), adv. (tam-quam, for **RR.** see tam *and* quam), *so as, just as, as if, as when.*

Tanais, is, m., a river in Scythia; *the Don.*

tandem, adv. (fr. ta, pron. stem, 3d pers., ta-m, ta-n+da, pron. stem de, acc. de-m,=tan-dem, *so far* (in time), *to that), at last, finally, at length, yet again.*

tangō, tetigī, tactum, 3 (**R.** STAG, *to grasp, tag,* ta-n-g-ere), *to touch, come in contact with; to tread; to impress, touch; to lay hold of, seize.*

Tantalis, idis, daughter *of Tantalus;* Niobe, Met. VI, 211.

Tantalus, ī, m., 1, son of Jupiter, father of Pelops, and of Niobe ; see notes on Met. VI, 173, X, 41 ; 2, grandson of the T. just mentioned, and son of Niobe, Met. VI, 240.

tantum, adv. (tantus), *so much, only, merely,* with nē, *only that not,* with non and verum, *not only—but, not only—but also.*

tantum-modo, adv., *only, merely.*

tantus, a, um, adj. (**R.** same as tam, ta, ta-ntu-s), *so great, so much, such, such great;* neut., tantum, *so much, so;* gen. of price, tanti, of so much, *such a price,* used with sum, *to be worth so much.*

tardē, adv. (tardus), *slowly, tardily.*

tardus, a, um, adj. (**R.** TAR, TRA, *to move,* tar-du-s), *slow-moving, slow, sluggish, dull, tardy, late.*

Tartarus, ī, m., pl. Tartara, ōrum, n. (**R.** (fr. Gr.), TAR, *tremble, make tremble, terrify*), terrible, the terrible (terrē-re fr. same **R.**), a deep abyss fabled to be under the infernal regions; *Tartarus,* as the abode of the lost ; by meton., *the lower world.*

Taurus, ī, m., 1, a range of mountains in Asia Minor; *the Taurus;* 2, (**R.** same as stō, sta, sta-vara, stau-ru-s, ταυρός, tau-ru-s, *a steer), a bull, steer;* 3, *the* constellation *Taurus.*

tectum, ī, n. (tegō), *a covering; a*

roof; ceiling; by meton., *a dwelling, a house, an abode, a home, a hiding-place, a room.*

tegimen, inis, n. (tegum-, syncopated to tegmen, fr. tegō), *a covering, garb, clothing, protection, defense, armor, a skin (a tegument).*

tegō, texī, tectum (R. STAG, *to cover,* steg, teg, teg-erc), *to cover, cover over, clothe; to surround, attend, defend, adorn, veil, to hide, conceal;* part., tectus, *covered, protected, sheltered, hidden, secret.*

tēla, ae, f. (fr. texō (texla), tĕla), *the web; the warp; the loom;* see note, Met. VI, 54.

Tēlemus, I, m., son of Eurymus, a seer; Met. XIII, 770.

tellus, ūris, f. (R. TAR, TAL, *to lift, weigh, to make like* or *level*, tal, tel, tellu-s, *level* or *surface* of the earth), *the earth, land, soil, ground; a land, district, country, region.*

tēlum, I, n. (R. TAK, *to cut, hew,* tec, tec-lu-m, tĕ-lu-m), *a weapon, missile, javelin, dagger, sword.*

temerārius, a, um, adj. (temerē, fr. R. TAM, *to be stunned, be beside one's self*, tem-ere, temer-ārius), *inconsiderate, thoughtless, heedless, rash.*

temerō, 1 (temere, see temerārius), *to treat rashly, to defile, stain, pollute;* part., temerātus, *stained, unclean, impure.*

tēmō, ōnis, m. (R. TAK, *to hew, cut,* tec, tec-mōn), *the pole* of a chariot; *beam* of a plow.

temperiēs, ēī, f. (tempus, wh. see), *a right mingling* of heat and cold, *a mild climate,* an agreeable *temperature; moderation.*

temperō, 1 (tempus), to mingle in right proportion, *to rule, moderate, govern; to temper.*

tempestīvus, a, um, adj. (tempus, (wh. see), tempes-tas, tempestāt, īvu-s, tempest-īvu-s), suited to the time or occasion, *timely, seasonable, opportune, fitting.*

tempestīvē (tempestīvus), adv., *seasonably, opportunely; happily.*

templum, i, n. (R. TAM, *to cut off,* tem, tem-u-lu-m, tem-lu-m, tem-p-lu-m), a place *cut off,* set apart, for uses of augury, a free space, then a sacred place, *a sanctuary, temple.*

temptō (tentō), 1 (fr. tendō), *to put to a trial, attempt, prove; tempt.*

tempus, oris, n. (R. TA, TAN, *to stretch, span,* tan-p, tam-p, temp-us, *time* as a *span;* but others take it fr. TAM, tem, *to cut off,* same R. as templum), *a time, opportunity, season; a period; a right time, an occasion; the time, the age; the times, circumstances; the temple* on the head, *the temples.*

tendō, tetendī, tentum, tensum, 3 (R. same as tempus, ta, tan, ten-dō), *to stretch, span, extend,* stretch out; *tend, strive for, hasten.*

tenebrae, ārum, f. pl. (R. same as temere, tem, then (m to n), ten-e-brae), *darkness, gloom; terror.*

tenebrōsus, a, um, adj. (tenebrae), *full of darkness, dark; gloomy.*

Tenedos, I, f., an island in the Aegean, off the Trojan coast.

teneō, uī, tentum, 2 (R. same as tendō, ta, tan, ten-ēre), *to hold, hold fast, grasp, bear, keep; to possess; to reach; to hold back, restrain.*

tener, era, erum, adj. (R. same as teneō, ta, tan, ten, ten-er), *soft, tender; weak; youthful.*

tenor, ōris, m. (teneō), *a course, progress, tenor.*

tenuis, e, adj. (R. same as tener), *thin, fine, narrow, weak, tender.*

tenuō, 1 (R. same as tenuis), *to make thin, to thin, to make weaker, weaken.*

tenus, prep. (R. same as tendō), *as far as, up to.*

tepeō, 2 (R. TAP, *to be warm,* tep, tep-ēre), *to be warm.*

tepēscō, 3 (tepeō), *to grow warm.*

tepidus, a, um, adj. (tepeō), *warm, tepid.*

ter, num. adv. (R. same as trēs, tri, tirs, ters, ter), *thrice, three times.*

terebrō, 1 (R. TAR, *to move, to rub,* ter, ter-ere, terebra-re), *to bore, to bore through* or *into.*

teres, etis, adj. (terō), (rubbed, worn), *rounded, smooth, well rounded.*

tergeō, tersī, tersum, 2 (also tergō), (R. same as sternō, STAR, star-g, ster-g, terg-ēre), *to wipe off, to clean.*

tergum, I, n. (R. TARGH, *to move,*

TERGUS   TIMIDUS   323

hasten, terg-u-m), *the back ; the rear ; a hide, bull's-hide.*
tergus, oris, n. (tergum), *the back ; a hide.*
ternī, ae, a, num. adj. (ter), *three by three, three each ; threefold.*
terō, trīvī, trītum, 3 (for **R.** see terebrō), *to rub, to rub smooth ; to wear away ; to touch lightly, graze.*
terra, ae, f. (**R.** TARS, *to be dry,* ters, ters-a, terr-a), *dry land,* as opposed to the sea, *the earth ; earth, land, mainland, region ; soil ; the Earth.*
terrēnus, a, um, adj. (terra), *of the earth, earthy, earthen ; belonging to the earth, earthly.*
terreō, uī, itum, 2 (**R.** TAR, *to tremble, make tremble,* tars, ters-ēre, terr-ēre), *to terrify, frighten.*
terribilis, e, adj. (terreō), *terrible, frightful.*
terrigena, ae, comm. (terra, gignō), *one born of earth, earth-born.*
terror, ōris, m. (terreō), *terror ; a terror ; fright.*
tertius, a, um, adj. (ter), *the third.*
tesca, ōrum, n. (TUSKA, TESQUA, *empty, worthless,* tesca), *rough, wild regions, deserts, wilds, wilderness.*
testa, ae, f. (**R.** same as terra, tar, tars, ters, ters-ta, tes-ta), *baked clay, pottery, a tile, potsherds.*
testis, is, m. (**R.** TARS, *to hold, support,* ters, ters-ti, tes-ti-s), *a witness.*
testor, 1, v. dep. (testis), *to testify, bear witness to, declare ; to summon as a witness, call upon.*
Tēthys, yos, f., a sea-goddess, wife of Oceanus, and mother of Clymene.
texō, texuī, textum, 3 (**R.** TAK, *to cut, to set in order,* tak-s, tax, tex-ere), *to put together, to weave, braid.*
textum, I, n. (texō), *something woven, a fabric, texture.*
thalamus, I, m. (θάλαμος. fr. **R.** DHAR, DHRA, *to hold*), *a room, chamber, a bed-chamber ;* by meton., *marriage.*
Thalīa, ae, f., one of the Muses, the Muse of Comedy ; *Thalia.*
Thaumantis, idos, daughter of Thaumas ; Iris.
theātrum, I, n. (θεά-ο-μαι, *to see*), *a theatre ;* by meton., *the spectators.*

Thēbae, ārum, f., *Thebes,* capital of Boeotia.
Thēbais, idis, f. (Thēbae), a woman of Thebes ; in pl., Thēbaides, the women of Thebes.
Themis, idis, f., daughter of Uranus, and goddess of order and justice.
Thermōdōn, ontis, m., a river in Cappadocia.
Thermōdontiacus, a, um, adj., *of the Thermodon.*
Thēseus, eī (eos), son of king Aegeus of Athens, *Theseus.*
Thisbē, ēs, f., the maiden loved by Pyramus ; Met. IV, 55.
Thrācius, a, um, adj. (Thrācia), *of Thrace ; a Thracian.*
Thrāx, ācis, adj. (Thrācia), *a Thracian.*
Thrēicius, a, um, adj., *the Thracian ; Orpheus.*
Thymbrēius, a, um, adj., *Thymbreian, of the river Thymbris.*
thyrsus, I, m., *a stalk* of a plant ; a staff twined round with ivy ; *the Bacchic staff, the thyrsus.*
tiāra, ae, f., or tiāras, ae, m., an Eastern head-dress, worn by Orientals of rank, *a turban, a tiara.*
Tiberis, is, or idis, m. (Tibris, Tybris), the river Tiber, in Latium, now the Tevere ; *the Tiber.*
tībia, ae, f. (**R.** STA, *to stand, make to stand firm,* sta-bh, tib, tīb, tīb-ia, *the shin-bone, as something standing firm) ;* by meton., *a pipe* or *flute,* because made of bone.
Tibullus, I, m. ; see note, Am. I, 15, 28.
tignum, I, n. (**R.** TAK, *to hew,* tignu-m), *a beam, rafter.*
tīgris, idis, and is, m. and f., *a tiger.*
tilia, ae, f. (**R.** PAT. *to spread out, be open,* pat-ēre, patul-ia, patil-ia, ptil-i-a, til-ia), *the linden.*
timeō, uī, 2 (**R.** same as temerārius, TAM, *to be stunned, to be beside one's self,* tem, tim, tim-or, tim-ēre, primarily, *to be disturbed in one's mind*), *to fear, be afraid, to have fear of.*
timidē, adv. (timeō), *timidly, fearfully.*
timidus, a, um, adj. (timeō), *timid, fearful, frightened.*

timor, ōris, m. (for **R.** see timeō), *fear, fearfulness;* by meton., *object of fear, a terror.*

tingō (tinguō), tinxī, tinctum, 3 (**R.** TVAK, *to wash,* tak, tag, tig, ti-n-g-ere), *to wet, dip, bathe, color; tinge.*

tinus, I, m., a tree resembling the wild laurel, and having bluish berries.

Tiresias, ae, m., a Theban seer.

Tirynthius, a, um, adj., of the city *Tiryns,* in Argolis; *Tirynthian; the Tirynthian.*

Tītān, ānis, m., the Sun-god (Sōl), son of Hyperion.

Tītānia, ae, f., and **Tītānis,** idos, daughter of a Titan; 1, Pyrrha, as grand-daughter of Iapetus; 2, Latona, as daughter of Coëus.

titubō, 1 (etym. unc.), *to reel, stumble, stagger.*

titulus, I, m. (**R.** KI, *to notice, honor,* ti, ti-tu-lu-s, *means of honor), a name of honor, honor; a mark of honor, a title.*

Tityos (-us), I, m., a giant-son of Earth; see note, Met. X, 43.

Tmōlus (Timolus), I, name of a wine-growing region in Lydia.

toga, ae, f. (fr. tegō, fr. **R.** STAG, *to cover,* steg, teg, tog-a), *the toga,* the gown-like, outer garment of the Roman citizen.

tolerō, 1 (**R.** TAR, TAL, *to lift, carry,* tel, tol, tol-lo (tol-es, toler-u-s), tol-crā-re), *to bear, carry, tolerate.*

tollō, sustulī, sublātum, 3 (for **R.** see tolerō), *to lift* or *take up, to raise up; to carry away, to remove; to put aside.*

Tomītae, ārum, name of a town; see note, Tr. IV, 10, 97.

tondeō, totondī, tōnsum, 2 (**R.** TAM, TAN, *to cut,* ton-d-ēre), *to shear, cut, trim, strip.*

tonitrus, ūs, m. (tonō) *thunder.*

tonō, tonuī, 1 (**R.** TA, TAN, *to stretch, sound,* ten, ton, tōn-āre), *to sound, to thunder;* part., tonāns, sc. Juppiter, *the Thunderer.*

tormentum, I, n. (torqueō), *an instrument of torture, the rack; torture;* also *an engine* for throwing missiles, so called because thrown by means of *twisted* (torqueō) ropes.

torpeō, 2 (**R.** TARP, *to be stiff,* torp, torp-ēre), *to be stiff; to stiffen.*

torpor, ōris, m. (torpeō), *stiffness, numbness, torpor.*

torqueō, torsī, tortum, 2 (**R.** TARK, *to turn,* tar+k, torqu-ēre), *to turn, twist, wind; to throw, hurl.*

torreō, torruī, tostum, 2 (**R.** same as terra, tars, ters, tors, tors-ēre, torr-ēre), *to dry; to roast, to parch.*

tortilis, e, adj. (torqueō), *twisted around, encircling.*

torus, I, m. (**R.** STAR, *to strew, spread,* ster, stor, tor-u-s, *something spread out* or *spreading), a mattress, couch, bed, marriage-bed;* by meton., *marriage; a bolster, cushion; a bier;* also the (spreading) swelling *muscles,* especially of the neck; *the dew-lap* or *brawn;* see note, Met. IX, 82.

torvus, a, um, adj. (**R.** TARG, *to threaten,* torg-vu-s, tor-vu-s), *gloomy, grim, fierce, savage; angry; earnest.*

tot, num. adj. (**R.** TA, 3d pers. pron. stem ta + ti, to-t), *so many.*

totidem, adj., fr. tot, toti-dem (ta + da), *just so many, just as many, as many.*

totiēns, adj. (totiēs), tot-iēns, *so many times, as many times, so often.*

tōtus, a, um, adj., *ius in gen.,* I in dat. (**R.** TU, *to swell, grow,* tau, tav, tou, to, tō-tu-s, *full, whole), entire, whole; wholly; all, all together.*

trabea, ae, f. (**R.** TARPJA, *a cloak, mantle,* trab-ea), a robe woven in stripes, and worn by magistrates, *a trabea, a robe.*

trabs (trabēs), -is, f. (**R.** TARK, *to turn,* tarp, tarb, trab-es, trab-s), *a beam, timber; the trunk of a tree; a tree.*

Trāchin, īnis, a city in Thessaly.

Trāchīnius, a, um, adj., *of Trachin, Trachinian.*

tractō, 1 (trahō), *to touch, handle.*

tractus, ūs, m., *a drawing; a stretch.*

trādō (trans-dō), -didī, ditum, -dere, 3, *to give over, hand over, surrender; to communicate, teach.*

trahō, traxī, tractum, 3 (**R.** TARGH, *to move, set in motion,* tragh, trah-ere), *to draw, drag, carry away, to carry with* or *behind* or *after one's self; to attract; to receive, get; to draw in,*

breathe; to draw up, heave; to draw out; to extend; to spend; while away.
trāiciō (trāns, jaciō), jēcī, jectum, 3, *to pierce through.*
trāmes, itis, m., *a cross-way, path.*
trāns, prep. with acc. (**R.** TAR, tra, *to move, move one's self,* trā-rc, tra-ns, part. present, *passing over*), *over, across, through.*
trāns-eō, iī (īvī), itum, 4, *to go or pass over, cross, pass or go by, pass over to, change one's self; to spring over.*
trāns-ferō, tulī, lātum, 3, *to carry over.*
trānsiliō, īvī or uī, 4, *to leap over.*
transitus, ūs, m. (trānseō), *a passage over or across; a transition.*
trāns-mittō, mīsī, missum, 3, *to carry or send over or across, send.*
tremebundus, a, um, adj. (for **R.** see tremō, *and* -bundus, see Grammar, 333, note 2), *trembling, quivering.*
tremefaciō (tremō *and* faciō), fēcī, factum, 3, *to make tremble, to shake.*
tremō, uī, 3 (**R.** TAR, *to quiver, shake,* tar-m, trem, trem-cre), *to tremble, quiver, quake, shake with fear.*
tremor, ōris, m. (tremō), *a trembling, quivering, tremor.*
tremulus, a, um, adj. (tremō), *trembling, tremulous.*
trepidō, 1 (**R.** TARK, *to turn, hurl,* tarp, trep, trep-i-du-s, trepidā-re, meaning *hasty* (tripping?) *movement, through fear*), *to hurry to and fro in fear, to move tremulously; to tremble, quake, quiver.*
trepidus, a, um, adj. (for **R.** see trepidō), *in tremulous movement, hurrying, hastening, trembling; frightened, fearful.*
trēs, tria, adj. num. (**R.** TRI, *three,* treis, trēs), *three.*
tribulus, ī, m. (τρίβολος), 1, *an instrument used against the approach of cavalry, having three prongs, on which it rested, and a fourth thrown upward; a caltrop;* 2, *a species of thorn, land-caltrop.*
tribuō, uī, ūtum, 3 (**R.** TRI, *three,* + nnu, *to grow, become, be,* bu,=tri-bu, tri-bu-s (tri-be), meaning *three-* (or *tri-*) *being,* one of *three stocks* or *races* of free Roman citizens (Ramnes, Tities, Lu-ceres); then tribu-ere), *to divide, distribute, bestow, allow, grant.*
tricuspis, idis, adj. (tri *and* cuspis, etym. unc.), *three-pointed, three-tined.*
tridēns, ntis, adj. (tri *and* dēns), *three-toothed, three-pronged.*
trifidus, a, um, adj. (findō), *three-cleft, three-forked.*
triformis, e, adj. (forma), *three-formed, threefold, triple.*
triō, ōnis, m. (**R.** same as terō, cre, tar, ter, tir, tir-o(n), tri-ō(n)), *an ox, a steer;* in pl., Triōnes, the constellation of the Wain, having seven stars—five for the wagon and two for the *steers,* or the team; see note, Met. I, 64; but Max Müller makes triō originally striō,TĀRĀ, Skr. STAR, meaning *a star;* by meton. (Met. I, 64, septem-triō); *the north.*
triplex, icis, adj. (**R.** tri+park, plak, plec, plec-s, plex, see sim-plex), *threefold, triple; three.*
tristis, e, adj. (**R.** same as tremō, tar, ters, tris, tris-ti-s), *sad, mournful, gloomy, sorrowful.*
trīticeus, a, um, adj. (trīticum, fr. same **R.** as terō, tar, ter, ter-cre, trī-vī, trī-tu-m, trī-ti-cu-m, from the *rubbing* or *threshing* of the grain; *wheat*), *of or pertaining to wheat, wheaten.*
Trītōn, ōnis, m., *a sea-god, son of Neptune and Amphitrite; Triton.*
Trītōnia, ae, f., *a name of Minerva;* see note, Met. II, 782.
Trītōniacus, a, um, adj., *of Tritonia, Tritonian.*
Trītōnis, idis, f., same as Trītōnia; also as an adj., *of Tritonia, Tritonian.*
triumphō, 1 (for **R.** see triumphus), *to triumph, celebrate a triumph; exult, triumph over or in.*
triumphus, ī, m. (**R.** TRIAMPO, *a shout of joy,* triumpu-s, triumphu-s), *the triumph, triumphal procession; a triumph, victory.*
Trōjānus (Trōja), a, um, adj., *Trojan; the Trojans.*
truculentus, a, um, adj. (**R.** TRU, *to threaten,* tru-co, tru-c, tru-cu-lentu-s, truc-s, tru-x), *fierce, savage, wild.*
truncus, a, um, adj. (**R.** TARK, turk, *to break, tear,* tru-n-cu-s), *broken.*
truncō, 1, *to strip (leaves off).*
truncus, ī, m. (**R.** same as the adj.

truncus), *the trunk of a tree, the trunk of a human body, a headless trunk.*

trux, trucis, adj. (for **R.** see truculentus), *savage, wild, grim, fierce, defiant.*

tū, tuī, pers. pron. (**R.** TVA, tu), *thou ;* pl., vos, *ye* or *you.*

tuba, ae, f. (**R.** same as tībia, STA, *to stand, make firm,* sta-bh, stab, tīb, tob, tub-a, *a reed, a tube), a trumpet.*

tueor, tuitus (tūtus), v. dep. 2 (**R.** TU, *to behold, protect,* tu-o-r, tu-e-or), *to behold, contemplate, consider ; to protect, defend, guard.*

tum, adv. (**R.** TA, demon. pron. stem, 3d pers., tu-m, acc.), *at that time, then ; in that case ; thereupon, then again, then.*

tumefaciō (tumeō and faciō), -fecī, factum, 3, *to cause to swell, to swell.*

tumeō, 2 (**R.** TU, *to swell,* tu-mo, tumō-re), *to swell, be swollen ; to be puffed up.*

tumēscō, tumuī, 3 (tumeō), *to begin to swell, to swell.*

tumidus, a, um, adj. (tumeō), *swelling.* **tumulus,** I, m., *a mound.*

tunc, adv. (**R.** same as tum, tu, tu-m, tum-ce, tun-c).

tundō, tutudī, tunsum, and tūsum, 3 (**R.** STU, *to thrust,* stu-d, tud, tu-n-d-ere), *to beat, strike, thrust.*

tunica, ae, f., etym. unc., the undergarment of the Romans, *a tunic, frock.*

turba, ae, f. (**R.** STVAR, stur, *to press forward,* tvar-va, tur-ba), *a press, confusion, disturbance ; a crowd, throng.*

turbō, inis, m. (**R.** same as turba), *a whirl, whirling, eddy, whirlwind, storm, hurricane; a round, a circle.*

turbō, 1 (**R.** same as turba), *to disturb, confuse, agitate, alarm.*

turpis, e, adj. (**R.** TARK, tarp, *to be ashamed,* turp, turp-i-s), *shameful, base, foul, unseemly, disgraceful.*

turris, is, f. (**R.** TURSI, *a tower,* turri-s), *a tower.*

tūs (thūs), tūris, n. (**R.** DHU, *to smoke, to offer sacrifice,* tūs, thūs, fr. Gr. θύ-ος), *incense, frankincense.*

tūtēla, ae, f. (tueor), *protection ; defense ;* by meton., *protector, guardian.*

tūtō, adv. (tūtus), *safely, securely, without danger.*

tūtus, a, um, adj. (tueor), *safe, secure, protected, without danger, unharmed.*

tuus, a, um, possessive pron. (for **R.** see tū), *thine, thine own, your, your own ;* in pl. as subst., tuī, *your friends* (yours).

Tyanēius, a, um, adj., *of Tyana,* a city in Cappadocia.

tympanum, I, n., *a drum, timbrel,* used in the service of Bacchus, and of Cybele.

Typhōeus, eī, m., *a giant-son of Earth ;* see note, Met. V, 347.

tyrannus, I, m. (Gr. τύραννος), *a sovereign ; a ruler, a king.*

Tyriēius, a, um, adj., *of Tyriaeum,* a city in Phrygia.

Tyrius, a, um, adj., *Tyrian, of Tyre.*

Tyros (-us), I, *Tyre,* a city in Phoenicia.

U

uber, eris, n. (**R.** VADH, UDH, *to make fruitful,* ub, ub-er), *an udder ; the breast.*

uber, eris, adj. (see preceding word for **R.**), *fruitful, rich, fertile, productive.*

ubi, adv. (**R.** KA, pron. stem indef., kva, qua, quo + bi = quo-bi, cu-bi, u-bi), *where ; when, after, as soon as.*

ūdus, a, um, adj. (**R.** VAG, UG, *to be damp,* ugv, ugvu-s, uvu-s, ūvē-re, ūvidus, uv-du-s, ū-du-s), *damp, wet, moist.*

ulciscor, ultus sum, v. dep. 3 (**R.** VAR, *to guard, protect,* var-k, volc-i-sc-i, ulc-i-sc-l), *to avenge one's self, take vengeance ; to punish, recompense.*

ullus, a, um, gen. īus, dat. I, adj. pron. (**R.** I, pron. stem, 3d pers., aī, ai-na (oi-no-s, early Latin), u-nu-s, uni-cu-s, dimin. unu-lu-s = ul-lu-s), *any, any one,* mostly in negatives, e. g., haud ullus, *not any one.*

ulmus, I, f. (**R.** AR, *to lift up, grow,* al, or, ol, ul, ul-mu-s), *an elm, elm-tree.*

ulna, ae, f. (**R.** AR, *to bend,* al, ul, ul-na), *elbow ;* by meton., *arm ;* as a measure, *an ell.*

ulterior, us, adj. comp. (**R.** ANA.

pron. stem, 3d pers., ana-la, ollu-s (illu-s, ille), ul-s, *on that side*, ul-ter, era, erum, ulter-ior, ul-timu-s, ultrā, sc. parte, ultrō), (over there), *farther, on the farther side ; (ulterior) ;* superl., ultimus, a, um, *farthest, extreme* (ultimate).

ultor, ōris, m. (ulciscor), *an avenger; avenging.*

ultrā, prep., and adv. (see ulter), beyond, farther, on the other side ; *further, more, besides.*

ultrō, adv. (see ulter), beyond, furthermore, besides ; also (when nothing more is required), *of one's own accord, voluntarily, without solicitation.*

ululātus, ūs, m. (ululō), *a howling, howl, shriek.*

ululō, 1 (**R**. UL, *to howl*, ul-ul-a, ululā-re, ululā-tu-s), *to howl, shriek, cry out.*

ulva, ae, f. (**R**. same as ulmus, wh. see, ul-va), *coarse grass, sedge.*

umbra, ae, f. (**R**. AMB, *to envelope*, umb-ra), *shadow, shade ; darkness, gloom ; shading ; a shade, a ghost ; the Shade, the Shades.*

umbrōsus, a, um, adj. (umbra), *shady.*

ūmeō (humeō), 2 (**R**. same as ūdus, wh. see), *to be damp, to be wet.*

umerus, ī (hum-), (**R**. AM, *to be strong*, am-c-so-s, om-c-ro-s, um-c-ru-s), *the shoulder.*

ūmidus (hum-), (for **R**. see ūdus), a, um, adj., *wet, damp.*

ūmor, oris (hum-), (see ūdus), *moisture, dampness ; juice.*

unquam (umquam), adv. (un-qrum, un fr. unus, quam fr. quī, both wh. see), (any one time), *at any time, ever.*

ūnā, adv. (ūnus), (by one way), *at once, together, along with.*

uncus, a, um, adj. (**R**. AK, ANK, *to bend*, unc-u-s), *bent, crooked, hooked.*

unda, ae, f. (**R**. VAD, UD, ὕδωρ, *to well up, bathe*, u-n-d-a), *a wave, billow, sea ;* by meton., *water, the waters, the sea.*

unde, adv. (**R**. KA + **R**. DA; fr. kn, qua, quo, quī, quo-m, cu-m, cu-n, then (c) un ; fr. da, de ; = (c) un-de), *from what place, whence ; from whom, from what.*

undecimus, a, um, num, adj. (unus *and* decimus, for **R**. see those words), *the eleventh.*

undique, adv. (fr. unde *and* que), *from all sides, from every quarter, everywhere.*

unguis, is, m. (**R**. AGH, angh, *to strangle, bind, join*, ungu-i-s), *a nail, a claw.*

unguō (ungō), xī, ctum, 3 (**R**. AG, ANG, *to anoint*, ung, ungu-ere), *to anoint.*

ungula, ae, f. (**R**. AK, ANK, *to bend, crook*, unc-, ung-u-s, ungu-lu-s), *a claw, hoof.*

ūnicolor, oris, adj. (ūnus, color), *of one color.*

ūnicus, a, um, adj. (ūnus, fr. **R**. I, pron. stem, 3d pers., ai, ni-na (oinos, early Latin), ū-nu-s, ūni-cu-s), (one, one-ly), *only, single, the only one ; singular, remarkable, unique.*

ūnus, a, um, gen. unīus, dat. unī (for **R**. see ūnicus), *one, the one, single, a, the single ; only one, alone, one and the same.*

urbs, urbis, f. (**R**. VARDH, *to grow*, vardh-i, ūrdh-i, urb-s, = *something grown*), *a city ;* by meton., for the inhabitants of a city, *the city.*

urgeō (urgueō), ursī, 2 (**R**. VARG, *to turn, press*, urg, urg- (urgu)-ēre), *to press, to press hard* or *close ; pursue, attack ; urge, urge on.*

urna, ae, f. (**R**. VAS, *to shine, burn*, aus, ōs, ūs, ūs-ere, ūr-ere, ur-na, *a vessel of burnt clay*), *an urn, a jar ; a cinerary urn.*

ūrō, ussī, ustum, 3 (for **R**. see urna), *to burn, singe, burn up, consume.*

ursa, ae, f., *a she-bear.*

usquam, adv. (fr. **R**. ka, qua, quo (quī), cu, u- + bi, u-bi, ubi-s, s being locative, ub-s, us + quam, us-quam), *anywhere, at* or *in any place.*

usque, adv. (for **R**. see us-quam, us fr. ub-s + que = qued, old abl. of quis), *all the way to, even to, as far as ; all the time, ever, quite, even.*

ūsus, ūs, m. (ūtor), *the using, use, employment, application ; use, advantage ; experience, habit, intercourse ;* usufruct, see note, Met. X, 37.

ut, utī (fr. pron. stems, ka + ta, cu-te; (tei being locative), u-tī, ut), 1, adv., *how, as, since ; just as*, ut-sic, as—so =

though—yet ; after that ; 2, conj., *that, in order that, so that ; supposing that.*

uter, utra, utrum, gen. Ius, dat. I, pronom. adj. (fr. **R.** KA (quI), ka-tara, quo-tero, cu-tero), u-ter), *which of the two.*

uterque, utraque, utrumque, pronom. adj. (uter-que), *each of two, both.*

uterus, I, m. (**R.** UD, *upon, out,* uteru-s, u-teru-s), *the womb ; fruit of the womb, child, young.*

ūtilis, e, adj. (ūtor), *useful, serviceable, advantageous, profitable.*

ūtilitas, ātis, f. (ūtor), *utility, advantage, profit, service.*

ūtiliter, adv. (ūtilis), *usefully, with advantage.*

utinam, adv., oh that ! *would that!*
ūtor, ūsus sum, 3, v. dep. (**R.** AV, *to like, help,* av-ēre, av-ta, av-a-ti, av-a-ti-s, ov-i-t-i-s, o-i-ti-s, ū-ti-s (in early Latin, oitier, oisus)), *to help with, to use, make use of, enjoy, employ, take advantage of.*

utrimque, adv. (uterque), *on both sides, on each* (of two) *side, from both sides.*

ūva, ae, f. (**R.** VAG, UG, *to be wet,* ugvu-s, ūvu-s, ūvē-re, ugv-a, ūva), *the grape, grapes, cluster or bunch of grapes.*

uxor, ōris, f. (**R.** VAK, *to desire, love,* vac, voc-tor, early Latin voxor, uxsor, uxor), *a wife* (the loving one).

V

vacca, ae, f. (**R.** VAK, *to sound,* vāk (vāca), vacca, *the lowing), a cow.*

vacō, 1, etym. unc., *to be empty, free from, to be without ; to be without occupation, at leisure.*

vacuus, a, um, adj., *empty, free, at leisure : open.*

vādō, vāsum, 3 (**R.** GA, *to go,* gva, va-d, va-d-u-m, *a place where one may go* (a *going*-place), *ford,* vad-e-re), *to go firmly, to go, pass.*

vadum, I, n. (for **R.** see vādō), *a ford, shoal, shallow.*

vāgiō, 4 (**R.** VAK, *to sound,* vāg, vāg-Ire), *to cry, wail ; whimper.*

vagor, v. dep., 1 (for **R.** see vagus), *to rove about, roam, wander, stray.*

vagus, a, um, adj. (**R.** VAGII, *to move to and fro,* vag, vag-u-s, vaga-re, rī), *rambling, roving, roaming, straying ; uncertain, vagrant.*

valeō, uI, itum, 2 (**R.** BAL, *to breathe, be strong,* valē-re), *to be strong, sound ; to be well ;* valē, *farewell ; to be powerfull, vigorous ; to avail, have influence;* part., valēns, ntis, as adj., *strong, stout, vigorous (valiant).*

validus, a, um, adj. (valeō), *strong, vigorous, violent (valid).*

vallis (-ēs), is, f. (**R.** VAR, *to cover, surround,* val, val-le-s, val-li-s, *a covered, protected, place), a valley, vale.*

valva, ae, f. (**R.** VAR, *to wind, roll, fold,* val-v), *a folding-door.*

vānus, a, um, adj., etym. unc., *emp-ty, void, vain; null, groundless, without success ; deceptive, untrustworthy.*

vapor, ōris, m. (**R.** KVAP, *to smoke, steam,* vap, vap-os, -or), *steam, vapor ; warmth, heat.*

variō, 1, etym. unc., *to make various, variegate ; to vary ; to diversify ; to make one's self different.*

varius, a, um, adj., *various, varying, manifold, diverse, different.*

Varrō, ōnis ; see note. Am. I, 15, 21.

vārus, a, um, adj. (**R.** KAR, *bent, crooked,* kvar, cvar-u-s, vār-u-s), *bent outward, bent.*

vastātor, ōris, m. (vastus), *one that lays waste, a ravager, destroyer ; desolating.*

vastē, adv. (vastus), *vastly, immensely, violently.*

vastus, a, um, adj. (**R.** VASTA, *waste, desolate,* vastu-s), *waste ;* then with the idea of extent, *vast, immense, huge, powerful.*

vātēs, is, comm. (**R.** GA, *to sing,* gā, gvā, vā, vā-te-s), *a soothsayer, seer ; singer, bard, poet.*

vāticinor (vātēs, canō), to announce as seer ; *to prophesy ; to sing.*

-ve, conj. (**R.** VAR, *to choose,* val, vol, vol-ō, vI-s, vi-s,=ve), *or (you will or you please), or—or, either—or.*

vē-cors, rdis, adj. (vē fr. **R.** DVA, dvi, *two,* dva, dva-i, va-i, vē, *too little, not very, not,*+cor, *not very intelligent =unintelligent),* not having sense or intelligence, *senseless, silly, foolish, mad, insane.*

vehō, vexī, vectum, 3 (**R.** VAGH, *to move,* vag, veh, veh-ere), *to carry, bear; to drive;* in pass., vehī, *to be borne, to ride, sail, journey.*

vel, conj. (fr. volō, vel-le, see vŏ), *or (you will or please), either—or ; even.*

vēlāmen, inis, n. (vēlō), *a veil, covering ; garment.*

vellō (vellī), vulsī, vulsum, 3 **R.** VAR, *to draw, pull,* vel, vel-l-ere), *to pull, pluck ; to tear out or up.*

vellus, eris, n. (fr. vellō, as something *pulled off*), *wool shorn off, a fleece; a sheep-skin, fell ; a hide.*

vēlō, 1 (for **R.** see vēlum), *to cover, surround, veil, clothe.*

vēlōciter, adv. (vēlōx), *swiftly, rapidly.*

vēlōx, ōcis, adj. (**R.** VAL, *to go, move one's self,* vŏl, vēl-ōx), *swift, fleet.*

vēlum, I, n. (**R.** VAGH, *to move,* vag, veh, veh-s-lu-m, vec-s-lu-m, ve-s-lu-m, vēlum, *something moving), a sail;* by meton., for a ship, *a sail ; a covering, awning.*

velut, velutī, adv. (for **R.** see ve, vel, vel-utī), *as if, as when, just as, as, as it were, as though.*

vēna, ae, f. (**R.** same as vēlum, vagh, vag, veh, veh-na, vē-na), *a vein, an artery ;* a vein of water, *a stream;* also a vein of metal.

vēnābulum, ī, n. (vēnor, fr. **R.** VI, *to chase,* vai, vē-nā-rī), *a hunting-spear.*

vendō, vendidī, venditum, 3 (vēnumdō, venundō), *to give for sale, to sell.*

venēnifer, fera, ferum, adj., *poisonbearing, poisonous.*

venēnum, I, n., etym. unc., *poison.*

veneror, 1, v. dep. (**R.** VAN, ven, *to desire, value,* ven-ia, Ven-us, ven-es-u-s, vene-rā-rī), *to value, honor, venerate.*

venia, ae, f. (for **R.** see veneror), *grace, permission, favor, indulgence, pardon.*

veniō, vēnī, ventum, 4 (**R.** GA, *to go* or *come,* gva, va, ga-n, ve-n, ve-n-īre), *to come, to reach, arrive at, to come near, approach.*

venter, ventris, m. (**R.** GATARA, *belly,* ge-n-ter, gve-n-ter, ve-n-ter), *the belly ; stomach.*

ventus, ī, m. (**R.** VA, *to blow,* va-nt, ve-ntu-s), *wind.*

Venus, eris, f. (**R.** same as veneror), *grace, beauty ;* the goddess of love, *Venus ; love.*

vēr, vēris, n. (**R.** VAS, *to shine,* ves, ves-er, ve-er, vēr), *the spring, springtime, Spring.*

verbēnae (verbōna), ārum, f. (**R.** VARDH, *to grow,* verb, verb-es-na, verb-ē-na), *vervain ; herbs* or *branches* from a sacred place.

verber, eris, n. (**R.** same as preceding, vardh, vardh-as, verb-es, verb-er, *a bough, branch*), *a whip, a lash ; a thong.*

verberō, 1, *to strike, beat.*

verbōsus, a, um, adj. (verbum), *full of words, wordy ; prolix, verbose.*

verbum, I, n. (**R.** VAR, *to speak,* vardha, ver-bu-m), *a word, words.*

verēcundus, a, um, adj. (vereor), *modest, bashful ; respectful.*

vereor, veritus sum, v. dep., 2 (**R.** VAR, *to guard, protect,* ver, ver-ērī), *to feel awe, be awed ; to fear, dread.*

Vergilius, ī (iī), Publius Vergilius Maro ; *Vergil.*

vernus, a, um, adj. (vēr), *of* or *pertaining to spring, vernal.*

vērō, adv. (vērus), *in truth, truly, assuredly ; but.*

Vērōna, ae, f., a city in Cisalpine Gaul ; *Verona.*

verrō, verrī, versum, 3 (**R.** VAR, *to draw through, drag,* var-s, vers, verrere), *to sweep ; draw.*

versō, 1 (vertō), *to turn again and again, to turn.*

versus, ūs, m. (vertō), a turn, turning ; *a line, a verse ; verse, poetry.*

vertex (vor-), icis, m. (vertō), *a turn, whirl, whirlpool, an eddy ; the crown* of the head ; *head, top.*

vertīgo, inis, f. (vertō), *a turning, a whirling,* of the water ; *a whirling* of the head, *vertigo.*

vertō (vor-), vertī, versum, 3 (**R.** VART, *to turn,* vert-ere), *to turn, to turn away* or *around,* or *about, to turn up, overturn ; to change ; to overthrow.*

vērum (vērus), conj., *but, yet, however, still.*

vērus, a, um, adj. (**R.** VAR, *to believe,* vēr, vēr-u-s), *credible, true ; real,* *genuine;* subst. neut., *the true, the truth; truthful, veracious.*

vesper, -cris, and -crī, m. (R. vas, *to clothe, envelope,* ves, ves-ti-s, ves-per (k to p), ἕσπερος), *the evening* (vespers) ; *land of the evening ; land of the setting sun, the west.*

Vesta, ae, f. (R. vas, *to light, shine, burn,* ves, ves-ta, ἑστία, *the* (burning) *hearth ; Vesta,* as the goddess of the hearth, of home, of domestic purity and order ; in mythology, the daughter of Saturn ; the perpetually burning fire in the temple of Vesta, as the goddess of the national home or household, a symbol of the perpetuity of the national life, of Rome, as the Eternal City.

vester, vestra, vestrum, possess. pron. (fr. R. tva, tu, pl. sva, svo, vo-s, nom. and acc., te-vo-s, tuu-s, vos-, vester), *your, yours.*

vestīgium, ī (iī), n. (R. stigh, *to step,* stīg, preceded by vĕ, wh. see, ve-stīg-iu-m), *a trace, a track, footprint, a vestige ; footstep, step, the foot.*

vestīgō, 1 (vestīgium), *to trace, to track, follow one's track ; to search for, investigate.*

vestiō, īvī (iī), ītum, 4 (for R. see vestis), *to clothe ; cover.*

vestis, is, f. (R. vas, *to clothe,* ves, ves-ti-s), *a clothing, garment, robe ; drapery, hangings, tapestry, carpet.*

vetō, vetuī, vetĭtum, 1 (R. vat, *year,* adj. *old,* vet, vetā-re (inveterāre, -tum, *inveterate*), *to let grow old, let go for nothing, not to let take place*), to do away with ; *to forbid, prohibit, refuse.*

vetus, eris, adj. (R. same as preceding), *long standing, old, former, earlier, early.*

vetustas, ātis, f. (vetus), *age, long time, lapse of time ; old age.*

vexō, 1 (veho, vectum, vex-ō, *to carry, chase to and fro*), *to chase, shake ; to annoy, vex.*

via, ae, f. (R. same as vehō, vagh, vag, veh, veh-ja, veh-ia or veha, vea, via), *a way, road, street ; a course, journey, passage, voyage.*

viātor, ōris, m. (via), *a traveler, wanderer.*

vibrō, 1 (R. vip, *to quiver, tremble,*

vib, vib-ru-s, vibrā-re), *to put into quivering or swinging motion ;* to brandish, shake ; *quiver, wave ; to gleam.*

vīcīnia, ae, f. (vīcīnus), *nearness, vicinity, neighborhood.*

vīcīnus, a, um, adj. (R. vik, *to come, reach,* voik, vīc, vīc-u-s, vīc-īnu-s), (come to, reached), *near, neighboring, close by, in the vicinity or neighborhood ;* subst. neut. pl., vīcīna, *the neighborhood.*

vicis, gen., nom. not in use, vicem, vice, pl. vices, vīcibus, f. (R. vik, *to change,* vic-, vic-is), *change, changes, chances, vicissitudes ;* in vicem, *in turn ; a* (changing in succession) *place, office, duty, function.*

victor, ōris, m. (vincō), *a victor, conqueror ;* adj., *victorious.*

Victōria, ae, f. (vincō), *victory, conquest ; Victoria, goddess of victory.*

victrīx, īcis, f. (vincō), *a conqueror ;* adj., *victorious.*

victus, ūs, m. (vīvō), *means of living, subsistence, sustenance, food.*

video, vīdī, vīsum, 2 (R. vid, *to see, know.* vid-ēre), *to see, look upon ; pass.,* vidērī, *to be seen, to seem ;* part., vīsus, *seen, looked upon,* videndus, *visible, to be seen ;* subst. pl. neut., vīsa, *the sight, vision* (the seen) ; *to experience, to visit,* go to see.

viētus, a, um, adj. (vicō, fr. R. gi, *to overcome,* gvi, vi, vi-s, vi-u-s, vio, violāre, vīĕ, vīĕ-tu-s, *overcome with age*), *old, withered, weak.*

vigeō, 2 (R. vag, *to be strong,* veg, vig, vig-ēre), *to be strong, vigorous ; to bloom, to live.*

vigil, ilis, adj. (R. same as preceding word, vag, veg, vig, vig-il), *wakeful, awake,* watchful, *lively, vigilant ;* subst., *a watchman, sentinel, guard.*

vigilāx, ācis, adj. (vigil), *watchful, vigilant.*

vigilō, 1 (vigil), *to watch, to be watchful, vigilant.*

vigor, ōris, m. (vigeō), *strength, activity, force, vigor.*

vīlis, e, adj. (same R. as vehō, vagh, vag, veh-ō, veh-l-culu-m, veh-ili-s, ve-ili-s, vi-ili-is, vīli-s, *something that is vehicle-full, and so is cheap*), *cheap, common, worthless ; vile.*

villōsus, a, um, adj. (villus), *hairy.*
villa, ae, f., *a farm-house, villa.*
villus, I, m. (R. same as vallis, var, *to surround*, val, val-na, vil-lu-s), *coarse hair, hair* of animals.
vīmen, inis, n. (vieō, R. GI, gvi, vi-, vI-men), *a twig, osier;* coll., *bushes.*
vinciō, vinxī, vinctum, 4 (R. vi, *to wind, braid,* vi-k, vi-n-k, vinc-Ire), *to wind around, bind, join, make firm; to twine, encircle.*
vincō, vīcī, victum, 3 (R. vik, *to fight, strike,* vi-n-c-ere), *to conquer, overcome, be victorious; to surpass, excel, prevail.*
vinculum, vinclum, I, n. (vinciō), *a bond, fetter, band, a bond of union or of relationship.*
vindex, icis, comm. (R. same as venia, VAN, ven, vin, + R. DA, *to show, learn, speak,* di-k, dic (+dex), dic-is, = vin-dex, -dic-is, *a speaker in one's favor or behalf), a defender, protector; an avenger.*
vindicō, 1 (same R. as the preceding, vindex-dic, vindic-u-s, vindicā-re), *to claim, defend, protect, vindicate; to avenge, punish.*
vindicta, ae, f. (vindicō). *vengeance.*
vīnētum, i, n.. *a vineyard.*
vīnum, I, n (R. same as vīmen. vi, *to wind,* vī, vī-ti-s (*a winding* plant, *a vine*), vī-nu-m, cf. οἶνος), *wine.*
viola, ae, f. (R. same as preceding, vi, vio, vio-la), *a violet.*
violentus (fr. violō, wh. see), a, um, adj., *violent, fierce, wild, threatening.*
violō, 1 (R. GI, *to overcome,* gvi, vi, vi-s, vi-n-s, vio-, vio-lā-re, vio-lēre, violent-u-s), *to violate, injure, do violence to; to wound; to stain, outrage.*
vīpera, ae, f. (fr. R. of vīvō, wh. see, + R. of pariō, wh. see, = vivi-paru-s, *that brings forth live young,* vivi-pera, vī-pera), *a viper, snake.*
vīpereus, a, um, adj. (vīpera), *of vipers or snakes; venomous.*
vir, virī, m. (R. VIRA, *man, hero,* viro, vir), *a man; a hero;* in pl., *men, people; a husband.*
virāgō, inis, f. (R. same as vir), *an heroic or a masculine woman;* used of Minerva, Met. VI. 130, where see note.
vireō, uī, 2 (R. GHAR, *to be green,*

ghvar, var, viri-di-s, viri-du-s, viridā-re, virē-re), *to be green, grow green, to flourish;* part., virēns. *flourishing.*
virga, ae, f. (R. VARG, *to push, swell* (urg-urgēre), virg-a), *a (swelling) shoot, twig, sapling; a rod, a wand.*
virgineus, a, um, adj. (virgō), (R. same as preceding), *of a virgin.*
virgō, inis, f., *a virgin, maiden.*
viridis, e, adj. (for R. see vireō), *green.*
virtūs, ūtis, f. (fr. vir), *manliness; manhood; force, strength; courage; merit; excellence; virtue.*
vīrus, I, n. (R. vis, *to work, to be active,* vis-u-s, vīr-u-s), *poison, venom; virus.*
vīs, gen. and dat. not used, vim, vī; pl., vires, -ium, ibus, f. (R. GI, *to overcome,* gvi, vi, vi-s), *force, strength, power, might;* in pl., *forces, powers, virtues.*
viscus, eris, n. (R. VISKA, *soft,* viscus, *the soft parts of the body*), *the inwards; entrails; viscera; the flesh; the vitals;* the *vital point* in anything.
vīsō, vīsī, vīsum, 3 (videō), *to go to see, to behold; to visit; to examine.*
vīta, ae, f. (R. same as vīvō, GIV, *to live,* vīv, vīv-u-s (early Latin, veiv-o-s), vīvi-du-s, vīv-āx, vīv-ere (vivita), vī-ta), *life;* the *living* or *vital principle; way of life, living.*
vītiō, 1 (R. same as vīnum, vi, *to wind, wind around* or *into,* vi-t-iu-m, *something that winds into one, vice,* vitiā-re), *to vitiate; to injure, destroy, ruin.*
vītis, is, f. (R. same as vīnum, wh. see), *a vine, a grape-vine.*
vitium, I (iī), n. (for R. see vitiō), *a defect, fault, blemish;* an injurious thing; *vice, a vice.*
vītō, 1 (R. VIK, *to separate, to separate one's self,* vic, vicā-re, vici-tā-re, vī-tā-re), *to shun, avoid.*
vītrum, I, n. (R. same as videō, VID, *to see,* vid-tru-m, vī-tru-m, *something to see with* or *through), glass.*
vitta, ae, f. (R. vi, *to bind,* vi-ta, vitta), *a band, fillet.*
vīvō, vixī, victum, 3 (for R. see vīta), *to live, be alive; to subsist; to keep alive, continue in life.*

vīvus, a, um, adj. (vīvō), *alive, living; quick; fresh, flowing, natural.*

vix, adv. (R. same as vincō, vik, vic-s, vix), *with difficulty, with pains, hardly, scarcely.*

vōcālis, e, adj. (R. same as vocō, vak, *to sound,* voc, vocā-re, voca-bili-s, voc-āli-s), *sounding, sonorous; vocal.*

vocō, 1 (see vocālis for R.), *to call, to call upon, invoke; to name, to call by name.*

volātus, ūs, m. (volō, 1), *a flying, flight.*

volitō, 1 (volō, 1), *to fly to and fro, to flit, flutter.*

volō, 1 (R. VAL, *to go, move one's self,* vol, voiā-re), *to fly, fly about, flit.*

volō, velle, voluī (R. VAR, *to will,* vel, vol, vol-ō, ŏ before ll and I becomes ĕ, volis, vilis, vils, vīs, vol-t early Latin, *vul-t;* vol-u-mu-s, vol-tis, *vul-tis, vol-unt;* subj., vel-ie-m, *vel-i-m;* inf., vel-se, *vel-le;* imperf., volō-bam; subj., vel-se-m, *vel-le-m;* fut., *vol-a-m;* perf., vol-uī; part., vol-ō-ns), *to will; to wish; to be willing, to consent, allow, choose; to have in view, to purpose.*

voltus, see vultus.

volūbilis, e, adj. (volvō), *rolling, whirling.*

volucer, volūcris, volucre, adj. (R. same as volō, ūre, val, vol, vol-u-cer), *flying, winged.*

volūcris, f. (see preceding), *a flying creature; a fowl; a bird.*

volūmen, inis, n. (fr. volvō), *a rolling, winding, coiling, coil; a roll of writing; a volume, book.*

voluntās, ātis, f. (from volō, velle), *will, wish, desire; purpose; good will.*

voluptās, ātis, f. (R. same as preceding, val, vol, val-p, vol-o-p, vol-u-p, volup-tās), *pleasure, enjoyment, delight; lust.*

volūtō, 1 (volvō), *to keep rolling;* *to roll to and fro; to revolve* in one's mind.

volvō, volvī, volūtum, 3 (R. VAR, *to wind, whirl,* val, vol, val-v, vol-v-ere), *to roll, roll over, whirl; to be rolled; to revolve;* of time (as annus), part., volvens, *rolling, the rolling year.*

vōmer, eris, m. (R. VASMI, *plow-share,* vosmi, vōmi-s, vōm-er), *a plow-share.*

vomō, uī, itum, 3 (R. VAM, *to spew,* vom, vom-ere), *to vomit, belch forth.*

vōtum, I, n. (voveō), *a thing vowed; a vow; prayer, wish, promise; a votive offering.*

voveō, vōvī, vōtum, 2 (R. GU, *to sound, to speak out,* gvov, vov, vov-ēre), *to make known by speaking, to promise, vow, wish; to devote, dedicate.*

vōx, vōcis, f. (R. VAK, *to sound,* voc, vōc, vōx), *a sound, a voice, the voice, a song; a cry; a tone; a word, words, discourse.*

Vulcānius, a, um, adj., *of or pertaining to* Vulcan.

Vulcānus, I, m., son of Jupiter and Juno, *Vulcan,* the god of fire; by meton., *fire.*

vulgāris, e, adj. (vulgus), *general, common, ordinary; vulgar.*

vulgō, 1 (vulgus), *to make common, publish abroad, make known; to divulge.*

vulgus (volgus), I, n. (R. VARG, *to press, to include and exclude,* valg, vulg, vulg-us), *the crowd, the great multitude, the common people; the rabble.*

vulnus (volnus), eris, n. (R. VAR, *to pull, tear, wound,* vel, vol, vul, vul-nus), *a wound, a stroke, blow; a bite.*

vultus, ūs, m. (volnus), (R. VAR, *to will, wish,* vol, vul, vul-tu, vul-tu-s, *expression of will), expression, mien, aspect, countenance, face; a look, form, appearance.*

X

Xanthus, I, m., a river near Troy, also called Scamander.

Z

Zephyrus, I, m., *the west wind, the Zephyrus, Zephyr.*

Zētēs, ae, m., one of the winged sons of Boreas; *Zetes.*

zōna, ae, f., Gr. ζώνη, *a girdle, a belt; a zone* of the earth or of the heavens.

www.ingramcontent.com/pod-product-compliance
Lightning Source LLC
Chambersburg PA
CBHW031427230426
43668CB00007B/464